"This is one of the most important books on methodological issues in the study of Jesus and the Gospels to have appeared for a long time. It deserves to be widely read."

—**Richard Bauckham,** professor of New Testament studies and Bishop Wardlaw Professor, St. Mary's College, University of St. Andrews

"*The Jesus Legend* is the best book in its class. Authors Eddy and Boyd demonstrate mastery of the disciplines essential for critical assessment of the Gospels and competent investigation of the historical Jesus. Again and again they expose the dubious assumptions and underpinnings of the theories proffered by those who assume that Jesus either did not exist or that the New Testament Gospels give us little more than myth and legend. I recommend this book in the highest terms."

—**Craig A. Evans,** Payzant Distinguished Professor, Acadia Divinity College, and author of *Fabricating Jesus: How Modern Scholars Distort the Gospels*

"Eddy and Boyd provide a clearly written, carefully researched, and powerfully argued defense of the historical reliability of the Synoptic Gospels. What makes this book noteworthy is the careful treatment of underlying issues in historical methodology and philosophy. A pleasure to read and a wonderful resource for those who have encountered troubling skeptical claims about the Gospels."

—**C. Stephen Evans,** University Professor of Philosophy and Humanities, Baylor University

"I am gratified that my friends and colleagues Paul Eddy and Greg Boyd have taken my work as seriously as they have in this comprehensively researched book. Bravo for their repudiation of any bias of philosophical naturalism! Amen to their urging that the burden of proof is on whomever would reject any bit of gospel tradition as unhistorical. Other than this, I would dispute almost every one of their assertions—but that is why I recommend the book! What can you learn if you only reinforce your own viewpoint? I urge any reader of my books to read this one alongside them!"

—**Robert M. Price,** professor of biblical criticism, Center for Inquiry Institute, and fellow of the Jesus Seminar

"Eddy and Boyd have provided a thoroughly compelling cumulative argument—one of the very best available—for the reliability of the Synoptic Jesus tradition. Their book constitutes a superb treatment of the various issues, involving both fresh research and a brilliant synthesis of material from a variety of relevant disciplines (philosophy, anthropology, historiography, as well as New Testament, early Judaism, and Greco-Roman antiquity). It is far better argued and documented than the works of the vast majority of the skeptics it challenges."

—**Craig S. Keener,** professor of New Testament, Palmer Seminary

"Misinformation about the historical Jesus and the reliability of the New Testament Gospels runs rampant in the twenty-first century. Some of this comes from eccentric or flawed scholarship; some from purely fictitious novels. Eddy and Boyd have surveyed technical and popular writing alike, in meticulous detail, and present what can be concluded responsibly about the trustworthiness of the Synoptic Gospels and the portraits of Jesus they contain. They compile a detailed and erudite case that supports Christian faith, but without the simplistic and unwarranted generalizations that one often hears in grassroots evangelical circles. Highly recommended!"

—**Craig L. Blomberg,** distinguished professor of New Testament, Denver Seminary

"A most welcome survey and critique of modern-day imaginative reconstructions of the rise of Christianity that attempt to justify faith in the presupposition of a non-supernaturalistic Jesus. . . . Well-written and organized, containing a masterful command of the literature. Eddy and Boyd show the difference between an open historical investigation of the life of Jesus and much of today's fictional writing that claims to be historical research concerning the origin of Christianity. A very useful introduction for college and seminary students."

—**Robert H. Stein,** senior professor of New Testament interpretation, The Southern Baptist Theological Seminary

THE JESUS LEGEND

A Case for the Historical Reliability of the Synoptic Jesus Tradition

PAUL RHODES EDDY
AND GREGORY A. BOYD

Baker Academic
Grand Rapids, Michigan

© 2007 by Paul Rhodes Eddy and Gregory A. Boyd

Published by Baker Academic
a division of Baker Publishing Group
P.O. Box 6287, Grand Rapids, MI 49516-6287
www.bakeracademic.com

Printed in the United States of America

Library of Congress Cataloging-in-Publication Data
Eddy, Paul R.
    The Jesus legend : a case for the historical reliability of the synoptic Jesus tradition / Paul Rhodes
    Eddy and Gregory A. Boyd.
        p. cm.
    Includes bibliographical references and indexes.
    ISBN 10: 0-8010-3114-1 (pbk.)
    ISBN 978-0-8010-3114-4 (pbk.)
    1. Synoptic problem. 2. Bible. N.T. Gospels—Criticism, interpretation, etc. I. Boyd, Gregory A.,
    1957– II. Title.
    BS2555.52.E33 2007
    226′.067—dc22   2007006639

Dedicated to

Jim Beilby
and
Roger Forster

I would like to dedicate this work to Jim Beilby, my colleague, collaborator, and close friend. His philosophical acumen, editing skills, and willingness to engage my rough drafts have enhanced my academic work over the years. His financial wisdom has challenged me to be a better steward. His honest and self-sacrificial friendship has been a blessing to my life. Thank you, Jim.

—Paul

I would like to dedicate this work to Roger Forster, founder and head of Ichthus Fellowship, centered in London. For fifty years Roger has tirelessly and selflessly served the Kingdom with intellectual brilliance and Christ-like sacrifice. Roger, I never knew what it was to respect and want to emulate another living human being until I met you. Thank you.

—Greg

CONTENTS

Assessing the Evidence**

  8. The Genre and Nature of the Canonical Gospels: *Did the Gospel
     Authors Intend to Write Historically Reliable Accounts?*   309
  9. Evaluating the Synoptic Gospels as Historical Sources:
     Methodological Issues and Preliminary Considerations   363
 10. The Synoptic Tradition and the Jesus of History: *Completing a
     Cumulative Case for the Reliability of the Synoptic Portrait(s) of
     Jesus*   407

     Index of Scripture and Ancient Writings   455
     General Index   465

ACKNOWLEDGMENTS

There are a number of people to whom we are indebted for various forms of input into, and encouragement and support of, this project. Jim Beilby, Michael Holmes, Erik Leafblad, Jeff Lehn, and Stewart Kelly each provided valuable reflections on early drafts of various chapters. Opportunities for correspondence with James Dunn and Theodore Weeden strengthened aspects of the chapters on oral tradition.

I (Paul) want to express my appreciation to Bethel University for supporting my sabbatical during the research phase of this project, and to my aunt Judie and uncle Tim O'Brien for offering me the gift of their Punta Rassa hide-away during that time (ah, precious Sanibel!). I also want to thank the Bethel University Alumni Association for providing two research grants in support of this project. We are grateful to Betty Bond and the Bethel University Interlibrary Loan Department for their tireless dedication in tracking down countless volumes related to this book—and their patience with us along the way!

I (Greg) want to express my appreciation to my skeptical colleague Robert Price, with whom I have had the pleasure and honor of publicly debating numerous times. Price makes one of the strongest cases for the legendary Jesus thesis, and our numerous debates have helped both Paul and I sharpen our case for the reliability of the Gospels.

We are both thankful for the presence and support of our ecclesial community, Woodland Hills Church, in St. Paul, MN, where we have the privilege of serving on the executive pastoral team together. A word of thanks must go to our fellow executive team member, Janice Rohling, for her tireless patience with us whenever the conversation turns to things theological!

As always, a special word of thanks goes to our precious families—and especially our wives, Kelly Eddy and Shelley Boyd—for their unending love and their gracious support of our academic ventures.

Finally, we would like to express our deep appreciation to two close friends, Jim Beilby and Roger Forster, to whom we dedicate this book.

ABBREVIATIONS

ABD	*Anchor Bible Dictionary*
ANF	*Ante-Nicene Fathers*
ANRW	*Aufstieg und Niedergang der römischen Welt: Geschichte und Kultur Roms im Spiegel der neueren Forschung,* part 2, The Principate, edited by W. Haase and H. Temporini (Berlin: de Gruyter, 1974–)
Antiquities	Josephus, *The Antiquities of the Jews*
BAR	*Biblical Archaeology Review*
CBQ	*Catholic Biblical Quarterly*
DDD	*Dictionary of Deities and Demons in the Bible*
EQ	*Evangelical Quarterly*
ExpT	*Expository Times*
HTR	*Harvard Theological Review*
JAAR	*Journal of the American Academy of Religion*
JBL	*Journal of Biblical Literature*
JETS	*Journal of the Evangelical Theological Society*
Jewish War	Josephus, *The Wars of the Jews*
JJS	*Journal of Jewish Studies*
JR	*Journal of Religion*
JSHJ	*Journal for the Study of the Historical Jesus*
JSJ	*Journal for the Study of Judaism*
JSNT	*Journal for the Study of the New Testament*
JSNTSup	Journal for the Study of the New Testament: Supplement Series
JSOT	*Journal for the Study of the Old Testament*
JSOTSup	Journal for the Study of the Old Testament: Supplement Series
JSSR	*Journal for the Scientific Study of Religion*

JTS	*Journal of Theological Studies*
LCL	Loeb Classical Library
Legat.	Philo, *Legatio ad Gaium (On the Embassy to Gaius)*
Life	Josephus, *The Life of Flavius Josephus*
Migr.	Philo, *De migratione Abrahami (On the Migration of Abraham)*
NovT	*Novum Testamentum*
NovTSup	Novum Testamentum Supplements
NTS	*New Testament Studies*
Quaes. Gen.	Philo, *Quaestiones et solutiones in Genesis (Questions and Answers on Genesis)*
SBL	Society of Biblical Literature
SBLDS	Society of Biblical Literature Dissertation Series
SBLSP	*Society of Biblical Literature Seminar Papers*
SJT	*Scottish Journal of Theology*
TynB	*Tyndale Bulletin*
WUNT	Wissenschaftliche Untersuchungen Neuen Testament
ZAW	*Zeitschrift für die alttestamentliche Wissenschaft*
ZNW	*Zeitschrift für die neutestamentliche Wissenschaft und die Kunde der älteren Kirche*

INTRODUCTION

The Case for the Legendary Jesus

The primary objective of this book is to investigate the extent to which the portrait(s) of Jesus in the canonical Gospels—particularly the Synoptic Gospels—are generally to be judged as reliable history, on one hand, or as fictional legend, on the other. This latter option will be referred to throughout this book as the "legendary Jesus" thesis.[1] For reasons that will become clear as we proceed, our task will require us

1. The term "legend" has various meanings in different contexts. In some academic circles, i.e., certain sectors of folkloristics, the term has come to refer to a transmitted story set in the relatively recent, or at least the historical, past that, though believed to be true by the teller, may or may not be rooted in actual history. On the multiple uses and definitional complexities of the term "legend"—including its relationship to "history"—see L. Degh and A. Vazsonyi, "Legend and Belief," in *Folklore Genre*, ed. D. Ben-Amos (Austin: University of Texas Press, 1976), 93–123; R. A. Georges, "The General Concept of Legend: Some Assumptions to Be Reexamined and Reassessed," in *American Folk Legend: A Symposium*, ed. W. D. Hand (Berkeley: University of California Press, 1971), 1–19; H. Jason, "Concerning the 'Historical' and the 'Local' Legends and Their Relatives," in *Toward New Perspectives in Folklore*, ed. A. Paredes and R. Bauman (Austin: University of Texas Press, 1972), 134–44; E. Oring, "Legend, Truth, and News," *Southern Folklore* 47 (1990): 163–77; T. Shibutani, "Legendary Accounts and Historiography," in *Improvised News: A Sociological Study of Rumor* (Indianapolis: Bobbs-Merrill, 1966), 155–61; Y. Zerubavel, "The Historic, the Legendary, and the Incredible: Invented Tradition and Collective Memory in Israel," in *Commemorations: The Politics of National Identity*, ed. J. R. Gillis (Princeton: Princeton University Press, 1994), 105–23. On the very similar category of the "memorate," see L. Degh and A. Vazsonyi, "The Memorate and the Proto-Memorate," *Journal of American Folklore* 87 (1974): 225–39. In this work, we will use "legend" in its more popular sense of a substantially nonhistorical/fictional story. From D. F. Strauss to Rudolf Bultmann to Robert Funk and the Jesus Seminar, the use of the term "legend" in New Testament studies generally appears to function as shorthand for an ostensive historical account that is, in fact, (at least largely) fictional. See D. F. Strauss, *The Life of Jesus*, 4th ed., trans. M. Evans (New York: Blanchard, 1860), 2; R. Bultmann, *The History of the Synoptic Tradition*, trans. J. Marsh (Oxford: Blackwell, 1963), 244–45; R. Funk and the Jesus Seminar, *The Acts of Jesus: What Did Jesus Really Do?* (San Francisco: HarperSanFrancisco, 1998), 15–17.

to consider recent findings from a number of disciplines, including ethnography, folkloristics, and orality studies. The thesis we will be defending is this: If, with its reports of the supernatural, one is able to remain sincerely open to the *possibility* (not merely the "logical" possibility, but the genuine historical possibility; see chap. 1 below) that the portrait(s) of Jesus in the Synoptic Gospels is historically reliable, then, given an appropriate historical method and the evidence at hand,[2] one is justified (on purely historical grounds) in concluding that the Synoptic portrait(s) of Jesus is quite historically *plausible*—in fact, that it is the *most historically probable* representation of the actual Jesus of history.[3] At the very least, we contend, the

---

At the start we should also note that our focus is primarily on the Synoptic Gospels. We have chosen largely to leave the Gospel of John aside in terms of detail and distinctives. We do so not because we think John's work is inherently less reliable than the Synoptics, but because this Gospel is so different from the other canonical Gospels that it requires a significantly different line of consideration when assessing its historicity. This would have made an already sizable work significantly longer. Among recent studies that have concluded with a generally favorable assessment of the historical reliability of the Fourth Gospel see C. L. Blomberg, *The Historical Reliability of John's Gospel: Issues and Commentary* (Downers Grove, IL: InterVarsity, 2001); C. S. Keener, *The Gospel of John: A Commentary*, 2 vols. (Peabody, MA: Hendrickson, 2003). For an impressive recent study that calls into question the all-too-common "de-historicization of John," and the "de-Johannification of Jesus," see P. N. Anderson, *The Fourth Gospel and the Quest for Jesus: Modern Foundations Reconsidered* (New York: Clark, 2006).

2. Throughout this work we will make reference to historical "evidence." We do so, we trust, not from a naive evidentialist perspective that presumes that evidence speaks for itself in some preinterpreted, decontextualized fashion. Rather, as recent interdisciplinary studies on evidentiary matters suggest, evidence and evidentiary standards are always approached and evaluated from within a concrete sociocultural-linguistic context. This is the case for historical evidence no less than it is for legal and other forms of evidence. On the context-dependent variability of evidentiary standards even within a single society, see S. U. Philips, "Evidentiary Standards for American Trials: Just the Facts," in *Responsibility and Evidence in Oral Discourse*, ed. J. H. Hill and J. T. Irvine (New York: Cambridge University Press, 1992), 248–59.

3. Some Christian readers may be disappointed that we are arguing only that it is *plausible/most probable* that the Synoptic portrait of Jesus is *substantially* rooted in history. They might rather have hoped we would argue it is *certain* that the Gospel portrait of Jesus is *completely rooted* in history. As shall become clear in the next chapter, however, given the constraints of historical method and the limitations of finite human knowledge, purely historical considerations alone can never get beyond probabilistic conclusions. We should also mention that, because we are approaching this topic from a critical historiographical standpoint, we will be treating the Synoptic Gospels as we would any other ancient document. Historiographically speaking, the fact that these works are recognized as canonical and "inspired" by the historic orthodox church is neither here nor there. This has important implications. The authors of this book are theologically trained evangelical Christians. However, although we certainly bring our own presuppositions to the task (see below), for the purposes of this particular study we have attempted to operate from a standpoint of critical historiographical inquiry. Given this methodological delimitation, our claims in this book will be much more modest than if we were writing a theological textbook on the nature of Scripture. For example, while it might be *theologically* problematic to countenance certain inaccuracies or fabricated elements in the Gospels, this does not trouble our more minimal *historiographical* thesis: namely that the Synoptic Gospels are—generally and substantially speaking—rooted in history. It is also important to note that the recognition that historical claims are always, at best, probabilistic in nature in no way creates a problem for Christian *faith*—at least when this faith is properly understood. In the biblical context, faith is primarily a covenant term that signals active trust in the character and promises of one's covenant partner. For helpful statements on this matter of faith and history, see N. T. Wright, *The New Testament and the People of God* (Minneapolis: Fortress, 1992), 93–96; J. D. G. Dunn, *Jesus*

cumulative case for the general reliability of the Synoptic presentation(s) of Jesus is such that the a posteriori burden of proof (on which see chap. 9) rests on those who contend that this portrait is generally unreliable.

One of the main purposes of this book is to draw together an array of interdisciplinary studies that in one way or another have bearing on the question of the historicity of the Synoptic Jesus tradition. In particular, a major impetus for this work is that the often relevant findings of contemporary interdisciplinary studies on orally oriented ancient cultures have generally not been integrated into historical-Jesus research as widely and thoroughly as one might hope. Much of the fuel for the legendary-Jesus thesis is drawn from anachronistic approaches to the early Jesus tradition, approaches that are tied to a modern, literary paradigm. Our contention is that when the early Jesus tradition is assessed from an orally oriented perspective—and in concert with an appropriate historical methodology—the legendary-Jesus thesis becomes difficult to maintain.

In this introduction we want to prepare the way for this endeavor. First, we will address a fundamental objection that could be raised against our thesis: that in our postmodern world it is naive to think we can attain, or should even attempt to attain, anything like an "objective" understanding of history. In the course of responding to this objection, we will offer a few cursory words about the method we will employ in this work (to be further fleshed out in chap. 1 and applied most systematically with respect to the Synoptics in chaps. 9 and 10). Following this we will clearly delineate the view(s) to be engaged in this study, namely, the "legendary-Jesus thesis." We will provide an overview of eight major lines of argumentation that are typically proffered by defenders of the legendary-Jesus thesis. This outline will serve as a framework both for fleshing out the cumulative case that can be made for the legendary-Jesus perspective, and for constructing a cumulative critical case in response, one that supports the general reliability of the Synoptic portrait(s) of Jesus.

The Postmodern Challenge to Historiography

The "Linguistic Turn"

In our postmodern climate, there is significant skepticism toward the classic historiographical assumption that it is (at least in theory) possible to arrive at something like an objective understanding of the past. According to many today, the ideal of "objective history" is not only an impossible goal to attain, but even an

---

Remembered (Grand Rapids: Eerdmans, 2003), 102–5; A. G. Padgett, "Advice for Religious Historians: On the Myth of a Purely Historical Jesus," in *The Resurrection: An Interdisciplinary Symposium on the Resurrection of Jesus*, ed. S. T. Davis, D. Kendall, and G. O'Collins (New York: Oxford University Press, 1997), 287–307. Finally, while we will often use the phrase "Synoptic portrait of Jesus" in this book, it should be assumed that "portrait(s)" is thereby intended. We in no way intend to downplay the distinctives of the three Synoptic Gospels' presentations of Jesus.

unrealistic and unhelpful goal to aspire to. Since our thesis is that an assessment of all the relevant evidence favors the conclusion that the portrait of Jesus in the Synoptic tradition is rooted in history, we need to address this hyperskeptical postmodern view of historiography.

Since what has been called the "linguistic turn," initiated by Saussure and developed in a radical, poststructuralist direction by Derrida, Foucault, and others, the postmodern critique of reason has threatened to turn historiography (and other fields) into a virtual subdiscipline of rhetoric and literary theory. According to these thinkers, it is language, and only language, "all the way down." No ancient or modern text can be understood to have an external reference point beyond itself, regardless of what the author of the text intended. People may think they are talking about what actually happened in the past, but in fact they are merely using language in ways that fit social conventions and further present social and personal purposes.

Consequently, as Hayden White argues, we must accept that "historical narratives are verbal fictions, the contents of which are as much invented as found and the forms of which have more in common with their counterparts in literature than they have with those in the sciences."[4] White is not talking about any *particular* historiography here. He is talking about historical writing as such: *any* history, *any* time, *any*where. Similarly, Keith Jenkins argues that, in light of the postmodern, linguistic turn, "history now appears to be just one more foundationless, positioned expression in a world of foundationless, positioned expressions."[5]

Assessing the Radical Postmodern Perspective

It is important to acknowledge that the postmodern turn has made some important contributions to contemporary historiography (as well as to other fields).

---

4. H. White, "Historical Texts as Literary Artifact," in *Tropics of Discourse: Essays in Cultural Criticism* (Baltimore: Johns Hopkins University Press, 1978), 82. See also his first famous salvo: *Metahistory: The Historical Imagination in Nineteenth-Century Europe* (Baltimore: Johns Hopkins University Press, 1973). Other strong postmodern critics of any sort of objectivity in historiography include: F. R. Ankersmit, *History and Tropology: The Rise and Fall of Metaphor* (Berkeley: University of California Press, 1994); idem, "Hayden White's Appeal to the Historians," *History and Theory* 37 (1998): 182–93; R. Barthes, "The Discourse of History," *Comparative Criticism: A Yearbook* 3 (1981): 3–28; K. Jenkins, *Re-thinking History* (New York: Routledge, 1991); H. Kellner, *Language and Historical Representation: Getting the Story Crooked* (Madison: University of Wisconsin Press, 1989); A. Munslow, *Deconstructing History* (New York: Routledge, 1997).

5. K. Jenkins, "Introduction" to *The Postmodern History Reader*, ed. K. Jenkins (New York: Routledge, 1998), 1. For discussions from a variety of perspectives on the relationship of postmodernism and historiography, see D. Attridge, G. Bennington, and R. Young, eds., *Post-Structuralism and the Question of History* (New York: Cambridge University Press, 1987); G. G. Iggers, *Historiography in the Twentieth Century: From Scientific Objectivity to the Postmodern Challenge* (Hanover: Wesleyan University Press, 1997); P. Novick, *That Noble Dream: The "Objectivity Question" and the American Historical Profession* (New York: Cambridge University Press, 1988); E. A. Clark, *History, Theory, Text: Historians and the Linguistic Turn* (Cambridge, MA: Harvard University Press, 2004). In the last chapter of her book, Clark applies the insights of postmodern historiography to ancient Christian history.

While there is little in this movement that is, philosophically speaking, truly original, the movement as a whole has forced us to wrestle with the fact that truth-claims can sometimes (if not often) be about things other than the quest for accurately recovering the past (e.g., power politics, etc.). The postmodern sensibility has highlighted the significant role subjective and social factors play in all our cognitive disciplines. Consequently, the postmodern turn has, at the very least, served to sharpen our awareness that historical claims are never purely objective, are always probabilistic, and thus are open to further questioning.[6] And this fact should serve to make us more humble and more self-critical when making and defending historiographical truth-claims.[7]

Despite this positive contribution, however, the hyperskeptical conclusions some have drawn from the postmodern turn are fraught with difficulties and have been subjected to heavy criticism.[8] Two of these problems warrant our attention.

6. See R. E. Frykenberg, *History and Belief: The Foundations of Historical Understanding* (Grand Rapids: Eerdmans, 1996) for an example of a scholar wrestling with this awareness in the context of the Christian faith.

7. In chap. 1, we will suggest that many within the guild of historical-critical biblical scholars have not taken certain implications of the postmodern turn seriously enough. It is worth noting that this postmodernist intuition about history is hardly new. As long ago as the late eighteenth century, Goethe's Faust expressed a similar sentiment to his assistant Wagner: "The times of the past are to us a book that is sealed with seven seals. What you call the spirit of the past—why that's your own spirit reflecting back at you"; Goethe's *Faust*, cited in E. D. Hirsch, "Back to History," in *Criticism in the University*, ed. G. Graff and R. Gibbons (Evanston, IL: Northwestern University Press, 1985), 191. In the early nineteenth century, James Bronterre O'Brien warned: "Have no faith in history, look upon it as a mass of fabrications, concocted, like modern newspapers, not with any regard to truth, or the interests of humanity, but to deceive the multitude, and thus to bolster up all the frauds and villainous institutions of the rich." O'Brien, *Poor Man's Guardian* (December 5, 1835), cited in T. Lummis, *Listening to History: The Authenticity of Oral Evidence* (Totowa, NJ: Barnes & Noble, 1987), 11. Likewise, in 1894 we find J. A. Froude remarking that history is like "a child's box of letters with which we can spell any word we please." *Short Studies on Great Subjects* (1894), cited in E. H. Carr, *What Is History?* (New York: Knopf, 1967), 30. Later in that century, Marx would go on to flesh out and radicalize this intuition, while Nietzsche would set the tone for the future postmodern project vis-à-vis history in no uncertain terms. In its essence, then, the radical postmodern critique of history is hardly new, and many of the weaknesses of this trajectory of thought identified in times past remain characteristic of its more recent incarnations.

8. As E. Breisach (*On the Future of History: The Postmodern Challenge and Its Aftermath* [Chicago: University of Chicago Press, 2003]) argues, the field of history has largely weathered the "crisis" of the radical postmodern critique. While chastened in a healthy manner—i.e., being weaned from any lingering historical positivism and the naive goal of *pure* historical objectivity—nonetheless, as Joyce Appleby, Lynn Hunt, and Margaret Jacob have stated in their recent and acclaimed book, human beings retain the "capacity to discriminate between false and faithful representations of past reality and, beyond that, to articulate standards which help both practitioners and readers to make such discriminations" (*Telling the Truth about History* [New York: Norton, 1994], 261). These three scholars opt for an approach that they term "practical realism" (see esp. pp. 247–51). For a number of other penetrating critiques of the radical postmodern challenge to history and/or recent statements of an appropriately critical-realist (philosophy of) historiography, see M. Bunzl, *Real History: Reflections on Historical Practice* (New York: Routledge, 1997); A. Cook, *History/Writing* (New York: Cambridge University Press, 1989); G. R. Elton, *Return to Essentials* (New York: Cambridge University Press, 1991); R. J. Evans, *In Defense of History* (London: Granta, 1997); J. Gorman, *Understanding History: An Introduction to Analytical Philosophy of History* (Ottawa: University of Ottawa

First, if we follow the radical fringe of the postmodern movement—especially those in the poststructuralist/deconstructionist camp—and thus jettison the possibility of arriving at, or even striving for, a more or less objective understanding of the past, we have to accept that we can no longer so much as speak about "good" versus "bad"—"legitimate" versus "illegitimate"—historiography.[9] Or, if we insist on speaking in this manner, we have to concede that we mean by this distinction nothing more than that we merely prefer one form of historiography—or one set of historical conclusions—over another. If we abandon the concept of objective history, we must, for example, grant a neo-Nazi propaganda tract denying the Holocaust ever happened the same hearing and status as a scholarly historical work meticulously chronicling the horrors of Nazi Germany. Such a conclusion is obviously absurd (tellingly, an observation that even radical postmodernists seem reluctant to challenge), yet one the postmodernist seems unable to convincingly refute.[10] As Michael Shermer and Alex Grobman note, "Ironically, it is with is-

Press, 1992); T. L. Haskell, *Objectivity Is Not Neutrality: Explanatory Schemes in History* (Baltimore: Johns Hopkins University Press, 1998); G. Himmelfarb, *The New History and the Old*, rev. ed. (Cambridge, MA: Belknap, 2004); Hirsch, "Back to History"; C. B. McCullagh, *The Truth of History* (New York: Routledge, 1998); R. Martin, *The Past within Us: An Empirical Approach to Philosophy of History* (Princeton: Princeton University Press, 1989); M. G. Murphy, *Philosophical Foundations of Historical Knowledge* (Albany: SUNY, 1994); L. Stone, "History and Post-Modernism," *Past and Present* 135 (May 1992): 189–204; A. Tucker, "A Theory of Historiography as a Pre-Science," *Studies in History and Philosophy of Science* 24 (1993): 633–67; K. Windschuttle, *The Killing of History: How Literary Critics and Social Theorists Are Murdering Our Past* (New York: Free Press, 1996); P. Zagorin, "History and Postmodernism: Reconsiderations," *History and Theory* 29 (1990): 263–74; idem, "Rejoinder to a Postmodernist," *History and Theory* 39 (2000): 201–9. For an enlightening series of interviews with various scholars along the spectrum on this issue, see E. Domanska, *Encounters: Philosophy of History after Postmodernism* (Charlottesville: University Press of Virginia, 1998). For an argument that poststructuralism has illegitimately wandered into the realm of the philosophy of historiography—in which it has no real business—see A. Tucker, "The Future of the Philosophy of Historiography," *History and Theory* 40 (2001): 37–56.

9. On the possibility and importance of distinguishing "legitimate" from "illegitimate" historiography, see Tucker, "Theory of Historiography," esp. 653–55.

10. It is noteworthy that, e.g., Hayden White adamantly argues against the Holocaust deniers, claiming that such a position is "as morally offensive as it is intellectually bewildering" ("The Politics of Historical Interpretation: Discipline and De-Sublimation," in *The Content of the Form: Narrative Discourse and Historical Representation* [Baltimore: Johns Hopkins University Press, 1983], 76). But, as Wulf Kansteiner has observed—given his theory—the epistemological grounds upon which he does so are problematic ("Hayden White's Critique of the Writing of History," *History and Theory* 32 [1993]: 273–95). For a perceptive and nuanced analysis of White's work, including a clear demarcation between White's thesis and that of the more radical, thoroughgoing postmodernist approach, see A. D. Moses, "Hayden White, Traumatic Nationalism, and the Public Role of History," *History and Theory* 44 (2005): 311–32.

White's notorious claim that doing history within a narrative framework always already distorts the subject matter has been countered by a number of thinkers. See, e.g., D. Carr, "Narrative and the Real World: An Argument for Continuity," *History and Theory* 15 (1986): 117–31; idem, *Time, Narrative, and History* (Bloomington: Indiana University Press, 1986); W. Dray, "Narrative and Historical Realism," in *On History and Philosophers of History* (New York: Brill, 1989), 131–63; N. Carroll, "Interpretation, History and Narrative," *Monist* 73 (1990): 134–66; L. Pompa, "Narrative Form, Significance and Historical Knowledge," in *Philosophy of History and Contemporary Historiography*, ed. D. Carr et al. (Ottawa: University of Ottawa Press, 1982), 143–57. From the perspective of a New Testament scholar, see

sues such as the Holocaust denial that all discussion of historical relativism ends. Ask deconstructionists if they think that the belief the Holocaust happened is as valid as the belief that it did not happen, and the debate quickly screeches to a halt."[11] And yet the radically skeptical postmodern approach to historiography offers no convincing resources by which to challenge the legitimacy claims of the Holocaust deniers. Here, the radical postmodern view of history is open not only to a *historiographical* critique, but to a *moral* critique as well.

If all historical narratives are "verbal fictions," if it is only "language all the way down," and if, therefore, no text has any external reference point, then finding "inappropriate" biases, propaganda, errors, and fabrications in any work, ancient or modern, is as impossible as it is irrelevant. A historical perspective can be judged to be biased and/or misguided only if it can be measured against other sources and/or by other methods one deems *more reliable*. But this, again, presupposes there is some way for us to step outside our "verbal fictions" and to some extent assess objectively the reliability of historical sources. If this is not possible, we are utterly trapped in our purely subjective perspectives and preferences.

Second, if White, Jenkins, Foucault, and others are right in insisting that texts cannot refer beyond themselves, it is not at all clear what these authors are *referring to* when they make the claim that no text can refer beyond itself. If their analysis is "correct" (measured against what?), they themselves must be judged as simply spinning their own preferred forms of "verbal fiction"—in which case neither they nor anyone else can judge them to be "correct." Again, to embrace their analysis is, at the same time, to subject it to its own critique, thus rendering it but one more "foundationless, positioned expression in a world of foundationless, positioned expressions"; thus their analysis cannot be said to be "correct" in any meaningful sense. Along these same lines, if all truth-claims are merely ideologically driven power plays, as radical postmodernists suggest, what are we to make of the truth-claim that "all truth-claims are merely ideologically driven power plays"? The claim itself must be taken to be nothing more than one more ideologically driven power play, in which case it constitutes no grounds for accepting the totalizing claim that all truth-claims are merely ideologically driven power plays. In short, the radical postmodern perspective is self-refuting. Consequently, and not surprisingly, their advocates are forced to trade in inconsistencies in the process of defending their claims. They must exempt themselves from their own critique in order to make their critique. One can claim that words cannot refer

---

G. R. Osborne, "Historical Narrative and Truth in the Bible," *JETS* 48 (2005): 673–88. To defend the use of narrative in historiography is not to imply that there are no potential problems in this realm. For an insightful discussion of the many ways in which scholars can fall into a number of logical fallacies when working with the narrative form, see D. H. Fischer, *Historians' Fallacies: Toward a Logic of Historical Thought* (New York: Harper & Row, 1970), 131–63.

11. M. Shermer and A. Grobman, *Denying History: Who Says the Holocaust Never Happened and Why Do They Say It?* (Berkeley: University of California Press, 2000), 29. On the issue of the Holocaust, see also the interviews with Georg Iggers and Jörn Rüsen in Domanska, ed., *Encounters*, 112, 186.

beyond themselves only by presupposing that the words involved in this claim at least *can* and *do* refer beyond themselves.[12]

Seeking Historical Truth in a Postmodern Context

In light of criticisms such as these, many scholars justifiably argue that the ideal of objectivity in historiography (and other fields) must not be abandoned. This is not to say that anyone is advocating a return to a naive, uncritical, "commonsense" view of the historical project such as was sometimes espoused in the past—namely, the view that historiography is simply a matter of "getting at the (uninterpreted) facts." Along with many others, we contend that it is entirely possible to do critical historiography in a way that embraces the legitimate insights of the postmodern linguistic turn without abandoning historical realism and/or the ideal of objectivity. As J. H. Hexter argued several years before White proposed his history-as-verbal-fiction theory, one can embrace the truth that historiography (like other cognitive endeavors) is inextricably tied to rhetoric without conceding it is *nothing but* rhetoric—that is, without abandoning the commitment to understand "the past as it actually was."[13] Similarly, Keith Windschuttle argues that there is no problem with the claim that "history is a form of literature." The problem arises only when one goes further and argues that "history is *nothing more* than a form of literature."[14]

In our postmodern context, we suggest that contemporary historians can still learn an important balance from Thomas Carlyle. Wrestling with the awareness that historical research is strongly influenced by subjective and sociological factors, he concluded:

> Such considerations truly were of small profit, did they, instead of teaching us vigilance and reverent humility in our inquiries into History, abate our esteem for them, or discourage us from unweariedly prosecuting them.[15]

---

12. Another interesting, ironic line of criticism should be noted. Some have suggested that the radical postmodern rejection of anything like objective "truth" may signal a last attempt of certain dominant forces in Western academia to have the final say on the matter. F. E. Mascia-Lees, P. Sharpe, and C. Ballerino Cohen have argued that "when Western white males—who traditionally have controlled the production of knowledge—can no longer define the truth . . . their response is to conclude that there is not a truth to be discovered" ("The Postmodernist Turn in Anthropology: Cautions from a Feminist Perspective," *Signs* 15 [1989]: 15). In a similar vein see also H. Gengenbach, "Truth-Telling and the Politics of Women's Life History Research in Africa: A Reply to Kirk Hoppe," *International Journal of African Historical Studies* 27 (1994): 619–27.

13. J. H. Hexter, *Doing History* (Bloomington: Indiana University Press, 1971), 75.

14. Windschuttle, *Killing of History*, 227. Similarly, F. Watson correctly observes: "Historical discourse's assumption of a subordinate relationship to a prior historical reality precludes a purely literary or rhetorical analysis which abstracts from the intention to speak truthfully about the past" (*Text and Truth: Redefining Biblical Theology* [Grand Rapids: Eerdmans, 1997], 42). For one example of a historian wrestling to find this middle ground, see Carr, "The Historian and His Facts," in *What Is History?* 3–35. Tucker wisely proposes that, while philosophy of historiography has in recent times "given way to literary theory as the major meta-historiographic discipline," the discipline would be far better served by taking its cue from recent lessons in the philosophy of science ("Theory of Historiography," 634–35).

15. T. Carlyle, "On History" (1830); cited in Haskell, *Objectivity Is Not Neutrality*, 1.

Considerations about the difficulty of striving for objective truth have value only if they serve to make us more vigilant and humble in striving for objective truth. Of course, the concept of "objective history" is an ideal, and as such, it can only be approached asymptotically. But it is this practically unattainable goal that alone renders intelligible our attempts to think and speak about the past as well as our most basic intuitions about this speaking and thinking (e.g., that not all historiographical perspectives are equally valid).[16]

N. T. Wright offers an insightful and balanced approach to this issue as it concerns historical-Jesus research when he writes: "The fact that somebody, standing somewhere, with a particular point of view, is knowing something does not mean that the knowledge is less valuable." Rather, he argues, this is simply *what it means* to know something. There is no knowledge that is not from "a particular point of view." He continues: "The fear that 'actual events' will disappear beneath a welter of particular people's perceptions" if we grant that subjective considerations factor into all our assessments "is . . . to be rejected as groundless." And he thus concludes:

> It must be asserted most strongly that to discover that a particular writer has a "bias" tells us nothing whatever about the value of the information he or she presents. It merely bids us be aware of the bias (and of our own, for that matter), and to assess the material according to as many sources as possible.[17]

Presuppositions and Methodology

This is in essence the methodological stance we shall assume throughout this book. We readily confess that, like everyone else, we approach this topic with a set of presuppositions and a priori commitments that influence our work. But we do not grant that this necessarily entails that neither we nor anybody else can make progress in moving asymptotically toward the ideal of "objective history." As Thomas Haskell has effectively argued, "objectivity is not neutrality."[18]

That which empowers scholars in principle to transcend their personal and sociological biases and make claims about reality is a resolute and uncompromising commitment to apprehend truth. As deconstructionists in particular have forcefully argued, it cannot be denied that it is easy for all of us to convince ourselves that we are looking for truth when in fact we are merely seeking security and/or

---

16. For a helpful discussion of historical "objectivity" after the postmodern critique, see T. L. Haskell, "Objectivity Is Not Neutrality: Rhetoric versus Practice in Peter Novick's *That Noble Dream*," in *Objectivity Is Not Neutrality*, 145–73. In this book, Haskell argues for a "sober fallibilism," and against the "presumptuousness on stilts" of radical postmodernism that argues "how things really are is that nothing but language or discourse is real" (p. 9).

17. Wright, *New Testament and People of God*, 89. We will discuss the biases of the Synoptic authors in chap. 9.

18. Haskell, *Objectivity Is Not Neutrality*.

power. For example, the most honest and insightful New Testament practitioners of the historical-critical method have always recognized that the method itself was never merely a tool for the doing of objective historiography. Rather, it was also—from the beginning—a "weapon of liberation" from ecclesial bondage.[19] However, to say it is "easy" to allow the historiographical enterprise to be used primarily as a mask for hidden, oppressive agendas is not to say it is "inevitable." The only way this self-serving subjectivism can be resisted, and thus the only way we can continue to claim with integrity that we are concerned with approaching, however asymptotically, objective truth, is by placing our commitment to pursue truth above everything else and then submitting our conclusions to the wider world for critical evaluation.

As we shall argue in chapter 1, this means that we must be willing to subject *everything*—including and especially our philosophical and religious presuppositions and a priori commitments—to the rigorous criticism of other truth-seekers. Everything must be considered fair game for conversation amid the community of critically minded scholars. Thus, while the historical-critical method has tended to operate with the unassailable naturalistic presupposition that miracles do not occur, we will argue that a *truly* critical historical method is one that allows this (and every other) foundational assumption to be subjected to criticism.[20] For example, a truly historical-critical method must, among other things, allow non-Western cultural perspectives that countenance the supernatural to challenge the Western naturalistic perspective.[21]

19. W. A. Meeks, "Why Study the New Testament," *NTS* 51 (2005): 157. See also the very frank confession of Helmut Koester on this matter: "Epilogue: Current Issues in New Testament Scholarship," in *The Future of Early Christianity: Essays in Honor of Helmut Koester*, ed. B. A. Pearson (Minneapolis: Fortress, 1991), 474.

20. Even to speak of "the" historical-critical method—as if there were a single agreed upon historical method within the New Testament guild—is, of course, problematic. As Meeks notes, the so-called historical-critical method "is not a *method* at all but a family of approaches and habits, a variable set of perspectives, in short a *practice*" ("Why Study," 159). On this point see also P. S. Minear, *The Bible and the Historian: Breaking the Silence about God in Biblical Studies* (Nashville: Abingdon, 2002), 189.

21. For example, African New Testament scholar S. Oyinbye Abogunrin argues that the African worldview is a much more similar—and appropriate—conceptual context from which to engage the New Testament than is the Western secular worldview. See "The Synoptic Gospel Debate: A Re-Examination from an African Perspective," in *The Interrelations of the Gospels*, ed. D. L. Dungan (Leuven: Peeters, 1990), 386–87; see also idem, "The Modern Search of the Historical Jesus and Christianity in Africa," *African Theological Journal* 9 (1980): 26. Here, New Testament scholars could learn from similar discussions/debates among contemporary historians of Africa. There is, for example, a growing awareness that secular Western (particularly certain ideologically driven social-scientific) presuppositions have largely controlled the doing of African history in the modern world—even for Africans themselves who may, in other realms of life, hold to vastly different perspectives. On this matter of "epistemological ethnocentrism," see W. MacGaffey, "Epistemological Ethnocentrism in African Studies," in *African Historiographies: What History for Which Africa?* ed. B. Jewsiewicki and D. Newbury (Beverly Hills, CA: Sage, 1986), 42–48; idem, "African History, Anthropology, and the Rationality of Natives," *History in Africa* 5 (1978): 101–20. The manner in which this sort of secular Western epistemological imperialism can invade one's work even without notice is truly remarkable. For example, while the historian of Africa

As we shall see throughout this work, this particular example of a truly critical approach is especially important in that the naturalistic assumption that the portrait(s) of the miracle-working Jesus in the Gospels *cannot be* rooted in history is, to a large extent, what leads legendary-Jesus theorists to conclude that the Gospels' portrait of Jesus *is not* rooted in history. As noted above, our counterargument is that if one will allow the Western naturalistic assumptions to be called into question, and thus if one remains open to the *genuine historical possibility* that the Synoptic portrait(s) of Jesus is substantially rooted in history, one will find there are compelling grounds for concluding that this portrait is historically *plausible*—that it is more probable than not that this general portrait is rooted in history.

At the same time, what is good for the goose is good for the gander. The authors of this work obviously bring their own religious and philosophical presuppositions to the enterprise. We must equally be willing to make these presuppositions and prior commitments clear and open them up for criticism. In brief, we believe that a personal Creator God exists. We also are convinced that God occasionally acts in the world in ways that fall outside the regular patterns of the natural order. That is to say, we are convinced that a spiritual (i.e., supernatural) realm exists and that, at times, personal agents within this realm act in ways that are evident, if unexpected, in the physical realm—that is, "miracles" can and do occur. For a variety of reasons, most of which shall be spelled out in this present work, we have also been convinced that the Jesus story told in the Christian Scriptures is rooted in history. Stemming from this and a host of other reasons, we have concluded that the Jesus of history is the very revelation of the Creator God. We believe, in other words, that the Gospels are not only historically grounded but also that their central message is *theologically* true.

Not only this, but we conduct our present research as individuals who have experienced (what we interpret to be) the reality of the risen Jesus in our lives. Indeed, our worldview has been powerfully shaped by our "religious" experience and by the Christian story as a whole. On top of all this, we readily confess that we approach this particular task as academics who have already had a good deal of experience wrestling with philosophical and historical objections to the Christian faith and who have, to our own satisfaction at least, discovered plausible answers for most of these objections. Thus, while we strive to approach our present research with a commitment to apprehending truth in the sense that we are genuinely open to having our presuppositions and commitments, as well as our particular findings, subjected to criticism—namely, we hope our quest for truth trumps our concern for security and/or power—we obviously are, in fact, far from neutral in how we now evaluate the evidence. Like everybody else, we approach our research with a bias.

Bogumil Jewsiewicki rightly decries this intellectual imperialism within modern approaches to African historiography, he does so on the basis of an alternative postmodern approach that is no less indebted to a secular Western (in this case poststructuralist) ideology. See his "Introduction: One Historiography or Several? A Requiem for Africanism," in *African Historiographies*, 9–17.

Yet, we do not believe the Christian faith bias we bring to our work jeopardizes our goal of asymptotically arriving at "objective history" any more than does the alternative bias of any other historian. The question is not whether we have biases: we all do. The question rather is, do we, as a matter of method and principle, strive to place our quest for truth ahead of our personal biases? Is our concern for truth in principle greater than, say, our concern for security and/or maintaining our current perspective at all costs? Do we allow our biases to predetermine our conclusions even in the face of clear and substantial counterevidence, or are we willing to allow evidence and alternative arguments to challenge our biases and possibly modify our conclusions? With our presuppositions and prior commitments on the table, we can only challenge ourselves with the always-asymptotic goal of arriving at as accurate a view of history as possible. The extent to which we are successful in following through on this challenge must be decided by the reader and the broader academic community.

What Constitutes the Legendary-Jesus Thesis?

The second thing we need to do before embarking on our investigation is to specify what constitutes the legendary-Jesus thesis we are engaging in this book. To accomplish this, it will prove helpful to break down the wide variety of views regarding the Jesus of history found in New Testament scholarship today into four broad (and admittedly overly simplistic) categories. This spectrum of viewpoints is, of course, ideal-typical in nature and is offered merely as a useful heuristic.

1. Scholars such as Bruno Bauer, Arthur Drews, and G. A. Wells have argued that the Jesus tradition is virtually—perhaps *entirely*—fictional in nature (i.e., "legendary" as we are using the term).[22] Indeed, it might be more accurate to refer to this position as the mythic-Jesus thesis rather than the legendary-Jesus thesis inasmuch as in common parlance "myth" tends to connote a story that is without any historical foundation, while "legend" tends to connote a fictitious story that revolves around an ostensibly historical figure. In any event, this view holds that we have no good grounds for thinking any aspect of the Jesus narrative is rooted in history, including the very existence of an actual historical person named Jesus. Some scholars we could include in this category, such as Robert Price, would back off this thesis slightly and argue that we simply lack sufficient

---

22. B. Bauer, *Kritik der evangelischen Geschichte der Synoptiker*, 2 vols. (Leipzig: Wigand, 1841). Bauer's work remains untranslated. On Bauer's critique of the Gospels and its influence, see Z. Rosen, *Bruno Bauer and Karl Marx: The Influence of Bruno Bauer on Marx's Thought* (The Hague: Nijhoff, 1977), 45–61. A. Drews, *The Christ Myth*, 3rd ed., trans. C. D. Burns (1810; repr., Amherst, NY: Prometheus, 1998). G. A. Wells, *The Historical Evidence for Jesus* (Buffalo, NY: Prometheus, 1982); idem, *The Jesus Legend* (LaSalle, IL: Open Court, 1996); idem, *The Jesus Myth* (Chicago: Open Court, 1999).

information to decide whether a historical Jesus existed. Here, a sort of "Jesus agnosticism" emerges.[23]

2. The work of scholars such as Rudolf Bultmann and Burton Mack suggests that we have enough evidence plausibly to conclude that an actual historical person named Jesus existed.[24] But, they insist, the reports we have of him are so unreliable and saturated with legend and "myth" that we can confidently ascertain very little historical information about him.

3. An increasingly common view among New Testament scholars today— especially scholars who stand in the post-Bultmannian tradition—is that historical research can indeed disclose a core of historical facts about Jesus. But, they argue, the Jesus we find at this historical core is significantly different from the legendary view presented in the New Testament. Most significantly, scholars in this group grant that the Gospels' reports about the authoritative claims made by Jesus as well as the miracles he performed—those aspects of the Gospels' portrait(s) of Jesus that shaped what came to be known as the orthodox Christian faith—are, by and large, part of the legendary, not the historical, Gospel material. Robert Funk and J. D. Crossan are well-known examples of scholars who espouse a version of this position.[25]

4. A fourth and final group of scholars argue that positions 1–3 are overly skeptical toward the Gospel material.[26] As with position 3, these scholars maintain that historical research can indeed disclose a good deal of reliable information about the historical Jesus. But, in contrast to position 3, scholars such as John Meier and N. T. Wright argue that the Jesus who can be recovered through responsible historical investigation is, generally speaking, fairly reflected in the portrait(s) of the Synoptic Gospels.[27] One important factor that commonly seems to distinguish

23. R. M. Price, *Deconstructing Jesus* (Amherst, NY: Prometheus, 2000), 17. Price further works through his "Jesus agnosticism" in idem, *The Incredible Shrinking Son of Man: How Reliable Is the Gospel Tradition?* (Amherst, NY: Prometheus, 2003).

24. R. Bultmann, *Jesus and the Word*, trans. L. P. Smith and E. H. Lantero (New York: Scribner, 1958), 8; idem, *Jesus Christ and Mythology* (New York: Scribner, 1958); B. Mack, *A Myth of Innocence: Mark and Christian Origins* (Philadelphia: Fortress, 1988); idem, *The Christian Myth: Origins, Logic, and Legacy* (New York: Continuum, 2003), esp. chaps. 1 and 2.

25. R. Funk, *Honest to Jesus: Jesus for a New Millennium* (San Francisco: HarperSanFrancisco, 1996); idem, "The Once and Future Jesus," in the Jesus Seminar's *The Once and Future Jesus* (Santa Rosa, CA: Polebridge, 2000), 5–25. J. D. Crossan, *The Historical Jesus: The Life of a Mediterranean Jewish Peasant* (San Francisco: HarperSanFrancisco, 1992); idem, *Jesus: A Revolutionary Biography* (San Francisco: HarperSanFancisco, 1995).

26. There are, of course, even more "conservative" positions taken on these matters, but with these positions typically there comes a general disregard for serious historical Jesus research. We will, therefore, not be placing these perspectives on our ideal-typical map.

27. J. P. Meier, *A Marginal Jew: Rethinking the Historical Jesus*, vol. 1: *The Roots of the Problem and the Person* (New York: Doubleday, 1991); idem, *A Marginal Jew*, vol. 2: *Mentor, Message, and Miracles* (New York: Doubleday, 1994); idem, *A Marginal Jew*, vol. 3: *Companions and Competitors* (New York: Doubleday, 2001). N. T. Wright, *New Testament and the People of God*; idem, *Jesus and the Victory of God* (Minneapolis: Fortress, 1996); idem, *The Resurrection of the Son of God* (Minneapolis: Fortress, 2003).

scholars in this camp from those in the previous group is the significant degree to which they take seriously the *Jewishness* (religiously as well as ethnically) of both Jesus and his cultural context.

This fourth grouping, like the others, is quite broad in terms of representative perspectives. One point at which proponents within this camp differ involves the manner in which they treat the ostensive supernatural elements within the Gospels' portrait(s) of Jesus. Still, despite the differences, there is something of a broad-based agreement among the scholars we would place in this camp. On the one hand, they agree that, by definition, the discipline of historiography within which they work deals with probabilities (not certainties) and stops with the description of events that are empirically attested in the historical record. On the other hand, they agree that the modern Western secular worldview is but one of many and that extraordinary events can and do occur in history that cannot be explained in terms of any human agency or natural force. They agree that to attempt to identify and discuss the "supernatural" agency behind such events is to move from the realm of history to that of theology and/or philosophy and therefore is not a project for the historian qua historian. However, they likewise agree that such matters are ripe for investigation and that the historical evidence can lead one to the conclusion that events interpreted within the Jesus tradition as miraculous did, in fact, occur in history—and did so in ways that cannot be reduced to metaphor, psychosomatics, and so on.[28] In brief, they do not believe

---

28. For representative statements to this effect, see Meier, *Marginal Jew*, 2:511–21; Wright, *New Testament and the People of God*, 92–93. Some scholars, of course, are difficult to place in our schema. For example, E. P. Sanders sounds like a thoroughgoing naturalist when he states that "the 'miracles' that actually happen are things we cannot yet explain, because of ignorance of the range of natural causes." Yet, when it comes to the resurrection of Jesus—stating that he regards the resurrection appearances of the disciples as "a fact," and that what "the reality was that gave rise to the experiences I do not know"—he seems to operate with an epistemological humility that could leave open the possibility of a supernatural agency. See *The Historical Figure of Jesus* (New York: Lane/Penguin, 1993), 143, 280. Similarly, although Marcus Borg states that he rejects the "supernatural intervention" explanation of Jesus's miracles, he is equally convinced that a reductionist (i.e., psychosomatic) interpretation is unable to account for the historical phenomena. See "Jesus before and after Easter: Jewish Mystic and Christian Messiah," in M. Borg and N. T. Wright, *The Meaning of Jesus: Two Visions* (San Francisco: HarperSanFrancisco, 1999), 66–67. Incidentally, Borg's two "problems" with the supernatural interventionist model (p. 259n35)—namely that it infers that God is "out there," thus "not normally here," and that it cannot explain why God intervenes sometimes and not others (i.e., the problem of evil)—have been cogently addressed by a number of scholars who find the supernatural model to be compelling. The first problem is easily solved by pointing out that the supernatural model does not require holding that to talk of God being "up in heaven" and "intervening on earth" necessarily implies a literal metaphysical statement of God's localization. Locating God "above" in this metaphorical manner offers a way to express his exalted status. Even the New Testament does not harden these categories—e.g., Acts 17:28 offers a different, more immanent image of God, in whom "we live and move and have our being." Borg's second problem has been carefully addressed by any number of theologians. Regarding the specific question of unanswered prayer, see, e.g., G. A. Boyd, *Satan and the Problem of Evil* (Downers Grove, IL: InterVarsity, 2001), chap. 7. Note: Boyd's articulation of the variables involved in the question of unanswered prayer does not depend on an "open" view of divine foreknowledge, as some have thought. Rather, this view can be entertained by any theology that allows

that critical historiography should be allowed to a priori *rule out* the possibility of an extraordinary occurrence, one that, in the specific sense just described, can legitimately be termed "supernatural." At the same time, they strive to be clear when they are talking as critical historians and when they have moved to the doing of theology.[29]

The goal of this book is to explore and defend the broad position of this last group of scholars over and against the various forms of what we are calling the "legendary-Jesus thesis." Thus, by "legendary-Jesus thesis" we are referring particularly to the views advocated by groups 1–3 outlined above. Again, we do not thereby want in any way to minimize the enormous differences that exist between the positions of these three groups. Indeed, we will emphasize these differences when appropriate. Yet, despite these significant differences, these three groups share one conviction in common, and it is this conviction we will be assessing throughout this book: namely, the conviction that the Synoptic portrait(s) of Jesus is substantially, if not entirely, legendary—that is, for the most part, it is historically inaccurate.

The Case for the Legendary-Jesus Thesis

It is time to provide an overview of the cumulative case that can be made for the legendary-Jesus thesis, and thereby, at the same time, offer an outline for our critical assessment of this view. At least eight major lines of argument commonly are employed by legendary-Jesus theorists in defense of their various perspectives.

Naturalism

As Van Harvey notes, it was commonplace for "naïve and mythologically minded" people in ancient times to attribute "unusual events of nature and history . . . to supernatural beings of all kinds." These people "lived in a mythological time . . . without any conception of natural order or law."[30] But times have changed, Harvey and others argue. Our post-Enlightenment, Western worldview is incurably naturalistic. We modern Westerners thus understand

---

for a general—as opposed to a meticulous—understanding of the operations of divine sovereignty. The question of contemporary historiography and the supernatural will be further explored in chap. 1.

29. Many within this camp would argue that the historical evidence for the trustworthiness of the Gospels' portrait of Jesus is an important part of the evidentiary basis by which one can confidently move beyond the historical evidence itself and embrace the theological claims of the Gospel authors—e.g., that Jesus performed his miracles by the power of God, that he was the Son of God and Savior of the world, etc. However, they would tend to make it clear that, in doing so, one has moved beyond the mere bounds of historiographical inquiry and is making use of resources that fall within the domains of theology and philosophy.

30. V. A. Harvey, *The Historian and the Believer: The Morality of Historical Knowledge and Christian Belief* (Philadelphia: Westminster, 1966), 10.

nature, as well as history, to operate according to natural laws of cause and effect.[31]

Hence, while modern Westerners might yet find spiritual value in ancient myths and legends, they cannot any longer accept them as historical, whether they are found in a cherished sacred book like the Bible or any other source. In the words of Harvey, "We cannot see the world as the first century saw it. . . . We have, as it were, bitten of the apple. . . . [O]ur eyes have been opened and our memories are indelibly stamped with the new vision of reality."[32] There simply is no place for supernatural interventions in this "new vision of reality." In the words of Jesus Seminar founder Robert Funk, the ancient view that "God interferes with the order of nature from time to time in order to aid or punish is no longer credible."[33]

Not only do modern Westerners find it impossible to believe in supernatural occurrences, it is argued, but as a matter of principle they should not accept explanations that appeal to the supernatural even if we *could* still believe in them. Most progress made in the modern sciences has been the result of a community of academics relentlessly looking for natural explanations, refusing to accept appeals to supernatural forces. To reverse this stance and accept appeals to supernatural influence would be to undermine the heart of modern science and functionally return to the "naive" and "mythical" mind-set of antiquity. There is, therefore, a sort of intellectual, even ethical, obligation—at least on the part of scholars and scientists—to commit to accepting only naturalistic explanations for events.[34]

There are other reasons for embracing naturalism as well, according to various scholars. First, the only way we can understand the past is by drawing analogies with the present (this is, in essence, Troelsch's famous "principle of analogy"). Since it is assumed that people do not experience supernatural occurrences in the present, it arguably follows that we have no analogical way of assessing reports of supernatural occurrences in the past. As a matter of principle, therefore, they must be dismissed.

31. We do not want to minimize the significantly different ways the physical sciences and the historical and sociological sciences are naturalistically oriented. Explaining human behaviors in terms of motivations is very different from explaining physical causes and effects. When throughout this book we claim that certain Western historians employ a "naturalistic" methodology, we do not thereby necessarily want to attribute to them the view that all human behavior can be exhaustively reduced to the laws of physics. We mean only that they rule out on an a priori basis any appeals to the supernatural, just as the physical sciences do.

32. Harvey, *Historian and Believer*, 115.

33. R. Funk, "Twenty-one Theses," *Fourth R* (July–August 1998): 8. Similarly, Bishop John Shelby Spong argues, "The miracle stories of the New Testament can no longer be interpreted in a post-Newtonian world as supernatural events performed by an incarnate deity" ("Christ and the Body of Christ," in *Once and Future Jesus*, 75).

34. "It was," Van Harvey argues, "just the [critical] assessment of fantastic reports—reports of the 'impossible'—in the light of knowledge produced by the sciences that accounts for the emergence of the very important categories of myth and legend which play such a crucial role in modern historical inquiry" (*Historian and Believer*, 75).

Second, some have argued that accepting that a law of nature has been momentarily suspended—that is, that a "miracle" has occurred—is intrinsically irrational, regardless of what supposed evidence can be marshaled for it. As David Hume argued, the probability that a reported miracle took place must be measured against the probability that it did not, and all our experience weighs in on the side that it did not. So, for example, the probability that Jesus actually rose from the dead must be assessed as one fractioned against all known instances of people confirming the natural law that dead people do not come back to life. In other words, it must be considered incalculably improbable, such that no conceivable historical evidence or argumentation could possibly suggest otherwise.

All this implies that a scholarly approach to the New Testament cannot, in principle, accept as historical the supernatural aspects of the Gospel portrait(s) of Jesus. We must rather interpret these stories as legendary, essentially no different from the multitude of other fabricated legends we find in all ancient cultures. We will further develop and assess this line of argument in chapter 1 ("Miracles and Method").

Hellenistic Judaism

Often, it is not difficult to explain how ancient people came to believe the myths and legends they embraced. Myths and legends typically fit well with the cultural beliefs of the people who hold them, while serving a discernible sociological function. Thus, a great deal hangs on whether one thinks the religious/cultural milieu of first-century Judaism—especially the Galilean Judaism out of which the Jesus movement arose—was conducive to the sort of fabricated myth-making that legendary-Jesus theorists assume can account for the claims we find in the Gospels. For example, does the idea of a miracle-working *divine man* fit the cultural beliefs of first-century Palestinian Jews? The legendary-Jesus thesis is much more plausible if we can answer this question in the affirmative than if we must answer it in the negative.

Christian apologists have traditionally argued for a negative response to this question. First-century Judaism—including Galilean Judaism—was not conducive to embracing the notion of a divine man. After all, it has been argued, first-century Jews were, on the whole, creational monotheists for whom the very idea of a man in some sense sharing Yahweh's exalted status was anathema. It is partly for this reason that Christian apologists have argued that we need to look beyond common sociological explanations to account for how the early Jewish Christian view of Jesus as the miracle-working embodiment of Yahweh-God arose.

Legendary-Jesus theorists, however, have argued that recent historical evidence has rendered this line of argumentation unpersuasive. Often, they maintain that the evidence instead suggests that the religio-cultural worldview of first-century Jews, including Galilean Jews, was not very different from the worldview of their first-century pagan neighbors.

For example, we now possess literary and archaeological evidence that some ancient Jews practiced magic and astrology. Among other things, we have found ancient synagogues decorated with Zodiac symbols and other pagan depictions. A Galilean synagogue has been unearthed that contains a floor mosaic of the Greek god Helios surrounded by a twelve-month Zodiac wheel. This suggests that ancient Palestinian Jews were much more hellenized, even paganized, than many previously thought.

Just as significantly, there is some literary evidence that the once unassailable line between Yahweh and created beings had become somewhat blurred prior to the time of Jesus. High-ranking angels, exalted patriarchs, and personified divine attributes (e.g., Wisdom) were sometimes spoken of in terms that traditionally were reserved for Yahweh alone. We also find examples of Jews referring to various heroes as supernaturally empowered "divine men" (*theios aner*), a concept that was used in Greco-Roman contexts to refer to people who were believed to share in both human and divine qualities. This arguably suggests that the once rigid monotheism of some ancient Jews had become more "flexible" by the time of Jesus.

In light of considerations such as these, legendary-Jesus advocates argue, it seems we have little reason to think it more unlikely that certain first-century Jews evolved and embraced a legend about a miracle-working divine man than that pagans did so. We thus need not look beyond shared sociological forces to explain the birth of Christianity. We will develop and assess this line of argumentation in chapter 2 ("A Jewish Legend of 'Yahweh Embodied'?").

Legendary Parallels to the Jesus Story

A number of scholars go beyond the general argument that first-century Judaism was a conducive environment for a legend about a divine man to arise and argue that we can plausibly identify the specific religious and cultural sources that gave rise to the Jesus legend. For example, Robert Price argues that the ancient Mediterranean world "was hip-deep in religions centering on the death and resurrection of a savior god."[35] He goes on to catalog a variety of examples to show that the "Christ cult" that arose was just another example of these ancient death-and-resurrection religions.

While many have defended the legendary-Jesus thesis on the basis of parallels with ancient Greco-Roman legends and myths, others have defended it on the basis of alleged parallels between the Gospel story of Jesus and various "hero myths"

35. Price, *Deconstructing Jesus*, 86; cf. 92. Examples include the gods Aleyan Baal, Tammuz/Dumuzi, Osiris, Attis, Dionysus, Mithras, and even the Corn King. For Price's discussion of the various Greco-Roman gods that can be used to explain the rise of the Christ cult, see *Deconstructing Jesus*, 86–92. For others who explicitly appeal to the work of the history of religions school, see E. Doherty, "The Jesus Puzzle: Pieces in a Puzzle of Christian Origins," *Journal of Higher Criticism* 4 (1997): 74–75; idem, *The Jesus Puzzle: Did Christianity Begin with a Mythical Christ?* (Ottawa: Canadian Humanist Pub., 1999); and D. Dormeyer, "Beatitudes and Mysteries," in *Ancient and Modern Perspectives on the Bible and Culture: Essays in Honor of Hans Dieter Betz*, ed. A. Yarbro Collins (Atlanta: Scholars Press, 1998), 352.

found throughout history. Indeed, some scholars, such as Price, incorporate elements of both approaches.

One way of analyzing hero myths that has been useful for legendary-Jesus theorists comes from the English folklore specialist Lord Raglan.[36] In Raglan's analysis, hero myths tend to have a number of features in common. For example, the hero's mother is often a royal virgin; his father is usually a king; the circumstances of the hero's conception often are unusual in some way; the hero is often regarded as a "son of a god"; and frequently there is an attempt to kill the hero in his infancy.

Many scholars find strong parallels between Raglan's "hero myth" analysis and the Jesus story of the New Testament. Alan Dundes, for example, argues that all but five of Raglan's list of twenty-two hero myth traits are exemplified in the Jesus story, which ranks Jesus closer to Raglan's ideal hero paradigm than many other legendary heroes.[37] Price goes even further when he argues that "every detail of the [Christ] story fits the mythic hero archetype, with nothing left over." From this Price surmises that it is "arbitrary to assert that there must have been a historical figure lying in back of the myth."[38]

Along similar lines, some scholars argue that the biblical Jesus is largely, if not totally, legendary on the basis of parallels to the Jesus story found in various religious movements throughout history. For example, in the second century CE a cult arose around a man named Apollonius. His followers claimed he performed miracles, even raising a girl from the dead. Some claimed he appeared

36. The theory that there is a distinct genre of myth that surrounds heroes goes back to Edward Taylor. See E. Taylor, *Primitive Culture*, 5th ed., vol. 1: *The Origins of Culture* (1871; repr., New York: Harper, 1958). For a brief history of the hero myth theory, see R. A. Segal, "Introduction: In Quest of the Hero," in O. Rank, Lord Raglan, and A. Dundes, *In Quest of the Hero* (Princeton: Princeton University Press, 1990), vii–xli. To date, three influential theories of the hero myth have been proposed, each suggesting a particular pattern. First, Otto Rank (a Viennese psychoanalyst; 1884–1939) developed a Freudian interpretation of the hero myth that emphasized the myth as a covert symbolic fulfillment of the Oedipal wish. See O. Rank, "The Myth of the Birth of the Hero," in Rank, Raglan, and Dundes, *In Quest of the Hero*, 3–86. Second, Joseph Campbell (American scholar of myths; 1904–87) offered a Jungian-influenced analysis of the hero myth. The hero myth functions to discover and express a latent side of one's personality. See Campbell, *The Hero with a Thousand Faces*, 2nd ed. (1949; repr., Princeton: Princeton University Press, 1972). Third, taking his cue from the theory of myth-ritualist scholar James Frazer that the ritualized killing of a king was believed to ensure the community's well-being, Lord Raglan (an English folklorist; 1885–1964) constructed a hero myth theory that requires a king. For Raglan, the hero myth—like all myths—is not about any psychological process, but rather is about human beings trying to understand and control their physical environment and the gods responsible for it. See Lord Raglan, "The Hero: A Study in Tradition, Myth, and Drama (Part II)," in Rank, Raglon, and Dundes, *In Quest of the Hero*, 89–175. Since it requires a king, Raglan's hero pattern has been used most often in trying to explain Jesus.

37. Dundes, "The Hero Pattern and the Life of Jesus," *Protocol of the Twenty-fifth Colloquy, Center for Hermeneutical Studies in Hellenistic and Modern Culture, 12 December, 1976* (Berkeley, CA: Center for Hermeneutical Studies in Hellenistic and Modern Culture, 1977), 10.

38. Price, *Deconstructing Jesus*, 259–61. Bultmann appeals to similar mythic hero parallels from the Hellenistic world (*History of the Synoptic Tradition*, 236–41). See also Mack, *Myth of Innocence*, 119.

after his death. And some of his devotees worshipped him as a god.[39] Similarly, in the seventeenth century a man named Sabbatai Svi was hailed as the Messiah, was reported to have done miracles, and was even worshipped as divine by many of his Jewish followers during (or shortly after) his lifetime.[40] So too, an early twentieth-century faith healer in the Congo named Kimbangu is reported to have performed many miracles, including raising people from the dead, and was worshipped as divine by some of his followers during his own lifetime.[41]

According to some legendary-Jesus theorists, phenomena like these demonstrate that there is nothing really unique in the fact that soon after Jesus's death some of his followers report that he did miracles and even came to worship him as God. Hence, we have no more reason to accept the early Christian reports about Jesus as historical than we do reports offered by followers of Apollonius, Sabbatai Svi, Kimbangu, or any other such figure. We shall further develop and assess these lines of argumentation in chapter 3 ("One among Many Legends?").

Silence in Non-Christian Sources

If Jesus performed the feats attributed to him in the Gospels, should we not expect that he would have caught the attention of at least a few pagan writers? Instead, some scholars argue, we find little or no mention of Jesus outside the New Testament. For some—especially the most radical fringe of legendary-Jesus theorists (viz. group 1)—this suggests the miracle-working figure of the Gospels is purely a legend, essentially no different from the mythological savior figures of other ancient mystery religions.

Of course, Christian scholars have long noted that while references to Jesus in non-Christian sources may be meager, they are there to be found. Josephus, Tacitus, Suetonius, Pliny the Younger, Thallus, Celsus, Lucian of Samosata, Mara bar Serapion, and certain Jewish rabbinic traditions all contain some references to Jesus and/or the early Christian movement. Indeed, traditionally it has been argued that some of the information found in these sources corroborates certain aspects of Jesus's life as recorded in the Gospels. Against this, however, the more radical legendary-Jesus theorists argue that each of these references is historically suspect. Some of the passages can be shown to be Christian interpolations, and those that are not interpolations are merely passing on hearsay—what Christians at the time were claiming about Jesus. There is, therefore, no solid evidence of Jesus's existence in any ancient non-Christian sources. We will explore and assess this line of argumentation in chapter 4 ("A Conspiracy of Silence?").

39. On Apollonius see Philostratus, *The Life of Apollonius of Tyana*, trans. F. C. Conybeare (Cambridge, MA: Harvard University Press, 1912).

40. For Price's use of Svi see *Incredible Shrinking*, 29, 133. On Svi see G. Scholem, *Sabbatai Sevi: The Mystical Messiah 1626–1676* (Princeton: Princeton University Press, 1973).

41. Price makes mention of Kimbangu; see *Incredible Shrinking*, 29. On Kimbangu see M.-L. Martin, *Kimbangu: An African Prophet and His Church*, trans. D. M. Moore (Grand Rapids: Eerdmans, 1975).

Silence in Paul

An argument that is especially prevalent among the most radical fringe of legendary-Jesus theorists—namely, defenders of the *mythic*-Jesus thesis—centers on the claim that Paul makes little or no reference to the historical Jesus. According to G. A. Wells, for example,

> [Paul's] letters have no allusion to the parents of Jesus, let alone to the virgin birth. They never refer to a place of birth . . . They give no indication of the time or place of his earthly existence. They do not refer to his trial before a Roman official, nor to Jerusalem as the place of execution. They mentioned neither John the Baptist, nor Judas, nor Peter's denial of his master. . . . These letters also fail to mention any miracles Jesus is supposed to have worked, a particularly striking omission, since, according to the gospels he worked so many.[42]

Scholars such as Wells, Doherty, and Price argue that Paul's view of Jesus was not anything like the recent, contemporary Galilean figure we find in the Gospels. His view of Jesus—which is the earliest view we have—was rather that of a vague cosmic savior figure who existed in the unknown, distant past and/or the mythic spiritual realm. Indeed, the Pauline Christ was actually quite close to the sorts of divinities we find in ancient mystery religions. According to these scholars, this makes it difficult to avoid the conclusion that the earliest Christians viewed Jesus as a sort of vague deity who became historicized as a rather recent figure only after Paul—as oral traditions were passed on and especially when the Gospels were written.

Just as significant for some legendary-Jesus theorists is the alleged claim that Paul rarely if ever quotes Jesus. Indeed, they argue that Paul seems completely unaware of the later Christian notion that Jesus was an ethical teacher.[43] For example, Paul does not cite Jesus when he is dealing with topics that, according to the Gospels, Jesus explicitly taught on. This suggests to some that when Paul wrote there was no memory of Jesus as a teacher. Rather, this too was part of the mythological development of Jesus in the oral traditions of the early church and in the writing of the Gospels. We will further explore this line of argument in chapter 5 ("The 'Silence' of Paul?").

The Free-Form Fabrication of the Oral Jesus Tradition

Regardless of where they stand within the spectrum of views on the historical Jesus, all scholars agree that at least some (if not *all*) of the content of the Gospels initially circulated among the Christian communities in oral form. Legendary-Jesus theorists typically argue that, since oral transmission is inherently free-form

---

42. Wells, *Historical Evidence*, 22.
43. Doherty, *Jesus Puzzle*, 27.

and unstable—and thus historically unreliable—this process of oral transmission was conducive for the development of legendary stories about Jesus.

This argument is grounded in certain basic convictions about the early oral Jesus tradition that have been operative among New Testament critics since the early part of the twentieth century. More specifically, there are six assumptions that have been widely held by scholars who specialize in analyzing the oral forms of literature represented in the Gospels (viz. form critics). Those assumptions are as follows:

- The earliest Christian communities were most likely composed of uneducated and illiterate folk. In any case, they were more interested in preaching the gospel than in writing things down. Thus, they relied solely on oral transmission to pass on the Jesus tradition. This allowed the Jesus tradition to evolve more freely than it otherwise would have.

- Oral traditions cannot pass on lengthy, unified narratives. Hence the narrative framework of the Gospel material should be understood to be mostly, even entirely, the fictitious creation of the Gospel authors.

- Early Christian communities had little or no biographical interest in the life of Jesus but rather were preoccupied with preaching their message of salvation to the world and addressing needs within their communities. Hence, the Gospels tell us more about the "life situation" (*Sitz im Leben*) of the early Christian communities than they do about Jesus.

- Oral traditions are formed and revised primarily by communities, not individuals. If there were any eyewitnesses of the historical Jesus in the early Christian communities, they played little to no regulative role in the transmission of the oral Jesus tradition. Together, these phenomena allowed the tradition to evolve in a highly free-form fashion.

- Oral traditions evolve according to discernible "laws." Hence, we can in many cases work back from the Gospels to discern the original "forms" the Gospel material took and see what role they played in the early church. When we carry this out, we discover once again that the Gospels tell us more about the *Sitz im Leben* of early Jesus communities than they do about Jesus.

- The early church relied heavily on the "inspired revelations" of early church prophets. Much of the material found in the Gospels can be understood as deriving from these "revelations" received and spoken as a means of keeping Jesus relevant to the ever-evolving early Christian communities. This perspective obviously reinforces the conclusion that the Gospel material primarily reflects the life of the early church, not the life of Jesus.

Again, a significant focus of this book involves bringing a variety of interdisciplinary studies surrounding orality to bear on the issue of the nature and reliability of the Jesus tradition. Along these lines we will consider and assess the first three of these six form-critical assumptions in chapter 6 ("Ancient Literacy and Oral Tradition") and address the remaining three in chapter 7 ("Historical Remembrance or Prophetic Imagination?").

The Historical Unreliability of the Gospels

The final set of arguments used to support the legendary-Jesus thesis concerns the written Gospels themselves. One important set of considerations revolves around whether the Gospel authors intended their works to be historical. A number of legendary-Jesus scholars argue that they did not, that their works were rather intended to be read as fictional accounts. Some scholars argue that the Gospels are examples of ancient novels and others that they are examples of Hellenistic mythic epics (e.g., along the lines of Homer's *Odyssey* and *Iliad*) or Jewish midrash. Still other legendary-Jesus scholars concede that the genre of the Gospel may be ancient biography or historiography but nevertheless argue that this does little to buttress our confidence in the reliability of these works since both of these ancient genre were largely unreliable. We assess these arguments in chapter 8 ("The Genre and Nature of the Canonical Gospels").

The Burden of Proof and Beyond

Finally, various legendary-Jesus scholars offer an assortment of other considerations that, to their way of thinking, further support the view that the Jesus of the Synoptic Gospels is substantially, if not entirely, legendary. The simple fact that these works contain reports of supernatural occurrences—the kind of reports we customarily dismiss as legendary when we find them elsewhere—means that these works must be regarded as inherently implausible. Hence, those who consider the Gospels to be historically reliable must bear the burden of proof. From this perspective, it is clear that the Gospels are heavily biased and thus cannot be trusted to pass on anything like reliable history. Moreover, these texts contradict one another and lack serious external corroboration by other literary or archaeological evidence. Hence, it is claimed, we have every reason to conclude they are not works that can be trusted to pass on reliable reports about the Jesus of history. We will consider this set of arguments in chapter 9 ("Evaluating the Synoptic Gospels as Historical Sources") and chapter 10 ("The Synoptic Tradition and the Jesus of History"). We turn now to begin this line of assessment. And the place to start, of course, is with the issue of historical methodology.

Part I

Historical Method
and the Jesus Tradition

Miracles, Parallels, and First-Century Palestine

The New Testament accounts of Jesus present him as a radically unique individual. Indeed, according to the Gospel authors, his uniqueness extends to the realm of the supernatural, for Jesus is presented as the miracle-working, resurrected Son of Man/God. Part 1 of this work explores the question of whether—and, if so, in what manner and to what extent—these claims about Jesus can or cannot be investigated within the context of a critical historiography.

Scholars who contend that the portrait of Jesus in the Gospels is substantially legendary—those we are categorizing as "legendary-Jesus theorists"—uniformly argue that one cannot be a critical historical scholar while also accepting supernatural explanations for past events. While mythologically minded people of previous ages routinely explained unusual occurrences by appealing to supernatural forces, it is no longer possible for post-Enlightenment, critically minded scholars to do so. Thus, whatever critical scholars make of the Jesus tradition, legendary-Jesus theorists argue that, as a matter of principle, they cannot accept the reportedly supernatural occurrences of the Gospels as reflective of the actual past. Rather, these reports of supernatural events associated with Jesus clearly must be judged to be legendary (i.e., fictional) creations. We will discuss the complexities of this question in chapter 1.

If we accept that a truly critical approach to history requires us to a priori rule out all claims of supernatural occurrences in history, how are we to account for the swift rise of faith in Jesus as a miracle-working, resurrected divine savior in a first-century Jewish context? Here much depends on how one understands the first-century Jewish context. Legendary-Jesus theorists sometimes argue that the first-century Jewish context was actually a fairly natural environment for a legend about a wonder-working divine man to arise, for Judaism was significantly hellenized at this time. If so, we need not suppose there was anything so unique in the rise of the Jesus story that the sorts of explanations offered in the Gospels themselves are required to explain it. We will explore this issue in chapter 2.

Finally, many legendary-Jesus scholars argue that New Testament claims associated with Jesus are not without precedent in history and thus are not that difficult to explain. It is argued that throughout history we find other instances where recent figures reportedly made divine claims, performed miracles, and even rose from the dead. In chapter 3 we will investigate the case for accepting that certain legends parallel the Jesus story and that this helps us explain the Jesus tradition in purely natural, sociological/comparativist terms.

1

MIRACLES AND METHOD

THE HISTORICAL-CRITICAL METHOD
AND THE SUPERNATURAL

The Gospels claim that Jesus and his disciples performed miracles such as healing the sick and disabled, casting out demons, and even raising the dead.[1] To the
thinking of many historical-critical scholars, this is enough to demonstrate that

1. Some scholars are understandably hesitant to discuss the issue of miracles within the categories of
"natural" vs. "supernatural." Two criticisms tend to emerge here. First, these classifications can foster the
modernist bifurcation of reality into two artificially constructed realms that are separated by an unbridgeable gulf. Second, with respect to biblical studies, these categories represent an anachronism that would
be largely unrecognizable to ancient people. See, e.g., N. T. Wright, *The New Testament and the People of
God* (Minneapolis: Fortress, 1992), 97; J. P. Meier, *A Marginal Jew: Rethinking the Historical Jesus*, vol. 2:
Mentor, Message, and Miracles (New York: Doubleday, 1994), 524–25n5. However, instead of dropping
these common categories, we will use them with three qualifications assumed.

First, while the modernist project tended to construe the realms as self-contained and mutually
exclusive, there is no reason to think this is the case. One can speak of a conceptual boundary without
imagining an impenetrable barrier. In fact, developments in modern physics offer intriguing prospects
for imagining the fluid interaction between these two worlds (e.g., see the discussion of the Divine Action Project below).

Second, once the idea of a hard and fast barrier between the "natural" and "supernatural" worlds is
removed from the distinction, one can find common ground between these contemporary notions and
similar ideas in the ancient world. As we will discuss below, many ancient peoples were far more savvy
about the "miraculous" than we often give them credit for. In any case, it is safe to say that ancient peoples
in general were quite aware of the difference between the idea/experience of common, predictable (i.e.,

they are substantially legendary. The purpose of this chapter is to argue that this conclusion is unwarranted, for the historical-critical method that leads to it is problematic on a number of counts. In its place we will propose the outlines of a critical historiographical methodology that avoids these problems and therefore remains open to the possibility that reports of supernatural occurrences are, in some cases, reliable. We will call this the "open" historical-critical method.

We will begin by presenting a succinct history and overview of the main lines of argumentation that have been used in support of the classical historical-critical method. We will then offer a critique of the foundational assumption of the histori-cal-critical method, one that forces it to rule out supernatural events as a matter of principle, lay out the main elements of the open historical-critical method we are proposing as an alternative, and respond to four objections that can be raised against it. Having assessed the foundational assumption of the historical-critical method, we will offer a critique of the foundational principle used to defend this method—what is called the "principle of analogy." In its place we will offer an alternative formulation of the principle of analogy that is superior for a number of reasons and does not necessarily rule out the possibility of allowing for historical explanations that include supernatural occurrences. We will then conclude this chapter by drawing together elements of our assessment of the classical historical-critical method while developing further five important aspects of the alternative critical methodology we are advocating.

Naturalism and the Historical-Critical Method

The Rise of Modern Western Science

From the sixteenth to the eighteenth centuries the Western view of the world underwent a radical transformation. We discovered that by treating the universe as a closed system of natural causes and effects operating according to invariant laws, we could understand, predict, and more effectively use nature to our own

"natural") regularities on one hand, and the idea/experience of occasional, unpredictable, and extraordinary (i.e., "supernatural") events on the other.

Third, when we speak of a "supernatural" occurrence throughout this work, we are not thereby including the theological interpretation of the event given by those who record the event, whether this be the Gospel authors or someone else. The theological interpretation given for a supernatural event goes beyond the domain of critical historiographical reasoning, as we shall later argue. Rather, as we shall use the term, a "supernatural occurrence" is simply an event that cannot be plausibly explained in naturalistic terms alone. It is an event that, as far as we can tell, outstrips natural cause-and-effect explanations. We would point out that, while this disciplinary distinction is important to maintain, a good case can be made that once the historiographical enterprise has identified the plausibility of a supernatural occur-rence in history, the question of explanation remains. Thus, in such a case, it is a short logical jump from the conclusions of historiography to the idea of a personal, supernatural agency—i.e., God or some other spirit-entity. On this matter see L. Pearl, "Miracles: The Case for Theism," *American Philosophical Quarterly* 25 (1988): 331–37.

advantage. The remarkable technological advances and increased standard of living the scientific approach to the world has brought us testifies to its general validity and practicality.

The scientific revolution made a profound impact on our understanding of history and therefore of the Bible. Among other things, it greatly affected the understanding of the supernatural on the part of many Western intellectuals. If nature uniformly operates by predictable laws of cause and effect, what are we to make of alleged reports of miracles? To many, the only rational and responsible answer was to reject them. Why should our understanding of history be less scientific than our understanding of the world? Hence, from the seventeenth century on, the general attitude among intellectuals toward ancient reports of supernatural events such as we find in the Gospels was that, as a matter of principle, they had to be judged as fictitious. They might be explained away as myth, as legend, as propaganda, as the result of emotional hysteria, or as hallucinations. But under the impact of the naturalistic, scientific worldview that had come to dominate the outlook of many Western intellectuals, they had to be explained away.

Hume's Case for Naturalism

This general outlook is called "naturalism," for it assumes that everything in the world, and in history, can be explained by appealing to "natural" laws. No appeals to supernatural forces are necessary. Perhaps the most famous philosophical critique of miracles was given by the eighteenth-century Scottish philosopher David Hume. Hume defined a miracle as "a transgression of a law of nature by a particular volition of the Deity, or by the interposition of some invisible agents."[2] With this definition in hand, Hume concluded that it is always irrational to believe a miracle has occurred. To Hume's way of thinking, one must weigh the probability of a claim that a "transgression" of a natural law (a miracle) had occurred against all confirmations of the relevant natural law. The result, of course, was that the alleged "transgression" was always ridiculously improbable and thus, according to Hume, irrational to accept. In Hume's words:

> There must, therefore, be a uniform experience against every miraculous event, otherwise it would not merit this appellation. And as a uniform experience amounts to a proof, there is here a direct and full *proof*, from the nature of the fact, against the experience of any miracle.[3]

2. D. Hume, *An Enquiry concerning Human Understanding*, ed. L. A. Selby-Bigge (1748; repr., Oxford: Clarendon, 1902), 115. How precisely to interpret Hume's argument against miracles is a controversial matter. In recent times, a probabilistic, Bayesian interpretation has been proposed by some. See, e.g., J. H. Sobel, "On the Evidence of Testimony for Miracles: A Bayesian Interpretation of David Hume's Analysis," *Philosophical Quarterly* 37:147 (1987): 166–86; R. D. Holder, "Hume on Miracles: Bayesian Interpretation, Multiple Testimony, and the Existence of God," *British Journal for Philosophy of Science* 49 (1998): 49–65. Where one comes out on this debate is of no real consequence to the gist of this chapter.

3. Hume, *Enquiry*, 115.

For example, consider the claim that Jesus rose from the dead. According to Hume, this claim "transgresses" the consistent empirical observation (the "natural law") that death is irreversible. The claim must therefore be weighed against every observed instance of this law being confirmed—that is, against every instance of people remaining dead. Viewed in this light, the probability of the claim that Jesus rose from the dead is one to the total number of people who have ever died and remained dead. This way of construing the matter obviously makes it irrational to believe that Jesus rose from the dead. Indeed, if accepted, Hume's argument renders all possible historical arguments in favor of Jesus's rising from the dead virtually irrelevant. For no conceivable historical evidence could possibly overturn such an overwhelmingly improbable claim—if, again, Hume's argument is valid.

Troeltsch and the Historical-Critical Method

The general application of the scientific method to the study of history came to be known as the historical-critical method. Like the natural sciences, the historical-critical method operates on the basis of methodological naturalism. That is, the a priori rejection of the supernatural is built into its methodology.[4] For this reason, and to distinguish it from the alternative historical-critical method we shall be proposing later on, we shall henceforth refer to it as the naturalistic—or the classical—historical-critical method. The basic reasoning behind it is that just as the empirical sciences are methodologically committed to looking for natural causes for all phenomena, so critical historians should be methodologically committed to looking for natural explanations for all historical events. And just as advances in science come only by the refusal of scientists to accept supernatural explanations, so, it is argued, advances in our understanding of history come only by critical historians refusing to accept supernatural explanations. However improbable a natural explanation for an event may seem, therefore, it is, as a matter of principle, always to be preferred over a supernatural one. Clearly, as Ernst Troeltsch realized, a "whole world view lies behind the historico-critical method."[5] It is a worldview that assumes that the world is closed to supernatural influences. It is the worldview of naturalism.

Troeltsch articulated three principles that should govern all truly critical historical investigation. These three principles—but especially the second, as we shall see—have exercised an incalculable influence on the application of the historical-critical method among academic historians, including New Testament

4. For helpful discussions of methodological naturalism in the context of historical studies, see R. Martin, *The Elusive Messiah: A Philosophical Overview of the Quest for the Historical Jesus* (Boulder, CO: Westview, 1999), chap. 6, esp. 107–10; D. A. Yerxa, "A Meaningful Past and the Limits of History: Some Reflections Informed by the Science-and-Religion Dialogue," *Fides et Historia* 34 (2002): 13–30.

5. Cited in E. Schillebeeckx, *Jesus: An Experiment in Christology*, trans. H. Hoskins (1974; repr., New York: Seabury, 1979), 38.

scholars. Each of these three principles reinforces the assumption that claims of the miraculous simply cannot be accepted by critical historians.[6]

First, Troeltsch argued for "The Principle of Criticism." This principle holds that all claims about the past can only be more or less probable, never certain. The principle itself is so obvious it would hardly warrant mentioning except for the fact that, when it is combined with Hume's previously mentioned argument regarding the massive improbability of miraculous occurrences, this principle has the effect of reinforcing the assumption that naturalistic explanations are—by definition—always more probable than explanations that involve supernatural occurrences. In other words, if historical explanations are always a matter of probability, and if the probability of a violation of a law of nature is to be assessed by weighing it against all confirmations of that law, then miracles always, by definition, have a probability approaching zero.

Second, and most important, Troeltsch argued for "The Principle of Analogy." This principle holds that our understanding of the past must always be analogically rooted in our experience of the present. Since Troeltsch and most other critical historians assumed people never experience supernatural events in the present, this principle led to the conclusion that it is outside the bounds of critical historiography to ever appeal to the supernatural.

Third, Troeltsch argued for "The Principle of Correlation." This principle explicitly holds that every event must be understood within a nexus of natural causes and effects. In the thinking of Troeltsch and many others, this was a foundational assumption for all truly "critical" history. In the words of Troeltsch's contemporary, F. H. Bradley, "The inevitability of law, and what loosely may be termed as causal connection, is *the condition* which makes history possible, and which, though not for her to prove, she must nonetheless *presuppose* as a principle and demonstrate as a result worked out in the whole field of her activity."[7]

For Bradley, as for Troeltsch and most other modern critical historians, the assumption that all things are governed by natural law is what makes a critical and

6. Ernst Troeltsch's three principles are delineated in his famous 1898 essay, "Historical and Dogmatic Method in Theology," in *Religion in History*, trans. J. L. Adams and W. F. Bense (Minneapolis: Fortress, 1991), 11–32, esp. 13–15. See also E. Troeltsch, "Historiography," in *Encyclopedia of Religion and Ethics*, ed. J. Hastings (New York: Scribner's Sons, 1955), 6:716–23. For two insightful philosophical analyses of Troeltsch's principles and how they have been played out in the historical-critical method, see C. S. Evans, *The Historical Christ and the Jesus of Faith: The Incarnational Narrative as History* (Oxford: Clarendon, 1996), 184–202; A. Plantinga, "Two (or More) Kinds of Scripture Scholarship," in *Behind the Text: History and Biblical Interpretation*, ed. C. Bartholomew et al. (Grand Rapids: Zondervan, 2003), 19–57. See also R. A. Harrisville and W. Sundberg, "Ernst Troeltsch: The Power of Historical Consciousness," in *The Bible in Modern Culture: Baruch Spinoza to Brevard Childs*, 2nd ed. (Grand Rapids: Eerdmans, 2002), 146–68.

7. F. H. Bradley, "The Presuppositions of Critical History," in *Collected Essays* (Oxford: Clarendon, 1969), 21 (emphasis added). As R. G. Collingwood has reminded us, the context out of which Bradley's essay emerged was "the condition of Biblical criticism as developed by the Tübingen school, notably F. C. Baur and David Strauss" (*The Idea of History* [Oxford: Clarendon, 1946], 135). With respect to universal "laws" in nature, see also the influential article by C. G. Hempel, "The Function of General Laws in History," *Journal of Philosophy* 39 (1942): 35–48.

scientific approach to history possible. This assumption, Bradley argues, does not have to be proven: *it is presupposed*. Not surprisingly, the results "worked out in the whole field of her activity" serve to demonstrate the validity of the assumption. The great New Testament scholar, Rudolf Bultmann, advocates the same perspective when he writes, "The historical method includes the presupposition that history is a unity in the sense of a closed continuum of effects. . . . This closedness means that the continuum of historical happenings cannot be rent by the interference of supernatural, transcendent powers and that therefore there is no 'miracle' in this sense of the word."[8]

For Bultmann, and many within the post-Bultmann stream of scholarship, one is a "critical" scholar only if one presupposes that history is a closed continuum of natural causes and effects. To be open to the idea that this "closedness" could be "rent by the interference of supernatural . . . powers" is to violate a working assumption of the historical-critical method.

Van Harvey's Case for a Naturalistic Historiographical Methodology

A more recent thinker who has further explored the naturalistic commitments of the historical-critical method is Van Harvey. In his influential work, *The Historian and the Believer*, Harvey puts forth a sustained argument that he believes substantiates the naturalistic approach to history.[9]

To begin, Harvey argues that, in contrast to modern people, ancient people were generally "naive and mythologically minded folk without any conception of natural order or law. They lived in a mythological time in which unusual events of nature and history were attributed to supernatural beings of all kinds."[10]

Because of this, he notes, miraculous claims are found in almost all religious traditions, especially surrounding their religious founders. The question Harvey poses is: What should be the stance of the critical historian toward these miraculous claims? We may summarize Harvey's argument by highlighting four points.

First, adherents of one tradition typically believe the miraculous claims attributed to their founder and/or that are part of their tradition, while rejecting the miracle claims of other traditions. Such a biased approach is clearly unac-

---

8. R. Bultmann, "Is Exegesis without Presuppositions Possible?" in *Existence and Faith*, trans. S. M. Ogden (Cleveland: Meridian/New York: World, 1966), 291–92. See also idem, "The Problem of Miracle," *Religion in Life* 27 (1958): 63–75. Many of Bultmann's students simply inherited this sort of presupposition from him. E. Käsemann, e.g., proclaims the "defeat of the concept of miracle" in "Is the Gospel Objective?" in *Essays on New Testament Themes*, trans. W. J. Montague (Naperville, IL: Allenson, 1964), 48.

9. V. A. Harvey, *The Historian and the Believer: The Morality of Historical Knowledge and Christian Belief* (Philadelphia: Westminster, 1966). Although Harvey wrote this book in the 1960s, its articulation of the approach that historical inquiry of the Bible should take continues to be treated as a methodological given for many scholars today. See, e.g., J. V. Hills, "The Jewish Genius: Jesus according to John Meier," *Forum*, n.s., 1 (1998): 343n12; R. Hoover, review of *Jesus under Fire, Journal of Higher Criticism* 3 (Fall 1996): 310–15. See also V. A. Harvey, "New Testament Scholarship and Christian Belief," in *Jesus in Myth and History*, ed. R. J. Hoffmann and G. A. Larue (Amherst, NY: Prometheus, 1986), 193–200.

10. Harvey, *Historian and Believer*, 10.

ceptable for critical historians, for the integrity of their work depends on their striving to be objective in their investigations. According to Harvey, therefore, critical historians must adopt a uniform approach to all miraculous claims and thus conclude, as a matter of methodological principle, that they are all myth, legend, or intentional fabrication.

Second, according to Harvey, accepting any miraculous claim as historical would put us back in the "naive and mythologically minded" stage of human development. Going back to this uncritical mind-set would in principle undermine all the advances of science and history we have made in the last two centuries. Indeed, we can now discern many ancient claims as mythological only because of our resolute commitment to naturalism. "It was," Harvey argues, "just the [critical] assessment of fantastic reports—reports about the 'impossible'—in the light of knowledge produced by the science [*sic*] that accounts for the emergence of the very important categories of myth and legend which play such a crucial role in modern historical inquiry."[11]

In other words, if we allow for the miraculous in any tradition, we undermine our ability to assess with integrity the miraculous claims of *any* tradition as mythological. Instead, in "the light of knowledge produced by . . . science," we should assume that *all* miraculous claims are mythological, legendary, or fabricated.

Third, Harvey argues that it simply is not possible for modern Westerners to go back to a precritical mind-set. No one can step outside of one's cultural presuppositions. Consequently, modern Western people simply cannot escape the naturalistic assumptions that (he believes) structure our contemporary Western worldview. He writes:

> It is impossible to escape from the categories and presuppositions of the intellectual culture of which one is a part, the common sense of one's own time. . . . These necessarily condition the perception and conception of all those who live in a culture. . . . We are in history as fish are in water, and our ideas of possibility and actuality are relative to our time.[12]

As applied to modern people's understanding of the Gospels, this means that "we *cannot* see the world as the first century saw it. . . . We have, as it were, bitten of the apple, and our eyes have been opened and our memories are indelibly stamped with the new vision of reality."[13] The point is reminiscent of Rudolf Bultmann's famous declaration: "It is impossible to use electric light and the wireless and to avail ourselves of modern medical and surgical discoveries, and at the same time to believe in the New Testament world of spirits and miracles."[14]

11. Ibid., 75.
12. Ibid., 114.
13. Ibid., 115 (emphasis in text).
14. R. Bultmann, "New Testament and Mythology," in *Kerygma and Myth*, ed. H. W. Bartsch, trans. R. H. Fuller (London: SPCK, 1953), 5.

In another context Bultmann puts the matter even more starkly:

> The idea of miracle as an event "contrary to nature" has become impossible for us today because we understand natural events in terms of natural law, that is, we think of miracle as an infraction of the laws of nature; and such an idea we can no longer entertain. This is the case, not because such an event would contradict all experience, but because the very idea of law, which for us is necessarily involved in our idea of nature, is not a demonstrated idea but a presupposed one, and because we cannot free ourselves from this presupposition simply by choosing to do so.[15]

According to this line of thinking, not only is there no reason to believe that the laws of nature are ever "transgressed," but also that modern Western people could not with integrity accept such "transgressions" *even if we wanted to*. We are functionally locked into the naturalistic worldview we have inherited from the scientific revolution.

Finally, Harvey goes even further and argues that, even if the laws of nature were occasionally miraculously suspended, we modern Western people would have no way of historically assessing them. Harvey defines a miracle as "an event alleged to be absolutely unique, which is to say, an event to which no analogies or warrants grounded in present experience can apply."[16] Since Harvey accepts Troeltsch's principle that all historical understanding must be analogically rooted in present experience, alleged "absolutely unique" events must remain unintelligible to modern people, for we do not experience miracles today. And if we have no way of rendering miracles intelligible, we certainly have no way of assessing their plausibility. Hence, Harvey concludes, critical historians are warranted in ruling out miracles on a methodological basis.

Methodological Naturalism and the Historical Jesus

Clearly, to the extent that one shares the assumption of a thorough-going methodological naturalism, one must judge, on an a priori basis, that major portions of the Gospels' portrait of Jesus are nonhistorical. Burton Mack, for example, argues that "the emergence of Christianity and its literature can be understood without recourse or caveats with regard to miracles, resurrections, divine appearances, presences, or unusual charismatic phenomena."[17]

15. Bultmann, "Problem of Miracle," 63–64. It is not only modern biblical scholars who write this way, but theologians as well. For two classic examples of twentieth-century systematic theologians who tell us what modern people can, and can no longer, believe about miracles, see L. B. Gilkey, "Cosmology, Ontology and the Travail of Biblical Language," *Journal of Religion* 41 (1961): 194–205; G. D. Kaufman, "On the Meaning of 'Act of God,'" *HTR* 6 (1968): 175–201. In the third section of this chapter, we shall explore the paradox of a guild of scholars proclaiming that the modern Western worldview renders incredible many things that the majority of modern Western people continue to find very credible.

16. Harvey, *Historian and Believer*, 225.

17. B. Mack, *A Myth of Innocence: Mark and Christian Origins* (Philadelphia: Fortress, 1988), 23. For a critique of Mack's and John Dominic Crossan's naturalistic explanation of early Christianity, see

This is not so much a conclusion Mack *arrives at* as it is a declaration of a methodological stance *he assumes*. It is not that Mack embarked on his investigations with an open mind toward the possibility that the reports of miracles in the Gospels were historically reliable. Rather, as Troeltsch, Harvey, Bultmann, and many others have advocated, Mack presupposed the naturalistic worldview at the start. Hence, the goal of Mack's historical-critical investigations of the New Testament are to explain the emergence of Christianity without any appeal to the supernatural. Given the anti-supernaturalistic presuppositions of the naturalistic historical-critical method, it could not be otherwise.

Similarly, Robert Funk, the late founder of the Jesus Seminar, discloses the philosophical assumptions he brought to his New Testament research when he wrote:

> The God of the metaphysical age is dead. There is not a personal god out there external to human beings and the material world. . . . The notion that God interferes with the order of nature from time to time in order to aid or punish is no longer credible, in spite of the fact that most people still believe it. Miracles are an affront to the justice and integrity of God, however understood. Miracles . . . contradict the regularity of the order of the physical universe. . . . God does not interfere with the laws of nature.

Not surprisingly, Funk went on to argue, "The resurrection of Jesus did not involve the resuscitation of a corpse. Jesus did not rise from the dead, except perhaps in some metaphorical sense."[18] Other reports of miracles in the Gospels were assessed along similar lines by Funk, as they are by most members of the Jesus Seminar and certainly all legendary-Jesus theorists. Given the assumption of naturalism that lies at the foundation of their critical methodology, it is unlikely that their research could have discovered anything else.

Along the same lines—though he maintains that we can know a significant amount about the historical Jesus from the Gospels and denies that he is a "naturalist"—John Dominic Crossan rejects the supernatural aspects of the Gospels as legendary.[19] For example, speaking of the story of Jesus raising Lazarus from the dead, Crossan says, "I do not think this event ever did or could happen. . . . I do not think that anyone, anywhere, at any time brings dead people back to life."[20] So too, Crossan reinterprets Jesus's miracles to be mythological expressions

---

G. Boyd, *Cynic Sage or Son of God? Recovering the Real Jesus in an Age of Revisionist Replies* (Grand Rapids: Baker Academic, 1995), esp. chap. 5.

18. R. Funk, "Twenty-one Theses," *The Fourth R* (July–August 1998): 8.

19. Crossan denies the label "naturalism" in P. Copan, ed., *Will the Real Jesus Please Stand Up? A Debate between William Lane Craig and John Dominic Crossan* (Grand Rapids: Baker Academic, 1998), 45–46. Nonetheless, in the very same debate Crossan states, "But it's a theological presupposition of mine that God does not operate [by miraculous intervention]" (p. 61).

20. J. D. Crossan, *Jesus: A Revolutionary Biography* (San Francisco: HarperSanFrancisco, 1994), 94–95.

of Jesus's revolutionary acceptance of people such as lepers who were ordinarily shunned. "Miracles are not changes in the physical world," he argues. They are rather "changes in the social world." Hence, "by healing the illness without curing the disease, Jesus acted as an alternative boundary keeper in a way subversive to the established procedures of his society."[21] Despite his denial, and in keeping with Troeltsch's principle of correlation, it certainly seems that Crossan is resolutely committed to understanding all of history within a nexus of natural causes and effects.[22]

Given the naturalistic assumption of the historical-critical method as it has usually been practiced within the guild of historical-critical scholars, the "discovery" that the miraculous reports found in the Gospels are not historical and that we can account for them by naturalistic means is hardly surprising. If one presupposes that the miraculous reports found in the Gospels cannot be historical, one has no recourse but to discover that these reports are nonhistorical and to search for naturalistic explanations for them. This, we submit, is a primary methodological assumption behind virtually all versions of the legendary-Jesus thesis.

The Principle of Analogy and Methodological Naturalism

One final aspect of the naturalistic historical-critical method requires consideration prior to the method's assessment, for this aspect plays a decisive role in the defense of the method. Perhaps the most fundamental justification given for the application of methodological naturalism to the study of history centers on Troeltsch's principle of analogy. It is primarily because naturalistic scholars believe present human experience is uniformly devoid of the supernatural that they feel justified in assuming, as a matter of principle, that all miraculous reports in the past should be explained in naturalistic terms. As Harvey argued, that for which we have no analogy cannot be understood, let alone assessed as plausible.

An appreciation for the role of the principle of analogy within a naturalistic methodology comes as one notices its circular nature. It is a circularity that manifests itself in a variety of ways in the naturalistic, historical-critical enterprise. In essence, the practical import of this principle is that we cannot accept reports of miracles in the past because we do not experience miracles in the present. But, as a matter of fact, we have many reports of miracles happening in the present (see below). How then can it be claimed that we have no experience of miracles in the present by which to analogically understand and assess miracles in the past? It

---

21. Crossan, *Revolutionary Biography*, 82. So too he writes, "The so-called nature miracles . . . are not about Jesus' physical power over the world, but about the apostle's spiritual power over the community" (p. 170). Specifically with respect to healing in the first-century context, this interpretation, we submit, is decisively unconvincing. Marcus Borg points out a central problem here: "Can 'healing illness' without 'curing disease' make much sense in a peasant society? Are peasants (or anybody else, for that matter) likely to be impressed with the statement 'your illness is healed' while the physical condition of disease remains?" (*Jesus in Contemporary Scholarship* [Valley Forge, PA: Trinity, 1994], 43n88).

22. On Crossan and objectivity, see Martin, *Elusive Messiah*, 101.

would seem the answer is that reports of miracles in the present day are not taken as a serious possibility because it is a common deliverance of the modern world that miracles do not occur. In other words, this line of reasoning presupposes the truth of naturalism in order to arrive at a naturalistic interpretation of all miracle claims, which, of course, constitutes circular reasoning.

We will see that some form of this circular reasoning lies at the foundation of most of the arguments put forth in defense of a naturalistic methodology. It reveals, among other things, just how inextricably tied the naturalistic historical-critical method is to an a priori worldview. It demonstrates how profoundly right Bultmann was when he noted that this method was unequivocally committed to the presupposition that history is a unity in the sense of a closed continuum of natural cause and effect. Indeed, for all intents and purposes, the naturalistic historical-critical method is nothing over and beyond a methodical application of this commitment. And the use of Troeltsch's principle of analogy to justify this methodical application is itself little more than another expression of this commitment.

For this reason, our critique of the naturalistic historical-critical method will center on issues that surround the unequivocal nature of this commitment. In the next section we focus on the nature of the commitment itself, and in the third section of this chapter we will focus on the principle of analogy used to justify it.

Metaphysics, Historical Method, and the Supernatural

In this section we will first consider the naturalistic historical-critical method in terms of the metaphysical nature of its foundational commitment and suggest a more open-minded alternative. We will then respond to four objections that might be raised against our alternative methodological proposal.

Empirical Generalizations and Metaphysical Assumptions

As we have already intimated, the most fundamental objection that can be raised against the classical historical-critical method is that it is inextricably tied to a questionable metaphysical assumption—the assumption of naturalism.

To begin, we need to consider the distinction between empirical observations, on the one hand, and metaphysical claims, on the other. The claim that nature tends to operate, and thus history tends to unfold, according to natural patterns of cause and effect is an empirical observation. The claim that the natural world and its history constitute a "closed continuum" of natural causes and effects is a metaphysical claim. We experience the regularity of the world. We do not experience "a closed continuum." The first claim is descriptive, simply reporting what we find in the world. The second is prescriptive, stipulating what we *must*—and *must not*—find in the world. The empirical claim does not rule out exceptions.

The metaphysical claim does.[23] The empirical claim is a factual report. The metaphysical claim is a statement of faith.

From our earlier discussion it should be clear that the naturalistic historical-critical method, as understood by most Western critical scholars, is driven by the metaphysical claim, not the empirical claim. Only on this basis could this historical methodology be used to rule out supernatural occurrences on an a priori basis.[24] Our contention is that, while the empirical description of the world generally as operating with regularity is warranted and needed in our critical investigation of history, the metaphysical claim is neither needed nor warranted. Similar to the renowned philosopher of history R. G. Collingwood, we argue that investigating historical matters with an a priori metaphysical commitment to naturalism actually undermines the "scientific" nature of the investigation. Science is in principle rooted in the quest to draw general conclusions about the world from empirical observations, Collingwood argues, not to prescribe how the world must operate on the basis of a priori metaphysical assumptions. He writes,

> On the one side, [critical history] claims that scientific thought reveals to us laws of nature to which there cannot be exceptions; on the other, it holds that this revelation is based on induction from experience, and therefore can never give us universal knowledge that is more than probable. . . . Hence in the last resort the attempt to base history on science breaks down; for although there might be facts which are inconsistent with the laws of nature as we conceive them (that is, miracles might happen), the occurrence of these facts is [to the critical historian] so improbable that no possible testimony would convince us of it. This impasse really wrecks the whole theory.[25]

Collingwood's point is that when a metaphysical assumption renders a class of possible events so improbable that no amount of evidence—"no possible testimony"—could convince us of their occurrence, our claim to being "scientific" is compromised. We are no longer drawing probabilistic conclusions *from* evidence. We are instead superimposing a metaphysical assumption *upon* evidence.

23. Scholars define "metaphysical" differently, and we could here enter into a very complicated, philosophical discussion and debate on how "metaphysical assumptions" and "empirical generalizations" are related. For our present purposes, however, it is sufficient to hold to the minimalist distinction that empirical generalizations allow for exceptions whereas metaphysical assumptions do not. Put differently, metaphysical assumptions are *prescriptive* in a way empirical generalizations are not.

24. This is hardly a new critique of the historical-critical method. As long ago as the early nineteenth century, for example, August Tholuck (*Die Glaubwürdigkeit der evangelischen Geschichte*, 2nd ed. [Hamburg: Perthes, 1838]) argued that D. F. Strauss's rejection of miracles was based upon questionable philosophical presuppositions and a definition of "miracle" as inherently impossible.

25. Collingwood, *Idea of History*, 139. We are not suggesting that Collingwood was intending to retrieve the miraculous as an historical explanation in the modern world. Clearly, in context, this statement was meant to support his distinctive idealist view of historiography. Nonetheless, one can take his point here and train its sights on a different target.

Or, more accurately, we are dictating at the start what is and is not allowed to count as evidence.

Of course, since the work of Thomas Kuhn and what has come to be called "the postmodern turn," we all recognize that neither modern science nor modern history has ever operated as a purely disinterested, "objective" enterprise.[26] Our plausibility structures—our assessment of what is "reasonable" or "plausible"—regarding any specific area of life is always informed by our broader worldview and its religio-philosophical presuppositions.[27] Thus, we are not faulting naturalistic historical-critical scholars for failing to abide by a purely empirical, presupposition-free, method. We can all agree there is no such thing.

What we *are* concerned with, however, is how determinative the naturalistic presupposition is for the findings of the classical historical-critical method. Stated otherwise, we are concerned with what Bultmann acknowledged to be an *unequivocal* commitment to naturalism. When nothing is allowed to count as evidence against a presupposition, and when nothing is allowed to call into question one's metaphysical commitments, the commitment to the presupposition is, for all intents and purposes, a religious commitment to a dogma. And this hardly seems consistent with a discipline that calls itself critical and that strives to be as objective and unbiased as possible in its assessment of evidence. As Matthew Ratcliffe has demonstrated (in another context),

> "Methodological naturalism" ultimately amounts to an interpretive background that *determines* the kind of things one is prepared to admit as possible constituents of reality. . . . [It] places a limit on the range of acceptable phenomena and it can reinterpret and accommodate anything that doesn't at first seem to fit. . . . [I]f held inflexibly, it amounts to *dogmatic enforcement of a metaphysical lens* through which the world is interpreted.[28]

It is this "inflexible" naturalism of the classical historical-critical method that requires serious rethinking.

An Open Historical-Critical Method

Most within the guild of historical-critical scholarship identify the historical-critical method with this unequivocal commitment to the presupposition of

26. T. Kuhn, *The Structure of Scientific Revolutions* (Chicago: University of Chicago Press, 1962).

27. With respect to historical method, this point is well stated by J. Vansina, "Knowledge and Perceptions of the African Past," in *African Historiographies: What History for Which Africa?* ed. B. Jewsiewicki and D. Newbury (Beverly Hills, CA: Sage, 1986), 28.

28. M. Ratcliffe, "Scientific Naturalism and the Neurology of Religious Experience," *Religious Studies* 39 (2003): 341–42 (emphasis added). Just how difficult it can be for contemporary academics to escape from a thoroughgoing naturalism is seen in the attempts of some to relativize their own Western naturalistic worldviews in the name of a postmodern pluralistic methodology—yet in the end naturalism still trumps all other perspectives on reality! See, e.g., P. F. Craffert and P. J. J. Botha, "Why Jesus Could Walk on the Sea But He Could Not Read and Write," *Neotestamentica* 39 (2005): 5–35.

naturalism. For such scholars, talk about a *naturalistic* historical-critical method is redundant, and talk about a historical-critical method that is not unequivocally committed to naturalism is a contradiction in terms. Be that as it may, we want to suggest that it is possible to embrace a rigorously critical historiographical methodology that is not driven by the naturalistic assumption. Indeed, in the remainder of this chapter we will contend that a historical-critical methodology that is open to the possibility of the supernatural is more rigorously critical than any method that is, on an a priori basis, closed to this possibility. We will refer to this alternative methodology as the "open historical-critical method," for it is not unequivocally committed to naturalism but is open to the possibility that evidence may suggest that events have taken place that defy plausible naturalistic explanations and thus may be referred to as *super*natural events.[29] Here we will simply offer the broad outlines of this approach, which we will flesh out further in the final section of this chapter.

Given the empirical observation that the world generally operates by natural laws of cause and effect, it is reasonable when investigating history to first look for natural explanations for events and to exercise caution when entertaining explanations that involve appeals to the supernatural. And, given this empirical observation, it is certainly reasonable to prefer natural explanations over supernatural explanations, all other things being equal. In other words, it makes sense to be committed to a historiographical approach wherein one expects to find natural causes for events in history. What does not seem reasonable, however, is to be *unequivocally* committed to an approach that a priori imposes a naturalistic interpretation on all of history, adopting a stance that goes beyond empirical observations of how the world in fact generally operates and making metaphysical claims for how the world *must* operate—all under the guise of the "unavoidable conclusions" of the natural sciences and/or a critical historiographical method.[30]

In light of this, we submit that what is needed is a historical-critical methodology that is committed to looking for natural explanations for all events but is

29. Decades ago, T. A. Roberts argued for what many adherents of the classical historical-critical method have only assumed: that with respect to historical investigation of the Gospels, "there is only one method open to us, the method of scientific historiography. There is no other" ("Gospel Historicity: Some Philosophical Observations," *Religious Studies* 1 [1966]: 198). One can generally affirm this statement while suggesting that one *version* of a "scientific historiography" is more appropriate than another, which is our point here. Roberts would, no doubt, take issue with our openness to the supernatural by arguing that the notion of a supernatural event strains the capabilities of language to describe it (see pp. 199–201). However, we would respond by noting that Roberts himself does a fine job of describing just such an event (i.e., his shape-shifting cat-dog, p. 200). Roberts has confused *description* with *explanation*, and on this basis his philosophical-linguistic argument against allowing for the supernatural in a critical historiography is shown to be misguided.

30. B. C. van Fraassen effectively argues that no metaphysical account of natural "laws" can succeed. He calls for the replacement of the idea of "laws of nature" with an approach to the natural sciences based upon the construction of models to represent the phenomena; see *Laws and Symmetry* (New York: Oxford University Press, 1989). We are indebted to Stewart Kelly for bringing van Fraassen's work to our attention.

also, as a matter of principle, open to the possibility that evidence may at times require us to entertain the possibility that an event cannot be plausibly explained exclusively in naturalistic terms. This open historical-critical method would be "critical" in that it always looks for "natural" cause-and-effect relationships to explain events, always applies standard critical criteria to the evaluation of ancient texts and artifacts, and always prefers plausible natural explanations for historical phenomena over ad hoc appeals to the supernatural. But at the same time it would be "open" in that it would not reject appeals to the supernatural on an a priori basis. This is the methodology we will attempt to employ throughout this work.

In our estimation, this methodology is not *less critical* than the naturalistic historical-critical method; rather, it is *more critical*. For, as we will argue more fully below, this method requires that Western scholars be critical of their commitments to their own culturally conditioned naturalistic presuppositions.[31] It requires Western scholars to adopt a stance of epistemological humility and acknowledge that their own culturally conditioned worldview may have something to learn from the worldviews of other cultures—worldviews that allow for supernatural occurrences. It requires that scholars not be uncritically committed to any metaphysical stance, but rather, in the name of critical scholarship, always bring a certain inquisitiveness to their presuppositional commitments. Because of this, the open historical-critical method could help ensure that historical-critical scholars remain committed to following the evidence, *wherever it leads*, rather than narrowly stipulating what can and cannot count as evidence on the basis of certain presuppositions.

Of course, there are a number of issues that need to be addressed regarding this proposed "open" historical-critical method. We will address some of these in the course of our assessment of the naturalistic historical-critical method and in part 4 of this work. For the moment, we simply want to set the stage for what is to follow by putting this open alternative on the table as an approach that is at once critical and yet not dogmatically closed to the possibility of supernatural occurrences. We turn now to four objections that might be raised against our proposed approach to critical historiography. In the course of discussing these four objections, we will address several of the arguments put forth in the defense of an a priori stance against the category of the supernatural.

A Naturalist's Response to the Charge of Dogmatism

The charge that to rule out a priori the possibility of supernatural occurrences is inconsistent with a truly "scientific" approach to history is not a new one.

---

31. A similar appeal to openness in the name of critical scholarship is made by D. P. Fuller in "The Fundamental Presupposition of the Historical Critical Method," *Theologische Zeitschrift* 24 (1968): 100. See also R. J. Sider, "The Historian, the Miraculous, and Post-Newtonian Man," *SJT* 25 (1972): 309–19, esp. 317.

However, the charge has taken on additional force in our postmodern climate as we have become more acutely aware of the socially constructed elements of our inherited worldviews (about which more will be said below). In light of this, some methodological naturalists have adjusted the way they express their stance toward the supernatural. Indeed, some have begun to maintain that, as a matter of fact, the naturalistic historical-critical method does not rule out the possibility of the supernatural on an a priori basis. It does not hold that supernatural events are impossible, simply that they are much less probable that natural events. Hence, the first response a defender of the naturalistic historical-critical methodology might give to our proposed alternative is that we are not saying anything the standard historical-critical method does not already grant.[32]

This line of argumentation has been put to use by one of the leading apologists for the Jesus Seminar, Robert Miller. Miller grants that certain supernatural claims are historically "possible."[33] To say this would seem to suggest that Miller is espousing a version of the "open" historical-critical method we have proposed. However, by "historically possible" Miller merely means an event that "involves no conceptual contradictions." In other words, he argues, "something is possible if we can imagine it."[34] Given this definition of "historical possibility," it is not surprising to find Miller quickly confessing that to claim an event is possible in this sense is "not very helpful in historical matters."[35]

Miller notes, for example, that the claim that an elephant flew on its own power is "historically possible," for it obviously involves no conceptual contradiction and can therefore be imagined. But granting this possibility gets us nowhere in trying to assess whether an elephant *actually flew*. To assess this, Miller argues, we need to distinguish between something being historically *possible*, on the one hand, and something being historically *probable*, on the other. Miller writes:

> To be historically possible, something only needs to be imaginable. However, for something to be historically probable means that there is some evidence for it. Not everyone in the historical Jesus discussion seems aware of this distinction, for we

32. From Collingwood's critique of Bradley, Harvey learned the importance of this more modest approach. He writes that "*all* truly historical events are unique and that neither [natural] law nor present experience [e.g., the principle of analogy]" can be used as an a priori standard against them; *Historian and Believer*, 73. Harvey seems not to have noticed, however, that this qualification, if carried through consistently, undermines his defense of the a priori rejection of miracles for historical-critical reconstructions of the past. We shall critique Harvey's concept of miracles as "absolutely unique" events shortly.

33. This would seem to follow from Miller's discussion of historical "possibility" vs. "probability"; see *The Jesus Seminar and Its Critics* (Santa Rosa, CA: Polebridge, 1999), 39. Similarly, Robert Price suggests that the critical historian must stop short of claiming that miracles are historically impossible (*The Incredible Shrinking Son of Man: How Reliable Is the Gospel Tradition?* [Amherst, NY: Prometheus, 2003], 19–20).

34. Miller, *Jesus Seminar*, 39.

35. Ibid.

often read statements like "It is quite possible that Jesus _____" or hear questions like "Isn't it possible that Jesus _____?" Fill in the blank with any scenario you like, no matter how bizarre: the answer will always be yes.[36]

So, in response to the question, "Are supernatural events possible?" Miller would contend that, in cases where the proposed event is at least imaginable, the naturalistic scholar can and should in good faith answer "Yes." Hence, it seems this method is not as unequivocally committed to naturalism as we have alleged and thus not in need of an alternative critical methodology that is open to the possibility of the supernatural. But, in fact, Miller's concession that miracles are "historically possible" accomplishes nothing of the sort, for in conceding this he has conceded nothing more than that supernatural occurrences are not logical contradictions. (Why he uses the phrase "historically possible" instead of the clearer and more customary phrase "logically possible" is a mystery.) But no one has ever alleged that this was the problem with the naturalistic historical-critical method. The problem is that the unequivocal commitment of historical-critical scholars to a naturalistic presupposition is such that it rules out at the start the possibility of genuine supernatural occurrences *in actual history*. Despite its aspiration for being "scientific," this method is actually quite unscientific insofar as it predetermines what it will *not* find in its historical investigations on the basis of a presupposed dogmatic conviction.

Miller may argue that the difference between a historical possibility and a historical probability is that there is evidence for the former, but not for the latter. So it is that supernatural events are possible but not probable. What Miller seems not to notice, however, is that the naturalist's a priori stance toward supernatural events renders their occurrence so improbable that no historical data would ever be allowed to count as evidence for them. The unequivocal commitment to a metaphysical assumption effectively ensures that a report about the supernatural will never be considered "historically probable." *This* is the problem that "wrecks the whole theory," and while it may sound better in our post-Collingwood, postmodern climate to concede that miracles are "historically possible," Miller has done nothing to alleviate the problem.

Our contention is that a truly critical historical methodology is one that is critical of the Western academic assumption of a thoroughgoing naturalism and is therefore genuinely open to finding supernatural occurrences in history—not merely conceding that they are logically possible. As noted in the introduction, the central claim of this work is that if someone is open to the *genuine historical possibility* that the portrait of Jesus in the Synoptics is substantially rooted in history, that one will find there are many compelling reasons to accept that this portrait is not only *possibly* rooted in history, but that it is *plausibly*—even *probably*—rooted in history.

36. Ibid.

Can We Step outside Our Worldview?

A second objection that might be raised against our proposed open historical-critical methodology is that it is naive. It could be argued that it does not take seriously the inevitable role cultural presuppositions play in how one views the world, and therefore in how one investigates history. As we saw above, scholars like Harvey argue that "it is impossible to escape from the categories and presuppositions of the intellectual culture of which one is a part."[37] On this basis it is argued that modern people—or at least modern academics—"cannot see the world as the first century saw it."[38] As Bultmann put it, modern people who use modern technology simply cannot "believe in the New Testament world of spirits and miracles."[39] In this light, it seems that Western scholars cannot help but be locked into the naturalistic worldview of the West, and thus cannot help but judge all supernatural reports to be examples of fabrication. There are, we submit, at least three problems with this response.

First, the claim that the contemporary Western worldview is one that inevitably sees reality in exclusively naturalistic terms simply is false, as we will argue more fully below. This is undoubtedly the predominant worldview among *secularized Western academics*, but it demonstrably is not, and has never been, the worldview of modern Western people in general.[40]

Second, while it obviously is true that people are strongly conditioned by the categories and presuppositions of their culture, it strikes us as an exaggeration to claim we are so locked into our cultural presuppositions that we cannot to some degree step outside of them. Were we completely unable to transcend our culturally conditioned categories, we could never critically reflect on these categories, and the writing of history would amount to mere autobiography. Yet it seems we can do this and should do this—especially if we are to claim to be engaging in a scholarly discipline that is critical and that strives for objectivity.

Along these same lines, were we completely unable to transcend our cultural presuppositions, it would be impossible for anyone to adjudicate between competing truth-claims found in differing worldviews. We could never claim that one worldview is, in any respect, more reflective of reality than another on any matter. For example, we would have to concede that cultural perspectives that view other people groups as subhuman, that assume women are property of males, that practice female genital mutilation and other barbaric patriarchal rites, and that view the earth as sitting on the back of a giant tortoise have as much validity as cultural perspectives that view all humans as equal and the cosmos in modern scientific terms. This seems broadly counterintuitive, to say the least.

What is more, if we hold that we can never transcend our cultural presuppositions, how can we explain "conversions" from one worldview to another? Many of

---

37. Harvey, *Historian and Believer*, 114.
38. Ibid., 115.
39. Bultmann, "New Testament and Mythology," 5.
40. On this point see Meier, *Marginal Jew*, 2:520–21.

those who are now unequivocally committed to naturalism held to a worldview that was open to the supernatural before they received their academic training. They "converted" to naturalism. Conversely, as we will see below, a surprising number of scholars who once embraced the Western naturalistic worldview have "converted" to a worldview that is open to supernatural occurrences, often as a result of personal encounters with what they perceive to be supernatural agencies. Such conversions from one worldview to another are hard to explain if people are as locked into the categories of their worldview as Harvey and others have suggested.[41]

Ironically enough, it is not even clear that Harvey and others who espouse this perspective actually believe it themselves. For if they did believe it, how could they judge *their* perspective—that all reports of the supernatural are fictitious—to be more true to reality than the view of "naive" and "mythologically minded" people who accept some of these reports as factual? Their judgment is intelligible only if these scholars have transcended their own worldview enough to enter into and understand the "mythological" worldview of ancient people and have in fact imaginatively stood outside of both worldviews to adjudicate between them.

Even more puzzling is this: if Harvey is correct in asserting that we in the West are so locked into our naturalistic worldview that "we cannot see the world as the first century saw it"[42] and thus cannot believe in miracles, and if Bultmann is correct in asserting that we are so locked into our worldview that "it is impossible to use electric light and the wireless . . . and at the same time to believe in the New Testament world of spirits and miracles,"[43] one wonders why Harvey and Bultmann have to write books to convince other modern Westerners of this fact. If they are correct, this much would already be obvious to all of us who are allegedly locked inside this

41. It seems apparent that Harvey, Bultmann, and others who share their convictions have bought into a simplistic model of strong conceptual and/or cultural incommensurability—a model that has been shown to be flawed. In this respect, biblical scholars and historians in general could benefit from the philosophical insights of D. Davidson and others of his persuasion. See Davidson's classic essay, "On the Very Idea of a Conceptual Scheme," *Proceedings and Addresses of the American Philosophical Association* 47 (1974): 5–20; also idem, "The Structure and Content of Truth," *Journal of Philosophy* 87 (1990): 279–328. (Note that one can appreciate Davidson's critique of the idea of the philosophical incommensurability of conceptual schemes whether or not one accepts his theory of truth.) As Nancy Frankenberry rightly notes, "The road to relativism is paved with good intentions, and nowhere more so than in connection with religious claims" ("American Religious Empiricism and Impulses to Relativism" [paper read at the 1989 Annual Meeting of the American Academy of Religion, Anaheim, CA], 1). For a variety of studies serving to unmask the myth of a strong conceptual/cultural relativism from different angles, see S. Coakley, "Theology and Cultural Relativism: What Is the Problem?" *Neue Zeitschrift für Systematische Theologie und Religionsphilosophie* 21 (1979): 223–43; F. G. Downing, "Our Access to Other Cultures, Past and Present (or The Myth of the Culture Gap)," *Modern Churchman* 21 (1977): 28–42; idem, "Interpretation and the 'Culture Gap," *SJT* 40 (1987): 161–71; R. P. C. Hanson, "Are We Cut Off from the Past?" in *Studies in Christian Antiquity* (Edinburgh: Clark, 1985), 3–21; A. McGrath, "On Being Condemned to History," in *The Genesis of Doctrine: A Study in the Foundations of Doctrinal Criticism* (New York: Blackwell, 1990), 81–102.
42. Harvey, *Historian and Believer*, 115.
43. Bultmann, "New Testament and Mythology," 5.

worldview. It seems that even these scholars inadvertently acknowledge that we are not as locked into our naturalistic worldview as they insist. In any event, there seems to be no cogent reason for supposing that Western scholars cannot intentionally strive to become open-minded toward the possibility of supernatural occurrences, whether in the past or the present. Hence there seems to be no compelling reason to suppose that the open historical-critical method we are proposing is, in this sense, inherently naive.

Can Secular Westerners Analogically Assess Miracles?

A third objection that might be raised against our proposed open historical-critical method is that even if we can in principle transcend our cultural presuppositions, we have no way of assessing claims about events for which we have no analogy in our present experience. As we saw Harvey argue earlier, miracles are supposedly "absolutely unique" events that the modern, naturalistic scholar cannot understand, let alone assess in terms of their plausibility. Hence, it could be argued, a methodology that suggests modern scholars remain genuinely open to the possibility of miracles occurring is naive and unfeasible. We offer three responses to this objection.

First, we readily grant that Troeltsch, Harvey, and others are correct in insisting that we can understand things only by analogically drawing on our present experience. That for which we have absolutely no analogy is utterly meaningless. We therefore agree that if an "absolutely unique" event were to take place, we would have no way of analogically understanding it and thus no way of assessing the plausibility of reports that it occurred. What is not clear, however, is why we should consider supernatural occurrences to be "absolutely unique" events for which modern people can find no analogies.

Things are said to be *analogous* when they are like each other in certain respects and unlike each other in other respects. So, even if an allegedly supernatural event differs from a person's experience in the respect that the person has never personally witnessed one, there are, most likely, other respects in which the alleged event would be somewhat similar to other events in this person's experience. At the very least, to identify it as an allegedly supernatural *event* is to suggest that it has enough in common with natural events to still be deemed an "event." The event may be unique, but it is not "*absolutely* unique."[44] Hence, there is no reason

44. For a survey, analysis, and defense of the concept of "unique events" from the perspective of a critical historiography, see A. Tucker, "Unique Events: The Underdetermination of Explanation," *Erkenntnis* 48 (1998): 59–80. The historiographical work of Tucker and others on this matter demonstrates that the moratorium on the concept of the historically "unique," imposed upon New Testament studies by the history of religions approach (either in its earlier or more recent forms), is without merit. For a recent example of this misguided banishment of the "unique," see J. Z. Smith, *Drudgery Divine: On the Comparison of Early Christianities and the Religions of Late Antiquity* (Chicago: University of Chicago Press, 1990). Smith fears that to grant an event the status of "unique" would be to jeopardize a place for analogy and thus robust comparison. But, again, this is to fall victim to the unhelpful, practically indefinable category of the "*absolutely* unique."

to assume that a person who has never experienced a supernatural event would not be able to analogically grasp the reality of such an event.

Consider, for example, the claim that Jesus rose from the dead. It is doubtful (though not impossible) that any reader of this book has ever witnessed a dead person coming back to life. But does this mean a resurrection constitutes what Harvey calls "an absolutely unique" event and thus that we cannot arrive at an analogical understanding of this event or assess the plausibility of reports about this event? If so, we would have to conclude that modern Western Christians are talking nonsense in claiming to believe in this event, for one cannot coherently believe in something that is essentially unintelligible. Even more puzzling, we would have to conclude that critics are talking nonsense in denying the resurrection, for one cannot coherently deny belief in something about which one can attribute no meaning. In truth, however, no one is talking nonsense, for there simply is no problem analogically understanding the claim "Jesus rose from the dead"—despite the probability that none of us has ever personally experienced such an event. The claim is unlike our experience in certain respects, but it intersects with our experience in other respects, giving us the ability to analogically understand and even assess this alleged event.

Though some readers undoubtedly have no conscious experience of God or any other invisible agent ever doing things, all of us obviously have experienced *physical* agents doing things. To say that God or any other supernatural agent acted in human history—raised Jesus from the dead, for example—is analogous to saying a human being acted in history, except that supernatural agents would be (among other things) invisible. We can understand the concept of invisible agents acting in the world by drawing analogies with our experience of visible agents acting in the world. In the same way, though it is probable none of us has witnessed a person coming back to life, we can surely imagine what an event like this might look like by drawing on analogies from our experience. We could, for example, imaginatively reverse the dying process. Hence, it seems that even the resurrection does not really constitute an "*absolutely* unique" event that is beyond the ability of secularized people to understand and assess.[45]

As a matter of fact, we would argue that it is not supernatural events that are meaningless because they are "absolutely unique" events; it is rather the concept of "absolutely unique" events that is meaningless. Any event that was in *every* respect *unlike* all other events would not be something we could even recognize as an "event." (Conversely, the concept of an "absolutely similar" event is also

45. It is worth recalling at this point that an open historical-critical assessment of the probability of a supernatural occurrence does not need to—in fact, cannot—determine what "invisible agent" might have performed a given "miracle." A historical-critical approach need only, and can only, assert that the evidence indicates that *something* other than natural causes brought about this event. The critical historian thus need only be able to imagine some nonnatural agency/force impinging upon history. Harvey and others notwithstanding, we insist that even the most secularized critic is capable of imagining this and thus assessing the probability of a claim that an event occurred that involved supernatural forces.

meaningless, for that which is in *every* respect *like* something else is *identical* with this "something else.") Different events are differing *events* only because they have some things in common. But they are *differing* events only because they have some things unique to themselves. Hence, we submit that our understanding of any particular event involves analogically assessing the ways in which it is similar to, and different from, other events.

When Harvey argues that modern Western people cannot understand or assess miracles because they are "absolutely unique" events, he is, in essence, simply saying that modern people cannot understand or assess miraculous events because miraculous events are not events. In other words, he is claiming that miracles are meaningless to modern Western people because miracles are meaningless to modern Western people. He is, in short, ruthlessly applying Troeltsch's principle of analogy in a circular manner. As we noted above, and as we shall discuss more fully below, this circular use of Troeltsch's principle undergirds much of the reasoning marshaled in defense of the naturalistic perspective.

As extraordinary as supernatural events may be to certain modern Western people, they are not impossible for such people to analogically understand. Hence, it is not naive or unfeasible to claim that critical scholars should remain open to the possibility that they may, in rare circumstances, have to appeal to supernatural events in order to plausibly reconstruct the past.

In fact, more often than not it is extraordinary events—events that are significantly on the *dissimilar side* of the similar-dissimilar spectrum that links and differentiates all events—that are most influential in the flow of history. They are often deeds and events that, precisely because they are extraordinary, stretch our imaginative abilities to understand them. Allowing ourselves to be stretched as we strive to understand and appreciate the uniqueness of history-defining events lies at the heart of the discipline of critical historiography.

In this light it seems to us that Richard Niebuhr was onto something significant when he argued that, far from being an unintelligible event "outside" of history, as so many of his historical-critical contemporaries were arguing, the miracle of the resurrection of Jesus was actually a supreme example of the challenge of doing critical history. The challenge of analogically understanding the uniqueness of the resurrection, Niebuhr argued, is a prototype of the challenge of understanding the uniqueness of all significant historical events. Yet, the uniqueness can be understood analogically precisely because it is not "*absolutely* unique."[46]

The open historical-critical method we are proposing simply stipulates that there is no justifiable, a priori point at which critical historians should shut down their analogical imagination. If we are striving to be truly critical, we must commit to being critical of the way in which our own cultural presuppositions condition our perspective on the world, and critical of our narrow, culturally conditioned

---

46. R. R. Niebuhr, *Resurrection and Historical Reason: A Study of Theological Method* (New York: Scribner, 1957).

proclivities vis-à-vis reconstruction of the past. If we are striving to make truth-claims about the way the world actually is and/or the way history has actually unfolded, as opposed to simply re-expressing our cultural conditioning, we must be willing to let other cultural perspectives—and the perhaps surprising historical evidence that accompanies them—stretch our imaginations beyond the conceptual restrictions our culture inevitably places upon us.

Hume and the Improbability of Miracles

A fourth objection that might be raised against the open historical-critical method we are proposing arises from Hume's critique of miracles discussed above. One could argue that, as alleged "transgressions" of the "laws of nature," the probability of any report of a supernatural occurrence being factual is weighed against all known confirmations of the law in question. Thus, regardless of the evidence one might marshal in support of a miraculous report, the probability of the report being factual is always so incredibly low that it is never reasonable to seriously consider it, no matter how implausible alternative, naturalistic explanations for the event in question might seem. Hence, it seems the open historical-critical method is asking historians to remain open to explanations that are intrinsically more improbable than naturalistic explanations, which is tantamount to asking them to be irrational. There are a number of problems with this line of reasoning, two of which warrant mentioning in this context.

One problem with Hume's line of reasoning is that he seems to associate rational thinking with *adding up* evidence rather than *weighing* evidence. To rationally determine whether one has been randomly dealt a perfect bridge hand, for example, one wouldn't simply add up all the possible alternative hands one could have been randomly dealt and compare it with the odds of getting a perfect bridge hand (1,635,013,559,600 to 1).[47] Were this the case it would obviously never be rational to accept that one had been dealt a perfect bridge hand—even if, as a matter of fact, one was holding one! The way a rational person goes about determining whether he or she has been randomly dealt a perfect bridge hand is by looking at the empirical evidence. Is the person in fact holding a perfect bridge hand? Is there any evidence the cards were not shuffled randomly? And so on.

Second, if carried through consistently, Hume's methodology would render it unreasonable to conclude that *anything* unusual *ever* happens, since, by definition, there are far more usual events than unusual ones. A historian would thus be justified in denying, for example, the mind-boggling exploits of Alexander the Great or Napoleon Bonaparte—despite the fact that there is overwhelming evidence most of the activities attributed to these men are

47. The illustration is taken from N. Geisler, *The Baker Encyclopedia of Christian Apologetics* (Grand Rapids: Baker Academic, 1999), 459.

generally accurate.[48] In fact, Hume's methodology would justify denying that a miracle occurred even if one witnessed it personally. Clearly, to assess whether something has happened in history, whether something ordinary or remarkably extraordinary—even supernatural—one must *weigh*, not merely *add up*, evidence.

It seems obvious that Hume would never have recommended evaluating reports about the fantastic exploits of Alexander the Great or Napoleon, or reports that one had been randomly dealt a perfect bridge hand, in the same way he recommended assessing reports of miracles. How could a philosopher as astute as Hume have committed such an obvious blunder?

So far as we can see, the only plausible explanation is that Hume's naturalistic worldview allowed for people to occasionally perform outrageous feats and for people to occasionally be dealt an outrageously lucky hand, but it did not allow for miracles to ever occur. Hume *brought to* his historical reasoning a resolved belief that miracles do not occur rather than trying to reach a conclusion about whether miracles ever occur *on the basis of* historical reasoning. Thus, as inevitably happens when one approaches evidence with an unequivocal commitment to a foregone conclusion, *everything* becomes evidence for the foregone conclusion. The conclusion determines the evidence that is used to support the conclusion, as well as the very admissibility of the evidence itself.

Hume's reasoning about miracles, it seems, was filtered through his a priori convictions about the probabilistically inviolable laws of nature, which rendered it virtually certain that miracles do not occur. Not surprisingly, Hume was overwhelmed by the massive "evidence" of miracles not occurring—for every natural event was now viewed in light of the a priori virtual certainty that miracles do not occur. Apparently unaware of how his conclusion was determining the evidence, Hume goes on to cite the overwhelming evidence to draw his conclusion. But obviously, the only reason the overwhelming occurrence of natural events in history was considered as evidence to be added up against the possibility of miracles was because Hume viewed each natural event in history against the contrasting backdrop of his a priori virtual certainty that miracles do not occur.

We have here yet another variation of the circular use of the principle of analogy. As with Harvey's argument about the "absolutely unique" nature of miracles, Hume's argument against miracles is actually nothing more than a proclamation of his own psychological certainty that miracles do not occur. Hume's experience of the world was such that it led him to believe miracles do not occur, and this certainty led him to find in history nothing other than what would reaffirm his certainty that miracles do not occur. As we shall discuss later, the open historical-critical method we are advocating offers a way to avoid this circularity by calling on scholars to exercise

---

48. See Richard Whately's refutation of Hume on this basis in his pamphlet, "Historical Doubts concerning the Existence of Napoleon Bonaparte," in *Famous Pamphlets*, 2nd ed., ed. H. Morley (New York: Routledge, 1890).

epistemic caution, even with respect to matters about which they are psychologically certain, and thus calls on them to remain open to the possibility that the world and its history may not be exhaustively captured in the naturalistic worldview.

The Principle of Analogy Reconsidered

We have examined the foundational assumption that drives the content of the naturalistic historical-critical enterprise and found it wanting. We must now assess the foundational principle that seems to drive the defense of the classical historical-critical enterprise—the principle of analogy in its Troeltschean form. As we have already noted, we accept the principle of analogy so far as it goes. All understanding of history must be analogically derived from the present. That for which we have no analogy is that about which we cannot think. What is problematic, however, is the way in which naturalistic scholars use this analogy to defend their unequivocal commitment to understanding history in strictly naturalistic terms.

In what follows we will first offer two brief preliminary observations about the questionable manner in which many naturalistic scholars use the principle of analogy. We will then embark on two much more lengthy discussions that address the limited scope of human experience naturalistic scholars draw from as they defend their secularized reconstructions of the past.

The Negative Use of the Principle of Analogy

While one is certainly justified in drawing on present human experience to make a case for what might have happened in the past, there seems to be no justification for drawing on present human experience to make a case for what *could not* have happened in the past. As a number of scholars have argued, while a positive application of the principle of analogy is justified and necessary, a negative application is not.[49] There is nothing in present human experience that indicates that our present experience exhausts what humans are capable of experiencing. Therefore, there is nothing in present human experience that warrants limiting all human experience to our present experience.

One might respond to this point by arguing that the principle of analogy rules out postulating experiences in the past that go beyond what we have directly experienced in the present. Hence, the negative application of the principle of analogy is justified. But as we noted earlier, this line of reasoning fails. All experiences, including alleged experiences of the supernatural, are *like* all other experiences in some respects and *unlike* other experiences in

---

49. So argues W. Pannenberg in "Redemptive Event and History," in *Basic Questions in Theology*, trans. G. H. Kehm (Philadelphia: Fortress, 1970), 1:39–53; T. Peters, "The Use of Analogy in Historical Method," *CBQ* 35 (1973): 475–82.

differing respects. And it is precisely this tension between the similarities and dissimilarities of various experiences that the principle of analogy misses. Even the most secularized person is able to imaginatively entertain what it would be like to experience a supernatural occurrence—an event that defied natural explanation. And so, such a person is unjustified in arguing that a supernatural event could not have happened in the past because no such event can be conceived of in the present.

Of course, proposed reconstructions of the past are certainly easier to believe when they comport easily with our present experience than when they do not. But there is nothing in our present experience that stipulates that everything in the past must be easy for us modern Western people to believe. Thus there is nothing in our present experience that warrants the metaphysical assumption that nothing can take place that disagrees with the way we presently experience the world. And, therefore, there is nothing in our present experience that justifies ruling out the possibility that historical evidence might on occasion lead us to suppose that events happened in the past that are quite different from our present experience. In short, there is nothing that justifies the negative application of the principle of analogy.

A False Dichotomy

Our second preliminary observation is that the naturalistic use of the principle of analogy to rule out miracles is predicated on the postulation of a radical dichotomy between the worldview of ancient people and the modern, Western worldview. We are told that the reason people in the past could believe in and claim to experience miracles, while modern Western people supposedly cannot, is because, unlike us, ancient people were "naive and mythologically minded." Ancient people supposedly had little to no awareness of the laws of nature, no sense of critical history, and thus could not clearly separate fact from fiction. Their world was so different from ours, Harvey suggests, that the gulf between us—as it concerns the question of the supernatural—is too vast to cross with any analogy rooted in contemporary experience.

Unfortunately for this perspective, there is mounting evidence that this alleged dichotomy between the worldview of ancient people and the worldview of modern Western people is itself a piece of modern mythology. For all their differences from the modern Western world, ancient people—as well as primordial groups today—were not nearly as uniformly "naive and mythologically minded" as many modern scholars have tended to assume. Two points may be made in this regard.

First, it should be acknowledged that the pervasive Western academic assumption that nonliterate or semiliterate cultures could not clearly distinguish myth from history was never based on solid empirical evidence. It is, in fact, largely an unwarranted Western, academic assumption. As we will explore in chapters 6 and 7, recent orality studies have demonstrated that orally dominant cultures (cultures in which reading plays little or no role) were and are often quite intentional in keeping fictional aspects of the oral tradition distinct from nonfictional elements when it comes to certain genres.[50]

Moreover, it is now undeniable that orally dominant cultures—such as first-century Palestinian culture—can be remarkably competent in passing on historical remembrances over extended periods of time without substantial alteration of the essential content. Indeed, as remarkable as it sounds, some specialists in the field of orality studies are now arguing that, in at least certain significant respects, these nonliterate cultures can be at least as competent in reporting on the essential aspects of the past as contemporary, literate historians.[51]

It is thus becoming increasingly evident that the common Western academic assumption that ancient, orally dominant cultures were not interested in actual history and/or were incapable of keeping factual historical remembrances distinct from myth is itself a grand myth propagated by modern Western scholars who were simply ignorant of the facts.

A closely related second point concerns the sensibilities of historians in the ancient world. They were not nearly as uncritical as some modern scholars seem to suppose. While most ancient historians certainly did not share the hyperskepticism of some contemporary Western scholars toward the supernatural, there was, as Glenn Chestnut has documented, "a good deal of skepticism within the Graeco-Roman historiographical tradition."[52] From Herodotus to Polybius to Pliny the

50. For critical discussions on both sides of the issue, see R. Dorson, "Introduction: Folklore and Traditional History," in *Folklore and Traditional History*, ed. R. Dorson (The Hague and Paris: Mouton, 1973); P. Pender-Cudlip, "Oral Traditions and Anthropological Analysis: Some Contemporary Myths," *Azania* 7 (1972): 12; J. Miller, "Introduction: Listening for the African Past," in *The African Past Speaks: Essays on Oral Tradition and History*, ed. J. C. Miller (Hamden, CT: Archon, 1980), 1–59; R. G. Willis, *On Historical Reconstruction from Oral Traditional Sources: A Structuralist Approach* (Chicago: Northwestern University Press, 1976), 2–16; A. Kaivola-Bregenhoj, "Varying Folklore," in *Thick Corpus, Organic Variation and Textuality in Oral Tradition*, ed. L. Honko (Helsinki: Finnish Literature Society, 2000), 101; W. E. Leuchtenburg et al., "A Panel of Historians Discuss Oral History," in *The Second National Colloquium on Oral History, at Arden House, Harriman, New York, November 18–21, 1967*, ed. L. M. Starr (New York: Oral History Association, 1968), 1–20.

51. For example, J. Handoo criticizes the "palace paradigm" associated with modern, Western, literate historiography as less reliable in significant respects than oral history ("People Are Still Hungry for Kings: Folklore and Oral History," in *Dynamics of Tradition: Perspectives on Oral Poetry and Folk Belief*, ed. L. Tarkka [Helsinki: Finnish Literature Society, 2003], 70). Social anthropologist E. Tonkin writes: "Oral history is not intrinsically more or less likely to be accurate than a written document" (*Narrating Our Pasts: The Social Construction of Oral History* [New York: Cambridge University Press, 1992], 113). For more on this matter, see chap. 6 below.

52. G. Chestnut, "The Pagan Background," in *The Christian and Judaic Invention of History*, ed. J. Neusner (Atlanta: Scholars Press, 1990), 38. See also: A. H. McDonald, "Herodotus on the Miraculous," in *Miracles: Cambridge Studies in Their Philosophy and History*, ed. C. D. F. Moule (New York: Morehouse-Barlow, 1965), 83–91; T. R. Tholfsen, "Thucydides and Greek Rationalism," in *Historical Thinking: An Introduction* (New York: Harper & Row, 1967), 18–26. With respect to Plutarch, B. S. MacKay points out that, for all of his convictions about the workings of the Deity in the world, there was "no such thing for him as Miracle in the popular sense" ("Plutarch and the Miraculous," in *Miracles*, 98). L. H. Feldman has observed that when recounting the miraculous in

Elder, miracle claims were generally regarded with suspicion. Indeed, Thucydides virtually rejected all appeals to the miraculous as an appropriate historical explanation. "Drawing on the rich intellectual resources of the humanistic and scientific rationalism of fifth-century Athens," T. R. Tholfsen notes, Thucydides developed a historiographical method characterized by "freedom from mythopoetic ways of thinking, critical realism, an 'eager generality,' and an inclination to penetrate rationally to the underlying order of things."[53]

Even more significant for our purpose (for it potentially affects our view of the gullibility of the authors of the Synoptic Gospels), it appears that when it comes to the question of belief in miracles, people in the first century were, on the whole, not very different from people in modern Western culture. Downing writes:

> We have no widespread evidence for any widespread *firm* belief in "magic" or in "miracle" whichever term is chosen, in the world where the Christian movement began. . . . [T]he level of belief—or suspension of disbelief—seems to have been not much different from what we find today for belief in alternative medicines, belief in ley-lines, belief in visitors from outer space, or belief in the free market economy.[54]

This observation comports well with Robert Grant's conclusion that "the least credulous period of antiquity was the late Hellenistic age."[55] Thus it seems that the divide between the worldviews of "modern" and "ancient" people was not nearly as extreme as many modern Western scholars would have us believe. Ancients were generally not as "naive and mythologically minded" as many moderns have thought, and, as we shall explore more fully below, most modern people are not nearly as secularized as many Western scholars seem to assume.[56] This observation obviously calls into question the claim that historically minded, critically thinking modern people can no longer believe in supernatural occurrences in the way ancient, mythologically minded, uncritical people could.

---

the Bible, "Josephus tends to down-grade miracles or to present scientific-like explanations of them or to give the reader the choice as to how to interpret them" (*Studies in Josephus's Rewritten Bible* [Boston: Brill, 1998], 568–69). On the broader question of the treatment of miracles by Greco-Roman historians, see the "report in progress" of J. S. Lown, "The Miraculous in the Greco-Roman Historians," *Forum* 2 (1986): 36–42.

53. Referring, of course, to his *History of the Peloponnesian War*; Tholfsen, "Thucydides," 18.

54. F. G. Downing, "Magic and Skepticism in and around the First Christian Century," in *Making Sense in (and of) the First Christian Century* (Sheffield: Sheffield Academic Press, 2000), 221. Two decades earlier, A. E. Harvey had made essentially the same point: "There is, for example, no justification for assuming that [Jesus's] contemporaries were a great deal more credulous than ourselves" (*Jesus and the Constraints of History* [Philadelphia: Westminster, 1982], 101–2).

55. R. M. Grant, *Miracle and Natural Law in Graeco-Roman and Early Christian Thought* (Amsterdam: North-Holland, 1952), 41. On the wide-ranging skepticism in antiquity, see pp. 41–60.

56. Relevant to this is Leclerc's observation that "to proscribe the history of a time because fables have had a part in it is to proscribe the history of all times" (Leclerc contra Niebuhr; cited in Paul Veyne, *Did the Greeks Believe in Their Myths?* trans. P. Wissing [Chicago: University of Chicago Press, 1988], 132n11).

Miracles and the Global Human Experience

Having briefly addressed two preliminary issues regarding the naturalist's use of the principle of analogy, we turn to a third, more substantial, criticism. While historians can and must attempt to understand the past by drawing analogies from present human experience, a great deal hangs on how broadly or narrowly one defines "present human experience."

Given how myopic and culturally conditioned every individual's perception and experience of the world is, and given how different the perception and experience of the world is from culture to culture, one would think it ill advised to define "present human experience" too narrowly. To the contrary, one might think a scholarly discipline that strives to be critical, objective, and unbiased would define "present human experience" relatively broadly. The last thing one might expect is for critical scholars striving for objectivity to restrict the pool of "present human experience" they draw from to understand the past *to a single slice of one culture* (i.e., the academic elite of the modern Western culture).

Remarkably enough, however, this is precisely how modern historiography has tended to operate. And, it seems, it is largely this arbitrary restriction of present human experience that has fueled the a priori rejection of the supernatural in modern historiography. Western naturalistic scholars in general understand and experience the world as devoid of supernatural elements, and so they argue that there is no analogy in the present to warrant accepting supernatural occurrences in the past. But the whole line of reasoning falls apart if one simply steps outside the narrow confines of the secularized experience of some Western scholars, for present human experience on a global scale is saturated with reported experiences of the supernatural.

Consider, for example, one commonly reported cross-cultural, supernatural phenomenon—demonization. This phenomenon is found throughout history up to the present time in a remarkably wide variety of cultures.[57] There are a number of things that typically characterize demonized people across cultures, and some of these characteristics are hard to explain on strictly naturalistic terms.[58] Interestingly

57. See E. Bourguignon, "Spirit Possession Belief and Social Structure," in *The Realm of the Extra-Human: Ideas and Actions*, ed. A. Bharatic (Paris: Mouton, 1976), 17–26; A. R. Tippett, "Spirit Possession as It Relates to Culture and Religion," in *Demon Possession*, ed. J. W. Montgomery (Minneapolis: Bethany Fellowship, 1976). Bourguignon has reported the "striking finding" that of 488 societies sampled, drawn from all of the "six major ethnographic regions into which the *Ethnographic Atlas* divides the world," spirit possession beliefs appeared in 74 percent ("Spirit Possession," 19).

58. E. D. Wittkower, "Trance and Possession States," *International Journal of Social Psychiatry* 16 (1970): 156; P. Stevens Jr., "Spirit Possession: Non-Pharmacological Bases for Understanding a Cultural Universal" (paper presented to the Jesus Seminar, Rutgers University, New Brunswick, NJ, October 1992). H. Salmons and D. J. Clark have remarked: "What is interesting, though, is that even in a Western culture in which demoniacal belief is not an active part of orthodox religious practice, such syndromes still arise, and similarities occur between patients from widely differing cultures" ("Cacodemonomania," *Psychiatry* 50 [1987]: 53).

enough, most of these features also parallel New Testament reports of demonization and exorcism.[59] Some of these cross-cultural characteristics are the following:[60]

- Demonized people are sometimes "seized" by a demon, causing them to fall into seizures or trances.

- Demonized people frequently engage in uncontrollable and uncharacteristic outbursts of violent behavior, sometimes exhibiting strength seemingly beyond their natural capacities.

- Demonized people sometimes recite information whose acquisition is difficult to explain by natural means.

- Demonized people sometimes exhibit a temporary ability to speak in languages they did not learn.

- Demonized people on occasion manifest bizarre physical behavior that seems to go beyond anyone's natural capacities—for example, fantastic facial contortions and physically improbable limb rotations.

- People involved in exorcisms sometimes report objects moving, or even flying, in the vicinity of the demonized person.[61]

59. There is, however, a significantly distinct element to the exorcistic ministry of Jesus, his earliest disciples, and a good sector of the early postapostolic church. They tend to differ from what we find elsewhere in at least three respects: the simplicity and non-ritualistic nature of their exorcistic method; the exclusive reliance on the authority of Jesus to expel the demon(s); and, reportedly, the comparative speed and unprecedented success by which they were able to carry out this expulsion. On the exorcistic ministry of Jesus and/or the early church, see G. Twelftree, *Jesus the Exorcist: A Contribution to the Study of the Historical Jesus* (Peabody, MA: Hendrickson, 1993); G. Boyd, *God at War: The Bible and Spiritual Conflict* (Downers Grove, IL: InterVarsity, 1997), 202–3; J. Rousseau, "Jesus, an Exorcist of a Kind," in *SBLSP*, ed. E. H. Lovering Jr. (Atlanta: Scholars Press, 1993), 148–49; E. Yamauchi, "Magic or Miracle? Diseases, Demons and Exorcisms," in *Miracles of Jesus*, ed. D. Wenham and C. Blomberg (Sheffield: JSOT Press, 1986), 131–42.

60. Beyond the sources mentioned above, see T. K. Oesterreich, *Possession: Demonical and Other*, trans. D. Illerson (Secaucus, NJ: Citadel, 1974); M. Shuster, *Power, Pathology, Paradox: The Dynamics of Evil and God* (Grand Rapids: Zondervan, 1987); M. Kraft, *Understanding Spiritual Power: A Forgotten Dimension of Cross-Cultural Mission and Ministry* (New York: Orbis, 1995); J. R. Nevius, *Demon Possession* (1894; repr., Grand Rapids: Kregel, 1968); J. Lhermitte, *True and False Possession* (New York: Hawthorne Books, 1963); F. D. Goodman, *How about Demons? Possession and Exorcism in the Modern World* (Bloomington and Indianapolis: Indiana University Press, 1988); W. Sargant, *The Mind Possessed* (Philadelphia: Lippincott, 1974); W. Wink, *Unmasking the Powers: The Invisible Forces That Determine Human Existence* (Philadelphia: Fortress, 1986); M. S. Peck, *People of the Lie* (New York: Simon & Schuster, 1983), 182–253; idem, *A Glimpse of the Devil: A Psychiatrist's Personal Accounts of Possession, Exorcism and Redemption* (New York: Free Press, 2005); M. Martin, *Hostage to the Devil* (New York: Bantam, 1977); and G. Dow, "The Case for Demons," *Churchman* 94 (1980): 199–208. The following list and subsequent discussion is also informed by the authors' own experiences with exorcism as well as firsthand interactions with others involved in similar experiences.

61. Jamie Bulatao, for instance, claims that while he believes most cases of purported possession can be explained in naturalistic, psychological terms, he has personally encountered four cases where the demonic phenomenon "was not only occurring inside the person but actually manifested itself by external events" that seemed inexplicable in natural terms—including the hurling of stones by an apparently unseen force. He justifiably concludes that "these phenomena present a challenge to human understanding" ("Local

To the thinking of most who witness phenomena like these—and the authors of this work count themselves among them—attempts to explain some of these phenomena in strictly natural terms are implausible, to say the least. The same could be said about a host of other supernatural phenomena that "present human experience" includes—if we step outside the shallow pool of experience represented by the naturalistic Western worldview.[62]

It is not uncommon for people in non-Western cultures to claim to have encountered angelic and/or demonic beings, experienced instantaneous healings, witnessed deceased people coming back to life, or witnessed supernatural occurrences of other kinds. Clearly, outside the narrow experience of secularized Western scholars, "present human experience" is not by any means devoid of the supernatural.

Now, if our goal is to do our historical research in as objective a manner as possible, it would seem we should strive to apply the principle of analogy in a similarly objective manner—and therefore we should consider cross-cultural experiential data. Unfortunately, Western naturalistic scholars rarely take supernatural claims found in non-Western cultures seriously. Instead, they treat reports of the supernatural in other cultures the same way they treat reports of the supernatural in the past. Typically they dismiss such reports as hearsay, legend, hallucination, psychosomatic hysteria, exaggeration, intentional fabrication, or something of the sort.[63] Belief in supernatural occurrences today, as much as in

---

Cases of Possession and Their Cure," *Philippine Studies* 30 [1982]: 424–25). See also Scott Peck's book, *A Glimpse of the Devil*, which includes descriptions of two exorcisms in which he was personally involved. For Edith Turner's (wife and colleague of the famed anthropologist Vic Turner) experience in Africa of an exorcism involving (by Western scientific standards) seemingly impossible phenomena, see *Experiencing Ritual: A New Interpretation of African Healing* (Philadelphia: University of Pennsylvania, 1992), 149–50; and esp. idem, "The Reality of Spirits," *ReVision* 15/1 (1992): 28.

62. See C. S. Keener, *The Gospel of John: A Commentary*, 2 vols. (Peabody, MA: Hendrickson, 2003), 1:263–67.

63. For example, some scholars have attempted to account for at least some of the cross-cultural commonality of behaviors associated with possession and exorcism by noting the common characteristics of certain physical and psychological maladies (e.g., epilepsy, disassociative identity disorder) and the common primitive inclination to regard such afflictions in superstitious ways. See, e.g., C. Goldberg, *Speaking with the Devil: A Dialogue with Evil* (New York: Viking/Penguin, 1996); J. B. Cortés and F. M. Gatti, *The Case against Possessions and Exorcisms* (New York: Vantage Press, 1975); S. McCasland, *By the Finger of God* (New York: Macmillan, 1951); B. Hebblethwaite, "Review of Richards, *But Deliver Us From Evil*," *Theology*, 78 (1975): 293. Others have attempted to explain them in purely reductionistic, psychosocial categories. See, e.g., J. E. D. Esquirol, "Demonomania," in *Vampires, Werewolves, and Demons: Twentieth Century Reports in the Psychiatric Literature*, ed. R. Noll (New York: Brunner/Mazel, 1992), 159–86; G. Obeyesekere, "The Idiom of Demonic Possession: A Case Study," *Social Science and Medicine* 4 (1970): 97–111; M. Pattison, "Psychosocial Interpretations of Exorcism," *Operational Psychiatry* 8 (1977): 5–19; and N. P. Spanos and J. Gottlieb, "Demonic Possession, Mesmerism, and Hysteria: A Social Psychological Perspective on Their Interrelationships," *Journal of Abnormal Psychology* 88 (1979): 527–46. Still others attempt to explain them away as individual psychological disorders. See, e.g., G. Taylor, "Demoniacal Possession and Psychoanalytic Theory," *British Journal of Medical Psychology* 51 (1978): 53–60; W. H. Trethowan, "Exorcism: A Psychiatric Viewpoint," *Journal of Medical Ethics* 2 (1976): 126–37; V. K. Varma,

the past, is evidence of a "naive and mythological" mind-set, according to most naturalistic scholars.

We do not wish to dispute that some, if not the majority, of these reports may be explained in naturalistic terms. But what justification is there for assuming that *all* such reports of the supernatural can be reductively explained in naturalistic terms? At least in some instances there is rather compelling evidence that events transpired that defy the regularities of nature as we now understand them. The primary reason Western naturalistic scholars do not take this evidence seriously, dismissing it instead as the fictive imaginings of "naive and mythologically minded people," is because it conflicts with their own experience.

This leads us, once again, back to the element of circular reasoning that lies at the heart of the secular scholar's application of the principle of analogy to justify a priori ruling out the supernatural in history. The naturalistic scholar declares that present human experience is devoid of the supernatural and thus uses the principle of analogy to rule out the possibility of finding supernatural occurrences in the past. But, as we have just argued, the only reason naturalistic scholars find present human experience to be devoid of the supernatural is because they limit the pool of present human experience to that which coincides with their own very small slice of human experience. On this basis, the conclusion is made that supernatural events do not occur in the present. And on this basis, it is argued that supernatural events cannot occur in the past—*because they do not occur in the present.* It may look like the principle is used to arrive at the conclusion, but in fact it is the conclusion that drives the principle. For apart from assuming that supernatural events do not and cannot occur, the principle of analogy, on its own, could never lead to the conclusion that such events do not and cannot occur.

This reductive, effectively circular use of the principle of analogy amounts to little more than a dogmatic declaration that the naturalistic, scientific, Western worldview encompasses all reality and that worldviews that are open to the supernatural are misguided—"naive and mythologically minded." In essence, this is tantamount to an unwarranted assertion of cultural imperialism. It is a declaration that the modern, scientific, Western worldview is superior to all other worldviews, ancient or contemporary. Of course, it cannot be denied that the naturalistic, scientific, Western worldview has brought about remarkable advances in technology that have improved the standard of living for those fortunate enough to have access

---

M. Bouri, and N. N. Wig, "Multiple Personality in India: Comparison with Hysterical Possession State," *American Journal of Psychotherapy* 35 (1981): 113–20; C. A. Ward and M. H. Beaubrun, "Psychodynamics of Demon Possession," *Journal for the Scientific Study of Religion* 19 (1980): 201–7; and F. D. Whitwell and M. G. Barker, "'Possession' in Psychiatric Patients in Britain," *British Journal of Medical Psychology* 53 (1980): 287–95. We of course do not deny there are many cases that can be plausibly and entirely explained in these categories. In our own estimation, we have witnessed some of these cases ourselves. However, we find these categories of explanation to be altogether inadequate in accounting for certain phenomena associated with demonization and exorcism.

to them. It can, therefore, be plausibly argued that this worldview is, in certain respects, *more useful* than other worldviews. But does this limited pragmatic advantage warrant the assumption that this naturalistic worldview is more accurate than other worldviews vis-à-vis the question of whether supernatural occurrences take place or not? Does it justify Western scholars dismissing all whose experience conflicts with the naturalism of their own worldview as "naive and mythologically minded"? We see no reason to answer these questions in the affirmative.

On this matter we believe naturalistic historical-critical scholars have something vital to learn from certain contemporary, Western ethnographers. For several decades now, an increasing number of academics in the fields of cross-cultural studies, especially anthropology, have been calling into question the long-standing tendency of Western scholars to reinterpret in naturalistic categories events that are interpreted as supernatural by the indigenous people who experience them. This dogmatic, naturalistic approach, they argue, is *ethnocentric*, for it assumes at the outset that the ethnic perspective of the West is the standard by which others may be judged. More specifically it has been described as *Eurocentric*, for it assumes that white-dominated European culture is the standard by which others are to be judged. And it has been appropriately described as *chronocentric*, for it assumes that the perspective of our modern times is the standard by which all times and cultures are to be judged.[64]

Against this, many Western ethnographers are now arguing that an accurate understanding of other cultures can be arrived at only if we begin by seriously entertaining the possibility that the culture being studied is, in fundamental ways, on the same level as our own. They are calling for a "new democratized epistemology" wherein the worldviews of other cultures are taken seriously as rival interpretations of a shared reality.[65] While affirming the technological benefits that the naturalistic, scientific, Western worldview has brought us, and while not relinquishing the validity of critical reason so valued by Western academia, these individuals are arguing that this worldview should no longer be used as the comprehensive and ubiquitous measuring stick of the truthfulness of all other perspectives.

64. Along these lines see, e.g., G. E. Marcus and D. Cushman, "Ethnographies as Texts," *Annual Review of Anthropology* 11 (1982): 25–69; P. Stoller, "Eye, Mind and Word in Anthropology," *L'Homme* 24 (1984): 91–114; J. R. Bowlin and P. G. Stromberg, "Representation and Reality in the Study of Culture," *American Anthropologist* 99 (1997): 123–34; R. Feleppa, "Emics, Etics, and Social Objectivity," *Current Anthropology* 27 (1986): 243–55. On the issue of chronocentricism, Thomas Oden rightly calls into question "the myth of modern superiority, the pretense of modern chauvinism that assumes the intrinsic inferiority of all premodern wisdoms" (*Requiem: A Lament in Three Movements* [Nashville: Abingdon, 1995], 132–33).

65. D. Rose, *Living the Ethnographic Life* (Newbury Park, CA: Sage, 1990), 46. As we shall argue more fully below, accepting this methodology need not entail wholesale cultural relativism. It only entails that one's own cultural perspective not be assumed a priori to be the correct perspective in every respect. Westerners do have much to teach other cultures. But we also have much to learn. The awareness of the spiritual world embodied in many non-Western cultures is one area where we believe we have much to learn.

The implications of this "new democratized epistemology" are significant for cross-cultural studies. It is bringing about a new sort of "radical ethnography, one that gets you close to those you study at the risk of going native and never returning." It suggests a methodology that stipulates that Western ethnographers no longer uncritically accept "the received assumptions," rooted in the "academic texts, methods, and corporate academic culture" in which they were trained.[66] This new approach calls for an epistemological humility that places the Western scholar in a position to actually have the scholar's own worldview challenged, perhaps learning something about the nature of reality from the culture he or she is exploring.

John Bowlin and Peter Stromberg put the matter starkly:

> It should regularly occur [to us Western ethnographers] that good ethnography encourages us to conclude that beliefs and warrants held by members of another society track the truth better than our own. An ethnography sufficiently humble about matters of belief must concede this possibility and should regard this kind of critical revision of our own beliefs as a welcomed consequence of careful inquiry.[67]

It is with this epistemological humility in mind that some Western ethnographers are now encouraging their colleagues in other disciplines to consider appeals to the supernatural as potentially valid. Indeed, a surprising number of those who have adopted this stance have done so as a result of having personally experienced supernatural events in their fieldwork. Such scholars have found that when we set aside the traditional assumptions of Western secularity and superiority, we discover that the Western perspective is actually defective—or at least deficient—in certain crucial respects. There is, among other things, a supernatural dimension to reality that our naturalistic, scientific perspective on the world tends to blind us to.[68]

It is just this epistemological humility that seems to be lacking in much historical-critical New Testament scholarship today. While most scholars in our postmodern context concede that worldviews involve elements of social constructs, naturalistic historical-critical New Testament scholars have often seemed unwilling to treat their own worldview in this fashion. Their own naturalistic perspective too often functions as the privileged vantage point and thus remains immune to criticism. While all worldviews are acknowledged to be involved to some degree in social construc-

---

66. Ibid., 12.

67. Bowlin and Stromberg, "Representation and Reality," 130.

68. Such phenomena are witnessed by Western academics more frequently than one would infer from the academic literature. Fear of ostracization in the academic community makes many hesitant to report their experiences. See P. Stoller, "Eye, Mind and Word," 93; idem, "Beatitudes, Beasts, and Anthropological Burdens," *Medical Anthropology Newsletter* 13 (August 1982): 2; L. Ramanucci-Ross, "On Analyses of Event Structures as Philosophical Derivations of the Investigating Cultures," in *Essays in Humanistic Anthropology*, ed. B. Grindal and D. Warren (Washington, DC: University Press of America, 1979), 57–58, 60.

tion, those of "naive and mythologically minded" people seem to be treated as more socially constructed—less reflective of "reality"—than the secularized perspective of the Western academy, which often is treated as the path by which to know reality. Hence no evidence in non-Western or ancient cultures that certain events defy naturalistic explanation is allowed to seriously challenge this perspective.

As the sociologist Peter Berger notes in response to a previously cited statement of Rudolf Bultmann, in much New Testament scholarship, "the electricity- and radio-users are placed intellectually above the Apostle Paul." The irony of this inconsistency is "funny," according to Berger. For, he continues:

> What is good for the first century is good for the twentieth.... Each [worldview] has its appropriate plausibility structure, its plausibility-maintaining mechanisms. If this is understood, then the appeal to *any* alleged modern consciousness loses most of its persuasiveness.... One has the terrible suspicion that the Apostle Paul may have been one-up cognitively, after all. As a result of such considerations an important shift takes place in the argument on the alleged demise of the supernatural in contemporary society.[69]

According to Berger, if we are consistent in viewing *all* worldviews as, among other things, involving social constructs, we will not take the alleged "demise of the supernatural" in contemporary society as an indication that we are necessarily moving toward a superior view of reality. It may just as well be an indication that we are moving toward an inferior, impoverished view of reality. If we are consistent, we will concede that the naturalistic, scientific, Western worldview is as socially constructed, as culturally myopic, as all other worldviews. And this means we must remain open to the possibility that, for example, the Gospel writers and others living and moving within a first-century Jewish worldview may in some respects be "one-up" on us, epistemologically speaking. At the very least, it means we should operate in epistemological humility, putting ourselves in a position to learn from, rather than simply to stand in judgment over, the range of experiences—natural and even supernatural—testified to by other people, ancient and contemporary.

The Alleged Naturalism of the Western Worldview

This brings us to our second substantial criticism of the way in which scholars often employ the Troeltschean principle of analogy to defend their unequivocal commitment to naturalistic explanations of the past. We have thus far left unexamined the common claim that the Western worldview is devoid of the supernatural. It is on this basis that naturalistic scholars argue that the principle of analogy requires that we do not allow for miracles in our reconstructions of the past. We now want to argue that this claim is patently *false*.

69. P. L. Berger, *A Rumor of Angels: Modern Society and the Rediscovery of the Supernatural* (Garden City, NY: Doubleday, 1969), 51–52.

The undeniable fact is that the majority of Western people have never stopped believing in and occasionally experiencing what they perceive to be supernatural occurrences.[70] Indeed, though many continue to announce the "demise of the supernatural" in Western culture, all indications are that the belief in, and experience of, the supernatural is, if anything, *increasing* in contemporary Western culture.[71]

For example, in 1989 George Gallup Jr. reported that 82 percent of the American populace affirmed that, "even today, miracles are performed by the power of God."[72] So too, a 1998 Southern Focus Poll found that 83.1 percent of its respondents believed that "God answers prayers," with 33.6 percent reporting that they had personally experienced having "an illness cured by prayer."[73] Not only this, but it is undeniable that Western culture at the present time is experiencing a significant surge of people publicly reporting experiences of healings, angelic or demonic encounters, and so on. Whatever else one makes of this, at the very least it suggests that the "modern, Western worldview" is not nearly as committed to naturalism as scholars such as Bultmann, Harvey, Funk, and others have suggested.

The stark clash between what naturalistic scholars say the Western worldview should entail, on the one hand, and what the majority of Western people in fact believe and experience, on the other, suggests that when scholars proclaim that the Western worldview is incurably naturalistic, their intent is not so much to *describe* what the Western worldview *is* as it is to *prescribe* what the Western worldview *should be*. When Bultmann confidently proclaimed that it is "impossible to use electric light and the wireless" and yet "believe in the New Testament world of spirits and miracles,"[74] he obviously knew that many Western people in his day had no difficulty whatsoever using lights while believing in spirits and miracles. His point clearly was not about what modern people in fact believe, but about what he believes modern people should believe. He was, in effect, announcing that if ordinary Western people were not "naive" and "mythologically minded"—if they

70. As R. Mullin has demonstrated; see *Miracles and the Modern Religious Imagination* (New Haven: Yale University Press, 1996).

71. A quick look through the popular media over the last few decades substantiates this claim. See, e.g., B. Kantrowitz et al., "In Search of the Sacred," *Newsweek*, November 28, 1994, 52–62; E. Tayler, "Desperately Seeking Spirituality," *Psychology Today* 27 (November/December 1994): 54–68; J. Adler et al., "Special Report: Spirituality 2005," *Newsweek*, August 29/September 5, 2005, 46–65. With respect to the existence of spirits, see the report on the angel craze of the 1990s, "Angels Among Us," *Time*, December 27, 1993, 56–65. See also G. Gallup Jr. and J. Castelli, *The People's Religion: American Faith in the 90s* (New York: Macmillan, 1989).

72. Gallup and Castelli, *People's Religion*, 58. A 1995 *Time* magazine poll found that 69 percent of Americans believe in miracles; J. Bonfante et al., "The Message of Miracles," *Time*, April 10, 1995, 65.

73. This last poll—published in the *Journal for the Scientific Study of Religion*—revealed the startling fact that when it comes to belief in "paranormal phenomena . . . better-educated people are actually more likely to believe" (T. W. Rice, "Believe It or Not: Religious and Other Paranormal Beliefs in the United States," *JSSR* 42 [2003]: 95–106 [quotes from p. 98, 101]). How this is to be reconciled with the "critical" perspective that belief in the supernatural is a characteristic of "naive" and "mythologically minded" people is not quite clear.

74. Bultmann, "New Testament and Mythology," 5.

were enlightened and understood what critical scholars such as himself understood about the Western worldview—they would find it as impossible to use lights and continue to believe in spirits and miracles as he does.

Similarly, consider Robert Funk's announcement that "the notion that God interferes with the order of nature from time to time in order to aid or punish is no longer credible, *in spite of the fact that most people still believe it.*"[75] Now, one might wonder how a scholar can declare that a belief is no longer credible while in the next breath conceding that most people continue to find it credible. Again, it seems that Funk, like Bultmann, is not describing what people in Western culture in fact find impossible to believe. Rather, he is prescribing what he believes people in Western culture *should* find impossible to believe—if they were not so "naive and mythologically minded."[76]

We noted previously the ethnocentrism inherent in the restriction of the pool of present human experience to modern Western culture alone. Now, however, it seems the restrictions are actually much more limited than that. Not only is the pool of present human experience limited to contemporary Western culture, but within this context it is also limited to the *secular academic subculture within this single culture.* This understanding and experience of the world as devoid of the supernatural not only conflicts with the vast majority of people around the globe and throughout time; it contrasts as well with the majority of people in the modern Western culture itself. Ironically, this dogmatic naturalistic stance is declared to represent truly "critical" scholarship—a scholarship that purportedly strives to be as self-critical and unbiased in its approach to history as possible.

It is important for us to realize that it is not simply common people who continue to resist the alleged "demise of the supernatural" in Western culture. An increasing number of academics are among the majority who believe in, and sometimes reportedly experience, the supernatural—a fact that makes the continued practice of dismissing the supernatural on the part of naturalistic scholars all the more curious.

The last several decades have brought a virtual explosion of interest in the supernatural within certain quarters of the Western academy. From philosophical assessments of miracles,[77] to dialogues between physicists and theologians on

75. Funk, "Twenty-one Theses," 8 (emphasis added).

76. One can understand this tendency within the historical-critical tradition as a carrying on of the grand "scientific" enterprise—in the heroic tradition of the pre-Socratic *physiologoi*—to explain all phenomena naturalistically and rationalistically, while the surrounding masses wallow in myth and mystery. As Gregory Vlastos pictures the *physiologoi* of old, so, it seems, it is tempting for the guild of historical-critical New Testament scholars to imagine themselves as "a handful of intellectuals against the world" (*Plato's Universe* [Seattle: University of Washington Press, 1975], chaps. 1–3).

77. For various contemporary perspectives on miracles, all of which take the notion seriously, see F. J. Beckwith, *David Hume's Argument against Miracles: A Critical Analysis* (Lanham, MD: University Press of America, 1989); R. D. Geivett and G. R. Habermas, eds., *In Defense of Miracles: A Comprehensive Case for God's Action in History* (Downers Grove, IL: InterVarsity, 1997); J. Houston, *Reported Miracles: A Critique of Hume* (New York: Cambridge University Press, 1994); R. A. H. Larmer, *Water into Wine?*

the notion of divine action,[78] to advances in the study of the paranormal,[79] to cutting-edge research on contemporary religious experience,[80] a wide variety of Western academics in our postmodern world are taking seriously the very ideas that Funk, Bultmann, Harvey, and the majority of legendary-Jesus theorists judge to be nothing more than the vestigial remains of an outdated, naive, premodern worldview. Even within the natural sciences—the very group of scholars popularly known as tough-minded, naturalistic empiricists—there is a growing percentage who profess faith in a personal God, in the reality of life after death, and even in the possibility of miracles.[81]

Most noteworthy, perhaps, are the numerous academics who have "converted" from a naturalistic worldview to a worldview that is open to the supernatural, often based on undeniable experiences they have had with what they perceive to be supernatural occurrences. We noted previously that an increasing number of ethnographers fall into this category. Typically taking place during fieldwork in non-Western, and/or non-first-world settings, Western academics have reported personal experiences that defy natural explanation. These encounters serve in

An Investigation of the Concept of Miracle (Montreal: McGill-Queen's University Press, 1988); Pearl, "Miracles"; R. Swinburne, The Concept of Miracle (New York: Macmillan, 1970); T. C. Williams, The Idea of the Miraculous: The Challenge to Science and Religion (New York: Macmillan, 1990). On the history of the debate on miracles, see R. M. Burns, The Great Miracles Debate: From Joseph Glanvill to David Hume (East Brunswick, NJ: Associated University Press, 1981); C. Brown, Miracles and the Critical Mind (Grand Rapids: Eerdmans, 1984).

78. Especially noteworthy here is the Divine Action Project (DAP), cosponsored by the Vatican Observatory and the Center for Theology and the Natural Sciences (Berekely, CA). Between 1988 and 2003, the DAP brought together an impressive array of scientists and theologians to reflect on this question. A number of published volumes came out of this project. For a recent description and assessment of the DAP, see W. J. Wildman, "The Divine Action Project, 1988–2003," Theology and Science 2 (2004): 31–75. Wildman's "Kantian skepticism" vis-à-vis the project is engaged by several thinkers in Theology and Science 2/2 (October 2004). See also S. T. Davis, "God's Action," in Defense of Miracles, 163–77; J. P. Moreland, "Science, Miracles, Agency Theory and the God-of-the-Gaps," in Defense of Miracles, 132–48; A. Plantinga, "Divine Action in the World (Synopsis)," Ratio, n.s., 14 (2006): 495–504.

79. See, e.g., M. Stoeber and H. Meynell, eds., Critical Reflections on the Paranormal (Albany: SUNY, 1996).

80. See, e.g., T. Beardsworth, A Sense of Presence (Oxford: Religious Experience Research Unit, Manchester College, 1977); C. David, The Evidential Force of Religious Experience (New York: Oxford University Press, 1989); D. Hay, Exploring Inner Space: Scientists and Religious Experience (New York: Penguin, 1982); M. Maxwell and V. Tschudin, Seeing the Invisible: Modern Religions and Other Transcendent Experiences (London: Arkana/Penguin, 1990); K. E. Yandell, The Epistemology of Religious Experience (New York: Cambridge University Press, 1993).

81. E. J. Larson and L. Witham, "Scientists Are Still Keeping the Faith," Nature 386 (April 3, 1997): 435–36. This survey notes that the percentage of scientists who believe in a personal God remains virtually unchanged from that reflected in a poll taken in 1916 (p. 435). The surprising continued belief in the supernatural on the part of common folk and academics alike has led certain sociologists to begin debating why the process of secularization in the West and around the globe has not occurred as it was expected to do. See J. Sweeney, "Recent Trends in British Sociology of Religion," Irish Theological Quarterly 69 (2004): 295–301.

some sense to "crack" their naturalistic paradigm, forcing them to the conclusion that there is more to reality than the scientific worldview allows for—things that other cultures often report.[82]

But it is not only in the field of ethnography that academics have "converted" to a more open-minded worldview. On the basis of experiences with supernatural evil in his counseling experience, the late, acclaimed psychotherapist Scott Peck came to believe in a personal devil who sometimes supernaturally afflicts people.[83] So too, on the basis of religious experiences, some biblical scholars—such as Jesus Seminar members Marcus Borg and Walter Wink—have come to be much more open to the reality of things beyond the commonly experienced natural order.[84]

Wink in particular recounts his experience in a way that addresses the issue at hand. Wink had a "religious" experience that fundamentally altered the paradigm within which he carried out his historical-critical research. The experience, he writes, "has colored everything I do as a biblical scholar." From this he makes the following significant observation:

> Historical research depends on analogy to understand the past. If we have limited analogues—if for some reason our life is truncated, or too narrow, or filled with anxiety about over-stepping the permissible, then our capacity to understand the past will suffer as a result. . . . As a result of my own experience, I have no trouble believing in the plausibility of some events that to some of my fellow scholars simply seem impossible. . . . Because of . . . [my] experiences with spiritual healing, I have no difficulty believing that Jesus actually healed people, and not just of psychosomatic diseases.[85]

Wink goes on to make an insightful observation about why so many Western scholars come to skeptical conclusions about narratives that report miracles.

> Other scholars, who have never experienced such healing, either in themselves or others, may find themselves totally rejecting the historicity of the healing stories. . . . This judgment, however, would be made not on historical grounds, but on the basis of their worldview, which is materialism. . . . *People with an attenuated sense of what is possible will bring that conviction to the Bible and diminish it by the poverty of their own experience.* . . . I am beginning to understand that no scholar can construct a picture of Jesus beyond the level of spiritual awareness that she or he has attained.

82. Two classic examples are L. Peters, *Ecstasy and Healing in Nepal* (Malibu, CA: Undena, 1981), and Turner, *Experiencing Ritual*, 149–50; idem, "Reality of Spirits," 28. As noted earlier, it seems anthropologists confront the supernatural much more frequently than one would think, given how rarely these reports are published.

83. Peck, *People of the Lie*; idem, *Glimpse of the Devil*.

84. Statements on this matter by Borg and Wink come out in two very personal accounts published in the Westar Institute's *Fourth R* magazine. See M. Borg, "Me and Jesus: The Journey Home," *Fourth R* (July/August 1993): 7–9; W. Wink, "Write What You See," *Fourth R* (May/June 1994): 5–9.

85. Wink, "Write What You See," 6.

No reconstruction outstrips the reconstructor. We cannot explain truths we have not yet understood.[86]

The fact that a certain group of scholars have an impoverished sense of the supernatural is, in our view, not surprising. Nor is the fact that these scholars would find it more difficult than others to accept the miracle accounts of the Gospels particularly problematic. Given how our personal experience influences our overall belief structures, this is, to some degree, inevitable.

What is problematic, however, at least on a methodological level, is the tendency within the naturalistic sector of the guild to canonize their "impoverished experiences" of the supernatural as the standard of critical scholarship. Rather than conceding that their experience is limited and their secular perspective but one of many, there is a tendency to transform their own experience and perspective into a metaphysical given—the one perspective that purportedly reflects the way the world really is. Ironically, this single perspective is enthroned in the midst of a discipline whose stated intention is the maintenance of a truly *self-critical* approach to the doing of historiography.

Becoming Consistently Critical

We trust it is clear that our complaint throughout this chapter has not been with critical historiography per se—unless one equates "critical" with "naturalistic," as has often been the case with respect to practitioners of the classical "historical-critical method" of post-Enlightenment biblical studies. We fully accept that unless one approaches history with a critical eye toward all historical claims, unless one strives to be as objective as possible in assessing historical evidence, and unless one prefers (all other things being equal) natural explanations over explanations that make supernatural appeals, one has no way to distinguish reliable history from myth, legend, propaganda, or simply bad historical reporting. Our complaint, rather, is that the classical historical-critical method has not been *critical enough*. While modern, Western, secular scholars have been very critical of the allegedly "mythological" worldview of ancient peoples, they have not to date consistently and aggressively applied critical reason to *their own* naturalistic worldview.

86. Ibid., 6, 7 (emphasis added). Incidentally, these and other considerations have caused Wink to decide to "ignore the Seminar's data-base and voting tabulations" when doing his own historical reconstruction of Jesus (p. 9). For several interdisciplinary explorations of religious experiences that make use of "altered states of consciousness" research and that focus on experiences of the resurrected Jesus, see J. J. Pilch, "Appearances of the Risen Jesus in Cultural Context: Experiences of Alternate Reality," *Biblical Theology Bulletin* 28 (1998): 52–60; P. H. Wiebe, *Visions of Jesus: Direct Encounters from the New Testament to Today* (New York: Oxford, 1997); idem, "Altered States of Consciousness and New Testament Interpretation of Post-Resurrection Appearances," *McMaster Journal of Theology and Ministry* 4 (2001), www.mcmaster.ca/mjtm/4–4.html. See also L. T. Johnson, *Religious Experience in Earliest Christianity* (Minneapolis: Fortress, 1998); Ratcliffe, "Scientific Naturalism," 323–45.

Peter Berger is among a number of scholars who have argued that it is time for the scholarly critical enterprise to become consistent. That is, it is time for "critical" Western scholars to employ the critical moment in an equal-opportunity manner—applying it to their own worldview. It is time Western scholars relinquish the arbitrarily assumed, metaphysically privileged status of the modern, naturalistic worldview and, at the very least, entertain a new "democratized epistemology." When the critical methodology is applied consistently, Berger argues, it "bends back on itself." The result is that the "relativizers are relativized" and the alleged "debunkers" of supernatural reports are themselves "debunked." The privileged epistemological perspective of the modern, Western scholar is finally brought to an end.

According to Berger, this does not necessarily result in a "total paralysis of thought," as though no one would any longer be warranted in making *any* truth claims vis-à-vis worldview issues. But it does result in a "new freedom and flexibility in asking questions of truth."[87] David deSilva argues along similar lines when he calls for a paradigmatic change in New Testament circles.

> What is crucial is that secularist New Testament scholars reflect on the dangerously Fundamentalistic enterprise in which they have been engaging for some time, namely the maintenance work of legitimating world-constructions rather than true critical investigation.... The challenge is to be critical of a commonly-held, taken-for-granted world-construction which has assumed the stature of absolute reality, when it is in fact no more than an on-going social construction.... In effect, the program of demythologization begun by Bultmann with the New Testament reaches its true conclusion here, in the "demythologization" of a secularized worldview.[88]

Thomas Oden, a former Bultmannian, expresses a similar concern when he writes:

> The hermeneutic of suspicion has been safely applied to the history of Jesus but not to the history of the historians. It is now time to turn the tables. The hermeneutic of suspicion must be fairly and prudently applied to the critical movement itself. This is the most certain next phase of biblical scholarship—criticism of criticism.[89]

87. Berger, *Rumor of Angels*, 52–53.

88. D. A. deSilva, "The Meaning of the New Testament and the *Skandalon* of World Construction," *EQ* 64 (1992): 20–21.

89. T. Oden, *Systematic Theology*, 3 vols. (San Francisco: Harper & Row, 1989), 2:226. Similarly, Elizabeth Schussler Fiorenza (in her 1987 presidential address to the SBL) writes: "A-political detachment, objective literalism, and scientific value-neutrality are the rhetorical postures that seem to be dominant in the positivistic paradigm of biblical scholarship. The decentering of this rhetoric of disinterestedness and presupposition-free exegesis seeks to recover the political context of biblical scholarship and its public responsibility. The scientific ethos of biblical studies was shaped by the struggle of biblical scholarship to free itself from dogmatic and ecclesiastical controls.... The pretension of biblical studies to 'scientific' modes of inquiry that deny their hermeneutical and theoretical character and mask their historical-social location prohibits a critical reflection on their rhetorical theological practices in their

When we apply "the hermeneutic of suspicion" to the "critical movement itself," as Oden calls for, we find that it is not quite as scientific, objective, and critical as it claims to be. To the contrary, it is largely driven by a metaphysical assumption buttressed by a form of cultural and intellectual elitism. It is time for the critical enterprise to turn its critical ideal on the area it has to date been most remiss in applying it, where it is now most needed, where it is most difficult to apply, and where it will affect the most paradigmatic change—namely, *on its own naturalistic presumption.*[90]

Freedom and Flexibility without Absolute Relativism

The "freedom and flexibility" Berger speaks of—the freedom and flexibility that arises when we bring the postmodern awareness that worldviews involve social constructions to the naturalistic worldview—is precisely what we have been calling for as it concerns the historical-critical approach to reports of supernatural occurrences. While one is certainly justified in looking for plausible naturalistic explanations and, all other things being equal, preferring these over explana-

---

sociopolitical contexts" ("The Ethics of Biblical Interpretation: Decentering Biblical Scholarship," *JBL* 107 [1988]: 11–12).

    Interestingly enough, this criticism has been around for some time—though, it seems, with little effect in some circles. In his famous presidential address to the American Historical Association in 1950, Samuel Eliot Morison reminded his colleagues that "skepticism is properly a two-edged sword in the hands of the historian; and if one edge of the two is keener than the other, it should be turned against oneself" ("Faith of a Historian," *American Historical Review* 61 [1951]: 268).

    90. D. Georgi writes: "Historians, including biblical critics, are not known for exposing themselves to the same kind of historical criticism that they apply to everything and everyone else. The historical situation of contemporary exegetes and their social location usually remain uninvestigated and thus—from a historical-critical and socio-historical perspective—unquestioned" ("The Interest in Life of Jesus Theology as a Paradigm for the Social History of Biblical Criticism," *HTR* 85 [1992]: 51). See also P. Minear, "Gospel History: Celebration or Reconstruction," in *Jesus and Man's Hope,* ed. D. G. Miller and D. Y. Hadidian (Pittsburgh: Pittsburgh Theological Seminary, 1971), 2:18. We suspect that one primary reason that the historical-critical method of biblical studies has been inadequately self-critical when it comes to their a priori rejection of the miraculous is because, from the very rise of this modern discipline, deistic and/or secular biblical scholars saw themselves as locked into ideological combat with the church, from which they were consciously and explicitly attempting to "liberate" the Bible. Few scholars are as forthwith about this explicit and ongoing bias as Helmut Koester, who says, "I am not advocating a value-free, objective agenda for the work of highly trained technicians who have no questions. It is too easily forgotten that the historical-critical method was by no means such an agenda. Rather, it was designed as a hermeneutical tool for the liberation from conservative prejudice and from the power of ecclesiastical and political institutions. Those who fear that the historical-critical method threatens their control over the religious orientation and theological judgment of their constituencies are absolutely correct" ("Epilogue: Current Issues in New Testament Scholarship," in *The Future of Early Christianity: Essays in Honor of Helmut Koester,* ed. B. A. Pearson [Minneapolis: Fortress, 1991], 474). We submit that after two hundred years of the historical-critical method functioning as a one-sided liberation movement, it is time to widen its scope. Today, a truly "equal opportunity" historical-critical method should be as quick to unmask dogmatic secularism as dogmatic ecclesialism.

tions that too quickly appeal to the supernatural, epistemological humility in our postmodern context requires that we reject an a priori totalizing methodological naturalism. It suggests we should instead embrace some form of what we have termed an *open* historical-critical method.

As Berger noted above, adopting the stance of epistemological humility need not, and should not, result in wholesale relativism—"a total paralysis of thought." To the contrary, the very concession that one worldview may be defective or deficient in certain respects as compared to another worldview presupposes a critical-realist interpretation of worldviews. It presupposes we are not absolutely "locked into" our worldviews, as Harvey assumes. While a truly critical approach to history must be one that self-critically takes into account our own culturally conditioned perspective, the very act of relativizing our perspective in relation to another and of critically adjusting our perspective in light of our encounter with other perspectives, presupposes that we have access—if always through some finite human perspective—to a reality that itself stands over and against our collective cultural perspectives. In other words, a truly "critical-realist" approach to history presupposes that there exists an objective reality that can, in principle, be appealed to as we critique our own and others' perspectives.[91]

A democratized epistemology thus does not entail wholesale relativism. It simply means that we are "flexible and free" with regard to our own presuppositions. It means, among other things, that we must strive to understand ancient and/or contemporary primordial cultures on their own terms and acknowledge that our own worldview partakes in elements of social construction as much as theirs. It means that we should never invalidate elements of another culture's perspective simply because it disagrees with our own. It means we should remain open to having our own cultural perspective challenged by the perspective and experiences of others. This stance, we submit, constitutes a truly critical stance—one that strives to be self-critical and open-minded in its quest for truth. As applied to historical matters, it constitutes what we are calling an "open historical-critical method."

We will conclude this chapter by bringing together elements of our critique of the naturalistic historical-critical method as we flesh out several implications of an open historical-critical method.

91. On a critical-realist approach to historiography in the context of biblical studies, see Wright, *New Testament and the People of God*, pt. 1; B. F. Meyer, *Critical Realism and the New Testament* (Alison Park, PA: Pickwick, 1989). In our postmodern world, the issue of worldview evaluation is not a simple or uncontroversial matter. Nonetheless, we are persuaded that broad worldview criteria—i.e., internal consistency, external coherence, explanatory power, and pragmatic ability—do exist and can be fruitfully used in the collective human enterprise of worldview analysis. On plausible criteria for worldview assessment, see A. F. Holmes, *Contours of a Worldview* (Grand Rapids: Eerdmans, 1983), 45–53; H. Netland, *Dissonant Voices: Religious Pluralism and the Question of Truth* (Grand Rapids: Eerdmans, 1991), 180–95.

Toward an *Open* Historical-Critical Method

There are five facets of an open historical-critical method that warrant further attention before we embark on an assessment of the legendary-Jesus thesis throughout the remainder of this book.

A Global Pool of Experience

First, as we have argued already, an open historical-critical method requires that we intentionally draw from as broad a pool of present human experience as possible when seeking analogies for our reconstructions of the past. No longer should scholars feel justified in calling their work "critical" when they foreclose the nature of the conclusions they will find in their historical research by arbitrarily restricting the pool of experience they base their analogies upon to the myopic experience of their own secularized academic subculture. We believe the historical-critical approach to history should mirror the open approach being increasingly embraced by a growing number of contemporary Western ethnographers. And the open historical-critical approach to history should draw extensively from the findings of these ethnographers. If we are to continue to claim to strive for objectivity in our research, the pool of experience we root our analogies in, while remaining "critical," must be global—as opposed to myopically ethnocentric—in scope.

Again, the "democratized epistemology" we advocate being applied to historical studies does not require that we uncritically accept claims of supernatural occurrences in the present as we build on the pool of present human experience for our analogical understanding of the past. Nor does it mean that we uncritically accept claims of supernatural occurrences in the past. Knowing that the world generally operates according to statistical regularities of natural forces, we certainly should exercise appropriate caution toward ancient and contemporary reports that these regularities (i.e., "laws") have, in any given instance, been suspended. But at the same time, knowing that the naturalistic Western worldview most likely does not capture the whole of reality, we must humbly acknowledge that present and past phenomena, in certain cases, may not plausibly be explained by appealing to natural laws alone.

A central claim of this work is that if one remains genuinely open to the historical *possibility* that the portrait(s) of Jesus in the Synoptic Gospels is substantially rooted in history, then, given an appropriate historical method and the evidence at hand, one is justified in concluding that this portrait is historically *plausible*, even that it is *most probably* grounded in history. We are suggesting that the appropriate historical method is an open historical-critical method that can deal with the supernatural occurrences associated with Jesus in a manner that, while "critical," is nonetheless "open" to finding that the properly interpreted evidence points in the direction of these extraordinary phenomena having occurred in actual history. To make the same point from another direction, we submit that when the a priori conviction of naturalism is subtracted from the legendary-Jesus thesis and the historical evidence is reinterpreted accordingly, one finds there is no compelling reason to accept this thesis.

Holding Assumptions Tentatively

Second, and closely related to this, the open historical-critical method requires that all participating scholars understand that a central aspect of their critical, scholarly activity is making their governing assumptions explicit and available for debate. A truly critical scholarly enterprise is one in which presuppositions (religious, philosophical, methodological) are fair game for assessment. No longer can we accept the prevailing tendency among the guild of Western, naturalistic scholars to reserve the honorary title of "critical scholarship" for those who embrace the "closed" view of the world and its history. Truly critical scholars will humbly acknowledge that even their most cherished, fundamental assumptions about the world *may be wrong*. This means that we can no longer neatly separate historical-critical debates about the interpretation of pieces of historical evidence from philosophical debates about the nature of reality. Indeed, to be truly critical in our investigations, everything must be considered fair game.

Of course, through their life experience and personal research, most scholars become *psychologically certain* of various assumptions they make about the world and its history. A variety of factors, including individual psychological constitutions and personal experiences, factor into the plausibility structure of individual scholars—especially on the issue of whether events that defy natural explanation can happen. So it is that the authors of this work are as psychologically certain that supernatural occurrences *can* occur as some other scholars are that they *cannot*. That two different scholars can feel equally psychologically certain about mutually incompatible truth-claims does not undermine the goal of striving for objectivity—*if* scholars will grant at the start that they may be wrong even on matters about which they are psychologically certain. As long as we maintain an epistemological humility and refrain from transforming our psychological certainty into an unassailable metaphysical a priori, we can, in principle, continue asymptotically to strive for objective truth. As long as we remain tentative about our assumptions and our commitment to truth takes precedence over our desire for the reaffirmation of those things of which we are psychologically certain, there is hope that together we can make progress toward the apprehension of actual history, even as we grant that this goal is always approached in an asymptotic fashion.

The fact that there are plenty of cases in which scholars who were once psychologically certain of one paradigm but subsequently "converted" to another shows that we need not, and should not, be locked into the subjectivism of our psychological certainty. The open historical-critical approach we are advocating builds this insight into its methodology by postulating that all assumptions be held tentatively. The conviction of this work is that if scholars can remain open to the genuine possibility that supernatural events can occur, they will find historical evidence associated with the Gospels (and elsewhere) that such events most likely do occur.

Assuming an A Priori Stance of Burden Bearing

Our third observation follows from the second. As we shall discuss later, there is a good deal of debate over where the "burden of proof" should rest as critical historians carry out their investigations. Is it upon the historian who wants to claim that a historical work is reliable? Or is it upon the historian who deems such a document to be unreliable? Not surprisingly, the issue has been especially intense as it concerns works that include supernatural occurrences.

As we shall argue more fully in chapter 9, the historiographical method we are advocating suggests a way around this impasse by recognizing that several insights from conflicting sides of the burden-of-proof debate have something important to offer. One important principle here is that, in one sense, the burden of proof rests upon any scholar making *any* claim about history, whether it be in defense of, or in opposition to, any particular historical document and—we would add—regardless of whether or not this document contains reports of supernatural occurrences.[92]

This means that critical scholars should in principle assume an a priori stance wherein they bear the burden of demonstrating any claim they make. Any judgment the historian makes that breaks neutrality must be defended, and this defense should encompass not only the historian's particular evidentiary reasoning but also, where relevant, the religio-philosophical assumptions that undergird this line of reasoning. Again, in a truly critical scholarly enterprise, everything must be considered fair game.

This a priori stance of burden bearing does not mean that scholars must grant all logically possible historical explanations equal weight prior to the examination of the evidence. Such an absurd posture would undermine historical-critical thinking as much as it would science, since there is always a theoretically infinite number of ways data can be explained. As the work of a number of thinkers suggests, unless our a priori intuitions about reality can be trusted to weed out the vast majority of *logically possible* explanations and present to us a much smaller range of *plausible* explanations, no branch of science, including critical historiography, would be possible.[93] What the ideal of mutual a priori burden bearing does suggest, however, is that *viable* competing historical explanations—that

---

92. D. H. Fisher calls this "the rule of responsibility" (*Historians' Fallacies: Toward a Logic of Historical Thought* [New York: Harper, 1970], 48, 63).

93. So far as we can discern, the decisive turn here was taken by Charles Peirce. Beginning with his famous early essay, "The Fixation of Belief," and continuing through his career, Peirce stressed the role that a prior intuition and "guessing" had on the direction of one's reasoning. The essay, with an accompanying discussion, can be found in D. R. Anderson, *Strands of System: The Philosophy of Charles Peirce* (West Lafayette, IN: Purdue University Press, 1995), 68–117. For discussions on the role of intuition, prior probability, and human reasoning, see M. Polanyi, *Personal Knowledge: Towards a Post Critical*

is, explanations that other informed, sane people find plausible—should not be ruled out of court at the start simply on the grounds that the explanation clashes with the presuppositions of one's plausibility structure.[94]

In other words, this a priori stance does not require that scholars attempt the psychologically impossible and epistemologically disastrous task of abandoning their a priori plausibility structures. But in the name of epistemological humility and the ideal of objectivity, it does require that scholars attempt the psychologically possible and epistemologically advantageous task of self-critically reflecting upon their own plausibility structures in light of those of others. In essence, this stance simply stipulates that critical scholars be open-minded and humble enough to try to seriously entertain claims that others find plausible, regardless of the fact that their own plausibility structures prejudice them against such claims. Additionally, they ought to be willing to place the assumptions that prejudice them against such claims on the table for scholarly analysis and debate.[95]

The Messiness of an Open Historical-Critical Methodology

Fourth, it must be acknowledged that an open historical-critical method such as we are advocating makes the work of historical-critical reconstruction of the past a great deal messier than it has characteristically been imagined in the post-Enlightenment West. How could it not be? Such a method calls for the dethronement of the Western, naturalistic worldview from its privileged position as arbiter of all things historical, and asks that it be as critically scrutinized as any other worldview. It calls for a democratized epistemology that must take seriously perspectives and understandings of the past and present that Western scholars have tended to summarily dismiss. It insists that the religio-philosophical presuppositions that lie behind one's historical methodology—presuppositions that have been taken for granted by many members of the modern, Western academic community—now be placed on the table for analysis and evaluation

---

Philosophy (Chicago: University of Chicago Press, 1962); J. Baron, *Thinking and Deciding*, 3rd ed. (New York: Cambridge University Press, 2000).

94. We refer to "other informed, sane people" instead of other "scholars" to guard against the intellectual elitism and ethnocentrism that has tended to plague the community of naturalistic historical-critical scholars. The epistemological humility that is intrinsic to the democratized epistemology we are advocating bids the (post)modern, Western scholarly community to rethink its privileging of the experience of its membership in the face of the reported majority experience of the broader human community. For an excellent analysis that offers both insights on, and resources for, the sort of appropriately humble (though realist) critical historiography that we are suggesting here, see A. Tucker, "A Theory of Historiography as a Pre-Science," *Studies in History and Philosophy of Science* 24 (1993): 633–67; idem, *Our Knowledge of the Past: A Philosophy of Historiography* (New York: Cambridge University Press, 2004).

95. It is important to note that it is not merely critical historians focusing on the New Testament who have generally failed to expose and explore their presuppositions. As Jonathan Gorman notes, practicing historians in general "rarely make explicit [the] central presuppositions of their writings" (*Understanding History: An Introduction to Analytical Philosophy of History* [Ottawa: University of Ottawa Press, 1992], x).

with respect to their influence upon one's historiographical conclusions.[96] It suggests that a truly interdisciplinary engagement—one that includes ethnography, philosophy, metaphysics, and (a)theology—take place around these important issues associated with the critical historiographical enterprise.[97] Most certainly, the methodology we are advocating is messy business.

At the same time, we must realize that, in one sense, this messiness has always been there. It is just that the naturalistic historical-critical method as practiced paved the way for scholars conveniently to ignore it. The apparent tidiness of the classical historical-critical method to date has been achieved ironically by an inability to focus the skeptical eye inward at itself. With this less than self-critical perspective established, there was no longer any need to debate the presuppositions that drove their work. If a scholar did not operate according to the naturalistic presuppositions of the scholarly guild, that scholar simply was not considered an earnest member of the guild and thus did not need to be taken seriously. Nor was there any need *seriously* to entertain the counter-experience of anyone outside this guild—namely, the vast majority of Western and non-Western people who believe in, and often claim to experience, the supernatural.

In this light, it is hardly surprising that the naturalistic historical-critical method looks a good deal tidier than the open historical-critical method we are advocating. But as an increasing number of scholars are coming to realize, this very tidiness significantly undermines the claim to being "critical" and to be striving for an objective approach to history. The method is tidy largely because—with respect to the supernatural—it is circular. Once the circle is broken, things get

96. To take just one example from a sister discipline, one from which New Testament historians might profit, contemporary historians of the African continent are being faced with a sustained critique of the way in which modern, Western secular historical methodologies have been imperialistically enthroned—with their questions, their interests, their intuitions—as the historical arbiters of Africa's past. A chief source of the methodological conflict is the often casual dismissal by Western historians of the historical value of oral history/tradition. See, e.g., N. E. Nziem, "African Historians and Africanist Historians," in *African Historiographies*, 20–27; J.-P. Chretien, "Confronting the Unequal Exchange of the Oral and the Written," in *African Historiographies*, 75–90; E. J. Alagoa, "African Oral Traditions and Oral History from Within and Without," in *Oral Tradition and Oral History in Africa and the Diaspora: Theory and Practice*, ed. E. J. Alagoa (Lagos, Nigeria: Centre for Black and African Arts and Civilization, 1990), 2–8; G. N. Uzoigwe, "On Values and Oral Tradition: Towards a New Field of Historical Research," in *Oral Tradition and Oral History in Africa*, 42–50; F. B. O. Akporobaro, "African Oral Traditions, Truth and the Creative Imagination," in *Oral Tradition and Oral History in Africa*, 232–39.

97. As many within the historical disciplines have noted, there has been an unfortunate divorce between the philosophy of history and the actual practice of critical historiography for quite some time now. Much of the reason for this revolves around the fact that the philosophy of history had, prior to this, come to be associated with grand system makers such as Hegel and Marx—speculative philosophical systems of history that now generally stand in ruins. One can acknowledge the unfortunate cul-de-sacs into which past grand-scale philosophies of history have led and yet still recognize the importance of the enterprise when done appropriately. For a brief but helpful orienting discussion on the demise of speculative philosophy of history and its replacement by critical philosophy of history (with its various internal debates), see R. Martin, *The Past within Us: An Empirical Approach to Philosophy of History* (Princeton: Princeton University Press, 1989), 7–11.

messier. But it is this messiness that, methodologically speaking, ought to be welcomed.

At the same time, while an open historical-critical methodology is certainly messier than the naturalistic historical-critical method, it need not be chaotic. This method will foster an envisioning of the world and its history as potentially much more complex and ambiguous than the view afforded by a bare naturalism. Critical reason not only can remain intact but also can be applied even more consistently, for it is now applied to the naturalistic historical-critical enterprise itself. There is an inevitable messiness to engaging in historical-critical research in a manner that is genuinely open to discovering supernatural occurrences in history. However, it is a messiness that—on the formulation we are proposing—signals a critical enterprise striving to stay true to its task.

The Limitations of the Open, Historical-Critical Method

It is important to make explicit two limitations of an open historical-critical method—though, in truth, they are limitations that attach to the naturalistic historical-critical method as well.

We have granted that, all other things being equal, scholars should prefer naturalistic to supernaturalistic explanations. Given the empirical fact that the world generally operates according to natural "laws" (descriptively—as opposed to prescriptively—speaking, of course) of cause and effect, it *should* require significantly more evidence to convince us that an event has taken place that involves the suspension of these known regularities than it does to convince us that an event has occurred in keeping with these regularities. The first limitation of the open method we are advocating is that it has no clear and obvious way of objectively assessing what "significantly more" in the previous sentence entails.

The approach we are advocating does require scholars to explicitly expose and defend the presuppositions (the foundational premises of their philosophy of historiography) that orient their work as historians and to willingly adopt an a priori burden-bearing stance. These principles can help to keep the messiness of the method from degenerating into chaos. Yet, at the end of the day, there is an irreducibly worldview-dependent aspect in assessing such data that cannot be avoided. Whether one finds any particular claim that a supernatural event has occurred compelling or not depends to a significant degree on the prior probability that one's plausibility structure assigns to such events. And this plausibility structure is inevitably conditioned by a host of variables, some of which are nonrational and decidedly subjective in nature. Hence, while we all should strive to hold the assumptions that comprise our plausibility structure tentatively and thus strive to not prejudge matters prior to our investigations, and while we must all be ready to put our presuppositions—including our plausibility structures and their prior probability estimations—on the table as part of our case for any conclusion we come to, there is a point beyond which debate will be relatively ineffective.

This limitation, however, is hardly unique to the open historical-critical method. Every judgment a historian makes about any purported event is conditioned by the prior probability the historian's plausibility structure assigned to the event. Indeed, this much is true of all scientific judgments as well. How scientists evaluate evidence for or against a particular theory depends on the prior probability they hold toward the theory in question. And this prior probability is rooted in a plausibility structure that is conditioned by, among other things, some nonrational, subjective factors that cannot easily be assessed.

So, in science and in history there may come a time when the debate ends and we simply have to confess, "This is just the way I see it." Despite this unavoidable subjective element, however, the goal of objectivity need not be abandoned, either in historiography or in science. While all decisions regarding the plausibility of an explanation ultimately involve subjective factors that cannot be rationally ascertained, people who are committed to rationality can exercise an influence on others who are committed to rationality. We share the common goal of wanting to arrive at the most plausible way of explaining data and thereby constructing the most plausible way the past unfolded or, in science, way the world operates. It is this commonality that makes rational discourse possible and that keeps us from being hopelessly locked in our own subjective perceptions. But it is also this commonality that requires that we subject *everything*—including the assumptions and biases we all bring to any weighing of evidence—to the critical eye of the interpersonal cognitive structures of reason.[98]

The second limitation of the open historical-critical method—though this too is a limitation for any critical approach to history—is this: while in theory it can bring us to the point of concluding that a supernatural occurrence *probably* occurred, it cannot conclude that a supernatural occurrence *certainly* occurred. Still less can it provide the *theological meaning* of the event even if it is granted that it occurred. The nature of the critical historiographical enterprise is such that it can never go beyond statements of probability, and its disciplinary parameters end before questions about the transcendent source and/or theological meaning of a plausibly supernatural occurrence can be answered.[99]

98. See Tucker's insightful discussion of theories of historiography as "prescience." Here, Tucker offers a convincing analysis of models of historiography, including the fact that competing models tend to form "schools" that are characterized by "historical incommensurability" (which is decidedly different from "philosophical incommensurability"), etc. See "Theory of Historiography," esp. 636–53.

99. This is not to say that historical research cannot offer a plausible account of how Jesus himself interpreted his own miracles. In fact, Graham Twelftree has provided what, in our view, is a solid case for understanding Jesus's own theological account of his miracles. For a summary of his findings, see *Jesus the Miracle Worker: A Historical and Theological Study* (Downers Grove, IL: InterVarsity, 1999), 346–48. All we are saying here is that historical research alone cannot demonstrate that Jesus's own interpretation of his supernatural acts is the metaphysically correct one. To investigate this question, one must necessarily move from the discipline of historiography to that of philosophy and/or theology. However, as one moves to assess this wider question, it would seem foolish to do so while ignoring Jesus's own explanation.

For example, along with N. T. Wright, we believe it is reasonable to conclude on the basis of an open historical-critical approach that there is no purely natural explanation that can plausibly account for all of the data surrounding the events that led to the early Christian claim that Jesus rose from the dead.[100] Thus, historiographically speaking, we conclude it is more probable than not that something on the order of a supernatural occurrence took place after Jesus's death that led to the reports in the tradition of his bodily resurrection. We submit that a historical-critical method that is not arbitrarily closed to the possibility of supernatural occurrences can take us this far. Something beyond the natural nexus of cause and effect—something *super*-natural—most likely took place. But to ask whether the early Christian *theological interpretation* of this event is correct takes us outside the domain of critical historiography.

Speaking merely as critical historians, we cannot say that it was God who raised Jesus from the dead in order to attest that Jesus is the Son of God and that his death has conquered sin, the devil, and the grave. As we noted in the introduction, and in the interest of putting all cards on the table, we confess that we in fact believe this early Christian interpretation to be true. And one of the reasons we believe this interpretation to be true is that we are convinced that the early Christian claim cannot be explained plausibly in strictly naturalistic terms. Still, the theological question takes us beyond the concerns of historical evidence and historical-critical reasoning per se, and into the wider vistas of religio-philosophical considerations.

When we argue for the general reliability of the Synoptic Jesus tradition in this work, therefore, it must be understood that we are arguing for the probable conclusion that the events recorded about Jesus in these works are rooted in history, not that the theological meaning that the Gospel authors attached to these works necessarily is correct. We are convinced that the interpretation(s) of the Gospel authors are, in fact, correct, but, again, this is a deliverance not of our critical historiography but of our theological reasoning within the context of a Christian theistic worldview.

Summary

The legendary-Jesus theory is significantly rooted in an assumption of naturalism. In this chapter we have offered considerations that we believe demonstrate

100. We find the sustained historical argument of N. T. Wright vis-à-vis Jesus's resurrection to be convincing. Wright concludes his massive study by stating: "The proposal that Jesus was bodily raised from the dead possesses unrivaled power to explain the historical data at the heart of early Christianity" (*The Resurrection of the Son of God* [Minneapolis: Fortress, 2003], 718). In fact, although Wright would reject the term "supernatural," we find his study to be a good example of both the sort of open historical-critical method we are advocating, and of how a New Testament historian can properly follow such a method to the point of concluding for the historicity of just such a supernatural (our language) occurrence.

that this assumption—as an unquestioned presupposition—is unwarranted and inconsistent with the goal of engaging in a truly critical investigation of history that strives for objectivity. In its place we have advocated an open historical-critical method that, among other things, is open to the possibility that evidence from history might require scholars to conclude that an event that defies plausible naturalistic explanation—a *super*-natural occurrence—has happened. This type of methodological openness to the supernatural has been proposed recently by Aviezer Tucker—in our estimation one of the most insightful contemporary philosophers of historiography. In Tucker's words, "A low posterior probability of any hypothesis, including a miracle hypothesis, is no sufficient reason for rejecting it. It is rational to go on accepting and using a low-probability hypothesis as long as there is no better explanation for the evidence."[101]

This open approach to critical historiography will form a part of the method-ological backdrop for the remainder of this book.[102] It will, for example, play at least an implicit role in the next chapter, as we investigate certain aspects of the cultural milieu of first-century Palestinian Judaism, the time and place where the Jesus movement arose. To this issue we now turn.

---

101. A. Tucker, "Miracles, Historical Testimonies, and Probabilities," *History and Theory* 44 (2005): 381. While we find the broad strokes of Tucker's methodological approach to be quite in line with our own, we would take issue with his actual historical assessment of the New Testament data at a number of points.

102. Our concerns in this chapter focus broadly on the question of critical historical method and the supernatural. In applying the open critical method to the more specific question of the miracles of Jesus, we believe that one is led to conclude that the evidence for supernatural occurrences within the ministry of Jesus is quite solid. While space considerations do not allow us to assess the historicity of any particular miracle reported in the Gospels, these questions have been explored in several recent studies, the most exhaustive of which is Twelftree's *Jesus the Miracle Worker*. We find that our methodological conclusions in this chapter comport well with Twelftree's more specific conclusions about the miracles of Jesus. As a summary statement of his findings Twelftree writes: *"There is hardly any aspect of the life of the historical Jesus which is so well and widely attested as that he conducted unparalleled wonders. Further, the miracles dominated and were the most important aspect of Jesus' whole pre-Easter ministry"* (p. 345 [emphasis in original]).

2

A JEWISH LEGEND
OF "YAHWEH EMBODIED"?

HOW OPEN TO "PAGAN" INFLUENCE
WAS FIRST-CENTURY JUDAISM?

In chapter 1 we argued that how one assesses the historicity of the Jesus story found in the Gospels and echoed in other New Testament writings is significantly influenced, if not determined, by the presuppositions one brings to the question. If one assumes at the start that the Jesus story found in the Gospels cannot be rooted in history—for they "just know" that miracles do not occur—then of course they will not find any arguments to the effect that this story *is* rooted in history compelling. They will rather explain the origin and content of this story in purely naturalistic terms—the most plausible explanation being that this story is legendary in nature. This naturalistic assumption, we have argued, is not philosophically defensible and is not reflective of a truly "critical" approach to history. The issue of whether the general contours of the Jesus story found in the Gospels and echoed in other New Testament writings is legendary or historical must be decided in dialogue with the full range of evidence, not on a presuppositional basis alone. The remainder of this book, therefore, will explore evidence relevant to this issue.

The first historical question we explore involves the rise of belief in, and worship of, Jesus as divine within early Christian circles. Where, when, how, and why did this belief/practice originate among the early Christians? But before we can begin to address this question, we must first consider an important and fairly recent shift in scholarly thought on a matter that has direct bearing on our problem.

A Tale of Two Schools

The Old History of Religions School

In order to understand why in this chapter we are focusing on the question of the nature of first-century Judaism, we must first set the context by considering two quite different schools of thought concerning the question: Where, when, how, and why did the belief in, and worship of, Jesus as divine originate? One common scholarly response—a view we can designate as the "hellenization thesis"—argues that, as first-century monotheistic Jews, Jesus and his early followers would never have entertained the notion of a divine man. Rather, this idea only evolved as the Jesus movement left its Palestinian Jewish matrix and syncretistically mixed with Hellenistic philosophical and/or religious ideas that characterized the wider pagan-Gentile world, where a variety of deities abounded in many forms.[1]

1. The "hellenization thesis" has a long history. The second-century philosopher Celsus ridiculed Christians by comparing their worship of Jesus with the cult set up by the emperor Hadrian for his boyfriend Antonius (Origen, *Against Celsus*, III, 36). There is evidence that one strand of Jewish polemic against early Christianity made its case by casting Jesus in terms of the pagan Adonis cult; see H. I. Newman, "The Death of Jesus in the *Toledot Yeshu* Literature," *JTS* 50 (1999): 59–79. Moving to the Reformation era, in his book *On the Errors of the Trinity* (1531), Michael Servetus criticized the "Hellenistic" terms used by Trinitarian Christians to explain their understanding of God. The same line of argument is picked up in the next century by the British Unitarian John Biddle, who traces the corrupting forces of Hellenism to the Platonic legacy of Justin Martyr (*A Confession of Faith Touching the Holy Trinity, According to the Scripture* [London: Thomason, 1648]). At the turn of the nineteenth century, Joseph Priestly's *The Doctrines of Heathen Philosophy Compared with Those of Revelation* (Northumberland: Binns, 1804) presents a similar case. On Biddle, Priestly, and other expressions, see J. Z. Smith, "On the Origin of Origins," in *Drudgery Divine: On the Comparison of Early Christianities and the Religions of Late Antiquity* (Chicago: University of Chicago Press, 1990), 1–35. At the turn of the twentieth century, the classical liberal theologian Adolph von Harnack offered his own now-famous version of this same thesis. In volume one of his *History of Dogma*, Harnack writes: "The great distinction here consists essentially in the fact that the Gnostic systems represent the acute secularizing or hellenizing of Christianity, with the rejection of the Old Testament, while the Catholic system, on the other hand, represents a gradual process of the same kind with the conservation of the Old Testament. . . . It is therefore no paradox to say that Gnosticism, which is just Hellenism, has in Catholicism obtained half a victory" (*History of Dogma*, trans. Neil Buchanan [Boston: Little, Brown & Co., 1901], 1:226–27). For Harnack, the doctrines of the deity of Christ and the Trinitarian God were "dogma"; and dogma was simply "a work of the Greek spirit on the soil of the Gospel" (*History of Dogma*, 1:17). For critical assessments of Harnack's hellenization thesis, see E. P. Meijering, *Die Hellenisierung des Christentums im Urteil Adolph von Harnacks* (Amsterdam: North Holland, 1985); W. Rowe, "Harnack and Hellenization in the Early Church" [an essay review of Meijering's *Die Hellenisierung*], *Philosophia Reformata* 57 (1992): 78–85; and several pertinent essays in W. E. Helleman, ed., *Hellenization Revisited: Shaping a Christian Response within the Greco-Roman World* (Lanham, MD: University Press of America, 1994).

The most sophisticated and influential version of the hellenization thesis was forged within the German *Religionsgeschichtliche Schule* of the late nineteenth and early twentieth centuries—now often referred to as the "old history of religions school."[2] Here, the crowning literary achievement in several ways is Wilhelm Bousset's 1913 work *Kyrios Christos*. Bousset envisions two forms of pre-Pauline Christianity: that typified by the early Palestinian-Jewish community on the one hand, and that found in the "Hellenistic-Gentile" communities on the other. This dichotomy is all-important for Bousset's thesis of christological development. He writes: "The great and decisive turning point in the development of Christianity is marked by its transition to Gentile-Christian territory in its very earliest beginnings. No other event approaches this in importance."[3] Rudolph Bultmann adopted this history of religions approach, and has drawn out the christological implications of Bousset's work: "In any case, the earliest [Palestinian-Jewish] Church did not cultically worship Jesus, even if it should have called him Lord; the Kyrios-cult originated on Hellenistic soil."[4]

Although many of the specifics of the old history of religions school have been largely abandoned today, similar methodological approaches—including the focus on Greco-Roman religion as the impetus for the notion of Jesus's deity—are still being proffered in the contemporary discussion. In recent years, no one has stated the thesis more baldly than Burton Mack in his 1988 study of early Christianity, *A Myth of Innocence*. He argues that:

> One of the more startling differences between the [Jewish reform] Jesus movements and the [Hellenistic] Christ cult is that a mythology sprang up about Jesus as a divine being. This mythology focused on Jesus' resurrection. . . . Jesus the Cynic-sage . . . was erased in the process.[5]

2. On the old history of religions school, see W. Baird, *History of New Testament Research*, vol. 2: *From Jonathan Edwards to Rudolf Bultmann* (Minneapolis: Fortress, 2003), 238–53.

3. W. Bousset, *Kyrios Christos*, trans. J. E. Steely (Nashville: Abingdon, 1970), 12. For a critical response to Bousset's approach, see Hurtado, "New Testament Christology: A Critique of Bousset's Influence," *Theological Studies* 40 (1979): 306–17.

4. R. Bultmann, *Theology of the New Testament*, trans. K. Grobel (New York: Scribner, 1951), I:51. The essence (if not the details) of Bultmann's perspective lives on through the work of his students. See, e.g., H. Koester, "Epilogue: Current Issues in New Testament Scholarship," *The Future of Early Christianity: Essays in Honor of Helmut Koester*, ed. B. A. Pearson (Minneapolis: Fortress, 1991), 467–76. Though clearly more developed in certain respects (e.g., contemporary psychological exegesis, etc.), often contemporary German Protestant scholarship continues to assume some form of the hellenization thesis by which to explain the rise and development of Christology. See, e.g., W. Zager, *Jesus und die fruhchristliche Verkundigung: Historische Ruckfragen nach den Anfangen* (Neukirchen-Vluyn: Neukirchener, 1999).

5. B. Mack, *A Myth of Innocence: Mark and Christian Origins* (Philadelphia: Fortress, 1988), 100. Mack is self-consciously indebted to a sociological theory of religion as developed by J. Z. Smith wherein religion is reduced to a mode of mythmaking in service to social formation. See *Myth of Innocence*, 20n9; and more recently, idem, *The Christian Myth: Origins, Logic and Legacy* (New York: Continuum, 2003), chaps. 4 and 5. As a historian of religions, Smith continues to work within the same broad methodological stream as did the old school, if in a much more tamed and careful manner; see *Drudgery Divine*. For a

Though less radical in his conclusions, Maurice Casey presents a similar form of the hellenization thesis in his aptly titled 1991 work *From Jewish Prophet to Gentile God*.[6] Here, he argues for a three-stage development of early Christianity. In the first two stages—Christianity as a Jewish subgroup and an influx into this initially Jewish Christianity of Gentiles who by-passed conversion to Judaism—a strong commitment to Jewish monotheism prevented the divinization of Jesus. In the final stage, however (first represented in the New Testament by the Gospel of John), Christianity has become a "Gentile religion," wherein monotheism is compromised, and thus Jesus is eventually divinized and worshipped.[7]

The New History of Religions School

A growing number of scholars in recent years have begun to challenge this hellenization thesis. These scholars, identified by some as something of a "new history of religions school," claim that Second Temple Palestinian Judaism—or, perhaps more accurately, "Judaisms"—may well offer the very type of fertile conceptual seedbed required to understand the rise and development of Christology in the early church.[8] Two of the earliest forays in this new direction are represented by Martin Hengel's 1975 work *The Son of God* and Alan Segal's 1977 *Two Powers in Heaven*.[9] Among others, scholars associated with this "new school" include Margaret Barker, Richard Bauckham, David Capes, Peter Carrell, Timo Eskola, Crispen Fletcher-Louis, Jarl Fossum, R. T. France, Charles Gieschen, William

---

more recent example of a chastened articulation of the hellenization thesis, see D. Zeller, "New Testament Christology in Its Hellenistic Reception," *NTS* 46 (2001): 312–33.

6. M. Casey, *From Jewish Prophet to Gentile God: The Origins and Development of New Testament Christology* (Louisville: Westminster/Knox, 1991). Casey nicely summarizes and defends his thesis in "The Deification of Jesus," *SBL Seminar Papers* 1994, ed. E. H. Lovering Jr. (Atlanta: Scholars Press, 1994): 697–714.

7. Casey, *Jewish Prophet*, 97.

8. Hengel first used the term "new *Religionsgeschichtliche Schule*" in his endorsement appearing on the back cover of L. W. Hurtado's, *One God, One Lord: Early Christian Devotion and Ancient Jewish Monotheism* (Philadelphia: Fortress, 1988). Since that time, a number of scholars have adopted the designation. See, e.g., J. Fossum, "The New *Religionsgeschichtliche Schule*: The Quest for Jewish Christology," in *SBLSP 1991*, ed. E. H. Lovering Jr. (Atlanta: Scholars Press, 1991): 638–45. See also Hurtado's insightful musings on the movement in *Lord Jesus Christ*, 11–18. Barry Bandstra has dubbed this movement a "New Quest for Jewish Christology" (review of Margaret Barker's *The Great Angel*, *Perspectives* 9 [February 1994]: 20). As will become clear later in this chapter, not everyone associated with the new school critique of the hellenization thesis believes that a purely "history of religions" approach can exhaustively explain the rise of early Christian devotion to Jesus.

9. M. Hengel, *The Son of God: The Origin of Christology and the History of Jewish-Hellenistic Religion*, trans. John Bowden (Philadelphia: Fortress, 1976); A. Segal, *Two Powers in Heaven: Early Rabbinic Reports about Christianity* (Leiden: Brill, 1977). Both Hengel and Segal have continued to produce important work on this topic. See Hengel's helpful survey of the question, "Early Christianity as a Jewish-Messianic, Universalistic Movement," in *Conflicts and Challenges in Early Christianity*, ed. D. A. Hagner (Harrisburg, PA: Trinity, 1999), 1–38.

Horbury, Larry Hurtado, Carey Newman, Paul Rainbow, Loren Stuckenbruck, and N. T. Wright.[10]

While there are a number of intramural debates within the new school itself, one primary conviction serves to bind these scholars together—namely that the attempts of the old school to explain the development of a high (i.e., divine) Christology within early Christianity fundamentally in terms of a (relatively late) hellenization/paganization process are seriously flawed. To summarize the primary points of critique: first, the specific arguments of the Old School regarding the processes by which Hellenistic philosophy and/or pagan religion supposedly

---

10. M. Barker, *The Great Angel: A Study of Israel's Second God* (Louisville: Westminster/Knox, 1992); R. Bauckham, "The Worship of Jesus in Apocalyptic Christianity," *New Testament Studies* 27 (1980–81): 322–41; idem, *God Crucified: Monotheism and Christology in the New Testament* (Grand Rapids: Eerdmans, 1998); idem, "Biblical Theology and the Problem of Monotheism," in *Out of Egypt: Biblical Theology and Biblical Interpretation*, ed. C. Bartholomew et al. (Grand Rapids: Zondervan, 2004), 187–232; D. P. Capes, *Old Testament Yahweh Texts in Paul's Christology*, WUNT 2:47 (Tübingen: Mohr Siebeck, 1992); P. R. Carrell, *Jesus and the Angels: Angelology and the Christology of the Apocalypse of John* (New York: Cambridge University Press, 1997); T. Eskola, *Messiah and the Throne: Jewish Merkabah Mysticism and Early Christian Exaltation Discourse*, WUNT 2:142 (Tübingen: Mohr Siebeck, 2001); C. Fletcher-Louis, *Luke-Acts: Angels, Christology and Soteriology*, WUNT 2:94 (Tübingen: Mohr Siebeck, 1997); J. Fossum, *The Name of God and the Angel of the Lord*, WUNT 36 (Tübingen: Mohr Siebeck, 1985); idem, "New *Religionsgeschichtliche Schule*"; idem, *The Image of the Invisible God: Essays on the Influence of Jewish Mysticism on early Christology* (Göttingen: Vandenhoeck & Ruprecht, 1995); R. T. France, "The Worship of Jesus: A Neglected Factor in Christological Debate?" *Christ the Lord: Studies in Christology Presented to Donald Guthrie*, ed. H. H. Rowdon (Downers Grove, IL: InterVarsity, 1982), 17–36; C. A. Gieschen, *Angelomorphic Christology: Antecedents and Early Evidence* (Leiden: Brill, 1998); W. Horbury, *Jewish Messianism and the Cult of Christ* (London: SCM, 1998); L. Hurtado, *One God, One Lord*; idem, *At the Origins of Christian Worship: The Context and Character of Earliest Christian Devotion* (Grand Rapids: Eerdmans, 1999); idem, *Lord Jesus Christ: Devotion to Jesus in Earliest Christianity* (Grand Rapids: Eerdmans, 2003); idem, *How on Earth Did Jesus Become a God? Historical Questions about Earliest Devotion to Jesus* (Grand Rapids: Eerdmans, 2005); C. C. Newman, *Paul's Glory Christology: Tradition and Rhetoric* (New York: Brill, 1992); P. A. Rainbow, "Monotheism and Christology in 1 Corinthians 8.4–6" (DPhil diss., Oxford, 1987); idem, "Jewish Monotheism as the Matrix for New Testament Christology," *Novum Testamentum* 33 (1991): 78–91; L. Stuckenbruck, *Angel Veneration and Christology: A Study in Early Judaism and in the Christology of the Apocalypse of John*, WUNT 2:70 (Tübingen: Mohr Siebeck, 1995); N. T. Wright, *The Climax of the Covenant: Christ and the Law in Pauline Theology* (Minneapolis: Fortress, 1992); idem, *The New Testament and the People of God* (Minneapolis: Fortress, 1992); idem, *Jesus and the Victory of God* (Minneapolis: Fortress, 1996). See also three important collections of essays: C. C. Newman, J. R. Davila, and G. S. Lewis, eds., *The Jewish Roots of Christological Monotheism: Papers from the St. Andrews Conference on the Historical Origins of the Worship of Jesus* (Leiden: Brill, 1999); K. J. O'Mahony, ed., *Christian Origins: Worship, Belief and Society* (New York: Sheffield Academic Press, 2003); and L. T. Stuckenbruck and W. E. S. North, *Early Jewish and Christian Monotheism* (New York: Continuum, 2004). Some familiar with this discussion may notice that the name of James Dunn is missing from our list. Dunn is a particularly interesting quotient in this conversation. On the one hand, his position aligns more naturally in some ways with that of, say, Maurice Casey in that he, too, holds that a high Christology only developed relatively late in the first-century. On the other hand, his theory challenges the hellenization thesis in important ways. See J. D. G. Dunn, *Christology in the Making: An Inquiry into the Origins of the Doctrine of the Incarnation*, 2nd ed. (Grand Rapids: Eerdmans, 2005); also the relevant essays in idem, *The Christ and the Spirit: Christology* (Edinburgh: Clark, 1998).

influenced early Christian thought and practice have, in the long-run, failed to convince most contemporary scholars.[11]

Second, the clear evidence of the *rapid speed* with which devotion to Jesus arose within the early Christian communities counts against the hellenization thesis. For example, consider the evidence associated with Paul and his letters. Most scholars agree that Paul wrote his epistles between the end of the fourth decade and the beginning of the sixth decade of the first-century. Already in Paul's letters we have evidence that Jesus is being thought of and worshipped as divine in a sense similar to Yahweh-God himself.[12] But in actuality, Paul's letters push the date of such devotion to Jesus even earlier than Paul himself. For example, what appears to be the remnant of a pre-Pauline hymn about Jesus, one already reflecting a high Christology, can be detected in Philippians 2:6–11.[13] Larry Hurtado highlights the implications of such hymns:

> The singing/chanting of such odes is one of several phenomena that demonstrate the remarkable and innovative nature of early Christian worship, in which Jesus was programmatically included in the "devotional pattern" of early Christian circles along with God, and in ways otherwise reserved for God. I contend that this incorporation of Jesus into the devotional pattern as a subject and recipient of corporate devotion is perhaps the most significant religious innovation that marks earliest Christian worship, especially in the context of Second Temple-Jewish religious tradition, which formed the immediate matrix out of which earliest Christianity developed.[14]

Again, the evidence associated with Paul pushes things even earlier when one considers, first, that Paul's conversion most likely took place within a few years of Jesus's execution, and, second, that its seems quite likely that the reason the zealous, pre-Christian Paul was persecuting the early Jewish-Christian movement

11. We will examine a number of these arguments in detail below; see esp. chap. 3.

12. While a few scholars (e.g., Casey, Dunn) take issue with this claim, the evidence that Paul worshipped and regarded Jesus as divine is significant. See, e.g., R. Bauckham, "Paul's Christology of Divine Identity," www.foranswer.org/Top_JW/Richard_Bauckham.pdf; D. Capes, *Old Testament Yahweh Texts*; idem, "YHWH Texts and Monotheism in Paul's Christology," in *Early Jewish and Christian Monotheism*, 120–37; L. Hurtado, *Origins of Christian Worship*, 91–92; idem, *Lord Jesus Christ*, 98–153; Rainbow, "Monotheism and Christology"; Wright, *Climax of the Covenant*, chaps. 4–6. See also the relevant sections in M. Harris, *Jesus as God: The New Testament Use of Theos in Reference to Jesus* (Grand Rapids: Baker Academic, 1992).

13. While some see nothing more in this passage than a purely human "Adam Christology" (e.g., Dunn, "Christ, Adam and Preexistence," in *Where Christology Began: Essays on Philippians 2*, ed. R. P. Martin and B. Dodd [Louisville: Westminster/Knox, 1998], 74–83), others have effectively made the case for the presence of a high Christology. See R. Bauckham, "Paul's Christology," 12–15; L. Hurtado, "A 'Case Study' in Early Christian Devotion to Jesus: Philippians 2:6–11," in *How on Earth*, 83–107; and Wright, *Climax of the Covenant*, 56–98.

14. Hurtado, "A 'Case Study,'" 86–87. We find the work of Hurtado to represent one of the most thorough and persuasive lines of thought within the new school and thus depend heavily on his analysis and assessment.

had to do, among other things, with "his outrage over their claims about Jesus and their reverence of him."[15] All of this provides evidence that, shortly after his execution, Jesus's early Jewish followers were recognizing and worshipping him as divine, yet within a creational monotheistic context.[16]

This evidence for the seemingly immediate rise of a very high Christology among Jesus's earliest Jewish followers is supported by what can now be recognized as solid evidence for *eyewitness tradition* within the early Jesus tradition, rooted in remembrances of Jesus's pre-Easter Palestinian ministry.[17] *Thus, it appears that we can trace the pattern of identifying the risen Jesus with, and worshipping the risen Jesus as, in some sense the very embodiment of Yahweh-God back even to the immediate Palestinian Jewish followers of Jesus.* In the words of Richard Bauckham: "The earliest Christology was already the highest Christology."[18]

This observation that the people among whom this devotional practice arose were, by and large, *practicing monotheistic Jews* constitutes a third line of critique of the standard hellenization/paganization thesis. Again, as Hurtado notes: "The named disciples who made up Jesus' own entourage (men and women) were all Jews from Roman Judea (mainly Galilee, it appears)," and even when consideration is made of Paul's circles, "the named figures . . . are mainly fellow Jewish Christians."[19] Hurtado draws the inevitable conclusion: "It is simply not very credible, therefore, to allege influence of the pagan religious environment as the crucial factor generating devotion to Jesus as divine."[20]

Fourth and finally, there is the undeniable fact that, across the board, the New Testament documents retain an unflinching commitment to Jewish creational monotheism and a rejection of pagan polytheism—the very polytheism that the Old School claims as the generative matrix of early Christianity's high Christology.[21] Hurtado plainly summarizes the implications of these four lines of evidence:

15. L. Hurtado, "Devotion to Jesus and Second-Temple Jewish Monotheistic Piety," in *How on Earth*, 34. On the wider Jewish polemic against early Christianity, see G. N. Stanton, "Jesus of Nazareth: A Magician and a False Prophet who Deceived God's People," in *Jesus of Nazareth, Lord and Christ: Essays on the Historical Jesus and New Testament Christology*, ed. J. B. Green and M. Turner (Grand Rapids: Eerdmans, 1994), 164–80 and Hurtado, "Pre-70 C.E. Jewish Opposition to Christ Devotion," *JTS* 50 (1999): 35–58.

16. Along these lines, see also M. Hengel, "Christology and New Testament Chronology," in *Between Jesus and Paul: Studies in the Earliest History of Christianity*, trans. J. Bowden (Philadelphia: Fortress, 1983), 30–47. We take the term "creational monotheism" from Wright, *The New Testament and the People of God*, 248–50. On the importance of this concept in arriving at an understanding of ancient Jewish monotheism that does not fall into anachronism, see below.

17. We will explore the evidence for the remnants of eyewitness testimony within the Synoptic Jesus tradition in chap. 7 below.

18. Bauckham, *God Crucified*, viii.

19. Hurtado, "Devotion to Jesus," 38, 39.

20. Ibid., 41.

21. Some within the new school have gone on to proffer a suggestion concerning the religio-philosophical presuppositions at work within the old school's hellenization thesis. Margaret Barker, for

Both the chronological and the demographic data make it extremely dubious to attribute the level of devotion to Jesus that characterized earliest Christianity to syncretistic influences from the pagan religious context. Devotion to Jesus appeared too early, and originated among circles of the early Jesus movement that were comprised of—or certainly dominated by—Jews, and they seem no more likely than other devout [monotheistic] Jews of the time to appropriate pagan religious influences.[22]

If the new school's critique of the old school and its hellenization thesis is on target—and the evidence certainly suggests that it is—*scholars must now explain the rise of the early Christian understanding and worship of the risen Jesus within a first-century—even Palestinian—Jewish context.* As Martin Hengel has aptly put it: early Christianity, with its high Christology, "grew *entirely* out of Jewish soil," and thus "whatever pagan influences have been suspected in the origins of Christianity were mediated without exception by Judaism."[23]

In light of the above considerations, whether or not the early Jesus tradition (that would eventually inform the Synoptic Gospels' portrait[s] of Jesus) can be plausibly accounted for by the legendary thesis largely hinges on the plausibility of supposing that a group of first-century Palestinian Jews would have been inclined imaginatively to create, embrace, and propagate a fictive legend about a miracle-working divine man who was to be given the worship due Yahweh-God.[24] A fundamental consideration affecting our assessment of this issue centers on the nature of the cultural milieu in question. Was first-century Palestinian Jewish culture an environment in which we might expect a legend about a miracle-working divine man to arise and spread? More specifically, since we know that multitudes of pagans in the first-century Mediterranean world believed in legends of this type, one question we need to investigate is, "How open to 'pagan' influences was first-century Judaism?" Were the earliest Jewish Christians sufficiently like their pagan neighbors in terms of their religious worldview to render it more likely than not that their view of Jesus was the result of a similar mythical imagination?

---

example, argues that a "hidden agenda" drives this thesis. This agenda fuels an attempt "to show that [Jesus's] 'divinity' was a later development and an unfortunate one at that." Following an earlier suggestion of Hengel (*Son of God*, 5–6), Barker identifies the force behind this agenda as "an alliance between Jewish and [liberal] Protestant scholars ... ; the former wished to reclaim Jesus for Judaism, but obviously only on their terms, and the latter felt unhappy with the more mysterious and supernatural aspects of the Gospel stories" (*Great Angel*, 1–2).

22. Ibid., 42.

23. Hengel, "Early Christianity," 1, 2–3 (emphasis in text).

24. While some scholars see something less than a high Christology within the Synoptic tradition, others have demonstrated its presence. See, e.g., M. E. Boring, "Markan Christology: God-Language for Jesus?" *NTS* 45 (1999): 451–71; S. J. Gathercole, *The Preexistent Son: Recovering the Christologies of Matthew, Mark and Luke* (Grand Rapids: Eerdmans, 2006); and Wright, *Jesus and the Victory*. See also C. J. Davis, *The Name and Way of the Lord: Old Testament Themes, New Testament Christology* (Sheffield: Sheffield Academic Press, 1996).

To fully appreciate how much hangs in the balance on this question, we need to call attention to a notable peculiarity of the early Jesus movement. On the one hand, the movement was predominantly Jewish. The categories the earliest Christians employed to understand and communicate their faith were inherently Jewish. Indeed, the New Testament as a whole makes little sense if divorced from the Old Testament. But, on the other hand, the center of the earliest Christians faith seems very *non*-Jewish, if not *anti*-Jewish, for these earliest disciples worshipped a contemporary Jewish man as their Lord, alongside God the Father. It is hard to imagine any belief and practice that ostensibly could be more antithetical to monotheistic Judaism than this.

This conflict needs explanation. What is the sufficient historical explanation for how a band of first-century Palestinian (predominantly Galilean) Jews came to abandon some of their most deeply held religious convictions—indeed, *the central tenet* of their traditional faith—and worshipped a Jewish contemporary of theirs as, in some sense, "Yahweh *embodied*?"[25] Of course, one explanation—the traditional Christian explanation—begins by appreciating how extraordinary the Jesus event must have been to inspire such a radical shift in the faith in his followers. *If* Jesus made the claims, lived the life, and performed the miracles the Gospels attribute to him, and *if* Jesus died on the cross and rose from the dead as the Gospels claim, and *if* his earliest Jewish followers personally experienced these momentous events—*particularly the resurrected Jesus*—*then* the radical worldview reorientation these followers experienced begins to make sense.[26]

But is there a way of plausibly accounting for the transformed worldview of the earliest Jesus followers without accepting all of this? All legendary-Jesus advocates of course argue that there is, and for a growing number, their alternative explanation begins with the claim that, as a matter of fact, *there is no radical change in worldview to account for.* According to some of these scholars, first-century Judaism was in fact not nearly as "monotheistic" as has been customarily assumed. To the contrary, they maintain that popular first-century Judaism was significantly influenced by Hellenistic pagan culture.

According to Erwin Goodenough, for example, first-century Jews were "as thoroughly saturated with Hellenistic ideas as they were loyal to the Torah."[27] This saturation infected not merely the Jews of the Diaspora but also of Palestine, including Galilee. Indeed, in the eyes of Burton Mack, "Galilee was in fact

---

25. The term is used of Jesus's sense of vocation by Wright, *Jesus and the Victory*, 642, 653.

26. Among those who argue that a reductive, "history of religions" approach *alone* is unable to account for the rise of these early Christian phenomena, but rather that appeal must be made to remarkable religious experiences and/or the revolutionary thought of Jesus himself, see L. Hurtado, *Lord Jesus Christ*, 72; C. C. Newman, "Resurrection as Glory: Divine Presence and Christian Origins," in *The Resurrection: An Interdisciplinary Symposium on the Resurrection of Jesus*, ed. S. Davis, D. Kendall, and G. O'Collins (New York: Oxford University Press, 1997), 88; Wright, *Jesus and the Victory*, chap. 13; and B. Witherington, *The Christology of Jesus* (Minneapolis: Fortress, 1990), 275–77.

27. E. R. Goodenough, *Jewish Symbols in the Greco-Roman Period*, 13 vols. (New York: Pantheon, 1953–68), 1:256.

an epitome of Hellenistic culture on the eve of the Roman era."[28] Because of this intense hellenization, many legendary-Jesus theorists argue, we have reason to believe that the religious worldview of first-century Jews, including those of Palestine itself, in certain respects may not have been that different from their Gentile neighbors.

For example, Margaret Barker argues that, right up to the first-century, Second Temple Judaism had never fully divested itself of ancient Canaanite influence. Specifically, she claims that El, the high God, and Yahweh, one of El's divine sons, were originally two distinct divine beings and that they were only fused in certain streams of Judaism after the Exile. Other forms of Judaism, however, retained the ancient pagan notion of two distinct gods right up and into the first century.[29] On Barker's thesis, the early Christians had merely to identify God the Father with the Jewish high God El/Elohim, and Jesus with El's divine son, Yahweh. Thus the "two gods" of Israel are transformed into the two Christian gods, Father and Son—the first two members of what eventually becomes the Trinity.[30] Thus, ironically, although Barker vehemently criticizes the old school's hellenization thesis, her own position ultimately attributes the early rise of a high Christology among Christians to lingering pagan elements within pre-Christian Judaism.

Barker's thesis is a clear example of one line of thought within the new school, wherein Second Temple Jewish monotheism is seen as a highly "flexible" phenomenon, one quite capable of embracing other divine beings alongside Yahweh in terms of both conception and worship. A similar perspective has recently led Paula Fredriksen to suggest that the term "monotheism" be given a "mandatory retirement" with regard to ancient Judaism. In her words, "what henotheism describes is really just normal ancient monotheism. . . . [Contemporary scholars would do well] if 'monotheism' were retired as a term of art for thinking about ancient religion."[31] In such light, some suggest, we have little reason to think Palestinian Jews would have found it significantly more difficult to accept a legend about a divine man than their Gentile neighbors.

In sum, the more influenced by pagan (i.e., polytheistic) ideas we believe the worldview of first-century Palestinian Judaism was, especially in Galilee where the Jesus movement arose, the less conflict we will see between the first disciples' faith and first-century Judaism itself. Consequently, the easier it will be to account for the early Christian view of Jesus in strictly legendary terms. Conversely, the less

28. Mack, *A Myth of Innocence*, 66.

29. Barker, *Great Angel*, 10. For further development of her thesis, see *The Risen Lord: The Jesus of History and the Christ of Faith* (Edinborough: Clark, 1996) and idem, "The High Priest and the Worship of Jesus," in *Jewish Roots of Christological Monotheism*, 93–111.

30. See Barker, *Great Angel*, 190.

31. P. Fredriksen, "Mandatory Retirement: Ideas in the Study of Christian Origins Whose Time Has Come to Go," *Studies in Religion/Sciences Religieuses* 35 (2006): 243. In contemporary parlance, "henotheism" is often used as a synonym for "monolatry," with both terms signifying exclusive devotion to one god combined with a belief in more than one god. On the history and use of these two terms see N. MacDonald, "The Origin of 'Monotheism,'" in *Early Jewish and Christian Monotheism*, 213–15.

influenced by pagan concepts we believe first-century Judaism to be, the more conflict we will see between the first disciples' faith and first-century Judaism, and the more difficult it becomes to explain their view of Jesus on strictly sociological grounds. Clearly, a great deal hangs on the question of the *extensiveness*—and the *nature*—of hellenization in first-century Palestinian Judaism, especially in the Galilee where Christianity originated.

This is the issue we shall explore in this chapter. We will begin by reviewing the case that has been made for concluding that first-century Palestinian Judaism was thoroughly hellenized, that, in certain quarters, its religious sensibilities had taken on significant pagan elements, and that first-century Jewish monotheism had consequently become "flexible" enough to begin conferring upon created beings the status of deity. We will then begin our response by offering two general arguments that suggest that, as a matter of fact, first-century Jews, including Galilean Jews, were not significantly affected by pagan Hellenism *in terms of their religious worldview*. Following this, we will respond to the eight arguments most frequently used to demonstrate that first-century Judaism was, religiously speaking, significantly hellenized. And we will conclude by responding to various arguments that have been put forth suggesting that first-century Jewish monotheism had become flexible enough to account quite easily for the rise of the early Christian view of Jesus as the embodiment of Yahweh.

The Case for a Hellenistic, Paganized First-Century Palestinian Judaism

Eight Arguments Supporting the "Hellenization" Thesis

"Hellenization" generally refers to the absorption of Greek culture by other cultures. Insofar as a culture's language, politics, education, arts, philosophy, and/or religion reflects distinct aspects of Greek culture, the culture can be said to be hellenized.[32] No one disputes that vast portions of the Mediterranean and Near Eastern worlds became significantly hellenized after the conquests of Alexander the Great in the fourth century BCE. The question is: to what degree—and, more important, *in what sense(s)*—did first-century Palestinian Judaism experience hellenization?

For much of the nineteenth and twentieth centuries, it was commonly accepted that while Palestinian Jews tended to resist hellenization, the pagan peoples of the

---

32. Jonathan Goldstein notes six traits that are characteristic of a Hellenistic environment: presence of a Greek population, use of Greek language, rational philosophies among the intelligentsia, dramatic epic and lyrical poetry, education in the context of a Greek gymnasium, and the presence of distinct architectural works (i.e., a gymnasium, stadiums, and theaters). See "Jewish Acceptance and Rejection of Hellenism," in *Jewish and Christian Self-Definition*, vol. 2: *Aspects of Judaism in the Graeco-Roman Period*, ed. E. P. Sanders et al. (Philadelphia: Fortress, 1981), 67. In recent years, some scholars have raised questions about the very definition of "Hellenism" as an ideological construct. See, e.g., P. S. Alexander, "Hellenism and Hellenization as Problematic Historiographical Categories," in *Paul beyond the Judaism/Hellenism Divide*, ed. T. Engberg-Pedersen (Louisville: Westminster John Knox, 2001), 63–80.

empire embraced the Hellenistic ethos, leaving the Jews of the Diaspora somewhere in between.[33] While this view can still be found today, it has suffered a significant challenge in recent decades. In his landmark study, *Judaism and Hellenism*, Martin Hengel persuasively argued that as early as the third century BCE even Palestinian Judaism reflected significant Hellenistic influences.[34] Indeed, he has argued that it may no longer be useful to contrast Hellenistic Judaism with a supposed *non*-Hellenistic Judaism, for all mid- to late-Second Temple Judaism was, to one degree or another, hellenized. Even a group as sectarian and separatistic as the Qumran community may well reflect Hellenistic influences, as is evidenced, for example, by the presence of astrological texts in their library.[35]

There are at least eight lines of evidence that have been offered to support the claim that Palestinian Jews in general, and Galilean Jews in particular, were significantly hellenized.

Greek Language

Evidence suggests that Greek was spoken throughout Galilee from the third century BCE onward. To many, this fact alone demonstrates a significant Hellenistic influence in this area.[36]

---

33. From the time of the Tübingen School, the "Hellenism vs. Judaism" divide has provided scholars with a fertile (Hegelian) dichotomy with which to work. For a brief history and critique, see W. A. Meeks, "Judaism, Hellenism, and the Birth of Christianity," in *Paul beyond the Judaism/Hellenism Divide*, 17–27. In recent years, scholars have tended to reject this dichotomy in terms of its strict compartmentalization. See D. B. Martin, "Paul and the Judaism/Hellenism Dichotomy: Toward a Social History of the Question," in *Paul beyond the Judaism/Hellenism Divide*, 29–61.

34. M. Hengel, *Judaism and Hellenism: Studies in Their Encounter in Palestine during the Early Hellenistic Period*, 2 vols., trans. J. Bowden (Philadelphia: Fortress, 1974). See also idem, "Judaism and Hellenism Revisited," in *Hellenism in the Land of Israel*, ed. J. J. Collins and G. E. Sterling (Notre Dame, IN: University of Notre Dame Press, 2001), 7. Martin Goodman refers to the recent "impressive consensus" among scholars that Hengel's thesis is correct ("Epilogue," in *Hellenism in the Land of Israel*, 302). Consensus, of course, does not mean that *all* agree; those who have questioned Hengel's thesis at one point or another include L. H. Feldman, "Hengel's *Judaism and Hellenism* in Retrospect," *JBL* 96 (1977): 371–82; idem, "How Much Hellenism in Jewish Palestine?" *Hebrew Union College Annual* 57 (1986): 83–111; F. Millar, "The Background to the Maccabean Revolution: Reflections on Martin Hengel's *Judaism and Hellenism*," *JJS* 29 (1978): 1–21; A. Momigliano, review of *Judentum und Hellenismus*, by Martin Hengel, *JTS* 21 (1970): 149–53. For a very helpful survey of the literature on Judaism and Hellenism up to 1990, see L. L. Grabbe, *Judaism from Cyrus to Hadrian*, vol. 1: *The Persian and Greek Periods* (Minneapolis: Fortress, 1992), 147–70.

35. M. Hengel, "Qumran and Hellenism," in *Religion in the Dead Sea Scrolls*, ed. J. J. Collins and R. A. Kugler (Grand Rapids: Eerdmans, 2000), 46–56. There is always the problem of knowing whether texts found at Qumran represent views held by the community itself. With respect to the astrological texts, there is reason to believe they did reflect the community's own beliefs given the similar ideas found in the community Rule (1QS)—i.e., soteriological determinism based upon particular mixtures of the "two spirits" within each person, etc.

36. See E. M. Meyers and J. Strange, *Archaeology, the Rabbis and Early Christianity* (Nashville: Abingdon, 1981), 78; H. C. Kee, "Early Christianity in the Galilee: Reassessing the Evidence from the Gospels," in *The Galilee in Late Antiquity*, ed. L. I. Levine (New York: Jewish Theological Seminary of America; Cambridge, MA: Harvard University Press, 1992), 20–22.

Proximity of Gentile Cities to Galilee

Galilee was in close proximity to several predominantly Gentile Hellenistic cities just outside its borders, including the cities of the Decapolis, such as Scythopolis and Gadera.[37] Some scholars argue that this Gentile population would have had an inevitable hellenizing influence on the culture and a paganizing influence on the religion of Galilean Jews. Partly on this basis, for example, Gerald Downing and others have argued that the historical Jesus should be considered something of a cynic philosopher.[38] We know that certain famous cynic philosophers hailed from Gadera. The argument is that if cynic philosophy was prominent in a city *near* Galilee, it is plausible to assume it would have been present *within* Galilee.

The Presence of Hellenistic Cities within Galilee

Not only do we know of Hellenistic cities in close proximity to Galilee, but we also know that the cities of Tiberius (on the Sea of Galilee) and Sepphoris (four miles north of Nazareth) were built on the Hellenistic model.[39] Though most agree that the cities were largely Jewish in population, archaeology suggests that they were thoroughly Hellenistic in terms of style, administration, and public entertainment.

A Pagan Gentile Population within Galilee

According to many scholars over the last century, evidence suggests there were a significant number of Gentiles in first-century Galilee.[40] Some have even argued that Gentiles were a dominating presence at the time, citing Matthew's reference to "Galilee of the Gentiles" (Matt. 4:15; cf. Isa. 9:1) in support of their claim. Whatever the actual population numbers, it is argued that the religions and cultures of this

37. There seems to have been a significant Jewish population in these cities as well, a fact that some use to further argue that the Jewish population of Galilee would have been influenced by Hellenism. See Kee, "Early Christianity," 16–17.

38. For claims that Jesus should be viewed as a cynic (-like) sage, see, e.g., F. G. Downing, *Cynics and Christian Origins* (Edinburgh: Clark, 1992); B. L. Mack, "The Case for a Cynic-Like Jesus," in *The Christian Myth: Origins, Logic, and Legacy* (New York: Continuum, 2003), 41–58; J. D. Crossan, *The Historical Jesus: The Life of a Mediterranean Jewish Peasant* (San Francisco: HarperSanFrancisco, 1991), 421. For critiques of the cynic-Jesus thesis, see G. Boyd, *Cynic Sage or Son of God? Recovering the Real Jesus in an Age of Revisionist Replies* (Grand Rapids: Baker Academic, 1995); P. R. Eddy, "Jesus as Diogenes? Reflections on the Cynic Jesus Thesis," *JBL* 115 (1996): 449–69.

39. Some have even speculated that as local carpenters, Joseph and Jesus may have worked on the construction of Sepphoris. See Kee, "Early Christianity," 15; R. A. Batey, *Jesus and the Forgotten City: New Light on Sepphoris and the Urban World of Jesus* (Grand Rapids: Baker Academic, 1991), 70–71. Regarding Sepphoris, Kee writes, "All the features of a Hellenistic city were there, including a theater, hippodrome, and temples" ("Early Christianity," 15), while Batey is more specific, claiming that first-century Sepphoris included a temple dedicated to Augustus and to Rome (*Jesus and the Forgotten City*, 56).

40. Adolf von Harnack argued this a century ago; see *What Is Christianity?* trans. T. B. Saunders (Philadelphia: Fortress, 1957), 33–34. More recently see M. Borg, *Meeting Jesus again for the First Time* (San Francisco: HarperSanFrancisco, 1994), 26. The picture of Jesus developed by Crossan fits perfectly within such a vision of Galilee; see *Historical Jesus*.

Gentile presence could not have helped but influence the Jewish population. Largely on this basis, Robert Funk has argued that "Jesus' home was semi-pagan Galilee, whose inhabitants, because they were often of mixed blood and open to foreign influence, were despised by the ethnically pure Judeans to the south."[41] K. W. Clark continues in this vein of speculation: "Shrines to numerous deities must have existed in the larger cities of Gentile Galilee, especially in a Roman town like Tiberius, and would have been found even in the more Jewish towns. They represented the normal and traditional worship of the Gentile majority in Galilee."[42]

THE LOCATION AND TOPOGRAPHY OF LOWER GALILEE

A number of scholars argue that the location and terrain of Lower Galilee is such that it would have been a major trade route for Gentiles, making it a cosmopolitan environment. Since such environments are typically syncretistic, some scholars argue that the Jewish population of Galilee, to one degree or another, likely would have been characterized by a religious syncretism.

FOREIGN RULE IN GALILEE

Except during its relatively brief rule by the Jewish Hasmoneans (103–63 BCE), the Galilee of Second Temple Judaism was ruled by foreign pagan nations. The rule of the Romans over this area has sometimes been interpreted by scholars as an "occupation" or "annexation."[43] John Dominic Crossan has compared the Roman "occupation" of Palestine to Ireland's colonization under British rule.[44] Hence, these scholars argue, it would be shocking if Hellenistic ideas and culture did not thoroughly permeate Galilean culture and religion (just as Britain's culture and religion permeated Ireland).

THE TENSION BETWEEN GALILEE AND JUDEA

It is commonly argued that tensions existed between the Galilean Jewish population and the Judean temple-state. While most of this tension seems to have been political and socioeconomic in nature, some of it may have been religious. For example, Judean Judaism centered on the temple and the priestly system, while Galilean Judaism was far removed from the temple and the priestly system.[45]

---

41. R. Funk, *Honest to Jesus: Jesus for a New Millennium* (San Francisco: HarperSanFrancisco, 1996), 33. Burton Mack describes Galilee as a "land of mixed peoples" (*The Lost Gospel: The Book of Q and Christian Origins* [San Francisco: HarperSanFrancisco, 1993], 53).

42. K. W. Clark, "Galilee," *Interpreter's Dictionary of the Bible*, ed. G. A. Buttrick et al. (Nashville: Abingdon, 1962), 2:344–47.

43. See M. J. Borg, *Jesus: A New Vision* (San Francisco: Harper & Row, 1994), 83, 137; J. D. Crossan, *Jesus: A Revolutionary Biography* (San Francisco: HarperSanFrancisco, 1994), 89.

44. Crossan, *Historical Jesus*, 105.

45. R. A. Horsley, *Galilee: History, Politics, People* (Valley Forge, PA: Trinity, 1995), chap. 2; idem, *Archeology, History and Society in Galilee: The Social Context of Jesus and the Rabbis* (Valley Forge, PA: Trinity, 1996).

Some claim that the Galilean Judaism of Jesus's day did not even make use of synagogues, since we have no archaeological evidence of synagogues in Galilee prior to the destruction of the temple in 70 CE.[46] Some have concluded from this that Galilean Judaism, in sharp contrast to Judean Judaism, had no official leaders and no established communal worship patterns.[47]

Putting all this together, we are given a picture of a Galilean Jewish population that was geographically separated from, and to some extent in religious conflict with, Jerusalem's temple religion and leadership, while they themselves were without any self-identifying anchor in terms of a formalized religious pattern or leadership. Such a population, it can be argued, would have been quite vulnerable to pagan influences with respect to their religious beliefs and practices.

MAGIC AND ASTROLOGY

Finally, we have literary evidence that many Jews were interested in magic and astrology in certain locales, including, it seems, in Palestine itself.[48] Even more significant, a number of synagogues excavated in Palestine were decorated with zodiac symbols. At Sepphoris was found a mosaic depicting the god Dionysus riding a donkey, a depiction of Dionysus in a drinking contest with Heracles, and several bronze figurines, possibly of Pan and Prometheus, as well as a bull. With regard to Galilee in particular, an ancient synagogue unearthed at Hammath Tiberius, on the shores of the Sea of Galilee, had a floor mosaic of the Greek god Helios surrounded by a twelve-month zodiac wheel. Each of the zodiac and seasonal signs is identified in Hebrew.[49]

While most conclude that this evidence is admittedly post-AD 70, some scholars argue that it constitutes a basis upon which to surmise that first-century Palestinian Judaism was already religiously syncretistic, assimilating significant portions of Greco-Roman religion into itself.[50] If so, argue various legendary-Jesus theorists, it would have been as likely an environment as any for a Hellenistic legend about a wonder-working divine man to arise and thrive.

46. For a summary of the evidence and literature see Kee, "Early Christianity," 3–14. We shall raise questions about this claim below.

47. For example, ibid., 11–14.

48. For example, Merkavah's Hekhelot texts, the Qumran Horoscope text, etc. See J. H. Charlesworth, "Jewish Astrology in the Talmud, Pseudepigrapha, the Dead Sea Scrolls, and Early Palestinian Synagogues," *HTR* 70 (1977): 183–200; A. Lange, "The Essene Position on Magic and Divination," in *Legal Texts and Legal Issues: Proceedings of the Second Annual Meeting of the International Organization for Qumran Studies, Cambridge 1995*, ed. M. Bernstein, F. G. Martinez, and J. Kampen (New York: Brill, 1997), 377–435; P. Schäfer, *The Hidden and Manifest God: Some Major Themes in Early Jewish Mysticism*, trans. A. Pomerance (Albany: SUNY, 1992).

49. Charlesworth, "Jewish Astrology," 193–98; H. Shanks, "Synagogue Excavation Reveals Stunning Mosaic of Zodiac and Torah Ark," *BAR* 10/3 (1984): 32–44.

50. J. Neusner has summarized some of the post-70 evidence; see "Jewish Use of Pagan Symbols after 70 CE," *JR* 43 (1963): 285–94.

A "Flexible Monotheism" and "Divine Men"

There is one further set of considerations that is important for our assessment of the degree to which Judaism was paganized in the first century. It is argued that certain intertestamental texts demonstrate that significant portions of Second Temple Judaism had embraced a "flexible monotheism" that allowed for mythological figures to play a God-like role next to Yahweh.[51] We find many examples of high-ranking angels (e.g., Michael, Metatron), exalted patriarchs (e.g., Enoch, Moses), and personified divine attributes (e.g., Wisdom, etc.) being spoken of in terms that were commonly associated with Yahweh himself.[52] All indications are that these texts were circulated widely and reflect general Jewish sentiments in the century leading up to the time of Jesus. On top of this, we have a number of examples of Jews referring to various heroes as supernaturally empowered "divine men" (*theios aner*), a concept that was sometimes used in Greco-Roman contexts to refer to people who were believed to be both human and divine.

There is widespread disagreement over how to explain the development of these intermediary figures and "divine men" on Jewish soil, as well as over how significant they are for our understanding of the theology of Second Temple Judaism.[53] What is most significant for our purposes, however, is that some legendary-Jesus theorists have appealed to these types of intermediary figures to explain the rise of early Christianity.

For example, G. A. Wells and Earl Doherty have argued that the Jesus of Paul was simply one of these intermediary divine beings. In their view, the Gospels later created a historical narrative around Paul's mythological savior figure and thereby transformed him into a historical person.[54] Others have argued that New Testament authors modeled their understanding of Jesus after the Hellenistic concept of "divine men," depicting Jesus as a person who straddled the boundary

---

51. A term used by Bauckham, *God Crucified*, 2.

52. This threefold typology was proposed by L. Hurtado in *One God, One Lord: Early Christian Devotion and Ancient Jewish Monotheism* (Philadelphia: Fortress, 1988) and has been adopted by many in the discussion. Others, however, have gone on to propose additional categories. For example, James Davila adds two new categories to Hurtado's list of divine mediators: "charismatic prophets and royal aspirants" as well as "ideal figures" (e.g., the expected Davidic Messiah figure). See "Of Methodology, Monotheism and Mediation," in *Jewish Roots of Christological Monotheism*, 3–18.

53. For example, at the radical end of the spectrum one finds the position of Margaret Barker, who claims that right up to the first century, Second Temple Judaism had never fully divested itself of ancient Canaanite polytheistic influence; see *Great Angel*, 10. Christopher Rowland sees in these texts a monotheism that has begun to disintegrate under the impact of Hellenism; see *The Open Heaven: A Study of Apocalyptic in Judaism and Early Christianity* (New York: Crossroad, 1982), 111–12. For others who share a similar perspective about the flexibility of Jewish monotheism, see A. Chester, "Jewish Messianic Expectations and Mediatorial Figures and Pauline Christology," in *Paulus und antike Judentum*, ed. M. Hengel and U. Heckel (Tübingen: Mohr Siebeck, 1991), 17–89; Fletcher-Louis, *Luke-Acts*; Gieschen, *Angelomorphic Christology*; P. Hayman, "Monotheism—A Misused Word in Jewish Studies?" *JJS* 42 (1991): 1–15.

54. G. A. Wells, *The Jesus Myth* (Chicago: Open Court, 1999), esp. 95–111; E. Doherty, *The Jesus Puzzle: Did Christianity Begin with a Mythical Christ?* (Ottawa: Canadian Humanist Pub., 1999).

between God and humans.[55] If, under the influence of Hellenism, the monotheism of the Jews of this period had indeed become so "flexible" that beings other than Yahweh could be treated as gods and heroic people could be spoken of as "divine men," then we must grant that the legendary-Jesus thesis begins to look more plausible.

Summary

The eight arguments for a religiously hellenized Palestine, together with the more general argument for a highly flexible monotheism, form the basis for the contention of some legendary-Jesus theorists that first-century Galilee was the kind of place in which a legend about a miracle-working divine man naturally would have arisen. If this is true, we need not toil over how to explain the supposed revolutionary worldview shift of the first disciples of Jesus. While the early Christian view of Jesus as divine may have been distinct in certain respects, this sort of belief was perfectly consistent with the hellenized religious worldview the early Jewish disciples were steeped in. One need not postulate anything unusual—let alone supernatural—to account for it.

At first glance, the case for a paganized first-century Judaism and for a thoroughly hellenized first-century Galilee looks quite compelling. Our argument, however, is that once all the evidence is considered in detail, the case looks much less impressive. Indeed, we will argue that there are solid reasons for concluding that, however hellenized first-century Jews had become with respect to certain aspects of their culture, *Hellenism by and large did not affect their religious worldview*.

Jewish Resistance to Hellenization

We begin our response by making two general observations that suggest first-century Jews—including those in Galilee—were not significantly affected by Hellenism *in terms of their religious worldview*.

The Resilience of Local Cultures

Our first observation concerns the hellenization process as a whole. There is little doubt that Hengel has, for the most part, established his thesis of the widespread influence of Hellenism upon both Diaspora and Palestinian Jews during the Second Temple period. However, as an increasing number of scholars are arguing, this influence, though pervasive, seems to have been largely superficial.

55. See, e.g., F. Hahn, *The Titles of Jesus in Christology*, trans. H. Knight and G. Ogg (London: Lutterworth, 1969), 11–13, 288–99; D. Georgi, *The Opponents of Paul in Second Corinthians* (Philadelphia: Fortress, 1986). For a helpful summary of this view, see G. Paterson Corrington, *The "Divine Man": His Origin and Function in Hellenistic Popular Religion* (New York: Lang, 1986), 181–93.

For the vast majority of those within the empire, hellenization appears to have functioned more as a cultural veneer than it did a cultural transformer.

Tessa Rajak, for example, has offered compelling evidence suggesting that, with few exceptions, the hellenization of the Mediterranean world left indigenous cultures largely intact. To be sure, hellenization often affected the language, political structure, arts, architecture, entertainment, and intellectual life of the society. But the evidence also suggests that only rarely was the actual underlying culture—including its religious and philosophical worldview—of an indigenous people substantially *replaced*. In most cases, she argues, the indigenous culture seems to have continued on largely unaffected.[56]

Fergus Millar's extensive studies on the ancient Near East during the Hellenistic period have shown that in most instances the available data does not allow us to do the pre- and post-hellenization comparisons necessary to draw definitive conclusions about the extent to which a particular culture was or was not affected by hellenization.[57] Nevertheless, the evidence is sufficient to reveal that, at least in the case of older Near Eastern societies, the culture generally remained intact, howbeit glossed over in varying degrees with a rather superficial Hellenistic appearance.[58]

Evidence of the resilience of indigenous cultures in this period is found in the fact that local traditions were more often than not left intact. G. W. Bowersock highlights the significance of this when he argues:

> The persistence of all these local traditions has suggested that there was no more than a superficial Hellenization in much of Asia Minor, the Near East, and Egypt. . . . [Hellenism] was a medium not necessarily antithetical to local or indigenous traditions. On the contrary, it provided a new and more eloquent way of giving voice to them.[59]

Complementing this perspective, Peter Green has argued that the main impetus for particular regions adapting aspects of Hellenistic culture was not usually with the indigenous masses but with its rulers and administrative hopefuls who had something to gain by impressing Greco-Roman rulers with the appearance of loyalty to the project of hellenization. It is not surprising, therefore, that we usually find the most

56. T. Rajak, "The Hasmoneans and the Uses of Hellenism," in *A Tribute to Geza Vermes: Essays on Jewish and Christian Literature and History*, ed. P. R. Davies and R. T. White (Sheffield: Sheffield Academic Press, 1990), 265.

57. F. Millar demonstrates this lack with regard to the pre-Hellenistic Syrian evidence in "The Problem of Hellenistic Syria," in *Hellenism in the East*, ed. A. Kuhrt and S. Sherwin-White (London: Routledge, 1987), 110–33.

58. F. Millar, "Empire, Community and Culture in the Roman Near East: Greeks, Syrians, Jews and Arabs," *JJS* 38 (1987): 143–64; idem, "Problem of Hellenistic Syria."

59. G. W. Bowersock, "Paganism and Greek Culture," in *Hellenism in Late Antiquity* (Ann Arbor: University of Michigan Press, 1990), 6–7. On this point see also Alexander, "Hellenism and Hellenization," 71–72; Grabbe, *Judaism from Cyrus to Hadrian*, 1:161, 170.

significant Hellenistic influence in public arenas (politics, arts, and entertainment) while the indigenous culture of the common people, expressed in their local traditions and distinct religious beliefs and practices, seems quite unaffected.[60] There is a good deal of evidence suggesting that Jews generally responded to Hellenism by becoming more, not less, conservative in their religious convictions. Kraabel's archaeological work in Sardis provides a case in point. Not only did the Jews in this strongly hellenized environment not become pagan, but he argues that they actually became more intentionally, and more distinctly, Jewish. In his words,

> At Sardis at least, proximity appears to have produced clarity, and the enjoyment of a gentile culture did not automatically produce capitulation to "paganism;" the Jews are strong and self-confident, they have a firm grasp on their Judaism and they express it in their building, their inscriptions and even in their iconography. And that may have happened *because* there were so many pagans so very close.[61]

As we shall see below, this defiant Jewish response to Hellenism seems to have been quite widespread. While there are a few exceptions, throughout the Roman Empire "Jews refused to honor gods, shrines, and cults other than their own," according to Lester Grabbe. Even Jews who seemed to be "most at home in the Hellenistic world"—people like Philo or the author of Pseudo-Aristeas—"found themselves marked—and marked off—by this fact."[62]

Only on the assumption that Diaspora Jews generally remained loyal to their Jewish religious traditions can we explain the fact that, as a whole, they were granted the rare indulgence on the part of Roman emperors to be excused from the worship of pagan deities and participating in pagan religious activities. This assumption would explain the fact that Herod publicly defended the Jews' rights to remain distinctly Jewish—not worshipping pagan deities, keeping the Sabbath, attending synagogue assembly, and keeping kosher foods.[63] It would also explain the fact that within Palestine coins often were printed without the customary representation of the emperor on them,[64] done in deference to their sensitivity to anything that could violate the second commandment.

60. P. Green, *Alexander to Actium: The Historical Evolution of the Hellenistic Age* (Berkeley: University of California Press, 1990), esp. 312–35. This observation can stand alone from Green's otherwise controversial thesis about Hellenism.

61. A. T. Kraabel, "Paganism and Judaism: The Sardis Evidence," in *Melanges offerts a Marcel Simon: Paganisme, Judaisme, Christianisme, Influences et affrontements dans le monde antique*, ed. P. Broche (Paris: E. de Boccard, 1978), 13–33; citation from p. 32 (emphasis in text).

62. Grabbe, *Judaism from Cyrus to Hadrian*, 1:170. On the range of Jewish responses to pagan cults, see P. Borgen, "'Yes,' 'No,' 'How Far?': The Participation of Jews and Christians in Pagan Cults," in *Paul in His Hellenstic Context*, ed. T. Engberg-Petersen (Minneapolis: Fortress, 1995), 30–59. Notice how few concrete examples Borgen can produce of Jews who unambiguously participated in pagan cults.

63. *Antiquities* 16.29–58.

64. For example, the coins minted by Herod Antipas at Sepphoris; see J. L. Reed, *Archaeology and the Galilean Jesus* (Harrisburg, PA: Trinity, 2000), 122–23.

This is not to suggest that Diaspora Jews, and even Palestinian Jews, were not significantly influenced by Hellenism; all the evidence suggests that Hengel's thesis is correct—Hellenism is everywhere. But it does suggest, as Hengel himself argues, that this hellenization was more of a veneer than it was a significant cultural/religious shift for Jews (as well as for most other indigenous people groups).[65] We thus accept that many aspects of Jewish society were affected by Hellenism—even in Palestine. But we see no grounds whatsoever for believing that this influence extended into the religious beliefs and practices of Jews in general, or of Palestinian Jews in particular. To the contrary, the evidence suggests that *precisely because* they were surrounded by pagan culture, Jews were highly resistant to any encroachment of paganism upon their distinct monotheistic religious beliefs.

Jewish Resistance to Religious Syncretism

Our second general observation is that, while there is certainly considerable evidence that Jews in general were superficially affected by Hellenism, there is also strong evidence that they generally resisted Hellenism when it came to their religious beliefs and practices. To gain an accurate picture of Second Temple Judaism, we must consider both sets of evidence.[66]

As a preliminary point, it is worth noting that Jews were not the only ones who found aspects of Hellenistic culture objectionable. Many conservative Romans, especially among the upper classes, held aspects of Greek culture in contempt. Greek poetry, philosophy, entertainment, and even the Greek language were at various times rejected as inferior and/or offensive.[67] Thus, we should not think it

---

65. As J. D. G. Dunn notes, there is certainly evidence everywhere of "a syncretism that incorporates Jewish elements," but there is no evidence of a "Jewish syncretism" ("On the Relation of Text and Artifact: Some Cautionary Tales," in *Text and Artifact in the Religions of Mediterranean Antiquity*, ed. S. Wilson and M. Desjardins [Waterloo, ON: Canadian Corp. for Studies in Religion, 2000], 199). For other cautions about too easily resorting to the category of syncretism regarding Diaspora Judaism, see J. M. G. Barclay, *Jews in the Mediterranean Diaspora from Alexander to Trajan* (Edinburgh: Clark, 1996), esp. 119–23; L. H. Feldman, *Jew and Gentile in the Ancient World: Attitudes and Interactions from Alexander to Justinian* (Princeton: Princeton University Press, 1993), 65–69; I. Levinskaya, *The Book of Acts in Its First-Century Setting*, vol. 5: *The Book of Acts in Its Diaspora Setting* (Grand Rapids: Eerdmans, 1996), 197–203. For one perspective on difficulties with the very category of "syncretism" see D. Frankfurter, "Syncretism and the Holy Man in Late Antique Egypt," *Journal of Early Christian Studies* 11 (2003): 339–85.

66. At this point, many scholars will want us to add an *s* to the end of "Judaism." While we certainly recognize the diversity of ways in which one could be a first-century Jew, we want to equally emphasize that without something that constitutes a unified "Judaism," the addition of an *s* pluralizes nothing in particular. In this chapter, we are focusing on the broad common Judaism that unified the diversity of its various expressions. What we have in mind here is nicely articulated by Wright in *New Testament and the People of God*, chaps. 8–10.

67. Goldstein, "Jewish Acceptance and Rejection." Lester Grabbe discusses several forms of Hellenistic resistance that accompanied aspirations of regaining political control of their land, including various forms of anti-Greek propaganda (*Judaism from Cyrus to Hadrian*, 1:163–64).

altogether exceptional that Jews resisted Hellenistic influences, even if the religious basis for their resistance was distinctive in the ancient world.

While many Jews rejected Hellenistic religious influences from the start, this rejection became much more widespread and took on a new fervency following the Maccabean revolt (168 BCE). Up to this point, we find evidence of religious syncretism among the Jews. In fact, it was an intentional effort on the part of various Jewish and Hellenistic leaders to reform Judaism and Jewish culture in a Hellenistic direction that led to this revolt. All indications are that the revolt was quite successful, for as Martin Hengel, John Collins, and others have argued, the evidence for religious syncretism among the Jews, especially in Palestine, virtually disappears after this time.

Hengel writes that between the time of the Maccabean revolt and the fall of Jerusalem "we find in Jewish Palestine no threatening Jewish assimilation to pagan beliefs and practices. This problem belonged to the past."[68] After the revolt, Hellenism "could not further threaten the religious and ethnic identity of the Jews." Rather, Hengel argues, it "strengthened it and made it more creative and fruitful."[69] Hengel thus concludes that it is *"impossible"* to conceive of first-century Palestinian Jews accepting elements of paganism, compromising their strict monotheism, or rejecting essential aspects of the Torah.[70]

John Collins concurs, noting that "the most striking thing about the Jewish encounter with Hellenism, both in the Diaspora and in the land of Israel, was the persistence of Jewish separatism in matters of worship and cult."[71] So too, Lester Grabbe points out that "in accommodating to Hellenistic culture the Jews always maintained one area that could not be compromised . . . religion. In the Greco-Roman world, only the Jews refused to honor gods, shrines, and cults other than their own."[72]

The Jews generally reacted intensely, if not fanatically, against any perceived pagan influence. For example, Josephus gives us an account of the Jews who stood up to Pilate's troops when he attempted to bring Roman standards into the city. When threatened with death, they bared their necks to the Roman swords, and Pilate backed down.[73] Such strong religious sentiments explain why political lead-

---

68. Hengel, "Judaism and Hellenism Revisited," 24.

69. Ibid., 29.

70. Hengel writes: "What is *impossible* [within first-century Jewish Palestine] can be listed quickly: a blatant pagan cult, i.e., a clear break with the first commandment (and the second), an obvious and lasting failure to observe essential parts of the Torah, and specific desecration of the temple" (*The "Hellenization" of Judaea in the First Century after Christ* [London: SCM, 1989], 54).

71. J. J. Collins, "Cult and Culture: The Limits of Hellenization in Judea," in *Hellenism in the Land of Israel*, 55.

72. Grabbe, *Judaism from Cyrus to Hadrian*, 1:170. So too Jonathan Goldstein writes, "The Jews . . . found their self-definition in the Torah, which sufficed to distinguish them from any pagan, Greek or non-Greek" ("Jewish Acceptance and Rejection," 86). See also Cohen, "Hellenism in Unexpected Places," in *Hellenism in the Land of Israel*, 236–37; Erich Gruen, "Jewish Perspectives on Greek Culture and Ethnicity," in *Hellenism in the Land of Israel*, 85.

73. *Antiquities* 18.3.1.55–59; *Jewish War* 2.9.2–3.169–74.

ers customarily treated Jews and Gentiles differently. With few exceptions, they respected Jewish religious sensitivities. Herod refused to build pagan temples or gymnasiums in Jewish areas and refused to build an amphitheater in Jerusalem.[74] And, as we have seen, in some regions heavily populated by Jews, special coins were printed without the representation of the emperor in deference to the Jewish sensitivity to graven images. Such evidence hardly squares with the view that the Jews of the first century were syncretistic in their religious worldview. From this same time period, we have "outsider" testimony that confirms this picture. The first-century BCE historian Diodorus Siculus reports that the Jews, alone, avoided dealings with other people, and regarded other folk as their "enemies."[75]

Particular Arguments for a Religiously Hellenized Palestine: A Response

We turn now to consider the eight arguments reviewed above that suggest first-century Jews were most likely significantly hellenized, religiously speaking. We will argue that when considered closely these arguments do not succeed in overturning the conclusion that Palestinian Jews strongly resisted Hellenism and other pagan influences in the realm of religious matters. We shall offer brief responses to each of the previously outlined arguments.

Greek Language

It cannot be disputed that Greek was used, to one degree or another, throughout Palestine from the third century BCE on. This constitutes undeniable evidence that by Jesus's day Palestine had, to some extent, experienced hellenization. This fact, however, does not tell us to what degree Jesus's Galilee in particular made use of Greek, or how much significance should be read into the fact that the Greek language was used in certain contexts. In our estimation, the use of Greek actually is quite insignificant as it concerns our primary issue at hand—the question of Hellenistic influence upon *the religious thought-world* of first-century Jews.

First, the actual inscriptional evidence for the use of Greek in first-century Galilee is quite meager. For instance, the only evidence in hand today of Greek inscriptions originating in Galilee from the first thirty years of the first century (the time of Jesus) is a market weight from Tiberius and some coins produced under Herod Antipas—coins that reveal a decidedly Jewish religious culture (see below).[76] Thus, as Mark Chancey reminds us, we currently live with a "general

74. E. P. Sanders, "Jesus' Galilee," in *Fair Play: Diversity and Conflict in Early Christianity, Essays in Honour of Heikki Raisanen*, ed. I. Dunderberg, C. Tuckett, and K. Syreeni (Boston: Brill, 2002), 21.

75. *Bibliotheca Historica*, Fragments of Book 34.1.

76. M. A. Chancey, "The Use of Greek in Jesus' Galilee," in *Greco-Roman Culture and the Galilee of Jesus* (New York: Cambridge University Press, 2005), 135.

ignorance about who used Greek, how often, and in what circumstances" in the first-century Galilean world.[77]

What seems much more certain, however, is that, while Greek was used in Galilee and the wider Palestinian world, Aramaic remained the lingua franca. As we would expect, given the fact that Palestine was under Hellenistic rule, royal inscriptions were written in Greek. Yet, as Lester Grabbe notes, "there was no attempt to make Greek the sole language of administration."[78] In fact, "the use of Greek seems to have been confined to a particular segment of the population, namely, the educated upper class," and "the number of Jews outside the Greek cities who were fluent in Greek seems small."[79]

Finally, within Palestine, religious literature continued to be written in Semitic languages. When the Hebrew Bible was translated for use in synagogue services, it was Aramaic that was chosen, not Greek.[80] Regardless of how widespread the use of Greek was among Palestinian Jews of Jesus's day—and the evidence itself is too uncertain to support decisively the claim that it was widespread—*there is no evidence to suggest that the use of Greek would have inclined the Jews toward Hellenistic religious ideas.*

Proximity of Gentile Cities to Galilee

How significant is it that Galilee was in close proximity to several Gentile cities just outside its borders? Several considerations lead us to conclude that the influence of these nearby cities upon Palestinian Judaism was, religiously speaking, negligible.

First, in light of the discussion above on the nature of hellenization in the empire, one should not be quick to conclude that the Gentile cities surrounding Galilee were hellenized to the point of losing their own indigenous Eastern flavor. Eric Meyers makes an observation that too often has not been considered:

> The oriental cities of the Decapolis and other gentile cities should not be viewed solely as purveyors of Greco-Roman culture but rather as eastern cities with a hellenistic overlay that often facilitated the expression of aspects of Semitic religion and practice, including Judaism. Jewish remains from the Roman period are well known from Gerasa (Jerash), Gadara (Umm Qeis), Abila, and possibly Capitolias (Beit Ras).[81]

77. Ibid., 164.

78. Grabbe, *Judaism from Cyrus to Hadrian*, 1:157.

79. Ibid., 158.

80. See H. Koester, "*Introduction to the New Testament*, vol. 1: *History, Culture, and Religion of the Hellenistic Age* (Philadelphia: Fortress, 1982), 224. The situation would have been different for Greek-speaking Jews of the Diaspora, of course. From the third century BCE onward, the Hebrew Bible was being translated into Greek. Jews of Alexandria, Asia Minor, and Rome would have made use of these translations.

81. E. Meyers, "Jesus and His Galilean Context," in *Archaeology and the Galilee: Texts and Contexts in the Graeco-Roman and Byzantine Periods*, ed. D. Edwards and T. McCollough (Atlanta: Scholars Press, 1997), 62.

Second, this argument is based on "the misperception that proximity equals influence." In fact, as E. P. Sanders reminds us, "places that are close physically may be very remote socially and mentally." Sanders suggests that modern scholars imagine such "proximity-as-influence" through the lenses of our contemporary, pluralistic, much-traveled world. In the first century, however,

> peasants worked from dawn to dusk six days a week and rested on the sabbath. For holidays they went to Jerusalem. Paganism up close would have scared or offended them. The desire for cosmopolitanism that modern scholars have should not be attributed to ancient Jews below the elite.[82]

Aryeh Kasher's important study, *Jews and Hellenistic Cities in Eretz-Israel*, confirms Sanders's point. It appears that the relationships between Jews and Gentiles within the Greek cities of Palestine were often anything but friendly.[83] We conclude, therefore, that the inference that Galilee must have been open to significant Hellenistic/pagan influences *on matters of religion* simply because it was in proximity to major Hellenistic cities is misguided speculation.

The Presence of Hellenistic Cities within Galilee

What are we to make of the fact that the Galilean cities of Tiberius and Sepphoris were built on the model of the Hellenistic city? Once again, this factor would seem to have little bearing on the receptivity of Palestinian Jews to Hellenistic religious ideas. All the evidence suggests that while the cities were Hellenistic in design, in terms of religious orientation they remained fundamentally Jewish in nature. Here, several points are worthy of notice:

- Aside from the Roman soldiers garrisoned in Sepphoris during the Jewish revolt, Josephus never mentions Gentile inhabitants, pagan temples, or Hellenistic institutions at this locale. Later rabbinic traditions corroborate this picture of a distinctly Jewish first-century Sepphoris.[84]
- While the style of the pottery in Sepphoris is Hellenistic, the pottery remains of the ancient city testify to the religiously Jewish nature of its inhabitants. In the Jewish purity system, certain types of vessels could become ritually

---

82. Sanders, "Jesus' Galilee," 38. See also L. H. Feldman's critique of Hengel at this point, review of *The "Hellenization" of Judaea in the First Century after Christ, JSJ* 22 (1991): 142–43.

83. A. Kasher, *Jews and Hellenistic Cities in Eretz-Israel: Relations of the Jews in Eretz-Israel with the Hellenistic Cities during the Second Temple Period (332 BCE–70 CE)* (Tübingen: Mohr Siebeck, 1990).

84. *Jewish War*, 3.2.4.31–32; rabbinic sources: Tosefta, *Yoma* 1.4; Tosefta, *Sotah* 13.7. For discussion of these points see M. Chancey and E. M. Meyer, "How Jewish Was Sepphoris in Jesus' Time?" *BAR* 26 (2000): 24; S. S. Miller, "Hellenistic and Roman Sepphoris: The Historical Evidence," in *Sepphoris in Galilee: Crosscurrents of Culture*, ed. R. M. Nagy et al. (Raleigh: North Carolina Museum of Art, 1996), 22. See also S. Schwartz, "The 'Judaism' of Samaria and Galilee in Josephus's Version of the Letter of Demetrius I to Jonathan (*Antiquities* 13.48–57)," *HTR* 82 (1989): 377–91.

impure, but stone vessels could not. It is now recognized that their presence—or absence—can be used as a Jewish identity marker. More than a hundred stone vessels have been recovered at the Sepphoris excavations, and this strongly suggests the population was religiously Jewish. So too, the archaeological evidence indicates that the Jews of Sepphoris continued to honor levitical prohibitions on eating pork and continued to practice ritualistic bathing.[85]

- We possess two coins from Sepphoris, dated 68 CE, that have no human representation. This suggests that Roman authorities continued to honor the Jews' sensitivity to graven images at Sepphoris. As Sean Freyne notes, "This can only mean that the total ethos, as distinct from certain centers, was still thoroughly Jewish, even if architectural designs and pottery styles taken in isolation could suggest the opposite."[86]

- There is no evidence of pagan temples, cultic objects, or inscriptions to pagan deities in Sepphoris or Tiberius dating from the first century.[87] The first sign of a pagan temple in Sepphoris is from the early third century.[88]

- Regarding Sepphoris's famous theater, it is worth noting that its dating is disputed. In Eric Meyer's judgment, "the theater in all probability was not yet constructed" in Jesus's day.[89] With Meyer, other scholars have concluded that it was most likely built after the Jewish revolt, either in the late first or early second century.[90]

- All the archaeological evidence for a significant Gentile presence in Sepphoris dates from after the Jewish revolt in 66–70 CE, and most of it is after the Jewish revolt of 135—thus after both Jesus and the rise of Christianity.[91]

In sum, the evidence suggests that the Hellenistic aspects of Sepphoris during the time of Jesus were largely superficial and did not impinge upon the religious life of the Jewish people who lived there. The population as a whole was "Torah-true in religious orientation."[92] We therefore concur with Sanders's broader conclusion

85. These lines of evidence are nicely summarized in Chancey and Meyer, "How Jewish Was Sepphoris," 25–27.

86. S. Freyne, *Galilee: From Alexander the Great to Hadrian 323 B.C.E. to 135 C.E.: A Study of Second Temple Judaism* (Wilmington, DE: Glazier, 1980), 144. On the general avoidance of figural art on the coinage of first-century Galilee, see Chancey, "The Coinage of Galilee," in *Greco-Roman Culture*, 166–92.

87. Chancey and Meyer, "How Jewish Was Sepphoris?" 27.

88. Sanders, "Jesus' Galilee," 6–7.

89. E. M. Meyer, "Roman Sepphoris in Light of New Archaeological Evidence and Recent Research," in *The Galilee in Late Antiquity*, 325.

90. Chancey and Meyer, "How Jewish Was Sepphoris?" 28.

91. Ibid., 28–31.

92. E. M. Meyer, "The Challenge of Hellenism for Early Judaism and Christianity," *Biblical Archaeologist* 55 (June 1992): 88; see also the similar conclusions of Chancey, "The Cultural Milieu of Ancient Sepphoris," *NTS* 47 (2001): 127–45; J. L. Reed, "Galilean Archaeology and the Historical Jesus," in

that "there were no cities in Antipas' Galilee that were, in population and culture, 'Hellenistic' or 'Greco-Roman.'" To be sure, "to some degree the entire Roman empire was 'Hellenized.'" But "Jewish Palestine was one of the least Hellenistic areas for the good and simple reason that the Jews did not want to be Hellenized [at least religiously speaking], and all the rulers, from Pompey to Antipas, accepted this fact."[93]

Yaacov Shavit accurately summarizes the overall picture archaeology gives us of Palestinian life during the Second Temple period when he writes:

> It seems right to claim that the Jews of Palestine of that time lived within the Hellenistic world, but were not an integral part of it. The Jewish village (or city) was different from the Hellenistic village (or city): it contained no temples, altars, or idols . . . it had no gymnasium or stadium. The daily routine, the rhythm of the year, public life, the historical consciousness, the legal system—all these were palpably different in essence and form. There were no mixed marriages, laws of impurity and purification effectively separated or determined clear lines of demarcation between populations. . . . Jewish life was distinctive and separate from the life of the Gentile neighbors.

Shavit thus concludes that "no matter how blurred the boundaries may be between Jews and non-Jews in various matters," they only serve to emphasize "the deep chasm that existed between Judaism and pagan Hellenism" on religious matters.[94]

A Pagan Gentile Population within Galilee

It is true that the population of first-century Galilee included Gentiles.[95] But are there any grounds for concluding that this segment of the population was a majority and/or that it significantly influenced Galilean Jews, especially on religious matters? The evidence suggests an answer in the negative.

Jonathan Reed has shown that the once common assumption that Galilee continued to be populated by a Gentile majority under Hasmonean rule is simply not born out by the archaeological evidence. Indeed, there is little evidence

---

Jesus Now and Then: Images of Jesus in History and Christology, ed. M. Meyer and C. Hughes (Harrisburg, PA: Trinity, 2001), 119–21; J. F. Strange, "Recent Discoveries at Sepphoris and Their Relevance for Biblical Research," *Neotestamentica* 3 (2000): 137–38; Sanders, "Jesus' Galilee," 27–33. See also the detailed discussions on Tiberius and Sepphoris in Chancey, "Myth of a Gentile Galilee" (PhD diss., Duke University, 1999).

93. Sanders, "Jesus' Galilee," 33.

94. Y. Shavit, *Athens in Jerusalem: Classical Antiquity and Hellenism in the Making of the Modern Secular Jew*, trans. C. Naor and N. Werner (Portland: Littman Library of Jewish Civilization, 1997), 326–27. Lawrence Schiffman has gone so far as to argue that, if anything, the Galilean *halakah* was more strident and conservative in nature ("Was There a Galilean Halakah?" in *Galilee in Late Antiquity*, 143–56).

95. For a survey of paganism in first-century Palestine, see S. Safrai and M. Stern, eds., *The Jewish People in the First Century: Historical Geography, Political History, Social, Cultural and Religious Life and Institutions* (Philadelphia: Fortress, 1976), 2:1065–1100.

of a significant Gentile population even prior to Hasmonean rule.[96] During the Hasmonean period, Aristobulus I gave the Gentile population in Galilee a clear option: "live as Jews or leave."[97]

Nor does the argument that Matthew's reference to "Galilee of the Gentiles" (Matt. 4:15) provides evidence of a majority Gentile population carry any weight. Matthew was quoting a passage from Isaiah (Isa. 9:1) for his own theological and literary purposes. His purpose was not to describe the population of Galilee at the time of his writing. Hence, as Mark Chancey concludes in his insightful study of Matthew's reference: "The phrase 'Galilee of the Gentiles,' appearing only once in a first-century C.E. source, and then, in a quote of an eighth-century B.C.E. source, tells us nothing about the region's population."[98]

We thus conclude that Gentiles were a minority population in first-century Galilee. But is there any evidence that this minority population significantly influenced the Jewish majority *in religious matters*? Again, the evidence suggests the answer is *no*. As noted above, from the Maccabean revolt and the rise of the Hasmonean dynasty until the fall of Jerusalem in 70 CE, all the evidence indicates that first-century Galilean Jews practiced relatively conservative forms of Judaism. Sean Freyne has shown that this much is revealed in Josephus's writings alone.[99] Jonathan Reed has demonstrated that archaeological evidence confirms this perspective. The most significant pieces of evidence are the following:

- Ceramic wares found in Galilee are carved from a distinctive soft chalk limestone. This type of vessel was particularly amenable to Jewish ritual purity requirements. Reed notes, "Such artifacts are unique to Jewish sites in the first century CE."[100]

- Stepped plastered pools have been discovered in a number of affluent Galilean homes, as well as in public spaces in a number of Galilean villages. There is little doubt that these pools are *miqvaoth*—ritual bathing pools unique to

96. Reed, "Identity of the Galileans," in *Archaeology and the Galilean Jesus*, 33. The most common theory of which group of pagan Gentiles might have settled in Galilee prior to the Hasmoneans is the Itureans, who originated in Syria and would have moved south into Galilee. However, the archaeological evidence reveals that those elements that characterize Iturean material culture (e.g., small unwalled farmsteads, pagan temples, and their distinctive pottery) have not been found in any sector of Galilee. See Reed, "Identity of the Galileans," 38–39.

97. Chancey, "Myth of a Gentile Galilee," 252. See *Antiquities* XIII, 318–19.

98. Chancey, "Myth of a Gentile Galilee," 258; for his study of this phrase, see 255–58.

99. S. Freyne, "Galilee-Jerusalem Relations According to Josephus' *Life*," *NTS* 33 (1987): 607. On the correspondence of the available literary evidence with the archaeological evidence, see Reed, "Identity of the Galileans," 53–55. On the need to take seriously both literary and archaeological evidence when reconstructing Judaism's past, see Dunn, "On the Relation of Text and Artifact."

100. Reed, "Galilean Archaeology," 117.

Jewish religious life.[101] As Reed again notes, "these structures are ubiquitous around Jerusalem and wherever Jews lived."[102]

- Galilean excavation sites reveal a consistent lack of pork bones. This is uniquely characteristic of Jewish sites where the levitical prohibition of pork was followed.[103]

- Galilean burial sites commonly reveal tombs designed with special shafts for second burials. That is, the first burial would take place, and then sometime later a second burial would follow in which the bones were collected and placed inside a stone box (ossuary). This type of second burial was characteristic of Jewish practices from the late first century BCE until the temple destruction in 70 CE.[104] In addition, burial sites are generally found outside the city precincts, in a typically Jewish fashion.[105]

- Coins minted by Herod Antipas in first-century Galilee at Tiberius "avoided human representation of any kind," while the coins of his brother Philip—who ruled in pagan cities—had both his own and the emperor's images upon them, as was typical of coinage in the empire.[106] As we noted earlier,

101. See Chancey and Meyers, "How Jewish Was Sepphoris?" 26–27; S. Freyne, "Galilean Questions to Crossan's Mediterranean Jesus," in *Galilee and the Gospels: Collected Essays* (Tübingen: Mohr Siebeck, 2000), 220; Strange, "Recent Discoveries at Sepphoris," 127; Reed, *Archaeology and the Galilean Jesus*, 45–47, 49, 134. Some have disputed that these pools at Sepphoris are *miqvaoth*. First, most do not contain an additional water-storage reservoir. In this view, unless an additional water-storage pool (*otzar*) is attached, then the ritual requirements of "living (i.e., flowing) water" would not be met. Second, in many of these homes there is no additional bathing facility for common use. Thus, these stepped pools may well have functioned as bathtubs rather than as religiously significant *miqveh*. See, e.g., H. Eshel, "A Note on 'Miqvaot' at Sepphoris," in *Archaeology and the Galilee*, 131–33; idem, "The Pools of Sepphoris: Ritual Baths or Bathtubs?—They're Not Ritual Baths," *BAR* (July/August 2000): 42–45; P. F. Craffert, "Digging Up *Common Judaism* in Galilee: *Miqva'ot* at Sepphoris as a Test Case," *Neotestamentica* 34 (2000): 39–55. However, these criticisms have been convincingly answered. See E. M. Meyers, "The Pools of Sepphoris: Ritual Baths or Bathtubs?—Yes, They Are," *BAR* (July/August 2000): 46–49; R. Reich, "The Great Mikveh Debate," *BAR* (March/April 1993): 52–53.

102. Reed, "Galilean Archaeology," 117.

103. On lack of pork bones as strong evidence for a Jewish population, see Reed, "Identity of the Galileans," 44, 47, 49; B. Hesse and P. Wapnish, "Can Pig Remains Be Used for Ethnic Diagnosis in the Ancient Near East?" in *The Archaeology of Israel: Constructing the Past, Interpreting the Present*, ed. N. Silberman and D. Small (Sheffield: Sheffield Academic Press, 1997), 238–70.

104. Reed, "Galilean Archaeology," 117; idem, *Archaeology and the Galilean Jesus*, 47–49. On ossuary burial and recovered boxes, see C. A. Evans, *Jesus and the Ossuaries* (Waco: Baylor University Press, 2003). There is debate as to whether ossuary burial is predicated upon Jewish belief in resurrection and afterlife. For relevant bibliography and a case in the negative, see E. Regev, "The Individualistic Meaning of Jewish Ossuaries: A Socio-Anthropological Perspective on Burial Practice," *Palestine Exploration Quarterly* 133 (2001): 39–49. In either case, the use of these burial shafts and ossuaries "are uniquely Jewish" (R. Hachlili and A. Killebrew, "Jewish Funerary Customs during the Second Temple Period, in the Light of the Excavations at the Jericho Necropolis," *Palestine Exploration Quarterly* 115 [1983], 129).

105. Meyer, "The Challenge of Hellenism," 88.

106. Freyne, *Galilee*, 143–44. See Reed, *Archaeology and the Galilean Jesus*, 122–23; Chancey, "Coinage of Galilee."

this aspect of the numismatic record can best be explained by the desire to avoid violation of the second commandment of the Torah, which prohibits graven images.

- In all of the first-century archaeological sites to date, pagan temples are completely absent.[107] This absence of pagan temples shows that "the Hasmoneans did not tolerate public displays of paganism, and even under the Herodians none have been present, seemingly indicating their sensitivity to the general [Jewish] populace."[108]

Such evidence strongly suggests that the Gentile population in Galilee exercised no significant influence, religiously speaking, on Galilean Jews. Indeed, without denying the presence of Hellenistic elements in public life, the surprising feature of first-century Palestinian Judaism is how thoroughly they *resisted* Hellenistic influences at the fundamental level of religious worldview. Louis Feldman puts the matter starkly when he writes:

> The question is not so much how greatly Jews and Judaism in the land of Israel were Hellenized, as how strongly they resisted Hellenization. In other words, what was the power of Judaism that enabled it to remain strong despite the challenge of Hellenism and later of Christianity? The answer may lie in its paradoxical self-confidence and defensiveness, its unity and diversity, its stubbornness and flexibility.

Feldman goes on to offer as an analogy the Jews of Eastern Europe who, for hundreds of years, carried on dealings with the Gentile "Christian" population and yet "maintained their own distinctive language, Yiddish . . . together with their religious laws and customs."[109] With Feldman, we submit that this paradoxical "stubbornness and flexibility" accounts for the otherwise puzzling fact that first-century Jews did assimilate aspects of Hellenism, but rarely in terms of their *religious convictions*.

The Location and Topography of Lower Galilee

Is there any warrant for the conclusion that the location and topography of lower Galilee would have made it a major trade route in the ancient world and thus have exposed its population to a wide variety of attractive Hellenistic religious influences? We submit there is little reason to think so.

107. Reed, "Galilean Archaeology," 118–19.
108. Reed, "Identity of the Galileans," 43. As Reed correctly notes (pp. 43–44n54), this complete absence of pagan sites is more telling than the relative absence of identifiable first-century synagogues, since the public square or private homes most likely functioned at this time as precursors to synagogue structures. See S. Hoenig, "The Ancient City-Square: Forerunner of the Synagogue," in *ANRW* 2.19.1:448–76. Although, on the identifiable presence of several first-century Galilean synagogue structures, see below.
109. Feldman, "How Much Hellenism in Palestine?" 111.

First, our estimations regarding the nature of the religion of Galilee's population must be rooted in archaeological and literary evidence, not speculation. And, as we have seen, the evidence suggests that Galileans remained staunchly conservative in their religious beliefs and practices. Thus, even if Galilee had a constant stream of mercantile Gentiles passing through it, we should conclude that this simply supplies further confirmation of how resistant first-century Palestinian Judaism was to Hellenistic religious influences.

Second, there is simply no reason to accept the common depiction of first-century Lower Galilee as a burgeoning center for ancient trade. To the contrary, as Mark Chancey has demonstrated, the evidence suggests that "by the first century CE, the chief routes bypassed Galilee." He goes on to argue that "nothing in the literary or archaeological record suggests that Galilee was practically overrun with visiting gentiles, despite scholarly claims to the contrary."[110]

Foreign Rule in Galilee

It is true that Galilee was ruled by Rome in the first century, but is it accurate to describe this rule as an "occupation" or "annexation," along the lines of Britain's occupation of Ireland, as John Dominic Crossan does? And can we speculate on the basis of this supposed "occupation" that Galilee must have been significantly hellenized, even on religious matters? The answer to both questions is a decisive no.

Generally speaking, Galilee was not "occupied" by Rome in any usual sense of the term. Indeed, this was not Rome's general policy toward *any* nation. As E. P. Sanders notes, "Rome ruled by terror, not by military occupation."[111] Troops were sent into unstable territories to reestablish order—often using ferocious tactics. But these invasions were the exceptions, not the rule.

Most significant for our purposes, there were no troops stationed in Galilee in Jesus's day.[112] The legions in charge of maintaining order in Palestine were stationed in Syria, not Galilee. It is true that for a time roughly three thousand Roman soldiers were stationed in Judea to support Herod's son Archelaus. But even in this instance they tended to keep to themselves—within the walls of the Antonia fortress or away in Caesarea—and thus, for the most part, away from the Jewish inhabitants.[113]

In any event, with an insignificant Gentile population to start with and with little military presence, it hardly seems accurate to describe Galilee as "occupied"

110. Chancey, "Myth of a Gentile Galilee," 250 (also 254). See also J. F. Strange, "First Century Galilee from Archaeology and from the Texts," in *Archaeology and the Galilee*, 39–48.

111. Sanders, "Jesus' Galilee," 10.

112. Mark Chancey provides a helpful assessment of this question. He concludes: "In the time of Jesus, there were no Roman army units, no colonists, and probably few, if any, Roman administrators in Galilee" ("The Roman Army in Palestine," in *Greco-Roman Culture*, 69).

113. Sanders, "Jesus' Galilee," 11.

or "annexed" by the Romans.[114] And so we must judge the argument for a strong Hellenistic influence on the basis of this alleged "occupation" as misguided.

The Tension between Galilee and Judea

How significant were the economic, cultural and religious tensions between Galilee and Judea? And how significant is the claim that we find no synagogues in Galilee prior to the destruction of the temple in 70 CE? Does it imply that Galilee was less Jewish and more vulnerable to pagan influences than Judea? In our estimation, it does not.[115]

A first consideration is Josephus's portrait of Galilee with respect to these issues. Freyne nicely summarizes what we find:

> An old and deep-seated attachment to Jerusalem and its temple, demonstrated particularly in fidelity to the pilgrimage, was capable of overcoming the social and economic tensions that existed between rural peasants from an outlying province and a ruling Jerusalem aristocracy who owned the better land and controlled the markets.[116]

114. Sanders sums it up well. "Those who write about Roman occupation can cite no evidence; they never say which legion occupied Galilee in Jesus' day" ("Jesus' Galilee," 12). See also Chancey, "Roman Army," 69.

115. The "Judea/Jerusalem vs. Galilee" dichotomy gains much of its force from socioeconomic speculations that appear far more indebted to an a priori neo-Marxist model of class conflict than they do to the actual first-century data. Such a model of "city vs. country" is assumed and plays a central role in works such as Crossan's *Historical Jesus* and Horsley's *Archaeology, History and Society in Galilee*. A number of archaeologists, however, have challenged the application of this model to first-century Galilee in light of the actual material culture that has been unearthed. Specifically, the model of urban exploitation of rural peasants is not so obvious from the actual remains. What John Lloyd argued vis-à-vis the wider empire, others have argued for Galilee in particular: "It would seem increasingly difficult to retain the view, still widely held, that the typical Roman town was a collection of amenities for the rich and their retainers, sucking in wealth from the countryside and returning to it very little. The sheer quantity of sites in the remoter countryside with centrally manufactured objects—tools and other metal works, amphoras, millstones, pottery, some of them imports from overseas—suggests a more vigorous economic role for the town and the large village, in trade and quite possibly in manufacture too" ("Archaeological Survey and the Roman Landscape: Forms of Rural Settlement in the Early Roman Empire," in *Roman Landscapes: Archaeological Survey in the Mediterranean Region*, ed. G. Barker and J. Lloyd [London: British School at Rome, 1991], 238). See also the contributions to G. M. Schwartz and S. E. Falconer, eds., *Archaeological Views from the Countryside: Village Communities in Early Complex Societies* (Washington, DC: Smithsonian, 1994); D. Edwards, "The Socio-Economic and Cultural Ethos of the Lower Galilee in the First Century: Implications for the Nascent Jesus Movement," in *Galilee in Late Antiquity*, 53–73; D. E. Groh, "The Clash between Literary and Archaeological Models of Provincial Palestine," in *Archaeology and the Galilee*, 29–38; E. M. Meyers, "An Archaeological Response to a New Testament Scholar," *Bulletin of the American Schools of Oriental Research* 297 (1995): 17–26; idem, "Jesus in His Galilean Context," 64.

116. Freyne, "Galilee-Jerusalem Relations According to Josephus' Life," 607. Burton Mack somehow claims to know the theological motives lurking behind Freyne's argument that first-century Lower Galilee was fundamentally Jewish—"He did this in order to establish the plausibility of strong loyalties to Jerusalem and, one suspects, claim a thoroughly Jewish context for Jesus and his message" (*A Myth of Innocence*, 65). Of course, the "let's-speculate-on-motives" sword is double-edged, for one could also hypothesize

Certainly the firsthand evidence of Josephus must be taken as more reliable than speculations some make about the hypothesized religious tension between Galilee and Jerusalem. What is more, as we have already shown, all the archaeological evidence suggests that Galilean Jews carried on the resistance to Hellenistic influences on religious matters that began with the Maccabean revolt. This too must be deemed more reliable than contemporary speculations.

Regarding the common claim that there is no evidence for the presence of synagogues in pre-70 CE Galilee, we must first note that *this is simply not the case*.[117] Several first-century synagogues have been discovered, including structures at Masada, Herodium, and Jerusalem.[118] With respect to Galilee itself, an excavation at Gamla has unearthed a first-century synagogue.[119] Also, the remnants of a basalt structure beneath the limestone synagogue discovered at Capernaum may well represent a prior first-century synagogue.[120]

Moreover, to do away with first-century Galilean synagogues, one must entirely reject as ahistorical the numerous claims of the Gospels regarding Jesus's teaching activity in synagogues all over Galilee (e.g., Matt. 4:23; Mark 1:39; Luke 4:15; John 18:20). Such a total rejection of the New Testament data reflects the unwarranted skepticism characteristic of a currently popular minimalism that refuses to countenance literary evidence unless it is corroborated by material remains. But, as a growing number of scholars are recognizing, such minimalism is simply bad methodology. In his recent monumental study of the ancient synagogue, Lee Levine questions such skepticism:

> Caution against such extreme skepticism should be maintained . . . chronologically they [the Gospels and Acts] are not so distant from Jesus' setting; the differences between the later part of the first century C.E. and ca. 30 C.E. is only a generation

that Mack's attempt to argue for a radically hellenized Galilee is fueled by his desires to cut ties to Jewish loyalties in order to claim a radically hellenized (read "Cynic") context for Jesus and his message.

117. At the 2001 meeting of the Lund Synagogue Project, Birger Olsson concluded that the "attempts in the 90s, especially by some American scholars, to date the synagogue institution and building in Palestine to ca. 200 C.E. . . . have not proven to lead to any valid conclusions" ("The Origins of the Synagogue: An Evaluation," in *The Ancient Synagogue from Its Origins until 200 C.E.*, ed. B. Olsson and M. Zetterholm [Stockholm: Almqvist and Wiksell, 2003], 132–33). See also R. Hachlili, "The Origin of the Synagogue: A Reassessment," *JSJ* 28 (1997): 34–47; K. Atkinson, "On Further Defining the First-Century C.E. Synagogue: Fact or Fiction? A Rejoinder to H. C. Kee," *NTS* 43 (1997): 491–502. On a pre-70 date for the famous Theodotus synagogue inscription—contra Kee's arguments for a fourth-century origin—see R. Riesner, "Synagogues in Jerusalem," in *The Book of Acts in Its Palestinian Setting*, ed. R. Bauckham (Grand Rapids: Eerdmans, 1995), 192–200. For a brief history of the wider debate, see B. Olsson, "The Origins of the Synagogue: An Introduction," in *Ancient Synagogue*, 27–36.

118. See L. I. Levine, *The Ancient Synagogue: The First Thousand Years* (New Haven: Yale University Press, 2000), 43; J. F. Strange, "Archaeology and Ancient Synagogues up to about 200 C.E.," in *The Ancient Synagogue*, 37–62; Riesner, "Synagogues in Jerusalem," 179–210.

119. Reed, "Galilean Archaeology," 119; Levine, *Ancient Synagogue*, 51–52.

120. Chancey, "Myth of a Gentile Galilee," 177; Strange, "Archaeology and Ancient Synagogues," 38–39.

or two. Furthermore, it is not at all clear that a Diaspora setting had an impact on these accounts. All the gospels, no matter when or where written, report much the same information regarding the Galilean synagogues. . . . It appears rather unlikely that all the gospel writers would refer time and again to Jesus' activity in an institution that never existed in his time. Such an assumption, that there were no synagogue buildings in Galilean towns and villages in the first century, thus appears unwarranted.[121]

In the debate on the existence of pre-70 Galilean synagogues, it is important to remember that most of the conflict is over the question of identifiable *building structures*. Thus, even if the position of H. C. Kee is correct—that prior to the Jewish revolt in 70 the "synagogue" referred not to an architecturally distinctive building but only a voluntary gathering place for worship—our case remains untouched.[122]

Even apart from this debate, the mere fact that we have little archaeological evidence of identifiable first-century synagogues in Galilee is no justification for drawing the conclusion that Galilee had no communal religious parameters and authority structure and that they were therefore more open to Hellenistic religious influences than the Jews of Judea. We know from Josephus as well as the New Testament that Galilean Jews regularly gathered for religious services. Whether they did so in homes, in buildings that would perhaps never be identified as synagogue structures (similar to early Christian house churches), or in public spaces (e.g., the city square) is irrelevant to the question at hand.[123] The paucity of identifiable structures certainly says nothing about how open or resistant the Jews of this area were to Hellenistic religious ideas. To answer this question we must stick with the available evidence. And, as we have seen, the evidence suggests they were remarkably resistant in this respect.

Magic and Astrology

What are we to make of the literary evidence that some Jews, including some in Palestine, were interested in magic and astrology? And what of the ancient synagogue remains within Palestine found to be decorated with zodiac symbols and even the Greek god Helios? Does this not suggest that, religiously speaking, first-century Galilean Judaism was in fact quite open to a syncretistic merger with

121. Levine, *Ancient Synagogue*, 44–45.
122. See Kee, "The Transformation of the Synagogue after 70 CE: Its Import for Early Christianity," *NTS* 36 (1990): 1–24; idem, "Defining the First-Century CE Synagogue: Problems and Proposals," *NTS* 41 (1995): 481–500. Although, note Olsson's conclusion: "The destruction of the temple seems not to be so important for the history of ancient synagogue as almost everybody suppose [sic]" ("Origins of the Synagogue: Evaluation," 137). A. T. Kraabel notes that, for various reasons, it often is difficult to identify Diaspora synagogues as well; "The Diaspora Synagogue: Archaeological and Epigraphic Evidence since Sukenik," *ANRW* 2.19.1:501–2.
123. Reed, "Identity of the Galileans," 43–44n54; Hoenig, "Ancient City-Square."

various religious aspects of Hellenistic paganism? In our view, the cumulative evidence suggests quite a different conclusion.

For several centuries in the modern era, a consensus was maintained that a serious Jewish interest in magic and astrology did not emerge until the Middle Ages. However, in the last several decades this once common view has been called into question.[124] While we agree that the old perspective was in need of reassessment given more recent discoveries (e.g., the Qumran texts), the fact remains that the clear evidence of late Second Temple Jewish interest in magic and astrology in no way suggests a fundamental openness to paganism.

First, with the exception of a very small number of Qumran texts, virtually all of the actual extant Jewish magical texts come from later centuries, up to the Middle Ages (e.g., the Cairo Genizah fragments).[125] There are, of course, references to Jewish magical interest and practice within other texts (e.g., the Hebrew Bible, intertestamental literature, the New Testament, and early rabbinic literature), but it is difficult to know how widespread this interest was, or where accurate depiction ends and polemical exaggeration begins.[126] As such, these sources can hardly tell us anything definitive about the extent to which the first-century Jewish population of Palestine showed an interest in astrology and magic. In fact, much of the "evidence" adduced for this portrait of first-century Judaism is largely irrelevant to the question at hand, since it generally reflects a later situation that is often anachronistically projected back onto the first-century context.

Regarding the relevant texts found in the Qumran library, it is not at all clear how significant they are for our understanding of the beliefs of the Qumran community.[127] Does the fact that this community's library included some astrological

---

124. See Charlesworth, "Jewish Astrology"; idem, "Jewish Interest in Astrology during the Hellenistic and Roman Period," in *ANRW* 2.20.2:926–27.

125. See P. Schäfer, "Jewish Magic Literature in Late Antiquity and Early Middle Ages," *JJS* 41 (1990): 75–91. J. C. Greenfield and M. Sokoloff note that only two Aramaic astrological omen texts have been found. See "Astrological and Related Omen Texts in Jewish Palestinian Aramaic," *Journal of New Eastern Studies* 48 (1989): 202.

126. On these two main lines of evidence see P. S. Alexander, "Incantations and Books of Magic," in E. Schürer, *The History of the Jewish People in the Age of Jesus Christ (175 B.C.–A.D. 135)*, rev. ed., ed. G. Vermes, F. Millar, and M. Goodman (Edinburgh: Clark, 1986), III/1, 343. For a rabbinic discussion on astrology, see Babylonian Talmud, *Shabbat* (156b).

127. The three Qumran texts—all from cave four—most often mentioned in this regard are 4Q186 (an encoded text widely known for decades as a "horoscope" text but more accurately regarded as a physiognomic text), 4Q561 (an Aramaic text reflecting the content of 4Q186), and 4Q318 (a brontologion, i.e., a text that purports to forecast the future based upon the proper interpretation of thunder). For helpful orientations, see P. S. Alexander, "Physiognomy, Initiation, and Rank in the Qumran Community," in *Geschichte—Tradition—Reflexion: Festschrift für Martin Hengel zum 70. Geburtstag*, ed. H. Cancik, H. Lichtenberger, and P. Schäfer (Tübingen: Mohr Siebeck, 1996), 1:385–94; J. Naveh, "Fragments of an Aramaic Magic Book from Qumran," *Israel Exploration Journal* 48 (1998): 252–61; M. O. Wise, "Thunder in Gemini: An Aramaic Brontologion (4Q318) from Qumran," in *Thunder in Gemini and Other Essays on History, Language and Literature of Second Temple Palestine* (Sheffield: Sheffield Academic Press, 1994), 13–50.

texts mean that the community altogether endorsed these texts? Perhaps they possessed them for polemical reasons. Or perhaps they endorsed certain aspects of the texts but not the overall worldview of the texts. The point is, we do not know which of these or other possible reasons led to the preservation of these texts at Qumran. The mere presence of the texts in this community's library does not itself tell us what the community thought about them.[128]

However, even if the majority view is correct in assuming the community did endorse these texts, this still does not constitute evidence that the Qumran community was *in general* open to pagan ideas. On other grounds we can conclude that clearly they were not.[129] And to whatever degree their interest in astrology and magic suggests a narrowly focused openness to such things, this certainly does not constitute evidence that first-century Judaism *in general* was open to pagan ideas. After all, the Qumran community was sectarian in nature and idiosyncratically esoteric with respect to certain of their beliefs and practices. More specifically, it is not difficult to imagine this community gravitating toward astrological texts given their strongly predestinarian theology.[130]

But what are we to make of the wider Jewish interest in magic and astrology? Several observations must guide this discussion if we are to arrive at a conclusion that does justice to the full range of evidence. First, there are the clear prohibitions within the Old Testament against divination and related practices (e.g., Deut. 18:9–22; Isa. 46:6–10). The ongoing relevance of these texts and their warnings are seen throughout Second Temple literature. For example, Deuteronomy 18:9–22 is included in the Qumran Temple Scroll. So too, in the *Book of Watchers*, magical and divinatory arts are taught to humanity by the fallen angelic watchers (*1 Enoch* 8:3). A similar etiology of, and warning about, these evil arts is offered in *Jubilees* (8:1–4; 11:7–8).[131]

---

128. For several perspectives that question the common assumption that the Qumran astrological/magical texts represented the views of the community itself, see M. Albani, "Horoscopes in the Qumran Scrolls," in *The Dead Sea Scrolls after Fifty Years: A Comprehensive Assessment*, ed. P. W. Flint and J. C. Vanderkam (Boston: Brill, 1999), 279–330; J. C. Greenfield and M. Sokoloff, "An Astrological Text from Qumran (4Q318) and Reflections on Some Zodiacal Names," *Revue de Qumran* 16 (1995): 507–25; M. R. Lehmann, "New Light on Astrology in Qumran and the Talmud," *Revue de Qumran* 8 (1975): 599–602.

129. A point emphasized—perhaps even overplayed—by Albani, "Horoscopes in the Qumran Scrolls," 315–17.

130. A point noted by a number of scholars; see, e.g., P. S. Alexander, "'Wrestling against Wickedness in High Places': Magic in the Worldview of the Qumran Community," in *The Scrolls and the Scriptures: Qumran Fifty Years After*, ed. S. E. Porter and C. A. Evans (Sheffield: Sheffield Academic Press, 1997), 330–33; R. T. Beckwith, *Calendar and Chronology, Jewish and Christian: Biblical, Intertestamental and Patristic Studies* (New York: Brill, 1996), 251–52. This perspective is supported by the fact that interest in things esoteric and magical within later Jewish contexts (e.g., Merkavah mysticism, etc.) often coincided with strongly predestinarian elements. See I. Gruenwald, "Two Types of Jewish Esoteric Literature in the Time of the Mishnah and Talmud," in *From Apocalypticism to Gnosticism: Studies in Apocalypticism, Merkavah Mysticism, and Gnosticism* (New York: Lang, 1988), 63; Schäfer, *Hidden and Manifest God*, 137–38.

131. For discussion see Lange, "Essene Position on Magic," 397–408.

Second, even when it might appear *to us* that Second Temple Jews were incorporating magical and divinatory practices, a case can be made that, to their own way of thinking, they were not syncretistically borrowing ideas from paganism but were simply practicing established aspects found within Judaism. There is, after all, precedent within the Old Testament itself for engaging in activities that border on the very type of divinatory practices that are otherwise proscribed. Obvious examples include dream interpretation (Gen. 40–41; Dan. 1:17–20) and the use of the Urim and Thummim to discern God's will (Exod. 28:30; Lev. 8:8; Deut. 33:8). Thus, long before Hellenism was a force in the Mediterranean world, certain divinatory-like practices were allowed while all others were forbidden. The crucial issue for ancient Jews was not whether one could "divine" God's will or some aspect of the future by "mantic" means, but whether the means and motives of this discernment were pagan in derivation and/or orientation.

J. C. VanderKam captures the essential point:

> Divination was no stranger to ancient Israel and to Judeans of the Hellenistic period. They clearly practiced various mantic techniques, forbade others, and placed all permissible ones within the framework of their monotheistic theology. Opposition to pagan divination centered on the fact that it was pagan, not that it was mantic.[132]

This general observation clearly applies even to the Qumran community itself. At the end of a recent study of magic and divination at Qumran, Armin Lange concludes: "Thus, the Essene approach to magic and divination is characterized by dualism and eschatology. The few forms of magic and divination practiced by them were either sanctioned by the Torah or by the priestly traditions."[133]

There is, therefore, no good reason to use the meager evidence for "divination" we find in first-century Judaism to draw the conclusion that their religious worldview had been significantly hellenized in a pagan direction.

But what are we to make of the intriguing presence of seemingly pagan symbols in ancient Palestinian synagogues? To begin, it is worth noting that some scholars have argued that by the first century these ostensively pagan symbols had become common cultural currency and were therefore used by Jews only for decorative and/or calendar purposes. On the basis of a passage in *Targum Pseudo-Jonathan* (in reference to Lev. 26:1), E. E. Urbach has argued that Jews were forbidden to *revere* pagan images and symbols but not forbidden from using them *for decorative purposes*.[134] A number of scholars, including Moshe Dothan, director of the

---

132. J. C. VanderKam, *Enoch and the Growth of an Apocalyptic Tradition* (Washington, DC: Catholic Biblical Association of America, 1984), 75.

133. Lange, "Essene Position on Magic," 435. See also the relevant conclusions of Alexander, "'Wrestling against Wickedness,'" 335–37; G. J. Brooke, "Deuteronomy 18.9–14 in the Qumran Scrolls," in *Magic in the Biblical World: From the Rod of Aaron to the Ring of Solomon*, ed. T. Klutz (New York: Clark, 2003).

134. The passage reads, "You shall not set up a figured stone in your land, to bow down to it, but a mosaic pavement of designs and forms you may set it in the floor of your places of worship, so long as

excavation of the Hammath Tiberius synagogue, have concluded that the zodiac was used by the Jews as a liturgical calendar to reckon time for Jewish holy days and seasons. In either case, it had no independent religious significance.[135]

Others suspect there is more to the story than merely decorative considerations yet find no reason to conclude that we are dealing here with a Jewish-pagan syncretism. James Charlesworth, for example, argues that Jews had "from earliest times ... demonstrated a brilliance for borrowing symbols and remitting them in line with older intrinsic traditions."[136]

Two famous examples of this are Philo and Josephus. Both rejected astrological ideas, yet both appeal to zodiac symbols for symbolic purposes.[137] Hence, Charlesworth concludes, the *use* of "zodiacal images must not be equated with astrological *beliefs*."[138] Similarly, Hershel Shanks concludes:

> For these Jews ... there was no reason why their God could not work through the zodiac. ... For centuries, the calendar had been regarded as a reflection of godly regularity, and the zodiac may well have been a living symbol which many Jews adopted to represent this divine order.[139]

---

you do not do obeisance to it." Cited by E. E. Urbach, "The Rabbinical Laws of Idolatry in the Second and Third Centuries in the Light of Archaeological and Historical Facts," *Israel Exploration Journal* 9 (1959): 237. Even Goodenough himself commented that the zodiac's presence in synagogues does "not testify to the congregation's interest in, or use of, astrology" (*Jewish Symbols*, 8:168). Oddly, at another point, Goodenough says it is "impossible" to consider the zodiac signs as merely ornamental (1:256). For a discussion of the interpretive disagreement between Urbach and Goodenough, see Charlesworth, "Jewish Astrology," 195–97. Goodenough's thesis of a widespread sacramental paganism and an "empire-wide, anti-rabbinic, mystical Judaism"—based on the Jewish use of these types of symbols—has been appropriately challenged. See, e.g., M. Smith, "Goodenough's *Jewish Symbols* in Retrospect," *JBL* 86 (1967): 53–68 (quote from p. 65).

135. M. Dothan, *Hammath Tiberius—Early Synagogues and the Hellenistic and Roman Remains* (Jerusalem: Israel Exploration Society/University of Haifa, 1983), 48–50. Here, Dothan follows the proposal of M. Avi Yonah, "The Caesarea Inscription of the Twenty-Four Priestly Courses," in *The Teachers Yoke: Studies in Memory of Henry Trantham* (Dallas: Baylor University Press, 1968), 46–57. R. Hachlili concurs ("The Zodiac in Ancient Jewish Art: Representation and Significance," *Bulletin of the American Schools of Oriental Research* 228 [1977]: 61–77). For challenges to this view, see L. A. Roussin, "The Zodiac in Synagogue Decoration," in *Archaeology and the Galilee*, 83–96; Shanks, "Synagogue Excavation," 43.

136. Charlesworth, "Jewish Astrology," 195. See also Chancey, "Greco-Roman Art and the Shifting Limits of Acceptability," in *Greco-Roman Culture*, 193–204.

137. See *Migr.*, 32; *Jewish War*, 5.5.4; 6.5.3 for their repudiation of astrology. Philo appeals to the zodiac in his Old Testament exegesis (*Quaes. Gen.* 4.164), and Josephus identifies the temple bread loaves with the zodiac circle (*Jewish War*, 5.5.5). Charlesworth adds, "Zodiacal symbols were sometimes demythologized from non-Jewish religions and remythologized in Jewish categories." A good example is the Jewish tradition of thirty-six hidden just men, upon whom hangs the daily fate of the world. This Jewish idea may have originated in the astrological belief in thirty-six stellar gods. If so, then "an astrological belief was reminted into a Jewish idea" (Charlesworth, "Jewish Astrology," 184, 185).

138. Charlesworth, "Jewish Astrology," 195 (emphasis added).

139. Shanks, "Synagogue Excavation," 43. Similarly, Eric Meyer concludes: "The minimalist position suggests a simple borrowing of motifs and use within a completely Jewish context" ("Ancient Synagogues in Galilee: Their Religious and Cultural Setting," *Biblical Archaeologist* 43 [Spring 1980], 106).

For our purposes, the most significant observation is that all the synagogue remains cited as evidence for a paganized first-century Judaism date from *after* the first century. For example, the Hammath Tiberius mosaic—the earliest of all—dates from the late second century at the earliest, while the Sepphoris Dionysus mosaic is third century.[140] Most of the remaining evidence dates from the fourth century or later.[141] Given that the Jewish world of Palestine changed drastically after 70 CE, we have no reason to think that artifacts from the third to the sixth century provide us with any reliable clues as to the nature of Judaism in the first century. At the very least, it is unwarranted to allow speculation on the basis of late artifacts to overturn the first-century evidence that demonstrates that the Palestinian Judaism of this time was, by nature, very resistant to paganism. Thus, even for those who interpret the synagogue mosaics as evidence of pagan religious influence and a monotheistic compromise, any extrapolation of this thesis to the pre-70 Palestinian world comes only with considerable anachronism.[142]

How "Flexible" Was First-Century Jewish Monotheism?

Finally, we must consider the claim that Second Temple Jews had come to embrace a "flexible monotheism" that was capable of ascribing godlike status to intermediary beings. Is this evidence that the Judaism out of which Christianity was birthed had assimilated pagan ideas to the point of compromising its traditional monotheism? More specifically, is it plausible to suppose that the early Christians viewed Jesus merely as one of these exalted beings, as many legendary-Jesus theorists contend? Could the Jesus of the Gospels be just one of the many "divine man" figures the ancients occasionally believed in? When a fair assessment is made of all the evidence, we believe each of these claims can be shown to be problematic.

Divine Beings and the Old Testament

First, scholars often exaggerate the difference between the view of intermediary beings in the intertestamental period and the view of intermediary beings prior to this time. In point of fact, "gods," "angels," "heavenly hosts," and other intermediary beings play a significant role throughout the Old Testament, far more so than many seem to realize. In the Old Testament, as in the intertestamental period, these beings are sometimes spoken of in very exalted terms and are viewed

140. Shanks, "Synagogue Excavation," 39; Chancey, "Myth of a Gentile Galilee," 25.
141. Charlesworth, "Jewish Astrology," 195, 198.
142. Chancey has recently pointed out the wider problem of the all too common "recontextualization [of Jesus] within late second- or even third-century C.E. Galilee" and the anachronism this involves ("Galilee and Greco-Roman Culture in the Time of Jesus: The Neglected Significance of Chronology," *SBLSP 2003* 42 [Atlanta: Scholars Press, 2003], 173–87).

as agents who to some extent affect what God does and what transpires in world history.[143]

We do not by any means deny that interest in intermediary beings intensifies in the intertestamental period. Nor do we deny that certain intermediary beings receive roles and attributes that go beyond what we find in the Old Testament. But none of this is altogether new, nor does it represent a departure from a robust "monotheism." As Gregory Boyd has argued elsewhere, if admitting a significant role to "gods" alongside the Creator God constitutes a denial of robust monotheism, then robust monotheism has rarely, if ever, existed, and never at any period in Jewish history prior to the Middle Ages.[144] Our claim here is that ancient Jewish *creational monotheism* is, in its own way, as robust as the *philosophical monotheism* of the Middle Ages and beyond, while allowing for the existence of other spirit beings.

Jewish Creational Monotheism

This leads directly to our second point. The distinguishing mark of traditional Jewish monotheism is its commitment to confess and worship only one God as Creator of all that exists. This "creational monotheism" never ruled out—indeed, it always presupposed—the existence of a multitude of spirit beings alongside the eternal Creator-God.[145] What is interesting about the intertestamental texts in question is that, though they ascribe remarkable status to certain intermediary beings, *they never back off from this core creational-monotheistic commitment*. Never are intermediary beings conceived as competing with the singular eternality, authority, and glory of the Creator. Hence, never is there any suggestion that an intermediary being should be *worshipped in the same way* as the one true God.[146] In the words of Richard Bauckham,

> However diverse Judaism may have been in many other respects, this was common: only the God of Israel is worthy of worship because he is sole Creator of all things

143. See G. A. Boyd, *God at War: The Bible and Spiritual Conflict* (Downers Grove, IL: InterVarsity, 1997), 114–42. For two excellent recent treatments of the "divine council" concept in the Old Testament, including relevant bibliography, see M. S. Heiser, "The Divine Council in Second Temple Literature" (PhD diss., University of Wisconsin–Madison, 2004); R. A. Johnson, "The Old Testament Background for Paul's Use of 'Principalities and Powers'" (PhD diss., Dallas Theological Seminary, 2004).

144. See Boyd, *God at War*, 119–29.

145. Again, we take the term "creational monotheism" and its definition from Wright, *New Testament and the People of God*, 248–50. With it, one could also talk of "providential monotheism" and "covenantal monotheism," as does Wright (pp. 250–52). Just how strict a form of monotheism this represents is a matter of discussion, within the generally agreed bounds articulated below. Larry Hurtado has done significant work on this issue and claims—we would argue rightly so—that a historically accurate definition of first-century Jewish monotheism can only be arrived at inductively by asking how first-century Jews, who claimed such monotheism as their own, actually expressed their religious beliefs within this context. See Hurtado, "First-Century Jewish Monotheism," *JSNT* 71 (1998): 3–26, esp. 5–8.

146. See Hurtado, "First-Century Jewish Monotheism"; idem, *One God, One Lord*; Bauckham, *God Crucified*; L. T. Stuckenbruck, *Angel Veneration and Christology*; idem, "'Angels' and 'God': Exploring the Limits of Early Jewish Monotheism," in *Early Jewish and Christian Monotheism*, 45–70.

and sole Ruler of all things. Other beings who might otherwise be thought divine are by these criteria God's creatures and subjects.[147]

We thus conclude that while the *language about* intermediary beings had become more flexible in the intertestamental period, the actual creational monotheism of the Jews of this period had not. If anything, their ongoing contact with paganism made them more, not less, resistant to the suggestion that any being could be worshipped in the same way as Yahweh.

The Meaning of "Divine Men"

Third, while it is true that some Jewish authors referred to various heroes of the faith as "divine men" (*theios aner*), it is also true that no Jewish author ever refers to another human as "God" (*theos*) *in the same manner used of Yahweh-God.* Nor is there any suggestion that a human could be *worshipped* such as we find in Greco-Roman religion. The Jews were repulsed by this concept, all the more so because they were surrounded by it.[148] Never is the absolute distinction between God and his creation compromised, a point that emphasizes how surprising it is that early Christians were willing to apply the title "God" to Jesus and to pray to and worship him as such.

Still, does the fact that some Jews were willing to refer to others as "divine men" not suggest that Second Temple Judaism was at least *moving in the direction* of accepting that a human could somehow participate in Yahweh's distinct status as God? Can we see this development as laying the groundwork for the sort of "divine man" novelty we find with the early Christians? Two points will suffice to show that there is little reason to suppose this.

First, as Carl Holladay has shown in his meticulous study of the concept, the term *theios aner* had a wide range of meaning in the ancient Hellenistic world. It could literally mean a "divine man," as it does at times with Greek writers. But it could also simply refer to an "inspired man," a "man, in some sense, close to God," or simply an "extraordinary man."[149] With such a broad semantic range, one must exercise extreme

147. Bauckham, *God Crucified*, 11.

148. "The fact is that Hellenization seems, in some instances, to have made it more difficult for Jews to conceive of a *divine* man" (C. Holladay, Theios aner in *Hellenistic Judaism: A Critique of the Use of This Category in New Testament Christology* [Missoula, MT: Scholars Press, 1977], 238 [emphasis in text]). See also Bauckham, *God Crucified*, 17; Hurtado, *One God, One Lord*, 51–69.

149. Holladay, Theios aner in *Hellenistic Judaism*, 237. D. L. Tiede, Barry Blackburn, and others have argued that some confusion about the concept of *theios aner* has resulted from the fact that scholars have used this category to bring together a very diverse array of depictions of extraordinary men. Blackburn argues: "'The miracle-working *theios aner*' is really a twentieth-century abstraction encompassing a wide array of figures, mythical and historical, whose diversity becomes apparent when one analyzes their social roles, the nature of their divinity, and the types and techniques of the miracles or miraculous powers ascribed to them" (Theios Aner *and the Markan Miracle Traditions*, WUNT 2:40 [Tübingen: Mohr Siebeck, 1991], 263). See also D. L. Teide, *The Charismatic Figure as Miracle Worker*, SBLDS 1 (Missoula, MT: Scholars Press, 1972), 245–46; A. J. Malherbe, "Greco-Roman Religion and Philosophy and the New Testament,"

care to examine the overall context of any given usage to determine the author's meaning. Holladay argues that Jews never used *theios aner* in the literal sense of the term. To the contrary, from a careful study of Josephus, Philo, and Artapanus, Holladay concludes that, within a Jewish context, the term was most likely used with an *ethical* connotation and is best translated as "godly man," "holy man," or "wise man." [150]

Second, when used by pagans, *theios aner* was usually associated with supernatural power, a point that is emphasized by some legendary-Jesus theorists to explain the Gospel's portrayal of Jesus as a wonder-worker. Yet, as Holladay, D. L. Tiede, Barry Blackburn, and others have shown, Jewish authors rarely associate the term with supernatural power, and even when they do so it is strictly in keeping with supernatural feats already ascribed to them in Scripture. Indeed, they tend to underemphasize the miracles of their heroes when compared with what the Old Testament says about them and are careful to make clear that the hero's supernatural power comes from God, not from any intrinsic power of the hero.[151] In this respect the Jewish usage contrasts significantly with the pagan *theios aner* tradition.

We conclude that the occasional use of *theios aner* by Jews in no way suggests that they were indulging in a pagan-inspired compromise of their creational monotheism. As such, it does not help us to understand how the early Jewish disciples could have talked about, and even worshipped, a recent contemporary of theirs as, in some sense, Yahweh embodied.

Summary

In this chapter we have seen that there is no compelling reason to suppose that first-century Jews as a whole—including Galilean Jews—were open to a revision of their basic religious convictions via pagan ideas. Related to this, we have seen

---

in *The New Testament and Its Modern Interpreters*, ed. E. J. Epp and G. W. MacRae (Philadelphia: Fortress, 1989), 14–15; and esp. Blackburn, Theios Aner *and the Markan Miracle Traditions*, 13–96.

150. For Holladay's conclusions on Josephus, see Theios aner *in Hellenistic Judaism*, 100–102; on Philo see pp. 194–98; and on Artapanus, see pp. 231–32. Holladay's work has been criticized for drawing conclusions that outstrip the evidence. See, e.g., W. R. Telford, review of Theios aner *in Hellenistic Judaism, JTS* 30 (1979): 246–52; Corrington, *The "Divine Man,"* 41–45. Nonetheless, Holladay's assessment of the generally negative attitude of Hellenistic Judaism toward the pagan tendency to blur the Creator/creature distinction has been confirmed by the more careful studies of those within the new history of religions school; i.e., exalted patriarchs were commonly extolled, but were not divinized in an ontological sense similar to Yahweh, nor were they worshipped as such. See, e.g., Bauckham, *God Crucified*, 3–4, 11; Hurtado, *One God, One Lord*, 30–33, 90–92, 123–24; idem, "First-Century Jewish Monotheism," 25; Stuckenbruck, *Angel Veneration and Christology*; idem, "An Angelic Refusal of Worship: The Tradition and Its Function in the Apocalypse of John," *SBLSP 1994*, ed. E. H. Lovering Jr. (Atlanta: Scholars Press, 1994), 679–96; C. Arnold, *The Colossian Syncretism: The Interface between Christianity and Folk Belief at Colossae* (Tübingen: Mohr Siebeck, 1995).

151. Holladay, Theios aner *in Hellenistic Judaism*, 195; Tiede, *Charismatic Figure*, 134, 245–46; See also Blackburn's extensive study, Theios Aner *and the Markan Miracle Traditions*, 229–32, and idem, "'Miracle Working THEIOI ANDRES' in Hellenism (and Hellenistic Judaism)," in *Gospel Perspectives*, vol. 6: *The Miracles of Jesus*, ed. D. Wenham and C. Blomberg (Sheffield: JSOT, 1986), 185–218.

that there are no grounds for supposing that the monotheism of first-century Jews had become so "flexible" that we might expect a legend about a man being identified as God to arise. To the contrary, all the evidence suggests that, while Jews in Palestine and elsewhere were hellenized in certain, largely superficial, ways, they were opposed to the religious concept of a man being God. Thus they seem to constitute about as unlikely a population for a legend about "Yahweh embodied" to arise as one can imagine.

Yet in this very context, during the reign of Pilate and Herod, when Caiaphas was high priest, we find a Jewish movement arising that worships a recent contemporary alongside and in a similar manner as Yahweh-God. To call this development "novel" is a significant understatement. In truth, it constitutes nothing less than a massive paradigm shift in the first-century, Palestinian Jewish religious worldview. As such, it cries out for a sufficient historical explanation. What can account for first-century Palestinian Jews—Jews who were intensely resistant to any encroachment of paganism into their faith—worshipping one of their Jewish contemporaries as God? To simply dismiss this radical new faith as a legend is inadequate, for now we must ask: what explains this radical new legend arising among these monotheistic Jewish disciples?

The explanation the New Testament itself gives as to what compelled the earliest disciples to embrace this radical new faith in Jesus Christ centers on his identification with Yahweh, substantiated by his life, his miracles, and *especially by his resurrection from the dead.*[152] According to Luke's account of the first Christian sermon, Peter proclaims to his fellow Jews: "Jesus of Nazareth [was] a man attested to you by God with deeds of power, wonders, and signs that God did through him among you, as you yourselves know. . . . God raised him up, having freed him from death . . . and of that all of us are witnesses" (Acts 2:22, 24a, 32b).

In his historical assessment of the origins of early Christian devotion to Jesus, Hurtado arrives at a conclusion reminiscent of Peter's explanation. He concludes that certain "revelatory experiences" led to the "mutation" within Jewish-Christian thought and practice that allowed for the cultic worship of Jesus alongside Yahweh-God. In his estimation, these resurrection experiences "involved an encounter with a figure recognized as Jesus but also exhibiting features that convinced the recipients that he had been clothed with divinelike glory and given a unique heavenly status."[153]

With this, it seems, we find ourselves faced with a plausible explanation for the rise of a high Christology within a first-century monotheistic Jewish context.

---

152. On this point see the following: C. C. Newman, "Resurrection as Glory: Divine Presence and Christian Origins," in *The Resurrection: An Interdisciplinary Symposium on the Resurrection of Jesus*, ed. S. Davis, D. Kendall, and G. O'Collins (New York: Oxford University Press, 1997), 88; Wright, *Jesus and the Victory of God*, 631–53; idem, *The Resurrection of the Son of God* (Minneapolis: Fortress, 2003), 710–18; C. J. Davis, *The Name and Way of the Lord: Old Testament Themes, New Testament Christology* (Sheffield: Sheffield Academic Press, 1996). See also the forthcoming work by R. Watts, *Jesus and the Mighty Deeds of Yahweh*.

153. Hurtado, *Lord Jesus Christ*, 70, 72. On the unique identification of Jesus with Yahweh-God in the early Jewish-Christian context, see also Eskola, *Messiah and the Throne*, 375–90.

3

ONE AMONG MANY LEGENDS?

DO "PARALLELS" RELATIVIZE THE JESUS OF HISTORY?

Thus far we have addressed the naturalistic view of the world and the claim of a religiously hellenized first-century Judaism that legendary-Jesus theorists build on to make their case. In this chapter we will address a third common aspect of the legendary-Jesus theory, namely, the contention that the presence of many parallels to the Jesus story as told in the New Testament reveals it to be just one among many similar mythological accounts found in the ancient world and throughout history. Some legendary-Jesus theorists go on to argue that the earliest disciples borrowed from other pagan and/or Jewish legends in embellishing their own story of Jesus.

First, we will provide an overview of various claims that the Jesus story parallels and even borrows from certain myth and legend-creating movements in history.[1] We will assess each of these claims, beginning with the claim that the Jesus story can be understood along the lines of ancient Greco-Roman mystery religions. We shall then respond to the analysis of the Jesus story as a paradigmatic hero-myth and follow this with a response to the argument that the early Jesus movement parallels other legend-creating movements in history. We will conclude this chapter

---

1. We remind the reader that for the purposes of this work the only distinction we are making between "legend" and "myth" is that "legends" purportedly are about (relatively recent) historical figures while "myths" generally are not.

with a discussion of the sense in which the Jesus story should, and should not, be understood as myth.

The Case for Jesus Story Parallels

The History of Religions School

While the claim that aspects of the Christian view of Jesus parallel, even are indebted to, ancient pagan legends and myths has a long history, it gained a new prominence with the birth of the history of religions school (*Religionsgeschichtliche Schule*) in the late nineteenth and early twentieth centuries.[2] Centered at the University of Göttingen, this group of German scholars believed that all "new" religious perspectives and practices could be explained as a natural outgrowth of previous religious phenomena reworked in new cultural settings to address new social needs.

According to this school of thought, the original Christians were simply Jewish believers who believed Jesus was the Messiah. Jesus perhaps worked some "miracles" (faith healings), but he was in no way "divine." According to the history of religions school, this earliest, Ebionite-like view of Jesus could be entirely understood and explained as a natural outgrowth and modification of traditional Jewish beliefs to meet new social and religious needs in the early first century.

The religion of Paul, however, could not be understood in this fashion. Among other things, Paul taught that Jesus was a divine savior figure who was to be worshipped, and there was no clear Jewish precedent for this novelty. To understand the rise of the religion of Paul, therefore, the history of religions school turned to influences within the wider Greco-Roman pagan environment. Their thesis was that the view of Jesus as divine savior figure and other Pauline distinctives could be understood as a Jewish appropriation of certain themes found in the ancient pagan world, and especially in Greco-Roman mystery religions.[3]

2. On the history of religions school, beyond the sources cited in chap. 2, see W. G. Kummel, *The New Testament: The History of the Investigation of Its Problems*, trans. S. Gilmour and H. C. Kee (Nashville: Abingdon, 1972), 206–324; K. Rudolph, "*Religionsgeschichtliche Schule*," in *The Encyclopedia of Religion*, ed. M. Eliade (New York: Macmillan, 1987), 12:293–96; H. Koester, "The History-of-Religions School, Gnosis, and Gospel of John," *Studia Theologica* 40 (1986): 115–36. The claim that the Christian view of Jesus parallels other myths goes back at least to Celsus in the second century (Origen, *Against Celsus* 2.55–56). Some early Protestants used a version of this argument as a polemic against Roman Catholicism. They claimed that Roman Catholic sacramental theology could be traced back to magical views found in ancient Greco-Roman mystery religions. One of the first to offer this critique was Isaac Casaubon in his 1614 work, *De rebus sacris et ecclesiasticis exercitationes*. On the consideration of the influence of ancient mystery religions on early Christianity from the Renaissance period into the nineteenth century, see E. Wind, *Pagan Mysteries in the Renaissance* (New Haven: Yale University Press, 1958).

3. This point presupposes the "radical early Christian diversity thesis," the idea that early Christianity was not a united movement, but from the beginning was characterized by a number of very diverse communities, each with its own understanding of who Jesus was and what following him entailed. Most contemporary

Scholars such as Wilhelm Bousset, Richard Reitzenstein, Samuel Angus, and Alfred Loisy developed this broad thesis in their own distinct ways.[4] In his famous book, *The Golden Bough*, Sir James Frazer added an important component when he argued that one could find direct parallels to the death and resurrection of the divine Jesus in the ancient "dying and rising gods" such as Adonis, Attis, Osiris, and Tammuz/Dumuzi.[5] According to Frazer, these various dying and rising gods were ultimately vegetation deities, whose cults served to ensure the continuation of the cycles of nature.

The themes of personal salvation and eternal life were also believed to have been appropriated in part from the mystery religions, as was Paul's "sacramental" theology—his views of baptism and communion. For example, the Cybele-Attis cult and the Mithraic cult practiced something similar to a baptismal initiation rite in which a person was bathed in the blood of a bull. So too in the Mithraic cult devotees regularly ate a sacred meal of bread and drank a cup of water. Through such practices, devotees believed they established a connection to their god and received salvation. The argument was that Paul appropriated these themes and modified them in creating his own "Christ-cult."[6]

---

forms of this view are influenced by Walter Bauer's famous work, *Orthodoxy and Heresy in Earliest Christianity*, 2nd ed., ed. R. A. Kraft and G. Krodel, trans. Philadelphia Seminar on Christian Origins (Philadelphia: Fortress, 1971). Bauer, of course, had predecessors. F. C. Baur and the Tübingen school—whose ideas were indebted to an unabashed Hegelianism—proposed the idea of a radical tension in early Christianity embodied in the antagonism between Jewish (e.g., Peter) and Hellenistic (e.g., Paul) factions. More recent incarnations of this perspective include J. M. Robinson and H. Koester, *Trajectories through Early Christianity* (Philadelphia: Fortress, 1971); and R. Wilken, *The Myth of Christian Beginnings: History's Impact on Belief* (Garden City, NY: Doubleday, 1971). For several important critical assessments of Bauer's thesis, see M. Desjardins, "Bauer and Beyond: On Recent Scholarly Discussions of *Hairesis* in the Early Christian Era," *Second Century* 8 (1991): 65–82; J. Lebreton, review of *Rechtglaeubigkeit und Ketzerei* by W. Bauer, *Recherches de Science Religieuse* 25 (1935): 605–10; J. McCue, "Orthodoxy and Heresy: Walter Bauer and the Valentinians," *Vigiliae Christianae* 33 (1979): 118–30; H. E. W. Turner, *The Pattern of Christian Truth: A Study in the Relations between Orthodoxy and Heresy in the Early Church* (London: Mowbray, 1954); and esp. T. A. Robinson, *The Bauer Thesis Examined: The Geography of Heresy in the Early Christian Church* (Lewiston, NY: Mellen, 1988).

4. W. Bousset, *Kyrios Christos*, trans. J. E. Steely (Nashville: Abingdon, 1970); R. Reitzenstein, *The Hellenistic Mystery-Religions*, trans. J. E. Steely (Pittsburgh: Pickwick, 1978); S. Angus, *The Mystery Religions and Christianity* (1925; repr., New York: University Books, 1967); A. Loisy, "The Christian Mystery," *Hibbert Journal* 10 (1912): 45–64. Rudolf Bultmann argued that gnostic redeemer myths played a more formative role in Paul's theology and even more so in the theology of the Gospel of John. See R. Bultmann, *Theology of the New Testament*, trans. K. Grobel (New York: Scribner's Sons, 1951, 1955), 2:6, 12, 66.

5. J. G. Frazer, *The Golden Bough: A Study in Magic and Religion*, 3rd ed. (New York: Macmillan, 1922), part 4. For brief introductions to these gods, see S. Ribichini, "Adonis," in *DDD*, 2nd rev. ed., ed. K. van der Toorn, B. Becking, and P. W. van der Horst (Boston: Brill, 1999), 7–10; M. H. van Voss, "Osiris," in *DDD*, 649–51; B. Alster, "Tammuz," in *DDD*, 828–34; J. Z. Smith, "Dying and Rising Gods," in *Encyclopedia of Religion*, 4:521–27. For a brief history of this line of thought, see J. Z. Smith, "On Comparing Stories," in *Drudgery Divine: On the Comparison of Early Christianities and the Religions of Late Antiquity* (Chicago: University of Chicago Press, 1990), 89–99.

6. In a 1968 article, J. R. Hinnells argues for a direct line of influence from Zoroastrian-based Mithraism to early Christianity ("Christianity and the Mystery Cults," *Theology* 71 [1968]: 20–25).

An Outdated Program Resurrected

The history of religions school was extremely popular in academic circles for several decades, but owing to trenchant critiques by such scholars as Samuel Cheetham, H. A. A. Kennedy, J. Gresham Machen, A. D. Nock, Bruce Metzger, and Günter Wagner, it eventually fell out of fashion.[7] Despite this general demise, the history of religions school has been making a surprising comeback in some quarters, especially among those scholars who advocate the more radical versions of the legendary-Jesus thesis.[8]

Scholars such as Burton Mack, Robert Price, Kurt Rudolph, and J. Z. Smith are arguing once again for the view that all new religious phenomena can be exhaustively understood along sociological lines. As social groups try to define themselves over and against other groups, they argue, they appropriate and modify religious motifs to legitimize and defend their distinct identities. And, as with the older history of religions school, they argue that the motifs the early (Pauline) Christians adopted were taken from Hellenistic religion and mythology.[9] To be sure, their claims are generally more cautious and nuanced than the old history of religions approach, but they certainly share a strong family resemblance.

For example, Burton Mack argues that Paul's view of Jesus as a divine figure who gives his life for the salvation of others had to originate in a Hellenistic rather than a Jewish environment. Mack writes, "Such a notion [of vicarious human suffering] cannot be traced to old Jewish and/or Israelite traditions, for the very notion of a vicarious human sacrifice was anathema in these cultures. But it can be traced to a strong Greek tradition of extolling a noble death."[10]

More specifically, Mack argues that a Greek "myth of martyrdom" and the "noble death" tradition are ultimately responsible for influencing the hellenized Jews of the Christ cults to develop a divinized Jesus.[11] Though he stops short of

7. S. Cheetham, *The Mysteries, Pagan and Christian* (New York: Macmillan, 1897); H. Kennedy, *St. Paul and the Mystery Religions* (London: Hodder and Stoughton, 1913); J. G. Machen, *The Origin of Paul's Religion* (New York: Macmillan, 1925); A. D. Nock, *Early Gentile Christianity and Its Hellenistic Background* (New York: Harper, 1964); B. Metzger, "Methodology in the Study of the Mystery Religions and Early Christianity," in *Historical and Literary Studies: Pagan, Jewish and Christian* (Grand Rapids: Eerdmans, 1968); G. Wagner, *Pauline Baptism and the Pagan Mysteries* (Edinburgh: Oliver and Boyd, 1967). On the demise of the history of religions school, see H. Riesenfeld, "Mythological Background of New Testament Christology," in *The Background of the New Testament and Its Eschatology*, ed. W. D. Davies and D. Daube (Cambridge: Cambridge University Press, 1956), 18.
8. See R. Nash, *Christianity and the Hellenistic World* (Grand Rapids: Zondervan, 1984), 10.
9. Not surprisingly, the "Christianity-as-pagan-myth" thesis also continues to make the rounds in the world of provocative, popular literature on the Bible. See, e.g., B. G. Walker, "Jesus Christ," in *The Woman's Encyclopedia of Myths and Secrets* (San Francisco: HarperSanFrancisco, 1983), 464–71; T. Freke and P. Gandy, *The Jesus Mysteries: Was the "Original Jesus" a Pagan God?* (New York: Harmony, 1999).
10. B. Mack, *The Lost Gospel: The Book of Q and Christian Origins* (San Francisco: HarperSanFrancisco, 1993), 216–17.
11. See B. Mack, *A Myth of Innocence: Mark and Christian Origins* (Philadelphia: Fortress, 1988), 98–101, 105. Here, Mack builds on the work of S. Williams, *Jesus' Death as Saving Event* (Missoula, MT: Scholars Press, 1975); and D. Seeley, *The Nobel Death* (Sheffield: JSOT, 1998).

explicitly calling Paul's Christ cult "a mystery religion" per se, he claims that the table gatherings (communion) of the Christ cults were fashioned "on the model of the mystery religions."[12]

Along the same lines, Robert Price argues that the ancient Mediterranean world "was hip-deep in religions centering on the death and resurrection of a savior god."[13] He then catalogs a wide variety of examples to explain the rise of the Christ cult through Paul—including the gods Baal, Tammuz/Dumuzi, Osiris, Attis, Dionysus, Mithras, and even the Corn King.[14] From these he concludes that the Christ cult formed by Paul was "a Mystery cult" pure and simple.[15]

Jesus as Mythic Hero

A number of scholars also find strong parallels between Jesus and various hero myths. The argument is not that there is a direct line of historical influence between any particular hero myth and the early Christians, such as is sometimes argued for Paul and the mystery religions. Rather, the argument is that the shared features between hero myths and the Jesus story of the Gospels implies that the Jesus of the Gospels belongs to this broad, cross-cultural, mythic paradigm.

For example, using Lord Raglan's widely acclaimed analysis of hero myths, Alan Dundes argues that Jesus meets the criteria for a mythic hero more closely than some of the commonly cited examples of this mythic pattern.[16] Robert Price goes so far as to argue that *every* aspect of the Jesus story found in the Gospels fits the "mythic hero archetype, with nothing left over."[17] With such a strong

---

12. Mack, *The Lost Gospel*, 220.

13. R. M. Price, *Deconstructing Jesus* (Amherst, NY: Prometheus, 2000), 86; see also 92.

14. For Price's discussion of the various Greco-Roman gods that can be used to explain the rise of the Christ cult, see *Deconstructing Jesus*, 86–92. D. G. Bostock has recently argued that the Egyptian god Osiris provided Paul with the model upon which he constructed his theology of the resurrection ("Osiris and the Resurrection of Christ," *ExpT* 112 [2001]: 265–71). Bostock concludes: "In spirit and in letter his doctrine of the resurrection is derived from Egyptian religion, not from Judaism or from Hellenism" (p. 271).

15. "A Christ religion modeled after a Mystery cult *is* a Mystery cult, a Christ cult worthy of the name" (Price, *Deconstructing Jesus*, 93). In context, Price is chiding Mack for using the name "Christ cult" while stopping short of explicitly linking it to the mystery cults, as the old school had done. Other examples of scholars who explicitly appeal to the work of the history of religions school are Earl Doherty, "The Jesus Puzzle: Pieces in a Puzzle of Christian Origins," *Journal of Higher Criticism* 4 (1997): 74–75; see also idem, *The Jesus Puzzle: Did Christianity Begin with a Mythical Christ?* (Ottawa: Canadian Humanist Pub., 1999); and Detley Dormeyer, "Beatitudes and Mysteries," in *Ancient and Modern Perspectives on the Bible and Culture: Essays in Honor of Hans Dieter Betz*, ed. A. Yarbro Collins (Atlanta: Scholars Press, 1998), 352.

16. Dundes says that Jesus is "closer to Raglan's ideal hero paradigm than Jason, Bellerophon, Pelops, Asclepius, Apollo, Zeus, Joseph, Elijah, and Siegfried" (A. Dundes, "The Hero Pattern and the Life of Jesus," *Protocol of the Twenty-fifth Colloquy, Center for Hermeneutical Studies in Hellenistic and Modern Culture, 12 December, 1976* (Berkeley, CA: Center for Hermeneutical Studies in Hellenistic and Modern Culture, 1977), 10.

17. Robert Price, "Christ a Fiction" (1997), www.infidels.org/library/modern/robert_price/fiction .html. See also idem, *Deconstructing Jesus*, 259–61; and Mack, *Myth of Innocence*, 119.

correspondence between Jesus and universally acknowledged mythic figures, the suggestion that the Jesus story is rooted in history while the other hero stories are not seems highly implausible to some.

Jesus and Other Legendary Religious Figures

Yet a third group of parallels sometimes cited as evidence that the biblical Jesus is largely, if not totally, legendary are found in various religious movements throughout history. The argument is that we have examples of historical figures being quickly enveloped in legend and sometimes even being worshipped as divine by their followers. Therefore, it is argued, even if we grant that Jesus was a historical figure, we should not be overly surprised that legends were told about him and even that he was worshipped as divine. This sort of thing happens on occasion.

Among the most frequently mentioned examples of this phenomenon are the first-century philosopher and purported healer Apollonius of Tyana and the seventeenth-century Messiah figure Sabbatai Svi.[18] Recently, some have added two twentieth-century figures to the list: an African healer named Simon Kimbangu and Menachem Mendel Schneerson, the Lubavitcher (Chabad) Rebbe who died in Brooklyn, New York, in 1994.[19] Miracle stories resembling those in the Gospels surround all of these figures, and they were hailed as, in some sense, divine by some of their followers soon after their deaths, if not during their lifetimes. According to some legendary-Jesus theorists, figures and movements such as these provide strong parallels with the early Christian movement and demonstrate that the stories about, and a worshipful attitude toward, Jesus is hardly unique.

The question we must now consider is: Do the alleged parallels between mystery religions, hero myths, and miracle-working, divinized figures in history, on the one hand, and the portraits of Jesus in Paul and the Gospels, on the other, suggest that the origin of the Christian faith can be explained plausibly in terms of the legendary thesis—as just one more example of rampant mythmaking in the ancient Greco-Roman world?

18. With the mention of Apollonius of Tyana, we meet what many consider to be a paradigmatic example of the Greco-Roman "divine man" (*theios aner*) phenomenon (discussed in the previous chapter). Pythagoras and Asclepius are also common candidates for this category.

19. For introductions to these four figures, see respectively E. L. Bowie, "Apollonius of Tyana: Tradition and Reality," in *ANRW* 2.16.2:1652–99; W. D. Davies, "From Schweitzer to Scholem: Reflections on Sabbatai Svi," *JBL* 95 (1976): 529–58; S. Rabey, "The People's Prophet [i.e., Kimbangu]," *Christian History* 32/3 (2003): 32–34; D. Berger, "The Rebbe, the Jews, and the Messiah," *Commentary* 112/2 (September 2001): 23–30. In our estimation, no one makes a better case for a legendary Jesus based on these parallels than Robert Price. See, e.g., Price, *The Incredible Shrinking Son of Man: How Reliable Is the Gospel Tradition?* (Amherst, NY: Prometheus, 2003), 29, 68, 133, 138–41, 179, 275, 280.

Jesus and the Greco-Roman Mystery Religions

It should be recognized up front that there are a number of interesting similarities between certain aspects of Christianity and the Greco-Roman mysteries. These similarities have been acknowledged from early on by both Christian (e.g., Justin Martyr) and non-Christian (e.g., apparently Celsus) thinkers alike.[20] The question, however, is whether these are merely intriguing similarities or whether they represent telling "parallels," suggestive of some direct, if unconscious, influence or even conscious borrowing. Suffice it to say that the following considerations lead us to conclusions quite different from those that characterize the various legendary-Jesus theses.

The Jewish Antipathy toward Paganism

First, in the light of the previous chapter, we need to question seriously whether it is historically probable that the apostle Paul borrowed motifs from Greco-Roman mythology and pagan mystery religions to create a new "Christ cult." In our estimation, the assumption is highly unlikely. Paul was an orthodox Jew—a Pharisee no less (Phil. 3:5)—living between the Maccabean revolt and the destruction of the temple in 70 CE. As we have seen, there is no evidence that Jews were open to Hellenistic religious ideas during this time. To the contrary, the evidence suggests that Jews were, generally speaking, intensely resistant to pagan ideas at this time, precisely because they were surrounded by them.[21]

All indications are that the earliest Christians shared this aversion to paganism. In fact, as Carlos Contreras argues, the "pagan world which, according to their apocalyptic expectations, is going to disappear soon, is almost entirely ignored" by the early Christians.[22] Hence, any thesis claiming that Paul and/or other early Christians developed a new religion on the model of the pagan mysteries is a priori unlikely, and thus carries a heavy burden of proof.

The Dating of the Mystery Religions

A second obstacle to any attempt to understand first-century Christianity in the light of ancient Greco-Roman mystery religions is that virtually all of our evidence for these religions comes from the second to the fourth centuries. Martin Hengel has put the matter forcefully:

> It should be remembered that we have more detailed accounts about the real "oriental" mystery deities or their cults only from the second and third centuries AD. . . . one can only hope that in the end it will also come to the notice of New Testament exegesis, so worn-out cliches which suppose crude dependence of earliest Chris-

20. Justin Martyr, *1 Apology*, 66.4; *Dialogue with Trypho*, 70.1; Origen, *Against Celsus*, 6.22.
21. A point also noted by Metzger, "Methodology in the Study of the Mystery Religions," 7.
22. C. A. Contreras, "Christian Views of Paganism," in *ANRW* 2.23.2:975.

tianity between AD 30 and AD 50 on the "mysteries" may give way to a more pertinent and informed verdict.[23]

Trying to explain a first-century religious movement by appealing to evidence for a "parallel" phenomenon a century or more later is questionable, to say the least. True, it is not unreasonable to assume that there were first-century precursors to the mystery cults of the second century and beyond. But this is an argument from silence, and in any case we are left with nothing conclusive about these precursor movements. Hence, any argument that Christianity was influenced by, let alone modeled after, these precursors must be judged as unwarranted speculation grounded in anachronism.

The crucial point here is that if there was any line of influence, it would seem more reasonable to argue that it was from Christianity to the mystery religions rather than the other way around. Bruce Metzger has pointed out that, in the face of the growing threat of Christianity, pagan religions were forced to "take steps to stem the tide. One of the surest ways would be to imitate the teaching of the Church by offering benefits comparable with those held out by Christianity."[24]

The Early Misdiagnosis of Mystery Religions

Third, recent scholarship has shown that the history of religions view of mystery religions was mistaken on a number of points. Mystery religions were more diverse theologically than originally thought. They were not nearly as widespread as was initially believed. And it now appears that they were not as evangelistically orientated as was originally assumed.[25] Hence, even if something close to the mystery religions existed at the time of Paul, and even if for the sake of argument we accept that Palestinian Judaism was open to pagan religious ideas, we still would have little reason to suppose that Paul would have been intimately acquainted with these religions and/or that they would have exercised any significant influence on his thinking.

The Prevalence of "Mystery" Language

Fourth, while it is true that Paul and (to a lesser degree) other New Testament authors sometimes use terms that were later used in mystery religions, it is also true

23. M. Hengel, *The Son of God: The Origin of Christology and the History of Jewish-Hellenistic Religion*, trans. J. Bowden (Philadelphia: Fortress, 1976), 27. Hengel notes the conclusion of L. Vidman: "The great wave of the oriental mystery religions only begins in the time of the empire, above all in the second century" (p. 27). See also Metzger, "Methodology," 6; D. H. Wiens, "Mystery Concepts in Primitive Christianity and in Its Environment," *ANRW* 2.23.2:1256–57. On Mithraism, see K. Rudolph, "Mystery Religions," in *The Encyclopedia of Religion*, 10:236.

24. Metzger, "Methodology," 11.

25. Abraham J. Malherbe, "Greco-Roman Religion and Philosophy and the New Testament," in *The New Testament and Its Modern Interpreters*, ed. E. J. Epp and G. W. MacRae (Philadelpha: Fortress, 1989), 12; Wiens, "Mystery Concepts."

that these terms were used fairly widely throughout the Greco-Roman world, even in Jewish circles, prior to the rise of the mysteries themselves. Thus, the presence of "mystery-like language" in the New Testament in no way suggests that New Testament authors were aware of, let alone dependent on, these religions.[26]

The Problem of "Parallelomania"

Fifth, the search for parallels is prone toward subjectivism, as a number of scholars have shown. One tends to read into accounts the commonalities one is looking for. R. F. Littledale demonstrated this point in an ingenious way when he presented a satire arguing that Max Mueller, a great twentieth-century Oxford scholar in comparative religions who championed the solar myth theory, was not an actual historical figure. Treating Max Mueller the way some legendary-Jesus theorists treat Jesus, Littledale argued that Mueller was actually an "Oxford Solar Myth" on the grounds that there were so many parallels between his life and the solar myth pattern![27] Employing a similar satirical method, Douglas Bush made the case that Jane Austen's *Pride and Prejudice* was packed full of covert references to such mythic beings as Dionysus, Hercules, Hylas, the Earth Goddess, Venus, and Adonis.[28] His point, of course, is that one can read parallels into just about anything if parallels is what one is looking for.

This concern caused Samuel Sandmel to write a now-famous article titled "Parallelomania." By this term, Sandmel meant to signal "that extravagance among scholars which first overdoes the supposed similarities in passages and then proceeds to describe source and derivation as if implying literary connection flowing in an inevitable or predetermined direction."[29] Under this definition, much of the theorizing behind the claims of the mystery religions' influence upon early Christianity—

---

26. Martin Hengel argues: "We must distinguish between the real cults and a widespread mystery language.... As the examples of Artapanus, the Wisdom of Solomon and Philo show, [this generic mystery language] has also been taken over by the synagogues of the Diaspora." Hence he concludes, "Evidence of [mystery language] in the New Testament still does not mean direct dependence on mystery cults proper" (*The Son of God*, 28). Malherbe argues that the "conclusion ... that the mystery language has acquired a generic quality and an almost universal appeal and that its use in no way shows direct dependence on specific mysteries ... seems to have carried the day" ("Greco-Roman Religion," 12).

27. He concluded, "Few solar myths are so detailed and various, and, perhaps, there is none which brings together in so concentrated a focus the special characteristic of Sanskrit, Hellenic, and Norse fable" (R. F. Littledale, "The Oxford Solar Myth," in *Echoes from Kottabos*, ed. R. Y. Tyrrell and Sir E. Sullivan [London: Grant Richards, 1906], 290).

28. Douglas Bush, "Mrs. Bennet and the Dark Gods: The Truth about Jane Austen," *Sewanee Review* 64 (1956): 591–96.

29. S. Sandmel, "Parallelomania," *JBL* 81 (1962): 1. The same concern has been raised by those who question the tactic—common within the history of religions school, both old and new—of describing similarities in terms of "analogy" but then going on to build theories that implicitly treat these very same similarities as "genealogy." See A. Deissmann, *Light from the Ancient East*, 4th ed., ed. L. R. M. Strachan (Grand Rapids: Baker Academic, 1978), 265–67; J. Riches and A. Millar, "Conceptual Changes in the Synoptic Tradition," in *Alternative Approaches to New Testament Study*, ed. A. E. Harvey (London: SPCK, 1985), 46.

claims that have fueled various expressions of the legendary-Jesus thesis—can now be confidently identified as clear-cut examples of just such "parallelomania."

The Tenuousness of the Alleged Parallels

Sixth, as soon as we become critical of reading parallels into the evidence, we discover that the differences between Christianity and the mystery religions are far more pronounced than any similarities. While there are certainly parallel *terms* used in early Christianity and the mystery religions, there is little evidence for parallel *concepts*. For example, as we have noted, both Christianity and the mystery religions spoke of salvation—as do many religions throughout history. But what early Christians meant by this term had little in common with what devotees of mystery religions meant by it. To site just one difference, there was in the mystery religions nothing similar to Paul's idea that disciples participate in the death and resurrection of their Savior and are adopted as God's children by placing their trust in him.[30]

Along the same lines, while many religions practice something like a "ceremonial washing"—usually expressing the universal awareness of our need to be spiritually cleansed—few today are impressed with the supposed parallel between (say) the early Christian view of baptism and the Mithraic practice of washing an initiate in bull's blood. And while many religions practice ceremonial meals, few scholars today are convinced by the alleged parallel between the Christian celebration, which remembers and celebrates a historical event, and various meals shared in mystery religions. Thus, there is today a wide-ranging consensus that detailed assessments of the purported sacramental parallels—a paradigmatic example of which is Günter Wagner's comparison of Paul and the mysteries regarding baptism—have shown the thesis of Christian dependence upon the mysteries to be a speculative claim devoid of substance.[31]

The Absence of "Dying and Rising Gods"

Seventh, while a number of scholars in the early twentieth century adopted Frazer's thesis that the early Christian notion of the death and resurrection of the divine Jesus is indebted to a ubiquitous pagan "dying and rising god" theme, most scholars today give it little credence. Two lines of consideration lie behind this broad consensus.

First, most scholars now agree that Frazer's classification of "dying and rising gods" is largely a scholarly construct that is not born out of the actual historical evidence. Ironically, one of the leading voices among those who continue to champion

---

30. "The Hellenistic mysteries did not know of sons of God who died and rose again, nor did the mystic himself become a child of the god of the mysteries" (Hengel, *Son of God*, 25). On the significant differences in the areas of regeneration and salvation, see Wiens, "Mystery Concepts," 1271–74, 1278–79.

31. Wagner, *Pauline Baptism and the Pagan Mysteries*; A. D. Nock, "Hellenistic Mysteries and Christian Sacraments," *Mnemosyne*, n.s., 5 (1952): 177–213; Wiens, "Mystery Concepts," 1268–71.

a Greco-Roman oriented history of religions approach to early Christianity—Jonathan Z. Smith—has also been a leading voice in proclaiming the demise of the "dying and rising gods" thesis. In his well-known article "Dying and Rising Gods," Smith concludes: "The category of dying and rising gods, once a major topic of scholarly investigation, must now be understood to have been largely a misnomer based on imaginative reconstructions and exceedingly late or highly ambiguous texts."[32] This rejection of the existence of a "dying and rising gods" pattern among ancient Mediterranean religions has become a virtual consensus over the last half century.[33] And, obviously, if there is no identifiable concept of "dying and rising gods," then the Christian claims about Jesus can hardly be indebted to them.

What led to this great reversal? Simply this: In the case of each proposed "dying and rising god," further study revealed that either there was no death, no resurrection, and/or no "god" to begin with. In the case of the two different mythic traditions of Adonis—once heralded as the paradigm example of a "dying and rising god"—in one myth there is no death, and in neither is there a resurrection. Rather, Adonis undergoes *bilocation*, spending part of the year in the upper world and part in the lower world. As Jonathan Z. Smith observes, Adonis is connected with resurrection only much later, and in texts clearly influenced by Christianity.[34] With regard to Attis, both mythic traditions include his death, but neither records his rebirth. Moreover, "Attis is not, in his myth, a dying and rising deity; indeed he is not a deity at all."[35]

Turning to the Egyptian god Osiris, there is no resurrection per se. The god is murdered and his body dismembered and scattered. The pieces of his body are

32. J. Z. Smith, "Dying and Rising Gods," 4:521.

33. Frazer's case for the "dying and rising gods" myth came under serious attack by Roland de Vaux in a 1933 article, "Sur quelques rapports entre Adonis et Osiris," reprinted in *Bible et Orient* (Paris: Cerf, 1967), 379–405. Critiques by Paul Lambrechts and Günter Wagner followed. See Lambrechts, "La 'resurrection' d'Adonis," *Annuaire de l'institut de philologie et d'histoire orientales et slaves* (Brussels) 13 (1955): 208–40; Wagner, *Pauline Baptism and the Pagan Mysteries*. Since the 1960s, the critiques have only multiplied. See, e.g., K. Baker, "The Resurrection of Jesus in Its Graeco-Roman Setting," *Reformed Theological Review* 62 (2003): 1–13; H. M. Barstad, *The Religious Polemics of Amos* (Leiden: Brill, 1984), 84n45, 48–51; W. Burkert, *Structure and History in Greek Mythology and Ritual* (Berkeley: University of California Press, 1979), 99–102; L. McKenzie, *Pagan Resurrection Myths and the Resurrection of Jesus* (Charlottesville, VA: Bookwrights, 1997); M. S. Smith, "The Death of 'Dying and Rising Gods' in the Biblical World: An Update, with Special Reference to Baal in the Baal Cycle," *Scandinavian Journal of the Old Testament* 12 (1998): 257–313; idem, *The Origins of Biblical Monotheism* (New York: Oxford University Press, 2001), 104–31. For an excellent survey of the attack on Frazer's category, see T. N. D. Mettinger, "The 'Dying and Rising God': A Survey of Research from Frazer to the Present Day," in *David and Zion: Biblical Studies in Honor of J. J. M. Roberts*, ed. B. F. Batto and K. L. Roberts (Winona Lakes, IN: Eisenbrauns, 2004), 373–86. Ironically, after concluding in this essay that the twentieth-century history of the "dying and rising gods" thesis has been one of "initial triumph and subsequent demise" (p. 386), Mettinger has produced a monograph in its defense; see *The Riddle of Resurrection: "Dying and Rising Gods" in the Ancient Near East* (Stockholm: Almqvist and Wiksell, 2001).

34. J. Z. Smith, "Dying and Rising Gods," 522. See also M. S. Smith, "Death of 'Dying and Rising Gods,'" 282–86; Mettinger, "'Dying and Rising God,'" 379–83; Barstad, *Religious Polemics of Amos*, 149–50.

35. J. Z. Smith, "Dying and Rising Gods," 523.

eventually recovered, gathered, and rejoined, and the god rejuvenated. However, he does not return to his original mode of existence but goes to the underworld, where he becomes a powerful god of the dead. Thus Smith concludes: "In no sense can Osiris be said to have 'risen' in the sense required by the dying and rising pattern."[36]

Regarding Tammuz (Akkadian)/Dumuzi (Sumerian), the situation is a bit more complex. Tammuz plays a role in the famous Mesopotamian myth of "Ishtar's (or Inanna's) Descent to the Underworld." In this myth, Tammuz/Dumuzi ends up in the underworld and—it was thought—is brought up again when Ishtar/Inanna descends to resurrect him. During the summer month of Tammuz, there was a period of mourning for the god's descent (a ritual mourning that is mentioned in Ezek. 8:14). Up until the middle of the twentieth century, it was yet possible to think that Tammuz/Dumuzi was "resurrected" by Ishtar (or Inanna) because the ending of the Akkadian version is so obscure. In the middle of the twentieth century, however, a Sumerian version of the story was found intact, as well as the text known as "Death of Dumuzi." From this version we learned that Inanna (queen of heaven) was killed in an attempt to gain rule over the underworld. She was revived, but only on the condition that she found a substitute to take her place in the underworld. She returned to her abode to find Dumuzi apparently reveling in her demise, and in anger she had him killed and sent to the underworld in her place. Hence, Inanna's descent did not lead to Dumuzi's rising; *it led to his death*!

Some yet held out hope for seeing Dumuzi as a resurrected deity on the basis of a Sumerian descent text discovered in 1963. This text says that Dumuzi was allowed to spend half the year in the realm of the living while his sister took his place in the underworld, and then vice versa. But, as Smith notes, this hardly constitutes an example of a rising god. "The myth emphasizes the inalterable power of the realm of the dead, not triumph over it. . . . Such alternation is not what is usually meant in the literature when speaking of a dying and rising deity."[37]

Attempts to identify other "dying and rising gods" have not fared any better. Contenders such as Baal, Demeter/Isis, Dionysus, Heracles, Marduk, Marqart, and the "unknown Phonecian god" have all fallen short of the mark.[38] Despite

---

36. J. Z. Smith, "Dying and Rising Gods," 524. See also M. S. Smith, "Death of 'Dying and Rising Gods,'" 270–72.

37. J. Z. Smith, "Dying and Rising Gods," 526. E. M. Yamauchi concurs; see "Tammuz and the Bible," *JBL* 84 (1965): 283–90. Alster offers further support when he points out the absence of any cultic ritual celebrating a resurrection. Although one version of the myth states that Dumuzi "came up," Alster argues that "this does not refer to the resurrection of the god to the realms of the living. What is meant is Dumuzi's participation in a ritual, in which the spirits of the dead were invoked and manifested themselves for a short time" ("Tammuz," 833). See also M. S. Smith ("Death of 'Dying and Rising Gods,'" 272–77), who questions whether Dumuzi was a god at all (p. 273).

38. On Baal see Barstad, *Religious Polemics of Amos*, 150–51; J. C. L. Gibson, "The Last Enemy," *SJT* 32 (1979): 160; J. Z. Smith, "Dying and Rising Gods," 522–23; M. S. Smith, *The Ugaritic Baal Cycle* (New York: Brill, 1994), 1:69–73; N. H. Walls, *The Goddess Anat in Ugaritic Myth* (Atlanta: Scholars Press, 1992), 5–6, 67–71. On Demeter/Isis see Baker, "Resurrection of Jesus," 5–6. On Dionysus see

the lingering protestations of a very few, the wide-ranging consensus has aligned itself with J. Z. Smith's conclusion: "The category of dying and rising deities is exceedingly dubious. It has been based largely on Christian interest and tenuous evidence. As such, the category is of more interest to the history of scholarship than to the history of religions."[39]

Our second argument related to the "dying and rising gods" motif is that, even if the pattern could be substantiated, this still would not demonstrate that the mythic theme influenced early Christian thought about Jesus. The differences are far too significant to warrant such a conclusion. In the Christian tradition, for example, Jesus's resurrection is tied to his humanity. None of the allegedly resurrected gods of this pattern are human. Likewise, Jesus is clearly a historical person in the Christian tradition, not a mythical deity. Moreover, the background for the early Christian understanding of Jesus's resurrection is Second Temple apocalyptic Judaism, not a pagan "dying and rising God" myth.[40]

Even among the relatively small number of scholars who still contend for the existence of a "dying and rising god" motif in the ancient world, it is not uncommon to find them stopping short of claiming that such myths influenced early Christianity. For example, T. N. D. Mettinger grants the existence of the "dying and rising gods" theme in the ancient world but nevertheless argues:

Baker, "Resurrection of Jesus," 4–5. On Heracles see M. S. Smith, "Death of 'Dying and Rising Gods,'" 280–82. On Marduk see J. Z. Smith, "Dying and Rising Gods," 523–24; Barstad, *Religious Polemics of Amos*, 148–49. On Marqart see M. S. Smith, "Death of 'Dying and Rising Gods,'" 277–79. And on the "unknown Phonecian god" see M. S. Smith, "Death of 'Dying and Rising Gods,'" 286–87. Incidentally, the old notion of a pre-Christian gnostic redeemer myth assumed by Bultmann (*Theology of the New Testament*, 2:6, 12–13, 66) also has been shown to be fundamentally flawed. On its demise see Koester, "History-of-Religions School," 120–22; K. Rudolph, "Early Christianity as a Religious-Historical Phenomenon," in *The Future of Early Christianity: Essays in Honor of Helmut Koester*, ed. B. A. Pearson (Minneapolis: Fortress, 1991), 9–10.

39. J. Z. Smith, "Dying and Rising Gods," 526. Barstad concludes that Frazer's category was "strongly influenced by the wish to demonstrate that Christianity was not an innovation, but that all its essential features are to be found in earlier religions. It has been maintained, in fact, that this was the major intention of the whole Golden Bough, and I believe this is correct" (*Religious Polemics of Amos*, 150). See also E. E. Evans-Pritchard, "Religion and the Anthropologists," in *Essays in Social Anthropology* (London: Faber & Faber, 1962), 29–45.

Among the few voices who still argue for the "dying and rising gods" are Price, *Incredible Shrinking Son of Man*, 273–74, 286–88; idem, review of J. Z. Smith's *Drudgery Divine*, *Journal of Higher Criticism* 3 (1996): 137–45; and Mettinger, *Riddle of Resurrection*, though even Mettinger is tentative at points (e.g., Adonis, Eshmun). J. S. Burnett has assessed Mettinger's case as "plausible but at best tenuous"; online review of *Riddle of Resurrection*, *Review of Biblical Literature* 04 (2005), 5, www.bookreviews .org/pdf/2958_4897.pdf. D. B. Redford recognizes the problems but worries that we may have "thrown out the baby with the bath water" (*Egypt, Canaan, and Israel in Ancient Times* [Princeton: Princeton University Press, 1992], 44).

40. See N. T. Wright, *The Resurrection of the Son of God* (Minneapolis: Fortress, 2003), 80–81, 146–206.

There is, as far as I am aware, no *prima facie* evidence that the death and resurrection of Jesus is a mythological construct, drawing on the myths and rites of the dying and rising gods of the surrounding world. While studied with profit against the background of Jewish resurrection belief, the faith in the death and resurrection of Jesus retains its unique character in the history of religions.

And so, with respect to explaining the "unique" nature of the early Christian view of Jesus's resurrection, Mettinger concludes, "The riddle remains."[41]

Jesus as a Recent Historical Figure

One of the most fundamental differences between the portraits of Jesus in the Gospels and Paul, on the one hand, and the savior figures of the mystery religions, on the other, is that Jesus is depicted as *a recent historical figure*. As James Dunn notes, "the [alleged] parallel between the Christian faith and these ... mythical formulations breaks down precisely at this point."[42] In the mystery religions, the death and resurrection of a god took place in a timeless, mythical realm. Sallust said of the Attis myth, "This never happened, but always is." "In direct antithesis" to this, as Dunn again notes, "the NT writers proclaim: 'This *did* happen.'" He thus concludes, "Even if the same sort of mythical language has been used to describe the 'Christ event' and Christian experience and hope of salvation in the NT, the point to be noted is that by its reference to Jesus the Hellenistic, unhistorical myth has been broken and destroyed as myth in that sense."[43]

An important consideration is the extremely short period of time that elapsed between Jesus's death and the divinity claims that were made by his monotheistic Jewish followers. Recall, for example, that the *brother* of Jesus (James) was still alive when Paul wrote his letters that depict Jesus as the Lord, Creator, and Savior of the world.[44] This has always posed a challenge to scholars: How does one account for the fact that a recent historical person was so quickly recognized and worshipped as divine by first-century Jewish monotheists—including his own brother? As Richard Horsley and Neil Silberman admit, the speed with which this took place is "something of a puzzle."[45] Even Burton Mack—who reduces all of the early Christian doctrinal claims to sociologically driven mythmaking— admits that, at this point, the early Jesus movement is quite unlike any other Jewish religious phenomenon:

41. Mettinger, *Riddle of Resurrection*, 221.

42. J. D. G. Dunn, "Demythologizing—The Problem of Myth in the New Testament," in *New Testament Interpretation: Essays on Principles and Methods*, ed. I. H. Marshall (Grand Rapids: Eerdmans, 1977), 294.

43. Ibid.

44. The attempts of some to dispute that James was the biological brother of Jesus shall be addressed in chap. 5.

45. R. A. Horsley and N. A. Silberman, *The Message and the Kingdom: How Jesus and Paul Ignited a Revolution and Transformed the Ancient World* (Minneapolis: Fortress, 2002), 111.

Early Christian imagination was not more fantastic than that of Jewish authors writing during the same period, *except for one thing*. Christian fantasies were used to claim significance for new social formations *by mythologizing a founder of very recent memory*. This conjunction of myth and history creates the riddle of Christian origins.[46]

Mack is unable to provide a compelling answer to this puzzle, given that he has a priori rejected the reason given by the early Christian community itself— namely the resurrection. But with N. T. Wright and others, we would suggest that something like this is precisely what is required for a plausible historical explanation of the data.[47]

The Evidence of Historical Reliability

Finally, a significant difference between the view of Jesus in the New Testament and all mythological savior figures is that *we have good evidence that the Synoptic portrait(s) of Jesus is historically reliable*. As we shall see, we have compelling reasons from recent orality studies to view the oral tradition expressed in the Synoptic Gospels as solidly grounded in history (chaps. 6–7) and other reasons for concluding the works themselves are generally reliable (chaps. 8–10). No one even attempts to argue for the historical reliability of any allegedly parallel story derived from the mystery religions. One primary reason for this is that most of the deity figures within the mysteries are purely mythological entities, for whom even the adherents of these ancient religions would never have claimed a mundane historical existence similar to Jesus, the carpenter's son from Nazareth.

Jesus and the Hero Myth

There are also a number of problems with the argument for a legendary Jesus based on alleged parallels with "hero myths."

46. B. Mack, "The Christ and Jewish Wisdom," in *The Messiah*, ed. J. H. Charlesworth (Minneapolis: Fortress, 1992), 209 (emphasis added). Merrill Miller, who, like Mack, holds to a strong reductionistic sociological interpretation of religion, nonetheless concurs: "The appeal to Jesus enhanced the novelty precisely by making sense of it in terms of the unprecedented authority and power of a contemporary teacher. That surely was a novelty. Other Jewish movements reimagined and repositioned figures of lore. The mythologizing or remythologizing went on with figures from the past in order to meet the cultural and social challenges of the present. For Jesus and Christ people the mythologizing attached itself to a contemporary" ("How Jesus Became Christ: Probing a Thesis," *Continuum* 2 (1993): 270). How and/or why we find this anomaly among, of all people, first-century monotheistic Jews is never quite explained but merely assumed per sociological thesis.

47. Wright, *Resurrection of the Son of God*, 710–18. See also C. Newman, "Resurrection as Glory: Divine Presence and Christian Origins," in *The Resurrection: An Interdisciplinary Symposium on the Resurrection of Jesus*, ed. S. Davis, D. Kendall, and G. O'Collins (New York: Oxford University Press, 1997), 88.

The Problem of Circular Reasoning

First, a "hero pattern" is created by abstracting certain features out of various stories. Such an abstraction necessarily presupposes a judgment about what is important and unimportant to include within the pattern. As such, the creation of patterns can easily fall prey to circular reasoning. One may find telling similarities among various stories because one is convinced from the start that telling similarities must exist in order to explain the data. Yet, as we noted above with regard to the alleged parallels with mystery religions, it may be that the differences between the stories are just as telling—if not more so—than the apparent similarities. Hence, as the renown folklorist Dan Ben-Amos argues, the creation of such a list "accounts for similarities but ignores differences."[48] Indeed, even when stories allegedly have a "trait" in common, the specific trait often has to be "fudged" to fit into a more general pattern.[49]

Hero Patterns in Oral Traditional Societies

Second, simply because a story exhibits a high number of "hero-myth" traits does not mean it is unhistorical, especially when the story was transmitted orally prior to being written down. From his years of analysis of oral traditions, the famed Albert Lord has discovered that "traditional narrators tend to tell what happened in terms of already existing patterns of story." Hence, he argues, it would not be surprising if aspects of the portraits of Jesus in the Gospels fit the mythic pattern. He writes:

> When I say that an incident in the gospel narrative of Jesus' life fits in a mythic pattern, there is no implication at all that this incident never happened. There is rather an implication that traditional narrators chose to remember and relate this incident because an incident of similar essence occurred in other traditional stories known to them and their predecessors. That its essence was consonant with an element in a traditional mythic (i.e., sacred) pattern adds a dimension of spiritual weight to the incident, but it does not deny . . . the historicity of the incident.[50]

48. D. Ben-Amos, "Response [to Dundes]," in *Protocol of the Twenty-fifth Colloquy*, 68–69. See also Samuel Sandmel's comments in this regard, "Response [to Dundes]," in *Protocol of the Twenty-fifth Colloquy*, 61.

49. M. P. Cootes, "Response [to Dundes]," in *Protocol of the Twenty-fifth Colloquy*, 42. Similarly, in a characteristically pointed critique, Morton Smith questions Dundes's argument. "Professor Dundes claims that [the hero pattern] agrees with the life of Jesus in seventeen of its 22 points. But eight of these come from the infancy narratives, and seven of the remainder are false. . . . And of the remaining points, several are forced" ("Response [to Dundes]," in *Protocol of the Twenty-fifth Colloquy*, 63).

50. A. B. Lord, "The Gospels as Oral Traditional Literature," in *The Relationships among the Gospels: An Interdisciplinary Dialogue*, ed. W. O. Walker (San Antonio: Trinity University Press, 1978), 39. In their responses to Lord's essay, both Charles Talbert ("Oral and Independent or Literary and Interdependent? A Response to Albert B. Lord," in *Relationships among the Gospels*, 99–100) and Leander Keck ("Oral Traditional Literature and the Gospels: The Seminar," in *Relationships among the Gospels*, 117–18) affirm Lord's important insight here, one that is often overlooked by critical biblical scholars. M. H. Beissinger

Historical Heroes

Another reason one cannot conclude that a hero story represents an ahistorical myth simply because it fits the "hero-myth pattern" is that stories that are known to be historical often reflect this pattern quite well. Indeed, they often do so *better* than fictional hero tales. If we employ it consistently, the suggestion that ostensively historical narratives conforming to the hero-myth pattern are to be judged as ahistorical myth leads to serious problems.

For example, Francis Lee Utley has effectively—if satirically—employed this type of reasoning to argue that we have more reasons for judging Abraham Lincoln to be a mythological figure than we do Oedipus, Theseus, or Moses—for Lincoln fits the "hero-myth pattern" better than they![51] Others have made similar tongue-in-cheek cases for the historical nonexistence of Winston Churchill and Napoleon.[52] Similarly, Charles Murgia has argued that President Kennedy fits the pattern better than many acknowledged myths, concluding that "conformity does not necessarily mean that the events did not occur."[53] So too, based on his fit with the hero-myth pattern, one could argue that William ("Braveheart") Wallace, the famed medieval warrior who led a revolt that freed the Scots from British rule, is merely a legendary figure. Yet, on the basis of evidence, historians do not doubt that he lived and that most of the nearly unbelievable feats attributed to him are rooted in history. All of this reveals how easy it is to reduce a historical figure to "just another fictional example of a mythic pattern" by proposing a seemingly impressive list of supposed "mythic parallels."

The point is that sometimes history actually produces living "heroes" of one type or another. Thus, even if we grant that Jesus's life corresponds to many of the characteristic traits of hero myths, there is no warrant for concluding on this basis that he is nothing more than a mythic hero figure. Whether the extant reports of Jesus, Lincoln, Churchill, Napoleon, Kennedy, or Wallace are historical must be decided on the basis of the actual evidence at hand, not on the basis of how well they do or do not fit a pattern somebody has abstracted out of a multitude of stories.

---

has recently offered a comparative analysis of the "initiatory hero" theme in Romanian oral epic (i.e., Gruia in the Novac cycle) and the Jesus story of the New Testament. Nothing she says, however, necessarily leads one to conclude that the Jesus story is therefore ahistorical myth; see "Rites of Passage and Oral Storytelling in Romanian Epic and the New Testament," *Oral Tradition* 17 (2002): 236–58.

51. F. L. Utley, "Lincoln Wasn't There, or Lord Raglan's Hero," *CEA Chap Book* (Washington, DC: College English Association, 1965; supplement to *The CEA Critic* 22 [June 1965]).

52. See J.-B. Peres, "How Napoleon Never Existed, or the Great Error, Source of an Infinite Number of Errors to Be Seen in the History of the Nineteenth Century" (originally written in French in 1827), English translation available at www.tektonics.org/lp/nappy.html; Justin Martyr [pseud.], "Some Notes on Alleged Parallels between Christianity and Pagan Religions; And, a Proof that Winston Churchill Did Not Exist," also available at www.tektonics.org/copycat/pagint.html.

53. C. E. Murgia, "Response [to Dundes]," in *Protocol of the Twenty-fifth Colloquy*, 52. Murgia goes on to argue, "There is very little in this world, heroic or non-heroic, legendary, historic, or contemporary, into which such symbolism cannot be read. Therefore the mere possibility of symbolism proves nothing" (p. 53).

Deviations from the Hero Pattern

Finally, if the Jesus story originated largely as a hero myth, one wonders why certain crucial aspects of the hero-myth pattern were excluded. For example, one wonders why Jesus is never depicted as a militarily oriented warrior/king—one of the most common features of the pattern. One also wonders why so much of what the Synoptics include about Jesus does not fit the hero-myth pattern. For example, Jesus is depicted as a teacher, a servant, and a miracle-worker, but these are not typical traits of the pattern. These differences add further weight to the claim that the Jesus story of the Synoptic Gospels cannot be explained away as an ahistorical hero myth.

Early Christianity and Legend-Creating Movements

Things do not fare much better for the legendary-Jesus thesis when we consider the alleged parallels between the early Christians and various legend-creating movements throughout history. While a cursory glance at the alleged parallels may give the appearance of telling similarities, a closer inspection reveals differences that render the proposed parallels problematic. In what follows we will assess the claim that movements arising around Apollonius, Sabbatai Svi, and Kimbangu parallel, and help explain, the movement that arose around Jesus.[54]

54. We will not include a detailed response to two Jewish phenomena that have been offered by some as instructive parallels to Jesus and the early Jesus movement. First, Geza Vermes and others have argued that Jesus is best viewed in light of the category of "Galilean holy men" or *hasidim*, men known for their spontaneously and miraculously answered prayers. As concrete examples of this category, Vermes offers Honi the Circle-Drawer (first century BCE) and Hanina ben Dosa (first century CE). See G. Vermes, *Jesus the Jew: A Historian's Reading of the Gospels* (Philadelphia: Fortress, 1973), 69–78. See also W. S. Green, "Palestinian Holy Men: Charismatic Leadership and Rabbinic Tradition," *ANRW* 2.19.2:619–47. Among other things, the dating of the extant material on these two figures is problematic. All of our evidence is post-Jesus, in most cases centuries later—i.e., after what seems to be a mention of Honi ("Onias") in Josephus (*Antiquities* XIV, 2, 1), there is no mention of either figure until the Mishna. As Meier rightly points out, the evidence of Honi and Hanina is so late and so spare that, alone, it does not provide a basis for the category of "Galilean holy men," to which Jesus might belong and/or be compared with. See J. P. Meier, *A Marginal Jew: Rethinking the Historical Jesus*, vol. 2: *Mentor, Message, and Miracles* (New York: Doubleday, 1994), 581–88.

Second, some argue that the recent messianic fervor and amazing claims surrounding the deceased Lubavitcher Rebbe Menahem Mendel Schneerson represent a telling parallel to the Jesus tradition. See, e.g., J. Marcus, "The Once and Future Messiah in Early Christianity and Chabad," *NTS* 46 (2000): 381–401; Price, *Incredible Shrinking Son of Man*, 179, 275, 280. The parallels are indeed interesting. These include: miracle claims, the idea that the rebbe is in some sense a collective soul containing all Israel, the application of Deut. 18:15 ("to him you shall listen") to the rebbe, and the explicit identification of the rebbe as Messiah by many within the Chabad community. In fact, there is evidence that the rebbe acknowledged he was Messiah, if only tacitly. On these and other aspects of the rebbe, see Lubavitcher Rebbe, *Wonders and Miracles: Stories of the Lubavitcher Rebbe* (Kfar Chabad, Israel: Maareches Ufaratsta, 1993); A. Gotfryd, *Living in the Age of the Moshiach* (New York: Mendelsohn, 2000); H. Lenowitz, *The Jewish Messiahs: From the Galilee to Crown Heights* (New York: Oxford

Apollonius of Tyana

It is true that, similar to Jesus, a late first-century wonder-worker named Apollonius reportedly performed miracles, appeared after his death, and was even suggested to be a god. Does this mean that the claims made for Apollonius and those made by the earliest followers of Jesus are on the same plane in terms of historical grounding? For the following reasons, we think not.

First, we have only one source for the life of Apollonius—Philostratus's *Life of Apollonius*—written more than a century after he lived.[55] Between the death of Apollonius (ca. 96–98, under Emperor Nerva) and Philostratus's *Life* (ca. 217–220), there is a virtual silence about Apollonius. In the case of Jesus, we have four Gospels, Paul's letters, and a number of other Christian and non-Christian sources that attest to aspects of his life. The earliest source of information about Jesus is Paul's collection of epistles, written twenty to thirty years after Jesus lived and that passes on traditional material that predates Paul. Moreover, even on a relatively late dating, the Gospels were all written within seventy years of Jesus's life. Hence, the amount of material and the dating of the material we have for Jesus can hardly be compared with what we have in the case of Apollonius.

Second, Philostratus, a trained rhetorician and sophist, was commissioned by the empress Julia Domna to write a laudatory biography of Apollonius. The project was clearly intended to rehabilitate Apollonius's questionable reputation as a magician and fraud. The Gospel authors had no such clear financial and/or

University Press, 1998); A. Ravitzky, *Messianism, Zionism, and Jewish Religious Radicalism* (Chicago: University of Chicago Press, 1996). Since his death in 1994, some within the movement have begun to speak of his "occultation," while others have proclaimed his "resurrection." Even more interesting is that some of his followers have begun to identify the rebbe with God, using terms such as "our Master, Teacher, and Creator," suggesting that it is appropriate to "bow down" to the rebbe, and even applying the divine Name (Exod. 3:14) to the Lubavitcher Messiah; see D. Berger, "The Rebbe, the Jews, and the Messiah," *Commentary* 112/2 (September 2001): 28. Are these remarkable parallels with the Jesus tradition telling? We believe so. But what the parallels tell us has little to say about the rise and/or nature of the Jesus tradition. Rather, we find numerous reasons to conclude that in these recent messianic developments within the Chabad movement, we are witness to the unquestionable influence of Christian christological convictions upon a contemporary Orthodox Jewish movement. At some points, the borrowing is as obvious as the Lubavitcher claim that the Messiah will come "in the twinkling of an eye" as cited in J. Marcus, "Modern and Ancient Jewish Apocalypticism," *JR* 76 (1996): 19. Compare this to 1 Cor. 15:52 and the broader theme in the Gospels (e.g., Matt. 24:42–44). As David Berger, a professor of Jewish history at Brooklyn College and Yeshiva University, has pointed out, there is no place in Jewish messianism for a dead Messiah. The only place one finds this Jewish oxymoron is within the Christian tradition. Thus, in Berger's words, with the Chabad messianists, "Orthodox Judaism has effectively declared that, with respect to this fundamental issue of principle, Christians were correct all along and Jews profoundly mistaken." In effect, Chabad "award[s] victory to Christianity" ("Rebbe, the Jews, and the Messiah," 24, 26). Berger elaborates on these concerns in *The Rebbe, the Messiah, and the Scandal of Orthodox Indifference* (Oxford: Littman, 2001). The point is that, although the Chabad movement tells us nothing about the rise of the early Jesus tradition, the Jesus tradition provides a crucial piece in explaining recent developments within Chabad.

55. F. C. Conybeare, ed., *Philostratus: The Life of Apollonius of Tyana*, 2 vols. (Cambridge, MA: Harvard University Press, 1912).

political motives. Indeed, they were writing in a hostile environment in which they knew they could be persecuted for their professed faith.

Third, a wide range of historical problems attach to Philostratus's *Life*. Historical anachronisms abound to the point that Kee concludes that "what Philostratus reports tells us a great deal about the author and his time—that is, at the turn of the third century—but provides no unassailable evidence about Apollonius and his epoch."[56] Likewise, Maria Dzielska rejects much of Philostratus's portrayal of Apollonius, based upon "the extent of fabrication, fiction, and historical falsity contained in this book."[57]

The genre question also comes into play at this point. While Philostratus's *Life* certainly has elements of Greco-Roman biography, it also contains elements that characterize ancient romance novels—including erotic escapades, "often with homoerotic overtones."[58] Thus, while few have gone so far as to reject a historical Apollonius altogether, most scholars are rather skeptical about the historicity of major aspects of the image offered by this one source written well over a century after the figure it depicts.[59]

In fairness it should be pointed out that similar criticisms have been leveled at the canonical Gospels, including historical anachronisms, blatant geographical blunders, and even classification within the genre of ancient romance novels. Each of these arguments will be explored in detail in subsequent chapters (chaps. 8–10). Suffice it for the present to simply anticipate our later conclusion: in sharp contrast to Philostratus's *Life*, there are plausible responses to these criticisms against the Synoptics. Conversely, we shall also argue that there are a multitude of other considerations that strongly suggest the Synoptic Jesus tradition is generally reliable.[60]

56. H. C. Kee, *Miracle in the Early Christian World: A Study in Sociohistorical Method* (New Haven: Yale University Press, 1983), 257.

57. M. Dzielska, *Apollonius of Tyana in Legend and History* (Rome: L'erma, 1986), 185.

58. Meier, *Marginal Jew*, 2:578. See also Bowie, "Apollonius of Tyana," 1663–64. Meier provides an excellent assessment of the Apollonius material vis-à-vis the miracles of Jesus (*Marginal Jew*, 2:576–81 and notes).

59. Beyond Dzielska and Kee, see Bowie, "Apollonius of Tyana"; E. R. Dodds, *Pagan and Christian in an Age of Anxiety* (New York: Cambridge University Press, 1965), 59; J. Ferguson, *The Religions of the Roman Empire* (Ithaca, NY: Cornell University Press, 1970), 181–82; B. F. Harris, "Apollonius of Tyana: Fact or Fiction?" *Journal of Religious History* 5 (1969): 189–99; M. Hengel, *Nachfolge und Charisma* (Berlin: Töpelmann, 1968), 30; E. Koskenniemi, *Apollonius von Tyana in der neutestamentlichen Exegese: Forschungsbericht und Weiterführung der Diskussion*, WUNT 2:61 (Tübingen: Mohr Siebeck, 1994); Meier, *Marginal Jew*, 2:578–80; E. Meyer, "Apollonius von Tyana und die Biographie des Philostratos," *Hermes* 52 (1917): 371–424. Note especially Koskenniemi's monograph, which argues forcefully that, on philological grounds, Philostratus's *Life* is shown to be more about third-century fiction than first-century history. On the other hand, for an insightful—and less skeptical—discussion of the difficulties of assessing the historical value of Philostratus's *Life*, see G. Anderson, "Philostratus on Apollonius of Tyana: The Unpredictable on the Unfathomable," in *The Novel in the Ancient World*, ed. G. Schmeling (New York: Brill, 1996), 613–18.

60. In his significant study of the traditions of Apollonius and Jesus, Gerd Petzke favorably compares the two traditions as historical sources; see *Die Traditionen Über Apollonius von Tyana und das Neue Testament* (Leiden: Brill, 1970); see also idem, "Die historische Frage nach den Wundertaten Jesu," *NTS*

Fourth, and following from our last point, the credibility of Philostratus's *sources* for Apollonius's life has been seriously questioned. Foremost among them is a diary given to Philostratus by Julia Domna purportedly written by a disciple and traveling companion of Apollonius named Damis. Howard Clark Kee summarizes the problems here: "The material allegedly drawn from Damis is so full of historical anachronisms and gross geographical errors that one could not have confidence in Damis as a reporter if there actually was a diary."[61] For these reasons, Kee and others have concluded that Damis and the diary are both literary creations rather than historical realities.[62]

Beyond the supposed Damis diary, Philostratus relied heavily on later accounts about Apollonius. The alleged "resurrection" parallel belongs to these later stories and amounts only to a report about a doubting disciple who, perhaps in a dream, sees the spirit of Apollonius (*Life*, 8, 31). We submit that this provides little parallel with the resurrection accounts in Paul and the Gospels. These stories have at their centerpiece Jesus appearing to a number of people while they are awake, in bodily form (i.e., the tomb is empty), over a period of weeks.

Fifth, to his credit, Philostratus often couches his account in tentative language (e.g., "it is reported that . . ." "some believe . . ."). For example, in his famous account of Apollonius's raising a girl from the dead (*Life*, 4, 45), Philostratus acknowledges that *some* believed the girl was actually dead while *others* believed only that she was close to death. By contrast, the Gospels exhibit no such tentativeness with respect to Jesus's miracles. Often, they read like they are passing on tradition rooted in eyewitness testimony and, as we shall later argue, they give us substantial reason to conclude that this is precisely the case.

Finally, and most important for the issue at hand, we must remember that all the material about Apollonius arose after Christianity had been around for almost two centuries. Legendary-Jesus theorists sometimes write as if the parallels between Philostratus's *Life of Apollonius* and the Gospels renders the Jesus tradition questionable. The anachronism seems to go unmentioned. Philostratus's *Life* was not composed until almost two centuries after Jesus and well over a century after the last canonical Gospel had been written. If the presence of one of these traditions calls into question the integrity of the other, it is the Jesus tradition that renders the Apollonius tradition questionable.

---

22 (1975–76): 180–204. However, as Meier has noted (*Marginal Jew*, 2:579), this favorable comparison is made possible only by "opting for the meager portrait of the historical Jesus common in the Bultmannian tradition on the one hand, while allowing a fairly confident assessment of the traditions of Apollonius on the other. A more confident assessment of the Jesus traditions and more skepticism about the historical value of the Apollonius traditions would have yielded notably different results" (for Meier's critique of Petzke's assessment see pp. 578–80).

61. Kee, *Miracle in the Early Christian World*, 256.

62. Beyond Kee see F. Copleston, *A History of Philosophy*, vol. 1: *Greece and Rome, Part II* (Garden City, NY: Image/Doubleday, 1962), 193; Dodds, *Pagan and Christian*, 59; Ferguson, *Religions of the Roman Empire*, 181–82; Hengel, *Nachfolge*, 30.

Along these same lines, we know that already by the second century, pagan writers (e.g., Celsus, Galen) were familiar with, and making reference to, the Gospels. It seems highly likely, therefore, that Philostratus knew of—and even borrowed from—the Jesus tradition. In fact, some scholars have argued that what motivated Empress Julia Domna's commissioning of Philostratus's *Life* was her desire for a creative polemic against the Christian Gospels and the portrait of Jesus found therein.[63] One does not have to go this far to recognize the likelihood that Philostratus borrowed from the Gospels to some degree. Meier's characteristically measured conclusion is worth noting: "I suggest instead that, in the ecumenical and eclectic climate of the circle of Julia Domna, Philostratus possibly borrowed some miracle stories from the Gospels to help him flesh out his portrait of Apollonius as a great philosopher and miracle-worker."[64] With Meier, therefore, we submit that, while both Jesus and Apollonius are depicted as healers, it is "difficult to speak in any detail of the first-century Apollonius as a parallel figure to Jesus of Nazareth."[65]

Sabbatai Svi

It is true that many followers of Svi acknowledged him to be the Messiah.[66] Some told stories of him performing miracles. And a few believed he was preserved from death. To what extent does this movement provide a relativising parallel to the movement that arose around Jesus? For the following reasons, we find the alleged parallels to be less than telling.

First, and most tellingly, it appears that the teachings and actions of Svi (and his prophet, Nathan of Gaza) were significantly influenced by elements of the Jesus tradition itself. In the most exhaustive contemporary study of Svi, Gershom Scholem notes the following aspects that seem to reflect the influence of the Christian tradition: the revealing of a "new law," characteristic exegesis and vocabulary, the choosing of twelve to represent a new Israel, and seeing the messiah as in some sense divine. In fact, Scholem concludes that Svi "may even have meditated on the possibility of a mysterious connection between Jesus and himself."[67] In any case, given the timeframe of Svi and the obvious parallels with the Jesus tradition, it seems clear that, whatever similarities with Jesus he shared,

---

63. Ferguson, *Religions of the Roman Empire*, 181–82; M. Scramuzza and P. L. MacKendrick, *The Ancient World* (New York: Holt, Rinehart and Winston, 1958), 693.

64. Meier, *Marginal Jew*, 2:580. Copleston's assessment is similar; see *History of Philosophy*, 1:193.

65. Meier, *Marginal Jew*, 2:580. Even at the level of the comparable healing miracles, significant and telling differences emerge between the traditions of Apollonius and Jesus. See W. T. Shiner, *Follow Me: Disciples in Markan Rhetoric* (Atlanta: Scholars Press, 1995), 239.

66. The most well-known study of Svi in recent times is G. G. Scholem, *Sabbatai Sevi: The Mystical Messiah, 1626–1676*, trans. R. J. Zwi Werblowsky (Princeton: Princeton University Press, 1973).

67. G. G. Scholem, *Sabbatai Sevi: The Mystical Messiah, 1626–1676*, trans. R. J. Zwi Werblowsky (Princeton: Princeton University Press, 1973), 217; on the parallels with the Jesus tradition, see 166–67, 217, 220–24.

most can be accounted for by the fact that they were borrowed (consciously or not) from the Christian tradition.[68]

Second, Svi's life was characterized by chronic depression, hypochondria, and mental illness—so much so that, as Scholem notes, he was "known as a sick man" who exhibited "strange behavior" during his manic phases. Among other episodes, he once purchased a large fish, dressed it up as a baby, and kept it in a cradle. Scholem points out that, quite unlike Jesus, Svi was unable to attract a permanent circle of followers, "obviously because of his psychopathological traits."[69]

Third, the miracle tradition associated with Svi is unimpressive. While certain miracle stories were attached to him, his own prophet claimed that Svi was a messiah by whom God would test Israel to see whether they would "believe without any sign or miracle."[70] When Svi himself was interrogated by a sultan's physician as to whether he could do miracles, he denied any such ability.[71] Sometime after Svi's death, rumors began to circulate that he had been delivered from death and taken to heaven. Unlike the Jesus tradition, there are no reports of anyone actually having seen Svi after his death, and the reports that are available appear to be shrouded in myth (i.e., a dragon supposedly guarded the way to his tomb).[72]

Fourth, when Svi was arrested by the sultan and offered the choice of either being martyred or converting to the Muslim faith, he chose to save his own life, renounce his Judaism, and convert to Islam.[73] The contrast of Jesus's willingness to go to the cross for his convictions is instructive.

Finally, though Svi was widely regarded as the Messiah, he was never worshipped as divine. By contrast, from early on Jesus was worshipped alongside Yahweh, and this by people who were raised in a strictly monotheistic environment that strongly opposed any blurring of the lines between the Creator God and humans, as we saw in the previous chapter.

68. Robert Price has suggested that the religious phenomenon associated with Svi demonstrates that legends about miracle working messiahs can arise "virtually overnight," thus providing a plausible explanatory parallel to the Jesus legend; *Incredible Shrinking Son of Man*, 29. Price's analogy, however, misses the really serious differences. Given the surrounding Christian context, the Svi movement had the Jesus model to draw from—a messiah figure who did miracles, was viewed as divine, etc. Such a model could catalyze a similar interpretation of Svi almost overnight. As we have noted in chap. 2, however, the first generation Jewish Christians had no such culturally available and attractive messianic model waiting for them—and yet they settled upon just such a one shortly after Jesus's death. *This* is the type of rapid development that requires an explanation.

69. Scholem, *Sabbatai Sevi*, 147, 159; on the fish episode, see 161. Of course, at one point in his ministry, Jesus's sanity was questioned by his family (Mark 3:21). Yet unlike Svi, Jesus was able to gather a permanent group of disciples, many of whom eventually would die for their faith in him. And again, quite unlike Svi, Jesus has become perhaps the single most admired figure in human history—hardly a person that strikes one as emotionally unstable.

70. Ibid., 238.

71. Ibid., 680.

72. Ibid., 920.

73. On Svi's apostasy, see ibid., 673–86.

Thus, there are enough significant differences between these two movements to conclude that explaining the historical data associated with the rise of Christianity is a more complex undertaking than explaining how Svi's short-lived messianic movement came into being.

Simon Kimbangu

In our estimation, one of the most compelling parallels to the early Jesus movement concerns an African miracle-worker named Kimbangu.[74] Kimbangu is reported to have healed the sick and even to have raised the dead. Some followers consequently worshipped him as God, even during his own lifetime. For those holding to a naturalistic worldview such as Robert Price, this movement provides an argument against the uniqueness of Christianity, for it shows how quickly people can accept legends and how prone they can be to exalt another human as divine. Without denying that those within polytheistic cultures (unlike first-century Jews) can, in some sense, be prone to deifying fellow human beings, we shall argue that the case of Kimbangu is in no way an instance of such a phenomenon. Hence we deny that his case counts as a real analogy to that of Jesus. To the contrary, when all the evidence is fairly examined, we believe that, ironically, the case of Kimbangu actually testifies in its own way to the qualitative uniqueness of the Jesus tradition.

Beginning on April 6, 1921, with the healing of a woman, Kimbangu reportedly performed various miraculous healings—on one occasion even raising a child from the dead.[75] Because we do not share the naturalistic assumption that such things cannot happen (see chap. 1), we are open to acknowledging that miracles did take place when the evidence suggests such. With respect to some of the miracle claims associated with Kimbangu, the evidence strikes us as worthy of serious consideration. To immediately dismiss his followers' reports of these miracles as "superstitious" is not to deal fairly, or critically, with the evidence. It also leaves unexplained what caused the immediate followers of Kimbangu to circulate such claims and why some of them went so far as to exalt him as God. In this respect there is arguably something of a parallel between the birth of the movement that grew up around Kimbangu and the movement that grew up around Jesus. But the parallel is not necessarily about how quickly legends can arise. Rather, the parallel, we suggest, is that *in both instances it appears that an appeal to the supernatural forms part of a plausible historical account of the data at hand.*

However, does the exaltation of Kimbangu to a divine status among some of his followers provide an instructive parallel to the early Jesus movement? Three considerations lead us to conclude that it does not. First, the worldview of the Congo people Kimbangu ministered to was steeped in the notion that the spiri-

---

74. On Kimbangu see Rabey, "People's Prophet"; M.-L. Martin, *Kimbangu: An African Prophet and His Church*, trans. D. M. Moore (Grand Rapids: Eerdmans, 1975).

75. Rabey, "People's Prophet," 32.

tual realm was populated with numerous deities. As such, these people—much like the wider first-century pagan world—would have little difficulty identifying a miracle-working human being as a divine entity. Again, by contrast, the world-view of the first-century Jewish people Jesus ministered to was resistant to the notion that a man could be God. If it is difficult to explain the reports and divine titles associated with Kimbangu without accepting that he performed some sort of miraculous feats (and we suspect that it is), how much more difficult is it to explain the reports and divine titles associated with Jesus by first-century Jews, unless we accept that he performed the kind of feats attributed to him?

Second, while it was claimed that Kimbangu miraculously raised a child from the dead, no one ever claimed that Kimbangu *himself* rose from the dead (he died in prison on October 12, 1951). This contrasts sharply with the early Christian message that was centered on the claim that Jesus's tomb was empty and that he repeatedly appeared to a multitude of disciples. What is more, according to the reports, it was this fact that ultimately convinced the earliest disciples, against their deeply held cultural and religious presuppositions, that Jesus was indeed the divine Son of God. If we deny that these reports are rooted in the actual experience of Jesus's followers, we are once again put in the difficult position of explaining why the reports were made at all, as well as of explaining what it was that led the earliest Jewish disciples to embrace, against all their cultural assumptions, the conviction that a contemporary of theirs was to be identified with the Creator God.

Third, and perhaps most important, Kimbangu was *a Christian pastor* who understood his miracles to be a demonstration of *Jesus's* divine authority, not his own. Related to this, Kimbangu adamantly *disclaimed* all titles to divinity, and the vast majority of his followers honored this disclaimer. Today, the remnant of Kimbangu's movement (composed of several million members)—the Church of Jesus Christ on Earth through the Prophet Simon Kimbangu (EJCSK)—denies even that he is the African Messiah. This contrasts sharply with the Gospels' depiction of Jesus presenting himself as Messiah and performing miracles to demonstrate *his own* unique authority. Not only this, but as is clear from Paul's writings, the belief that Jesus was Lord, Creator, and Savior of the world was widely shared by the early followers of Jesus.

In light of this, we conclude that the case of Kimbangu does not at all demonstrate that Christianity can be understood simply as one of a number of superstitious movements. In the name of Jesus, it seems that Kimbangu performed a number of miracles. Some of his followers who were not adequately grounded in the Christian faith mistakenly began to attribute divinity to Kimbangu. Given their polytheistic religious background, we can easily understand their mistake. But what is not as clear is how this fact counts against the uniqueness of the Jesus story. To the contrary, it suggests, on the one hand, the possibility that miracles can and do occur, and, on the other, that the Kimbangu tradition is something less than a solid parallel to the first-century Palestinian Jesus tradition.

Myth Become Fact

Thus far we have argued that the attempt to undermine the uniqueness and/or to establish the merely legendary nature of the early Jesus tradition by finding mythic parallels is unconvincing. The differences between the New Testament's story about Jesus and Greco-Roman mystery religions, ahistorical hero-myths, and/or legend-creating movements throughout history are far more telling than their similarities. Moreover, in sharp contrast with ahistorical legends and myths, we shall later demonstrate that we have good historical grounds for believing that the depiction(s) of Jesus in the Synoptic Gospel tradition is generally reliable (chaps. 6–10).

Still, one could argue, there is a general "mythological pattern" that the story of Jesus fits into, however loosely. The Christian story of God coming to earth, doing miracles, and dying and rising again to rescue humanity from an evil enemy (the devil) at least echoes what we find in other places. Let us grant that our case thus far has established that the *precise way* early Christians speak of these matters has no real parallel. Still, the simple fact that the Jesus story is about God visiting us and/or about a God who does something along the lines of dying and rising is not altogether unique. The history of religion and mythology is full of "incarnation-like" stories and "resurrection-like" stories. So, one could argue, if we assume that all these analogous "incarnations" and "resurrections" are mythological, we should similarly concede that the Christian version of these stories is mythological, its unique features notwithstanding.

To address this objection we shall assume a very different approach from the one we have taken thus far. Whereas we have to this point defended the distinctness of the Jesus tradition, we will now highlight a broader commonality that it shares with some other "incarnation-like" and "resurrection-like" myths. We suggest that, in a much broader sense than we have considered thus far, the Jesus story *is* in fact "mythic"—but not *merely* mythic. Semantics, of course, is all-important here. What we want to argue is that, on one set of definitions, the categories of "myth," "truth," and even "history" are not mutually incompatible. To the contrary, in the Jesus story one could argue that we find the interpenetration of these very categories; we find "true myth."

On "True Myth"

To begin, we must first consider broadening an all-too-common definition of "myth."[76] There has been a tension in the Western tradition, going all the way back to the ancient Greek skeptics (fifth century BCE), between understanding myth as a story that discloses reality, on the one hand, and as "what other people believe

---

76. Dunn rightly notes, "The basic problem of myth is the problem of definition" ("Demythologizing," 285). Similarly, Paul Ricoeur points out that scholars cannot agree on a definition of "myth" ("Myth," in *Encyclopedia of Religion*, 10:261). Ricoeur's own definition—"an expression of the sacred in words"—would allow for our sense of "true myth" (p. 261).

as true but I know is false," on the other.[77] Since the Enlightenment, the second view has been dominant in Western culture. As we saw in chapter 1, it has been especially prominent in historical-critical scholarship with its judgment on ancient and contemporary non-Western worldviews as "naïve and mythologically minded."[78] But there is insight to be gained by broadening our understanding of myth and applying it to the question of whether Jesus is a "mythic figure" in the sense that the story about him *discloses reality*.

The narrow rationalistic understanding of myth as fiction has rightfully been subjected to a great deal of criticism on a number of fronts in the last several decades. Among other things, it has been argued that this perspective is rooted in a modern Eurocentric presupposition that enthrones the Western worldview (as interpreted by certain intellectuals) as judge over all other worldviews. Accordingly, it assumes that science and reason are the only means by which reality can be known. Hence it concludes that all stories that do not conform to this way of knowing can only be primitive distortions of, as opposed to revelations of, reality.

One unfortunate consequence of this rationalistic interpretation of myth is that it does not allow a person to let myth speak to him or her *on its own terms*. It cannot take seriously the idea of a distinctly mythic truth—a "true myth." In the words of Wolfhart Pannenberg, the rationalistic perspective

treats the form of thought which it describes as "mythical," not as something irreducibly distinct and unique, but as the expression of something else, e.g., natural

77. J. Creed, "Uses of Classical Mythology," in *The Theory of Myth: Six Studies*, ed. A. Cunningham (London: Sheed and Ward, 1973), 19. See also P. Veyne, *Did the Greeks Believe in Their Myths? An Essay on the Constitutive Imagination*, trans. P. Wissing (Chicago: University of Chicago Press, 1988).

78. The modern origins of this understanding of myth (though he used the term "fable") can be traced to Bernard Fontenelle's (1657–1757) *De l'origine des fables*. He was the first Enlightenment thinker to propose a comprehensive theory of myth that argued for its roots in the naïveté and "childishness" of the ancients and contemporary "savages." Although Fontenelle's text was not published until 1724, there is good evidence to conclude that it was written by 1680, thus making it the earliest modern theory of myth; see R. A. Johnson, *The Origins of Demythologizing: Philosophy and Historiography in the Theology of Rudolf Bultmann* (Leiden: Brill, 1974), 132n2. On the rise of the Enlightenment understanding of myth, see also Ricoeur, "Myth," 268–70; W. Pannenberg, "The Later Dimensions of Myth in Biblical and Christian Tradition," in *Basic Questions in Theology*, trans. G. H. Kehm (Philadelphia: Fortress, 1970–1971), 3:7–15. This rationalist understanding of myth was adopted and developed by the German philologist C. G. Heyne. It was applied to biblical studies by his student J. G. Eichorn, and, through him, influenced other biblical scholars such as J. P. Gabler and G. L. Bauer. It was eventually applied with full force to the Gospels by scholars such as D. F. Strauss and Bruno Bauer, the latter of whom went so far as to question the historical existence of Jesus. On the rise and development of the application of myth and legend to the New Testament texts, see the sections on Eichorn, Gabler, G. L. Bauer, and Strauss in W. Baird, *History of New Testament Research*, vol. 1: *From Deism to Tübingen* (Minneapolis: Fortress, 1992); Christian Hartlich and Walter Sachs, *Der Ursprung des Mythosbegriffes in der Modernen Bibelwissenschaft* (Tübingen: Mohr, 1952); C. A. Evans, "Life-of-Jesus Research and the Eclipse of Mythology," *Theological Studies* 54 (1993): 3–36. On Bruno Bauer's extreme historical skepticism toward the Gospels, see Z. Rosen, *Bruno Bauer and Karl Marx: The Influence of Bruno Bauer on Marx's Thought* (The Hague: Nijoff, 1977), chaps. 5–6.

processes. . . . It no longer looks at the conceptions and phenomena described as "mythical" to see what their own distinctive importance is, their own characteristic truth.[79]

When we allow myth to communicate its "own characteristic truth," we experience it as disclosing profound aspects of ourselves and the world. We experience it *as true* in terms of what it discloses about our deepest hopes and intuitive anticipations of reality. True myth has the power to move us beyond our "mundane" experience of the world and put us in touch with realities we might otherwise remain unaware of. True myth can thereby enrich our lives, broaden our horizons, transform our self-awareness, and affect our social relations.

The Jesus Tradition and "True Myth"

The question of the relationship between the Christian view of Jesus and mythic savior figures changes if we have in mind this broadened conception of myth rather than the rationalistic understanding of myth as "that which is not historically true." With the rationalistic definition, the issue is restricted to whether the New Testament view of Jesus is historically reliable. And the answer to this question hangs upon things like the relative proximity of the parallels to the Jesus story and the question of the historical influence of these parallels on New Testament authors. We have thus far argued that a fair assessment of the evidence suggests that the case for judging the New Testament portrait of Jesus as "mythic" *in this sense* and *on this basis* is weak.

If we adopt a broader definition of myth, however, the question is no longer one of historical truth but of *spiritual meaning*. More precisely, the question is: Does the Jesus story as expressed in the Gospels and in Paul disclose reality in a manner that is in certain fundamental respects similar to the way other mythic savior stories disclose reality? The answer, we submit, is a decisive "yes." Indeed, in this sense, not only do we believe "the Christ myth" to be similar to certain pagan myths but we also believe the "Christ myth" *fulfills* these pagan myths.[80] It "incarnates" all that is true in all similar myths. Hence, while we maintain that Jesus is not mythical in the first sense of the term, with the second sense of the term we argue that the Jesus story epitomizes myth.

Moreover, far from constituting an argument against the historicity of the New Testament view of Jesus, the existence of mythic parallels, *understood as disclosures of ourselves and reality*, is precisely what we would expect if the New Testament portrait *is* historically true. After all, the New Testament itself declares that Jesus is the light that illuminates all people (John 1:4, 9). While the New Testament teaches that God

79. Pannenberg, "Later Dimensions of Myth," 14–15.
80. Pertinent here is Don Richardson's category of "redemptive analogies" as discussed in his *Eternity in Their Hearts*, rev. ed. (Ventura, CA: Regal, 1984). See esp. part 1: "A World Prepared for the Gospel: The Melchizedek Factor."

was decisively revealed in the historical person of Jesus (e.g., John 14:8–11), it also teaches that God is Lord of all people and is at work everywhere and at all times to reveal himself to people (e.g., Acts 17:25–28).[81] It is not surprising, therefore, that we find mythical echoes of the true story in the minds and hearts of various peoples.

C. S. Lewis states this perspective well when he writes,

> Theology, while saying that a special illumination has been vouchsafed to Christians and (earlier) to Jews, also says that there is some divine illumination vouchsafed to all men.... We should, therefore, expect to find in the imagination of the great Pagan teachers and myth makers some glimpse of that theme which we believe to be the very plot of the whole cosmic story—the theme of incarnation, death, and rebirth.[82]

The differences we find between the mythic saviors and the Jesus of the New Testament are precisely what we would expect if the Jesus story in the New Testament is grounded in history. Again, Lewis argues:

> The Pagan stories are all about someone dying and rising, either every year, or else nobody knows where and nobody knows when. The Christian story is about a historical personage, whose execution can be dated pretty accurately.... It is not the difference between falsehood and truth. It is the difference between a real event on the one hand and dim dreams or premonitions of that same event on the other. It is like watching something come gradually into focus; first it hangs in the clouds of myth and ritual, vast and vague, then it condenses, grows hard and in a sense small, as a historical event in first-century Palestine.[83]

From this vantage point, Lewis argued that Jesus was "Myth became Fact." In Jesus, "the essential meaning of all things came down from the 'heaven' of myth to the 'earth' of history."[84] The dreams of finding salvation in the so-called dying and rising of a god are perfectly expressed, and become historically true, in the New Testament story of Jesus Christ.

81. This ostensive tension in the New Testament between the universal love of God and the particularity of the saving work of Jesus Christ has led to various perspectives within orthodox Christianity on the controversial question of the "destiny of the unevangelized," etc. While some seem to suggest that the only traditional perspective is that of a "restrictivist" view, in fact Christian tradition has included what John Sanders has called a "wider hope" perspective from the beginning (e.g., Justin Martyr et al.). On "restrictivism" and the "wider hope" perspectives in Scripture and tradition, see J. Sanders, *No Other Name: An Investigation into the Destiny of the Unevangelized* (Grand Rapids: Eerdmans, 1992). On four perspectives that have been espoused by self-proclaimed evangelicals, see G. A. Boyd and P. R. Eddy, *Across the Spectrum: Understanding Issues in Evangelical Theology* (Grand Rapids: Baker Academic, 2002), chap. 12.

82. C. S. Lewis, "Is Theology Poetry?" in *The Weight of Glory, and Other Essays* (New York: Macmillan, 1980), 128.

83. Ibid., 128–29. Here, Lewis has apparently accepted the existence of the category of "dying and rising gods." Even if one rejects this clear-cut category per se, as we have, his essential point still stands.

84. Ibid., 129–30.

In some respects, J. R. R. Tolkien makes the case even more poignantly. Tolkien explains that the "peculiar quality of the 'joy' in successful Fantasy [mythology]" is due to "a sudden glimpse" of an "underlying reality or truth." The joy of this sudden glimpse is the "far-off gleam or echo of evangelium [good news] in the real world"—in Jesus Christ. He continues:

> The Gospels contain a fairy-story, or a story of a larger kind which embraces all the essence of fairy-stories. They contain many marvels—peculiarly artistic, beautiful, and moving: "mythical" in their perfect, self-contained significance; and among the marvels is the greatest and most complete conceivable eucatastrophe [eruption of joy].

Yet, the story of Jesus in the New Testament is not *only* a fairy story, according to Tolkien, but a fairy story incarnated in real time and space. In the person of Jesus, an all-embracing fairy story

> has entered History and the primary world; the desire and aspiration of sub-creation has been raised to the fulfillment of Creation. The Birth of Christ is the eucatastrophe of Man's history. The Resurrection is the eucatastrophe of the story of the Incarnation. The story begins and ends in joy. It has pre-eminently the "inner consistency of reality." There is no tale ever told that men would rather find was true, and none which so many skeptical men have accepted as true on its own merits.

And from this Tolkien concludes, "[The Christian] story is supreme; and it is true. Art has been verified. God is the Lord, of angels, and of men—and of elves. Legend and History have met and fused."[85]

In the Jesus story, our most profound intuitions about ourselves, about reality, and about God—the stuff expressed by "true myth" as well as art—are fulfilled. Far from being an argument against the historicity of the New Testament "myth," the existence of broadly parallel myths, understood in this fashion, *argues in its favor.*[86] In other words, while there are no grounds for concluding that the Jesus story is an example of *ahistorical legend*, as other mythic stories are, there are very good grounds for concluding that the Jesus story is *mythically true* just as some other mythic stories are—but to a superlative degree.

Of course, all of this leaves open the question of why we should believe that, of all myths ever created, the Jesus story is the one that fuses "legend and history." To be sure, the superlative beauty and inner consistency of the Jesus story argue in its favor, as Tolkien noted. But this alone is insufficient to convince most that the story is historically factual. Our task in the remainder of this book will be to investigate this question in the course of assessing still other observations and arguments raised by legendary-Jesus theorists.

85. J. R. R. Tolkien "On Fairy-Stories," in *Leaf and Tree* (Boston: Houghton Mifflin, 1965), 71–72.
86. C. S. Lewis, "Myth Became Fact," in *God in the Dock: Essays on Theology and Ethics*, ed. W. Hooper (Grand Rapids: Eerdmans, 1970), 67.

Part 2

OTHER WITNESSES

ANCIENT HISTORIANS AND THE APOSTLE PAUL

The canonical Gospels present Jesus as a remarkable, miracle-working Messiah figure. If this portrait is generally accurate, would we not expect to find some record of this amazing ministry outside the Gospels? Part 2 of this work investigates this issue.

Scholars who fall within the legendary-Jesus spectrum—especially the Christ myth theorists—typically argue that there is little-to-no independent information regarding a historical Jesus to be found in early non-Christian sources. Hence, the relative silence of non-Christian writers in the ancient world regarding Jesus is evidence that the Gospel portrait of him is most likely the stuff of later legend rather than history. We will investigate this perspective in chapter 4.

Some scholars who hold that the Jesus of the canonical Gospels is substantially legendary also argue that Paul, the first Christian writer, has little—or nothing—to say about the historical Jesus. Indeed, Christ myth theorists argue that Paul views Jesus as a cosmic savior figure, along the lines of a mystery-religion deity, not a historical person in the recent past. They argue that it was only later, when the Gospels were written, that a fictitious historical narrative was imposed on this mythical cosmic savior figure. We shall investigate the merits of this case in chapter 5.

4

A CONSPIRACY OF SILENCE?

WHAT ANCIENT NON-CHRISTIAN SOURCES SAY, AND DO NOT SAY, ABOUT JESUS

As we have noted, some legendary-Jesus theorists argue that, while it is at least possible, if not likely, an actual historical person named Jesus existed, he is so shrouded in legendary material that we can know very little about him. Others (i.e, Christ myth theorists) argue that we have no good reason to believe there ever was an actual historical person behind the legend. Yet some within both camps make much of the claim that there is little or no credible information about the historical Jesus to be found in first- and second-century non-Christian sources or in Paul, the earliest Christian source. Surely if a miracle-working prophet like the Jesus of the Gospels actually existed, it is argued, Paul and pagan contemporaries would have mentioned his feats and his teachings. Instead, they argue, we find a virtual silence. And this strongly suggests that the miracle-working teacher of the Gospels is mostly, if not entirely, legendary.

The next two chapters are devoted to considering these arguments. This chapter will investigate the alleged silence of non-Christian sources, and the next chapter the alleged silence of Paul. Our argument in these two chapters is that, as a matter of fact, both Paul and certain non-Christian sources do relate data about Jesus. While there is not a wealth of information from these sources, there is some, and the relatively little we find generally aligns with the view of Jesus provided in the Gospels. Additionally, there are plausible explanations for why there is a relatively small amount of information in these sources.

Christian scholars have long noted that a number of ancient non-Christian literary sources make mention of Jesus, including Josephus, Tacitus, Suetonius, Pliny
the Younger, Thallus, Celsus, Lucian of Samosata, Mara bar Serapion, and certain
Jewish rabbinic traditions. They have argued that not only do these sources attest
to Jesus's existence in history but also that some of them offer information that
serves to corroborate certain aspects of Jesus's life as recorded in the Gospels.

Against this, various legendary-Jesus theorists argue that each of these sources
is historically suspect. The passages that seem to speak of Jesus are either passing
on hearsay of what Christians claimed to be true, or they can be shown to be later
interpolations introduced into the text by Christians.

What we have, then, is what the Christ myth theorist Earl Doherty calls "a
conspiracy of silence."[1] He writes: "The Gospel Jesus and his story are . . . missing
from the non-Christian record of the time. Philo of Alexandria, the Jewish historian Justus of Tiberius, Pliny the Elder as collector of reputed natural phenomena,
early Roman satirists and philosophers; all are silent."[2]

This silence, it is argued, is not at all what we would expect if the Gospel portraits of Jesus are at all accurate. According to Michael Martin,

> Pagan witnesses indicate that there is no reliable evidence that supports the historicity of
> Jesus. This is surely surprising given the fact that Jesus was supposed to be a well-known
> person in the area of the world ruled by Rome. One would surely have supposed that
> there would have been *some* surviving records of Jesus if he did exist. Their absence,
> combined with the absence of Jewish records, suggests that [the negative evidence
> principle] applies and that we are justified in disbelieving that Jesus existed.[3]

To corroborate this "conspiracy of silence," some legendary-Jesus theorists
make much of the fact that the second-century apologist Justin Martyr seems to
respond to an objection that Jesus never existed. On their reading, Justin's Jewish dialogue partner Trypho argues that Christians accept "a groundless report"
and have therefore "invent[ed] a Christ for yourselves."[4] Some legendary-Jesus
theorists see this passage as ancient evidence that at least some early opponents
of Christianity argued for Jesus's nonhistoricity.[5] Since opponents of Christianity

1. E. Doherty, "The Jesus Puzzle: Pieces in a Puzzle of Christian Origins," *Journal of Higher Criticism*
4 (1997): 68.

2. Ibid., 69.

3. M. Martin, *The Case against Christianity* (Philadelphia: Temple University Press, 1991), 52. T. Freke
and P. Gandy give a list of twenty-seven ancient authors, including Arrian, Damis, Juvenal, Plutarch,
Quintilian, Seneca, and Velerius Maximus, and wonder why Jesus is mentioned in none of them (*The
Jesus Mysteries: Was the "Original Jesus" a Pagan God?* [New York: Harmony, 1999], 133).

4. Justin Martyr, "Dialogue with Trypho," in *The Ante-Nicene Fathers*, ed. A. Roberts and J. Donaldson
(Buffalo, NY: Christians Literature, 1885), 1:199.

5. On the basis of this remark, for example, Herbert Cutner claims that we know that "some Jews
about the year 150 A.D. *did* deny the historicity of Jesus in no uncertain terms" (*Jesus: God, Man, or
Myth? An Examination of the Evidence* [Mokelumne, CA: Health Research, 1986], 201).

were making this argument in the second century, while first- and second-century sources are silent, it is argued that we have good reason to suspect that the Jesus of the Gospels is largely, if not entirely, legendary.

Our response to this argument shall proceed along the following lines. We begin by addressing two important preliminary questions. Should we have expected pagan writers to notice Jesus? And is there any evidence that ancient critics of Christianity claimed that the figure of Jesus was largely or entirely an outright fabrication? Following this we shall examine all the extant references to Jesus in pagan sources. Following the procedure of Craig Evans, we will consider these sources in three groups.[6]

First, we shall consider what Evans terms "dubious sources"—sources that most scholars judge to contain no independent information about Jesus. We will then consider "sources of minimal value"—sources that may contain some independent information about Jesus, but the information is minimal and/or questionable. Finally, we shall consider three references found in two "important sources"—sources that provide significant information about Jesus and of which we can be relatively confident about. Because of their importance we shall consider these three references in some depth. We will first consider a reference to early Christians found in the early second-century Roman historian, Tacitus. We will then consider the first of two references to Jesus found in Josephus, a reference known as "the James Passage." And, finally, we will examine the most famous—and most controversial—reference to Jesus found in a non-Christian source, a reference in Josephus known as the *Testimonium Flavianum*.

Two Preliminary Words

Would Pagan Writers Have Noticed Jesus?

Before we examine what, if anything, noncanonical sources have to say about Jesus, we need to address two preliminary questions. The first concerns whether we should expect Jesus to have been noticed by pagan writers, assuming the Gospels'

---

6. C. A. Evans, "Jesus in Non-Christian Sources," in *Studying the Historical Jesus: Evaluations of the State of Current Research*, ed. B. Chilton and C. A. Evans (New York: Brill, 1994), 443. The fact that we follow Evans's threefold categorization of the evidence should not be taken to mean that our evaluation of the evidence necessarily accords with his on every point. For helpful discussions of these non-Christian sources, see F. F. Bruce, *Jesus and Christian Origins outside the New Testament* (Grand Rapids: Eerdmans, 1974); Evans, "Jesus in Non-Christian Sources," 443–78; R. T. France, *The Evidence for Jesus* (Downers Grove, IL: InterVarsity, 1986), 19–58; G. R. Habermas, *The Historical Jesus: Ancient Evidence for the Life of Christ* (Joplin, MO: College Press, 1996), 187–228; M. Harris, "References to Jesus in Classical Authors," in *Jesus Traditions outside the Gospels*, ed. D. Wenham (Sheffield: Sheffield Academic Press, 1982), 275–324; J. P. Meier, *A Marginal Jew: Rethinking the Historical Jesus*, vol. 1: *The Roots of the Problem and the Person* (New York: Doubleday, 1991), 56–111; and esp. R. E. Van Voorst, *Jesus outside the New Testament: An Introduction to the Ancient Evidence* (Grand Rapids: Eerdmans, 2000), 19–134.

accounts of his ministry are rooted in history. Though we will argue shortly that the claim that no reliable non-Christian source mentions Jesus is mistaken, at the outset it must be conceded that there is relatively little mention of Jesus in these sources. The question is: How significant is this fact? Our contention is that it is not at all significant, for it is not at all surprising. Three points can be made here.

First, there is a problem with the assumption that if the Gospel accounts are true, Jesus would have been something of an international figure whom people in the first century would generally have been aware of. There is simply no reason to assume this. While the Gospels certainly speak of "crowds" occasionally following Jesus in Galilee, there is no reason to think that his reputation would have expanded much beyond this region. We must remember that information in the ancient world generally was disseminated by word of mouth and therefore traveled slowly and usually haphazardly.

But it is not even clear that Jesus would have captured the attention of most people in the region of Galilee. We must bear in mind that the early first century was a time of intense social and political unrest within Palestine. We know from Josephus and other sources that there were a number of religious and political movements and figures vying for people's loyalties.[7] So, while it is likely that many people in Galilee had heard about this miracle-working preacher who was delivering a radical new message, and while large crowds would have attended a sermon here or there (e.g., Mark 6:32–44), it is also likely that for many Jesus was just another "voice in the crowd." It seems unreasonable, then, to assume that Roman historians in the first or second century would have heard about Jesus.

Second, even if Roman historians had heard about Jesus, we have no reason to suppose they would have been interested in him. During this period, there were countless religious figures and movements existing throughout the Roman Empire, with new ones arising all the time. Why would any Roman writer be interested in this one? As John Meier notes, "Jesus was a marginal Jew leading a marginal movement in a marginal province of a vast Roman Empire." As such, it would be surprising if "any learned Jew or pagan would have known or referred to him at all in the 1st or early 2nd century."[8]

Third, we must remember that most of the literature of the ancient world has been lost. For example, the writings of the Roman historian Tacitus exist in only two manuscripts, and it is believed they contain only about half of what he actually wrote.[9] This leaves open the possibility that Jesus was in fact referred to by

7. See R. A. Horsley and J. S. Hanson, *Bandits, Prophets, and Messiahs: Popular Movements at the Time of Jesus* (San Francisco: Harper & Row, 1985).

8. Meier, *Marginal Jew*, 1:56. For discussion see France, *Evidence for Jesus*, 19. Even the leading contemporary Christ myth theorist, G. A. Wells, acknowledges this point. See G. A. Wells, *The Jesus Myth* (Chicago: Open Court, 1999), 196. Having acknowledged this insight, Wells chooses not to use the absence of Jesus in other non-Christian texts as an argument and instead moves directly to an attempt at debunking Josephus et al.

9. France, *Evidence for Jesus*, 19–20.

various ancient writers but that these works or sections of their works were lost. This is, of course, an argument from silence. But then again, the entire argument by legendary-Jesus theorists at this point is one from silence.

Trypho as a "Christ Myth" Theorist?

A second preliminary question we must address concerns a cryptic sentence written by a second-century critic of Christianity named Trypho. In the course of answering the critique of Trypho—a non-Christian Jew—Justin Martyr records him as saying that Christ, "if indeed he has been born, and exists anywhere—is unknown." Trypho adds that Christians have accepted "a groundless report" and have "invent[ed] a Christ for [themselves]."[10] What makes this reference significant is that some scholars interpret Trypho as denying that Jesus existed. This interpretation then grounds the argument that perhaps other non-Christians in the ancient world doubted Jesus's historical existence. This, some argue, lends credence to the view of the most radical legendary-Jesus theorists, who insist the Jesus figure of the Gospels is entirely mythological. Two considerations demonstrate the weakness of this line of argumentation.

First, even if we grant for the moment that Trypho doubted Jesus's existence, this hardly constitutes a credible argument for Jesus's nonhistoricity. This would be the only place where we learn of such a charge in the ancient world, and we have no reason to conclude that it reflects a widespread sentiment. What is more, even if Trypho is doubting Jesus's existence, his doubt is expressed over a hundred years after the time Christians claim Jesus lived and died—a fairly safe time for someone hostile to Christianity to concoct a "Jesus never existed" theory, since by this time all eyewitnesses would have been dead.

Second, and far more significant, there is no reason whatsoever to interpret Trypho's statement as suggesting that Jesus never existed. If read carefully, it becomes clear that his argument is not about *Jesus*, but about *the Messiah*, the "Christ." The passage we are concerned with reads as follows:

> But [the] Christ—if He has indeed been born, and exists anywhere—is unknown, and does not even know Himself, and has no power until Elias comes to anoint him, and make him manifest to all. And you, having accepted a groundless report, invent a Christ for yourselves, and for his sake you are inconsiderately perishing.[11]

Trypho is not denying that Jesus existed. He is simply denying that Jesus *is the Christ*, God's anointed Messiah. As a Jew, Trypho believes that if the one who is to be the Christ has already been born, he is yet unknown and in fact does not yet know that he is the Messiah. For, according to Trypho's particular brand of Judaism, the Messiah can have no power until Elijah appears and reveals him.

10. *Dialogue with Trypho*, ANF, 1:199.
11. Ibid.

Since Jesus was not revealed by Elijah, Trypho judges the Christian claim that Jesus was the Christ to be unfounded. He thus believes Christians have "invented a Christ for [themselves]" and are therefore "perishing." Trypho is not arguing that Christians invented *Jesus*. Indeed, his argument is actually predicated on Jesus's historical existence, for he is arguing that Christians invented a false conception of Christ and applied it to Jesus. The fact that Trypho assumes Jesus existed throughout the remainder of his debate with Justin Martyr further confirms our interpretation.[12]

Hence, we have no reason to think that Trypho, or anyone else in the first and second centuries, denied that Jesus existed. Given that Christianity had numerous enemies in the ancient world who wanted to expose it as a lie, the absence of this criticism is noteworthy, especially if Jesus was a fabricated figure, as Christ myth theorists contend. We are being asked to accept that the Jesus story was a fabricated myth, even though all the earliest opponents of this supposed myth presuppose it is *not* a fabrication in the very process of critiquing it.

Having addressed these two preliminary matters, we turn to an examination of specific references to Jesus in pagan sources. As noted above, we shall make use of Craig Evans's three categories of "dubious sources," "sources of minimal value," and, finally, three references that fall within his category of "important sources."

Dubious Sources

Rabbinic Traditions

The first "dubious" source is the rabbinic Jewish tradition.[13] Although a few Christian apologists claim that rabbinic Jewish sources provide us with historically relevant information about Jesus, there are three considerations that lead us to a more negative conclusion.

First, the earliest rabbinic sources date from the late second to the third century and the most celebrated material even later than this. This alone raises questions about the historical value of this material. To illustrate, we possess a rabbinic account of Jesus's life (*Toledot Yeshu*) that claims, among other things, that Jesus was born out of wedlock, grew up acting disrespectful toward Jewish leaders, and mastered magical practices to gain a following. It also claims that Jesus's body was found after his death. Were this a first- or even second-century document, it might be of historical interest. However, the *Toledot Yeshu* was compiled in the fifth century. True, *Toledot Yeshu* and other Jewish literature contain traditions that predate them, but the relatively late date and clear polemical focus of *Toledot Yeshu* and other rabbinic references to Jesus render them suspect as historical

---

12. See Van Voorst, *Jesus outside the New Testament*, 15n35.

13. On Jesus in the rabbinic writings, see J. Z. Lauterbach, "Jesus in the Talmud," in *Rabbinic Essays* (Cincinnati: Hebrew Union College, 1951), 473–570; Meier, *Marginal Jew*, 1:93–98.

sources. They tell us something about Jewish polemics against the early Christian movement, but nothing reliably about Jesus.[14]

Second, in a number of instances it is not entirely clear that the rabbinic text is even talking about Jesus. For example, some have tried to argue that Ben Pandera (or Pantere), Ben Stada, and even Balaam, referred to in various rabbinic writings, are actually references to Jesus (e.g., Babylonian Talmud *Sanhedrin* 67a; *Shabbat* 104b). But there is simply no solid evidence to support these speculations.[15]

Third, in those instances where it seems certain that an author *is* referring to Jesus, there are textual indications that the material is dependent upon earlier Christian claims and/or anti-Christian propaganda. For example, Jesus is presented as being illegitimately born of a tryst between Mary and a Roman soldier named Panthera. It is significant that Panthera appears to be a play on the Greek word for virgin (*parthenos*). Hence, many scholars conclude that this story is nothing more than a contrived attack on the Christian claim that Jesus was born of a virgin.[16]

While the rabbinic material gives us insight into how some Jews reacted polemically against the Jesus tradition, it does not represent early, independent, or historically reliable information about Jesus. The only truly significant point about this literature is that, though it sometimes credits Jesus's power to sorcery, magic, or the devil himself, it never denies that Jesus performed miracles—let alone that Jesus existed.

The Qur'an

A second source of dubious value is the Qur'an. The Qur'an mentions Mary (e.g., suras 4, 5, 19) and Jesus—or *Isa*—a number of times (e.g., on Jesus's miraculous birth, see 3:42–49; 66:12). However, there are significant reasons to call into

14. On the polemically inspired—as opposed to the historically inspired—version of Jesus's death in the *Toledot Yeshu*, see H. I. Newman, "The Death of Jesus in the *Toledot Yeshu* Literature," *JTS* 50 (1999): 59–79.

15. In his study of this topic, J. Maier concludes that the Mishnah and both Talmuds lack *any* authentic, direct reference to Jesus. See *Jesus von Nazareth in der talmudischen Überlieferung* (Darmstadt: Wissenschaftliche Buchgesellschaft, 1978). While we think this may be an overly pessimistic position on the question, it does highlight the problem of reading Jesus too easily into rabbinic tradition.

16. For example, Bruce, *Jesus and Christian Origins*, 57–58. One rabbinic text that has been seen as important by some scholars is a tractate in the Babylonian Talmud, *Sanhedrin* 43a. In this text, a certain Yeshu (i.e., Jesus) was said to have led Israel astray, and so he was hung on the eve of Passover. The text also claims that, prior to his execution, a herald called for forty days for someone to step forward to defend the accused, but no one did. As many have argued, this last claim is most likely a polemical rejoinder to the claim of the Gospels that Jesus experienced a rush to judgment, with a trial and execution that took less than twenty-four hours. Thus, as Meier notes, this text is most likely "simply reacting to the gospel tradition" (*Marginal Jew*, 1:97). For other treatments of Jesus in the rabbinic tradition, see E. Bammel, "Christian Origins in Jewish Tradition," *NTS* 13 (1967): 317–35; Evans, "Jesus in Non-Christian Sources," 443–50; M. Goldstein, *Jesus in the Jewish Tradition* (New York: Macmillan, 1950); J. Z. Lauterbach, "Jesus in the Talmud," 473–570; G. H. Twelftree, "Jesus in Jewish Traditions," in *Jesus Traditions outside the Gospels*, 310–24; Van Voorst, *Jesus outside the New Testament*, 104–34.

question the historical basis of a number of its claims about Jesus.[17] For one thing, the Qur'an dates from the seventh century, far too late to be taken seriously as a reliable *independent* source of information about Jesus. Second, the claim is made that Jesus did not die on a cross but was taken up to heaven by Allah (4:157–58). However, if there is any fact of Jesus's life that has been established by a broad consensus, it is the fact of Jesus's crucifixion. For the Qur'an to get it wrong at this most fundamental point raises serious questions about the historical reliability of *any* claim it makes about Jesus.

Sources of Minimal Value

We turn now to Evans's second category of non-Christian sources: sources that are of minimal value. These are sources that may confirm that Jesus existed and perhaps even parallel some aspects of the Gospel accounts, but the information is meager and uncertain. There are six sources that fit into this category.

Thallus

The first source is an obscure first-century writer named Thallus. In one of the surviving fragments of the work of the third-century Christian historian Julius Africanus, we find a reference to a Roman historian named Thallus who apparently wrote a now-lost three-volume chronicle of world history in the mid-50s.[18] In this fragment Julius is discussing the darkness that fell on the land during Jesus's crucifixion. In the course of his brief discussion, he makes an offhand reference

17. For helpful assessments of the Jesus material in the Qur'an and Islamic tradition, see Bruce, *Jesus and Christian Origins*, 167–86; Evans, "Jesus in Non-Christian Sources," 453–54; K. Zebiri, *Muslims and Christians Face to Face* (Rockport, MA: Oneworld, 1997), 59–67. From an Islamic perspective, see M. 'Ata'ur-Rahim and A. Thomson, *Jesus, Prophet of Islam*, rev. ed. (London: Ta-Ha, 1996); T. Khalidi, *The Muslim Jesus: Sayings and Stories in Islamic Literature* (Cambridge, MA: Harvard University Press, 2001).

18. The fragment (18) of Africanus's five-volume *History of the World* (i.e., to ca. 217) is preserved by the Byzantine historian Georgius Syncellus (ca. 800). For the extant fragments of Thallus, see F. Jacoby, *Die Fragmente der griechischen Historiker IIB* (Berlin: Weidmann, 1929), 1156–58. The main evidence for Thallus, aside from Julius, comes from Eusebius. All that remains of Eusebius's *Chronicle* are the Armenian fragments. For the critical edition, see J. Karst, ed., *Eusebius Werke*, vol. 5: *Die Chronik* (Leipzig: Hinrichs, 1911), 125. There is a dating problem here. Eusebius says that Thallus's history covered the period from the fall of Troy to the 167th Olympiad (i.e., 112–109 BCE). However, other sources give evidence that Thallus wrote well into the first-century CE. A number of scholars suggest that Eusebius simply made an error and that when the date is amended by two Greek letters (i.e., not the 167th, but the 207th Olympiad) we arrive at the dates 49–52 CE. This would coincide with the other sources. For discussion see M. Goguel, *Jesus the Nazarene: Myth or History?* (London: Fisher & Unwin, 1926), 91–92; Van Voorst, *Jesus outside the New Testament*, 22; Harris, "References to Jesus," 344. Some speculate that the Thallus Julius refers to is the Thallus who, according to Josephus, was a Samaritan resident of Rome who made a large loan to Agrippa (*Antiquities*, 18.6.4.167). This is purely conjecture, for it requires that Josephus's text, which records the man's name as "*Allos*," be amended to read "*Thallos*" (i.e., Thallus).

to Thallus, saying: "In the third book of his history Thallus calls this darkness an eclipse of the sun—wrongly in my opinion."[19]

In the eyes of some, this reference provides us with the earliest non-Christian reference to the crucifixion of Jesus. Specifically, from this perspective, it provides independent confirmation of the Gospel account of the unusual darkness that fell when Jesus was crucified (Matt. 27:45; Mark 15:33; Luke 23:44–45). According to others, however, it provides nothing of the sort.

For one thing, critics argue, it is not clear that Thallus was referring to the time of Jesus's crucifixion. This interpretation is provided by Julius. For another, even if Thallus was originally referring to the time of Jesus's crucifixion, the source of this information may have been the Christian tradition itself. In this case, Thallus was taking the Christian claim that darkness fell during Jesus's crucifixion as fact but offering an alternative explanation for it.[20] In either case, it is argued, Julius's reference to Thallus cannot be taken as providing any independent historical corroboration of the Gospel incident.

Two considerations make us hesitant to concede the critics' point. First, though it is not altogether impossible, it strikes us as highly unlikely that a Roman historian would take the claims of a recent and relatively minor religious sect so seriously that it would warrant a counterexplanation—*unless he believed it to be true on other grounds*. We must remember that Thallus was writing a mere two decades after the unusual "eclipse" allegedly took place.

Second, we think it very improbable that Julius provided the interpretation that the eclipse Thallus spoke of was the unusual darkness that fell during Jesus's crucifixion. Unlike us, Julius was aware of the full context of Thallus's quote. With this in mind, we have to ask why Julius argued that Thallus was *mistaken* in explaining away the darkness that occurred during Jesus's crucifixion? As Maurice Goguel has argued, if Julius had simply found a reference to an eclipse that corresponded to the time of Jesus's crucifixion, it seems he would have taken this as *confirming* the Christian tradition, not as a *counterexplanation* he had to argue against.[21]

For these reasons, it seems to us more likely than not that Thallus's remark constitutes the earliest evidence of Jesus outside the New Testament and plausibly the earliest non-Christian confirmation of an aspect of the Gospel account of the crucifixion.

Mara bar Serapion

Sometime between the late first century and the third century, a man named Mara bar Serapion wrote a letter to his son from prison. In it he warns his son, who apparently was a governing official, of the folly of persecuting wise and good

---

19. As cited in Harris, "References to Jesus," 343.

20. Wells, *Jesus Myth*, 285n1; Doherty, *The Jesus Puzzle: Did Christianity Begin with a Mythical Christ?* (Ottawa: Canadian Humanist Pub., 1999), 203.

21. Goguel, *Jesus the Nazarene*, 91–92.

men. He recounts the woes that fell on the Athenians after murdering Socrates. He speaks of the hardships that fell on the Samosians after putting Pythagoras to death. And, most significant for our purposes, he refers to the mistake the Jews made when they killed "their wise king, because their kingdom was taken away at that very time."[22] No one doubts that the reference to the loss of the Jewish kingdom refers to the destruction of Jerusalem and the scattering of the Jews in 70 CE. Hence, some argue that this letter gives us an independent reference to the death of Jesus.

Other scholars are not convinced of this, however. The reference to the "wise king" may be to someone other than Jesus. If Serapion wanted to refer to Jesus, they argue, why did he not do so by name, as he did Socrates and Pythagoras? But even if the reference is to Jesus, they contend, we know that some early Christians believed Jerusalem was destroyed as divine punishment for the crucifixion of Jesus, and so it may be that Serapion was simply passing on this unsubstantiated hearsay to his son. Related to this, the letter may be as late as the third century, by which time aspects of the Christian tradition had widely circulated throughout the Roman Empire. Thus, many argue that this passage cannot be treated as an independent attestation of Jesus's existence or of his death.

In response, it seems to us that the suggestion that Serapion is referring to someone other than Jesus is a stretch. We know both from New Testament authors and Josephus that Jesus was regarded by Christians and even some non-Christians as both "wise" and, in some sense, a "king" (Mark 15:26; *Antiquities* 18.3.3.63). Moreover, Serapion clearly assumed his son would know who he was referring to, otherwise his reference to this "wise king" has no point. How many Jews, martyred before the destruction of Jerusalem, were known by pagans throughout the Roman Empire in the second or third centuries as "wise kings"—to the point of possibly being household names, on a par with Socrates and Pythagorus? It would seem that Jesus is the only viable candidate.

The objection that Serapion may be dependent upon Christian sources for his information carries more weight, especially in light of the fact that the dating of this letter has not been firmly established. However, as we have already suggested, it is clear that Serapion was not himself a Christian. Immediately following his reference to Jesus being "a wise king," he says, "nor is the wise king [dead], because of the new laws he laid down." In this respect, Serapion argues, he is like Socrates, who lives on in the teachings of Plato, and Pythagorus, who lives on in the statue of Juno.[23] We submit that it is extremely unlikely that *a Christian* would have discussed with his son how Jesus continues to "live on" without mentioning the resurrection, or that he would have compared the postmortem life of Jesus to that of Socrates or Pythagorus. So, while we cannot rule out the possibility that Serapion is dependent on Christian teachings for his information, we have no

22. As cited in Van Voorst, *Jesus outside the New Testament*, 54.
23. Ibid.

reason to assume that he was. And even if this was the case, Serapion's letter at the very least suggests that some pagans between the first and third centuries did not question the existence of Jesus. Indeed, it suggests that some held him in a positive light and believed he was put to death unjustly.

Pliny the Younger

Pliny the Younger, the nephew and adopted son of Pliny the Elder, was a Roman senator, lawyer, and civilian administrator. He published nine books of letters in his own time. In about the year 110 CE, while governor of Bithynia, Pliny wrote to the Emperor Trajan asking him for advice on dealing with Christians in his territory. In the course of the letter, Pliny recounts information about Christians he had gathered from people who had defected from the faith under threat of death. He says,

> They [the former Christians] assured me that the sum total of their error consisted in the fact that they regularly assembled on a certain day before daybreak. They recited a hymn antiphonally to Christus as if to a god, and bound themselves with an oath not to commit any crime, but to abstain from theft, robbery, adultery, breach of faith, and embezzlement of property entrusted to them. After this it was their custom to separate, and then to come together again to partake of a meal, but of an ordinary and innocent one.[24]

Those legendary-Jesus theorists who deny Jesus's historical existence point out that this is a report about what Christians themselves believed about "Christ"—not as a historical figure, but as a mythical savior god. As G. A. Wells puts it,

> His letter demonstrates no more than that Christians existed in the early second century and worshipped Christ.... it represented what, by then, Christians believed, not what was necessarily historically the case.[25]

Hence, Wells and others argue that while this report gives us insight into the beliefs and practices of Christians in the early second century, it cannot be treated as providing any independent historical information.

This much is true. At the same time, however, it is interesting that Pliny notes that Christ was worshipped by Christians "as if" (Latin, *quasi*) he were a god. This may suggest that both Pliny and the former Christians he interrogated assumed that Jesus was a historical person. Pliny was simply reporting that Christians worship this man as a god.[26] Still, Pliny is dependent on the ex-Christians he interrogated

24. Book 10, Letter 96. As cited in Evans, "Jesus in Non-Christian Sources," 459.
25. Wells, *Jesus Myth*, 197.
26. Goguel, *Jesus the Nazarene*, 39–40; Harris, "References to Jesus," 346–47. However, A. N. Sherwin-White has shown that Pliny sometimes used *quasi* to mean "as" rather than "as if." And if this is Pliny's meaning in this passage, one cannot read his statement as presupposing that Jesus existed as a historical

for his information, so this reference provides no independent attestation to the historical existence of Jesus.[27]

This source is nevertheless valuable not only because it likely indicates that both Christians and non-Christians assumed Jesus was a historical person at the beginning of the second century, but also because it demonstrates that by this time the Christian movement had become numerous enough in the region of Bithynia to be problematic to its ruler. This is remarkable for a religion that had been around for less than eighty years and in varying degrees had been persecuted from its inception.

What is more, Pliny's testimony tells us that the Christians of this time worshipped Jesus as God, a point that confirms the view of Jesus given by the New Testament. Indeed, it tells us that some Christians were willing to die for this belief, even though the information Pliny gathered came from others who decided to defect from the faith to spare their lives.

Suetonius

In the fifth volume of his *Lives of the Caesars*, the Roman historian Suetonius refers to the expulsion of Jews from Rome during Claudius's reign in 49 CE. Writing in about 120 CE, he notes that Claudius "expelled the Jews from Rome, since they were always making disturbances because of the instigator Chrestus."[28] Some scholars argue that this reference to Chrestus is a reference to "Christ" (Jesus).

Objectors point out that the passage simply refers to some otherwise unknown troublemaker named Chrestus and argue that the attempt to link "Chrestus" with "Christ" is nothing more than unwarranted speculation.[29] But even if the reference is to Christ, others argue, Suetonius is probably dependent upon Christian hearsay for his information. As Doherty puts it, "Even if Chrestus refers to Christ, the original situation may have related to Roman Christians who followed a mythic Christ . . . [Suetonius] may have been influenced by Christian hearsay in Rome about the reputed founder of the movement."[30]

Of course, it is true that we do not know what Suetonius used for his source and thus cannot rule out his using Christian hearsay. But it seems unlikely that a Roman historian of the stature of Suetonious, who we know had access to Roman libraries and archives, would pay any serious attention to, let alone solely rely on, hearsay from

---

man (Sherwin-White, *Fifty Letters of Pliny* [Oxford: Oxford University Press, 1967], 177). On this point see Van Voorst, *Jesus outside the New Testament*, 28–29.

27. So concludes Evans, "Jesus in Non-Christian Sources," 459; France, *Evidence for Jesus*, 43; Meier, *Marginal Jew*, 1:92; Van Voorst, *Jesus outside the New Testament*, 29.

28. As cited in Van Voorst, *Jesus outside the New Testament*, 30.

29. See S. Benko, "The Edict of Claudius of A.D. 49," *Theologische Zeitschrift* 25 (1969): 406–18; H. D. Slingerland, *Claudian Policymaking and the Early Imperial Repression of Judaism at Rome* (Atlanta: Scholars Press, 1997). See also Doherty, *Jesus Puzzle*, 203; Martin, *Case against Christianity*, 51–52.

30. Doherty, *Jesus Puzzle*, 203. See also Wells, *Jesus Myth*, 197–98.

a discredited minor religious sect.[31] This supposition becomes even more unlikely when we consider that Suetonius is speaking of an edict from a Roman official that in all probability would have been recorded in official court documents.

It is also true that, while the identification of Chrestus with Christ is speculative, it is hardly an unreasonable conjecture. It is significant that Chrestus was a common name among Gentiles but never used by Jews, so far as we know.[32] At the same time, one can easily understand Suetonius mistaking a Jewish title ("Christ") he was unfamiliar with for a common Greek name and thus emending it to Chrestus.[33]

It is also significant that Luke tells us that the Jews were temporarily expelled from Rome by Claudius in 49 CE (Acts 18:2). It is very easy to surmise that Suetonius (or his source) mistakenly understood a riot that had broken out over the preaching of Christ as being instigated by Christ himself, whom, as we have suggested, he mistook to be the proper Greek name Chrestus. While certainty is impossible, at the very least we have here an early non-Christian source that confirms Luke's accuracy about the expulsion of Jews by Claudius.

Celsus

In the late second century, the Neoplatonist philosopher Celsus wrote the first known full-scale attack on Christianity, titled *True Doctrine*.[34] Celsus denigrates the idea of the virgin birth and claims that Jesus was illegitimately born when Mary committed adultery. He argues that Jesus grew up to be a small and ugly man, that he gathered a small following of sailors and tax collectors, and that he amazed them with displays of sorcery and magic, a craft Celsus says he learned in Egypt. Celsus further claims that Jesus taught his disciples to beg and steal for a living and that when he died, hysterical women reported a resurrection.[35]

We know from Celsus's own work that he was familiar with a number of New Testament texts as well as other Christian apologetic works. There is therefore little reason to suppose that Celsus had access to any independent sources of information about Jesus. Add to this the fact that his work is intensely polemical— often resorting to caricature and lampooning—and we must conclude that there is little of historical value in Celsus's work as it concerns Jesus.

31. On Suetonius's access to sources, see G. Kennedy, "Classical and Christian Source Criticism," in *The Relationship among the Gospels: An Interdisciplinarian Dialogue* (San Antonio: Trinity University Press, 1978), 141.

32. Van Voorst, *Jesus outside the New Testament*, 33. As Van Voorst notes, the name "Chrestus" is never found among Jewish inscriptions in Rome, as attested by D. Noy, *Jewish Inscriptions of Western Europe*, vol. 2: *The City of Rome* (New York: Cambridge University Press, 1995).

33. So argues Meier, *Marginal Jew*, 1:92. Other scholars who conclude that it is likely Suetonius is referring to Jesus include Evans, "Jesus in Non-Christian Sources," 457–58; Harris, "References to Jesus," 353–54; Van Voorst, *Jesus outside the New Testament*, 29–39.

34. While the work is lost, Origen preserved vast portions of it in his rebuttal, *Against Celsus*.

35. For a helpful summary, see Van Voorst, *Jesus outside the New Testament*, 66–67. This summary can be gathered from Origen, *Against Celsus*, 1.28, 32, 39, 62; 2.6, 32, 44–55; 6.75; 8.41.

The one point that is worth noting concerns Celsus's contention that Jesus was a sorcerer and a magician. This was a common explanation for Jesus's supernatural ministry among early opponents of Christianity, especially among Jews. According to the Gospels, even during his lifetime adversaries alleged that Jesus cast out demons through the power of the devil (e.g., Mark 3:22). What is significant is that no one in the ancient world seems to have flatly denied that Jesus performed miracles—let alone that he existed. Rather, they grant that he was a wonder-worker but offer a different manner of explanation for how he performed his feats. And this, it seems, is difficult to explain on the assumption that the Jesus story was nothing more than a recently created legend. If the Jesus story was in fact a recent legend, it seems the ancient critics could have, and most certainly would have, argued this point instead of wasting time offering counterexplanations for his miracles.

Lucian of Samosata

A final reference of minor importance comes from Lucian's work, *The Death of Peregrinus*, written sometime after 165 CE. In this work Lucian warns his readers about the dangers of the teachings of the Christians, for he holds that these teachings contributed to the ruin of Peregrinus. In the course of his warning, he refers to Christ as "that other whom [Christians] still worship, the man who was crucified in Palestine because he introduced this new cult into the world." And he continues:

> [The Christians'] first lawgiver persuaded them that they are all brothers of one another after they have transgressed once for all by denying the Greek gods and by worshipping the crucified sophist himself and living according to his laws. Therefore they despise all things equally and regard them common, without certain evidence accepting such things.[36]

Since Christian claims were well known in most quarters of the Roman Empire by the late second century, some legendary-Jesus theorists argue that we must assume that all Lucian's information was based on secondhand reports "of what Christians now believed about their origins."[37] It thus does not represent anything like independent, reliable information about Jesus.

We are not entirely convinced of this. It may be significant that the word Lucian uses for crucifixion (*anaskolopizein*) is not the common one, and certainly not the one used in the Gospels (*stauroun*). It literally means "to impale," which is not how any early Christian described Jesus's death. This deviation from Christian tradition may indicate that Lucian is relying on an independent tradition. As Craig Evans points out, it "suggests that Lucian's knowledge of Jesus, 'the man crucified in Palestine,' may not be limited to Christian tradition."[38]

36. As cited in Evans, "Jesus in Non-Christian Sources," 462.
37. Doherty, *Jesus Puzzle*, 200–201.
38. Evans, "Jesus in Non-Christian Sources," 462.

Tacitus

Having addressed the dubious sources and sources of minimal value, we now consider three references that fall within Evans's third category of non-Christian sources—"important sources." With Evans, we concur that these texts are the most convincing examples of ancient, independent, non-Christian sources about Jesus. We first consider a passage from the early second-century Roman historian, Tacitus.

Cornelius Tacitus was proconsul of Asia for two years (112–113 CE) and author of the *Annals* and the *Histories*, both of which survive today only in portions. The *Annals*, Tacitus's last and unfinished work, covers the period from Augustus through Nero (14–68 CE) and was composed in at least sixteen volumes. Only parts of books 1–4 and 12–15 have survived.

The portion of the *Annals* that is of interest to us (15.44) was most likely written around 115 CE. The passage comes in the context of a discussion of the great fire of Rome under Nero's reign. Here Tacitus reports:

> Therefore, to stop the rumor [that the burning of Rome had taken place by order], Nero substituted as culprits, and punished in the utmost refinements of cruelty, a class of men, loathed for their vices, whom the crowd styled Christians. Christus, the founder of the name, had undergone the death penalty in the reign of Tiberius, by sentence of the procurator Pontius Pilatus, and the pernicious superstition was checked for a moment, only to break out once more, not merely in Judea, the home of the disease, but in the capital itself, where all things horrible or shameful in the world collect and find a vogue.[39]

If Tacitus's statement can be trusted, it tells us three things about Jesus. First, it confirms that the time of his execution was during the reign of Tiberius (14–37 CE) and during Pilate's governorship (26–36 CE). Second, it confirms that Jesus's death was by execution order of the Roman governor of Judea, Pilate. And third, it claims that the movement was temporarily suppressed but broke out again even in Rome. The passage thus gives further evidence that in the span of three decades (since the time of Tiberius and Pilate) the Christian movement had grown to the point where it could be made a plausible scapegoat for a Roman emperor.[40] If this passage is authentic and reliable, therefore, it is of some significance in confirming certain aspects of the Gospels' record about Jesus.

Questioning Tacitus

Not all scholars agree that the Tacitus passage can be trusted, however. Four major arguments have been raised against the authenticity and/or reliability of this passage.

39. Tacitus, *Annals*, trans. C. H. Moore and J. Jackson, LCL, reprint ed. (Cambridge, MA: Harvard University Press, 1962), 283.
40. A point made by Meier, *Marginal Jew*, 1:91.

First, a few scholars have suggested that this passage could be a later Christian interpolation.[41] The fact that the passage is never quoted by later Christian writers is sometimes taken as evidence in support of this claim.

Second, Tacitus identifies Pontius Pilate as a "procurator" of Judea when we now know from an ancient inscription that the official term usually used for Pilate's position during his reign was "prefect."[42] "Procurator" was the term used in Tacitus's day and, it is argued, he anachronistically applied it to Pilate. Some argue that this calls into question his reliability as a historian and thus calls into question the information reported in this passage.

Third, Tacitus refers to the founder of the Christian movement as "Christus," the Christian title for Jesus, instead of "Jesus," his legal name. To some this suggests that Tacitus relied on "popular Christian mythology" for his information about Jesus's execution rather than reliable, independent information (e.g., official Roman records).[43]

Fourth, some argue that it is unlikely that the trial of a minor insurrectionist would have been recorded in Roman records. And even if it had, it is unlikely that Tacitus would have had access to these archives. Not only this, but even if Tacitus had such access, there is no reason to suppose he would have been motivated to investigate the Christian claim about Jesus's execution under Pilate. Hence, some conclude, we have compelling reasons to suppose that this passage in the *Annals* is based on nothing more than early second-century Christian hearsay.

There are several things that can be said in response to each of these arguments.

Is the Passage a Christian Interpolation?

There is no compelling reason to think the passage under consideration is an interpolation. While the earliest extant manuscript is dated to the eleventh century, the manuscript tradition of the *Annals* is nonetheless stable in its inclusion of the essential elements of this passage.[44] Moreover, there is nothing about the passage that suggests a Christian inserted it. To the contrary, it is rather difficult to imagine a Christian describing Christianity as a deadly "superstition" that fosters "shameful" acts. What is more, one would not expect a Christian interpolator to leave the account of Christian origins with Jesus's execution. Rather, one would

41. See, e.g., A. Drews, *The Christ Myth*, trans. C. D. Burns, 3rd ed. (Amherst, NY: Prometheus, 1998), 231–33.

42. The correct title was identified from the so-called "Pilate stone" found in Caesarea Maritima in 1962. See J. J. Rousseau and R. Arav, "Pontius Pilate's Stone," in *Jesus and His World: An Archaeological and Cultural Dictionary* (Minneapolis: Fortress, 1995), 225–27.

43. Doherty, *Jesus Puzzle*, 201.

44. While there is some discussion about the text in certain respects, nothing of note hangs upon it in this passage except the question of "Christians" vs. "Chrestians." The latter is found in the earliest available manuscript and almost certainly reflects the original. For a helpful discussion and bibliography, see Van Voorst, *Jesus outside the New Testament*, 42–44.

expect a Christian interpolator to at least allude to Jesus's resurrection, such as we find with the clear interpolation into Josephus's account of Jesus (see below).

The fact that the Tacitus passage is never cited by early Christian writers hardly supports the interpolation theory. It is not clear how well known Tacitus's work was to later Christian authors. But even if we assume it was known, it is hard to imagine what purpose Christian authors would have had for quoting a passage that is so demeaning to their faith. We thus find ourselves in agreement with John Meier when he concludes: "Despite some feeble attempts to show that this text is a Christian interpolation in Tacitus, the passage is obviously genuine."[45]

The Use of an Anachronistic Title

What are we to make of the fact that Tacitus identified Pilate by an anachronistic title? In our view, not much. First, our estimation of this or any other passage in Tacitus must be made in light of our assessment of Tacitus's trustworthiness as a historian in general. Interestingly, there is virtually unanimous agreement among scholars that Tacitus was, by ancient standards, a very careful historian.[46] He read widely, used multiple sources when available, and held a healthy sense of caution toward his sources.[47] According to Arnaldo Momigliano, Tacitus was "a writer whose reliability cannot be seriously questioned."[48] Indeed, some scholars regard him as "the most accurate of all Roman historians."[49] Whatever else we make of his anachronistic ascription of Pilate's office, therefore, it should not be taken as evidence that he was generally unreliable.

Regarding the ascription itself, it is entirely possible that Tacitus was intentionally anachronistic for the sake of clarity. Since "procurator" was the accepted title of Pilate's position among Tacitus's audience, he may have used the term knowing

---

45. Meier, *Marginal Jew*, 1:90; see also Evans, "Jesus in Non-Christian Sources," 465.

46. Evans thus argues that it is far more likely that Tacitus's anachronism is due to whatever sources he is using rather than his sloppiness as a historian ("Jesus in Non-Christian Sources," 465). For a number of the following points on Tacitus as a historian, we are indebted to the article and bibliography of J. P. Holding, "Nero's Scapegoats: Cornelius Tacitus," www.tektonics.org/tekton_01_01_01_TC.html.

47. The older claim that Tacitus used only a single source is now generally rejected. See D. Dudley, *The World of Tacitus* (Boston: Little, Brown, & Co., 1968), 29; D. Martin, *Tacitus* (Berkeley: University of California Press, 1981), 211.

48. A. Momigliano, *The Classical Foundations of Modern Historiography* (Berkeley: University of California Press, 1990), 111–12.

49. R. Mellor, *Tacitus* (New York: Routledge, 1993), 40. Mellor notes that Tacitus's "deep skepticism served him especially well" (p. 37). He "consulted both obscure and obvious sources" (p. 32) and "distinguishes fact from rumor with a scrupulosity rare in any ancient historian" (p. 45). According to the Tacitian specialist Ronald Syme, Tacitus was precise in his documentation, his "prime quality" was "distrust," and he was "no stranger to industrious investigation" (*Tacitus* [Oxford: Clarendon, 1958], 1:398, 281). C. W. Mendell notes that in books 11 to 16 of the *Annals*—the section in which our passage falls—Tacitus "concerns himself with the evidence and source references to a greater extent than in the earlier books" (*Tacitus: The Man and His Work* [New Haven: Yale University Press, 1957], 207). On this point see also Mellor, *Tacitus*, 44.

full well that the position used to be titled "prefect." But it is even more likely that we are making too much of the distinction between "procurator" and "prefect" in the ancient world, for the evidence suggests that these terms were rather fluid in the first century.

For example, though the "Pilate stone" discovered at Caesarea Maritima gives Pilate the title "prefect," both Philo (*Legat.* 38) and Josephus (*Jewish War* 2.9.2.169) refer to him as "procurator" (Greek *epitropos*), just as Tacitus does. In fact, Josephus sometimes uses the two terms interchangeably.[50] In light of this, Murray Harris writes:

> It seems reasonable to suppose that there was a certain fluidity of terminology regarding the titles of the governor of Judea, at least in popular usage, during the period A.D. 6–66, but that from A.D. 6–41 the titles *praefectus* or *pro legato* predominated, while after the reconstitution of the province, from A.D. 44–66, the term procurator (= *epitropos*) became the common designation. During both periods, however, the unofficial term "governor" (*hegemon*) was also used, as it is in the New Testament of Pilate (e.g., Mt. 27:2; Lk 20:20; also Jos. Ant. [18.3.1.55]) and other Roman officials governing Judea (e.g., Acts 23:26; 26:30).

Hence, regarding Tacitus's alleged "mistake," Harris concludes, "We can scarcely accuse Tacitus . . . of being inaccurate or ill-informed on this point."[51]

Did Tacitus Rely on Hearsay?

No compelling case can be made that Tacitus is relying on hearsay in this passage simply because he referred to the founder of the Christian movement as "Christ" rather than by his proper name. For one thing, it is improbable that Tacitus, who elsewhere proves himself to be a reliable historian who routinely consults sources, would at this point rely solely on the hearsay of a group he himself identifies as a "pernicious superstition" and as evil.[52] Moreover, by the early second century "Christ" and "Jesus" could be used interchangeably, both by Christians and non-Christians. Thus we need not suppose that Tacitus's use of the title "Christ" reflects a sole dependency on Christians as his source of information.

Additionally, it is important to note that the passage we are concerned with is not about *Jesus* per se but about *Christians*. Tacitus only mentions "Christ"

---

50. To illustrate, Josephus refers to two different governors of Judea, Cuspius Fadus (ca. 44–46) and Porcius Festus (ca. 59–61) by both terms at different places (for Fadus see *Antiquities* 19.9.2.363, 20.1.1.2, and 20.1.2.14; for Festus see *Antiquities* 20.8.11.193 and *Jewish War* 2.14.1.271). In fact, "procurator" predominates in Josephus.

51. Harris, "References to Jesus," 349–50.

52. On Tacitus's use of sources, see Mendell, *Tacitus*, 211; Syme, *Tacitus*, 282; Mellor, *Tacitus*, 32–35. G. A. Wells cites a single source—the 1893 work of Philippe Fabia—to argue that Tacitus rarely consulted written sources; see *The Jesus of the Early Christians* (London: Pemberton, 1971), 187. The consensus of recent scholarship on Tacitus stands against him.

in order to explain the origin of the term "Christians." A reference to "Jesus" at this point would not have explained the term "Christian" and thus would have been completely beside the point.[53] We conclude, then, that Tacitus's use of "Christ" in no way undermines the independent historical value of this passage.

Related to this, there is no reason to suppose that Tacitus would not have been interested in substantiating his information about Christians and would not have had access to official documents to do so.[54] Tacitus consistently demonstrates a motivation to critically check his sources. We have no reason to suppose he would not have been so motivated here. In fact, three considerations lead us to conclude that, if anything, Tacitus would have been *more* motivated than usual to check out his sources on this topic.

First, the subject of the passage is an official action taken by a Roman emperor. Second, Tacitus consistently reflects an unusual fascination with, and animosity toward, "pretenders" and superstitions, particularly those connected with claims of having been raised from the dead.[55] And third, throughout his work Tacitus is very concerned with the happenings of members of the royal court, and there is some indication that several members of the royal family had aligned themselves with this "cult."[56]

All of this explains why Tacitus speaks so acrimoniously about the "pernicious superstition" of the Christian movement, even though he is clearly moved by the horrendous pain Nero inflicted on them. But it also suggests that, if ever Tacitus would have been concerned to check out his information, it would have been in a context such as the one we are considering.

Would Tacitus Have Had Access to Official Documents?

Tacitus may have had the motivation to carefully investigate his sources, but would he have had the means? A rather solid case can be made that he would have. We must remember that Tacitus was a person of some renown. He was a widely respected orator and held a number of esteemed governmental posts, including proconsul of Asia and Roman consulship. He was well connected, being friends with Pliny the Younger and married to a daughter of Britain's governor, Julius Agricola. If anyone would have had access to court documents, it would have been someone like Tacitus.

53. See Van Voorst, *Jesus outside the New Testament*, 46.
54. The following points are highlighted by Holding in "Nero's Scapegoats."
55. G. W. Bowersock, "Tacitus and the Province of Asia," in *Tacitus and the Tacitean Tradition*, ed. T. J. Luce and A. J. Woodman (Princeton: Princeton University Press, 1993), 5.
56. It is also not without significance that in the late 90s, Emperor Domitian's niece Domatilla and her husband Favius Clemens were accused of "atheism" as well as "being carried away into Jewish customs." Many scholars believe that they had in fact become Christians, since only Christians were commonly accused of being both atheists and Jewish. For discussion on this point, see S. Benko, *Pagan Rome and the Early Christians* (Bloomington: Indiana University Press, 1984), 15–16.

What we do know is that Tacitus had access to the *Acta Senatus*—the Senate's archives of its own activities—for he cites these archives twice in his work (*Annals* 5.4; 15.74), and his further use of them is implied by his detailed reports of Senate happenings.[57] Any official communications about Jesus's crucifixion, or even communications that incidentally mention the matter, may well have been found in these archives. It is therefore possible that Tacitus consulted such correspondence for his information about the crucifixion of Jesus under Pilate. At the same time, there were other sources that would have been readily available to Tacitus, including Rome's public libraries, the *Acta Diurna* (a daily gazette), biographies, letters, and speeches.

Since Tacitus does not tell us where he acquired his information (a practice that is typical for ancient historians), we can never move beyond an educated guess. What seems clear, however, is that, whatever his sources may have been, Tacitus consistently "distinguishes fact from rumor with a scrupulosity rare in any ancient historian."[58] A report of Tacitus "very seldom shows him to be false to fact." And "when the sources differ and the truth is hard to decipher, [Tacitus] takes refuge in ambiguous language or the balance of alternative and sometimes spiteful variants."[59]

We thus have every reason to assume that, had Tacitus been forced to rely solely on the rumors of a "pernicious superstition" for his report, he would have given us some indication of this fact. At the very least, we would have expected him to qualify his report by saying something like, "*Christians claim that* Christus, the author of their name, had suffered the death penalty." But he does nothing of the sort. His report of Jesus's crucifixion under Pilate is given with the same confidence, and in the same breath, as his report about Christians suffering under Nero. We have as much reason to trust Tacitus regarding the former report as we do the latter.

All these considerations suggest Tacitus is an independent—and thus important—non-Christian source about Jesus. Tacitus's report demonstrates that a mere thirty years after Jesus died (hence while many living witnesses of the founder were still alive) his followers were willing to be put to death for their faith, and in ways that were so barbaric it moved a very unsympathetic Roman historian to pity them.[60] Thus, Tacitus's report provides solid, independent, non-Christian evidence for the life and death of Jesus, the remarkable resolve of his earliest followers, and the astounding early growth of the movement he founded.

57. See Mendell, *Tacitus*, 21, 212; Syme, *Tacitus*, 278, 281; Mellor, *Tacitus*, 19–20, 33. Tacitus tells us he did not gain access to the *Commentarii Principis*—the court journal of the emperor (*Histories* 4.40).

58. Mellor, *Tacitus*, 45.

59. K. Wellesley, "Tacitus as a Military Historian," in *Tacitus,* ed. T. A. Dorey (New York: Basic, 1969), 65–66.

60. Tacitus writes (*Annals*, 15.45) that, in spite of their guilt, "there arose a sentiment of pity" for the Christians, due to the heinous nature of their tortures and the fact that they were less a threat to the state than an easy scapegoat for Nero.

Josephus's "James Passage"

The second important non-Christian source is undoubtedly the most signifi-cant. Flavius Josephus is the single most important Jewish historian of the ancient world. His two most important works are *The Antiquities of the Jews*, which traces Jewish history from creation to his own day, and *The Wars of the Jews (Jewish War)*, which chronicles Jewish history from the Maccabean revolt to the fall of Masada in 73 CE. While scholars agree that Josephus is often biased and self-serving in his writings, most also agree that he is in general a rather reliable historian.[61] As noted earlier, there are two passages in Josephus's *Antiquities* that mention Jesus.[62] In this section we will consider the shorter and less significant of the two. This passage—often referred to as "the James passage"—simply mentions Jesus in passing as a means of identifying his brother James. It reads,

> When, therefore, Ananus [the high priest] was of this [angry] disposition, he thought he had now a proper opportunity [to exercise his authority]. Festus was

61. Paul Spilsbury has recently argued that, while Josephus certainly assimilated himself to the inevitabilities of Roman rule, "he was not simply the imperial 'stooge' he is sometimes caricatured to have been." Rather, Josephus offered his fellow Jews "a coherent and workable theory about the legitimacy of Roman rule in the light of a biblical reading of the providence of God" ("Flavius Josephus on the Rise and Fall of the Roman Empire," *JTS* 54 [2003]: 21). With regard to Josephus's treatment of historical sources, P. Bilde notes the "surprising conclusion" that contemporary Josephan scholars have reached, that "he remains loyal towards his sources as far as their substance, main contents, and their most essential data are concerned" (*Flavius Josephus between Jerusalem and Rome: His Life, His Works and Their Importance* [Sheffield: Sheffield Academic Press, 1988], 196). Mireille Hadas-Lebel has recently argued that it is high time that we render Josephus his due as a significant historian of Rome. In fact, he argues that "the passages in *Ant* 18–20 devoted exclusively to Roman history do not suffer by comparison to parallel passages by Suetonius or Tacitus" ("Flavius Josephus, Historian of Rome," in *Josephus and the History of the Greco-Roman Period*, ed. F. Parente and J. Sievers [New York: Brill, 1994], 99). It is worth noting that these are the very chapters in which we find the two passages on Jesus.

62. In the early twentieth century, an Old Russian translation of *Jewish War* surfaced. It has come to be known as Slavonic Josephus. In the Greek texts of *Jewish War*, there is no mention of Jesus. But in Slavonic Josephus, *four* passages refer to Jesus. They include claims about Jesus's wondrous feats, the Jewish leaders' jealousy toward Jesus, the bribing of Pilate, the hanging of a tablet contain-ing charges against Jesus on the temple gate, and details about the empty tomb and resurrection. These four passages seem to be clear instances of Christian interpolations. For example, the first and longest passage reflects christological controversies that took place long after Josephus. The Slavonic text seems to use the New Testament at several points to develop its story of Jesus. The most obvious problem is the text-critical one. In all of its other forms, the various texts of *Jewish War* never mention Jesus. With the exception of Robert Eisler and George A. Williamson, no serious twentieth-century scholars have considered the authenticity of the Slavonic text a serious possibility. See R. Eisler, *The Messiah Jesus and John the Baptist*, trans. A. Krappe (London: Methuen, 1931); G. A. Williamson, *The World of Josephus* (Boston: Little, Brown, 1964), 308–9. For negative assessments of the authen-ticity of Slavonic Josephus, see S. Zeitlin, "The Hoax of the 'Slavonic Josephus,'" *Jewish Quarterly Review* 39 (1948–49): 171–80; Van Voorst, *Jesus outside the New Testament*, 85–88; Evans, "Jesus in Non-Christian Sources," 453.

now dead, and Albinus was but upon the road. So he assembled the sanhedrin of judges, and brought before them the brother of Jesus, who was called Christ, whose name was James." (*Antiquities* 20.9.1)[63]

If this passage is authentic, it not only confirms the existence of Jesus but also the New Testament's claim that James was the brother of Jesus. This latter point is especially significant because Paul mentions James, the brother of the Lord, as a contemporary of his (Gal. 1:19). This means that Paul would have viewed Jesus as a recent contemporary, thereby refuting the Christ myth theory that Paul thought of Jesus as a mythological figure who lived in the distant past. If authentic, the passage forces the question of how Jesus could have arisen to the status of the embodiment of Yahweh by means of legendary accretion while his brother was still alive—indeed, with his brother becoming *one of his followers*! This is not at all easy to explain, especially in a first-century Palestinian Jewish context. It forces us to consider strongly the possibility that Jesus was in fact the kind of figure presented in the Gospels.

The Case for the Inauthenticity of the "James Passage"

Not all scholars agree that this passage is authentic, however.[64] Some, including the evangelical scholar Graham Twelftree, suspect it is a Christian interpolation.[65] There are eight considerations that are offered by various scholars in support of this view.

THE MANUSCRIPT PROBLEM

The textual support for Josephus's *Antiquities* is sparse. We possess only a dozen manuscripts of *Antiquities*, and the three Greek manuscripts that are most reliable date from the thirteenth century. The large gap between the original and the extant copies of *Antiquities* makes it easy to suppose Christians inserted their own ideas at some point in the text's transmission.

THE MENTION OF CHRISTOS (MESSIAH)

Though Josephus mentions many "messiah" figures, he never uses the term "Christos" in his works except in connection with Jesus. As a pro-Roman historian, his avoidance of this term makes sense since this term was associated with political revolutionaries in some quarters. To some, this suggests that he did not pen either of the passages that mention Jesus.

63. *The Works of Josephus*, trans. W. Whiston (Peabody, MA: Hendrickson, 1987), 537–38.
64. For a general survey of views, see Paul Winter, "Excursus II—Josephus on Jesus and James: *Ant.* xviii 3, 3 (63–4) and xx 9, 1 (200–3)," in Emil Schurer, *The History of the Jewish People in the Age of Jesus Christ (175 B.C.–A.D. 135)*, rev. and ed. Geza Vermes and Fergus Miller (Edinburgh: Clark, 1973), 1:428–30.
65. Twelftree, "Jesus in Jewish Traditions," 297–301.

THE ISSUE OF "LEGOMENOS"

Some have argued that Josephus refers to Jesus as the "so-called Christ" and have argued that no Christian would have spoken of Christ in this way. Hence the passage is authentic. But others argue the term *legomenos* need not be translated in this way. The term can be translated as "called" or "said to be." This is its clear meaning in several New Testament passages (Matt. 1:16; 27:17, 22; John 4:25). The fact that these passages link the term with Jesus strengthens the suspicion that a Christian wrote this.[66]

THE ORDER OF JAMES AND JESUS

The fact that Josephus mentions Jesus before James suggests to some that this passage is a Christian insertion. As Christ myth theorist Earl Doherty puts it, "Why would Josephus think to make the Jesus idea paramount, placing it before the James one?"[67]

THE VIEW OF ANANUS

The passage involves a very negative assessment of Ananus the high priest. However, when Josephus mentions Ananus in his earlier work, *Jewish War* (4.5.2), he is quite positive about him. Tessa Rajak notes this "startling divergence from the previous assessment," and on this basis concludes against the authenticity of the James passage.[68] One can easily imagine a Christian interpolator writing a scathing assessment of the high priest who had executed James, a hero of the early church.

EVIDENCE OF TEXTUAL ALTERATION

The third-century theologian Origen reported that Josephus believed Jerusalem fell because God was punishing the Jews for killing James (*Against Celsus* 1.47). No extant text of *Antiquities* contains this commentary. This information seems to have been inserted into the version of the text Origen was using, and the only ones who held the perspective expressed in this insertion were Christians.[69] Even though this particular interpolation did not survive into our present text, it suggests that Christians were tampering with Josephus's texts, and thus indirectly casts suspicion on the "James Passage."

THE FLOW OF THE PASSAGE

The passage reads naturally without any reference to Jesus; nothing is lost if Jesus's name is removed. Since the story is about Ananus, not James, there would

---

66. See the discussions in Winter, "Excursus II," 430–31; Twelftree, "Jesus in Jewish Traditions," 300.

67. Doherty, *Jesus Puzzle*, 217.

68. T. Rajak, *Josephus: The Historian and His Society* (Philadelphia: Fortress, 1983), 131n73.

69. For discussion see G. A. Wells, *The Jesus Legend* (LaSalle, IL: Open Court, 1996), 54–55; idem, *Jesus Myth*, 220.

be no need for Josephus to include an additional qualifier on James. A Christian interpolator, however, would have obvious motive to add this qualifier.[70]

THE OPAQUENESS OF THE REFERENCE

Finally, it is not clear why Josephus would mention "Jesus, who was called Christ" as a way of clarifying who James is, for his audience arguably would have known no more about Jesus than they would have about James.

Arguments for the Authenticity of the "James Passage"

The case against the authenticity of the "James passage" is formidable, and to some decisive. Nevertheless, there are several considerations that, in the minds of many other scholars, suffice to defuse these objections and render it more probable than not that the passage is authentic.

THE MANUSCRIPT TRADITION

It is true that the manuscript evidence for *Antiquities* is scant, but it is not more so than for most other ancient works. Hence the appeal to the possibility of interpolations on the basis of the lack of a more robust manuscript tradition is not very compelling in and of itself.

THE NEUTRALITY OF THE TEXT

As Craig Evans has noted, it is significant that there is in this passage "nothing Christian, or positive, in the reference to James or Jesus. The whole point seems to be to explain why Ananus was deposed as High Priest."[71] If a Christian had added this passage, one would have thought that much more would have been made of James and especially of Jesus. Instead, as John Meier points out, all we have here is "a passing, almost blasé reference to someone called James."[72] Once the force of this observation is recognized, the burden of proof begins to shift toward those who claim it as a Christian interpolation.

THE NEGATIVE ASSESSMENT OF ANANUS

We saw above that Tessa Rajak and others argue that the negative assessment of Ananus in this passage contradicts Josephus's earlier positive assessment in *Jewish War* (4.5.2). This argument is not particularly strong, however. For one thing, we frequently find tensions between accounts of the same event in *Jewish War* and *Antiquities*, as a number of scholars have noted.[73] But even more important, we can detect an unmistakable negative shift in Josephus's general attitude toward

---

70. This argument is offered by Doherty, *Jesus Puzzle*, 216.

71. Evans, "Jesus in Non-Christian Sources," 469.

72. Meier, *Marginal Jew*, 1:57.

73. See, e.g., L. H. Feldman, "Introduction," in *Josephus, Judaism and Christianity*, ed. L. Feldman and G. Hata (Detroit: Wayne State University Press, 1987), 56.

Jewish religious and political leadership between these two works.[74] The negative view of Ananus in this passage is consistent with this general shift. Therefore, nothing of any significance can be read into it.

The Way James Is Designated

Early Christians did not refer to James in the matter-of-fact way this passage does—simply calling him "the brother of Jesus." Rather, they tended to use more laudable titles such as "the brother of the Lord" or "the brother of the Savior."[75] This observation favors viewing this passage as authentic.

The Manner of James's Martyrdom

The account of James's martyrdom in Josephus differs noticeably from the traditional Christian account. From Eusebius, Hegesippus, and Clement of Alexandria, we learn that early Christians believed James was first thrown from the battlement of the temple by scribes and Pharisees. They then began to stone him but were stopped by a priest. Finally, James was clubbed to death by laundrymen. In contradiction to this, Josephus says simply that James was stoned to death by order of the high priest Ananus. Moreover, according to the Christian tradition, James was killed just prior to Vespasian's siege of Jerusalem in 70 CE. According to Josephus, he died before the Jewish war broke out, around 62 CE. The fact that the Josephan account differs so dramatically from the traditional Christian narrative suggests that this passage is not a Christian interpolation.[76]

The Title "Christ"

Josephus's use of the term "Christ" for Jesus does not necessarily suggest a Christian interpolation, as some have argued. It is true that Josephus nowhere else uses this title, but we can easily imagine why he would use it when describing the brother of James. Josephus mentions twenty-one other people with the name Jesus. Indeed, in the very same section as the James passage, he mentions a certain "Jesus, the son of Damneus." It seems Josephus simply knew that the brother of James was "called Christ" by his followers and so distinguished him from the other persons named "Jesus" he had already mentioned.[77] The very fact that Josephus says *legomenou Christou* ("*called* Christ") rather than "Jesus the Christ" suggests we are dealing with a historian who merely wanted to identify James by specifying his well-known brother—a brother who had followers who believed he was the Christ—rather than with a Christian interpolator.

---

74. For discussion on this point, see Meier, *Marginal Jew*, 1:59.
75. For example, as in Gal. 1:19 and in Hegesippus, a second-century Christian historian cited in Eusebius's *Ecclesiastical History* 2.23.4. See also 1 Cor. 9:5—"brothers of the Lord."
76. For discussion see Meier, *Marginal Jew*, 1:58.
77. A point noted by Twelftree, "Jesus in Jewish Traditions," 300.

ORIGEN'S REFERENCE

Finally, in his work against Celsus (ca. 248), Origen refers to Josephus's passage on the death of James. Origen most likely would not have cited this in his public apology unless he was quite sure his pagan readership would have found the passage in *Antiquities*—official copies of which apparently were available in the Roman public library.[78] For these reasons we conclude that it is more probable than not that the James passage is authentic.

The *Testimonium Flavianum*

As important as the James passage is in Josephus, it pales in comparison to the next passage. Known as the *Testimonium Flavianum*, this passage has been the focus of an incredible amount of scholarly attention—and for obvious reasons.[79] In its extant form it reads,

> About this time there lived Jesus, a wise man, if indeed one ought to call him a man. For he was one who wrought surprising feats and was a teacher of such people as accept the truth gladly. He won over many Jews and many of the Greeks. He was the Messiah. When Pilate, upon hearing him accused by men of the highest standing among us, had condemned him to be crucified, those who had in the first place come to love him did not give up their affection for him. On the third day he appeared to them restored to life, for the prophets of God had prophesied these and countless other marvelous things about him. And the tribe of the Christians, so called after him, has still to this day not disappeared. (*Antiquities* 18.3.3)[80]

Here we have the most important Jewish historian in ancient times ostensibly acknowledging not only that Jesus existed, but also that he was wise, performed miracles, was the Messiah, was crucified, and even rose from the dead! The issue, of course, is whether—or to what extent—this passage comes from the hand of Josephus himself.

Arguments against the Authenticity of the Testimonium

Six major arguments have been raised against the authenticity of the *Testimonium Flavianum*. Most scholars find that these arguments prove that, at

---

78. Origen, *Against Celsus*, 1.47. On the presence of *Antiquities* in Roman libraries in Origen's day, see Eusebius, *Ecclesiastical History*, 3.9. This line of argument in defense of the authenticity of the James passage has been presented effectively by A. Whealey, *Josephus on Jesus: The Testimonium Flavianum Controversy from Late Antiquity to Modern Times* (New York: Lang, 2003), 2.

79. For an excellent treatment of the history of the debate surrounding the *Testimonium Flavianum*, see Whealey, *Josephus on Jesus*.

80. For the text see Josephus, *Antiquities*, trans. L. H. Feldman, LCL (Cambridge, MA: Harvard University Press, 1965), 48, 50.

the very least, certain aspects of this passage come from the hand of a Christian interpolator.

THE MANUSCRIPT PROBLEM

As with the James passage, it must at the start be acknowledged that there was plenty of time, opportunity, and motive for Christians to alter the Josephan text.

THE CONTEXT

Some argue that the passage does not naturally fit the context of book 18 of *Antiquities* in which it is found. This section is basically a list of episodes that criticize Pilate and/or the Jewish leaders of that time. In the *Testimonium*, however, there is no real criticism as such.[81]

THE CONTENT

The content of this passage is certainly not what we would expect a non-Christian historian to say about Jesus. The phrases that most strongly betray a Christian influence are the following:

- "...*if indeed one ought to call him a man.*" This is clearly an implicit allusion to Christ's deity, which no non-Christian Jew would have granted. It can easily be read as a Christian scribe's way of augmenting Josephus's original claim that Jesus was merely a "wise man."
- "*He was the Messiah.*" Only a Christian would have said this. Not only this, but it seems that Josephus did not even believe that the Messiah would be Jewish. Remarkably enough, he seems to have thought that his patron, the Roman general Vespasian, was the Messiah (e.g., see *Jewish War* 6.5.4).
- "*On the third day he appeared to them restored to life, for the prophets of God had prophesied these and countless other marvelous things about him.*" This whole sentence is filled with a distinctly Christian content. The phrase "on the third day" is not self-explanatory but attained formulaic status in early Christian circles as evidenced by both Paul and the Gospels. The claim that Jesus was restored to life is obviously a Christian confession of the resurrection. And the claim that Old Testament prophets foretold aspects of Jesus's life was a common Christian apologetic theme. If this came from the pen of the original Josephus, it seems we must accept that Josephus was a covert Christian—something no one accepts, and for good reason.
- "*And the tribe of the Christians, so called after him, has still to this day not disappeared.*" Josephus does not elsewhere use the term "tribe" (*phylon*) to

---

81. Thus Michael Martin writes, "It appears out of context, thereby breaking the flow of the narrative" (*Case against Christianity*, 49).

describe followers of a religious movement. However, Eusebius does refer to Christians as a "tribe," and this may reflect how Christians commonly referred to themselves.[82] If so, its appearance in Josephus's text supports the interpolation theory.

LACK OF A *TESTIMONIUM* PARALLEL IN *JEWISH WAR*

There is a section in his *Jewish War* in which Josephus covers the deeds of Pilate, and it parallels this section of *Antiquities* quite closely.[83] However, no mention of Jesus is made in *Jewish War*.

THE SILENCE OF EARLY CHRISTIANS

The first to mention the *Testimonium* is Eusebius in about 323 CE (*Ecclesiastical History*, 1.11). Earlier apologists like Irenaeus, Tertullian, and Origen are clearly familiar with *Antiquities* but never refer to this passage. This is difficult to explain except on the supposition that the *Testimonium* was not found in their copies of this work. Doherty asks, "If a figure of the stature of Josephus had said the things contained in the alleged 'authentic' *Testimonium*, can one really believe that every Christian commentator for over two centuries would regard nothing in it as worthy of mention?"[84]

Even more damaging, Origen twice noted that Josephus did *not* believe Jesus was the Messiah (*Against Celsus*, 1.45; *Commentary on Matthew*, 10.17). In the case of Origen, therefore, we have not just an argument from silence. We also have positive evidence that the *Testimonium* was not in his version of the *Antiquities*.

AN ANCIENT TABLE OF CONTENTS

While no text of the *Antiquities* predates the eleventh century, there is a table of contents based on a now-lost Latin translation of this work that dates to the fifth or sixth century. Curiously enough, it fails to mention the *Testimonium Flavianum*, which suggests at the very least that this passage was "much less remarkable" in the text the Latin translation was based on than it is in the manuscripts we possess today.[85]

Assessing the Authenticity of the Testimonium

On the basis of these considerations, we, along with most other scholars, take it as settled that the *Testimonium* is at least partly the product of Christian interpolation. But this does not mean that the entire passage is forged. To the contrary, there are a number of rather compelling arguments that, taken together, suggest we can reconstruct what Josephus originally wrote about Jesus in this passage.

82. Eusebius, *Ecclesiastical History*, 3.33.
83. *Jewish War*, 2.9.2–4.
84. Doherty, *Jesus Puzzle*, 209.
85. Feldman, "Introduction," 57.

THE JAMES PASSAGE SUPPORTS THE *TESTIMONIUM*

The *Testimonium* occurs before the James passage in *Antiquities*. The probable authenticity of the mention of Jesus in the James passage (see above) suggests at the very least that Josephus previously mentioned Jesus in the *Testimonium*.[86] Josephus refers to "the brother of Jesus, who was called Christ" as a way of specifying who James is. But this seems to presuppose that Josephus had informed his readers previously in the text about this particular Jesus.

GENERALLY AGREED CHRISTIAN INTERPOLATIONS

Once three obviously Christian elements are identified and removed from the *Testimonium*, the rest of the passage reads quite like something a first-century Jewish historian would write about Jesus. The three elements generally identified as showing clear signs of Christian interpolation are: (1) the allusion to Jesus's divinity; (2) the confession that Jesus was the Messiah; and (3) the acknowledgment that Jesus rose from the dead on "the third day" in accordance with Old Testament prophecy. If we remove these statements from the text, we arrive at the following:

> About this time there lived Jesus, a wise man. For he was one who wrought surprising feats and was a teacher of such people as accept the truth gladly. He won over many Jews and many of the Greeks. When Pilate, upon hearing him accused by men of the highest standing among us, had condemned him to be crucified, those who had in the first place come to love him did not give up their affection for him. And the tribe of the Christians, so called after him, has still to this day not disappeared.[87]

There is nothing in this passage that a Jewish historian could not have said about Jesus. Acknowledging that Jesus was a "wise man" and a doer of "surprising feats" would have been no problem for Josephus. As almost all contemporary scholars agree, Jesus was known as a teacher and a miracle-worker in the ancient world. Josephus is merely noting what likely would have been commonly known about Jesus of Nazareth in first-century Palestine. Also, there is little ground for thinking that the term "tribe" had to come from a Christian interpolator. Eusebius uses this term to describe Christians, but aside from this one instance, there is no known instance of Christians using this term as a self-designation.

AN ANCIENT ARABIC VERSION OF THE *TESTIMONIUM*

We now have a copy of a tenth-century Arabic translation of the *Testimonium* (from Agapius's *Book of the Title*), discovered and published several decades ago

---

86. As Craig Evans notes, "The reference to 'Jesus the one called Christ' [in the James passage] ... clearly implies a prior reference. In all probability the *Testimonium* is that prior reference" ("Jesus in Non-Christian Sources," 470).

87. This seems to be the most common reconstruction. See J. Klausner, *Jesus of Nazareth: His Life, Times and Teaching*, trans. H. Danby (New York: Macmillan, 1943), 55–56; Meier, *Marginal Jew*, 1:61.

by Shlomo Pines.[88] What is most interesting about this copy of the *Testimonium* is that the three passages that have been widely acknowledged as Christian insertions in the Greek text are either missing or seriously altered. The phrase, "if indeed one ought to call him a man," is completely absent. The phrase, "He was the Messiah," is relocated to the end and reads, "He was perhaps the Messiah." And the claim about Jesus's postmortem appearances after the third day is preceded by, "They reported that . . ."

All of this suggests that Agapius had access to a version of *Antiquities* that did not contain the three questionable portions as found in the Greek text. Thus, the Arabic text helps confirm the reconstructed version of the *Testimonium* offered above. Largely on this basis James Charlesworth concludes, "We can now be as certain as historical research will presently allow that Josephus did refer to Jesus in *Antiquities* [18.3.3]."[89]

NON-CHRISTIAN ELEMENTS IN THE RECONSTRUCTED PASSAGE

Not only does this reconstructed passage contain things that a Jewish historian could have said about Jesus, but it also contains things that a Christian interpolator most likely would *not* have said. The statement that Jesus "won over" many Jews *and Gentiles* seems inconsistent with a Christian interpolator. For the Christian tradition, as contained in the Gospels, gives no indication that Jesus ever evangelized the Gentiles—let alone that he was successful in doing so. The Gospels present Jesus as intentionally pursuing a Jewish mission during his lifetime (e.g., Matt. 10:5). As Meier notes, it seems much less likely that a Christian interpolator would have contradicted the Gospels' own picture of Jesus's ministry than that Josephus himself simply "retrojected the situation of his own day," wherein many among Jesus's followers were Gentiles.[90] In fact, "naïve retrojection is a common trait of Greco-Roman historians."[91]

In addition, the treatment of the role played by the Jewish authorities does not correspond with the Gospels. The Jewish leaders are said only to have "accused" Jesus, while it is Pilate alone who "condemned" him. This is in tension with the picture we are given in the Gospels in which Jewish leaders bear the primary responsibility for Jesus's execution.

Finally, the last sentence in the *Testimonium*, which reads, "And the tribe of the Christians, so called after him, has still to this day not disappeared," also seems to be something a Christian interpolator would not have said. As Meier notes, there seems to be an element of surprise in this sentence. Josephus is insinuating that, given Jesus's "shameful end . . . one is amazed to note . . . that this group of postmortem lovers is still at it and has not disappeared even in our day." There is

---

88. S. Pines, *An Arabic Version of the Testimonium Flavianum and Its Implications* (Jerusalem: Israel Academy of Sciences and Humanities, 1971).

89. J. Charlesworth, *Jesus within Judaism* (New York: Doubleday, 1988), 96.

90. Meier, *Marginal Jew*, 1:65.

91. Ibid.

in this a distinctly "dismissive if not hostile" tone, according to Meier.[92] This is not what we would expect from a Christian interpolator.

FLOW OF THOUGHT

Once these three elements are removed, the flow of the passage is restored. As Meier again notes, "Precisely these three Christian passages are the clauses that interrupt the flow of what is otherwise a concise text carefully written in a fairly neutral—even purposely ambiguous—tone."[93] With these three elements removed, there are no grounds whatsoever to consider the passage inauthentic on stylistic grounds.

THE CONTEXT OF *ANTIQUITIES* 18

Earlier we noted that some argue that the *Testimonium* does not fit the context in which it is found, a context in which Josephus is criticizing Pilate and Jewish leaders of his time. This argument lacks merit, however.

First, it has been observed that "the entire section of the *Antiquities* dealing with Pilate's term of office is uneven."[94] This is most likely due to the fact that Josephus is using a mixture of sources, both Palestinian and Roman.[95] Second, in the ancient world there was no use of footnotes for digression purposes. For example, a text dealing with some aspect of a person or theme could be expected to include other aspects related to the same subject at that point in the narrative. Thus, while book 18, chapter 3 is a section that emphasizes Pilate's rule in Judea, it is understandable why Josephus—wanting to add a comment about Jesus at some point—included the event in this context, since it was Pilate who crucified Jesus.

Finally, since we know a Christian interpolator has modified the text, it is possible that he removed unflattering comments Josephus made about Jesus. While acknowledging that Jesus was known as a wise man and wonder-worker, the original *Testimonium* may have painted Jesus as just another troublemaker during Pilate's reign.[96]

JOHN THE BAPTIST PASSAGE

Speaking of context, another strong argument favoring accepting a reconstructed version of the *Testimonium* as authentic concerns its relationship to the section that follows this passage. Shortly after his comments on Jesus, Josephus launches into a much more lengthy discussion of John the Baptist. If the whole

92. Ibid., 66.

93. Ibid., 61.

94. Winter, "Excursus II," 438. For a clear summary of the Pilate section, see Steve Mason, *Josephus and the New Testament* (Peabody, MA: Hendrickson, 1992), 163–64.

95. For discussion see Winter, "Excursus II," 438–39.

96. On this matter see the comments of G. Stanton, *Gospel Truth? New Light on Jesus and the Gospels* (Valley Forge, PA: Trinity, 1995), 126.

of the *Testimonium* was the work of a Christian interpolator, it seems he would have followed the Gospel pattern and placed it *after* the discussion on John the Baptist, whom all Christians regarded as a forerunner of Jesus.[97] It also seems he would have created an account that at least paralleled the Baptist discussion in terms of length.[98] The fact that the *Testimonium* is short and located before the account of the Baptist suggests that the Christian interpolator did not take great liberties with rearranging the *order* of Josephus's text, but rather simply modified the passage while leaving it in its original location.

THE SILENCE ABOUT JESUS IN JOSEPHUS'S *JEWISH WAR*

What are we to make of the fact that the passage in *Jewish War* that parallels the *Antiquities* passage in which the *Testimonium* is found fails to mention Jesus? In our estimation, very little. In general, Josephus offers more detail in *Antiquities* than he does in comparable passages in *Jewish War*. So it is not particularly surprising that Jesus is mentioned in the former but not the latter. Also, we must remember that there was more than a twenty-year span of time between these two works. The Christian movement experienced significant growth in these two decades. Hence, Josephus had more reason to mention the founder of this movement in the latter work than he did in the former one.

RESPONSE TO THE "PATRISTIC SILENCE" ARGUMENT

One of the most challenging arguments against the *Testimonium*'s authenticity is that it goes unmentioned by early Christian writers for several centuries. Even in its reconstructed form we might have expected it to have caught the attention of early Christian writers, especially since a number of them cite Josephus on other matters.[99] How is this to be explained? Three considerations lessen the force of this objection.

First, this is a classic example of an argument from silence. As such, it must be considered tenuous. The fact that no Christian writers prior to Eusebius mention the *Testimonium* does not prove that it did not exist. They simply may have had no reason for mentioning it in the writings that have survived. The strength of this consideration increases when we consider that the *Testimonium*, once divested of its interpolated elements, would have little apologetic value in the early church. It provides early non-Christian confirmation that Jesus existed and had a reputation for being a wise teacher and a wonder-worker. But no one in the ancient world denied this.

---

97. On this point, Feldman states: "One would have expected that an interpolator would have modified Josephus' passage about John the Baptist so as to make the occasion of John's death accord with the Gospels and to indicate that he was a forerunner of Jesus" ("Introduction," 56).

98. So argues Meier, *Marginal Jew*, 1:66.

99. On the use of Josephus in the early church, see M. E. Hardwick, *Josephus as an Historical Source in Patristic Literature through Eusebius* (Atlanta: Scholars Press, 1989).

In fact, when divested of its interpolated elements, the *Testimonium* arguably gives a somewhat negative portrait of Jesus and the early Christians.[100] We have already commented on Josephus's amazement that Christians are "still around to this day," even after their leader suffered such a shameful fate. We might now add that the Greek term *epegageto* ("won over" or "gained a following") can have a pejorative connotation of duping someone or bringing something bad upon someone.[101] The suggestion may be that this wonder-worker (trickster) seduced people to join a misguided movement.

The reconstructed *Testimonium* fails to mention that Jesus is the Messiah. Indeed, if the negative reading of this passage is correct, it actually constitutes an argument *against* his being the Messiah. This suffices to explain why early Christians did not cite the *Testimonium*. It also explains the previously mentioned fact that Origen complains that Josephus does not believe Jesus was the Messiah (*Against Celsus*, 1.45; *Commentary on Matthew*, 10.17). Ironically, this very complaint is further evidence for something like the reconstructed *Testimonium*. For, as Feldman notes, "it makes no sense for Origen to express wonder that Josephus did not admit Jesus to be the Messiah if he did not even mention him."[102]

Further confirmation comes from Jerome. We know that Jerome knew about the *Testimonium* (seemingly without the interpolated elements) because he mentions it explicitly (see *De Viris Illustribus*, 13.14).[103] Yet he never makes any use of it. Indeed, he never mentions it again—though he cites Josephus over ninety times in his writings. Had Jerome not mentioned the *Testimonium* this one time, critics would have counted him among the number of those whose silence supposedly proves the *Testimonium* did not exist. As it stands, his one reference proves that he did know it existed but simply saw no reason to refer to it—and certainly not as an apologetic. We have every reason to suppose that other early church fathers treated it in a similar fashion.

In light of these considerations, we side with the majority of scholars today who conclude that something like the reconstructed version of the *Testimonium* was penned by Josephus. Thus, in her recent survey of Josephus research, Helen Bond observes: "Most scholars have accepted . . . our present text as a Christian-

100. Some have proposed that the original passage contained even more negative elements, which have been excised by the Christian interpolator. See Bruce, *Jesus and Christian Origins*, 38–40; Van Voorst, *Jesus outside the New Testament*, 94–95.

101. So notes Evans, "Jesus in Non-Christian Sources," 470.

102. L. H. Feldman, "The *Testimonium Flavianum*: The State of the Question," in *Christological Perspectives: Essays in Honor of Harvey K. McArthur*, ed. R. F. Berkey and S. A. Edwards (New York: Pilgrim, 1982), 183. Whealey agrees (*Josephus on Jesus*, 13).

103. It is likely that Jerome knew of the *Testimonium* from the copy of Eusebius available to him. The common claim by Christ myth theorists that Eusebius could be responsible for the *Testimonium* is undercut by the observation that fourth-century versions seem to be "independently transmitted by Pseudo-Hegesippus into *De excidio Hierosolymitano* and by Eusebius into his *Historia Ecclesiastica*" (Whealey, *Josephus on Jesus*, 41).

ized version of a Josephan original. . . . What we have in our present text, then, is very similar to what Josephus actually wrote about Jesus."[104]

Summary and Conclusion

Having analyzed all relevant non-Christian sources in terms of their information about the historical Jesus, we may draw twelve plausible conclusions.

1. Despite the insistence of some legendary-Jesus theorists, Trypho did not doubt that Jesus existed, though he did vehemently deny that he was "the Christ."
2. While we do not have a wealth of references to Jesus in non-Christian sources in the ancient world, we have as much or more than we should expect, given the marginal status of Jesus and the early Christian movement in the first-century Roman Empire.
3. While there is nothing in early rabbinic tradition that independently confirms or denies either the historical existence of Jesus or any aspect of the Gospel tradition, it is significant that, as hostile as this tradition was to the claims of early Christianity, it never denies that Jesus existed or even that he was a miracle-worker.
4. In Thallus we have a probable confirmation that an unusual darkness came over the earth when Jesus was crucified.
5. The letter of Mara bar Serapion arguably demonstrates that pagans between the first and third centuries did not question the existence of Jesus. In fact, it likely demonstrates that some held him in a positive light and believed he was put to death unjustly.
6. Pliny's letter informs us that, despite widespread persecution, Christianity had spread even to rather remote regions of the Roman Empire by the turn of the century. His letter suggests that both Christians and non-Christians assumed Jesus existed and that Christians worshipped Jesus as "a god." And his letter indicates that while some Christians defected from their faith under threat of death, others were willing to die for it.
7. Suetonius appears to corroborate Luke's account of the expulsion of Jews under Claudius in 49 CE. With respect to Jesus, while it is possible that Suetonius represents nothing more than Christian hearsay, it is also possible that he offers an independent attestation of Jesus's existence.
8. As much as Celsus opposed the Christian faith, he does not charge that the stories of Jesus were simply made up. He grants that Jesus existed and that he was a wonder-worker. Had the story of Jesus been substantially legend-

104. H. K. Bond, "New Currents in Josephus Research," *Current Research in Biblical Studies* 8 (2000): 179.

ary, it is difficult to explain why neither Celsus nor anyone else thought of raising this objection against the Christian movement.

9. It is possible that Lucian of Samosata provides us with an independent tradition regarding Jesus's crucifixion.

10. Tacitus provides us with independent, non-Christian confirmation of Jesus's crucifixion, that it occurred during the reign of Tiberius (14–37 CE) and under Pilate's governorship (26–36 CE). He also shows us that within three decades of Jesus's death there was a strong Christian presence in some quarters of the Roman Empire—enough so that Nero could use them as a plausible scapegoat for political purposes. And he tells us that many of these Christians were willing to suffer and die for their faith.

11. Josephus's "James Passage" confirms that James, a recent contemporary of Josephus, was the brother of Jesus. This undercuts the attempts of Christ myth theorists to argue that Paul and the early Christians thought of Jesus as a mythological deity who existed in the distant past. This in turn forces the question of how, within a first-century Palestinian Jewish context, an ordinary Jewish carpenter could be mythologized to the point of being regarded as divine while his brother was still alive.

12. While the manuscript tradition of the *Testimonium* of Josephus clearly has been tampered with, a solid case can be made that the original passage depicted Jesus as "a wise man" who performed wonders, was crucified under Pilate, and whose followers inexplicably continued to follow him even after his death.

On this basis we conclude that there is no "conspiracy of silence" among early non-Christian sources concerning Jesus. At the very least, the evidence they provide dispels any suspicion that Jesus never existed. Beyond this, corroborative evidence is provided for early Christian claims with respect to Jesus's reputation as a teacher and miracle-worker and for the time and manner of his death.

5

The "Silence" of Paul?

What, If Anything, Did Paul Know about the Jesus of History?

In the last chapter we addressed the alleged silence of non-Christian references to Jesus in the first century. We now turn to the claim made by certain legendary-Jesus theorists—particularly those who argue for the more radical Christ myth theory—that Paul is virtually silent about, and largely uninterested in, the (supposed) Jesus of history. In this view, Paul's silence indicates that he did not view Jesus as a recent historical figure. Rather, these scholars argue that Paul viewed Jesus as a mythic deity who performed his saving work in the distant past and/or in the heavenly realm. The issue of Paul's awareness or ignorance of the earthly Jesus is important to the issue of the reliability of the Synoptic Gospels, for almost everyone agrees that Paul wrote his epistles before the Gospels were written. If Paul's writings indicate that he viewed Jesus as a mythic figure of the distant past/heavenly world, rather than as a recent contemporary, this suggests that the Gospel depiction of Jesus as a recent historical figure is fictional. Even for less radical legendary-Jesus theorists, Paul's apparent silence tends to be viewed as evidence that the early church had little interest in preserving accurate information about the life of Jesus.

We will first review the case made by Christ myth theorists for concluding that Paul did not view Jesus as a recent historical figure. We will then begin our response by reviewing four preliminary arguments that challenge this thesis. Next, we will argue more specifically that, in fact, Paul's writings reflect an awareness of, and concern for, the Jesus of history. We will follow this by arguing that Paul's writings also reflect a significant awareness of Jesus's teachings, as evidenced by what are likely conscious citations of the Jesus tradition, as well as a good number of possible "allusions" to, and "echoes" of, the Jesus tradition.

Despite the presence of this "Jesus-tradition" material in Paul, it cannot be denied that Paul rarely directly quotes Jesus—even on topics where it would seem to be to his advantage to do so. We will conclude by suggesting there is a plausible explanation for this. The import of our cumulative argument in this chapter is that, over and against the contention of certain legendary-Jesus theorists, Paul's writings not only support the existence of Jesus but also comport well with the essence of the Synoptic portrait(s) of him.

Paul and Jesus among the Skeptics

Paul's Lack of Historical Information

While New Testament scholars agree that Paul has relatively little to say about the life and ministry of Jesus, most grant that Paul viewed Jesus as a recent contemporary. The most extreme legendary-Jesus theorists, however—particularly the Christ myth theorists—deny this.[1] They argue that nothing in Paul's letters indicates that he believed Jesus was a contemporary of his. Rather, they contend, the Jesus of Paul's theology is a savior figure patterned after similar figures within ancient mystery religions. According to the theory, Paul believed that Christ entered the world at some point in the distant past—or that he existed only in a transcendent mythical realm—and died to defeat evil powers and redeem humanity.[2] Only later was Jesus remythologized as a Jewish contemporary. Thus, according to the theory, this supposition best explains the absence of Jesus material in Paul's letters. In the words of G. A. Wells:

1. For example, E. Doherty, *The Jesus Puzzle: Did Christianity Begin with a Mythical Christ?* (Ottawa: Canadian Humanist, 1999), 24–26, 74–75, 302–4; A. Ellegard, *Jesus—One Hundred Years before Christ: A Study in Creative Mythology* (Woodstock, NY: Overlook, 1999); M. Martin, *The Case against Christianity* (Philadelphia: Temple University Press, 1991), 52–56; G. A. Wells, *The Jesus Myth* (Chicago: Open Court, 1999), 49–78, 111–13.

2. For example, Doherty holds that Paul never saw Jesus as anything more than a "divinity *in the supernatural realm*" (*Jesus Puzzle*, 16 [emphasis in text]). Ellegard, on the other hand, argues that Paul identified Jesus with the Essene Teacher of Righteousness, who had lived sometime in the past. See *Jesus—One Hundred Years before Christ*; idem, "Theologians as Historians," *Scandia* 59 (1993): 171. Others grant that Paul knew Jesus to be a recent historical figure but that he went on to apply contemporary Greco-Roman mythological themes to Jesus, transforming him into a divine son of God whose death atones for the sins of the world. In this way, Paul—not Jesus—became the founder of Christianity. See, e.g., H. Maccoby, *The Mythmaker: Paul and the Invention of Christianity* (New York: Barnes & Noble, 1986), 16–17.

[Paul's] letters have no allusion to the parents of Jesus, let alone to the virgin birth. They never refer to a place of birth. . . . They give no indication of the time or place of his earthly existence. They do not refer to his trial before a Roman official, nor to Jerusalem as the place of execution. They mention neither John the Baptist, nor Judas, nor Peter's denial of his master. . . . These letters also fail to mention any miracles Jesus is supposed to have worked, a particularly striking omission, since, according to the gospels he worked so many.[3]

According to these thinkers, all these historical aspects of the Jesus story were invented and placed in the Gospels after Paul wrote his letters.

Paul's Words "from the Lord"

Related to this is the claim that Paul never quotes the earthly Jesus. Some even argue that Paul seems completely unaware of the later Christian notion that Jesus was an ethical teacher. To be sure, there are several places where Paul mentions that he is passing on information he received "from the Lord" (1 Cor. 7:10–11; 9:14; 11:23–25; 14:37; 2 Cor. 12:9; 1 Thess. 4:15–17), but these are to be understood not as references to the actual words of the Jesus of history, but as personal revelations Paul believed he, or others, had directly received from the spiritual Christ.

Legendary-Jesus theorists point out that the belief that people could receive personal revelations from Christ was widespread in the early church. Paul and his congregations simply believed that his revelations carried a special "apostolic" authority. In support of this interpretation, some legendary-Jesus theorists appeal to 1 Corinthians 14. Here we find Paul giving instructions about the proper protocol for people sharing "spiritual gifts" within the church, including personal revelations they had received (1 Cor. 14:26–36). He concludes his teaching by saying, "Anyone who claims to be a prophet, or to have spiritual powers, must acknowledge that what I am writing to you is a command of the Lord" (1 Cor. 14:37).

Most agree that in this instance Paul is not claiming to be passing on a command that went back to the earthly Jesus, for there is no evidence Jesus ever addressed the issue of how to use spiritual gifts. Rather, it appears that Paul is passing on a revelatory command he believed he received from the risen Christ, a revelation that had the authority to specify how all other revelations were to be shared.[4] Anyone who was to be regarded as a prophet or to have special powers within Paul's congregations had to operate in conformity with Paul's apostolic revelation. Paul emphasizes his authority by insisting he *did not* receive the gospel from other people; he got it directly through personal revelation (Gal. 1:12). According to some legendary-Jesus theorists, this is how we should uniformly understand Paul's claim to be passing on teachings he received "from the Lord."

3. G. A. Wells, *The Historical Evidence for Jesus* (Buffalo, NY: Prometheus, 1982), 22.
4. See Wells, *Historical Evidence*, 30; Doherty, *Jesus Puzzle*, 29–30.

Paul's Lack of Citations

The most significant aspect of Paul's writing that betrays a lack of awareness of Jesus as a teacher, according to legendary-Jesus theorists, is his consistent failure to cite the historical Jesus as an authority *when it would have been to his advantage to do so*. He sometimes gives teachings that sound something like sayings (allegedly) later put in the mouth of Jesus by the Gospel authors. But, according to legend-ary-Jesus theorists, "he seems to have no idea that he is imitating any preaching of Jesus" when he utters these words.[5]

For example, when trying to resolve a dispute about what is and is not proper for Christians to eat, Paul declares that there is nothing unclean in and of itself (Rom. 14:14). The Gospel of Mark presents Jesus as giving a similar teaching (Mark 7:17–23). If Paul was aware of this Jesus tradition, it is argued, he most certainly would have mentioned it. Backing up his own teaching with Jesus's authority would have buttressed the point he was making. In the words of Doherty,

> If ever there were a moment and an emotional argument when one would expect Paul to seize on Jesus' own declared position for support, this is it. His silence can only indicate that he is truly ignorant of such traditions as those found in Mark 7 where Jesus accuses the Pharisees of hypocrisy and tells the people, "Nothing that goes into a man from outside can defile him."[6]

So too, some legendary-Jesus theorists wonder why Paul never cites Jesus's confrontation with the Pharisees in his battle against the Judaizers. "Paul is greatly concerned to protect Galatian Christians from Christian teachers who were press-ing them to keep the Jewish law," Wells argues. And he concludes, "Had he known that Jesus had criticized it, he could hardly have failed to say so in this context."[7] Something similar could be said regarding Paul's teaching not to judge others (Rom. 14:13), his teaching on love (Rom. 13:8; Gal. 5:14), and his theology of the end times (1 Thess. 4:16–17). At times his wording is similar to words of Jesus we later find in the Gospels, yet he never cites Jesus as his source.

According to the most radical legendary-Jesus theorists, all of this is evidence that the portrait(s) of Jesus as a recent miracle-working teacher given in the Gos-pels is a legend that had not yet been invented at the time of Paul's writing. It is evidence that it is not Paul who is echoing the words of Jesus, but the authors of the Gospels who are echoing Paul (and other sources) as they put them into the mouth of their newly historicized, fictional Jesus. Hence, these legendary-Jesus theorists argue, the only Christ Paul was aware of was "a divine presence in Chris-tian communities, bestowing revelation and guidance, a channel to God and to knowledge of spiritual truths." And the only authoritative voice he was aware

5. Doherty, *Jesus Puzzle*, 27.
6. Ibid., 28.
7. Wells, *Historical Evidence*, 32.

of was "the voice of this spiritual Son which Christians hear, not the passed-on words of a former teacher."[8]

How solid is the case for these claims on the basis of Paul's alleged silence about the Jesus of history? In our estimation, it does not hold up under scrutiny. We turn first to the allegation that Paul thought of Jesus as a heavenly being who came to earth in the distant, mythological past.

Jesus as a Recent Contemporary of Paul

Four pieces of evidence pose serious problems for the Christ myth perspective.

The Reliability of the Gospels

First, for the legendary-Jesus theory to be true, the Synoptic Gospel tradition must be judged to be altogether historically unreliable. However, as we shall later argue over several chapters (chaps. 6–10), these works give us good reason to conclude that they are as generally reliable as we could hope any ancient document could be. To the degree that we consider the claims of the Synoptic Gospel tradition that Jesus lived and died in the first half of the first century accurate, to that degree we can assume that when Paul writes about "Jesus," it is to this recent historical person that he refers.

The Absence of Mystery Religions

Second, since the typical Christ myth thesis understands Paul's view of Jesus as patterned after the savior figures of the ancient mystery religions, this would require that knowledge of these mystery religions be both available and attractive to a first-century Jew—a Pharisee, no less (Phil. 3:5)—like Paul.[9] As we have already suggested, however, neither of these claims is likely (chaps. 2–3). We have no solid evidence that mystery religions existed in the first century in the form proposed by Christ myth theorists. And we have very good evidence suggesting that, even if they had been in existence, first-century Jews would have viewed them with contempt.

The Problem of James

An even more significant obstacle to those versions of the legendary-Jesus thesis that deny Jesus existed is that Paul explicitly refers to James as "the Lord's

8. Doherty, *Jesus Puzzle*, 30.
9. We find Hyam Maccoby's (*Mythmaker*, 15) claim that Paul was no Pharisee—rather that he was a former Sadducean police officer beneath the high priest, who later fabricated a Pharisee's pedigree to further enhance the effectiveness of his ministry—to be without a credible historical basis. As N. T. Wright concludes (in response to A. N. Wilson's similar line of argument): "It is historically out of the question that Saul of Tarsus should have been . . . a servant of the high priest" (*What Saint Paul Really Said: Was Paul of Tarsus the Real Founder of Christianity?* [Grand Rapids: Eerdmans, 1997], 170). All the evidence points to the preconversion Paul as a (Shammaite) Pharisee.

brother" (Gal. 1:19), a fact that is most probably confirmed by Josephus, as we saw in the last chapter. This fact alone undercuts the Christ myth theory. Clearly, if Paul knows the brother of Jesus is still alive when he is writing, he must have viewed Jesus as a person of recent history.

Though Wells admirably admits that "what seems to be the plain sense of the text [Gal. 1:19] does not support me," he nevertheless insists that James was not the biological brother of the Lord. Rather, he and several other legendary-Jesus advocates argue that the phrase "the Lord's brother" should be taken as a designation of "a small group or fraternity of Messianists not related to Jesus but zealous in the service of the risen one."[10] That is, they suppose that there were a number of subgroups within the early church with different designations, and one of them was designated "the brothers of the Lord."

In support of his claim Wells notes how the church at Corinth had factions that were divided according to people's special allegiances. Some claimed to belong to "Paul," others to "Cephas" or "Apollos," and, most significantly, some to "Christ" (1 Cor. 1:11–13). Wells speculates that the "brothers of the Lord" was the designation of this latter group. The fact that "brother" could in certain ancient contexts be used as a euphemism for a "principle servant" is cited in support of his contention.[11]

In our estimation, this position is clearly ad hoc, lacking anything like probative support. If we had any evidence of a special group of zealous servants within the early church known as "the Lord's brothers," our assessment might be otherwise—but we have none. To the contrary, as far as we know, *all* believers in the early church understood themselves to be called to be "zealous in the service of the risen one."

The fact that one of the divisive groups within Corinth identified themselves in a unique way with Christ hardly supports Wells's contention. In fact, it may count as further evidence against it, for Paul *castigates* the Corinthians precisely on this basis: their divisions were evidence of their immaturity and carnality (1 Cor. 1:10–15). It is difficult to imagine Paul being outraged by a special "Jesus fraternity" at Corinth while affectionately condoning James's participation in such a fraternity at Galatia. If "the Lord's brother" referred to a faction of zealous servants of Jesus, similar to the factions centered on Cephas, Paul, or Apollos, one wonders why we never hear of anyone being designated as "Cephas's brother," or "Paul's brother," or "Apollos's brother." We conclude that we have no good grounds for taking Paul's reference to "the Lord's brother" in any way other than its natural sense.

Witnesses of a Recent Resurrection

Fourth, the way Paul speaks of the resurrection suggests that he understands it to be a recent event. In the account of the resurrection that Paul (interestingly

10. Wells, *Historical Evidence*, 168.
11. Ibid., 167–68.

enough) had received and was passing on (1 Cor. 15:1–3), he notes that Jesus was buried, rose three days later, appeared to Cephas (Peter), to "the twelve," to five hundred—most of whom were still living when Paul wrote—then to James, to all the apostles, and finally to Paul himself (1 Cor. 15:4–8). The passage presupposes that most of those who saw the risen Lord *were still alive* at the time of Paul's writing. And this suggests that Paul believed that Jesus lived, died, and rose in the recent past.

Christ myth theorists attempt to skirt this conclusion by arguing that the "witnesses" to the resurrection listed in this passage experienced nothing more than "a simple vision" that had nothing to do with a historical event.[12] On this theory, the savior-deity who was resurrected at some point in the mythological past in a heavenly realm appeared in ecstatic visions to certain individuals now that "the end of the age" had come.

This suggestion, however, lacks plausibility. There is certainly nothing *in the text* to suggest a long span of time between Jesus's resurrection and the appearances Paul talks about. Wedging an indefinite span of time and a different realm between verse 4, when Christ died and rose, and verse 5, when he "appeared" to the disciples, seems very unnatural. The inclusion of James, "the Lord's brother," as one of those who saw the risen Lord positively rules out wedging an indefinite span of time between the resurrection and the appearances—unless, of course, one accepts the unlikely idea that this phrase does not refer to the Lord's biological brother—an idea we have concluded against (see above).

Moreover, we have good grounds for concluding that the leaders Paul lists in this passage were disciples of Jesus *while Jesus was alive*, as the Gospels report. For example, as we shall argue more fully below, Paul's reference to "the twelve" is difficult to explain except on the assumption that this category goes back to Jesus himself. It is worth remembering that on the basis of this passage, Rudolf Bultmann himself took issue with Paul for citing "witnesses" in a manner that led to the inevitable conclusion that the resurrection is a historical—rather than a mythical—event.[13] Clearly, Bultmann would have loved to find what the Christ myth theorists claim to see—or rather not see—in this passage. But he could not. In his landmark work on the resurrection of Jesus, N. T. Wright argues: "The list of witnesses, despite the anguished protests of Bultmann and his followers, is a clear indication that Paul does not suppose Jesus' resurrection to be a metaphorization of an experience of the disciples, or of some 'ineffable truth beyond history.'"[14]

On top of all this, the Christ myth understanding of the resurrection appearances has to accept that the "appearances" were psychological projections or hallucinations. There are numerous problems with this suggestion, however, not least of which is that it flies in the face of the first-century Jewish understanding

12. Doherty, *Jesus Puzzle*, 71.

13. R. Bultmann, *Kerygma and Myth*, ed. H.-W. Bartsch (London: SPCK, 1962–1964), 1:38–41, 83.

14. N. T. Wright, *The Resurrection of the Son of God* (Minneapolis: Fortress, 2003), 324. Here Wright is citing R. B. Hays, *First Corinthians* (Nashville: Abingdon, 1997), 257.

of resurrection. When Jews thought of resurrection, they thought of a *bodily* resurrection in history, not a mystical vision. More particularly, as N. T. Wright has established, there is no other way of understanding the New Testament's "resurrection" language.[15] If first-century Jews were psychologically to project and/or hallucinate about the resurrection of Jesus, we can only suppose they would have done so in categories that made sense in their cultural context. The categories used by the Christ myth theory to explain the resurrection reports are not those of first-century Judaism. The New Testament itself bears witness that first-century Jews did have a category by which to explain appearances of spiritual apparitions (e.g., Acts 12:15), but this is decidedly not the category they used to describe the resurrection of Jesus.

We thus conclude that the Jesus Paul proclaimed was not a legendary figure in the distant "mythological" past, but a recent contemporary Jew. And the implications of this are significant. This conclusion once again forces on us the need to explain how first-century, monotheistic, Palestinian Jews could have come to view a recent contemporary of theirs—and in the case of James, his own brother—as attaining to the anticipated "resurrection" as an individual, and as having a status worthy of worship.

If we had a cultural context that was conducive to legend making, and if we had several centuries, or at least several generations, to allow for a legend of this magnitude to develop, the legendary-Jesus theory undoubtedly would be more compelling. But we have neither. *Almost immediately after Jesus's death* we have monotheistic Jews—including his own brother—ascribing to him the status of "resurrected," of sharing in the identity of Yahweh, and of being worthy of worship. And this takes place in an environment that was generally hostile to any suggestion that a human could be equated with God. What, we must ask, could explain this?[16] What must the Jesus of history have been like to have convinced his disciples, and his own brother, that he was the presence of God on earth? The question itself—viewed from the standpoint of an "open" historical-critical method—begins to make the Gospels' portrait(s) of a resurrected Jesus look more plausible. As N. T. Wright argues, "The proposal that Jesus was bodily raised from the dead possesses unrivaled power to explain the historical data at the heart of early Christianity."[17]

15. See Wright, *Resurrection*, esp. 146–206, 372–74.

16. As we noted in chap. 2, what some are calling the new history of religions school has demonstrated that there were important elements in late Second Temple Judaism that could have paved the way for Christians to think in terms of the close identification of an exalted creature and Yahweh himself (e.g., archangels, exalted patriarchs, and personification of divine attributes). However, at two points these important conceptual resources stand in discontinuity with the early Christian claims about Jesus. First, Jesus is a recent contemporary figure, not a divine attribute, an angel, or an ancient patriarch of renown. Second, Jesus is presented as willingly receiving worship along with (or better, *as* the embodiment of) Yahweh. For all of the valuable insights that the new school offers in terms of continuity between early Christianity and other Second Temple Jewish theologizing, these two distinctives signal a quantum leap in Jewish religious thought.

17. Wright, *Resurrection*, 718.

Pauline References to the Life of Jesus

We turn now to the claim that there are no clear and specific references to the Jesus of history in Paul's writings. This claim, we submit, is simply incorrect.[18]

Pauline Allusions to the Jesus of History

From Paul's writings it is evident that he knew a significant amount of detail concerning the life of Jesus. He knew Jesus was born and raised as a Jew (Gal. 4:4) and that he was a descendant of Abraham and David (Gal. 3:16; Rom. 1:3). Paul knew Jesus had a brother named James (Gal. 1:19) and perhaps other brothers as well (1 Cor. 9:5). He knew by name a number of disciples who ministered with Jesus, and he knew that Jesus's disciple Peter was married (1 Cor. 9:5). Paul also knew that Jesus was betrayed (1 Cor. 11:23) and that he was executed by crucifixion (1 Cor. 1:17–18; Gal. 5:11; 6:12; Phil. 2:8; 3:18) with the help of certain Judean Jews (1 Thess. 2:14–15).[19] Paul was aware that Jesus instituted a memorial meal the night before his death (1 Cor. 11:23–25), and that Jesus was buried after his death and was resurrected three days later, a fact he refers to frequently and places a great deal of weight on (Rom. 4:24–25; 1 Cor. 15:4–8; cf. Rom. 6:4–9; 8:11, 34; 1 Cor. 6:14; 2 Cor. 4:14; Gal. 1:1; 1 Thess. 4:14). As we have noted, in a first-century Jewish context, this affirmation inherently implies the resurrection of a physical body in a historical sense.

Moreover, Paul knew that Jesus's earthly life was characterized by meekness, gentleness, self-sacrificial love, and humble service (2 Cor. 10:1; Phil. 2:5–7). Paul's central passion was to know and be conformed to Jesus Christ (Phil. 3:8–10), and he consistently held up Jesus's life—and his own life as modeled on Jesus's life—as examples to be emulated (1 Cor. 11:1). In this light, it cannot be regarded as a coincidence that Paul's own thought, attitude, and conduct paralleled closely what we find in the Jesus of the Gospels. Nor can it be considered a coincidence that Paul's healing ministry, his welcoming of sinners, his life of poverty, and humble service closely paralleled Jesus's life and ministry as recorded

18. For the sake of argument, we shall base our case of Paul's knowledge of Jesus's life and teaching on those letters that the vast majority of scholars affirm as Pauline. While we believe a good case can be made for accepting all canonical books attributed to Paul as coming from his hand, many scholars argue that Titus, 1 and 2 Timothy, Colossians, and Ephesians are not authentic (some would include 2 Thessalonians as well). The case we are making in this chapter is not affected by this issue. On the authorship of some of the disputed epistles, see I. H. Marshall, "Recent Study of the Pastoral Epistles," *Themelios* 23 (1997): 3–29. With respect to the Christ myth theory, to the degree one considers 1 Timothy as Pauline and/or reflective of Paul's own views, then 1 Tim. 6:13 becomes an important passage. Here we read that Jesus gave his testimony *before Pontius Pilate*. Christ myth theorists must dismiss the entire epistle as non-Pauline and/or argue that the phrase involving Pilate is an interpolation; see, e.g., Doherty, *Jesus Puzzle*, 299–302.

19. Legendary-Jesus theorists who hold that Paul did not see Jesus as a recent contemporary must, of course, argue that 1 Thess. 2:15–16 is an interpolation, since it clearly affirms that "the Jews" killed Jesus in an actual historical event. On the authenticity of this passage, see below.

in the Gospels.[20] Paul practiced what he preached, and at the foundation of what he preached was a body of knowledge about the ministry and character of the Lord he served.

The Need for Biographical Information

The presence of this historical material about Jesus seems to fly in the face of the contention that Paul viewed Jesus as a savior figure from the distant past and/or heavenly realms and/or knew next to nothing and cared little about his earthly life. How, for example, could Paul possibly have set conformity with Christ as the goal of his life, and how could he possibly have insisted that others do the same, if he knew and cared little, in concrete detail, about what it was he and other disciples were supposed to conform to? With Paul, as with all other first-century Hellenistic and Jewish models of character, the call to imitate the life of a person presupposed a significant shared body of knowledge about the life that person lived. In the words of Michael Thompson,

> The importance of imitation in pagan and OT thought, coupled with evidence from later Jewish traditions that a rabbi's example had decisive significance for his followers, supports the *a priori* expectation that Paul too would want to know all he could about his master.[21]

Moreover, only on the assumption that Paul and his congregations cared and knew about the life of the one they had devoted their own lives to can we explain the creation of the Gospels. The Gospels are, if not biographies per se, at least biographical in the sense that they "display a didactic concern to portray the character of their subject matter by recounting things he did and said."[22] In other words, they are structured for teaching purposes. But how are we to explain the felt need to provide instruction from the life of Jesus in the church shortly after

20. S. Kim, "Jesus, Sayings of," in *Dictionary of Paul and His Letters*, ed. G. F. Hawthorne, R. P. Martin, and D. G. Reid (Downers Grove, IL: InterVarsity, 1993), 490. Reprinted as idem, "The Jesus Tradition in Paul," in *Paul and the New Perspective: Second Thoughts on the Origin of Paul's Gospel* (Grand Rapids: Eerdmans, 2002), 259–92.

21. M. Thompson, *Clothed with Christ: The Examples and Teaching of Jesus in Romans 12:1–15:13* (Sheffield: Sheffield Academic Press, 1991), 69. James Dunn agrees when he writes: "Given the universal curiosity in the prominent or hero figure which is as evident in ancient writings as it is today, it would be surprising if those who claimed to have put their faith in this Christ were not a little curious about the character and content of his life and ministry prior to his death" ("Jesus-tradition in Paul," in *Studying the Historical Jesus: Evaluations of the State of Current Research*, ed. B. Chilton and C. Evans [New York: Brill, 1994], 156–57). In his provocative book, *Saint Saul: A Skeleton Key to the Historical Jesus* (Montreal: McGill-Queens University Press, 2000), historian D. H. Akenson takes a similar approach. One does not have to accept all of Akenson's novel thesis (that the Jewish war in 70 CE so radically changed things that the only credible sources on the historical Jesus are those written before this period—i.e., Paul's letters) or his particular interpretation of the Jesus tradition in the Pauline letters to appreciate the way he takes seriously the Jesus tradition in Paul.

22. Dunn, "Jesus-tradition," 158.

Paul's death if the extreme legendary-Jesus theorists are right in arguing there had been virtually no interest in, let alone a need for, such information before Paul's death? It seems much more reasonable to assume that from the start the earliest Christian communities felt a need to know about the historical person they had committed their lives to.[23]

The Case for 1 Thessalonians 2:13–16 as a Later Interpolation

Still, some legendary-Jesus theorists argue, there is only one reference in the authentic Pauline letters that positively *requires* us to accept that Paul viewed Jesus as a *recent* historical person. In 1 Thessalonians 2:13–16, Paul notes that the Jews who persecuted the churches of Judea were the same ones who "killed both the Lord Jesus and the prophets, and drove us out." Because of this, Paul says, they have "been filling up the measure of their sins; but God's wrath has overtaken them at last." Legendary-Jesus theorists of the extreme Christ myth variety admit that if this passage is authentic we cannot avoid concluding that Paul viewed Jesus as a contemporary figure. However, along with some others, they argue that this passage is a later interpolation. The theory seems to hinge on five lines of argument.[24]

1. It is argued that verses 13–16 interrupt the natural flow of Paul's thought. The passage as a whole reads better when verses 13–16 are extracted from it.[25]

2. It is argued that the language and style of this passage are atypical of Paul. The designation of the Jews as those who "killed both the Lord Jesus and the prophets" and as people who have constantly "been filling up the measure of their sins" is arguably un-Pauline, as is the language about God's wrath "overtaking them at last."

3. The reference to God's wrath overtaking the Jews "at last" can refer only to the destruction of Jerusalem and the scattering of the Jews in 70 CE. Since this event occurred after Paul's death, it seems it could not have been written by Paul.[26]

---

23. A standard form-critical objection to this thesis is that the (alleged) sayings, aphorisms, speeches, and deeds of Jesus were originally transmitted orally in the early church as independent units. Since it is assumed that oral traditions do not transmit long narratives, many form-critics assume that the narrative of Jesus's life was superimposed on these otherwise disparate units when the Gospels were written. As we shall see in the next chapter, recent research into the nature of oral traditions decisively refutes this standard form-critical assumption.

24. As examples of those who are not Christ myth theorists yet argue for the interpolation thesis, see B. A. Pearson, "I Thessalonians 2.13–16: A Deutero-Pauline Interpolation," *HTR* 64 (1971): 79–94; D. Schmidt, "I Thess 2:13–16: Linguistic Evidence for an Interpolation," *JBL* 102 (1983): 269–79. For the case that a wide variety of interpolations can be identified in Paul's letters (including this passage), see W. O. Walker, *Interpolations in the Pauline Letters*, JSNTSup 213 (Sheffield: Sheffield Academic Press, 2001).

25. Wells writes, "The natural continuation after 2:12 comes only with 2:17, where Paul is again speaking of his dealings with that church, so that verses 13 through 16 are easily detachable from the context in which they have been placed" (*Historical Evidence*, 25).

26. Doherty, *Jesus Puzzle*, 297.

4. This passage blames the Jews for Jesus's crucifixion, a theme frequently found in later Christian authors, while Paul places the blame on spiritual rulers and/or secular rulers (depending on one's interpretation of 1 Cor. 2:8).

5. Finally, it is argued that the theology of judgment expressed in this passage is inconsistent with the optimism we find in Romans 11, where Paul is confident that in the end, "all Israel will be saved" (v. 26).[27]

The Case for the Authenticity of 1 Thessalonians 2:13–16

In our opinion, each of the five arguments have significant problems, and thus the cumulative case itself fails to convince. We offer five responses.

1. It is no minor problem for a textual theory when there is no textual evidence to support it. Yet this is the case here. Every ancient copy of 1 Thessalonians we have contains verses 13–16. The claim that this passage is an interpolation often rides on the coattails of a wider claim regarding a variety of Pauline interpolations, again generally without manuscript evidence.[28] However, as I. Broer has effectively argued, the evidence from early Christian writings (e.g., 1 Clement, Ignatius, Polycarp) suggests that the relatively widespread knowledge of the Pauline letters would naturally have served to hamper the easy acceptance and/or creation of interpolations.[29]

2. There is little to be said in favor of rejecting these verses on syntactical grounds. It is true that verses 12 and 17 can be seamlessly joined together. But for an author as given to parenthetical expressions as Paul is, this observation carries very little weight. It is also true that these verses seem stylistically uncharacteristic of Paul, but it is not clear that they are so to an extent that would warrant the conclusion that they are not Paul's own words.[30]

If an explanation is required, it seems more likely that it is to be found in the parallels that exist between these verses and teachings found in Matthew and Luke (Q). David Wenham and others have shown that the teaching about the Jews killing the prophets, about them filling up the full measure of their sins, and about God's wrath overtaking them in the end all have significant parallels in Q (Matt. 23:32–36 // Luke 11:48–51). On this basis Wenham has made a strong case for viewing Paul as echoing a preexisting Jesus tradition in verses 15–16.[31] Obviously, this would explain the stylistic differences.

27. Doherty, *Jesus Puzzle*, 298; Wells, *Historical Evidence*, 24–25.

28. See, e.g., Walker, *Interpolations*; W. Munro, *Authority in Paul and Peter: The Identification of a Pastoral Stratum in the Pauline Corpus and I Peter* (New York: Cambridge University Press, 1983).

29. I. Broer, "'Der ganze Zorn ist schon über sie gekommen': Bemerkungen zur Interpolationshypothese und zur Interpretation von I Thess. 2, 14–16," in *The Thessalonian Correspondence*, ed. R. F. Collins (Leuven: Leuven University Press, 1990), 142–45.

30. Schmidt's linguistic arguments have been convincingly answered by J. Weatherly, "The Authenticity of 1 Thessalonians 2:13–16: Additional Evidence," *JSNT* 42 (1991): 91–98; and J. W. Simpson, "The Problems Posed by I Thessalonians 2:15–16 and a Solution," *Horizons in Biblical Theology* 12 (1990): 52–54.

31. D. Wenham, *Paul: Follower of Jesus or Founder of Christianity?* (Grand Rapids: Eerdmans, 1995), 319–26.

3. There is no reason to assume that the reference to God's wrath overtaking the Jews refers to the destruction of Jerusalem. To be sure, we can perhaps understand why people *after* this event would view it as such and perhaps associate the warning of this passage with that event. But it is odd to suppose that a Jewish author prior to 70 CE could not have spoken of God's wrath overtaking his people without having this event in mind. In fact, since Paul speaks of God judging people by abandoning them to idolatry, giving them over to their ungodly cravings, hardening them in their unbelief, or sending a spirit of delusion on them (e.g., Rom. 1; 9; 2 Thess. 2:11), it is not even clear that the reference to God's wrath must be understood as an observable event in history.

Yet, even if we assume the reference must be to some observable event, there is no reason to assume it must be the destruction of Jerusalem. Some have suggested that it refers to the expulsion of the Jews from Rome under Claudius in 49 CE.[32] But it is not even certain that the author of these passages is assuming the event—if it is such—has already happened at the time of his writing. The phrase "at last" (*eis telos*) literally means "to (or until) the end" and, as with other aspects of this passage, it parallels Jesus's eschatological discourse (Matt. 24:13 // Mark 13:13).[33] The phrase thus may communicate the conviction that God's wrath has turned on the Jews *until* the end of the age, the parousia. As was characteristic of the early church, Paul believed that this end was already upon them and would soon culminate in a cataclysmic, apocalyptic event. But we need not read him as presupposing that the final expression of God's wrath had already occurred at the time of his writing.[34]

4. The contention that this passage cannot come from Paul because it blames the Jews for Christ's death is hardly compelling. There is simply no reason to suppose that Paul could not have believed that several groups—including some Jews and some secular authorities and/or spiritual powers—were responsible for bringing this event about. Indeed, this seems to be precisely how the early church understood the matter. Jon Weatherly notes that "all four canonical Gospels and Acts ascribe responsibility for Jesus's death to Jews and Romans (e.g. Mark 10:32 and parallels; Luke 22:3; Acts 4:27–28), and there is little reason to think that Paul's view was necessarily more narrow."[35]

Likewise, the charge that the perspective of this passage is too "anti-Semitic" to have come from Paul is less than effective. Recently, Jeffrey Lamp has read 1 Thessalonians 2:13–16 in light of *Testament of Levi* 6 and concluded:

Both the context of I Thess 2:13–16 and the comparison with Testament of Levi 6 strongly suggest that the use of generalizing language neither consigns all individuals

32. Ibid., 322.
33. Ibid., 324; see the references in n. 82. Wenham suggests that Paul "may have been assuming that his readers were familiar with the thought of 'wrath' to come on the Jews" and that "his obscurity could in part be because he was alluding to a tradition that they knew" (p. 322).
34. Weatherly, "Authenticity," 90–93.
35. Ibid., 82.

within the group of "the Jews" to perdition nor implies that all individuals within this group are guilty of any or all points of Paul's indictment against the group.[36]

5. Finally, even if the theology of this passage seems inconsistent with the theology of Romans 11, this does not mean that Paul did not write both. It is not uncommon for authors to phrase matters in ways that seem inconsistent to later readers—particularly in historically occasioned documents such as Paul's epistles. And even if we grant that the theology of 1 Thessalonians 2 is in fact inconsistent with the theology of Romans 11, one could still argue this does not constitute grounds for denying that Paul wrote both. Is it not possible that Paul's theology evolved between the time he wrote his epistle to the Thessalonians and the time he wrote his epistle to the Romans?[37]

There is, however, little reason to suppose these two passages stand in contradiction to each other. It is true that in Romans Paul envisioned a time when Israel as a nation would come to trust in their Messiah and be saved (Rom. 11:26). But it is also true that in this very same letter Paul expresses the conviction that God was already judging Israel as a nation for its unbelief (Rom. 9–10; 11:7–10). Paul's language in Romans 11 seems just as severe toward Israel as the language of 1 Thessalonians 2:13–16. Moreover, in Romans 11 Paul specifically cites the (Q) theme of Israel stoning and killing the prophets (11:2–10), just as he does in 1 Thessalonians 2:15–16.

Unless we are willing to suppose that Paul flatly contradicted himself within the span of several verses in Romans 11, it seems we have no grounds for supposing he is contradicting himself in saying all Israel will be saved in Romans 11 while saying that the unbelieving Jews are being judged in 1 Thessalonians 2.[38] Whatever Paul specifically had in mind when he said "all Israel will be saved," it clearly does not rule out his *also* believing that their sin has "been filling up" and that they were already being judged for their rebellion.

For all these reasons, we conclude that it is reasonable to maintain the authenticity of 1 Thessalonians 2:13–16. And we therefore see this passage as providing solid evidence that Paul viewed Jesus as a recent contemporary in history.

A Networked Visionary

In light of what has been argued thus far, it seems evident that Paul believed Jesus was a recent contemporary and knew a good bit about his life. There is no reason to think that Paul had any contact with Jesus during Jesus's ministry, which

36. J. S. Lamp, "Is Paul Anti-Semitic? *Testament of Levi* 6 in the Interpretation of I Thessalonians 2:13–16," *CBQ* 65 (2003): 427.

37. Simpson, "Problems," 42–43.

38. It might be significant in this regard to note that Paul's statement in 1 Thessalonians is specifically about Jews in Judea who killed Jesus, stoned the prophets, and hindered the progress of the gospel. It is not directed toward Jews *as a whole*. On the significance of the geographical specificity of 1 Thessalonians 2:15–16, see Weatherly, "Authenticity," 85.

means the only plausible explanation as to how Paul acquired this information was that he was networked with a church tradition that went back to the earthly Jesus. According to many legendary-Jesus theorists, however, Paul's theology and mission was informed and fueled almost exclusively by his own "personal revelations." These scholars argue that Paul's citations of instructions "from the Lord" are to be understood in this light, not as allusions to teachings given by the Jesus of history and passed on in the church tradition. What are we to make of this argument?

It cannot be denied that Paul leveraged a good deal of authority on his personal revelations. But this in no way implies that personal inspiration was the only source Paul drew on when writing his epistles. It is important to note that Paul always assumed that the faith he came to embrace and preach was the *same faith* he had earlier sought to destroy (Gal. 1:23; see also 1 Cor. 15:11). This means that Paul did not *create* the Christian faith he preached; to a significant extent, at least, *he inherited it*.[39]

After his conversion, Paul met with other church "pillars" in Jerusalem for the purpose of ensuring that what he believed and preached was consistent with what they had been believing and preaching from the beginning (Gal. 2:1–9). And, while we need not assume they saw eye to eye on every point (e.g., Gal. 2:11–14), Paul and his colleague Barnabas were given "the right hand of fellowship" (Gal. 2:9). Indications are that the church leaders supported Paul and he supported them, even to the point of raising funds on their behalf (2 Cor. 8–9) and citing the Judean Christians as exemplary models to be imitated (1 Thess. 2:14).

We should not be surprised, therefore, when we find Paul on occasion acknowledging that he was passing on teachings he had received from others (1 Cor. 11:2; 15:3; 1 Thess. 4:1–2; 2 Thess. 3:6; cf. Col. 2:6; Gal. 1:18).[40] Many other times Paul indicates that he is reminding his audience of teachings they already received, a point that is reinforced by the frequency of Paul's rhetorical question, "Do you not know?" (e.g., 1 Cor. 3:16; 5:6; 6:2, 3, 9, 15). All of this suggests that the faith of Paul and his audiences was informed and shaped by an authoritative tradition they all submitted

---

39. The "Jesus vs. Paul" dichotomy has been a staple of certain sectors of critical scholarship for some time. For a helpful overview of a good portion of the debate, see V. P. Furnish, "The Jesus-Paul Debate: From Baur to Bultmann," in *Paul and Jesus: Collected Essays*, ed. A. J. M. Wedderburn and C. Wolff (Sheffield: Sheffield Academic Press, 1989), 17–50. See also S. G. Wilson, "From Jesus to Paul: The Contours and Consequences of a Debate," in *From Jesus to Paul: Studies in Honour of Francis Wright Beare* (Waterloo, ON: Wilfried Laurier University Press, 1984), 1–21. For two exemplars of the discontinuity view, see R. Bultmann, "The Significance of the Historical Jesus for the Theology of Paul," in *Faith and Understanding*, trans. L. P. Smith (London: SCM, 1969), 1:220–46; G. Lüdemann, *Paul: The Founder of Christianity* (Amherst, NY: Prometheus, 2002). For several cases for continuity between Jesus and Paul, see Wenham, *Paul*; Wright, *What Saint Paul Really Said*; I. H. Marshall, "Jesus, Paul and John," *Aberdeen University Review* 173 (Spring 1985): 18–36; S. Freyne, "The Jesus-Paul Debate Revisited and Re-Imaging Christian Origins," in *Christian Origins: Worship, Belief and Society*, ed. K. J. O'Mahony, JSNTSup 241 (New York: Sheffield Academic Press, 2003), 143–63.

40. Dunn, "Jesus-tradition," 157.

to. As Michael Thompson notes, this certainly demonstrates that Paul "had no desire to break away and establish separate 'Pauline' churches, but rather was concerned to preserve the unity (and thus the central tradition) of the body of Christ."[41]

The significance of these considerations is that they stand against the idea shared by many scholars, that early Christianity was not a generally unified movement but was rather a conglomeration of radically diverse movements with little more than a vague—and diversely understood—conception of Jesus in common. Moreover, these considerations refute the common legendary-Jesus conviction that Paul was the creator of Christianity—in the form of a new "Christ cult."[42] Again, we are not denying that Paul believed he received revelations directly from the risen Jesus. But nowhere does he suggest that his knowledge of Jesus is *limited* to these personal revelations. And he everywhere reflects the conviction that the revelations he received were consistent with the teachings the Christian churches had been passing on from the beginning.

References to the "Jesus Tradition" in Paul

If we do not assume at the outset that Paul was an isolated visionary who was opposed to receiving and passing on traditional material, we can begin to identify a significant amount of material in his letters that plausibly reflects what has come to be called "the Jesus tradition." This "tradition" refers to the body of knowledge about the ministry and teachings of Jesus that circulated primarily via oral performance in the early church. As we will argue in the next chapter, most likely from fairly early on, various portions of this tradition were occasionally "textualized" in written form. Eventually, a major stream of this Jesus tradition was inscribed in the Synoptic Gospel tradition.[43] There is solid evidence that commonalities exist between certain aspects of Paul's teachings and the Synoptic Jesus tradition that cannot plausibly be regarded merely as coincidental.[44]

We must at the outset acknowledge that it is very possible to push this thesis too far. Some scholars in the past have read into Paul parallels with the Jesus tradition that are now unanimously regarded as wildly implausible.[45] We must also grant

41. Thompson, *Clothed with Christ*, 67. We will explore the central role of strong tradition bearers and/or performers of oral tradition (tradents) and teachers in chaps. 6–7.

42. On the "Christ cult" category, see B. L. Mack, *A Myth of Innocence: Mark and Christian Origins* (Philadelphia: Fortress, 1988), 98–123; R. M. Price, *Deconstructing Jesus* (Amherst, NY: Prometheus, 2000), 75–95.

43. As we will see in the next two chapters, a good deal hangs on our understanding of the nature, scope, and reliability of this pre-Gospel oral and/or written tradition.

44. James Dunn rightly argues that a number of a priori considerations should lead us to expect that there is "a high degree of probability that Paul must have both known and cared about the ministry of Jesus," *The Theology of Paul the Apostle* (Grand Rapids: Eerdmans, 1998), 188; see 185–89 for specifics.

45. The most famous example of this is perhaps A. Resch, who in 1905 claimed to have found 1158 allusions to tradition deriving from Jesus. See *Der Paulinismus und die Logia Jesu* (Leipzig: Hinrichs,

at the outset that some similarities may indeed be simply coincidental, especially when we can plausibly account for them by appealing to the shared Jewish and/ or Hellenistic culture of Paul and the Gospel authors. When it comes to Paul and the Jesus tradition, we must be as cautious of "parallelomania" as we are of "parallelophobia."[46] Moreover, even when we are relatively sure a connection between Paul and the Gospel tradition exists, we cannot rule out the possibility that, in some instances, the line of influence may be from Paul to the Gospel tradition rather than the other way around. There is certainly no a priori reason for thinking that Paul could not have helped shape the transmission of the Jesus tradition.

Still, we submit that when the evidence is viewed with care, a strong case can be made that Paul, at certain points, relied on an oral Jesus tradition that preceded him. This case in turn argues that Paul knew about, and cared about, the teaching tradition stemming from Jesus as it was passed on to his disciples and transmitted within the church. And it thereby refutes the view that Paul viewed Jesus as a mystery-religion–type savior figure who lived in a distant past Paul knew and cared little about.

Following Seyoon Kim, we will break down possible instances of Jesus tradition in Paul into two broad categories: (1) certain/probable references, and (2) possible echoes.[47] While assessments of the matter vary significantly, under Kim's analysis there are over twenty-five instances where "Paul certainly or probably makes refer-

---

1905). In this context, Wenham rightly cautions us from falling into "parallelomania," on one hand, or "parallelophobia," on the other (*Paul*, 25). The only hope of avoiding either is to identify and adopt an appropriate methodology by which to identify quotations, allusions, and echoes.

46. Wenham, *Paul*, 25.

47. Kim, "Jesus Tradition in Paul," 259. Another helpful approach has been developed by Thompson, who offers a methodological proposal by which to distinguish between quotations, allusions, and echoes; see *Clothed with Christ*, 29–36. The methodology and conclusions that follow have been shaped by a number of studies, including: D. C. Allison, "The Pauline Epistles and the Synoptic Gospels: The Pattern of the Parallels," *NTS* 28 (1982): 1–32; idem, *Scriptural Allusions in the New Testament: Light from the Dead Sea Scrolls* (North Richland Hills, TX: Bibal, 2000); D. L. Dungan, *The Sayings of Jesus in the Churches of Paul* (Philadelphia: Fortress, 1973); Dunn, "Jesus-tradition"; idem, "Paul's Knowledge of the Jesus Tradition: The Evidence of Romans," in *Christus Bezeugen: Festschrift für Wolfgang Trilling*, ed. K. Kertelege, T. Holtz, and C.-P. März (Leipzig: St. Benno, 1989), 193–207; idem, *Theology of Paul*, esp. 182–206; T. Holtz, "Paul and the Oral Gospel Tradition," in *Jesus and the Oral Gospel Tradition*, ed. H. Wansborough (Sheffield: Sheffield Academic Press, 1991), 380–93; J. Murphy-O'Conner, "The Origin of Paul's Christology: From Thessalonians to Galatians," in *Christian Origins*, 120–23; F. Neirynck, "Paul and the Sayings of Jesus," in *L'Apotre Paul*, ed. A. Vanhoye (Paris: Gembloux, 1986), 265–321; S. J. Patterson, "Paul and the Jesus Tradition: It Is Time for Another Look," *HTR* 84 (1991): 23–41; D. M. Stanley, "Pauline Allusions to the Sayings of Jesus," *CBQ* 23 (1961): 26–39; C. Stettler, "The 'Command of the Lord' in 1 Cor 14,37—a Saying of Jesus?" *Biblica* 87 (2006): 42–51; W. A. Strange, "The Jesus-Tradition in Acts," *NTS* 46 (2000): 59–74; C. Tuckett, "Paul and Jesus Tradition: The Evidence of I Corinthians 2:9 and Gospel of Thomas 17," in *Paul and the Corinthians: Studies on a Community in Conflict, Essays in Honour of Margaret Thrall* (Boston: Brill, 2003), 55–73; Wenham, *Paul*; N. T. Wright, "The Paul of History and the Apostle of Faith," *Tyndale Bulletin* 29 (1978): 61–88. In our estimation, the best single work on the topic of references to Jesus throughout the Pauline corpus is Wenham's *Paul: Follower of Jesus or Founder of Christianity?*

ence or allusion to a saying of Jesus," and "over forty possible echoes of a saying of Jesus."[48] Although entering into the often complex issues that surround these alleged parallels would take us well beyond the scope of this work, it will be helpful for our purposes to briefly discuss a few instances in each category that seem most pertinent to refuting the more extreme forms of the legendary-Jesus thesis.

We shall first discuss four passages where Paul appears to be citing (in the sense appropriate to an orally dominant culture in which primarily "things," not necessarily "words," are remembered)[49] traditional Jesus material that can be connected to known teachings of Jesus in the Synoptic tradition. As such, they are among the strongest evidence against the legendary-Jesus perspective vis-à-vis Paul. We will then conclude this section by discussing examples of "possible echoes" of, and/or allusions to, the Jesus tradition in Paul.

1 Corinthians 11:23–26

For I received from the Lord what I also handed on to you, that the Lord Jesus on the night when he was betrayed took a loaf of bread, and when he had given thanks, he broke it and said, "This is my body that is for you. Do this in remembrance of me." In the same way he took the cup also, after supper, saying, "This cup is the new covenant in my blood. Do this, as often as you drink it, in remembrance of me." For as often as you eat this bread and drink the cup, you proclaim the Lord's death until he comes.

No one disputes that Paul's words here strongly parallel the account of the Last Supper found in all four Gospels, especially Luke's (Luke 22:17–20). The only question is: Are we to explain this commonality by supposing that Paul is here following an established oral Jesus tradition, later expressed in the Gospels? Or should we explain it by supposing that Paul (or some proto-Pauline hellenized "Christ cult") originated this teaching, and that it later found its way into the Gospels? Several arguments have been put forth arguing for the latter supposition. None of them are compelling in our estimation.

The old history of religions school argued that the Last Supper account in Paul was derived from sacred meal traditions found in the mystery religions. Several scholars have recently resurrected versions of this claim—some more nuanced than others.[50] This theory is extremely improbable, however.

48. Kim, "Jesus, Sayings of," 490.

49. Critics who argue that divergence of wording is evidence that quotation is not in view only betray the fact that they come to this judgment via post-Gutenberg, highly literate sensibilities and criteria. It has now been firmly established by contemporary orality studies that what is generally remembered in orally dominant contexts is essential propositional content rather than particular wording (things, not words, or "gist"). See F. A. Yates, *The Art of Memory* (Chicago: University of Chicago Press, 1966), 29–31; T. Lentz, *Orality and Literacy in Hellenic Greece* (Carbondale: Southern Illinois University Press, 1989), 92. See also J. P. Small, *Wax Tablets of the Mind: Cognitive Studies of Memories and Literacy in Classical Antiquity* (New York: Routledge, 1997), 193–96. Thus, while quotation may include verbatim wording, it need not.

50. A. J. M. Wedderburn, while cautious (see his final caveat on p. 829), has reopened the door to serious consideration of the influence of mystery religions on Paul, perhaps via earlier Hellenistic Chris-

All the extant evidence we have for the mystery religions dates well after the time of Paul, and there is no reason to think a (Pharisaic) Jew like Paul would have found them appealing, even if such traditions had been available to him. A. J. M. Wedderburn, who, methodologically speaking, is quite open to the possibility of the influence of mystery religions upon early Christianity, poses the proper warning when he calls scholars to "be realistic as to how much Paul or any early Christian was likely to be in a position to know much about the mystery-cults and as to how he was likely to view anything which he knew to belong to such rites."[51] Additionally, the sacred meals of the mystery religions bear little resemblance to Paul's, or the Gospels', account of the Last Supper. Indeed, a number of scholars have noted that the New Testament accounts of the Last Supper are deeply rooted in Palestinian Jewish theology and culture.[52]

Geza Vermes has argued that the metaphor of eating someone's body and drinking someone's blood would have been foreign, and indeed shocking, in a Palestinian Jewish cultural setting. Therefore, this tradition must have originated in a non-Jewish environment.[53] This argument fails on a number of counts, however. For one thing, Vermes's argument seems to ignore the fact that the preconversion Paul was himself a Torah-true Jew (Phil. 3:4–6). If *he* was capable of embracing this teaching, we have every reason to suppose other Jews would have been capable of embracing it. Indeed, the fact that the teaching eventually found its way into the Gospels (including Matthew's) suggests the same thing.[54]

Actually, far from arguing against the metaphor's authenticity, the fact that the metaphor of eating a body and drinking blood would have been shocking to Torah-oriented Jews arguably counts *in favor* of viewing Paul's account of the Last Supper as being rooted in the life of Jesus. Jesus frequently used vivid, countercultural parables and metaphors designed to shock his Jewish audience. Unless this shocking metaphor was solidly rooted in the authority of the earthly Jesus, we are left with the question of how it found a traditional—even central—place among his early Jewish followers. As shocking as the imagery was, however, it nonetheless

tianity. See "Paul and the Hellenistic Mystery-Cults: On Posing the Right Questions," in *La Soteriologia dei culti orientali nell' Impero Romano*, ed. U. Bianchi and M. J. Vermaseren (Leiden: Brill, 1982), 817–33. More brazen examples include Doherty, *Jesus Puzzle*, 111–12; A. N. Wilson, *Paul: The Mind of the Apostle* (New York: Norton, 1997), 165–68. The basic orientation of both Mack (*Myth of Innocence*, 114–20) and Price (*Deconstructing Jesus*, 86–93) would fit well with this approach, though neither fleshes out this connection as fully as they might.

51. Wedderburn, "Paul and the Hellenistic Mystery-Cults," 829.

52. See, e.g., Wenham, *Paul*, 157; D. Daube, *He That Cometh* (London: London Diocesan Council, 1966); D. B. Carmichael, "David Daube on the Eucharist and the Passover Seder," *JSNT* 42 (1991): 45–67. This broader line of consideration—the fundamentally Torah-centered nature of first-century Palestinian Judaism and its aversion to pagan religious influence—has already been addressed in chaps. 2 and 3.

53. G. Vermes, *The Religion of Jesus the Jew* (London: SCM, 1993), 16.

54. Luke and Paul speak about "the new covenant in blood" while Matthew and Mark have Jesus say, "this is my blood." It is possible that Luke and Paul toned down the expression because of the offensiveness of the idea of drinking blood. See Wenham, *Paul*, 158n43.

finds its conceptual home within the world of a deeply Jewish covenant theology. The timing (Passover), the Old Testament allusion ("new covenant"; e.g., Jer. 31:31–34), the language ("remembrance" = covenant sign), and even the blood metaphor itself all make sense within a Jewish covenantal matrix.

Some legendary-Jesus theorists argue that when Paul says he "received from the Lord" the teaching he gives in this context, he is signaling that he obtained this information by direct revelation from the heavenly Christ, not from a supposed Jesus tradition. Indeed, they argue that it was this direct revelation that was eventually embedded in the historicized myth of Jesus found in the later Gospels. While this interpretation of Paul's expression is not impossible, we agree with the vast majority of scholars that there is little to recommend it. Three considerations count against it.

First, we have no other evidence that Paul or anyone else in the early church claimed to acquire information about *past historical events* through revelation. If this is what Paul is doing in this passage, it would appear to be the only time he does so—and this is reason enough to suspect that something else is going on.

Second, the text itself suggests Paul is relying on traditional material. He introduces his material with standard Jewish terminology for "receiving" and "handing over" sacred tradition (v. 23).[55] This suggests that Paul was passing on material *that had been passed on to him by others*. In this light, when Paul says he "received from the Lord" this teaching, it seems most natural to take him to be referring to his conviction that this traditional material *goes back to the Lord's own words and actions*. Through the tradition, now being mediated through Paul, the Corinthians were "receiving from the Lord" the teaching about the Last Supper. This conclusion is confirmed by the fact that Paul's words betray a "wholly fixed verbal form," as is seen when compared with Luke 22:19–20.[56]

Third, it seems highly improbable that a personal revelation of a supposed historical event could have gained such a deep and pervasive authority throughout the various streams of the early church.[57] While it is clear that the early church was charismatic, they were not uncritical of prophetic words (1 Cor. 14:29) and did not seem to place them on a par with the authority of the Old Testament or of Jesus.[58]

55. See B. Gerhardsson, *Memory and Manuscript: Oral Tradition and Written Transmission in Rabbinic Judaism and Early Christianity* (Lund/Copenhagen: C.W.K. Gleerup/Ejnar Munksgaard, 1961), 290–99.

56. Holtz, "Paul and the Oral Gospel Tradition," 383. See also Dunn, *Theology of Paul*, 606–8; Kim, "Jesus Tradition in Paul," 261; Stanley, "Pauline Allusions," 27.

57. The fact that the Lukan version is arguably independent of Mark, as is John's, strengthens this argument; see Wenham, *Paul*, 157.

58. Indeed, it does not seem the early Christians necessarily placed personal revelations on a par with authoritative writings from church leaders, such as Paul. How else can we explain the fact that Paul's *written* instruction about prophetic words were part of the criterion by which a "word" was regarded as of God or not (1 Cor. 14:27–33)? On this broader issue, see J. Dunn, "Prophetic 'I'-Sayings and the

1 Corinthians 7:10–11

To the married I give this command—not I but the Lord—that the wife should not separate from her husband (but if she does separate, let her remain unmarried or else be reconciled to her husband), and that the husband should not divorce his wife. To the rest I say—I and not the Lord—that if any believer has a wife who is an unbeliever, and she consents to live with him, he should not divorce her.

It seems reasonable to see in this passage a Pauline citation of a command prohibiting divorce that derives from the teaching of Jesus (i.e., Matt. 19:3–12 // Mark 10:2–12). The fact that Paul takes care to distinguish teaching he received "from the Lord" and his own (inspired) convictions on the matter reinforces this conclusion.

Besides the parallel convictions of Paul and the Jesus tradition on divorce, there are theological similarities between Paul and this aspect of the Jesus tradition as well. For example, both Paul and the Jesus of the Gospels ground their understanding of marriage and divorce in the Genesis concept of married couples becoming "one flesh" (1 Cor. 6:12–20). There are also strong verbal similarities. For example, Paul's teaching that the wife "should not separate" (*me choristhenai*) from her husband is very close to Jesus's declaration that, "What God has joined together, let no one separate" (*me chorizeto*). There are even significant structural similarities. For example, in both Paul and the Jesus tradition the prohibition on divorce is followed by a teaching discouraging remarriage.[59]

On this basis it seems reasonable to conclude that Paul not only was aware of a specific command in the Jesus tradition, but also was well acquainted with "his teaching on marriage as a whole, including its 'one flesh' principle and its relationship to the service of the kingdom of God."[60] In the words of D. L. Dungan, "Paul stands squarely within the tradition that led to the Synoptic gospels, and is of one mind with the editors of the gospels, not only in the way he understands what Jesus (the Lord) was actually commanding in the sayings themselves but also in the way he prefigures the Synoptic editors' use of them."[61]

Against this view, some scholars contend that Paul's acknowledgment that he received his command from the Lord means that he got this material not from earlier Jesus tradition, but from what he believed to be a personal revelation from the risen Christ.[62] With the majority of scholars, we deem this suggestion to be

---

Jesus Tradition: The Importance of Testing Prophetic Utterances within Early Christianity," *NTS* 24 (1977–78): 175–98.

59. See Wenham, *Paul*, 242–46. Also Kim, "Jesus Tradition in Paul," 260; Holtz, "Paul and the Oral Gospel Tradition," 383; J. P. Meier, *A Marginal Jew: Rethinking the Historical Jesus*, vol. 1: *The Roots of the Problem and the Person* (New York: Doubleday, 1991), 45–46.

60. Kim, "Jesus, Sayings of," 475.

61. Dungan, *Sayings of Jesus*, 139 (much of Dungan's argumentation in this book can stand apart from his neo-Griesbachian source-critical conclusions). Wenham concurs: "The case for Paul's dependence on the Jesus-tradition that we know from the synoptics is very strong here" (*Paul*, 244).

62. For example, Doherty, *Jesus Puzzle*, 29. Some more conservative scholars have come to this conclusion as well; e.g., P. Richardson, "'I Say, Not the Lord': Personal Opinion, Apostolic Authority and

quite unlikely. Among other problems, the phrase "but the Lord" can naturally be taken as a reference to the Jesus of history, mediated by the Jesus tradition (cf. 1 Cor. 9:14; 11:23). Moreover, it is difficult to imagine Paul distinguishing his own Spirit-inspired teaching (i.e., 1 Cor. 7:40) from teachings he received through Spirit-inspired personal revelation in the way that would be required by this passage.

Even more fundamentally, however, the legendary-Jesus theory asks us to believe that Paul's revelatory teaching was so authoritative in the early church that not only the content but also the theology, wording, and structure of his teaching became historicized myth in the Gospels. Even apart from the implausibility of seeing the Gospels as historicized myth (see chaps. 10–12), it is difficult to believe that any prophetic oracle could gain this much authority this quickly in the early church, as noted above. Hence, we see no good reason to deny that Paul is relying on, and distinguishing his own inspired opinion from, the Jesus tradition when he passes on this teaching on divorce and remarriage.

1 Corinthians 9:14

... the Lord commanded that those who proclaim the gospel should get their living by the gospel.

The subject matter in the broader context of this passage is the need for believers to restrict their own freedom for the sake of others (1 Cor. 8–10). To illustrate his point, Paul mentions that he did not receive any payment for his ministry even though, on Jesus's authority, he had a right to do so. In the course of giving this illustration, Paul defends his apostolic calling by responding to critics who apparently saw his refusal to accept payment as evidence that he was not a true apostle (9:3–23). Paul insists he is a true apostle, for he had seen the risen Lord (9:1, cf. 15:8). He therefore insists he has a right to "food and drink" (9:4) just as other ministers have (9:5–11, 13). But Paul (and Barnabas) chose to forgo this right so as to avoid putting any "obstacle in the way of the gospel of Christ" (9:12).

At this point Paul says that the Lord "commanded that those who proclaim the gospel should get their living by the gospel." Many scholars have argued that the teaching Paul is referring to is found in the Q material (Luke 10:7 // Matt. 10:10), where Jesus taught that "the laborer deserves to be paid." While the wording of Paul's citation is quite different from Q's, the case for Paul's reliance on a common Jesus tradition at this point is fairly strong.

First, Paul's application of the teaching in 1 Corinthians to the work of mission is the same as in Q. This suggests that Paul knew not only the saying in isolation, but also the broader missionary discourse tradition within which it is located.[63]

---

the Development of Early Christian Halakah," *TynB* 31 (1980): 71; O. Cullmann, "The Tradition," in *The Early Church*, ed. A. B. Higgins (London: SCM, 1956), 68–70.

63. Wenham, *Paul*, 193.

What is more, there are verbal cues in 1 Corinthians 9 that further suggest Paul was drawing on the same tradition as that reflected in Q. For example, the Q terms "work" and "hire" feature significantly in 1 Corinthians 9 (vv. 1, 6, 13), and Paul repeats the Q connection between reward and "food and drink" (v. 4, cf. v. 13). As Wenham notes, "The conjunction of ideas in [Paul and Q] . . . can hardly be coincidental."[64] It is true that Paul's wording is quite different from what we find in Q, but this sort of variation is typical of oral traditions, where the essential intention—the "gist"—of sayings and remembered events is valued much more than verbatim repetition.

As with the previously cited instances of Paul appealing to commands he received from the Lord, legendary-Jesus theorists have tried to argue that Paul is here giving a personal revelation that perhaps became imbedded in the mythologized narrative of Luke and Matthew. But this contention has significant problems. It faces the same difficulties we noted above in connection with the previous two references in Paul to the Jesus tradition. But this instance faces an additional difficulty.

In this passage Paul is quoting a command of the Lord *against himself*. Paul says, "The Lord commanded that those who proclaim the gospel should get their living by the gospel." "But," he then adds, "I have made no use of any of these rights" (v. 15). He is, in a sense, in violation of the Lord's "command." Indeed, it may have been this violation that led some of his critics to question the genuineness of his apostolic calling. In any event, Paul's argument presupposes that the command Paul is citing was *already known* both to his congregation and to his critics. In other words, it strongly suggests that we accept that Paul was relying on the Jesus tradition and that elements of this tradition had already been passed on to his congregation.

1 Thessalonians 4:15–17

> For this we declare to you by the word of the Lord, that we who are alive, who are left until the coming of the Lord, will by no means precede those who have died. For the Lord himself, with a cry of command, with the archangel's call and with the sound of God's trumpet, will descend from heaven, and the dead in Christ will rise first. Then we who are alive, who are left, will be caught up in the clouds together with them to meet the Lord in the air; and so we will be with the Lord forever.

While there is certainly no verbatim parallel between Paul's teaching here and anything we find in the Synoptic Gospels, there are a host of considerations that lead many scholars to conclude that Paul is in fact passing on an aspect of the Jesus tradition he had received from others and that he indicates this by noting that he is giving his teaching "by the word of the Lord."

---

64. Ibid. Here, 1 Tim. 5:18 also serves to support the connection. Even on the thesis that this text represents the work of a deutero-Pauline author, this author explicitly connects Paul's opinion on the matter (i.e., 1 Cor. 9:14) with Luke 10:7 and/or the tradition from which it is derived. See Holtz, "Paul and the Oral Gospel Tradition," 384.

Paul uses a number of vivid and distinctive apocalyptic images that are similar to the eschatological teachings found in the Gospels. The sounding of the trumpet (Matt. 24:31), the descent from heaven on the clouds with angels (Mark 13:26–27), the gathering of the elect, and perhaps even the notion of people being "caught up in the clouds" (arguably reminiscent of "one taken, one left" in Matt. 24:40, 41 // Luke 17:34, 35) are all found in the Synoptics.

Beyond this, a number of scholars have argued that the "cry of command" and the "archangel's call" parallel the Matthean parable of the virgins, which centers around a "cry" and uses the same unusual Greek phrase meaning "come out to meet him" (*eis apantesin*) (Matt. 25:6). Moreover, the warning to stay awake and be ready is found in both contexts (Matt. 25:13, cf. v. 5), as is the theme of "rising" to go away with the returning master (Matt. 25:7, 10).

The case for a connection to the Jesus tradition is further strengthened by the fact that similar parallels with the eschatological tradition found in the Gospels are found elsewhere in 1 and 2 Thessalonians. For example, Paul reminds the Thessalonians that the Lord would return "like a thief in the night," a point he (significantly enough) tells them they already knew "very well" (1 Thess. 5:2, 4). This distinctive imagery is found nowhere else in ancient Jewish literature, yet it directly parallels a Q tradition (Luke 12:39–40 // Matt. 24:43–44).[65] Similarly, it is hard not to hear Jesus's teaching about the need to stay alert (Luke 12:36–38) reflected in Paul's teaching on staying awake and remaining sober (1 Thess. 5:5–7).[66]

For these reasons, we are inclined to agree with Kim that,

> The several and clear echoes of Jesus' sayings in [1 Thess 4:15–17] seem to suggest that Paul must be conscious that the material he is using was Jesus material and therefore that with "the word of the Lord" here Paul is referring to the word(s) of the historical Jesus he is using rather than a prophetic oracle spoken in the name of the Lord.[67]

Still, could the parallels be accounted for by supposing that Paul influenced the Jesus tradition rather than the other way around? While there is no reason to suppose that Paul could not have influenced the Jesus tradition in some respects, it seems exceedingly unlikely that he originated *this* aspect of it.

First, for a number of reasons, it is explanatorily more efficient to see the line of influence coming from the Jesus tradition to Paul rather than the other way around. To give just one example, Paul ordinarily uses the word *koimao* for "sleep," yet in his teaching on not falling asleep in 5:6, he uses *katheudo*, the word used in Matthew's parable of the virgins. The easiest way to explain this variation is to suppose that Paul is at this point tapping into the eschatological tradition expressed in the parable of the ten virgins.

65. Kim, "Jesus, Sayings of," 476.
66. Wenham, *Paul*, 308n34.
67. Kim, "Jesus, Sayings of," 476.

Second, Paul sprinkles eschatological teaching throughout 1 and 2 Thessalonians. He elsewhere speaks of the Son appearing suddenly and gloriously, with angels (1 Thess. 1:6–10; 5:1–10), of God's coming judgment (1 Thess. 1:10; 2:16; 2 Thess. 1:4–10), of the need for believers to live righteously as they wait for the Lord's coming deliverance (1 Thess. 3:13; 4:1–10; 2 Thess. 1:5, 11–12), of the gathering of the saints in Christ at his coming (2 Thess. 2:1), and of events that will precede this coming (2 Thess. 2:3–12). Given how pervasive eschatological teaching is in these two letters, it seems most unnatural to suppose that in 1 Thessalonians 4:15–17 alone Paul is giving a prophetic oracle. The material in 4:15–17 is simply not that distinctive in relation to this other eschatological material. Rather, it seems that in 4:15–17, as elsewhere, Paul is passing on standard eschatological teaching in the church, and that some of this material—as in 4:15–17—is identified as more specifically tied to Jesus's own teaching. Moreover, the fact that 15b—the section that appears to contain the specific material drawn from Jesus—"fits only awkwardly into the logic of the statement" suggests that Paul faithfully retains the content (if not the wording) of the tradition without modifying it to more easily fit his particular needs.[68]

A final and important consideration is that Paul frequently tells the Thessalonians he is simply reminding them of a tradition *they already knew*—precisely as he is imparting his eschatological teaching. He notes how the Lord would avenge people who practice injustice "just as we have already told you beforehand and solemnly warned you" (1 Thess. 4:6). When it comes to the question of when this second coming would occur, Paul writes, "You do not need to have anything written to you. For you yourselves know very well that the day of the Lord will come like a thief in the night" (1 Thess. 5:1b–2). Similarly, just after telling the Thessalonians that he prays that they will appear blameless before God when he returns, Paul proceeds to tell them how to live blamelessly (1 Thess. 4:1–12), saying, "You know what instructions we gave you through the Lord Jesus" (v. 2). So too, when the second coming is addressed in the second epistle, we find: "Do you not remember that I told you these things when I was still with you?" (2 Thess. 2:5). And again: "So then, brothers and sisters, stand firm and hold fast to *the traditions that you were taught by us*, either by word of mouth or by our letter" (2 Thess. 2:15, emphasis added).

Significantly, the traditional eschatological material Paul is reminding the Thessalonians of is extensive, detailed, and is found nowhere else in the Pauline corpus (2 Thess. 2:1–12). Were it not for these passages, we would have no indication that Paul or his congregations believed any of this. Yet Paul explicitly tells us he was simply reminding them of "the traditions" he and they had received. This suggests that when Paul established congregations he probably passed on to them a great deal of traditional material that we remain uninformed of for the simple reason that Paul had no particular reason to mention it in his always-occasional extant letters.

68. Holtz, "Paul and the Oral Gospel Tradition," 386.

In any event, all of this provides good reason to conclude that Paul is not giving a new prophetic word in 1 Thessalonians 4:15–17. As elsewhere, he is recalling traditional material the Thessalonians already knew. The "word of the Lord" that Paul was referring to in this passage was the Jesus tradition that had been passed on to him and that he had in turn passed on to the Thessalonians.

Echoes and Allusions of the Jesus Tradition in Paul

Thus far we have seen that Paul reflects knowledge of the teachings of Jesus, knew him to be a person who lived in the recent past, and assumed that his audiences also knew a good deal about him—enough to model their lives after his. We have also seen that there is good reason to believe that, while Paul invested a significant degree of authority in his personal revelations, he also received and passed on established, authoritative, oral Jesus tradition. And we have seen that some of these traditions contained material about what Jesus taught, for Paul alludes to them at various points in his writings.

With all this in mind, it makes sense to further mine Paul's writings for other areas where his teaching may to some degree reflect the Jesus tradition. When we do so, we find that Paul's writings are full of ideas, phrases, and words that can plausibly be understood as "echoing" or "alluding to" the Jesus tradition. While some of these echoes and allusions may be explained as coincidence and perhaps others as Paul influencing the Jesus tradition rather than the other way around, the pervasiveness of these echoes reinforces the conviction that Paul was well acquainted with, and significantly dependent upon, the Jesus tradition that was later expressed in the Gospels.

Given space considerations, we cannot mention—let alone discuss—all the possible echoes of or allusions to the Jesus tradition in Paul's writings.[69] It will be helpful, however, to briefly illustrate this range of material by listing a few examples that have led many scholars to conclude that Paul and his congregations were well informed by traditions stemming from Jesus.

Among the distinctive parallels between Paul and Jesus (as represented by the Jesus tradition within the Gospels), we find both taught that:[70]

- God can be referred to as "Abba" (Rom. 8:15; Gal. 4:6 // Mark 14:36)
- we are to give to God what belongs to God (Rom. 12:1–2 // Mark 12:17)

69. We find Thompson's distinction between "allusions" and "echoes" to be most fruitful; see *Clothed with Christ*, 30. In Thompson's typology, an allusion is a passage "*intended* to remind an audience of a tradition they are presumed to know as dominical," while an echo signals a passage where "the influence of a dominical tradition upon Paul seems evident, but where it remains uncertain whether he was conscious of the influence at the time of dictating" (emphasis in text).

70. The following list is largely derived from Kim, "Jesus, Sayings of," 481. The list was arrived at by "critical comparisons of the vocabulary, form and/or content of Pauline statements with those of dominical logia preserved in the Synoptics" (p. 482). Other helpful contributions to the issue of allusions and/or echoes of Jesus tradition in Paul include Allison, "Pauline Epistles"; Dunn, *Theology of Paul*, 189–95; Holtz, "Paul and the Oral Gospel Tradition," 389–92; Thompson, *Clothed with Christ*.

- we are to bless those who do us wrong and love our enemies (Rom. 12:14; 19–21 // Luke 6:27–28; Matt. 5:44)[71]
- we are to live peacefully with all people (Rom. 12:18 // Mark 9:50)
- love fulfills the law (Rom. 13:8 // Mark 12:28–33)
- we must remain alert for the second coming (Rom. 13:11–14 // Luke 21:28, 31, 34)
- we are not to judge others (Rom. 14:1–13 // Matt. 7:1)
- no food is unclean in and of itself (Rom. 14:14, 20 // Mark 7:15)
- salvation is offered to Gentiles (Rom. 15:8–9 // Matt. 8:11)
- we are to be wise "as serpents" regarding what is good and innocent "as doves" regarding evil (Rom. 16:19 // Matt. 10:16)
- the kingdom is offered to those of low status in the world (1 Cor. 1:18–2:16 // Luke 10:21–24)
- ungodly people seek for a sign (1 Cor. 1:20–25 // Luke 11:29–32)
- the gospel will offend many (1 Cor. 1:23 // Matt. 11:6)
- we are called to be trustworthy stewards who will be judged by our master (1 Cor. 4:1–5 // Luke 12:41–46)
- we are to expect mistreatment in kingdom work (1 Cor. 4:12–13 // Luke 6:22–23)
- remaining single requires a special gift from God (1 Cor. 7:7 // Matt. 19:12)
- people must take care not to cause others to stumble (1 Cor. 8:13 // Mark 9:42)
- we are called to suffer and serve, not to be served (1 Cor. 9:19; 10:33; Phil. 1:27–2:11 // Mark 10:45, cf. 1 Cor. 11:1)
- faith can move mountains (1 Cor. 13:2 // Matt. 17:20)
- our earthly temple is "made with hands," but we shall inherit a temple "not made with hands" (2 Cor. 5:1 // Mark 14:58)
- kingdom work is accompanied by signs and wonders (2 Cor. 12:12 // Mark 6:7)
- knowledge of Jesus's identity comes from divine revelation (Gal. 1:1, 12–16 // Matt. 16:16–17)
- whoever rejects God's messenger rejects God (1 Thess. 4:8 // Luke 10:16)

71. The fact that Paul nowhere uses *kataraomai* ("curse") supports this conclusion. Dunn concludes, "Since the testimony of the Jesus tradition is clear that Jesus was remembered as saying something to this effect, it would be somewhat perverse to look for a different source of this distinctly Christian teaching. And since it is only in the Lukan and Romans form that we have the contrast drawn between 'blessing' and 'cursing,' the most obvious corollary is that it was indeed Jesus who provided the decisive moral impetus for the conduct here commended, and that the form known to Paul was expressed somewhat along the lines of the Lukan version" ("Jesus-tradition," 162). See also Wenham, *Paul*, 286–87.

- we must return evil with good (1 Thess. 5:15, cf. Rom. 12:17 // Matt. 5:39–40; Luke 6:29)
- cataclysmic events will precede the second coming (2 Thess. 2:1–12 // Mark 13)

Beyond these particular echoes or allusions, attention should be drawn to a number of theological parallels that permeate Paul's writings. Paul's distinctive understanding of God's grace, of salvation, and of outsiders being welcomed into the kingdom parallels material found in the Jesus tradition, including the substance of Jesus's "Kingdom of God" vision.[72] And, despite the claim of some that there is "no hint that Paul knew of the narrative tradition about Jesus," a number of scholars have demonstrated that within Paul's kerygmatic formulations (e.g., Gal. 3:13–14; 4:3–6; Rom. 3:24–26; 4:24–25; 5:6–10; 6:9–10; 8:3–4; 10:3–4) a sort of minisummary of the passion narratives in the Gospels can be discerned.[73]

The presence of these echoes and allusions confirms the conclusion we drew from his more explicit references: Paul was by no means unaware of the oral Jesus tradition. To the contrary, his thought seems to be permeated with it. And he gives us good reason to conclude that the same is true of the congregations he was writing to. As we shall show in the next two chapters, we also have good grounds from recent studies on oral tradition to view the early church as being saturated with orally transmitted material about Jesus's life and the content of his teachings and deeds.

72. For a good summary of the specifics see Kim, "Jesus Tradition in Paul," 275–79. Patterson has argued that one of the chief signs that Paul was aware of the Jesus tradition is that he champions a social radicalism similar to Jesus ("Paul and the Jesus Tradition," esp. 35–41). While this is true, a second argument proposed by Patterson is less convincing. He suggests that the primary reason Paul avoided the sayings tradition is tied to the fact that in texts like *Gospel of Thomas* (and Q), the sayings genre had been used in a way that neglected the death and resurrection of Jesus—elements of the gospel that were central to Paul. Patterson also argues that certain sayings found only in *Thomas* seem to lie behind some of Paul's material. For various reasons, we do not find these lines of argument persuasive. Among other things, the early date for Thomas assumed in this argument is problematic. Moreover, as Tuckett has shown in one important instance (1 Cor. 2:9 // *Thomas* 17), the textual evidence suggests that the flow of influence was from Paul to Thomas ("Paul and Jesus Tradition," 73).

73. See, e.g., R. Hays, *The Faith of Jesus Christ: An Investigation of the Narrative Substructure of Galatians 3:1–4:11* (Chicago: Scholars Press, 1983). C. H. Dodd argued in this direction in *The Apostolic Preaching and Its Development* (New York: Harper, 1935). See also L. Goppelt, who argues that the Jesus traditions are pervasive in Paul's writings, not as *geschichtlich* (narrative history) but as *heilsgeschichtlich* (salvation history) (*Theology of the New Testament*, ed. J. Roloff, trans. J. E. Alsup [Grand Rapids: Eerdmans, 1976], 362–90). On this issue see the recent collection of essays edited by Bruce Longenecker, *Narrative Dynamics in Paul: A Critical Assessment* (Louisville: Westminster Knox, 2002), and Hays's response, "Is Paul's Gospel Narratable?" *JSNT* 27 (2004): 217–39. See also B. Witherington, *Paul's Narrative Thought World: The Tapestry of Tragedy and Triumph* (Louisville: Westminster Knox, 1994). The all-too-common idea that Paul's thought was not anchored in a traditional Jesus narrative is not only problematic on textual grounds (as argued by Hays and others), but also flies in the face of what we now know to be true about both the structure of human thought in general and the orienting role played by extended narratives within orally dominant cultures in particular (see chap. 7 below).

Why Does Paul Not Explicitly Cite Jesus More Often?

Despite the presence of several apparently direct references and many echoes of, and allusions to, the Jesus tradition in Paul, we must nevertheless address the issue of why Paul seemingly cites Jesus's words so rarely, and especially why he fails to do so in contexts where doing so would greatly strengthen the argument he is making. We can begin to discern the possible answers to this perplexing question as we consider the issue in light of the similar phenomenon in the book of Acts.

The Lack of Citations of the Jesus Tradition in Acts

The vast majority of scholars grant that the author of the Gospel of Luke is also the author of the book of Acts. Indeed, the two works are generally understood as two volumes of one work. Yet, in the second volume, Luke chooses to make little use of the Jesus tradition that he obviously is so familiar with (as witnessed by the content of his first volume). As W. A. Strange observes, Luke fails "to provide any substantial teaching from Jesus which would assist the church in solving the problems that he describes in Acts. . . . When the church in Acts faces some perplexity, it does not base its decisions on the teaching of Jesus."[74]

We shall discuss how this curious phenomenon might be explained shortly. But however we explain it, we clearly cannot suggest that the lack of references to the Jesus tradition in Acts in any way reflects an ignorance of, or lack of interest in, that tradition on the part of the author. In Luke's own words, his Gospel was about "all that Jesus *did and taught* from the beginning until the day when he was taken up to heaven" (Acts 1:1–2, emphasis added).

The same principle, we suggest, must be applied to Paul. However we explain the scarcity of explicit citations of the Jesus tradition in Paul, we have no reason to follow those legendary-Jesus theorists who suppose it was because he was unaware of, or unconcerned about, Jesus's teaching. To the contrary, as with Acts, we have seen that we have good reason to suppose Paul was well aware of much of Jesus's teaching.

The Language of Traditional Referentiality

So why might Paul and Luke, in certain contexts, have avoided citing teachings from Jesus they were well aware of? There are, we believe, at least three related reasons. First, as James Dunn has argued, when Paul was writing, "the Jesus-tradition was not yet set in fixed and unyielding forms. Rather, it was *living* tradition, a tradition which was evidently adaptable to different needs and diverse contexts." The Jesus tradition, he argues, "was cherished not merely as something

---

74. Strange, "Jesus-Tradition in Acts," 69. Similarly, Kim notes that John's epistles and the book of Revelation contain few references to traditions found in the Gospel of John. Hence, he concludes, "The scarcity of Paul's explicit reference to Jesus-tradition can hardly mean his lack of knowledge of or interest in it" ("Jesus, Sayings of," 488).

said two or three decades earlier, but as a living word; not merely as a relic of a dead leader, but as still expressing the will of the living Lord."[75] As with the Old Testament (which Paul often alludes to rather loosely) the Jesus tradition "is to be recognized [in Paul] at the level of shaping thought, not so much as an external authority whose authority can be called on only by formal dictation."[76] Hence, Dunn concludes that both with allusions to the Old Testament and Jesus tradition,

> we are actually witnessing... the language of community discourse. We must imagine Christians who were steeped in the language and thought forms of the (Jewish) scriptures (the only scriptures they had), and who had been deeply impressed, their whole lives transformed and shaped afresh by the message of Jesus. In communities bonded by such common experience and language there is a whole level of discourse which consists of allusions and echo.... A community which can communicate only by citing explicit chapter and verse has no depth to it.[77]

As we shall see in the following chapters, this perspective fits perfectly with what scholars have been learning over the last several decades about how oral traditions function in predominantly oral cultures. Specifically, the groundbreaking work of Homeric scholar John Miles Foley has opened new vistas in our understanding of orally oriented texts and the notion of "traditional referentiality," wherein dense idiomatic expression is the assumption, and which "only the properly prepared audience is equipped to understand."[78] Foley notes that "traditional referentiality enables an extremely economical transaction of meaning, with the modest, concrete part standing for a more complex whole. *Pars pro toto* is the fundamental principle."[79] Thus, in an orally dominant context, each written text with its subtle allusions and echoes is but "a thin slice of the tradition's vast, rich, and unchartable narrative possibilities."[80]

It is this phenomenon of traditional referentiality that Dale Allison identifies when he observes that "much of the Bible is fundamentally elliptical. It says

75. Dunn, "Jesus-tradition," 174–75.

76. Ibid., 176.

77. Ibid., 177.

78. J. M. Foley, "What's in a Sign?" in *Signs of Orality: The Oral Tradition and Its Influence in the Greek and Roman World*, ed. A. E. MacKay (Boston: Brill, 1999), 7. On this important concept see also idem, *Immanent Art: From Structure to Meaning in Oral Epic* (Bloomington: Indiana University Press, 1991); idem, "Word-power, Performance, and Tradition," *Journal of American Folklore* 105 (1992): 275–301. This sort of insight has come with the interdisciplinary "turn to orality/performance" (on which see chap. 7) and as modern, highly literate scholars have begun to better understand the characteristic communicative dynamics at work in orally oriented contexts. For similar conclusions from the anthropological side of things, see R. Baumann and C. L. Briggs, "Poetics and Performance as Critical Perspectives on Language and Culture," *Annual Review of Anthropology* 19 (1990): 59–88, esp. 66–70, 75.

79. Foley, "What's in a Sign?" 11.

80. M. C. Amodio, *Writing the Oral Tradition: Oral Poetics and Literate Culture in Medieval England* (Notre Dame, IN: University of Notre Dame Press, 2004), 14. This observation, made with respect to the poetics of medieval England, applies equally to other orally oriented texts such as Paul's letters and the Gospels.

much in few words, in words that point beyond themselves, for the canonical writings are literature of inheritance, being deliberately interactive and full of allusive reciprocal discourse."[81] Thus, in the first-century Greco-Roman world, a world dominated by oral/aural sensibilities—even for the written text—and thus a world indebted to traditional referentiality, the elliptical manner in which Paul uses the Jesus tradition (in which he was no doubt steeped) is common communicative fare.

The Language of Exhortation

Second, Michael Thompson argues that Paul's lack of citation of the Jesus tradition is readily understood if we keep in mind that the purpose of Paul's letters was primarily exhortation, not argumentation. "Where argument ceased and exhortation began," he argues, "apostles had little need to cite sources." Hence, Thompson argues, "We should not necessarily expect explicit reference to [the Jesus tradition]."[82] Kim agrees when he writes, "In paraenesis, unlike in theological argument, one normally does not prove the truth of one's teaching, and so it is not required to cite its sources."[83]

The Jesus Tradition and Evangelism

Finally, the intriguing proposal of W. A. Strange regarding the parallel phenomenon in Acts complements the observations of both Dunn and Thompson. In investigating why Luke's Gospel is full of teachings that Acts never cites, Strange notices something. With few exceptions, every time some aspect of Jesus's life is referred to in Acts it is done *for evangelistic purposes*.[84] When the church is struggling with its own issues, however, the focus is on the *present* leading of the Spirit. On this basis, Strange argues that the early church understood "the function of the gospel material to be directed outwards, to serve the church's mission, rather than inwards, to give weight to partisan positions in Christian controversy."[85] The fact that we have several examples of the Gospels being used in evangelism in the second century, and no examples of them being used to settle theological controversies within the church until Irenaeus, further confirms this thesis.[86]

81. Allison, *Scriptural Allusions*, 4.
82. Thompson, *Clothed with Christ*, 71.
83. Kim, "Jesus, Sayings of," 489. Kim notes (ibid.): When "he was conscious of the opinions or attitudes contrary to his own teachings, he *did* refer or allude to Jesus' teachings in order to support his apostolic teachings with the Lord's authority" (e.g., Rom. 14:14; 1 Cor. 7:10–11; 9:14; Gal. 5:14).
84. See the detailed listing in Strange, "Jesus-Tradition in Acts," 60–64.
85. Ibid., 73.
86. Ibid., 73–74. If one wishes to add further considerations as to why Paul makes little explicit use of the Jesus tradition, N. T. Wright offers an insightful proposal. He argues that if Paul had repeated the Jesus tradition as many suggest he should have had he known it, "he would not have been endorsing Jesus, as an appropriate and loyal follower should. He would have been denying him. Someone who copies exactly what a would-be messiah does is himself trying to be a Messiah; which means denying the earlier claim." Rather, what we do find is "the *appropriate continuity* between two people living, and

This observation may well explain why Paul, as a rule, would not explicitly cite the Jesus tradition in his epistles. As Dunn and Thompson note, his purpose in writing various letters was not to evangelize but to exhort people who were already believers and to settle various church issues. It makes sense, therefore, that his writings are full of echoes of and allusions to the Jesus tradition that his congregations are steeped in, just as they are full of allusions to the Old Testament. Paul is speaking the language of "community discourse," as Dunn says, not the language of evangelism or apologetics.

Summary

This chapter has attempted to demonstrate the implausibility of the claim made by the more radical advocates of the legendary-Jesus thesis, namely that Paul did not view Jesus as a recent contemporary and/or that he reflects little knowledge of, or concern for, Jesus's life and teachings. We have argued that Paul knew he lived in the same generation as Jesus and that he reflects interest in, and awareness of, the life and teachings of Jesus. We have also suggested there are compelling reasons why Paul so rarely cites Jesus's teaching in an explicit fashion.

All of these considerations count strongly against the notion that Paul created a mythic Jesus that was later historicized in the Gospels. We concur with David Wenham when he writes:

> Paul would have been horrified at the suggestion that he was the founder of Christianity. For him the foundation of theology was Jesus; first, the Jesus whom he met on the Damascus road; second, the Jesus of the Christian tradition. He of course identified the two. Paul saw himself as the slave of Jesus Christ, not the founder of Christianity.[87]

Yet, if Paul indeed saw himself as an heir to a Jesus tradition that predated him, we are faced once again with the challenge of explaining how this tradition came into being so quickly and in the most unlikely of environments. If the teachings and stories, including Jesus's miracles and resurrection, are not rooted in history, where did they come from? If the teachings and stories are not rooted in history, what explains the fact that Paul and other first-century Jews—including Jesus's own brother—ascribed divine attributes to this recent contemporary (and brother) of theirs, while worshiping and praying to him? In our estimation, the attempt to explain this simply by appealing to the early church's imagination and legend-making tendencies is inadequate.

---

conscious of living, at different points in the eschatological timetable" (*What Saint Paul Really Said*, 180–81 [emphasis in text]).

87. Wenham, *Paul*, 409–10.

We readily grant that accepting that the Jesus tradition is rooted in history is not an easy path either. We are being asked to accept that the Synoptic portrait(s) of Jesus is substantially correct. It *is* a fantastic story, one that requires that we rethink the absoluteness of our Western naturalistic presuppositions. Yet given the implausibility of alternative explanations, we think it reasonable to consider this possibility. If indeed Jesus's claims and deeds were something like those intimated in Paul and expressly declared in the Gospels, and if indeed Jesus rose from the dead as his original followers claimed, then there is no difficulty explaining the faith of the early Christians. If, however, we assume that the Jesus of history was quite unlike the image(s) presented in the Gospels—or worse, if he did not exist at all—the origin of the faith of the early Christians remains a perplexing mystery.

Yet we are far from exhausting either the objections raised by legendary-Jesus theorists against the historicity of the first-century Jesus traditions or the grounds for accepting that the Jesus traditions are historically reliable. We have yet to examine the reliability of the oral Jesus traditions that found their way into the Synoptic Gospels, and we must still consider the reliability of the Gospels themselves. To these tasks we turn in the remaining chapters.

Part 3

BETWEEN JESUS AND THE GOSPELS

THE EARLY ORAL JESUS TRADITION

Few dispute that prior to the writing of the Gospels, tradition about Jesus circulated primarily by means of oral transmission. Hence, to a significant extent, one's estimation of the historical reliability of the Gospels will depend on one's estimation of the reliability of the oral traditions that preceded them. In part 3 of this work we investigate the issue of the nature and general reliability of precanonical oral and/or written traditions. This section is particularly important as there has been something of a revolution taking place the last several decades in orality studies that could—and we believe should—revolutionize our understanding of the oral traditions leading up to the writing of the Gospels.

In keeping with standard form-critical assumptions that have been prevalent in critical New Testament circles for much of the last century, most scholars who argue that the Jesus of the Gospels is substantially nonhistorical have contended that the pre-Gospel Jesus communities had to rely exclusively on oral transmission, since they were largely illiterate. Moreover, whatever else they deem to be historical or nonhistorical in the Gospels, they have tended to argue that, at the very least, oral transmission is incapable of passing on extended narratives. This leads to the form-critical conclusion that the overall narrative framework of the written Gospels is, at least to a substantial degree, a literary fiction designed to house the small, disconnected units of Jesus material. On top of this, legendary-Jesus theorists have generally argued that the early Christian communities had little interest in biographical information about Jesus, which is partly what allowed the oral traditions to expand in legendary directions so freely. In chapter 6 we will explore and assess these perspectives.

Also in keeping with standard form-critical assumptions, legendary-Jesus theorists argue that eyewitnesses to Jesus's ministry (if there were any) played little or no role in transmitting and regulating the oral Jesus tradition within the early Jesus communities. Moreover, they often argue that the ways in which these oral traditions were creatively modified and expanded with fictionalized elements can be traced with some confidence in accordance with discernable "laws"—or at least clear and reliable tendencies—of oral transmission. Finally, legendary-Jesus theorists generally argue that the sayings of Jesus circulating within the early Christian communities—including those communities whose views were eventually expressed in the written Gospels—are as likely to have originated in moments of "prophetic inspiration" within the post-Easter church as from Jesus himself. In chapter 7 we will consider and evaluate each of these claims.

6

ANCIENT LITERACY AND ORAL TRADITION

ASSESSING THE EARLY ORAL JESUS TRADITION

Most scholars acknowledge that the Gospel material was primarily, if not entirely, transmitted orally within the Christian communities for decades prior to the writing of the canonical Gospels. According to legendary-Jesus theorists, these early oral Jesus traditions were only loosely (or, in the case of Christ myth advocates, not at all) rooted in actual remembrances of Jesus and were very susceptible to legendary accretion. Word of mouth is not a trustworthy means of disseminating information in the best of circumstances, it is argued. And it is even less reliable when one is dealing with "naive and mythologically minded" people like the early Christians. Thus it is reasonable to conclude that much (if not all) of the Jesus material we find in the Gospels is rooted in the imagination of early Christians, as opposed to historical reality. How compelling is this perspective? This is the question we shall concern ourselves with in the next two chapters.

Our investigation shall center on six assumptions made by classical form-critical methodology, so an introductory word about this discipline is in order.[1]

---

1. It is important to note that the classical form-critical approach to the oral Jesus tradition (as represented by Rudolph Bultmann) certainly is not the only approach available to New Testament scholars today. Birger Gerhardsson and the "Scandinavian school" he represents have offered an alternative vision that portrays a much more conservative treatment of the oral Jesus tradition in the early church. Werner

Under the pressure of a new round of skepticism directed at the Gospel of Mark, source criticism seemed to have run its course as a tool by which to recover the historical Jesus. With the rise of form criticism in the early twentieth century, it seemed that a new tool for exploring even earlier Jesus tradition—oral tradition— was now available. Following the lead of Hermann Gunkel's form-critical work on Genesis, New Testament critics began to analyze the Gospels in terms of literary forms. From 1919 to 1921, three German scholars published works that served to define the field of Gospel form criticism—Karl Schmidt, Martin Dibelius, and, most importantly, Rudolf Bultmann.[2]

Form criticism serves to identify and investigate the multitude of diverse literary forms in the Gospels: parables, aphorisms, pronouncement stories (short narrative introductions plus a saying of Jesus), miracle stories, and so on. More specifically, form criticism attempts to determine the possible roles these forms played in the ever-evolving oral tradition leading up to the writing of the Gospels. By helping us recognize and exegete distinct literary forms, form criticism has unquestionably aided our understanding of the Gospels.

From the beginning, however, this discipline has tended to operate with a number of methodological assumptions that, in light of more recent interdisciplinary studies of orality, must now be judged to be seriously flawed. Among other things, these unfortunate assumptions about the nature of oral tradition have served to foster an undue skepticism with respect to oral historical narrative in general, and thus the oral Jesus tradition in particular. It is this set of methodological presuppositions of the form-critical enterprise that will be the subject of our investigation in this and the following chapter.

We will provide a brief overview of the three form-critical assumptions to be assessed in this chapter. Then we shall proceed to examine those three assumptions—that the period leading up to the written Gospels was a purely oral period;

Kelber has provided a third alternative that is indebted to twentieth-century interdisciplinary orality studies. More recently, Kenneth Bailey has articulated a fourth model drawn from his personal experience in the context of Middle Eastern village life. As will become clear throughout the next two chapters, our own view, like Kelber's, is deeply indebted to contemporary orality studies—although, at many points, we read the evidence and its implications for the oral Jesus tradition quite differently than does Kelber. In a number of ways our view comports nicely with Bailey's, and yet it is rooted in a much wider base of orality theory and field studies than is Bailey's quite limited anecdotal argument. Each of these views and representative bibliography will be discussed further below. While each of these views offers a viable alternative to approaching the oral Jesus tradition, the form-critical model as articulated by Bultmann has dominated New Testament studies for over eighty years. It has also been one of the chief influences behind the skepticism inherent in the legendary-Jesus thesis. For this reason we will focus our assessment on this widely influential paradigm.

2. K. Schmidt, *Der Rahmen der Geschichte Jesu* (Berlin: Trowitzsch, 1919); M. Dibelius, *From Tradition to Gospel*, trans. B. L. Woolf (New York: Scribner's, 1935); R. Bultmann, *The History of the Synoptic Tradition*, trans. J. Marsh (New York: Harper, 1963). For helpful introductions to the rise and nature of form criticism, see E. V. McKnight, *What Is Form Criticism?* (Philadelphia: Fortress, 1969); W. Baird, *History of New Testament Research*, vol. 2: *From Jonathan Edwards to Rudolf Bultmann* (Minneapolis: Fortress, 2003), 269–87.

that oral traditions are not capable of passing on extended narratives; and that the early church had little true biographical interest in their founder.

An Overview of Three Form-Critical Assumptions

The Assumption of a Purely Oral Period

The first assumption almost uniformly shared by form critics is that the traditions that lay behind the Gospels were transmitted almost exclusively in oral form. The assumption is that early Christians were an "unlettered people" who "had neither the capacity nor the inclination for the production of books." Hence, as the early form critic Martin Dibelius argues, we "must not predicate a true literary activity in the Christian Church of the first two or three decades."[3] This perspective has been reinforced by recent arguments suggesting that only a small fraction of first-century Palestinian Jews were literate.[4]

If the teachings and deeds of Jesus were not stabilized in writing for several decades, it is argued, there is a good deal of room for the collective memory of (or original mythological imaginings about) Jesus to be significantly altered. Hence, the view that the period leading up to the Gospels was mostly, if not entirely, one of oral transmission tends to support the thesis that the Jesus of the Gospels is enveloped in legendary fiction.

The Assumed Lack of a Coherent Narrative

A second form-critical assumption that has led many scholars to a negative assessment of the historical reliability of the Gospels is that oral traditions are mostly composed of small, disconnected units. To be sure, many scholars suspect that a pre-Gospel Passion narrative existed as a coherent extended unit prior to being incorporated into Mark's Gospel. But most also argue that the bulk of the

3. Dibelius, *Tradition to Gospels*, 9. So too, Werner Kümmel argues that, "It is incontrovertible that in the earliest period there was only an oral record of the narratives and sayings of Jesus" (*Introduction to the New Testament*, rev. ed., trans. H. C. Kee [Nashville: Abingdon, 1973], 55–56).

4. See, e.g., W. V. Harris, *Ancient Literacy* (Cambridge, MA: Harvard University Press, 1989); M. Bar-Ilan, "Illiteracy in the Land of Israel in the First Centuries C.E.," in *Essays in the Social Scientific Study of Judaism and Jewish Society*, ed. S. Fishbane and S. Schoenfeld (Hoboken, NJ: KTAV, 1992), 2:55; C. Hezser, *Jewish Literacy in Roman Palestine* (Tübingen: Mohr Siebeck, 2001). New Testament scholars who emphasize the low literacy rates within the world of ancient Palestine include J. Dewey, "Textuality in an Oral Culture: A Survey of the Pauline Traditions," *Semeia* 65 (1995): 39–40; R. A. Horsley, "The Oral Communication Environment of Q," in R. A. Horsley with J. A. Draper, *Whoever Hears You Hears Me: Prophets, Performance, and Tradition in Q* (Harrisburg, PA: Trinity, 1999), 125–27. While Werner Kelber—whose work has powerfully shaped contemporary New Testament scholarship's vision of orality—acknowledges that the world into which Christianity was born was significantly literate, the image he presents of the early Christian communities seems to be a subculture of a predominately illiterate, oral type. See *The Oral and the Written Gospel: The Hermeneutics of Speaking and Writing in the Synoptic Tradition, Mark, Paul, and Q* (Philadelphia: Fortress, 1983), 15–17.

Gospel narrative of Jesus's life and ministry was created de novo when the first Gospel (usually identified as Mark) was written.

As in many other matters pertaining to form criticism, a major voice for this perspective was the early form critic Rudolf Bultmann.[5] He understood the Jesus tradition to be an example of *Kleinliteratur*—unsophisticated traditions created by the simple masses responding to sociological needs and operating under the same "laws" as other folklore traditions.[6] Bultmann's assessment of folk traditions led him to conclude that ancient narrators do not give lengthy, unified accounts but rather create small, independent units of tradition (the "forms" identified by form criticism). As these units of tradition are passed along, they tend to be expanded, with details being added. Moreover, in time they tend to be loosely grouped together, forming larger units.[7]

Only when the decision was made to put the community's "memory" of Jesus into writing was an overall narrative of Jesus's life required and therefore created. The individual sayings (*logia*), aphorisms, pronouncement stories, parables, speeches, and miracle stories that had for decades been independently remembered and/or created and passed along were at this time fit into a mostly imagined narrative framework. Obviously, if the Bultmannian understanding of the oral Jesus tradition leading up to the writing of the Gospels is correct, the legendary-Jesus thesis becomes much more plausible.

The Assumed Lack of Biographical Interest

A third form-critical assumption, and one that characterizes most versions of the legendary-Jesus thesis, is that the earliest Christians had little to no interest in the actual details of the life of Jesus. Their interest, rather, was almost purely evangelistic. "They wanted nothing else than to win as many as possible to salvation in the last hour just before the end of the world," according to Dibelius. Thus, the "early Christians were not interested in history."[8] Even the written Gospels have "no historical-biographical interest," according to Bultmann.[9] And it is for this reason that it is impossible "to separate historical stories from legends" in them.[10]

The question we must now address is, how plausible is each of these three methodological assumptions? In what follows we will examine them in their

5. Of course, Bultmann and the other early form critics had inherited the skepticism of those like Wilhelm Wrede, Johannes Weiss, and Albert Schweitzer with respect to the Markan narrative framework.

6. For an articulation of the laws of the tradition as Bultmann views it, see Bultmann, "The Study of the Synoptic Gospels," in R. Bultmann and K. Kundsin, *Form Criticism: Two Essays on New Testament Research*, ed. F. C. Grant (New York: Harper & Row, 1962), 32–35.

7. Bultmann writes: "Even in the written collections the principle on which larger units are formed are at first no different from what they were in the oral tradition, i.e., it is simply a quite primitive process of adding one small unit to another, and in this similarity of content or some outward likeness (the use of some catchword) is the guiding principle, though now and then pure chance takes a hand" (*History*, 322).

8. M. Dibelius, *Gospel Criticism and Christology* (London: Nicholson and Watson, 1935), 16.

9. Bultmann, *History*, 372.

10. Ibid., 245.

respective order and argue that, in light of more recent interdisciplinary studies, each must now be judged as decidedly flawed.

The Assumption of a Purely Oral Period

As we have seen, the form-critical enterprise generally has assumed that there were few if any written documents that anchored the oral Jesus tradition in its first several decades. If this assumption holds, then one can more easily imagine early Christians revisioning and/or creating their views of Jesus. Later, we will dispute the claim that oral traditions that lack a written foundation are intrinsically and necessarily unreliable. At present, however, we wish to argue that there are no solid grounds for thinking that the Jesus traditions of the early church were purely oral in the first place. One's conclusions on this matter are related, in part, to one's prior estimation of the literacy level among first-century Palestinian Jews, and so to this question we now turn.

Harris's Thesis on the Low Literacy Rates of Ancient Cultures

The most persuasive case for the relative illiteracy of ancient Palestine (and of the ancient world in general) has been advanced by the historian William Harris in his book, *Ancient Literacy*. Thus we will use his work as a starting point for our response.

Rather than basing his estimation of literacy on epigraphic evidence—the classical approach that he deems unreliable on a number of counts—Harris employs a broader, comparativist approach. Put simply, Harris first establishes the conditions he believes are necessary for any culture to enjoy widespread literacy and then investigates whether various ancient cultures met these conditions.

Harris's methodology yields estimates of ancient literacy that are significantly lower than most previous estimates. Among other things, Harris contends that ancient cultures did not generally have a widespread need for writing, educational systems were not adequately developed to teach masses how to read, and reading material and writing supplies were too expensive for common people to acquire even if they could have learned to read and write. Hence, Harris claims that literacy in the ancient world was usually reserved for the relatively few powerful and wealthy.[11]

This holds true, he argues, for the ancient Greco-Roman world. Though many previous scholars have argued for a robust literacy rate from the fourth century BCE on—the period of hellenization—Harris argues that in most areas the literacy rate for adults would have been no more than ten to fifteen percent.[12] Har-

11. Harris, *Ancient Literacy*, 326–27. Harris draws from the earlier work of others such as L. Stone, "Literacy and Education in England, 1640–1900," *Past and Present* 42 (1969): 69–139.
12. Harris, *Ancient Literacy*, 328.

ris recognizes that "these conclusions will be highly unpalatable to some classical scholars," but nevertheless claims that his case is solidly rooted in comparativist data.[13] Though it counters the classical approach, Harris's methodology has caught on in academic circles, producing what one scholar has called a "fashionable skepticism" in many academic quarters regarding literacy in the ancient world.[14]

There can be no question that Harris's broad-based comparativist approach has brought the discussion of ancient literacy to a new level of sophistication. At the very least, his work has shown that formerly optimistic assessments about widespread literacy in the ancient world were often built upon slender and tenuous foundations. However, there are a number of considerations that call into question Harris's conclusions and their application to any particular locale in the ancient Greco-Roman world.

Questioning Harris's Methodology

It has been argued by some that Harris's comparativist methodology is, in important ways, flawed. In a word, Harris assumes that comparativist deductive assessments can tell us more about ancient literacy rates than can actual epigraphic evidence. While some see this methodological breakthrough as a "virtue,"[15] others see it as ignoring important details that could serve to undermine the application of Harris's thesis to any particular cultural setting. Nicholas Horsfall, for example, argues that, "given Harris' general approach to the evidence, the discovery of . . . solid bodies of [written] material, in however many provinces, is more or less irrelevant to him."[16] Similarly, Harlow Snyder has observed that this methodology exhibits a tendency "to press toward conclusions that seem to be established *a priori*, either on theoretical grounds or because the data may prove uncongenial."[17]

To scholars such as Horsfall and Snyder, broad-based, comparativist generalizations are not altogether illegitimate, but they must be balanced by the actual epigraphical evidence at hand.[18] And, as we shall see, when the epigraphical evidence

13. Ibid., 328–29.

14. William M. Schiedewind, "Orality and Literacy in Ancient Israel," *Religious Studies Review* 26 (2000): 331. In context, Schiedewind's phrase applies to scholarship on literacy in preexilic Judah, and yet it certainly characterizes much of the scholarly mood regarding the first-century question as well.

15. M. Beard, "Writing and Religion: Ancient Literacy and the Function of the Written Word in Roman Religion," in *Literacy in the Roman World*, ed. M. Beard (Ann Arbor: University of Michigan Press, 1991), 35.

16. N. Horsfall, "Statistics or States of Mind?" in *Literacy in the Roman World*, 60.

17. Snyder is commenting on Hezser's study, which employs Harris's methodology. H. G. Snyder, review of *Jewish Literacy in Roman Palestine*, by C. Hezser, *Review of Biblical Literature* 8 (2002): 4.

18. Related to this, many recovered ancient texts remain untranslated and/or unpublished. While this caveat causes many scholars to remain "optimistic about the centrality of literacy in the ancient world, and wary of the assumption that what we have is all there can be," for Harris such evidence is, on methodological grounds, rendered relatively insignificant. See A. Bowman, "Literacy in the Roman Empire: Mass and Mode," in *Literacy in the Roman World*, 120.

is given its due weight, our estimations about the literacy of the ancient world in general, and of the Greco-Roman world in particular, can change substantially.

Literacy among the Rural and the Poor?

Some scholars have challenged Harris's assumption (shared by others) that only the powerful and wealthy would have had access to the materials and education necessary for writing. For one thing, it is not altogether clear that the cost of materials like papyrus was as expensive as some have claimed.[19] Evidence against the common assumption of the universally prohibitive costs of writing materials in the ancient world has been discovered at sites such as the ancient (ca. 100) military fort at Vindolanda in Britain. This site evidences an amazing amount of writing on thin wooden leaves with a type of ink pen (as opposed to the better-known wax tablets with a metal stylus).[20] As Alan Bowman notes, "These leaf tablets must have been cheap (or free) and easy to make. They completely undermine the argument that writing materials were available only to the well-to-do."[21]

Nor is it clear that education was as inaccessible to lower classes as Harris and others claim. The clear evidence for writing among military personnel and slaves in the ancient world suggests that we must be cautious in concluding that lower classes were always illiterate.[22] Intriguingly, we have recovered a second-century clay tablet with a memo written in Latin by a bricklayer's assistant in a rural area. This provides concrete evidence, contra Harris's a priori speculations, that a poor, rural laborer could indeed possess literacy skills.[23]

Moreover, Alan Bowman and Alan Millard have argued that there is good evidence that ancient people assumed that certain written texts (e.g., publicly posted documents) would inform all segments of society, including rural villagers.[24] This

19. Colin H. Roberts and T. C. Skeat state that the "fruitlessly debated" question of the relative costs of papyrus and parchment is "unanswerable and meaningless" due to the fact that "objective criteria are almost wholly lacking" ("Papyrus and Parchment," in *The Birth of the Codex* [New York: Oxford University Press, 1983], 7).

20. On the texts found at Vindolanda, see A. K. Bowman and J. D. Thomas, "Vindolanda 1985: The New Writing-tablets," *Journal of Roman Studies* 76 (1986): 120–23; idem, "New Texts from Vindolanda," *Britannia* 18 (1987): 125–42; and esp. idem, *Vindolanda: The Latin Writing Tablets* (London: Society for the Promotion of Roman Studies, 1983); idem, *The Vindolanda Writing-Tablets:* Tabulae Vindolandenses *II* (London: British Museum, 1994). See also Bowman, *Life and Letters on the Roman Frontier: Vindolanda and Its People* (London: British Museum Press, 1994).

21. Bowman, "Literacy in the Roman Empire," 128. Few New Testament scholars have taken this evidence into account. One who has is G. Stanton, "Early Christian Preference for the Codex," in *The Earliest Gospels: The Origins and Transmission of the Earliest Christian Gospels—The Contribution of the Chester Beatty Gospel Codex P45*, ed. C. Horton (New York: Clark, 2004), 44–46.

22. Bowman, "Literacy in the Roman Empire," 123–27.

23. As documented in Horsfall, "Statistics or States of Mind?" 59.

24. See Bowman, "Literacy in the Roman Empire," 121–22. Alan Millard has done extensive research on the literacy level of ancient Israel and has arrived at much more optimistic conclusions than Harris, Hezser, or Bar-Ilan have. See Millard, "The Practice of Writing in Ancient Israel," in *Biblical Archaeologist* 35 (1972): 98–111; idem, "An Assessment of the Evidence for Writing in Ancient Israel," in *Biblical*

suggests, at the very least, that the "inability to read would not have been accepted
as a legitimate excuse for ignorance." It implies that "those who could not read
(or write) participated in literacy in some significant way."[25] Millard also argues
that the vast amount of personal letters, legal deeds, divorce certificates, writing
on coins, and ossuary inscriptions that were clearly not written by scribes strongly
suggests that literacy levels were relatively high and widespread.[26] All of this serves
to confirm the conclusion of Jeffrey Hurwit on literacy in the Greco-Roman world:
Given the evidence at hand, "it is difficult to imagine . . . an Archaic society in
which a limited literacy was simply a function of class."[27]

Does Literacy Depend upon Public Schools?

Harris's comparativist approach assumes that "an ample and expanding school
system" would have been necessary for literacy to flourish.[28] While no one can
doubt that public school systems support the growth of literacy, it does not follow from this that the absence of a public school system entails the absence of
literacy skills. It is entirely possible that reading and writing were taught at home
on a widespread basis, a possibility Harris himself entertains but gives little attention to.[29] After all, we posses ample evidence that it was commonplace in the
ancient world for fathers to teach their sons professional skills at home, and this
homeschooling naturally would have included literacy skills to the extent that
the vocational trade depended on it.[30]

Between Literacy and Illiteracy

Finally, Harris has been properly criticized for too often working with a functional dichotomy of "literate" and "illiterate," while paying insufficient attention
to the vast spectrum between these two poles. He gives short shrift to what, in

---

*Archaeology Today: Proceedings of the International Congress on Biblical Archaeology, Jerusalem, April
1984*, ed. Janet Amitai (Jerusalem: Israel Exploration Society, 1985), 301–12; idem, "The Question of
Israelite Literacy," *Bible Review* 3 (Fall 1987): 23–31; idem, "Literacy: Ancient Israel," in *Anchor Bible
Dictionary*, ed. D. N. Freedman (New York: Doubleday, 1992), 4:337–40; idem, *Reading and Writing
in the Time of Jesus* (Sheffield: Sheffield Academic Press, 2000); idem, "Zechariah Wrote (Luke 1:63),"
in *The New Testament in Its First Century Setting: Essays on Context and Background in Honour of B. W.
Winter on His 65th Birthday*, ed. P. J. Williams et al. (Grand Rapids: Eerdmans, 2004), 46–55.

25. Bowman, "Literacy in the Roman Empire," 121–22. Among those who were altogether illiterate,
we find evidence that they were quite adept at finding access to the literate world as required. In her study
of ancient illiteracy, Ann Ellis Hanson notes, "[Illiterates] turned first to literates among their close relatives and family members; next to friends, business associates, and other colleagues; finally to professional
scribes in government employ" (Hanson, "Ancient Illiteracy," in *Literacy in the Roman World*, 164).

26. Millard, *Reading and Writing*, 168.

27. J. M. Hurwit, "The Words in the Image: Orality, Literacy, and Early Greek Art," *Word and Image*
6 (1990): 194.

28. Harris, *Ancient Literacy*, 327.

29. Ibid., 307.

30. See the discussion in Horsfall, "Statistics or States of Mind?" 62–64.

fact, is a spectrum of degrees of literacy in the ancient Greco-Roman world—including the wide range of abilities that can be deemed "semiliterate." The world of semiliteracy covers a vast array of skill levels and includes those who could read but could not functionally write, those who could sign only their name, those deemed "slow writers" who could write simple texts if given the time necessary, and those who simply had poor handwriting skills.[31] Things are complexified further when one considers "phonetic literacy," as well as "nonrational" uses of writing (e.g., symbolic, magical, monumental, etc.).[32]

The Qumran Question

We come closer to the context of Jesus when we consider the vast literature produced and preserved by the Qumran community. Does this not indicate that reading and writing were potentially widespread in Palestinian Judaism during the Hellenistic period? Catherine Hezser, who follows the comparativist approach of Harris, thinks not. She argues that this community "cannot be considered representative of Palestinian Judaism as a whole."[33] But other than the fact that this literate community obviously does not fit the comparativist approach she works with, she offers no evidential basis for her conclusion. Snyder hits the mark when he responds to Hezser's claim by noting, "It is hardly sound practice to disregard evidence that does not conform to what Hezser has already judged to be 'representative.'"[34] If we do not begin by arbitrarily assuming the Qumran community was exceptional among Palestinian Jews in terms of education and literacy, it seems to count in favor of the conclusion that a fair portion of Palestinian Jews around the time of Jesus were, in fact, quite literate.

Jewish Literacy in First-Century Palestine

While there is solid evidence upon which to question the exceedingly low literacy rates in the Roman Empire proposed by Harris and others, there are even stronger grounds for concluding that literacy rates among Jews in Palestine were

31. For a helpful introduction to the world of ancient semiliteracy, see H. C. Youtie, "*Bradeos graphon*: Between Literacy and Illiteracy," *Greek, Roman and Byzantine Studies* 12 (1971): 239–61. See also Hanson, "Ancient Illiteracy," 158–97. For examples of those who could read but not write (from a different historical context but one that remains instructive) in the context of epic production, see H. Fromm, "Kalevala and Nibelungenlied: The Problem of Oral and Written Composition," in *Religion, Myth and Folklore in the World's Epics: The Kalevala and Its Predecessors*, ed. L. Honko (New York: Mouton de Gruyter, 1990), 99–102.

32. See R. Thomas, *Literacy and Orality in Ancient Greece* (New York: Cambridge University Press, 1992), 78–88, 92. On problems with attempts to establish literacy rates in the ancient world, see R. Thomas, *Oral Tradition and Written Record in Classical Athens* (New York: Cambridge University Press, 1989), 17–18. Here, Thomas argues that the question of the *extent* of literacy is a far less important question than "*how*, and with what degrees of sophistication, [writing] was used" in a given context (p. 10). In any case, contemporary assessments of ancient literacy are too often clouded by our own modern, post-Gutenberg conceptions of "literacy" (p. 15).

33. Hezser, *Jewish Literacy*, 426.

34. Snyder, review of *Jewish Literacy*, 4.

likely higher than the general first-century Greco-Roman population. Unlike most other people groups in the ancient Western world, the faith of Jews was firmly rooted in a collection of *writings*. This elevated the importance of reading to a level unparalleled among Gentiles in the ancient world. As John Meier notes,

> The very identity and continued existence of the people of Israel were tied to a corpus of written and regularly read works in a way that simply was not true of other peoples in the Mediterranean world of the first century. . . . To be able to read and explain the Scriptures was a revered goal for religiously minded Jews. Hence literacy held a special importance for the Jewish community.[35]

Similarly, Birger Gerhardsson argues, "The milieu in which Jesus and the original disciples ministered, and the milieu in which remembrances of Jesus' life and teaching were passed on, was one that revered the written word and thus valued literacy."[36]

Moreover, many scholars argue that there are good grounds for concluding that synagogues were prevalent in first-century Palestine—including Galilee. This point is noteworthy inasmuch as there is evidence to suggest that synagogues could function as schools for Jewish boys.[37] As discussed in chapter 2, both epigraphic evidence (e.g., Josephus, Philo, Luke-Acts) and archaeological evidence (e.g., the Theodotus inscription, the discovered remains of pre-70 synagogues at Gamla, Herodium, Masada, and Qumran) reveal the presence of synagogues in the Palestinian world of Jesus's day.[38] To be sure, in rural settings

35. J. P. Meier, *A Marginal Jew: Rethinking the Historical Jesus*, vol. 1: *The Roots of the Problem and the Person* (New York: Doubleday, 1991), 275. This emphasis on literacy among the Jews did not go unnoticed by other ancient people. For example, it is noted by Theophrastus, Megasthenes, and Clearchus of Soli. See C. S. Keener, *The Gospel of John: A Commentary* (Peabody, MA: Hendrickson, 2003), 1:101n165.

36. B. Gerhardsson, "The Gospel Tradition," in *The Interrelations of the Gospels*, ed. D. L. Dungan (Leuven: Peeters, 1990), 538.

37. On the educational role, etc., of the synagogue, see R. Riesner, *Jesus als Lehrer: Eine Untersuchung zum Ursprung der Evangelien-Ueberlieferung* (Tübingen: Mohr Siebeck, 1981), 123–206. Meier concurs with this observation (*Marginal Jew*, 1:277). Of course, as noted in chap. 2, the debate about the existence of pre-70 Palestinian synagogues continues unabated. In the current debate, as Stuart Miller points out, the "recent preoccupation with edifices" has distracted us from the type of focus and critical assessment that the literary sources deserve ("On the Number of Synagogues in the Cities of 'Erez Israel," *Journal of Jewish Studies* 49 [1998]: 64).

38. Again, a pre-70 dating of the Theodotus inscription (discovered in Jerusalem in 1913) has been most common; for arguments to this effect, along with a translation of the inscription, see Millard, *Reading and Writing*, 110–11; R. Riesner, "Synagogues in Jerusalem," in *The Book of Acts in Its Palestinian Setting*, ed. R. Bauckham (Grand Rapids: Eerdmans, 1995), 192–200. The writings of Josephus (*Life*, 277, 280; *Jewish War*, 2.14.4; *Antiquities*, 14.10.23, 19.6.3), Philo (*Legat.* 132), and Luke (e.g., Luke 13:10–17; Acts 6:9) all testify to the presence of pre-70 synagogues. For discussions of the archaeological remains at Gamla, Herodium, and Masada, see K. Atkinson, "On Further Defining the First-Century CE Synagogue: Fact or Fiction? A Rejoinder to H. C. Kee," *NTS* 43 (1997), 492–98; J. H. Charlesworth, *Jesus within Judaism: New Light from Exciting Archaeological Discoveries* (New York: Doubleday, 1988), 108–9; Riesner, "Synagogues in Jerusalem," 184–87. On the "rudimentary synagogue" in a small room

the synagogues of Jesus's day often may have been little more than a designated room in a private home, a gathering place, as the Theodotus inscription suggests, where the Law would be read and taught. But synagogues they would have been, nonetheless.

This implies that it is more likely than not that a strongly Jewish village such as Nazareth would have had a local synagogue of some kind, with this sort of educational purpose, functioning in the days of Jesus's youth.[39] In the words of Rainer Riesner, "In my opinion one cannot overstress the importance of the synagogal teaching system as a background for the formation and transmission of the Gospel tradition. The synagogues provided even in small Galilaean villages such as Nazareth a kind of popular education system."[40]

Was Jesus Literate?

This brings us to the question of whether Jesus and his disciples were literate. While in the nature of the case no absolute proof can be offered one way or the other, we submit that it is more reasonable to assume that at least some of them were, in fact, literate.

Turning first to the issue of Jesus's literacy, the previously mentioned evidence for a significant degree of literacy among Palestinian male Jews and the evidence for functional synagogues in small towns itself renders it quite conceivable that Jesus was literate.[41] But the probability is increased when we consider the Gospel tradition that consistently depicts Jesus as engaging in debates with scribes and Pharisees on scriptural interpretation. If we do not assume that this tradition was simply a creation of the early Christian community, it suggests that Jesus had the

---

at Qumran (locus 39), see N. Golb, *Who Wrote the Dead Sea Scrolls? The Search for the Secret of Qumran* (New York: Scribner, 1995), 24–25; also Atkinson, "On Further Defining the First-Century CE Synagogue," 499–500.

39. So argues R. Hachlili, "The Origin of the Synagogue: A Reassessment," *JSJ* 28 (1997): 45–46. Reinforcing this suggestion is the fact that Nazareth seems to have been a strongly Torah-true village. To date, archaeological excavations have found no sign of pagan symbolism in first-century Nazareth. In fact, a roughly fourth-century Hebrew inscription found at Caesarea in 1962 lists Nazareth as one of the villages in which the priestly classifications were retained after the Jewish war. This may well signal the fact that Nazareth had a reputation of stalwart Jewish piety. For a brief discussion see Meier, *Marginal Jew*, 1:308n137.

40. R. Riesner, "Jesus as Preacher and Teacher," in *Jesus and the Oral Gospel Tradition*, ed. H. Wansbrough (Sheffield: Sheffield Academic Press, 1991), 191. John Meier argues that, even in a town the size of Nazareth, "the existence of a synagogue with some educational program for Jewish boys is a likely hypothesis" (*Marginal Jew*, 1:277). In his impressive recent study of ancient literacy and education, D. M. Carr confirms these conclusions. He writes: "By the first century, however, we see multiple sites of probable synagogues, and these appear to be major sites for reading and education outside the temple" (*Writing on the Tablet of the Heart: Origins of Scripture and Literature* [New York: Oxford University Press, 2005], 243). See also W. M. Schniedewind, *How the Bible Became a Book: The Textualization of Ancient Israel* (New York: Cambridge University Press, 2004), 25, 211–12.

41. See J. D. G. Dunn, "Did Jesus Attend the Synagogue?" in *Jesus and Archaeology*, ed. J. H. Charlesworth (Grand Rapids: Eerdmans, 2006), 221–22.

educational training needed to debate rather technical interpretive points of the Law and tradition, a training that arguably would suggest the possession of literacy skills.[42] At the very least, that we have this tradition in the Gospels is enough to prove it was not implausible to the original audiences of the Gospels that a Jew from Nazareth would have this level of literacy.

Also supporting the literacy of Jesus is a passage in John that mentions, rather incidentally, that Jesus amazed crowds by his "learning" (*grammata oiden*)—a term that usually included reading skills (John 7:15). John Meier argues that this text "provides some indirect basis for supposing that Jesus could read and comment on the Hebrew Scriptures."[43] Similarly, Thomas Boomershine argues that, in light of the fact that there is "no obvious redactional motive" for this passage, the "most probable explanation" for its inclusion in the Gospel is that it "reflects a tradition of Jesus as literate."[44]

Also worthy of consideration is the tradition contained in Luke 4:16–30 that specifically recounts Jesus's reading from and commenting on the book of Isaiah. Many critical scholars take this narrative to be a creative elaboration of Mark's account of Jesus's preaching and rejection at Nazareth (Mark 6:1–4) and thus deny that it constitutes historical evidence of his literacy. But others argue that it was part of Luke's special "L" source and arguably represents an accurate remembrance of a literate Jesus.[45]

When one adds to this that the Gospels present Jesus as being recognized by others as a teacher—indeed, as a person whose whole thought world was saturated with the Old Testament—the case for Jesus's literacy becomes strong indeed. John Meier nicely sums up the case when he writes:

> If we take into account that Jesus' adult life became fiercely focused on the Jewish religion, that he is presented by almost all the Gospel traditions as engaging in learned disputes over Scripture and halaka with students of the Law, that he was accorded the respectful—but at that time vague—title of rabbi or teacher, that more than one Gospel tradition presents him as preaching or teaching in the synagogues (presumably after and on the Scripture readings), and that, even apart from formal disputes, his teaching was strongly imbued with the outlook and language of the sacred texts of Israel, it is reasonable to suppose that Jesus' religious formation in

42. Thomas Boomershine argues that this tradition is the most compelling evidence of Jesus's literacy ("Jesus of Nazareth and the Watershed of Ancient Orality and Literacy," *Semeia* 65 [1995]: 21).

43. Meier, *Marginal Jew*, 1:269.

44. Boomershine, "Jesus of Nazareth," 22.

45. Ulrich Busse argues the entire pericope is a Lukan creation in *Das Nazareth-Manifest: Eine Einführung in das lukanische Jesusbild nach Lk 4, 16–30*. SBS 91 (Stuttgart: Katholisches Bibelwerk, 1978), 113. For more moderate perspectives and discussions, see J. Holland, *Luke 1–9:20*, Word Biblical Commentary (Dallas: Word Books, 1989), 192–95; I. H. Marshall, *The Gospel of Luke: A Commentary on the Greek Text* (Grand Rapids: Eerdmans, 1978), 178–180; H. Conzelmann, *The Theology of Luke*, trans. G. Buswell (New York: Harper & Row, 1961), 31–32.

his family was intense and profound, and included instruction in reading biblical Hebrew.

From this we can conclude with Meier that it is quite probable that,

> [Jesus] was literate, and his literacy probably extended beyond the mere ability to sign one's name or conduct basic business transactions ("tradesman's literacy") to the ability to read sophisticated theological and literary works and comment on them ("scribal literacy"). Jesus comes out of a peasant background, but he is not an ordinary peasant.[46]

Were the Disciples Literate?

Turning to the issue of the literacy of Jesus's disciples, we must first acknowledge that there is no hint in the Gospels of the disciples recording Jesus's words in writing. Thus it seems "unlikely . . . that literacy was a requirement for discipleship."[47] On top of this, Acts 4:13 contains a tradition that John and Peter were "uneducated and ordinary men," a verse that has been taken as evidence that they were illiterate. Such a conclusion is possible but not required. The term *agrammatoi* need imply

---

46. Meier, *Marginal Jew*, 1:276, 278. See also P. Foster, "Educating Jesus: The Search for a Plausible Context," *JSHJ* 4 (2006): 7–33. On the centrality of Jesus as "teacher" in the Gospel tradition, see Riesner, *Jesus als Lehrer*; idem, "Jesus as Preacher and Teacher"; Samuel Byrskog, *Jesus the Only Teacher: Didactic Authority and Transmission in Ancient Israel, Ancient Judaism and the Matthean Community* (Stockholm: Almqvist and Wiksell, 1994). Boomershine concurs that "it is probable that Jesus was literate" ("Jesus of Nazareth," 22). Boomershine goes on to compare Jesus with Socrates, who "was another seminal figure who was fully literate but did not write"—i.e., from whom we know of no written texts (p. 24). See also Schniedewind, *How the Bible Became a Book*, 211–12. In a recent article, Tor Vegge suggests that the impressive level of literary style in the teachings of Jesus as recorded in the Gospels raises the question of whether they could truly reflect the actual speech style of the historical Jesus as he spoke to Galilean peasants; see "The Literacy of Jesus the Carpenter's Son: On the Literary Style in the Words of Jesus," *Studia Theologica* 59 (2005): 19–37. However, it seems to us that Vegge is working with an insufficiently robust spectrum of possibilities by which to categorize and assess literary styles within orally dominant contexts. In this sense, his approach could be helped by the sort of work done on this complex question by John Miles Foley; see "Oral Tradition into Textuality," in *Texts and Textuality: Textual Instability, Theory, and Interpretation*, ed. P. Cohen (New York: Garland, 1997), 1–24. Foley identifies a spectrum with "transcribed [oral] performance" at one end and "'literary' works with roots in oral tradition" at the other. However, there remains "a broadly defined middle area" that, we suggest, better characterizes the oral/aural-oriented Gospels (pp. 17–18). As George Kennedy notes, "The Gospel writer's purpose is not literary" ("Classical and Christian Source Criticism," in *The Relationships among the Gospels: An Interdisciplinary Dialogue*, ed. W. O. Walker [San Antonio: Trinity University Press, 1978], 137). Beyond this, it is also highly questionable that the average "Galilean peasant" was beyond the style characterized by the teachings of Jesus in the Gospels. One must beware of the all-too-common caricature of "oral peasant culture" and its supposedly simplistic, nonliterary, isolated "little tradition." Against the former see L. Vail and L. White, "The Invention of 'Oral Man,'" in *Power and the Praise Poem: Southern African Voices in History* (Charlottesville: University Press of Virginia, 1991), 1–39. Against the latter see S. J. Tambiah, *Buddhism and the Spirit Cults in North-East Thailand* (New York: Cambridge University Press, 1970), 370–72.

47. Boomershine, "Jesus of Nazareth," 22.

nothing more than that these two never received a formal education—a fact that is hardly surprising since they were fishermen.[48]

However, even if we grant that the literacy skills of Peter and John are uncertain, this says nothing of the other ten disciples and nothing of those among Jesus's wider circle of followers. At the very least, Matthew the tax collector would have had to have a "trade literacy" for his occupation (Mark 2:14; Matt. 9:9; 10:3). It is significant that Papius, who arguably received his information from the apostle John, mentions that "Matthew collected the oracles (*ta logia*) in the Hebrew language, and each interpreted them as best he could."[49] Given Matthew's presumed literacy and this early church tradition, Robert Gundry offers the quite plausible suggestion that Matthew "was a note-taker during the earthly ministry of Jesus" and that "his notes provided the basis for the bulk of the apostolic gospel tradition."[50]

But there is no reason to assume that Matthew was the only one among Jesus's original entourage who could write and thus who would have taken notes. Eusebius passes on a tradition that the young disciple Mark was Peter's interpreter and wrote accurately all that Peter remembered.[51] This may well refer to the practice of note-taking (*hypomnemata*). Moreover, Luke notes, quite incidentally, that "many" before him had attempted to write accounts of what went on among the early Christians (Luke 1:1).

On top of this, there are sayings in Paul's letters that parallel sayings in the Gospel traditions (see chap. 5). This may suggest that sayings were written down and circulated well before the Gospels were written. Even more forceful, however, are the strong verbal similarities between Matthew and Luke when recording material not found in Mark. These similarities can be accounted for most easily by supposing that Matthew and Luke shared a common written source (Q). And, as a number of scholars have noted, there is ample evidence of early collections of Old Testament proof-texts (testimonia) in written form that were apparently used in preaching and in apologetic settings in the early church.[52]

---

48. On this point it is worth noting that fishermen in the Mediterranean world of the first century were "hardly peasants, ranking instead with tax-gatherers, carpenters, and artisans as a sort of middle-income group that comprised much of the upper 10 percent of wage earning in antiquity" (Keener, *Gospel of John*, 1:101).

49. Cited in Eusebius, *Ecclesiastical History*, 3.39.16. The translation here is taken from S. McKnight, "Matthew, Gospel of," in *Dictionary of Jesus and the Gospels*, ed. J. B. Green, S. McKnight, and I. H. Marshall (Downers Grove, IL: InterVarsity, 1992), 527. The proper interpretation of this passage is much debated; for discussion see McKnight, "Matthew, Gospel of," 527–28. For a forceful defense of Papias's testimony as deriving from the apostle John, see R. H. Gundry, *Mark: A Commentary on His Apology for the Cross* (Grand Rapids: Eerdmans, 1993), 1026–45. His arguments are reproduced in idem, *Matthew: A Commentary on His Handbook for a Mixed Church under Persecution*, 2nd ed. (Grand Rapids: Eerdmans, 1994), 609–20.

50. R. H. Gundry, *The Use of the Old Testament in Matthew's Gospel* (Leiden: Brill, 1967), 182.

51. Eusebius, *Ecclesiastical History*, 3.39.15.

52. See M. C. Albl, *"And Scripture Cannot Be Broken": The Form and Function of the Early Christian Testimonia Collections* (Boston: Brill, 1999); Alessandro Falcetta, "Testimonies: The Theory of James Rendel Harris in the Light of Subsequent Research" (PhD diss., University of Birmingham, 2000). Falcetta

In light of all this, it does not seem that the earliest disciples were altogether illiterate or that the tradition leading up to the writing of the Gospels was purely oral. As Robert Stein argues, there is "no need to think that this material [of Jesus's teachings] was simply memorized by the disciples. Some of Jesus' teaching could well have been written down in brief notebook-like memoranda for use during their mission."[53]

This notion of note-taking is an important one. At a landmark 1978 interdisciplinary conference on the Gospels, the respected classicist George Kennedy pointed out that New Testament scholars have tended seriously to neglect—and without good reason—both the general likelihood of note-taking among Jesus's early disciples, and the specific external evidence contained in Papias for just such note-taking.[54] In response to Kennedy's challenge, Reginald Fuller concludes:

> Some of the conclusions of form criticism can and probably should be modified in significant ways. . . . Kennedy's introduction of the *hypomnemata* [i.e., note-

---

calls attention to a text in the John Rylands collection (Papyrus Rylands Greek 460), considered to be the earliest extant testimonia fragment; see "A Testimony Collection in Manchester: Papyrus Rylands Greek 460," *Bulletin of the John Rylands University Library of Manchester* 83 (2001): 3–19. In this regard see also Karl Paul Donfried, "Paul as Skenopoios and the Use of the Codex in Early Christianity," in *Christus Bezeugen: Festschrift fuer Wolfgang Trilling* (Leipzig: St. Benno, 1989), 254–56.

53. R. H. Stein, *The Synoptic Problem: An Introduction* (Grand Rapids: Baker Academic, 1987), 205. Related to this, see the now-classic study of Heinz Schuermann that demonstrated that the pre-Easter setting of Jesus's own ministry provides the proper context within which to make sense of much of the Jesus tradition: "Die voroesterlichen Anfaenge der Logientradition," in *Der Historische Jesus und der Kerugmatische Christus: Beitraege zum Christusverstaendnis in Forschung und Verkuendigung*, ed. H. Ristow and K. Matthiae (Berlin: Evangelische Verlangsanstalt, 1960), 342–70.

54. Kennedy, "Classical and Christian," 152. From the same year see also E. E. Ellis, "New Directions in Form Criticism," in *Prophecy and Hermeneutic in Early Christianity: New Testament Essays* (Tübingen: Mohr Siebeck, 1978), 242–47. Since that time, a growing number of New Testament scholars appear to be taking the idea of early writings among Jesus's followers quite seriously. As examples (and across the lines of liberal and conservative scholarship): J. M. Robinson: "The history of the synoptic tradition is no longer dependent only on the forms of oral transmission, but now has a series of written texts bridging much of the gulf back from canonical gospels to Jesus" ("A Written Greek Sayings Cluster Older than Q: A Vestige," *HTR* 92 [1999]: 61); B. W. Henaut: "The assumption of an early and exclusively oral phase of transmission terminating in written documents only after a lengthy passage of time . . . may not be warranted. The growing awareness of pre-synoptic written sources, a history of redaction within Q, and the inclusion in Paul's letters of some synoptic sayings and other parenesis warns that the literary phase of transmission may have started much earlier than is often thought" (*Oral Tradition and the Gospels: The Problem of Mark 4* [Sheffield: Sheffield Academic Press, 1993], 116–17); P. Head: "The emerging picture suggests that the production of written records would have had a place in the cultural milieu of the Galilean disciples of Jesus" ("A Further Note on *Reading and Writing in the Time of Jesus*," *EQ* 75 [2003]: 345); A. Millard: "The evidence indicates the presence of some people, not professional scribes, who could use writing in their daily business throughout Palestine, even in rural regions, able to make notes of a preacher's words if they wished" (*Reading and Writing in the Time of Jesus*, 181–82). Even Werner Kelber, a staunch supporter of the "orality" of the early church, concedes that the "concept of a predominantly oral phase is not meant to dispense with the existence of notes and textual aids altogether" (*The Oral and the Written Gospel*, 23).

taking] as an intermediate stage in the process of gospel composition demands a reassessment and a revision of the more skeptical historical assumptions of form and redaction criticism.[55]

While the nature of historical research means we can never rise above probability estimates, it seems we are on fairly secure ground in rejecting the standard form-critical assumption that the material about Jesus circulated in a *purely* oral form prior to the written Gospels. For our purposes, this is significant because it makes it more difficult to envision the pre-Gospel Jesus tradition being as susceptible to rampant and unrestrained "creative" activity—fictionalization and mythmaking—as the various forms of the legendary-Jesus thesis require.

The Assumed Lack of a Coherent Narrative

Our critique of the first form-critical assumption has led us to the conclusion that, in all likelihood, writing played some regulative role in the transmission of Jesus material within the early church. Whatever the scope of this role may have been, however, we must nevertheless agree with the scholarly consensus that the *primary* means of passing on the Jesus tradition in the early church would have been *oral*. Hence a great deal continues to hang on our estimation of the nature and general reliability of the early oral Jesus tradition.

Thus we turn now to the second form-critical assumption that has tended to undermine the reliability of the early church's oral tradition: the assumption that there was no shared, historically rooted, extended life-of-Jesus narrative within which the various pieces of the tradition fit until decades after Jesus, when a Gospel writer (usually identified with Mark) created a largely fictitious narrative framework within which to organize the disparate units of tradition. Indeed, one of the very first works of the form-critical fathers—Schmidt's *Der Rahmen der Geschichte Jesu*—refers in its very title to the general form-critical consensus that there was no historically rooted, pre-Gospel narrative "framework" to complement and contextualize the many small individual units of tradition that circulated in the early church. How should this common form-critical assumption be evaluated?

The Discovery of Long Oral Narratives

Early form critics such as Bultmann took it for granted that folk traditions consisted almost exclusively of short vignettes. How could longer narratives, to say nothing of epics, be remembered and transmitted intact orally? While this

---

55. R. H. Fuller, "Classics and the Gospels: The Seminar," in *Relationships among the Gospels*, esp. 178, 180. W. A. Meeks also responded positively to Kennedy's insights on this matter; see "Hypomnemata from an Untamed Sceptic: A Response to George Kennedy," in *Relationships among the Gospels*, 159–60. G. Stanton affirms this insight, suggesting that it is most likely that Paul himself kept notes in preparation for his epistolary activity; see "Early Christian Preference for the Codex," 47–48n40.

view is still prevalent today among many in New Testament circles, a significant number of folklorists, anthropologists, and ethnographers over the last several decades have justifiably abandoned it.[56] The reason for this reversal is that empirical evidence has shown it to be demonstrably wrong. A large number of fieldwork studies have "brought to light numerous long oral epics in the living traditions of Central Asia, India, Africa, and Oceania, for example." Hence, as the famed Finnish folklorist Lauri Honko recently noted: "The existence of genuine long oral epics can no longer be denied."[57] In fact, amazingly, scholars have documented oral narratives whose performance lasted up to twenty-five hours carried out over several days.[58]

The performances of oral narratives within orally dominant cultures tend to share fundamental characteristics.[59] Oral performances are almost always composed of a longer narrative plot line together with various smaller units that compose the bulk of the story in any given performance. Because of their length, the long narrative plot line is almost never played out fully in any single performance. Moreover, the degree of detail in which the narrative is played out varies consid-

56. L. Honko claims that discoveries over the last several decades have "shattered" and "obliterated" the classic view, which questions the existence of long oral narratives; see *Textualizing the Siri Epic* (Helsinki: Academia Scientiarum Fennica, 1998), 18. Yet the classic view persists. For example, Walter Ong—who has influenced the views of so many on issues related to orality—can be found arguing that "an oral culture has no experience of a lengthy, epic-sized, or novel-sized climactic linear plot, nor can it imagine such organization of lengthy material. In fact, it cannot organize even shorter narrative in the highly climactic way that readers of literature for the past two hundred years have learned more and more to expect" ("Oral Remembering and Narrative Structures," in *Analyzing Discourse: Text and Talk*, ed. D. Tannen [Washington, DC: Georgetown University Press, 1982], 15); see also idem, *Orality and Literacy: The Technologizing of the Word* (New York: Methuen, 1982), 143.

57. Honko, "Introduction: Oral and Semiliterary Epics," in *The Epic: Oral and Written*, ed. L. Honko, J. Handoo, and J. M. Foley (Mysore, India: Central Institute of Indian Languages, 1998), 9. This new awareness constitutes a "paradigm shift" according to Lauri Honko ("Text as Process and Practice: The Textualization of Oral Epics," in *Textualization of Oral Epics*, ed. L. Honko [New York: Mouton de Gruyter, 2000], 3–4). A historical recounting of this shift would have to include: Ruth Finnegan's observation in the 1970s on lengthy narration in Somali poetry (*Oral Poetry: Its Nature, Significance and Social Context* [Bloomington: Indiana University Press, 1992], 78–79); Roger Abrahams's work—in dependence upon Mary Catherine Bateson's theory of "praxa," or "chunks of knowledge"—with African-American oral traditions (Abrahams, *Deep Down in the Jungle*, rev. ed. [Chicago: Aldine, 1970]; idem, "License to Repeat and Be Predictable," *Folklore Preprint Series* 6/3 [1978]; 4–6); Bateson, "Ritualization: A Study in Texture and Texture Changes," in *Religious Movements in Contemporary America*, ed. I. I. Zaretsky and M. P. Leone (Princeton: Princeton University Press, 1974), 150–65; Dell Hymes's work with Native American oral traditions, e.g., the oral narrative "Seal (and) Her Younger Brother Lived There" (*"In vain I tried to tell you": Essays in Native American Ethnopoetics* [Philadelphia: University of Pennsylvania Press, 1981], chaps. 8–9); and Lauri and Anneli Honko's work with various oral epics in south India (*Textualizing the Siri Epic*). On African oral epics, see J. W. Johnson, T. A. Hale, and S. Belcher, eds., *Oral Epics from Africa: Vibrant Voices from a Vast Continent* (Bloomington: Indiana University Press, 1997).

58. Honko himself has witnessed one oral narrative whose performance ran seven days (*Textualizing the Siri Epic*, 15). On lengthy oral epic performances, see J. Brockington, "The Textualization of Sanskrit Epics," in *Textualization of Oral Epics*, 210–11.

59. On what follows, see Honko, *Textualizing the Siri Epic*, 193–94.

erably from performance to performance, depending largely on the particular situation of the audience. The narrative schematic itself functions as something of a "mental text" (to use Honko's phrase) within the mind of the performer, one that is "edited" for each particular performance. There is also a significant degree of flexibility in terms of the placement, order, and length of the smaller units of tradition that fill out the narrative in any given performance. This too largely depends on the purpose, context, and time constraints of the performance in the light of the situation of the community.

The Gospels as Performance Events in the Oral Style

These observations decisively refute the classic form-critical assumption that oral traditions, by nature, do not involve long narratives. Applying this conclusion to the Jesus tradition, there is no longer any justification for supposing the overall narrative framework of the Gospels to be a literary "fiction" imposed on previously autonomous, disconnected units of the oral Jesus tradition. But these observations also go a long way toward explaining the interesting balance between the general uniformity and specific flexibility that we find within the Gospels. They help explain the fact that, while we find the same general portrait of Jesus in the Synoptic Gospels, we also find remarkable variations in what each specific portrait includes and excludes, as well as in the order and specific form of the material that constitutes each portrait. This is to say that the Gospel writers themselves worked with something of an "oral conception"—that is, an oral-like "hermeneutic," an oral-like communicative style—when it came to the composition of their texts.[60]

This type of model goes a long way toward explaining the sort of variations we find within the Jesus tradition. On one hand, E. P. Sanders and Margaret Davies are (at one level) certainly correct when they claim that "on one point the form critics were surely right. They correctly observed that in the gospels one can see *individual and originally independent units*."[61] On the other hand, this single observation, left to stand alone, is very misleading. For Birger Gerhardsson is no less correct when he claims that "it was impossible already at the beginning to be content with only individual, episodal narratives about the activity of Jesus."[62] Viewed from outside the constraints of the modern, highly literate paradigm and guided by oral performance studies, we can embrace important elements of both of these claims. The individually identifiable units of tradition are, in fact, small, discrete units, and they can function relatively independently with respect to order (within limits) and even presence (i.e., within any given performance, oral

---

60. On the valuable insight of E. J. Bakker regarding the important distinction between an "oral medium" and an "oral conception," see Bakker, *Poetry in Speech: Orality and Homeric Discourse* (Ithaca, NY: Cornell University Press, 1997), 7–9; idem, "How Oral Is Oral Composition?" in *Signs of Orality: The Oral Tradition and Its Influence in the Greek and Roman World*, ed. A. E. MacKay (Boston: Brill, 1999), 29–33. We will explore and apply these crucial categories in chap. 10.

61. E. P. Sanders and M. Davies, *Studying the Synoptic Gospels* (Philadelphia: Trinity, 1989), 134.

62. Gerhardsson, "The Gospel Tradition," 536.

or written). However, at the same time, they were always-already envisioned within the schematic backdrop (the "mental text") of a lengthy narrative tradition about Jesus. For any given telling, how, where (within certain logical limits), and even whether they functioned in *that* particular oral—or written—performance of the wider tradition was always subject to the exigencies of the specific performance.

The knowledge we have acquired over the last several decades about the nature of oral performances within orally dominant cultures gives us a framework for understanding how this interesting unity-amid-diversity transpired. Whether spoken or not, the narrative framework of Jesus's life always formed something of a mental narrative text within the context of which early Christian tradents (i.e., tradition bearers) and their audiences understood the relatively numerous *logia*, aphorisms, pronouncement stories, and so on that played a significant role in any particular oral performance. As with oral performances observed today, we may assume that the contingencies of particular early Christian communities and/or the particular performance event itself determined which "forms" were selected and which portions of the overall narrative were told. And, just as in oral performances observed today, we may assume that there was significant flexibility as to the order and length of the individual forms that were included in any given oral performance. In short, viewing the early church as an orally dominant culture along the lines of similar cultures today explains nicely the general uniformity with specific flexibility we find in the Jesus tradition, both written and (we can safely surmise) oral.

Applications to New Testament Research

Over the last few decades, a number of New Testament scholars have begun to grasp the significance of these insights. One of the first to do so was Thorleif Boman.[63] Contrary to classical form-critical theory, and in line with recent folklorist studies, Boman made a compelling case that orally recounted historical narratives do not emerge out of independently circulating units of prior tradition. Rather, the narrative and the units *inextricably belong together*.[64] As Leander Keck notes, Boman's work suggests that,

> From the outset, oral tradition about historical persons embraces both individual items and an overall picture of the hero. If Mark is the bearer of oral tradition, he did not create a picture of Jesus out of miscellaneous items but rather transmitted a picture of Jesus that was already present in the oral tradition.[65]

63. T. Boman, *Die Jesus-Ueberlieferung im Lichte der neueren Volkskunde* (Goettingen: Vandenhoeck & Ruprecht, 1967). For two helpful reviews see M. D. Hooker's review in *JTS* 22 (1971): 566–68; and F. Wieden's review in *CBQ* 30 (1968): 430–32. Although Güttgemanns would soon scrutinize form-critical theory in light of newer studies of oral tradition (particularly the Parry-Lord thesis), he did not deeply explore the question of a pre-Markan narrative framework.

64. Boman, *Die Jesus-Ueberlieferung*, 21–31.

65. L. E. Keck, "Oral Traditional Literature and the Gospels: The Seminar," in *The Relationship among the Gospels*, 111. The general sense of the necessary and important role that an early common narrative

As the interdisciplinary data on the existence and nature of long oral narratives has continued to grow over the last few decades, Boman's argument has been increasingly confirmed. As a result, a growing number of New Testament scholars are abandoning the classical form-critical bias against an early orally transmitted Jesus narrative.

Joanna Dewey, for example, argues that the "form-critical assumption that there was no story of Jesus prior to the written Gospels, only individual stories about Jesus . . . needs to be reconsidered in light of our growing knowledge of oral narrative."[66] Dewey has pointed out that an oral narrative the length of Mark would take at most two hours to perform, which, as we have seen, is relatively short by the oral-narrative standards.[67] What is more, as oral narratives go, Mark's narrative would be relatively easy to remember and transmit. "Good storytellers could easily learn the story of Mark from hearing it read or hearing it told," she writes. And from this she concludes that, "given the nature of oral memory and tradition . . . it is likely that the original written text of Mark was dependent on a pre-existing connected oral narrative, a narrative that already was being performed in various versions by various people."[68]

We now have good reason to think that the relationship between the parts (the individual pericope of the Gospels that have been the sole focus of form criticism) and the whole (the broad narrative framework of Jesus's life, ministry, death, and resurrection) from early on would have been both much more fundamental and, at the same time, much more flexible than the modern, literate paradigm (under which classical form criticism has always labored) could ever imagine. Breakthrough theories such as Lauri Honko's concept of "mental text,"

---

would have played in the earliest Christian community had, of course, been recognized by some scholars for some time prior to Boman. See, e.g., A. Menzies, *The Earliest Gospel* (London: Macmillan, 1902), 29; C. F. D. Moule, "The Intention of the Evangelists," in *New Testament Essays: Studies in Memory of T. W. Manson*, ed. A. J. B. Higgins (Manchester: Manchester University Press, 1959), 172–73. C. H. Dodd pushed beyond the bare observation to propose a more detailed analysis of this narrative. See "The Framework of the Gospel Narrative," *ExpT* 43 (1931–32): 396–400; reprinted in idem, *New Testament Studies* (Manchester: Manchester University Press, 1953), 1–11. When Dodd's specific proposal was criticized in terms of certain specifics, many abandoned the entire project prematurely. More recently—and, we would add, with much fieldwork data from a wide range of orally dominant cultures to back him up—Stephen Hultgren has taken up the project again in a fruitful way in his recent *Narrative Elements in the Double Tradition: A Study of Their Place within the Framework of the Gospel Narratives* (New York: de Gruyter, 2002). For details on Hultgren, see below. A similar project, this time focusing on the recovery of a historically rooted framework for Jesus's ministry within the Fourth Gospel, has recently been outlined. See F. J. Moloney, "The Fourth Gospel and the Jesus of History," *NTS* 46 (2000): 42–58. Moloney builds on the foundation laid by the twentieth-century British group—Gardner-Smith, Hoskyns, Dodd, Robinson—who argued that the Fourth Gospel was independent of the Synoptics and/or that it contains a good deal of historically rooted data on the historical Jesus.

66. J. Dewey, "Oral Methods of Structuring Narrative in Mark," *Interpretation* 43 (1989): 44.

67. J. Dewey, "The Gospel of Mark as an Oral-Aural Event: Implications for Interpretation," in *The New Literary Criticism and the New Testament*, ed. E. S. Malbon and E. V. McKnight (Sheffield: Sheffield Academic Press, 1994), 146.

68. Dewey, "Gospel of Mark," 146–47, 158.

Egbert Bakker's idea of oral performance as "activation," and John Miles Foley's "metonymy" thesis applied to oral narratives have deepened our ability to understand how lengthy oral narratives can be retained and transmitted, and how they relate to the individual parts.[69]

Working with Paul Ricoeur's findings on narrative and representation, Jens Schroeter has argued that the narrative framework of the Gospel tradition has no less a claim to historicity than the individual sayings of Jesus.[70] This statement points toward a crucial observation, one that has emerged in recent interdisciplinary conversations around the concerns of history, epistemology, and narrative. The heart of the matter is this: *human beings, by their very epistemological nature, generally structure their experience of reality in the form of narrative.* We orient and live our lives by the stories we tell. As John Niles points out: "Oral narrative is and for a long time has been the chief basis of culture itself. . . . [S]torytelling is an ability that defines the human species as such, at least as far as our knowledge of human experience extends into the historical past and into the sometime startling realms that ethnography has brought to light."

Thus, Niles argues, it is not an overstatement to designate the human species as "*Homo narrans.*"[71] Part of the reason for this unavoidable narrativizing impetus is that the human experience is always-already bound up with the experience of

69. On "mental text"—i.e., the story lines, textual elements, and rules for oral reproduction that exist within the mind of any given tradent—see L. Honko, *Textualizing the Siri Epic*, 92–99; idem, "Epics along the Silk Road: Mental Text, Performance, and Written Codification," *Oral Tradition* 11 (1996): 1–17. On "activation"—the idea that within any single oral performance, a limited number of ideas from within the wide, communally shared narrative pool of concepts undergo "activation"—see E. J. Bakker, "Activation and Preservation: The Interdependence of Text and Performance in an Oral Tradition," *Oral Tradition* 8 (1993): 5–20. On "metonymy"—the idea of "parts standing for wholes," wherein entire epic-length oral narratives are implied in, and signaled by, shorter "parts" in performance—see J. M. Foley, *Immanent Art: From Structure to Meaning in Traditional Oral Epic* (Bloomington: Indiana University Press, 1991), esp. 5–13; idem, "Selection as *pars pro toto*: The Role of Metonymy in Epic Performance and Tradition," in *The Kalevala and the World's Traditional Epics*, ed. L. Honko (Helsinki: Finnish Literature Society, 2002), 106–27. In this last essay, Foley reminds those of us who live and move in the modern literate world that to even talk of "partial performances" or the performance of the "whole" work is to employ questionable concepts in the world of orality, concepts born from a literate mentality and its "latent textuality" (p. 113).

70. J. Schroeter, "*Von der Historizitaet der Evangelien: Ein Beitrag zur gegenwaertigen Diskussion um den historischen Jesus,*" in *Der historische Jesus: Tendenzen und Perspektiven der gegenwaertigen Forschung,* ed. J. Schroeter and R. Bruckers (Berlin: de Gruyter, 2002), 163–212.

71. J. D. Niles, *Homo Narrans: The Poetics and Anthropology of Oral Literature* (Philadelphia: University of Pennsylvania Press, 1999), 2–3. Niles is, of course, building on the seminal work of Ricoeur and others. See esp. P. Ricoeur, *Time and Narrative*, trans. K. McLaughlin and D. Pellauer, 3 vols. (Chicago: University of Chicago Press, 1984–1988). Thus Terrence Tilley correctly observes: "*Human* experience is *inherently* narrative in form" (*Story Theology* [Wilmington, DE: Glazier, 1985], 23, also 26–27). See also S. Crites, "The Narrative Quality of Experience," in *Why Narrative? Readings in Christology*, ed. S. Hauerwas and L. G. Jones (Grand Rapids: Eerdmans, 1989), 65–88. This conviction is further supported by studies of oral tradition. Although discrete units of tradition are used, "there has to be some hierarchical planning and organizing of the material in advance. In other words, the nervous system has to contain an overall structure within which individual units are slotted" (I. Pyysiäinen, "Variation from a Cognitive Perspective," in *Thick Corpus, Organic Variation and Textuality in Oral Tradition*, ed. L. Honko

time, and thus sequence and duration. The experience of sequence and duration, in turn, are most naturally structured and articulated in the form of what we designate as "narrative."[72]

So too, Pieter Botha, one of the leading New Testament scholars in terms of applying recent interdisciplinary studies on oral tradition to the Gospels, contends that "it is absurd to think that an extended narrative about Jesus became a reality outside the initial followers of Jesus and only after a long passage of time."[73] Rather, he argues, we have every reason to believe that the extended narrative of Jesus's life, as well as the individual sayings, aphorisms, parables, and speeches that find a place within this narrative, go back to the original community of Jesus followers.

As a final word on this matter, we should make mention of the work of Stephen Hultgren, who has recently argued that we can identify a common narrative framework not only in Mark but also in the supposedly narrative-free double tradition (the Q material).[74] Hultgren's thesis is the sort of thing we should expect to find, given what we now know about the fundamental nature of narrative within an orally dominant culture. Hultgren summarizes his conclusions as follows:

> Before any of our canonical gospels were written, there existed in the gospel tradition a common, coherent, and primitive narrative-kerygmatic framework that ran from the baptism of Jesus to his passion, death and resurrection. The narrative elements in the double tradition were not only fully embedded in this narrative-

---

[Helsinki: Finnish Literature Society, 2000], 188). On this point see also H. Gardner, *The Mind's New Science: A History of the Cognitive Revolution* (New York: Basic, 1987), 11–13.

This general insight has begun to profoundly affect the worlds of biblical studies and theological reflection as a wide range of narrative-oriented studies has exploded onto the scene over the last several decades. See, e.g., H. Frei, *The Eclipse of Biblical Narrative: A Study in Eighteenth and Nineteenth Century Hermeneutics* (New Haven, CT: Yale University Press, 1974); R. A. Krieg, *Story-Shaped Christology: The Role of Narrative in Identifying Jesus Christ* (New York: Paulist, 1988); and the various essays in Hauerwas and Jones, eds., *Why Narrative?* N. T. Wright has pushed this methodological issue to the foreground in *The New Testament and the People of God* (Minneapolis: Fortress, 1992), see esp. 47–80. Even here, however, Wright does not carry through his proposal as thoroughly as he could. He writes, for example, of the "strange, unstoried world" of Q and the Gospel of Thomas (p. 435). But whether any given text of Q began with the narrative of Jesus's baptism or not, the world of Q (and presumably Thomas) was no doubt deeply and profoundly "storied" in nature. To think otherwise simply because we cannot identify certain explicit narrative elements in the reconstructed text is to be blinded by our thoroughly literate, text-centric, post-Gutenberg sensibilities. It is to miss what John Miles Foley has pointed out that contemporary scholars so often miss—namely the communicatively economical world of orally dominant cultures, where metonymic representation reigns. See esp. Foley, "Selection as *pars pro toto*." F. G. Downing, for example, appears to be properly cognizant of this point; see "Words as Deeds and Deeds as Words," *Biblical Interpretation* 3 (1995): 141. Incidentally, while Miles's discussion is in the context of oral epic, he rightly notes that the basic theory of metonymy applies to a variety of traditional oral genre (p. 108).

72. Some argue that the very fact that history writing is inextricably bound to aspects of narrative construction (e.g., selection, linearity, etc.) that it is, in this process, rendered more like fiction than anything else. We will address this question in chap. 8.

73. P. Botha, "Mark's Story as Oral Traditional Literature," *Hervormde Teologiese Studies* 47 (1991), 323.

74. Hultgren, *Narrative Elements*, 311–25.

kerygmatic framework from the beginning of the gospel tradition, but they were in part constituent of that framework.[75]

All of this suggests that, for all its diversity and flexibility, the memory of Jesus passed on in the early church had "a high degree of unity and homogeneity" to it, a conclusion that squares well with the recent interdisciplinary findings on the existence and nature of oral narratives.[76] We therefore have good reason to conclude that the earliest Christians were concerned about, and privy to, a broad, shared vision of the ministry, death, and resurrection of Jesus from the beginning. Among other things, this conclusion explains how Paul could appeal repeatedly to the life of Jesus as a model for his audience to pattern their lives after, as we saw in the previous chapter. If the oral traditions of the early church embodied a broad, community-shared "mental text" of Jesus's life, such appeals make good sense.

When we recall our earlier point that we have every reason to suppose that at least some of the earliest disciples were literate and thus that the early church would not have had to rely exclusively on oral tradition in the first place, we begin to gain confidence that the oral traditions leading up to the Gospels were perhaps not as unreliable as many critical scholars of the past imagined. Related to this, we can safely reject the notion that the narrative framework of the Gospel was superimposed on previously disparate and unrelated Gospel material. This, in turn, renders less plausible the view that there was significant legendary accretion in the oral traditions leading up to the Gospels.

The Assumed Lack of Biographical Interest

A third form-critical assumption is that the earliest Christians were focused almost solely upon apocalyptically motivated evangelism and thus had little inter-

---

75. Hultgren, *Narrative Elements*, 310. As we saw in the last chapter, there is pervasive evidence of this pre-Gospel kerygmatic framework found in Paul's letters.

76. Ibid., 353. Interestingly enough, once the form-critical assumption of the absence of an oral Jesus narrative in earliest Christianity is abandoned, the musings of some early twentieth-century New Testament scholars begin to regain their plausibility. For example, in 1902 Allan Menzies suggested that in the creation of his Gospel, Mark "must have been guided by one who knew the life of Jesus not only as a set of isolated stories but as a connected whole inspired by a growing purpose" (Menzies, *The Earliest Gospel*, 29). In the 1930s, C. H. Dodd identified the broad outlines of this pre-Markan narrative, arguing that it is visible not only in Mark but also in certain speeches in Acts (e.g., Acts 10:36–43) and other New Testament passages (Dodd, "The Framework of the Gospel Narrative," 396–400; reprinted in idem, *New Testament Studies*, 1–11). For decades, Dodd's thesis has been subjected to searching criticism, with many scholars considering it to be laid to rest. See, e.g., D. E. Nineham, "The Order of Events in St. Mark's Gospel: An Examination of Dr. Dodd's Hypothesis," in *Studies in the Gospels*, ed. D. E. Nineham (Oxford: Blackwell, 1955), 223–39. Others, however, have remained convinced that Dodd was generally on the right track, even if his theory failed on certain particulars. See, e.g., F. F. Bruce, "Are the New Testament Documents Still Reliable?" in *Evangelical Roots: A Tribute to Wilbur Smith*, ed. K. S. Kantzer (Nashville: Nelson, 1978), 57. We submit that the "paradigm shift" regarding the existence and nature of longer oral narratives has rendered these older perspectives more plausible once again.

est in passing on historically rooted biographical information about Jesus. How is this assumption, one not unrelated to an early twentieth-century approach to folklore and oral tradition, to be assessed today?

What Do We Mean by "Biographical"?

We must note that a good deal hangs on what we mean by "biographical." For example, the form-critic Vincent Taylor argues that prior to the writing of the Gospels, "a Christianity had existed which was destitute of the biographical interest." This, he argues, is why "no one thought of recording the life of Christ" for the first decades of the church.[77]

Now, it might initially appear that Taylor was flat out denying that early Christians were interested in accurate information about Jesus's life. When Taylor fleshes out what he means by "biographical," however, it becomes clear he is not denying this at all. He is simply using the term "biographical" in a rather technical, modern sense. By "biographical interest" Taylor refers to "the desire to trace the course of a man's life, to show how one thing led to another, to depict the development of his personality." Taylor rightly notes that early Christians had "no interest" in doing *this*.[78]

But this says little more than that early Christians were not interested in certain technical specifics that modern biographers and historians are interested in. In this modern sense of the word, we have to grant that neither the oral narratives about Jesus nor the written Gospels are "biographical." Indeed, in this sense of the term, it is questionable whether *any* premodern account of a person's life should be considered fully "biographical." But this does not at all imply that the earliest Christians did not have a concern to accurately transmit historically rooted information about Jesus. To the contrary, a wide body of field-based research on orally dominant cultures suggests that we should expect quite the opposite.

Oral Traditions and Historical Concern

Much of the extensive work done on the transmission of oral traditions over the last half century directly challenges the assumption held by previous scholars that orally oriented cultures tend to be indifferent to the distinction between historical and fictional narratives. The view of an increasing number who work within the interdisciplinary world of orality studies is that certain oral genre—namely historically oriented genre—not only can be, but *tend to be*, concerned about accurately transmitting recollections of their historical past. While "folklore is present," according to Richard Dorson, a folklorist who has been at the forefront of this discussion, "so is historical content." "Even more importantly," he continues, "so are historical attitudes of the traditions bearers."[79]

77. V. Taylor, *The Formation of the Gospel Tradition* (London: Macmillan, 1935), 143–44.
78. Ibid., 144.
79. R. Dorson, "Introduction: Folklore and Traditional History," in *Folklore and Traditional History*, ed. R. Dorson (The Hague: Mouton, 1973), 9. We should note that orality scholars frequently distinguish between three forms of history in oral traditions: the recent past, the remote past, and the "middle

The anthropologist Patrick Pender-Cudlip makes the point even more force-fully. He argues that "oral tradents" (those entrusted with transmitting oral tradi-tions) demonstrate as much concern to "receive and render a precise, accurate and authentic account of the past" as do modern literate historians: "Both consist of supposedly authentic narratives of past events, both explain and express truths about the present through stories about the past, and both use the present as a model for reconstructing the past. Regarded in this light, the differences between them are mainly technical."[80]

Joseph Miller, a specialist on African history and oral tradition, goes so far as to describe "tellers of tales about the past in oral cultures" as "professional historians in the sense that they are conscious of history and evidence." Hence, he adds, "Oral historians are . . . no less conscious of the past than are historians in literate cultures."[81] Similarly, Annikki Kaivola-Bregenhoj observes that oral peoples ex-hibit a capacity to determine whether a narrative performance is "a fictitious story or a report of something that really happened, something to be taken seriously or a tall story."[82] It is not uncommon to find in orally dominant societies a clear

---

period." See, e.g., J. C. Miller, "Introduction: Listening for the African Past," in *The African Past Speaks: Essays on Oral Tradition and History*, ed. J. C. Miller (Hamden, CT: Archon, 1980), 35–39; idem, "The Dynamics of Oral Tradition in Africa," in *Fonti Orali: Antropologia e Storia*, ed. B. Bernardi, C. Ponti, and A. Triulzi (Milan: Angeli, 1978), 80; T. Spear, "Oral Traditions: Whose History?" *History in Africa* 8 (1981): 171–73; J. Vansina, "Oral Tradition, Oral History: Achievement and Perspectives," in *Fonti Orali*, 64–69; R. G. Willis, *On Historical Reconstruction from Oral Traditional Sources: A Structuralist Approach* (Chicago: Northwestern University Press, 1976), 2–16. Oral traditions about the recent past regularly lack the cosmological, mythological, and purely sociologically motivated elements of tradi-tions about "the remote past." See, e.g., Miller, "Dynamics of Oral Tradition," 80; Willis, *Historical Reconstruction*, 15. They also tend to provide causal connections between events and include personal remembrances. See Willis, *Historical Reconstruction*, 15; Miller, "Listening for the African Past," 22. It is this "recent past" aspect of oral traditions—sometimes designated as "oral history"—that many scholars now regard as generally historically reliable in terms of essential content. And it is this dimension that most interests us, since the remembrances of Jesus in the pre-Gospel decades would have been of a person in the very recent past.

80. P. Pender-Cudlip, "Oral Traditions and Anthropological Analysis: Some Contemporary Myths," *Azania* 7 (1972): 12. According to a number of contemporary scholars, the primary difference between oral histories and written histories is not their fundamental attitudes toward history, but in the respec-tive advantages and disadvantages inherent in each mode of communication. See Miller, "Listening for the African Past," 51.

81. Miller, "Listening for the African Past," 51, 52.

82. A. Kaivola-Bregenhoj, "Varying Folklore," in *Thick Corpus*, 101. As R. Law notes with respect to intentional historical narratives within oral societies, "It is important that each event occurred and can be linked to the feature of the present which it serves to explain or legitimate" ("How Truly Traditional Is Our Traditional History? The Case of Samuel Johnson and the Recording of Yoruba Oral Tradition," *History in Africa* 11 [1984]: 198). Here, Law points out that oral tradents tend to be concerned both about actual historical events of the past and the present sociological realities that they illuminate and/or legitimate. While many contemporary scholars of orality—particularly anthropologists and literary critics—tend to focus upon the latter and thus neglect or even outright deny the former, a properly balanced approach will recognize both concerns at work in the historical narrative genres of most orally dominant cultures.

conceptual and/or terminological differentiation between narratives considered
to be factual and those considered to be fictional. Ruth Finnegan, an anthropologist and leading voice in contemporary orality studies, notes that with regard to
African oral tradition, it is often the case that "more serious narrations concerned
with historical events may be distinguished as a separate literary form."[83]

A most significant expression of this historical awareness is that it is frequently
the case in predominantly oral settings that, within the context of the performance
arena, the audience shares in the responsibility of accurately preserving the essential
historical remembrances. That is, if an oral performer misrepresents the tradition—
sometimes in even relatively minor ways—the audience frequently corrects him
in the midst of the performance.[84] Hence, while the performer is entrusted with

83. R. Finnegan, *Oral Literature in Africa*, repr. ed. (Nairobi: Oxford University Press, 1979), 370.
On the relationship between oral history and Western academic history writing, Vansina writes: "Oral
history itself poses no major problems to the scholar. . . . It is now used especially by historians and political
scientists, although most anthropologists have life histories for their major informants as well. . . . For
[African history] it is essential" ("Oral Tradition, Oral History," 65). For largely positive, and yet prudently
careful, assessments of the historical value of oral history by a panel of historians, see W. E. Leuchtenburg
et al., "A Panel of Historians Discuss Oral History," in *The Second National Colloquium on Oral History,
at Arden House, Harriman, New York, November 18–21, 1967*, ed. L. M. Starr (New York: Oral History Association, 1968), 1–20. Here, we must remember that the panel is dealing with oral history as
transmitted and collected in the context of twentieth-century, North American individualism and the
oral history "interview" process. The nature of ancient oral transmission in a social setting of conscious
corporate solidarity would serve to further safeguard the general preservation of communally shared oral
remembrances, given the fact that, within the traditional performance arena, the audience tended to act,
at one and the same time, as both receptor and regulator of the tradition.

84. This phenomenon is well documented in a wide variety of settings; see, e.g., H.-J. Becken, "The
Use of Oral Tradition in Historiography: Some Pitfalls and Challenges," *Studia historiae eclesiasticae* 19
(1993): 87; I. Okpewho, *African Oral Literature: Backgrounds, Character, and Continuity* (Bloomington:
Indiana University Press, 1992), 183, 192; J. A. Robinson, "Personal Narratives Reconsidered," *Journal of
American Folklore* 94 (1981): 72; E. Tonkin, "The Boundaries of History in Oral Performance," *History in
Africa* 9 (1982): 278. This concept brings to mind, of course, Kenneth Bailey's much discussed proposal
of "informal, controlled oral tradition," based on his reported experience of the *haflat samar* ("a party
for preservation") in the context of Middle Eastern (i.e., Egyptian) village life. See Bailey, "Informal,
Controlled Oral Tradition and the Synoptic Gospels," *Asia Journal of Theology* 5 (1991): 34–54; idem,
"Middle Eastern Oral Tradition and the Synoptic Gospels," *ExpT* 106 (1994–95): 363–67. The most
powerful critique of Bailey's model to date has come from Theodore J. Weeden Sr. in several unpublished papers: "A Critique of Kenneth Bailey's Theory of Oral Tradition: A Flawed Theory [2 parts]."
This two-part critique is available online at http://groups.yahoo.com/group/crosstalk2/message/8301
and http://groups.yahoo.com/group/crosstalk2/message/8730. Weeden also presented the essence
of his critique in "Bailey's Theory of Oral Tradition: A Theory Repudiated by Its Evidence," a paper
read at the Historical Jesus Section of the Annual Meeting of the SBL, Philadelphia, November 21,
2005. Weeden's critique focuses upon certain aspects of Bailey's specific and personal examples of this
phenomenon. We agree that Weeden's careful investigative work has turned up questions for some of
Bailey's particular examples. Nonetheless, the fact that this phenomenon of what can broadly be called
an "informal, controlled oral tradition" is so widely reported in so many field studies of orally dominant
cultures confirms that the phenomenon itself is securely documented far beyond Bailey's experience—an
experience, by the way, that Bailey himself clearly admits is based not on carefully controlled fieldwork
but rather on anecdotes and his own personal impressions. Thus, while Weeden's critique is relevant to,

expressing and creatively adapting traditional oral material to each new setting, the collective memory of the community stands as a counterbalancing authority over each specific performance and over each individual tradent.

This means that in most oral communities there are checks and balances that ensure that the substance of historically oriented oral tradition is not distorted or lost. On the basis of this ongoing community influence, Jawaharlal Handoo has gone so far as to argue that oral histories are generally *more* reliable than written histories! The "strong internal controls over misrepresentation" that we find in oral communities provides a balance that is lacking in histories written from "the palace paradigm"—that is, from an individualist, elitist, and invariably ideologically driven perspective.[85]

In the view of a growing number today, Western folklorists and anthropologists of the past did not notice or take serious this resilient historical dimension of oral tradition largely because of their Western academic biases. Both fields tended to be dominated by the pervasive, modern, academic assumption that nonliterate people, ancient and modern alike, are uncritical of ostensively historical stories and reports, and that a concern for reliable history is a rather recent development of the West. The data collected by recent field studies demonstrate this assumption to be altogether unfounded. Indeed, to the thinking of many scholars, these findings expose this assumption to be rooted in Western chronocentric, ethnocentric bias.[86]

---

even problematic for, Bailey's specific case, it in no way calls into question the well-documented, cross-cultural array of similar phenomena.

85. J. Handoo, "People Are Still Hungry for Kings: Folklore and Oral History," in *Dynamics of Tradition: Perspectives on Oral Poetry and Folk Belief*, ed. L. Tarkka (Helsinki: Finnish Literature Society, 2003), 70. Social anthropologist Elizabeth Tonkin, who is in no way blind to the difficulties of retrieving reliable history from oral narratives, nonetheless states: "Oral history is not intrinsically more or less likely to be accurate than a written document" (*Narrating Our Pasts: The Social Construction of Oral History* [New York: Cambridge University Press, 1992], 113). In this light, many of the current criticisms of "oral history"—especially those that cavalierly contrast it with the superiority of written history—appear less than persuasive. For example, Patrick O'Farrell concludes that oral history is suspect in that it is always vulnerable to the distorting influences of memory, subjectivity, bias, and "myth"; see O'Farrell, "Oral History: Facts and Fiction," *Quadrant* 23 (1979): 4–8. One wonders whether O'Farrell has somehow found written histories that are free from subjectivity and bias, and, if not, whether the safeguards against the ever-present threat of historical distortion that are found in the modern, Western "literate" world of rugged individualism are any more effective than were the safeguards in the ancient world of communally focused oral transmission.

86. See Wright, *New Testament and the People of God*, 82–85. On the historical concern of ancient and/or oral cultures from a variety of disciplinary perspectives, see also S. O. Iyasere, "African Oral Tradition—Criticism as a Performance: A Ritual," in *Myth and History*, ed. E. D. Jones (New York: Africana, 1980), 169–74; Miller, "Listening for the African Past"; idem, "Dynamics of Oral Tradition"; A. W. Mosley, "Historical Reporting in the Ancient World," *NTS* 12 (1965): 10–26; Pender-Cudlip, "Oral Traditions"; J. M. Strijdom, "A Jesus to Think with and Live By: Story and Ideology in Crossan's Jesus Research," *Religion and Theology* 10 (2003): 267–95; E. Tonkin, "Investigating Oral Tradition," *Journal of African History* 27 (1986): 210; J. Vansina, *Oral Tradition as History* (Madison: University of Wisconsin Press, 1985). On the ancients as generally no more or less gullible than moderns, see F. G.

264

On account of this biased perspective, and in concert with the widespread use of functionalist and/or structuralist analyses of oral traditions, many folklorist and anthropological studies have failed to take seriously the possibility that the traditions they study could contain reliable historical information.[87] To the contrary, many have simply equated all oral traditions—including those genres intended to transmit historically rooted remembrances—with the entertainment-oriented, often fictional oral genre typically represented by Western categories of "folklore."[88] Thanks to the data collected in more recent studies, we now know just how myopic and genre-insensitive these previous studies often were. Orally dominant societies tend to be quite capable of distinguishing historically rooted information from entertainment-oriented fiction and generally have access to a variety of culturally shared oral genres designed to signal which is which.

The Importance of "Tradition" and "Teachers" in the Early Church

There is no reason to see the early church's oral traditions about Jesus as an exception to what we have more recently learned about historically oriented oral tradition in general.[89] To the contrary, we have every reason to suppose that early Christians would have been concerned with, and thus would have, generally speaking, accurately passed on, historical remembrances important to their social self-identity.

For example, as we saw in the last chapter, Paul's letters reflect a deep concern with passing on established traditions (e.g., 1 Cor. 11:2, 23; 15:1–3; Gal. 1:9; Phil. 4:9; Col. 2:6–7; 1 Thess. 4:1; 2 Thess. 2:15; 3:6). Indeed, Paul places remarkable weight on these traditions. In the words of Robert Stein,

> Such traditions were to be "held" on to (1 Cor. 15:1–2; 2 Thess. 2:15); life was to be lived "in accord" with the tradition (2 Thess. 3:6; cf. Phil. 4:9), for the result of

Downing, "Magic and Skepticism in and around the First Christian Century," in *Making Sense in (and of) the First Christian Century* (Sheffield: Sheffield Academic Press, 2000), 208–22; P. Merkley, "The Gospels as Historical Testimony," *EQ* 58 (1986): 332. On the perception of orality as inferior to writing, see R. Bauman, "Conceptions of Folklore in the Development of Literary Semiotics," *Semiotica* 39 (1982): 1–20; Finnegan, *Oral Poetry*.

87. For example, Richard Dorson writes: "Folklorists for their part also have been slow to widen their net beyond the conventional oral genres of tale, song, proverb, and riddle to recognize historical traditions as a legitimate and valuable target" ("Oral Literature, Oral History, and the Folklorist," in *Folklore and Fakelore: Essays toward a Discipline of Folk Studies* [Cambridge, MA: Harvard University Press, 1976], 138–39). See also D. Ben-Amos, "The Modern Local Historian in Africa," in *Folklore in the Modern World*, ed. R. Dorson (The Hague: Mouton, 1978), 330.

88. On the tendency among many folklorists to view all oral tradition under the rubric of "folklore," see J. Pentikainen, "Oral Transmission of Knowledge," in *Folklore in the Modern World*, 239–40.

89. Ruth Finnegan observes that while most anthropologists have moved beyond the "crude reductionism" of past structuralist and functionist methodology, it is still "sometimes being echoed by scholars in other disciplines drawing on the earlier anthropological work" ("Introduction; or, Why the Comparativist Should Take Account of the South Pacific," *Oral Tradition* 5 [1990]: 178). In our estimation, this observation definitely hits the mark regarding much New Testament scholarship. Much New Testament research remains significantly entrenched in now-antiquated perspectives on oral tradition.

this would be salvation (1 Cor. 15:1–2), whereas its rejection meant damnation (Gal. 1:9). The reason for this view was that this tradition had God himself as its ultimate source (1 Cor. 11:23).[90]

In accord with this emphasis on divinely governed tradition, early Christians stressed the importance of "teachers" (e.g., Acts 13:1; Rom. 12:7; 1 Cor. 12:28–29; Eph. 4:11; Heb. 5:12; James 3:1; *Didache* 15:1–2). Undoubtedly influenced by the example of Jesus's own teaching ministry, teachers seem to have played a central role within the early church and appear to have been the first paid ministers (Gal. 6:6; *Didache* 13:2). In a predominantly oral community such as the early church, the primary function of these teachers would have been to transmit faithfully the oral traditions, as James Dunn has argued.[91] The leading historian of Africa, Jan Vansina, notes how oral tradents function as a sort of "walking reference library" of oral traditions within orally dominant cultures, and we have every reason to believe that Jesus's immediate disciples would have played a similar role as the primary oral tradents of the earliest Christian community.[92]

The regulative role of teachers vis-à-vis the oral Jesus tradition in the early church has been largely neglected by critical scholarship for some time. One reason for this involves the form-critical assumption—one rooted in a now-obsolete, nineteenth-century Romantic literary theory—that the Jesus tradition, both in terms of its origin and ongoing transmission, was largely indebted to the "community" as a whole, as opposed to certain individual, specialized tradents. More recently, a wide variety of studies of orally dominant cultures have demonstrated that this Romantic notion has virtually no empirical grounding. To the contrary, what John Niles has termed the "strong tradition bearer"—the gifted and communally recognized individual tradent—has emerged as the primary custodian of oral tradition.[93] Niles points out that the older idea of "an ideal folk community—an undifferentiated company of rustics, each of whom contributes equally to the processes of oral tradition," is no longer tenable. Rather,

In any region where oral narratives have been collected systematically, certain performers stand out for their large repertory and authoritative style. . . . Collectors often seek out and record these outstanding tradition-bearers for the same reasons that other people like to listen to them: they perform whole songs and stories, not just fragments, and they perform them with verve and authority. Having a good

90. Stein, *Synoptic Problem*, 191.
91. J. D. G. Dunn, *Christianity in the Making*, vol. 1: *Jesus Remembered* (Grand Rapids: Eerdmans, 2003), 176.
92. Vansina, *Oral Tradition as History*, 37.
93. On "strong tradition bearers" see the excellent study of Niles, *Homo Narrans*, 173–93. This notion of Niles's is confirmed by David Rubin's impressive study of memory and oral tradition, wherein he discusses the important role of "expertise in remembering"; see *Memory in Oral Tradition: The Cognitive Psychology of Epic, Ballads, and Counting-out Rhymes* (New York: Oxford University Press, 1995), 167–70.

voice never hurts, but it is not their voice but their command of a large body of traditional lore that makes them stand out from others.[94]

Niles notes that among the important natural gifts required to be a strong tradition bearer is an unusually retentive memory, one that enables the individual tradent to "absorb whole narratives and internalize them when other people hear them and forget them."[95] And while many folklorists and anthropologists who focus on performance studies today emphasize the creative capacities of oral performers, Niles properly balances this point by noting that strong tradition bearers typically are "confident enough to power a tradition and yet affectionate enough, in regard to their sources, to want to steer the tradition along familiar lines."[96] This quality of faithfulness to the tradition is vastly more important when one is dealing with what the community perceives to be historically rooted narrative, as opposed to entertainment-oriented folktales—a point almost systematically overlooked in many studies of the nature and reliability of oral tradition.

Again, given what we now know about orally dominant cultures, there is no reason to suppose that *only* individual oral tradents—teachers, apostles, and so on—would have been concerned with the fidelity of orally transmitted material. If the early church was typical of predominantly oral cultures—and we have no reason to think it was not—then the community itself had a stake and responsibility in preserving the essential elements of the original oral history.[97] Perhaps something of this truth is manifested in Paul's several injunctions for believers to "test" prophecies and teachings (1 Cor. 14:29; 1 Thess. 5:19–22). In any event, the customary responsibility orally dominant communities generally assume regarding traditional material with historical import can only further buttress our estimation of the reliability of the transmission of the oral Jesus tradition.

Further Evidence of the Early Church's Historical Interest

There are other indications as well that the early church had an abiding concern in preserving the historical memory of Jesus. For example, there are the prevalent

94. Niles, *Homo Narrans*, 174. Niles's observations raise the important distinction between "active" and "passive" bearers of tradition; see p. 177.
95. Ibid., 185.
96. Ibid., 180.
97. We need to remember that, as Egbert Bakker has shown, "activation" of mutually shared ideas would have been a primary purpose of transmitting the oral Jesus tradition, not simply the sharing of new information (Bakker, "Activation and Preservation," 9). This perspective is foreign to contemporary scholars who tend to assume that the primary purpose of communication is to provide new information. This simply is not the case with oral performances in orally dominant cultures. Again, the categories of "active" and "passive" tradition bearers comes into play here. Although even here we must be careful. In the typical performance arena of an orally dominant culture, the supposed "passive" tradition-bearing role of the audience is, in fact, quite "active" by modern, Western standards, i.e., audience members usually show no hesitation in stepping in to comment upon and even correct the details presented by any given performer.

themes of "bearing witness" to Jesus (e.g., John 1:7–8, 15, 19, 32, 34; 3:26, 28; 5:32; Acts 1:8, 22; 2:32; 3:15; 5:32; 10:37–41; 13:31; 22:15, 18; 23:11; 26:16) and of "remembering" the ministry, death, and resurrection of Jesus within the early church (Luke 22:19; 1 Cor. 11:2, 24–25; 2 Thess. 2:5; 2 Tim. 2:8, 14). These reoccurring themes are difficult to reconcile with the classical form-critical assumption that the earliest Christians had no concern for accurate information about the life and teachings of Jesus.[98]

Both Paul and Luke (Luke-Acts) depict the "apostles" as providing links of continuity between the church and Jesus, with special emphasis being given to Peter, John, and James the brother of Jesus (e.g., Acts 1:15, 21–22; 2:14, 42; 3:1–11; 4:13, 19; 5:1–10, 15, 29; 8:14; 12:2; 1 Cor. 15:1–8; Gal. 2:9; Eph. 2:20).[99] Moreover, the very fact that the Gospels were written testifies to the interest of the early church in the life and ministry of Jesus. As we shall argue in chapter 8, these documents are in many respects written along the lines of ancient biographies—with significant Greco-Roman historiographical elements (esp. Luke)—and give us every reason to believe that they intend to pass on reliable historical information (e.g., Luke 1:1–2).

Finally, as Francois Bovon has recently demonstrated, "there was a natural and distinct tendency to memorialize the first Christian generation, the generation of the apostles and witnesses, both men and women."[100] That is to say, the early Christians were interested not only in the life of Jesus, but in the lives of the original apostles/witnesses as well. While the reasons for this interest may not be those that inspire a modern historian, they nonetheless served to motivate the early Christians to seek and retain reliable traditions about the first-generation heroes of the faith. These reasons include (1) the desire for an ethical model (alongside the lives of Old Testament saints and Jesus himself); (2) a concern to keep Jesus's love commandment—"to love is to remember"; (3) the need to preserve faithful doctrine in the face of alternative claims; and (4) the ability to trace church authority to the original apostles.[101] To these "historical reasons" Bovon adds a "theological one":

> As long as the Christians of antiquity tried to preserve the historicity of the revelation and the very real incarnation of their Lord, they could not avoid emphasizing the historical and human face of the communication of the gospel, that is to say, the actual value of the apostles themselves, including both their voices and their role as intermediaries.[102]

98. See Dunn, *Jesus Remembered*, 177–80. A. N. Dahl noted the importance of memory in the early church half a century ago; see "Anamnesis: Memory and Commemoration in Early Christianity," in *Jesus in the Memory of the Early Church* (Minneapolis: Augsburg, 1976). This essay, which Dunn considers sadly "neglected" (*Jesus Remembered*, 179n36), was originally published in 1946.

99. For discussion see Dunn, *Jesus Remembered*, 180–81.

100. F. Bovon, "The Apostolic Memories in Ancient Christianity," in *Studies in Early Christianity* (Grand Rapids: Baker Academic, 2005), 1.

101. Ibid., 1–2.

102. Ibid., 2.

As the first-century and the living apostolic witnesses passed on, later centuries brought a variety of wildly speculative imaginings about the lives of Jesus and the apostles. But, while the *historical reliability* of these later texts often is dubious, they nonetheless continue to give witness to the ongoing *historical interest* of the early Christians.

For all these reasons we conclude that the evidence strongly suggests that, contrary to the third form-critical assumption, the early church from the beginning had a rather significant historical (even "biographical," in the broad sense of the term) interest in the life, death, and resurrection of Jesus. It may be that certain contemporary New Testament scholars are not interested in historical questions,[103] but this same charge cannot seriously be leveled against the early tradents of the Jesus tradition.

Summary

In this chapter we have examined three form-critical assumptions that tend to support a negative estimation of the reliability of the early church's oral tradition and thus support the legendary-Jesus thesis. In the process, we have argued that there is no reason to conclude that Jesus and all his earliest disciples were illiterate and thus no reason to suppose that the Jesus tradition was transmitted exclusively by oral means. We also have argued that, based on recent investigations of orally dominant cultures, we can now conclude that such cultures are, without question, capable of transmitting exceptionally long oral narratives. And we have argued that historically oriented oral traditions tend to reflect a concern for history and are capable of passing on recent historical information in a generally faithful manner. Each of these points ought to increase our estimation of the historical reliability of the early church's Jesus tradition and thus decrease the plausibility of the legendary-Jesus thesis.

Our task in assessing the pre-Gospel oral traditions is not yet complete, however. There are three other assumptions that have tended to pervade form-critical studies and that argue against the reliability of this tradition. To these we now turn.

---

103. For example, Kelber admits that, with regard to his reassessment of form criticism, his interest "is primarily language, not history" (*The Oral and the Written Gospel*, 18).

7

HISTORICAL REMEMBRANCE
OR PROPHETIC IMAGINATION?

MEMORY, HISTORY, AND EYEWITNESS TESTIMONY
IN THE EARLY ORAL JESUS TRADITION

In the last chapter we examined the first three of six form-critical assumptions that have served to foster an undue skepticism regarding the reliability of the pre-Gospel oral Jesus tradition. In this chapter we will review and evaluate the remaining three: the assumption that eyewitnesses played no role in regulating the early oral Jesus tradition; the assumption that we can discern certain "laws" of oral transmission on the basis of literary evidence; and, finally, the assumption that a significant portion of the oral Jesus material may have come from "prophetic inspiration" rather than historical recollection.

Three Final Form-Critical Assumptions

Limited Role of Eyewitnesses

Owing to the influence of Bultmann, it has become a "basic article of belief" with most form critics that "the Gospel tradition owed the form in which it reached our evangelists almost entirely to community use and its demands, and hardly at all to direct intervention or modification on the part of eye-witnesses."[1] Appeals to eyewitnesses found in the Gospels, and especially the epistles, usually have been understood as apologetic fictions.

To be sure, some of the earlier form critics—most notably Vincent Taylor and Martin Dibelius—diverged from the Bultmannian perspective and insisted that the disciples of Jesus must have played some regulating role in the oral transmission of the Jesus tradition.[2] Not surprisingly, they generally came to more optimistic conclusions about the amount of historical material in the Gospels than did the Bultmannians. Unfortunately, Bultmann's influence has tended to far outweigh Taylor's and Dibelius's, and this has obviously been to the advantage of legendary-Jesus theories.

Assumed "Laws" of Oral and Written Traditions

Bultmann and many of the form critics who followed him assumed they could confidently draw conclusions about the original creation and early transmission of Jesus tradition on the basis of discovered "laws" about how folk traditions are created, orally transmitted, and creatively expanded.[3] Bultmann claimed that we have three "tools" by which we can discern these laws.

First, we can study how Matthew and Luke used Mark and Q and extrapolate these findings to the earlier oral tradition. Second, we can identify the pure "form"

---

1. D. E. Nineham, "Eye-Witness Testimony and the Gospel Tradition, I," *JTS* 9 (1958): 13.

2. M. Dibelius, for example, writes: "At the period when eyewitnesses of Jesus were still alive, it was not possible to mar the picture of Jesus in the tradition" (*From Tradition to Gospels*, trans. B. L. Woolf [New York: Scribner's, 1935], 293). See also idem, *Jesus*, trans. C. B. Hendrick and F. C. Grant (Philadelphia: Westminster, 1949), 25. Vincent Taylor even more emphatically states the case in his now-famous words: "It is on this question of eyewitnesses that Form-Criticism [e.g., as approached by Bultmann and company] presents a very vulnerable front. If the Form-Critics are right, the disciples must have been translated to heaven immediately after the Resurrection. As Bultmann sees it, the primitive community exists *in vacuo*, cut off from its founders by the walls of an inexplicable ignorance. Like Robinson Crusoe it must do the best it can. Unable to turn to anyone for information, it must invent situations for the words of Jesus, and put into his lips sayings which personal memory cannot check. . . . However disturbing to the smooth working of theories, the influence of eyewitnesses on the formation of the tradition cannot possibly be ignored. The one hundred and twenty at Pentecost did not go into permanent retreat; for at least a generation they moved among the young Palestinian communities, and through preaching and fellowship their recollections were at the disposal of those who sought information. . . . When all qualifications have been made, the presence of personal testimony is an element in the formative process which it is folly to ignore" (*The Formation of the Gospel Tradition* [London: Macmillan, 1935], 41–43).

3. R. Bultmann, *History of the Synoptic Tradition*, trans. J. Marsh (New York: Harper, 1963), 6–7. Bultmann developed his "laws" primarily by analyzing various stages of rabbinic material, Hellenistic stories, Greco-Roman "proverbs, anecdotes, and folktales," "folksongs," and certain Buddhist texts (ibid., 309). Methodologically, Bultmann was simply following the lead of Old Testament scholars like Hermann Gunkel, who had already applied the findings of folklore studies to various Old Testament materials. The question of Gunkel's inspiration is a complex one. Certainly he was influenced by the comparativist method of the history of religions school of which he was a member. It is in his later work that his dependency upon folklore studies becomes clear. On this matter see D. A. Knight, *Rediscovering the Traditions of Israel* (Missoula, MT: Society of Biblical Literature, 1973), 71–83.

of independent units of the Jesus tradition and thereby determine later, second-ary accretions. And third, we may observe tendencies "found frequently in the history of popular tradition." On this basis Bultmann and others believed they could confidently speculate on how various literary forms were initially created and later developed in the early Christian communities.[4]

Related to this, Bultmann and his followers believed they could discern the original life situation (*Sitz im Leben*) in which an oral and/or literary form was created and used. According to Bultmann, "Every literary category has its 'life situation,' a typical situation or occupation in the life of a community."[5] Indeed, according to Helmut Koester, "Form criticism begins with the presupposition that the beginning and the continuation of the tradition were the early Christian community."[6] This implies that the various independent units that comprise the Gospels, and thus the Gospels as wholes, tell us much more about the life situation of early Christian communities than they do about Jesus.

"Prophetic Inspiration" and Jesus Sayings

Closely related to these two assumptions is the conviction that the early church was very creative in producing Jesus material that would speak to its own needs and concerns. While various scholars emphasize Jewish and even Greco-Roman sources as providing material for the imaginative construction of the early Christian views of Jesus, most form-critical scholars identify prophetic inspiration as a primary source early Christians drew on. Bultmann argued that "the [early] Church drew no distinction between . . . utterances by Christian prophets and the sayings of Jesus in the tradition."[7] Prophets would speak "words from Jesus" and perhaps even tell "inspired" accounts of Jesus that eventually came to be as accepted in the community as tradition rooted in historical remembrance. Hence Bultmann argued that it is "perfectly clear that it was not the historical interest that dominated [in the early church] but the needs of Christian faith and life."[8]

The Jesus Seminar scholars reflect clear Bultmannian tendencies on this point when they write:

> We know that the evangelists not infrequently ascribed Christian words to Jesus—they made him talk like a Christian, when, in fact, he was only the precursor of the movement that was to take him as its cultic hero. . . . In a word, they creatively

4. It is significant that Bultmann believed he could apply these laws to written material as well as oral material (*History*, 6). Hence, concerning his final exposition of the history of the Jesus tradition, Bultmann concludes that "there is no definable boundary between the oral and written tradition" (ibid., 321). We shall conclude otherwise below.

5. Ibid., 4.

6. H. Koester, "Written Gospels or Oral Tradition?" *JBL* 113 (1994): 297.

7. Bultmann, *History*, 127; see also idem, "The New Approach to the Synoptic Problem" (originally published in 1926), in *Existence and Faith* (London: Collins-Fontana, 1964), 42.

8. R. Bultmann, "The Study of the Synoptic Gospels," in Bultmann and Karl Kundsin, *Form Criticism: Two Essays on New Testament Research*, ed. F. C. Grant (New York: Harper & Row, 1962), 64.

invented speech for Jesus. Storytellers in every age freely invent words for characters in their stories. This is the storyteller's license.[9]

In the light of this, many form critics conclude that the Gospels tell us much more about the communities that developed the material they contain than they do about Jesus. Bultmann even went so far as to conclude that "we can know almost nothing concerning the life and personality of Jesus."[10] Many legendary-Jesus theorists, of course, agree.

As in the previous chapter, we must now ask: How plausible are these three assumptions? And, once again, we will argue that, among other things, in light of more recent, field-based studies of oral traditions and orally oriented cultures, each of these assumptions is without warrant.

Eyewitnesses and the Transmission and Regulation of the Early Oral Jesus Tradition

Individuals, Communities, and Oral Transmission

The form-critical assumption that eyewitnesses played no real role in the transmission and regulation of the pre-Gospel oral Jesus tradition mirrors similar Romanticist views found in nineteenth- and early twentieth-century folkloristics and anthropology. These disciplines concluded that communities play a far more important role than individuals in the transmission of oral material. The needs of the community tended to determine the content of oral traditions rather than the claims of any individual. Hence, even if individual eyewitnesses had a role in *originating* an oral tradition, including the early church's, this model stipulated that they played little role in *how and why it was later transmitted.*

---

9. R. W. Funk, R. Hoover, and the Jesus Seminar, *The Five Gospels: The Search for the Authentic Words of Jesus* (New York: Macmillan, 1993), 29. So too Howard Teeple writes, "According to the theory of an authentic oral tradition, the flow of tradition was from the earthly Jesus to his disciples to the apostles in the church. Actually, the flow was in the opposite direction: from the apostles in the church to the earthly Jesus" ("The Oral Tradition That Never Was," *JBL* 89 [1970], 67). He argues that the theory of an authentic oral tradition that moved from Jesus's teaching to the disciples to the church and the New Testament is one of the most serious errors in biblical scholarship (p. 68).

10. R. Bultmann, *Jesus and the Word*, trans. L. P. Smith and E. H. Lantero (New York: Scribner's, 1958), 8. For the Jesus Seminar's view of oral tradition, see "From the Gospels to Jesus: The Rules of Oral Evidence," in *Five Gospels*, 25–34. Along similar skeptical lines, Barry Henaut concludes that "the oral phase of the Jesus tradition is now lost forever. . . . It is perhaps time to rewrite Bultmann's permissive into an imperative" (*Oral Tradition and the Gospels: The Problem of Mark 4*, JSNTSup 82 [Sheffield: Sheffield Academic Press, 1993], 295, 305). Similarly, Harm Hollander writes, "The oral phase behind our gospel texts and pre-gospel sources makes it, historically speaking, impossible for us to ascribe any saying to the historical Jesus" ("The Words of Jesus: From Oral Traditions to Written Record in Paul and Q," *Novum Testamentum* 42 [2000]: 354).

As we noted in the previous chapter, while this community-focused understanding of oral traditions is yet found in some quarters, folklore and anthropological studies carried out since the 1930s increasingly have shown it to be misguided.[11] Beginning with the fieldwork of Milman Parry and his student Albert Lord, and continuing on through the "turn to performance" of the last several decades, there has been a growing awareness of, and appreciation for, the role of the individual tradent in the oral traditioning process.[12] Indeed, the new paradigm generated by these more recent studies has transferred the primacy previously granted to the communities in the classic model to the individual performer. True, the community as ongoing audience of oral performances can itself perform an active custodial role when individual tradents veer significantly from the tradition, as we noted in the last chapter. But most folklorists now agree that the primary one entrusted to carry on and shape the tradition *is the individual oral tradent*.

This new research sheds important light on our understanding of the oral Jesus tradition. If the oral period of the early church functioned similar to the way we now know oral communities tend to operate, we should expect that those individuals who were closest to Jesus during his ministry would have played a significant role in the transmission of oral material about Jesus. This does not in any way deny that the material was, to some extent, shaped by the needs of the early faith

11. Many now realize that Western scholars tended to operate with a "devolutionary" paradigm that devalued the role of individuals in oral (or "folk") communities while romanticizing the creativity and authority of these communities as a whole. See A. Dundes, "The Devolutionary Premise in Folklore Theory," *Journal of the Folklore Institute* 6 (1969): 13–14. On the paradoxical devaluing of the individual and romanticization of the community in classic folklore studies, see R. Kellogg, "Oral Literature," *New Literary History* 5 (1973): 63. On this problem see also L. Honko, "The Kalevala and the World's Epics: An Introduction," in *Religion, Myth and Folklore in the World's Epics: The Kalevala and Its Predecessors*, ed. L. Honko (New York: Mouton de Gruyter, 1990), 2–3. The result of all this was that in the classical perspective, folklore was *by definition* considered to be the product of a community, not an individual. As Honko notes, "The moment a single author could be pointed out, the product would have ceased to be folklore, because collectivity was the dividing line between folk poetry and art poetry" (ibid., 3). As Leroy Vail and Landeg White have demonstrated, the diminishing of the role of the individual oral performer within Western academia continued on, ironically, even among some of the contemporary leading authorities on orality. See "The Invention of 'Oral Man,'" in *Power and the Praise Poem: Southern African Voices in History* (Charlottesville: University Press of Virginia, 1991), 1–39.
12. This recognition of the centrality of the individual performer came from several interdisciplinary quarters, including Homeric studies (i.e., the oral-formulaic theory), anthropology, folkloristics, orality studies, etc. For the pillar works of the oral-formulaic (Parry-Lord) theory, see M. Parry, *The Making of Homeric Verse: The Collected Papers of Milman Parry*, ed. A. Parry (Oxford: Clarendon, 1971); A. B. Lord, *The Singer of Tales* (Cambridge, MA: Harvard University Press, 1960). J. M. Foley, a former student of Lord's and one of the most influential thinkers in the oral-formulaic school, has significantly developed the Parry-Lord synthesis by merging oral-formulaic theory with insights drawn from folklorics and the anthropological "performative turn." See Foley, "Word-power, Performance, and Tradition," *Journal of American Folklore* 105 (1992): 275–301; idem, *Immanent Art: From Structure to Meaning in Traditional Oral Epic* (Bloomington: Indiana University Press, 1991). On this interdisciplinary merger, see also D. Hymes, "Ethnopoetics, Oral-Formulaic Theory, and Editing Texts," *Oral Tradition* 9 (1994): 330–70.

communities, for as we have seen oral tradents always shape their performances according to the particular situation of their audience. But it does at the very least mean that we would expect to see this material being transmitted by, among other "strong tradition bearers," eyewitnesses from among the original followers of Jesus.[13] And this makes it much more difficult to suppose that the oral Jesus tradition acquired a significant amount of fictionalized material in the process of transmission during the several decades prior to the writing of the Gospels.

This new research on the role of gifted individuals within the oral traditioning process not only renders it plausible that the Jesus material of the early church was preserved in a generally faithful manner by those who were eyewitnesses; it also answers several classical objections to the view that eyewitnesses played a regulative role in the early church. We shall consider two of these.

Eyewitnesses and Stylized Forms

One of the valid insights given to us by form criticism is that the Gospels are comprised of a number of distinct, identifiable "forms." Unfortunately, most form critics have assumed that these stylized forms could be the product only of a community creation process. In other words, it was assumed that eyewitnesses would not pass on personal material *in the more formal style* we find in the Gospels. Thus, the stylized forms in which we find the Gospel material has frequently been used as an argument against the notion that eyewitnesses lay behind this material.[14]

Recent fieldwork studies on oral tradition, however, have demonstrated that this assumption often does not hold. For example, in working with the Jlao Kru people of southeast Liberia, Elizabeth Tonkin has found that oral performers often recount personal experiences in the same formally stylized fashion as they do traditional material.[15] In this light, the formalized nature of the Gospel ma-

---

13. Again, on "strong tradition bearers"—a concept entirely neglected by the classic form-critical approach—see J. D. Niles, *Homo Narrans: The Poetics and Anthropology of Oral Literature* (Philadelphia: University of Pennsylvania Press, 1999), 173–93.

14. Nineham is representative of many critical scholars who assume that because the Jesus tradition is characterized by stylized "forms" we are dealing with "impersonal tradition of the community," as opposed to individual eyewitness testimony; see "Eye-Witness Testimony, I," 22.

15. E. Tonkin, "The Boundaries of History in Oral Performance," *History in Africa* 9 (1982): 280. Among others who have touched on the same phenomenon, see B. A. Stolz, "Historicity in the Serbo-Croatian Heroic Epic: Salih Ugljanin's 'Grcki rat,'" *Slavic and East European Journal* 11 (1967): 430; J. Vansina, "Memory and Oral Tradition," in *The African Past Speaks: Essays on Oral Tradition and History* (Hamden, CT: Archon, 1980). As A. B. Lord notes: "The story of a recent personage can also be regarded as traditional if the essential story pattern is one that has been used by storytellers in the given culture for a long time" ("The Gospels as Oral Traditional Literature," in *The Relationships among the Gospels: An Interdisciplinary Dialogue*, ed. W. O. Walker [San Antonio: Trinity University Press, 1978], 38). That is to say, one can faithfully transmit historical information in a manner that uses the stylized, formal structures associated with the "tradition" of that culture. Of course, the standards of descriptive accuracy and precision that constitute a "faithful" report may not be those of the modern Western academy, as we shall discuss at greater length later.

terial is not necessarily evidence that individual eyewitnesses were not involved in the transmission of this material.[16] This phenomenon is explained by the fact that stylized oral tellings is a natural result of multiple repetitive performances designed to make the material easily memorable for the audience. Robert Stein illustrates this point effectively when he notes that if Peter had publicly repeated a certain episode from Jesus's life—one he had personally witnessed—once a month between the time of Pentecost and the writing of Mark's Gospel (approximately thirty-five years on most reckonings), he would have told the same account roughly 420 times. Certainly Peter's personal remembrances would have become quite "stereotyped and generalized" in this process.[17] On top of this, there are good grounds for concluding that the disciples were interested in presenting material in ways their audiences could readily remember. This also would have contributed to the stylization of their material, since orally/aurally memorable forms and mnemonic devices would have been naturally employed in the performance arena. Hence, it seems Nineham and others have jumped to unwarranted conclusions in assuming that the stylized nature of the Gospel material counts against its being rooted in eyewitness testimony.

Eyewitness Testimony and the Question of Memory

Another criticism of the claim of eyewitness data within the Gospels attaches not to the Gospels themselves but rather to the nature of eyewitness testimony

16. Some form-critical scholars may respond to these recent folkloristic findings by insisting that they have little significance for our understanding of the Jesus tradition, since the assumptions of form criticism have been independently verified by the empirical study of the Jesus tradition itself. But, as a number of scholars have argued, the claim that form criticism has independently verified its assumptions is simply false. Rather, their assumptions have driven their conclusions. They assume that the stylized forms of the Gospels preclude eyewitnesses playing a regulatory role in the transmission of the Gospel material, and *on this basis* conclude that eyewitnesses played no such role. The recent findings that stylized forms do not rule out eyewitness material exposes the arbitrariness of the classic form-critical assumption and circularity of their methodology. Erhardt Güttgemanns's warning, given at the advent of the "revolution" in folkloristic studies decades ago, continues to apply: "New Testament studies should not take too lightly the scientific revolution taking place in folkloristics; it should not minimalize it by asserting—in contrast to the period when form criticism was being established—that the self-understandability of the general reference to the phenomenon of analogy in German folkloristics is irrelevant because the hypothetical assessment in the circular method in form criticism has become so certain by its verification in the entire synoptic material that it no longer needs renewed reflection about methodological foundations and their justification" (*Candid Questions concerning Gospel Form Criticism: A Methodological Sketch of the Fundamental Problematics of Form and Redaction Criticism*, trans. W. G. Doty [Pittsburgh: Pickwick, 1979], 56–57). This general point was emphasized by Thorleif Boman (*Die Jesus-Ueberlieferung im Lichte der neueren Volkskunde* [Goettingen: Vandenhoeck & Ruprecht, 1967], 10, 112) and more recently by H.-J. Schulz (*Die apostolische Herkunft der Evangelien* [Freiburg: Herder, 1993], chap. 4).

17. R. H. Stein, *The Synoptic Problem: An Introduction* (Grand Rapids: Baker Academic, 1987), 196. As T. F. Glasson has pointed out, both ancient and contemporary use of eyewitness anecdotes should have alerted form critics to their questionable assumptions on this matter; see "The Place of the Anecdote: A Note on Form Criticism," *JTS* 32 (1981): 142–50.

per se. The question of memory is crucial to that of oral tradition, for "oral traditions depend upon human memory for their preservation. If a tradition is to survive, it must be stored in one person's memory and be passed to another person who is also capable of storing and retelling it."[18]

Within the last several decades, a number of psychologists have argued that, due to the malleable nature of all human memory, eyewitness testimony itself is always suspect.[19] This perspective generally derives from a common view of human memory—one stemming from the memory experiments of Sir Francis Bartlett in the early 1900s—in which memory itself is understood as "(re)constructive" in nature; that is, a memory is never simply encoded, stored, and retrieved as a discrete whole, but rather is (re)created from various components in the recall process.[20] As psychologist Elizabeth Loftus describes it, the reconstructive theory of memory states that "retrieval of memory involves a process in which the initial memory content is modified as a result of interactions with other information already stored in memory."[21] Naturally, it is this presumed "modification" that leads to skepticism about the reliability of the memory functions of individual human beings. Drawing from this type of memory theory, John Dominic Crossan proclaims that "fact and fiction, memory and fantasy, recollection and fabrication are intertwined in remembering. . . . [N]obody, including ourselves, can be absolutely certain which is which, apart from independent and documented verification."[22] With this, Crossan seemingly can call into question the very possibility of a reliable early oral Jesus tradition.

18. D. C. Rubin, *Memory in Oral Tradition: The Cognitive Psychology of Epic, Ballads, and Counting-out Rhymes* (New York: Oxford University Press, 1995), 9–10.

19. See, e.g., C. R. Barclay, "Schematization of Autobiographical Memory," in *Autobiographical Memory*, ed. D. C. Rubin (New York: Cambridge University Press, 1986), 82–99; R. F. Belli and E. F. Loftus, "The Pliability of Autobiographical Memory: Misinformation and the False Memory Problem," in *Remembering Our Past: Studies in Autobiographical Memory*, ed. D. C. Rubin (New York: Cambridge University Press, 1996), 157–79; R. Buckhout, "Eyewitness Testimony," *Scientific American* 231/6 (1974): 23–31; E. F. Loftus, *Eyewitness Testimony* (Cambridge, MA: Harvard University Press, 1979); E. F. Loftus and K. Ketcham, "The Malleability of Eyewitness Accounts," in *Evaluating Witness Evidence: Recent Psychological Research and New Perspectives*, ed. S. M. A. Lloyd-Bostock and B. R. Clifford (New York: Wiley and Sons, 1983), 159–72; H. L. Roediger, "Memory Illusions," *Journal of Memory and Language* 35 (1996): 76–100 (this entire issue of *Journal of Memory and Language* is devoted to the subject of "Illusions of Memory").

20. F. C. Bartlett, *Remembering: A Study in Experimental and Social Psychology* (New York: Cambridge University Press, 1932); idem, "Some Experiments on the Reproduction of Folk Stories," in *The Study of Folklore*, ed. A. Dundes (Englewood Cliffs, NJ: Prentice-Hall, 1965), 243–58. For a more recent expression and application of this view, see C. R. Barclay and P. A. DeCooke, "Ordinary Everyday Memories: Some of the Things of Which Selves are Made," in *Remembering Reconsidered: Ecological and Traditional Approaches to the Study of Memory*, ed. U. Neisser and E. Winograd (New York: Cambridge University Press, 1988), 91–125.

21. E. F. Loftus, "Tricked by Memory," in *Memory and History: Essays on Recalling and Interpreting Experience*, ed. J. Jeffrey and G. Edwall (New York: University Press of America, 1994), 19.

22. J. D. Crossan, "Does Memory Remember?" in *The Birth of Christianity* (San Francisco: HarperSanFrancisco, 1998), 60.

This psychology-based skepticism about individual human memory has been complemented and intensified in recent years by sociological studies of "collective" or "social" memory.[23] Sociologist Barry Schwartz, a leading thinker on social memory, describes it as "a second-cousin of public opinion," or in simple terms, "the distribution throughout society of beliefs about the past."[24] In an important sense, social memory plays a similar role for society as that played by personal memory for the individual: "Social memory defines a group, giving it a sense of its past and defining its aspirations for the future."[25] Many who work with this cultural phenomenon have come to emphasize the ways in which social memory *distorts the past* in order to render it ideologically serviceable for the political *purposes of the present*. In the words of Maria Cattell and Jacob Climo: "Social, collective, historical memory is provisional, malleable, contingent. It can be negotiated and contested; forgotten, suppressed, or recovered; revised, invented, or reinvented."[26] Thus, once the early Jesus tradition is defined in terms of social memory, it comes under a new sort of skeptical scrutiny. Werner Kelber nicely captures this conviction:

> The deepest impulse driving the memorial composition of the gospels is the retrieval of the past for the benefit of the present. . . . This is why gospel narratives as cultural memories always reflect the condition of their production. Selection, organization, and composition of materials are informed not predominantly by responsibility vis-à-vis the past, but more by ethical, communicative, and rhetorical accountability toward the present.[27]

Space considerations prevent anything like a sustained response to what we shall call the "memoric skepticism" paradigm. However, we can summarize several considerations that serve to call into question this radically skeptical assessment of human memory—especially as it has been used to undermine the very possibility of a reliable early oral Jesus tradition.

23. The pioneer here was M. Halbwachs, *On Collective Memory*, ed. and trans. L. A. Coser (Chicago: University of Chicago Press, 1992). Helpful introductions to the issues involved with social/collective memory include: J. Assmann, "Collective Memory and Cultural Identity," *New German Critique* 65 (1995): 125–33; J. J. Climo and M. G. Cattell, eds., *Social Memory and History: Anthropological Perspectives* (New York: Altamira, 2002); J. Fentress and C. Wickham, *Social Memory* (Cambridge, MA: Blackwell, 1992); A. Funkenstein, "Collective Memory and Historical Consciousness," *History and Memory* 1 (1989): 5–26; A. Kirk, "Social and Cultural Memory," in *Memory, Tradition and Text: Uses of the Past in Early Christianity*, ed. A. Kirk and T. Thatcher (Atlanta: Society of Biblical Literature, 2005); P. Nora, "Between Memory and History: *Les Lieux de Memoire*," *Representations* 26 (1989): 7–24.
24. B. Schwartz, "The Cynical Science," unpublished manuscript, 1. We are grateful to Professor Schwartz for making available to us several of his recent essays on social memory, including this unpublished piece.
25. Fentress and Wickham, *Social Memory*, 25.
26. M. G. Cattell and J. J. Climo, "Introduction: Meaning in Social Memory and History: Anthropological Perspectives," in *Social Memory and History*, 4–5.
27. W. Kelber, "The Case of the Gospels: Memory's Desire and the Limits of Historical Criticism," *Oral Tradition* 17 (2002): 80.

In order to understand and assess accurately the new forms of memoric skepticism operative today, one must understand the intellectual influences and contexts that have given birth to them.[28] The "crisis of memory" that began to be widely announced in the 1980s and 1990s can trace its seeds to the general collapse of confidence in human knowledge that followed the debacle of World War I. It is no coincidence that the same time period that gave rise to memoric skepticism in its individual (F. C. Bartlett) and collective/social (Maurice Halbwachs) forms also fostered the rise of similar skepticism in historiography (Carl Becker), sociology of knowledge (Karl Mannheim), and New Testament studies (Rudolf Bultmann). As Schwartz notes: "These men appealed so greatly to the West because their views resonated so closely with the cynicism of the post World War I worldview and ethos: 'the world is not what it seems.'"[29]

This interdisciplinary spirit of skepticism included a strong suspicion—and commitment to the unmasking—of the always-already-present ideological/political motives behind claims of historical "truth." Over the decades, this trend has been fueled by such intellectual forces as Marxist historical analysis, poststructuralist deconstruction, Foucault's "genealogical" historiography, and a variety of other postmodern intellectual impulses and intuitions.[30] With each of these forces comes a bias *for* the new, the contingent, the aporia, and a bias *against* the traditional, the connected, and the stable. In such an intellectual context—one whose ethical-aesthetic sensibilities are naturally drawn to the promise of freedom, creativity, and the liberation from oppressive "historical" traditions offered by the memoric skepticism paradigm—

memory's notorious vagaries become its strengths, and the acknowledgment of what some historians have taken as evidence of memory's inferiority to "real" history emerges as therapeutic if not revolutionary potential. As Marita Sturken puts it: "It is precisely the instability of memory that allows for renewal and redemption." Memory is partial, allusive, fragmentary, transient, and for precisely these reasons it is better suited to our chaotic times.[31]

In such an intellectual context (and here the forces of postmodernism are fed by certain forces within the earlier currents of modernism and Romanticism),

28. Helpful sources for this exercise include D. Berliner, "The Abuses of Memory: Reflections on the Memory Boom in Anthropology," *Anthropological Quarterly* 78 (2005): 197–211; P. H. Hutton, "Placing Memory in Contemporary Historiography," in *History as an Art of Memory* (Hanover, NH: University Press of New England, 1993), 1–16; W. Kansteiner, "Finding Meaning in Memory: A Methodological Critique of Collective Memory Studies," *History and Theory* 41 (2002): 179–97; K. L. Klein, "On the Emergence of *Memory* in Historical Discourse," *Representations* 69 (2000): 127–50; J. Winter, "The Generation of Memory: Reflections on the 'Memory Boom' in Contemporary Historical Studies," *German Historical Institute Bulletin* 27 (2000): 1–15.
29. Schwartz, "Cynical Science," 3. See also B. Schwartz, "Christian Origins: Historical Truth and Social Memory," in *Memory, Tradition and Text*, 45–46.
30. See esp. Hutton, "Placing Memory," 1–10.
31. Klein, "Emergence of *Memory*," 138.

the ideas of reliable human memory and stable oral repetition are not merely concepts to be questioned—they are political/cultural threats to be resisted, rejected, and debunked.[32] On one hand, powerful ruling elites throughout history have used their own versions of "remembered tradition/history" to protect their ideological/political interests. On the other hand, even in less power-hungry contexts, the ideas of reliable memory and stable, "memorized" tradition can seem restrictive, passé, boring. One can easily catch these current cultural sentiments in a statement by John Dominic Crossan: "Jesus left behind him thinkers not memorizers, disciples not reciters, people not parrots."[33] This statement, which begins by contrasting "thinking" with "memorizing," and ends by identifying "disciples" and "people" with the former—and "reciters" and "parrots" with the latter—beautifully expresses a common and largely unquestioned bias against memory and memorization in our culture today.

The contemporary penchant for that which the memoric skepticism paradigm can deliver is, ironically, an example of ideologically driven theorizing about memory that owes as much (and perhaps more) to its own natural predilections as it does to objective, empirically derived evidence.[34] This is not to say that we have not learned important lessons on the complexities and weaknesses (and strengths!) of human memory or the socially influenced dynamics of communal remembering, for we clearly have. It is to say, however, that in emphasizing its more malleable and unreliable dimensions, such studies often have tended to downplay aspects that point to the stability and accuracy of human memory—particularly as memory would have been operating in the context of an ancient, orally dominant culture. All of this is to say that the memoric skepticism paradigm is an unsurprising child of its ideological time. This, alone, does not undercut its skeptical claims. But it does serve to raise suspicions as to its own extra-theoretical function in our contemporary cultural milieu. It also raises the question of whether its purported empirical base is as solid as the psychological experiments and sociological data cited by its proponents suggests. The considerations that follow, in fact, suggest otherwise.

First, ironically, though not surprisingly, the hyperskepticism that characterizes the memoric skepticism paradigm turns back on itself in an ultimately self-destructive fashion. The skeptical arguments upon which it depends are based upon "scientific" studies—psychological studies of individual memory, sociocultural studies of collective memory, and so on. The problem, of course,

32. For a clear example of resistance to the ideas of "remembering" and "repetition" (i.e., mimesis), see G. Stein, "Portraits and Repetition," in *Lectures in America* (Boston: Beacon Hill, 1935), 168–83. On the depreciation of memory in the modern world, see C. C. Park, "The Mother of the Muses: In Praise of Memory," *American Scholar* 50 (1980–1981): 56–58.

33. J. D. Crossan, *The Historical Jesus: The Life of a Mediterranean Jewish Peasant* (San Francisco: HarperSanFrancisco, 1991), xxxi.

34. This point is nicely articulated by S. Campbell throughout her *Relational Remembering: Rethinking the Memory Wars* (Lanham, MD: Rowman & Littlefield, 2003).

is that the scientific enterprise is always-already itself radically dependent upon human memory—both in its individual and social forms. From scientists "remembering" the details and results of their studies as they type them up, to the ever-present reality of "social memory" within the intellectual community of any given scientific subdiscipline, human memory is always at the heart of the scientific endeavor. As Sue Campbell writes, "We cannot, however, in our pursuit of the sciences of memory avoid reliance on memory. Researchers who study memory are tremendously reliant on their own memories and on the memories of their experimental subjects. . . . When memory is the faculty devalued . . . faith in science and scientists is, quite obviously, no remedy."[35] If we must inevitably be skeptical of human memory and its products, then we must equally be skeptical of all scientific findings—*including the findings that suggest human memory is malleable and unreliable.*

Second, despite the contemporary inclination toward images of episodic memory as (re)constructive, malleable, unstable, and unreliable, there are multiple lines of evidence that suggest human memory is—as a rule—dependable, stable, reliable, and quite adequately reflective of the past that it represents. We note here a few of these.

1. While the tradition of Bartlett and his reconstructive theory of memory has assumed highest profile in our current climate, the data from a competing tradition remains to be reckoned with. The memory experiments of Hermann Ebbinghaus at the end of the nineteenth century pointed toward the general reliability of human memory.[36] While the Bartlett tradition (i.e., an emphasis on the unreliability of memory) has, in general, been adopted within psychological and sociological circles as of late, other disciplines can be found moving in the wake of what we can call the Ebbinghaus tradition (i.e., an emphasis on the reliability of memory). One such discipline is that of oral history studies. In its early years, the oral history movement simply assumed the general reliability of memory and troubled itself little over methodological questions about the nature of human memory.[37] In recent decades, however, the question of the reliability of memory has been explored within the field. In this context, a number of studies have demonstrated the remarkable resilience and accuracy of the human memory.[38] Even more surprising is that some convinced memoric skeptics have announced a change

35. Ibid., 140. The self-defeating nature of the memoric skepticism paradigm is the primary topic of chap. 6 of Campbell's book.

36. H. Ebbinghaus, *Memory: A Contribution to Experimental Psychology* (New York: Dover, 1964).

37. An observation made by J. Neuenschwander, "Oral Historians and Long-Term Memory," in *Oral History: An Interdisciplinary Anthology*, ed. D. K. Dunaway and W. K. Baum (Nashville: American Association for State and Local History/Oral History Association, 1984), 324–32.

38. See, e.g., A. M. Hoffman and H. S. Hoffman, "Reliability and Validity in Oral History: The Case for Memory," in *Memory and History: Essays on Recalling and Interpreting Experience*, ed. J. Jeffrey and G. Edwall (New York: University Press of America, 1994), 107–30; P. Friedlander, "Theory, Method and Oral History," in *Oral History: An Interdisciplinary Anthology*, 135–36; T. Lummis, *Listening to History: The Authenticity of Oral Evidence* (Totowa, NJ: Barnes & Noble, 1987), 120–21.

of view based upon their own research. One notable example involves psychologist and autobiographical memory researcher William Brewer. For years, Brewer was a staunch advocate of a strong reconstructive view of memory in the Bartlett tradition. More recently, he has moved to what he terms "a partly reconstructive view of autobiographical memory"—one that "suggests that recent personal memories are *reasonably accurate copies of the individual's original phenomenal experiences.*"[39]

2. As a number of scholars have observed, experiments whose results support a skeptical view often can be seen as prejudiced toward the "discovery" of data supporting the paradigm. For example, Brewer and others have pointed out that "too much of the evidence for the reconstructionist position is either anecdotal or concerned with matters (e.g., memory for conversations) that . . . are not central to the study of autobiographical memory."[40] Moreover, the manner in which autobiographical memory experiments employ "foils" (i.e., misinformation units designed to test the subjects' recall ability) is all-important. In many cases the foils "involve only minor differences from original records, so that subjects incorrectly recognize large numbers of such foils." This data is then used to confirm the memoric skepticism paradigm. This questionable use of data "would surreptitiously enhance the appearance that autobiographical memories are frequently inaccurate and that they are therefore also frequently reconstructed."[41]

More relevant to our concerns is the observation that memory experiments in the Bartlett tradition generally are ill suited to gauge the reliability of human memory as it would operate within an ancient, orally dominant, community-centered context. Consider Bartlett's own memory experiments with Cambridge University undergraduate students in the 1920s and 1930s. First, this set of subjects reflects a loose collection of isolated, highly literate young people within a largely individualist social context—quite unlike the subjects one would find in an orally dominant context. A second concern is raised as one considers the nature of Bartlett's actual experiments. For example, one experiment involved having the students read a previously unknown story two times and then testing their recall. The vast differences between *silently reading an unfamiliar tale twice as an isolated individual*, on one hand, and *hearing commonly known, identity-shaping material spoken countless times by an array of tradents within a communal performance arena*, on the other, hardly need to be pointed out.[42] Third, experiments in the Bartlett tradition typically miss one of the central features that provide stability to the remembered tradition within an orally dominant environment—*the*

39. W. F. Brewer, "Memory for Randomly Sampled Autobiographical Events," in *Remembering Reconsidered*, 87 (emphasis added).

40. R. N. McCauley, "Walking in Our Own Footsteps: Autobiographical Memory and Reconstruction," in *Remembering Reconsidered*, 126.

41. Ibid., 127; here McCauley is reporting on Brewer's observations. See McCauley's own comments on this matter (pp. 134–35).

42. On these factors see the editor's introductory comments to Bartlett's "Some Experiments on the Reproduction of Folk Stories," 244–45. See also Rubin, *Memory in Oral Tradition*, 130–36.

active, custodial role of the always-present audience. As David Rubin—the premier contemporary researcher of the role of memory in oral tradition—has noted: "An audience knowledgeable in a tradition is a strong conservative force that keeps the [tradent] within traditional bounds by voicing its approval, by offering alternative versions it thinks are preferred, or even by providing corrections."[43] This custodial, "memory-regulating" phenomenon that is an intrinsic aspect of the oral performance context *is entirely missing from the radically individualistic context of contemporary memory experiments.*[44]

Bruce Rosenberg notes, "The Cambridge students made many more altera-tions in transmitting these tales than would be true of the native transmission of familiar material."[45] David Rubin broadens this observation beyond Bartlett's experiments: "The changes that occur when a passage is transmitted from person to person are much greater in psychology experiments than they are in oral tradi-tion."[46] Given these crucial differences, we must seriously question, for example, Crossan's use of Bartlett to support his generally skeptical view of the oral Jesus tradition.[47] This brings us to a related point.

3. In order to correctly assess the probable accuracy or inaccuracy of the memo-ries of the tradents of the early oral Jesus tradition, we must consider the *value and practical importance* placed upon memory and memorization in the ancient Medi-terranean world. While memorization generally is *devalued* in our postmodern culture today, it was, to the contrary, *highly valued* in the pre-Gutenberg world.[48] In the largely illiterate, pre-Gutenberg universe, people primarily depended upon memory for the preservation of their past. It is not surprising therefore that, within

---

43. Rubin, *Memory in Oral Tradition*, 135. On this point see also B. A. Rosenberg, "The Complexity of Oral Tradition," *Oral Tradition* 2 (1987): 86. Rubin's book represents the most thorough study to date of memory phenomena in relation to oral tradition. While many of Rubin's conclusions can be extrapo-lated to other oral genre, his book does focus on three primary types of oral tradition: epic, ballads, and counting-out rhymes. One of his most insightful observations throughout the book is the genre-specific nature of so many questions related to oral tradition.

44. Throughout his important study, *Memory in Oral Tradition*, Rubin explores a variety of other factors that serve to constrain and conserve oral tradition by its very nature (see esp. chaps. 2–8). The reader is strongly encouraged to refer to Rubin's work for further discussion of the multiple memory constraints and cues that are intrinsic to various oral genres.

45. Rosenberg, "Complexity of Oral Tradition," 85.

46. Rubin, *Memory in Oral Tradition*, 122.

47. Crossan, *Birth of Christianity*, 78–84.

48. On the importance of memory/memorization in the ancient and/or medieval world, see D. M. Carr, *Writing on the Tablet of the Heart: Origins of Scripture and Literature* (New York: Oxford Univer-sity Press, 2005); M. Carruthers, *The Book of Memory: A Study of Memory in Medieval Culture* (New York: Cambridge University Press, 1990); S. Crowley, "Modern Rhetoric and Memory," in *Rhetorical Memory and Delivery: Classical Concepts for Contemporary Composition and Communication*, ed. J. F. Reynolds (Hillsdale, NJ: Erlbaum, 1993), 31–44; Park, "Mother of the Muses"; J. P. Small, *Wax Tablets of the Mind: Cognitive Studies of Memories and Literacy in Classical Antiquity* (New York: Routledge, 1997); F. A. Yates, *The Art of Memory* (Chicago: University of Chicago Press, 1966); D. Zlotnick, "Memory and the Integrity of the Oral Tradition," *Journal of the Near Eastern Society* 16–17 (1984–1985): 229–41.

such cultures, mnemonic-based memory-aid systems were developed and taught. For example, among the Greeks,

> Plato's Hippias taught an elaborate system of mnemonics. The Roman historian Pliny tells us of [a] certain Greek named Charmades, who was able to recite "the contents of any libraries that anyone asked him to quote as if he were reading them." He then writes of the construction of *memoria technica*, a method invented by the lyric poet Simonides and perfected by Metrodorus of Scepsis, enabling anything heard to be repeated in the identical words.[49]

Similar feats of memory are commonly reported in both the ancient and medieval worlds. From Josephus to Thomas Aquinas—both of whom are said to have possessed remarkable memorization capabilities—the quality of a retentive memory was widely recognized and praised.[50] Memorization as an educational technique was ubiquitous in the ancient world. As any good oral teacher would do, Jesus himself clearly taught in ways that facilitated remembrance of his words. Consider the contrast offered by our contemporary culture's general inattentiveness to such matters of memory. As Thomas Butler observes:

> We have learned to process experience so quickly, that we are usually not even conscious of what we are doing. And we encode information according to some schema of which we are often unaware. . . . As for everyday life experiences, we most often have no filing system at all, leaving their later recollection to chance.[51]

In sum, the ancient, orally oriented world—unlike the Western, post-Gutenberg, (post)modern world within which contemporary memory experiments are conducted—offered a context within which memory was valued and memorization and its techniques were intentionally studied and practiced. We should not be surprised to find that such an environment provided a more conducive context for the possibility of accurate memory encoding, retention, and retrieval.

4. Finally, the use of contemporary social memory studies—at least those born from the a priori hyperskepticism characteristic of the postmodern social-scientific enterprise—to undercut the reliability of reports of recent events within an orally dominant, communally oriented context is faulty methodology. The circularity of this hyperskeptical enterprise, as well as its similarities to the post-Bultmannian trajectory of New Testament criticism, has been noted by Barry Schwartz:

> We need to recognize [social memory scholarship's] merits and avoid its pathologies, especially those it shares with biblical studies, lest it certify the very distortions we want to correct. These distortions result from a cynical "constructionist"

---

49. Zlotnick, "Memory," 236.
50. On Josephus, see *Life*, 2.5. On Aquinas, see the discussion in Carruthers, *Book of Memory*, 2–7.
51. T. Butler, "Memory: A Mixed Blessing," in *Memory: History, Culture and the Mind* (New York: Blackwell, 1989), 14.

project rooted in the valuable idea of memory being assembled from parts . . . but fixated on the circular assumption that constructed products are not what they seem precisely because they are constructed. No assumption, in my view, has done more to undermine the foundation of social memory scholarship or hindered its application to biblical studies.[52]

Schwartz goes on to express his concern about the effect of hyperskeptical social memory theory upon Gospel studies in no uncertain terms: "Theories that dismiss the Gospels as screens on which church leaders projected their agendas are instances of intellectual dandyism . . . but since they resonate with the taste of a cynical age, their burden of proof is light."[53]

Beyond Schwartz's concerns, there is the fact that, in service to its ideological leanings, postmodern social memory theory tends strongly to emphasize the distorting influences of social remembering, while virtually ignoring the truth/fact-enhancing aspects of this communal process (though it should be noted that even skeptical theorists occasionally acknowledge that social memory can in fact be "extremely accurate").[54] This neglect is not surprising, given the common announcement from social memory theorists that the "truth/fact question" is of little interest to them.[55] However, as Sue Campbell observes, what has been left largely unexplored is the way in which "relational remembering" can actually enhance our confidence in human memory. Campbell writes, "I contend that a discussion of the relational dimensions of remembering primarily in terms of the threat of memory distortion compromises our understanding of the sociability of memory."[56] In her book, *Relational Remembering: Rethinking the Memory Wars*, she goes on to offer a much-needed analysis of social/relational memory that seriously challenges the current hyperskeptical vision of such collective remembering.[57]

In light of these various considerations, we believe that human memory provides nothing like an insurmountable barrier to the reliable remembering and reporting of the recent past—particularly when we consider it within the context of

52. B. Schwartz, "Christian Origins," 43–44.

53. Ibid., 53.

54. See, e.g., Cattell and Climo, "Introduction," 26. See also Fentress and Wickham, *Social Memory*, xii. Even Daniel Schacter, a memory theorist known for his work on the distorting effects of memory, can offer a generally positive assessment of the matter: "On balance . . . our memory systems do a remarkably good job of preserving the general contours of our pasts and of recording correctly many of the important things that have happened to us" (*Searching for Memory: How Minds, Brains and Societies Reconstruct the Past* [New York: Basic, 1996], 308).

55. See, e.g., Cattell and Climo, "Introduction," 17, 27; Fentress and Wickham, *Social Memory*, xi–xii.

56. Campbell, *Relational Remembering*, 8.

57. Campbell's work in this regard is, broadly speaking, supported by that of C. A. J. Coady, who has provided a defense (complete with an appropriate epistemology) of testimony as a source of reliable knowledge. See *Testimony: A Philosophical Analysis* (Oxford: Clarendon, 1992). He specifically addresses the memoric skepticism position in its psychological form in chap. 15.

an orally dominant, communally centered culture such as the world of the early oral Jesus tradition.

The Assumed Perspicuity of Eyewitnesses

Another objection to the view that eyewitnesses played a regulative role in the oral period of the early church is that the Gospels lack the sort of perspicuity that (some think) typically characterizes eyewitness recounting. Now, we shall argue in a later chapter that we do in fact find the sort of detail in the Gospels that is quite compatible with eyewitness influence. But the more fundamental question is whether the assumption of perspicuity necessarily applies to oral performances of traditions rooted in personal reminiscence. The answer that recent studies of orality suggest is that it does not.

For a variety of reasons, oral cultures frequently use techniques that serve to veil or code information within the performance arena. At times this is due to the community's strong sense of identity and sensitivity to the distinction between "insiders" and "outsiders."[58] There is "a private side" to oral traditions, and as N. Tisani notes, it is most intense when a community's *religious* traditions are being performed.[59] What outsiders perceive as obscurity, if not nonsense, in an oral performance is frequently a metaphorically driven insider language employed to solidify the group's sense of identity over against other people-groups. This use of intentional obscurity, or even "anti-language," is most common when an orally dominant community exists as a minority group in a social context that is perceived as hostile.[60]

In light of this, we should not be too quick to use the lack of perspicuity in some Gospel material as evidence that eyewitnesses do not lay behind it. Early Christians certainly transmitted their oral and/or written material in an environment that was, in varying degrees, perceived by them as hostile. We know that, like many sectarian Jews before them, they sometimes coded teachings in, for example, apocalyptic imagery as a means of protecting the "insider/outsider" distinction. And the Gospel material itself tells us that Jesus intentionally taught

58. As Jan Vansina reminds us with regard to oral transmission of personal historical reminiscence, even in the best-case scenarios, "there still remain remembrances that can be told to anyone, others to intimates only, and some perhaps to no one" (*Oral Tradition as History* [Madison: University of Wisconsin Press, 1985], 9).

59. N. Tisani writes, "Oral tradition . . . can also be a medium that helps humans rise from the secular to the sacred realm. Usually such an undertaking is in the hands of the people who, in keeping with sacred mysteries, will use special language and codes. This is the private side of oral tradition, which is mainly made up of classified information to which there is limited and controlled access" (N. Tisani, "Classified Material in Oral Tradition: Its Survival and Transmission," in *Oral Tradition and Its Transmission: The Many Forms of Message*, ed. E. Sienert, M. Cowper-Lewis, and N. Bell [Durban, South Africa: University of Natal, 1994], 170).

60. For a discussion of this sociological category, see M. A. K. Halliday, "Anti-languages," *American Anthropologist* 78 (1976): 570–84; idem, *Language as Social Semiotics: The Social Interpretation of Language and Meaning* (London: Arnold, 1978).

in ways that would be unintelligible to those who did not have "ears to hear" (e.g., Matt. 11:15; 13:9–16, 43).[61]

Another reason for what appears to outsiders—especially modern, highly literate outsiders—as obscurity within an oral tradition involves the concepts of "activation" and metonymic reference mentioned above. In an orally dominant context, communicative economy is a central feature of the performance arena. As J. M. Foley explains, "Simply put, the composer and the audience communicate economically because they converse in a register heavily coded with traditional signification, within a performance arena that supports this specialized kind of transaction."[62] When a modern scholar, steeped in a highly literate register, approaches this type of orally oriented tradition, "the marked [oral] register is falsely construed as an unmarked variety of language."[63] What this means is that the modern reader tends to miss the metonymic signals that, in the original performance arena, naturally and unambiguously activated a wealth of communally shared ideas. The modern reader sees obscurity where, in the original oral context, there was none.

Thus, there are good reasons to suppose that the level of clarity, detail, and ostensive obscurity we find in the Gospels is about what we should expect from historical reminiscence that has become the basis for an orally dominant community's tradition that, among other things, serves to preserve its religious and social identity within an often hostile context. At the very least, recent studies of oral performances must caution modern scholars from making assumptions about what eyewitness material looks like when transmitted in non-Western, orally dominant cultures.

The Centrality of "Witnesses" in the Jewish Scripture and Tradition

The last several decades have seen a renewed emphasis on the need to understand Jesus and early Christianity within a first-century Jewish context.[64] In this light, it is significant to note that—beginning with its Scriptures—the Jewish tradition

---

61. Robert Gundry has recently made a strong argument that the Gospel of John makes extensive use of anti-language and double entendre for the same reasons. See *Jesus the Word according to John the Sectarian* (Grand Rapids: Eerdmans, 2002), 56–57.

62. J. M. Foley, "Selection as *pars pro toto*: The Role of Metonymy in Epic Performance and Tradition," in *The Kalevala and the World's Traditional Epics*, ed. L. Honko (Helsinki: Finnish Literature Society, 2002), 108.

63. Ibid., 109.

64. Concerning Jesus: e.g., E. P. Sanders, *Jesus and Judaism* (Philadelphia: Fortress, 1985); J. H. Charlesworth, *Jesus within Judaism* (New York: Doubleday, 1988); N. T. Wright, *The New Testament and the People of God* (Minneapolis: Fortress, 1992); C. A. Evans, *Jesus and His Contemporaries: Comparative Studies* (Leiden: Brill, 1995); S. McKnight, *A New Vision for Israel: The Teachings of Jesus in National Context* (Grand Rapids: Eerdmans, 1999). Concerning early Christianity, note the rise of the "new history of religions school," one that locates early Christianity and its theological development firmly within the context of a Jewish thought-world. See, e.g., L. W. Hurtado, *One God, One Lord: Early Christian Devotion and Ancient Jewish Monotheism* (Philadelphia: Fortress, 1988); idem, *Lord Jesus Christ: Devotion to Jesus*

as a whole put strong emphasis on the role of eyewitnesses. Only by appealing to credible eyewitnesses could one certify a claim as factual (e.g., Jer. 32:10, 12; Ruth 4:9–11; Isa. 8:2). Correlatively, bearing false witness was considered a major crime in ancient Judaism. Indeed, this was one of the explicit prohibitions of the ten primary stipulations of the Sinai covenant (Exod. 20:16). The Jewish law of multiple witnesses reflects the life-or-death importance of this command (Deut. 17:6–7; Num. 35:30).

It seems that this emphasis on the importance of eyewitnesses was quite explicitly carried over into the early church. The Sinai principle regarding multiple witnesses was retained (Mark 14:56, 59; John 5:31–32; Heb. 10:28) and made the basis of church discipline (Matt. 18:16; 2 Cor. 13:1; 1 Tim. 5:19). More broadly, the themes of bearing witness, giving a true testimony, and making a true confession are ubiquitous in the tradition of the early church (e.g., Matt. 10:18; Mark 6:11; 13:9–13; Luke 1:1–2; 9:5; 21:12–13; 22:71; John 1:7–8, 15, 19, 32, 34; 3:26, 28; 5:32; Acts 1:8, 22; 2:32; 3:15; 5:32; 10:37–41; 13:31; 22:15, 18; 23:11; 26:16; Rom. 1:9; 1 Cor. 1:6; 15:6; 2 Cor. 1:23; Phil. 1:8; 1 Thess. 2:5, 10; 1 Tim. 6:12–13; 2 Tim. 2:2; 1 Pet. 5:1; 2 Pet. 1:16; 1 John 5:6–11; Rev. 1:5; 2:13; 3:14; 6:9; 11:3; 17:6). As Robert Stein observes, the sheer pervasiveness of these themes in the early church testifies to "the high regard in which eyewitness testimony was held."[65]

More specifically, certain key individuals are singled out in the New Testament for their roles as faithful witnesses, teachers, and preservers of the Jesus tradition, for example, Peter, James, and John, as well as James the brother of Jesus (e.g., Acts 1:15, 21–22; 2:14, 42; 3:1–11; 4:13, 19; 5:1–10, 15, 29; 8:14; 12:2; 1 Cor. 15:1–8; Gal. 2:9; Eph. 2:20).[66] This emphasis on key individuals is not only consistent with ancient Judaism, but it is precisely what we should expect, given what we have learned from orality studies about the central role individual tradents play in orally dominant cultures.

It is difficult to explain this common appeal to eyewitness testimony in the New Testament if it is not rooted in historical fact. It seems we must accept as fact that "Jesus gathered around himself a group of committed disciples, some of whom were also prominent in the early church."[67] This conclusion would suggest that mechanisms were in place in the early church that would naturally limit the amount of legendary material that was introduced into the Jesus tradition. For, as

---

in *Earliest Christianity* (Grand Rapids: Eerdmans, 2003); R. Bauckham, *God Crucified: Monotheism and Christology in the New Testament* (Grand Rapids: Eerdmans, 1998).

65. Stein, *Synoptic Problem*, 193.

66. *Pace* J. P. Meier's skepticism (*A Marginal Jew: Rethinking the Historical Jesus*, vol. 3: *Companions and Competitors* [New York: Doubleday, 2001], 211–12), the evidence supports Dunn's conclusion that the tradition of Peter, James, and John as forming Jesus's inner circle among the twelve is best understood as reflecting the pre-Easter situation, as opposed to a post-Easter fabrication (J. D. G. Dunn, *Christianity in the Making*, vol. 1: *Jesus Remembered* [Grand Rapids: Eerdmans, 2003], 540n250).

67. Meier, *Marginal Jew*, 3:47.

Dibelius argued decades ago, during "the period when eyewitnesses of Jesus were still alive, it was not possible to mar the picture of Jesus in the tradition."[68]

The Work of Dunn, Byrskog, and Bauckham

A number of Jesus scholars have in various ways come to similar conclusions.[69] We shall briefly review the work of three of them.

One of the leading proponents of applying interdisciplinary studies of oral traditions to the Jesus tradition is James Dunn. In the light of recent folkloristic and anthropological research, Dunn argues that New Testament scholars need to move beyond Bultmannian form-critical assumptions and acknowledge the central role Jesus's immediate disciples would have played as eyewitnesses to his life and teaching. He contends that we must not forget "the continuing role of eyewitness tradents, of those recognized from the first as apostles or otherwise authoritative bearers of the Jesus tradition." He continues: "Such indications as there are from the pre-Pauline and early Pauline period suggest already fairly extensive outreach by such figures, both establishing and linking new churches, and a general concern to ensure that a foundation of authoritative tradition was well laid in each case."

Applying recent insights regarding individual oral tradents, Dunn concludes: "In focusing particular attention on the communal character of the early traditioning process we should not discount the more traditional emphasis on the individual figure of authority respected for his or her own association with Jesus during the days of his mission."[70]

Arguing along similar lines, Samuel Byrskog has recently provided us with one of the most exhaustive studies on the role of eyewitnesses in the early church.[71] Most significant for our present purposes, Byrskog approaches his work well-

---

68. Dibelius, *Tradition to Gospels*, 293.

69. Beyond the works discussed below, see also M. Hengel, "Eye-Witness Memory and the Writing of the Gospels," in *The Written Gospel*, ed. M. Bockmuehl and D. A. Hagner (New York: Cambridge University Press, 2005), 70–96.

70. Dunn, *Jesus Remembered*, 242–43. While Dunn wisely recognizes the role of eyewitnesses in the early tradition, on the one hand, and the important role played by the twelve disciples on the other (p. 540), he fails, to any significant degree, to explicitly connect the two and explore the ways in which they might have provided continuity between Jesus and the post-Easter tradition. This problem has led Samuel Byrskog to push Dunn on this point; see "A New Perspective on the Jesus Tradition: Reflections on James D. G. Dunn's *Jesus Remembered*," *JSNT* 26 (2004): 467–68.

71. Samuel Byrskog, *Story as History—History as Story: The Gospel Tradition in the Context of Ancient Oral History* (Tübingen: Mohr Siebeck, 2000). Byrskog's work can be seen as a development and maturation of the "Scandinavian" approach to the Jesus tradition, classically represented by Harold Riesenfeld and Birger Gerhardsson. Byrskog's earlier book, *Jesus the Only Teacher: Didactic Authority and Transmission in Ancient Israel, Ancient Judaism and the Matthean Community* (Stockholm: Almqvist and Wiksell, 1994), originally was crafted as a dissertation under the direction of Gerhardsson at Lund University. For a helpful overview of Byrskog's work, especially as it relates to the question of eyewitness influence on the Jesus tradition, see P. M. Head, "The Role of Eyewitnesses in the Formation of the Gospel Tradition: A Review Article of Samuel Byrskog, *Story as History—History as Story*," *TynB* 52 (2001): 275–94.

informed by recent interdisciplinary studies on ancient oral traditions and "oral history."[72] Byrskog first demonstrates that Greco-Roman social groups generally conform to the pattern of orally dominant cultures regarding their interest in accurately preserving the essence of past events relevant to their self-identity. He then argues that the early Christians fit this same pattern as is evidenced by their frequent appeals to eyewitness testimony.[73]

Of course, scholars in the Bultmannian tradition argue that these appeals to eyewitnesses are later fabrications crafted as apologetic ploys. But Byrskog effectively argues that there is no compelling reason to assume this. Eyewitnesses would have been both available and valued in the earliest communities. Appeals to them are rather sober and modest, especially when compared to other Greco-Roman authors of the period. And, while it is true that the frequency of appeals increases in later New Testament writings, it is also true that these appeals underlie the entire Jesus tradition from the start. Moreover, we naturally should expect the emphasis on eyewitnesses to increase as the distance between the audience and the event itself increases.[74] Hence, the frequency and nature of the New Testament's appeals to eyewitnesses is quite in line with what we should expect, given Old

72. Here, Byrskog joins a number of other Jesus scholars (e.g., see E. P. Sanders and M. Davies, *Studying the Synoptic Gospels* [Philadelphia: Trinity, 1989], 143; Wright, *New Testament and the People of God*, 423–24) in recognizing that, given the relatively short period of oral transmission between Jesus and the writing of the Gospels, technically we are in the realm not of "oral tradition" per se, but rather of "oral history." "Oral tradition" is commonly defined as oral transmissions that have been passed on for at least "several generations"; see David Henige, "Oral, but Oral What? The Nomenclatures of Orality and Their Implications," *Oral Tradition* 3 (1988): 232. The designation of "oral history"—at least since the rise of the "oral history movement" in the 1930s—refers to oral transmissions of events that have occurred within the life span of the narrator. On the oral history phenomenon in contemporary times, see P. Thompson, *The Voice of the Past: Oral History*, 2nd ed. (New York: Oxford University Press, 1988); L. M. Starr, "Oral History: Problems and Prospects," *Advances in Librarianship* 2 (1971): 275–304. Wright follows Sanders and Davies in emphasizing that the difference between oral tradition and oral history is that the former is characterized by formal, verbatim memorization of a teacher's sayings, while the latter merely reflects more informal, "often-repeated tales" of what someone said and did (*New Testament and the People of God*, 423). This, however, is a less-than-accurate representation of how these two terms are usually defined and distinguished in the interdisciplinary literature. This becomes clear once it is recognized, on one hand, that the personal reminiscences of "oral history" can be quickly stylized for easier memorization and communication, and, on the other hand, that, with regard to much of the "oral tradition" in various cultures, the tradents never aspire to anything like verbatim memorization of the material, with some even avoiding formal, stylized oral patterning. See respectively, Tonkin, "Boundaries of History in Oral Performance," 280; and D. W. Cohen, "The Undefining of Oral Tradition," *Ethnohistory* 36 (1989): 9–18, esp. 11–13, 15–16 (regarding the latter point, note also the findings of the oral-formulaic school with regard to certain forms of oral tradition and the absence of verbatim memorization).

73. More specifically, Byrskog makes a powerful case that the early Jesus tradition emphasized the role played by "the Twelve" (with Peter as the main spokesman), several women (with Mary Magdalene at the forefront), and certain family members of Jesus, particularly Mary and his brother James. These, he contends, were the primary oral tradents of the Jesus tradition. See Byrskog, *Story as History*, 91. On the influence of Peter and other specific individuals in the early church, see also Schulz, *Die apostolische Herkunft der Evangelien*, chap. 5.

74. See Byrskog, *Story as History*, chap. 5.

Testament precedent, the nature of ancient oral history, and the ever-increasing distance between the community and the events associated with Jesus.

Byrskog also raises the important question of why we should assume that because something serves an apologetic purpose, it therefore must have been fabricated. If the Jesus material was indeed entrusted to eyewitnesses, it would have been apologetically advantageous for early Christians to appeal to them. The claim that these appeals are fabricated for apologetic purposes has force only if one *assumes at the start* that these appeals *are not true*. Obviously, this is a classic case of circular reasoning.[75] A fair-minded approach would be to take the appeals at face value, unless we have convincing reason not to.

This brings us to what may be the crux of the issue. For many scholars, it seems that we have a very convincing reason for not accepting the early Jesus tradition as rooted in eyewitness recollection—namely the ubiquitous presence of supernatural and miraculous elements.[76] Long ago, Julius Wellhausen made this often hidden presupposition quite explicit when he wrote, "The miracle stories in the form in which they are presented in Mark are most resistant to being attributed to the most intimate disciples of Jesus," and therefore "none of them may come from an eyewitness."[77] Here, we submit, a historical decision about eyewitness influence upon the Jesus tradition is being decisively influenced by a metaphysical conviction about the possibility of supernatural occurrences. In light of our earlier proposal for an "open" historical method, we do not find this approach to be acceptable.

Finally, we must consider the recent work of Richard Bauckham on eyewitness testimony in the Gospel tradition.[78] Building upon some of the insights of Byrskog, Bauckham offers several additional lines of evidence for the presence and importance of eyewitness testimony in the early church. First, Bauckham mines Papias's famous statement about his connection to testimony rooted in eyewitness recollection. After assessing the various ways of approaching this claim, Bauckham concludes:

75. For a more extensive critique of the circular nature of some form-critical arguments in the Bultmannian tradition, see G. Boyd, *Cynic Sage or Son of God? Recovering the Real Jesus in an Age of Revisionist Replies* (Grand Rapids: Baker Academic, 1995), esp. chap. 5.

76. Martin Hengel concludes that the persistent rejection today of a link from Peter's eyewitness testimony to Mark's Gospel involves "an unacknowledged modern apologetic interest, characteristic of Protestant theology after the Enlightenment, namely offence at the numerous miracle stories in the Gospels" (*The Four Gospels and the One Gospel of Jesus Christ*, trans. J. Bowden [Harrisburg, PA: Trinity, 2000], 88).

77. Cited in Hengel, *Four Gospels*, 89.

78. See Bauckham, "The Eyewitnesses and the Gospel Tradition," *JSHJ* 1 (2003): 28–60. Bauckham has delivered a number of papers on this topic in recent years and has just released a full-scale study on the phenomenon of eyewitness testimony in the early Jesus tradition, *Jesus and the Eyewitnesses: The Gospels as Eyewitness Testimony* (Grand Rapids: Eerdmans, 2006), that will likely serve as a landmark statement on this topic. Given that we were in the later stages of the publication process when the book was released, we were unable to incorporate it within the body of the text.

We may therefore trust the most significant implication of what Papias says: that oral traditions of the words and deeds of Jesus were attached to specific named eyewitnesses. . . . Papias assumes that the value of oral traditions depends upon their derivation from still living witnesses who are still themselves repeating their testimony.[79]

Next, Bauckham explores the implications of the fact that, while the tendency in the Gospel tradition is to leave characters unnamed, some nevertheless are named. Bultmann would have explained this phenomenon by an appeal to the "law of increasing detail," wherein he assumes a developmental tendency in the tradition to add details (i.e., names) to earlier, more streamlined accounts.[80] Unfortunately for Bultmann's thesis, Bauckham has shown that the tendency within the Synoptic Gospels is in precisely *the opposite direction*. In fact, "in no case does a character unnamed in Mark gain a name in Matthew or Luke," while Matthew and Luke are found in several instances dropping the name of a character that is provided in Mark.[81] Rather, it appears that "the names in these Gospel narratives belong to the original form of the traditions."[82] In working through this data, Bauckham concludes that in many cases—for example, Cleopas (Luke 24:18), the named women at the crucifixion and tomb (Mark 15:40), Simon of Cyrene and his sons (Mark 15:21), and four recipients of Jesus's healings—"the named characters were eyewitnesses who not only originated the traditions to which their names are attached but also continued to tell these stories as authoritative guarantors of the traditions."[83]

In conclusion, given that the first-century Jewish world of the pre-Gospel oral Jesus tradition highly valued eyewitness testimony, we find it far more plausible that *the early church valued and preserved the essence of the personal remembrances of Jesus's original disciples* than that they neglected the actual eyewitnesses, only to manufacture fabricated testimonies at a later date. At the very least, we can now conclude that the standard form-critical arguments against the presence of a significant amount of eyewitness testimony within the oral Jesus tradition are deeply flawed.

The Alleged "Laws" of Oral Transmission

As noted previously, early form critics were generally confident they could understand the development of the oral Jesus tradition in terms of "laws" that

79. Bauckham, "Eyewitnesses," 35, 42.
80. Bultmann, *History*, 68, 215, 241, 283, 310, 345, 393.
81. Bauckham, "Eyewitnesses," 47. Bauckham rightly notes that something like Bultmann's "law" is more apparent in later, extracanonical Gospels.
82. Ibid., 49.
83. Ibid., 44. For a more detailed look at Bauckham's thesis, see pp. 417–19 below.

presumably govern all oral transmission. On this basis they believed they could confidently theorize how various aspects of the Jesus tradition were created and modified over time. The plausibility of the legendary-Jesus thesis is significantly enhanced or diminished by the plausibility of these supposed "laws." In what follows we will assess each of the three "tools" Bultmann used to arrive at these "laws."

The Two-Source Theory

By examining how Matthew and Luke use Mark and Q, Bultmann believed he could discover "laws of development" that could be extrapolated back to our understanding of the development of the oral tradition prior to the writing of the Gospels. This approach raises methodological questions on at least three counts.

First, it assumes the two-source hypothesis. While the majority of New Testament scholars continue to embrace some version of this hypothesis, it has been subjected to rather trenchant criticisms.[84] Obviously, to the extent that the two-source theory is vulnerable, any theory regarding the "laws of transmission" that is based on it is also vulnerable. With the majority of New Testament scholars today, we suspect that something like the two-source theory best explains the data of the Synoptic Gospels.[85] However, it remains a hypothesis at best, and any theory that rests upon it must always be recognized to be no less hypothetical.

Second, as E. P. Sanders has argued, Bultmann's approach is somewhat circular in that the two-source theory is significantly *based* on the assumed "laws of development," which are, in turn, partly *derived* from the two-source theory.[86]

Third and equally problematic, Bultmann and those who have followed his approach assume that one can arrive at laws that govern oral traditions from an

84. For critiques of the two-source theory—particularly Q—see A. Farrer, "On Dispensing with Q," in *The Two-Source Hypothesis: A Critical Appraisal*, ed. A. J. Bellinzoni (Macon, GA: Mercer University Press, 1985), 321–56; M. Goodacre, *The Case against Q: Studies in Markan Priority and the Synoptic Problem* (Harrisburg, PA: Trinity, 2002); M. Goodacre and N. Perrin, eds., *Questioning Q: A Multidimensional Critique* (Downers Grove, IL: InterVarsity, 2005); M. Goulder, *Luke—A New Paradigm*, 2 vols. (Sheffield: JSOT, 1989); A. J. McNicol, D. B. Peabody, and L. Cope, eds., *One Gospel from Two: Mark's Use of Matthew and Luke: A Demonstration by the Research Team of the International Institute for Gospel Studies* (Harrisburg, PA: Trinity; New York: Continuum, 2002).

85. While we continue to work with a form of the two-source theory, we are also convinced that even here recent orality studies have much to offer by way of corrective. Given the rhetorical culture of the first-century Mediterranean world (on which see chap. 8), the Synoptic interrelations are no doubt deeply indebted to oral traditional material as well. For example, Terence Mournet has recently demonstrated that a variety of pericopes typically attributed to the Q document can, in fact, be quite plausibly accounted for by oral forces, once they are understood against the background of contemporary folkloristic studies on the variability and stability of *orality*. See *Oral Tradition and Literary Dependence: Variability and Stability in the Synoptic Tradition and Q* (Tübingen: Mohr Siebeck, 2005). W. Kelber rightly has raised similar issues; see "The Case of the Gospels," 71, 78–81.

86. Sanders, *Tendencies of the Synoptic Tradition* (New York: Cambridge University Press, 1969), 26; see also 25.

analysis of *written* texts. Bultmann and other modern, highly literate form critics naturally worked within a "literary paradigm" in which it was assumed that oral traditions operate like written texts. Indeed, according to Bultmann, "There is no definable boundary between oral and written tradition."[87] This "literary paradigm" is evidenced by the vocabulary he uses to talk about oral traditions. For example, he frequently refers to "layers" of oral tradition, "editing" within the oral tradition, "strata" and "strands" of oral traditions, and so on.[88] Thus, in Bultmann's eyes, oral transmission follows the same "laws" as written transmission.[89]

If the explosion of research on orally dominant cultures over the last half century has demonstrated anything, it is how fundamentally mistaken this way of thinking is. In what has been called "the turn to orality/performance," scholars from a variety of fields have come to realize that there are significant differences between spoken and written (particularly typeset) media, as well as between oral and literate communicational "conceptions" and strategies.[90] While the differences between the dominantly oral and dominantly literate worlds have often been overplayed as something of an unbridgeable "great divide," it is true that we cannot adequately understand oral traditions by relying on analogies drawn from typeset texts and literate paradigms.[91]

Among other things, we now know that variations in oral tradition do not follow linear, unidirectional "laws" (as the literary paradigm assumes), but rather

87. Bultmann, *History*, 321.

88. Ibid., 321; idem, "The Study of the Synoptic Gospels," 25.

89. For Bultmann's summary discussion of these laws and the editing process with regard to the history of the Jesus tradition, see *History*, 307–43. Unfortunately, for all of its brilliance, E. P. Sanders's *Tendencies of the Synoptic Tradition* largely labors under the same mistaken paradigm and its assumption; see p. 8n2. It is, however, almost as difficult to fault Sanders here as it is Bultmann, since he was working on this study in the form of a dissertation at Union Theological Seminary from 1964 to 1966, the very years in which the "turn to orality" was just beginning to gain steam in other disciplines. On the negative repercussions of the "text critical" paradigm for the study of oral tradition, see L. Honko, "Thick Corpus and Organic Variation: An Introduction," in *Thick Corpus, Organic Variation and Textuality in Oral Tradition*, ed. L. Honko (Helsinki: Finnish Literature Society, 2000), 4–5, 7–13.

90. This "turn" has been an interdisciplinary phenomenon. From Homeric studies, the oral-formulaic theory of Parry and Lord was a major impetus. A front-runner from the anthropological sector was the late Victor Turner; see his posthumously published volumes *On the Edge of the Bush: Anthropology as Experience*, ed. E. L. B. Turner (Tucson: University of Arizona Press, 1985); and *The Anthropology of Performance* (New York: PAJ, 1986). See also R. Bauman, *Story, Performance, and Event: Contextual Studies of Oral Narrative* (New York: Cambridge University Press, 1986); R. Bauman and C. L. Briggs, "Poetics and Performance as Critical Perspectives on Language and Culture," *Annual Review of Anthropology* 19 (1990): 59–88; D. Conquergood, "Poetics, Play, Process, and Power: The Performative Turn in Anthropology," *Text and Performance Quarterly* 1 (1989): 82–95. With respect to folkloristics, see S. J. Bronner, "Art, Performance, and Praxis: The Rhetoric of Contemporary Folklore Studies," *Western Folklore* 47 (1988): 75–102. See also E. C. Fine, "Performance Praxis and Oral Tradition," *Oral Tradition* 18 (2003): 46–48; D. Pollock, "Oral Traditions in Performance," *Oral Tradition* 18 (2003): 263–65.

91. For a classic statement against the "great divide" mentality, see R. Finnegan, "Literacy versus Non-literacy: The Great Divide?" in *Modes of Thought: Essays on Thinking in Western and Non-Western Societies*, ed. R. Horton and R. Finnegan (London: Faber and Faber, 1973), 112–44.

follow far more complex, multidirectional paths. Oral variations "depend on the performance situation itself—and every performance is, to one degree or another, different from the next."[92] The same tradent performing the same oral text may offer a longer, more elaborate version today, and a shorter, more stylized version tomorrow, depending upon the particular audience, time constraints, and countless other factors that attach to each individual performance. These are the sorts of variables not captured by "the literary paradigm" and thus never considered by the Bultmannian form-critical enterprise.

The Identification of Pure "Forms"

Bultmann's second tool is no less suspect than his first. Bultmann and those who followed him assumed that each literary form had an original, pure type that could be identified. On this basis, he believed he could identify secondary accretions that developed as the original form was modified over time. The method is questionable on at least two counts.

First, as with the first tool, it appears Bultmann's methodology, to a significant degree, is circular. Obviously, in order to work *back* from a written text to discover the "original" oral form, one has to know *how* the unit developed orally prior to its being written. But just as obviously, one has to know the "original" oral form *before* one can discern how it developed orally on its way to being written. In other words, Bultmann *establishes* the supposed "laws of development" by distinguishing the "original" oral from the later written form by showing how the later developed from the former. But the only "original form" he knows of in the first place is the hypothetical one posited by *assuming* certain "laws of development" that led from the original to the written form.

Second, this tool is as rooted in an anachronistic literary paradigm as is the first. Bultmann and many others who have followed his lead assumed that "laws" governing the progression of written documents apply to oral texts. As we have already noted, however, we now know that *they tend not to*.

To illustrate, one of the most fundamental "laws" of oral development espoused by Bultmann is that shorter and simpler units are more primitive than longer and more complex ones, since texts tend to acquire material, not lose it, as they are transmitted. While this may be true of *written* texts, it is not necessarily true of *oral* texts. Within two decades of the publication of Bultmann's *History of the Synoptic Tradition*, Parry and Lord were already providing evidence from field studies demonstrating that no inherent connection can be made in oral traditions between the length and complexity of a form, on the one hand, and how early or late it was, on the other. In the words of Albert Lord, "Given the nature of oral traditional composition and transmission . . . [it] does not in any way necessarily follow that

---

92. L. Marander-Eklund, "Variation in Repeated Interviews: Stories of Childbirth," in *Thick Corpus,* 432. While Marander-Eklund's comment was made specifically in connection with orally transmitted childbirth stories, it applies across a wider oral context.

the shortest is the oldest and the longest the latest or that the crudest is the oldest and the most polished the latest. It may be, but it is not necessarily so."[93]

This general observation was confirmed with regard to the Synoptic tradition by E. P. Sanders in the 1960s. Sanders writes: "Some tendencies which have been thought to have been generally operative among transmitters of the early Christian tradition have been shown not to have been so common. Thus we have seen that the material did not necessarily grow in overall length."[94]

The Search for the Sitz im Leben

This last point also has serious implications for the classic form-critical attempt to locate the life situation (*Sitz im Leben*) of the community that supposedly gave rise to and/or shaped the original and subsequent forms of the oral Jesus material.[95] If we cannot confidently distinguish more primitive forms from more developed forms within oral traditions, it is difficult to be confident about locating the life situations that supposedly gave rise to and/or shaped these forms. Moreover, there is simply no evidence that the "life situation" of a community substantially changes, let alone gives rise to, the forms of its oral traditions in the first place.[96] In fact, recent research on oral traditions suggests we can draw no necessary correlation between "form" and "life situation." As Graham Stanton has argued, any "form" can be used in a variety of situations, and almost every situation can utilize a variety of forms.[97]

Burke Long sums up the matter when he observes that "the field data" from oral traditions forces the conclusion that "the relationship between genre and setting is not at all a simple matter of style, structure, and a little sociology." Rather, "it depends upon a host of factors related to the act of performance" in orally dominant settings.[98] In this light, "the field data stands in sharp contrast to a deeply held form critical assumption that every literary type has its definitive, essential setting, without which it ceases to be what it is."[99]

93. Lord, "Gospels as Oral Traditional Literature," 43.

94. Sanders, *Tendencies of the Synoptic Tradition*, 273–74; see also 68. An increasing number of scholars are realizing the adverse consequences both the "turn to orality" and the resultant demise of the "literary paradigm" for understanding oral traditions has for form criticism. For example, speaking specifically of the classic form-critical search for original forms of the Gospel material, Susan Niditch writes: "No longer are many scholars convinced that they can uncover original oral Ur-forms, nor that the most seemingly oral-traditional or formulaic pieces are earliest in date. . . . The most formulaic may be the latest in date" ("Oral Tradition and Biblical Scholarship," *Oral Tradition* 18 [2003]: 43).

95. For critical reflections on the form-critical search for the *Sitz im Leben*, see Güttgemanns, *Candid Questions*, 236–42; Boman, *Die Jesus-Ueberlieferung*, 112–13; Graham Stanton, "Form Criticism Revisited," in *What about the New Testament? Essays in Honor of Christopher Evans*, ed. M. Hooker and C. Hickling (London: SCM, 1975), 23; B. O. Long, "Recent Field Studies in Oral Literature and the Question of *Sitz im Leben*," *Semeia* 5 (1976): 35–49.

96. Boman, *Die Jesus-Ueberlieferung*, 112–13.

97. Stanton, "Form Criticism Revisited," 23.

98. Long, "Recent Field Studies," 44–45.

99. Ibid., 41–42. Long later observes, "Where oral literature thrives, we find diversity, plurality, variability. The idea of a single, original societal setting for a given literary genre often has little relevance

If taken to heart, this means that the attempt to envision the supposed development of the early church's life and theology on the basis of the alleged development of oral forms must be abandoned. In light of what we now know of oral traditions, no necessary correlation between forms and life situations can be confidently drawn.

The Alleged Universal Laws of Oral Transmission

Bultmann's third "tool" was a comparative analysis of folklore traditions. He and other early form critics believed that the "laws of development" they arrived at were significantly rooted in comparative studies of "popular oral tradition in general."[100] Their stated desire to understand the early church's oral tradition in light of oral traditions within contemporary orally dominant cultures was laudable. But there were serious limitations and misconceptions involved in this project, flaws that can now be judged as undermining the legitimacy of their conclusions.

While comparative studies may have helped the early form critics to identify formal units of the Jesus tradition, it is not without significance that they never actually carried out empirical research to arrive at their "laws of development."[101] Rather, following in the footsteps of Herman Gunkel, early New Testament form critics simply accepted the folklore theories of their day. Unfortunately, as we noted in the previous chapter, crucial aspects of these theories are now uniformly rejected by contemporary folklorists, and for good reason.

To illustrate, we need only to look at the most influential theorist of the late nineteenth and early twentieth centuries, Axel Olrik, who influenced both Gunkel and, at least indirectly, the early New Testament form critics, who patterned much of their work after Gunkel.[102] In keeping with the scientific spirit of the late nineteenth century, Olrik believed that all phenomena, including those associated with human behavior, could be exhaustively understood by analyzing them according to natural laws. Olrik was among the first to apply this scientific assumption to the

---

to the real situation. If I judge correctly, Biblical critics will find little support for their fundamental [form-critical] perspective. And this compromises many of their substantive historical and theological conclusions as well" (p. 37). See also his conclusion on p. 45.

100. G. Bornkamm, *Jesus of Nazareth*, trans. I. and F. McLuskey with J. M. Robinson (New York: Harper, 1960), 218. See the similar claim of W. G. Kümmel, *Einleitung in das neue Testament*, 13th ed. (Heidelberg: Quelle & Meyer, 1964), 21–22.

101. In his landmark study of the developmental tendencies within the Jesus tradition, E. P. Sanders assesses this question, and concludes: "The form critics did not derive laws of transmission from a study of folk literature, as many think" (*Tendencies of the Synoptic Tradition*, 26; see pp. 13–20 for his informative discussion of this question).

102. Olrik's famous essay "Epic Laws" was translated into German in 1909 and was utilized by Gunkel in the 1910 edition of his commentary on Genesis. Kümmel notes Gunkel's influence on the early form critics (*Einleitung in das neue Testament*, 21). On Gunkel's appreciation and citation of Olrik's "Epic Laws" essay, see B. Holbek, "Introduction," to A. Olrik, *Principles for Oral Narrative Research*, trans. K. Wolf and J. Jensen (Bloomington: Indiana University Press, 1992), xxii–iii, 156n1.

study of folklore.[103] His specific research was on Danish ballads and Danish and Icelandic sagas, but he believed he could describe laws that govern the development of all folklore by extrapolating from this limited field of research.[104]

Folklorists today are, to say the least, much less confident about the viability of such grand enterprises. Brynjulf Alver represents a contemporary critique of Olrik's approach when he writes:

> It would be a mistake unreservedly to accept Axel Olrik's epic laws as invariable in narratives. . . . Like so many of his generation, Olrik regarded his working hypotheses as universally valid axioms even though they were based on material mainly taken from a more or less local tradition, and his isolation of phenomena was related to his subjective conception of folklore. What Olrik really observed was some compositional tendencies in different genres of epic narrative tradition common within a limited geographical area.[105]

We now realize that Olrik and other folklorists of this period were far too confident in their ability to discover universal "laws" of oral transmission from relatively small fields of study. Indeed, the current scholarly consensus is that such universal "laws" simply do not exist. Even apart from empirical data, our postmodern context is justifiably suspicious of universal laws about human behavior. As we have already noted, many contemporary scholars are painfully aware of how easy it has been for Western scholars to project their own Western assumptions onto other cultures in the process of trying to understand them, and to do it in the name of having discovered a "law."

At the same time, the empirical data unequivocally lends credence to this postmodernist suspicion. Because our "sample field" is much more extensive than it was in the past, and because we can utilize recording devices that allow much more detailed analyses of oral performances than was previously possible, we now know that variations in oral performances do not conform to "laws of development" but are usually the result of contextual adaptation and/or spontaneous creativity. As Lena Marander-Eklund observes, oral variations "depend on the performance situation" itself—and every performance is, to one degree or another,

103. For discussion of these cultural forces, especially as an influence upon Olrik, see Holbek, "Introduction"; B. Alver, "The Epic Laws of Folk Narrative," in *Telling Reality: Folklore Studies in Memory of Bengt Holbek*, ed. M. Chesnutt (Copenhagen: University of Copenhagen, 1993).

104. For a helpful discussion see Holbek, "Introduction," xv–xxvi.

105. Alver, "Epic Laws of Folk Narrative," 203–4. Ironically, Olrik himself, at the end of his life, recognized that his laws did not apply to all oral narrative genres in the same way and/or to the same degree. He stated as much in chap. 6 of his work, *Principles for Oral Narrative Research*. Unfortunately, he died before this chapter could be finished. The chapter is titled "Concerning the Individual Genres of Folklore." See Olrik, *Principles for Oral Narrative Research*, 110–15. This has not prevented some contemporary scholars from continuing to appeal to Olrik's laws of folklore as if they stood unchallenged; see, e.g., M. S. Jaffee, *Torah in the Mouth: Writing and Oral Tradition in Palestinian Judaism 200 BCE–400 CE* (New York: Oxford University Press, 2001), 9–10, 163n15.

different from the next.[106] In the words of Annikki Kaivola-Bregenhoj, we have discovered that "variation is never mechanical"—that is, predictable according to a known "law"—and it is therefore "impossible to lay down any precise rules for its reasons and manifestations."[107]

E. P. Sanders has arrived at a similar conclusion regarding the variations in the Gospel tradition. "There are no hard and fast laws of development of the Synoptic tradition," he writes. Rather, "on all counts the tradition developed in opposite directions. It became both longer and shorter, both more and less detailed, and both more and less Semitic. For this reason," he continues, "*dogmatic statements that a certain characteristic proves a certain passage to be earlier than another is never justified.*"[108] Unfortunately, a great deal of the form-critical enterprise is rooted in such dogmatic assumptions.

The misguided form-critical perspective involving "laws" of oral tradition was very influential in leading form critics and others to adopt a highly skeptical view of the reliability of the pre-Gospel traditions about Jesus. Once we abandon this perspective, we have added another reason to reconsider the widespread skepticism toward the oral Jesus tradition.

Prophetic Inspiration and the "Memory" of Jesus in the Early Church

Finally, we must address the Bultmannian view that "the Church drew no distinction between . . . utterances by Christian prophets and the sayings of Jesus in the tradition."[109] We may call this view "the creative-prophets thesis," for it holds that early church prophets—inspired by the Spirit of the risen Christ—freely created material that was eventually retrojected back onto the Jesus of history. If in fact the early church could freely reimagine Jesus on the basis of "inspired speech," the plausibility of the legendary-Jesus thesis is obviously increased.[110]

106. Marander-Eklund, "Variation in Repeated Interviews," 432.

107. A. Kaivola-Bregenhoj, "Varying Folklore," in *Thick Corpus,* 126. Honko notes the problem: "The [earlier] researchers seem to have been largely unaware of the fact that the variation in their material did not reflect the real variation of folklore in its cultural contexts. For this, the density of variants was too thin" ("Thick Corpus and Organic Variation," 8). With the advent of portable sound recording equipment (with Milman Parry being one of the first to employ such technology in the field), the possibility of researchers collecting a "thick corpus" was finally possible, and with it a much more accurate picture of the true nature of oral traditions.

108. Sanders, *Tendencies of the Synoptic Tradition,* 272 (emphasis in text).

109. Bultmann, *History,* 127; see also idem, "The New Approach to the Synoptic Problem," 42.

110. Until Eugene Boring's comprehensive work on the creative-prophets thesis in the 1980s, Bultmann's view was for the most part simply reiterated rather than argued for in a systematic fashion, as Boring himself notes. See Boring, *Sayings of the Risen Jesus: Christian Prophecy in the Synoptic Tradition* (New York: Cambridge University Press, 1982); revised as *The Continuing Voice of Jesus* (Louisville: Westminster/Knox, 1991). For example, while Ernst Käsemann reformulates Bultmann's perspective ("Is the Gospel Objective?" in *Essays on New Testament Themes* [London: SCM, 1964], 60), his case remains largely one of assertion rather than a systematic argument, as David Hill has demonstrated ("On

The Issue at Hand

What can be said in response to this view? We should begin by acknowledging the possibility that a prophet in the early church could have spoken a word from "the risen Jesus" that was later construed as having originated with the earthly Jesus. In light of the fact that prophetic activity was common in the early church and given significant authority (1 Cor. 12–14; Eph. 2:20; 4:11; etc.), even some more conservative scholars find this possibility to be, at certain points, quite likely.[111] For example, Earle Ellis and James Dunn have argued that Matthew 18:20 likely originated as a post-Easter prophetic word, for Jesus's teaching seems to anachronistically presuppose Jesus's *spiritual* presence with his followers.[112]

The issue at hand is not whether or not it was *possible* some material in the Jesus tradition originated in prophetic inspiration. We grant that it is. Rather, we object to the suggestion that a significant portion (let alone the majority) of the Jesus tradition originated by this means.[113] We shall offer six considerations that we believe render this latter suggestion implausible.

---

the Evidence for the Creative Role of Christian Prophets," *NTS* 20 [1974]: 270–73). Most current New Testament scholars point to Boring's reformulation as having finally established that prophecy played a crucial role in forming the early church's view of Jesus. For example, W. Kelber, *The Oral and Written Gospel: The Hermeneutics of Speaking and Writing in the Synoptic Tradition, Mark, Paul, and Q* (Philadelphia: Fortress, 1983), 21. While we grant that Boring's work has unquestionably strengthened this position, we believe there remain compelling arguments against it, as we shall attempt to show.

111. Gerald Hawthorne, former New Testament professor at Wheaton College, has argued in this direction; see "The Role of Christian Prophets in the Gospel Tradition," in *Tradition and Interpretation in the New Testament: Essays in Honor of E. Earle Ellis for His 60th Birthday*, ed. G. Hawthorne with O. Betz (Grand Rapids: Eerdmans, 1987), 119–33. See also Dunn, *Jesus Remembered*, 187; E. E. Ellis, "Reading the Gospels as History," in *Christ and the Future in New Testament History*, NovTSup 97 (Boston: Brill, 2000), 51–54. Peter Richardson (following Oscar Cullmann) argues that Paul's quote of Jesus's words in 1 Cor. 7:10 stems not from a saying of the earthly Jesus, but rather derives entirely from a post-Easter, prophetically derived saying of the "exalted Lord" ("'I Say, Not the Lord': Personal Opinion, Apostolic Authority and the Development of Early Christian Halakah," *TynB* 31 [1980]: 71); and Craig Evans seems to entertain the possibility of the phenomenon in question ("Source, Form and Redaction Criticism: The 'Traditional' Methods of Synoptic Interpretation," in *Approaches to New Testament Study*, ed. S. E. Porter and D. Tombs [Sheffield: Sheffield Academic Press, 1995], 29–30).

112. Ellis, "Reading the Gospels," 254; Dunn, *Jesus Remembered*, 187. Other sayings—or aspects of them—that these scholars suggest may have arisen in the same fashion include: Matt. 11:28–30; Luke 11:49–51; 22:19b; as well as 1 Cor. 11:24 ("Do this in remembrance of me"), and Luke 9:23 (the addition of the modifying word "daily" to "take up your cross"). On a theological note, no one who believes that Jesus Christ is risen and can (or could) speak to his people through prophets should be disturbed by the prospect that portions of the Gospels originated in prophetic inspiration. As Hawthorne argues, "Just because a saying may have originated with a Christian prophet does not mean that it is of secondary importance, without authority or 'inauthentic.' Only the person who has no doctrine of inspiration can say this" ("Role of Christian Prophets," 130). Both Hawthorne and Ellis press the interesting point that, once one takes seriously the ongoing Christian claim that the exalted Jesus—the same Jesus who walked the earth in first-century Palestine—continued to speak through his Spirit-inspired prophets, then sayings derived in this manner are "no less authentic" than the words this same Jesus spoke during his earthly ministry. See Ellis, "Reading the Gospels," 254; Hawthorne, "Role of Christian Prophets," 130.

113. For a similar line of argumentation, see Hawthorne, "Role of Christian Prophets," 130.

Lack of Convincing Evidence

First, and perhaps most fundamental, there is simply no clear evidence that first-century Christian prophets spoke in the first-person voice of Jesus in the gathered communities.[114] Nor is there any evidence, either in the New Testament or in ancient Judaism, of prophetic speech being transformed later into historical "memory."[115] Being asked to embrace a theory for which there is no clear evidence and no clear cultural precedent is, at the very least, questionable.

The evidence instead indicates that early Christians followed the Old Testament precedent of associating prophecies with the prophet who uttered them, even when the prophecy was accepted as coming from God. As Dunn notes, "No OT prophetic book names Yahweh as its author."[116] So too, when the New Testament explicitly reports a prophecy, it identifies the prophet by name (e.g., Acts 11:27–28; 13:1; 21:9–14). Likewise, it seems early Christians distinguished Spirit-inspired speech (e.g., Acts 13:2; 21:11; 1 Cor. 12, 14) from the words of the risen Jesus (Acts 18:9–10; 23:11), as well as from the words of the earthly Jesus.[117] As we noted earlier, Paul was careful to distinguish his words from those of Jesus in 1 Corinthians 7:10–12. The distinction becomes all the more important when we note that Paul is, in this same context, arguing that he himself speaks with the authority of "the Spirit of God" (v. 40).[118] If an authority of the stature of Paul took care to distinguish his words from the historical Jesus—even while insisting that he was speaking with the Spirit's authority—how can we imagine lesser inspired prophets and other Christians being cavalier about such a distinction?[119]

On Revelation 2–3

It might seem that Revelation 2–3 counts against our first point, for here we do find Jesus speaking through John in the first person. Not surprisingly this passage has become foundational to the creative-prophets thesis, but our second argument against this thesis is that this is a very weak foundation. Two things may be said.

---

114. As Dunn notes (*Jesus Remembered*, 188).

115. As argued by W. Grudem, "The Gift of Prophecy in I Corinthians" (PhD diss., University of Cambridge, 1978), 230.

116. Dunn, *Jesus Remembered*, 188. Dunn follows F. Neugebauer on this point; see "Geistssprüche und Jesuslogien," *ZNW* 53 (1962): 222.

117. As noted by Dunn, *Jesus Remembered*, 188.

118. As we argued in chap. 5, the argument of those like Richardson ("'I Say, Not the Lord,'" 71) that the words of Jesus being quoted by Paul in 1 Cor. 7:10 refer not to Jesus's earthly teaching but rather to the words of the post-Easter risen Jesus spoken by a prophet does not best account for the data.

119. Related to this, Sanders raises the question of what would constitute a plausible *Sitz im Leben* for such an activity. See Sanders, *Jesus and Judaism*, 15–16. This is a point also emphasized by D. Aune, "Oral Tradition and the Aphorisms of Jesus," in *Jesus and the Oral Gospel Tradition*, ed. H. Wansbrough (Sheffield: Sheffield Academic Press, 1991), 223.

First, there is no reason to suppose that what John experienced in his vision at Patmos—and later recorded as the Revelation—was in any way typical of the experience of first-century Christian prophets. As David Hill notes,

> The author of Revelation stands closer to Old Testament prophecy than to what we know of Christian prophecy from the New Testament. . . . [T]he prophet-author of the Revelation is unique in his community, . . . it simply cannot be said, without other evidence, that Christian prophets in the primitive communities spoke as he did in the name of the risen Christ, nor that their prophetic consciousness may be discerned by examining his.[120]

For example, the prophets Paul addressed at Corinth spoke short, inspired words to a house church gathering at a particular point in time (1 Cor. 14). Clearly, this is no analogy to what John is doing in Revelation.

Second, and of decisive importance, John does not confuse the words of the risen Jesus with words from the earthly Jesus. In fact, one could argue that Revelation 2–3 argues *against* the creative-prophets thesis on just these grounds. The passage shows that "words of the risen Jesus" continued to be remembered as words of the *risen* Jesus given through *an identified human prophet*. They were not retroactively applied to the earthly Jesus.[121] In other words, this passage constitutes further evidence that early Christians followed the precedent of Judaism and thus retained the remembrance of the human prophet through whom the risen Jesus spoke.

An Ad Hoc Thesis

Third, it can be argued that the creative-prophets thesis is ad hoc. It becomes necessary only on the assumption that Jesus did not do and say much of what the Gospels attribute to him. If Jesus did not actually say and do what the early Jesus tradition "remembered" him saying and doing, we have to explain how the early church came to "remember" him in this way. The creative-prophets thesis helps us do this. But unless there are independent reasons for thinking Jesus could not have said and done what the early church claims to "remember" him saying and doing, and without independent arguments demonstrating that prophets functioned in this way in the early church, the thesis must be judged ad hoc in nature.

To illustrate, while we grant that it is possible to conceive of the early church reimagining (via prophetic inspiration) Jesus speaking about persecution to encourage itself in the face of impending persecution, it is also possible to conceive of the historical Jesus anticipating persecution and teaching about it, just as the Gospels report (e.g., Matt. 5:10–12; 10:16–31; 23:34–35). So too, while it is possible to conceive of the early church reimagining Jesus speaking about mission as

---

120. Hill, "Creative Role of Christian Prophets," 269.
121. A point emphasized by B. Witherington, *The Christology of Jesus* (Minneapolis: Fortress, 1990), 3.

a means of encouraging its own missionary activity, it is also possible to conceive of the earthly Jesus casting a missionary vision for his disciples in his lifetime, as the Gospels report (e.g., Matt. 28:19). The question is, why should we assume the former rather than the latter?[122] In most cases—as in these two examples—no obvious reason can be given. Only on the assumption that the latter possibility is not true is the former thesis even necessary. And this suggests, again, that the latter theory essentially is ad hoc in nature.[123]

Testing the Prophets

Fourth, for the creative-prophets thesis to stand, we have to conceive of early Christian prophecies having an enormous amount of authority in the early Christian communities. On this thesis the words of these prophets were accepted as having the same authority as words passed on from the earthly Jesus—to the point where they were retroactively put into his mouth. Unfortunately for this thesis, it does not seem early Christians granted prophets this much authority.[124]

Several times Paul instructs believers to critically test prophecies (e.g., 1 Cor. 14:29–32; 1 Thess. 5:19–22), a point taken to heart by later Christian writers.[125] As on many matters, here the early church was following the precedent of the Old Testament, which routinely recognized and warned against the possibility of false prophets (Deut. 13:1–5; 18:20–22; Jer. 14:13–16; 23:9–40; 28:12–17; Ezek. 13). James Dunn summarizes the situation well when he writes:

> A uniform feature both in the older Jewish and in early Christian prophecy is the recognition that inspiration could give rise to *false* prophecy. A prophetic utterance was *not* simply accepted at face value as a word from God. The need to *test* prophecy and to have tests for prophecy was recognized more or less from the beginning of Israel's reliance on prophecy.[126]

122. As Dunn argues, "Boring's logic works only if Jesus did not send out his disciples on mission, did not expect persecution for his disciples (even with the precedent of John the Baptist looming large), and did not regard his own message as having final eschatological significance" (*Jesus Remembered*, 188–89).

123. Boring admits that one's prior assumptions about the tradition process will largely determine one's conclusion on the question of creative prophets: "Any theory of prophetic expansion of the tradition implies a theory not only about Christian prophecy but about the nature of the tradition process itself" (*Sayings of the Risen Jesus*, 10). For this and a number of other reasons, Boring concludes by asking, "Has it been demonstrated in the preceeding pages that sayings of the Christian prophets can be identified within the synoptic tradition?" To his credit, he answers his own question with a "No" (p. 230).

124. Dunn, *Jesus Remembered*, 188; Hill, "Creative Role of Christian Prophets," 274.

125. See, e.g., *The Didache*, chaps. 11–12, in *The Apostolic Fathers*, trans. F. Glimm, J. Marique, SJ, and G. Walsh, SJ (Washington, DC: Catholic University of America Press, 1962), 1:180–81; and *Shepherd of Hermas*, 11th mandate, in *The Apostolic Fathers*, 1:280–81.

126. Dunn, *Jesus Remembered*, 189 (emphases in text). See also Dunn's detailed study of this phenomenon; "Prophetic 'I'-Sayings and the Jesus Tradition: The Importance of Testing Prophetic Utterances within Early Christianity," *NTS* 24 (1977–1978): 175–98.

The early church thus had a healthy hermeneutic of suspicion toward prophetic utterances.[127] The most fundamental criterion by which prophetic words would be tested, Dunn argues, is the received Jesus tradition. He writes, *"Any prophecy claiming to be from the exalted Christ would have been tested by what was already known to be the sort of thing Jesus would have said. This . . .* implies the existence in most churches of such a canon (the word is not inappropriate) of foundational Jesus tradition."[128]

In this light, we may conclude that even if certain prophetic words were later conflated with the words of the earthly Jesus within the Jesus tradition, they would not have distorted his essential message. For if they were not basically consistent with the received tradition, they would not have been accepted as true prophetic words in the first place.[129]

The Resistance of Oral Communities to Novelty

Our fifth argument against the creative-prophets thesis is closely related to the last point and arises from a discovery made about historically oriented oral narrative traditions discussed in the last chapter. We saw that while individual strong tradition bearers hold the primary responsibility for preserving and transmitting traditions within orally dominant communities, audiences also play a critical role in ensuring the basic continuity between each particular oral performance and the pool of tradition from which it emerges and to which it gives voice.[130] While oral

127. Dunn, *Jesus Remembered*, 190.

128. Ibid., 191 (emphasis in text). Dunn is not alone in positing the likelihood of something like a "canonical" oral Jesus tradition within the early churches that functioned, among other things, as a litmus test for prophetic utterances. Dibelius himself argued for regulatory collections of Jesus sayings (*From Tradition to Gospels*, 240–43). Arthur Baird, taking into account some of the work of Gerhardsson, has argued in a similar direction; see *Holy Word: The Paradigm of New Testament Formation* (Sheffield: Sheffield Academic Press, 2002). While Baird no doubt presses his point to speculative extremes, his vision of a regulative function for the words of the earthly Jesus within the early church points in the proper direction. Two confirming examples of Dunn's thesis are Rev. 3:20–21 and 16:15. Both passages provide sayings of the risen Lord. As David Hill notes, in both cases "what the Lord says by the Spirit is in fact a development or adaptation of something already in the tradition of Jesus sayings" ("Creative Role of Christian Prophets," 269). Specifically, Rev. 16:15 seems to be a development of Luke 12:39, while Rev. 3:20–21 seems to echo Luke 22:29 and possibly Luke 12:36.

129. Dunn, *Jesus Remembered*, 191–92.

130. The interdisciplinary studies that document the regulative role of the audience within orally dominant cultures are wide-ranging and voluminous. See, e.g., B. W. Andrzejewski and I. M. Lewis, *Somali Poetry: An Introduction* (Oxford: Clarendon, 1964), 46; H.-J. Becken, "The Use of Oral Tradition in Historiography: Some Pitfalls and Challenges," *Studia historiae eclesiasticae* 19 (1993): 87; R. Finnegan, *Limba Stories and Story-Telling* (Oxford: Clarendon, 1967), 66–69; idem, *Oral Literature in Africa* (Nairobi: Oxford University Press, 1970), 11; Foley, *Immanent Art*, 45; Honko, *Textualizing the Siri Epic* (Helsinki: Academia Scientiarum Fennica, 1998), 197; I. Okpewho, *African Oral Literature: Backgrounds, Character, and Continuity* (Bloomington: Indiana University Press, 1992), 183, 192; J. A. Robinson, "Personal Narratives Reconsidered," *Journal of American Folklore* 94 (1981), 72; S. Sowayan, *Nabati Poetry: The Oral Poetry of Arabia* (Berkeley: University of California Press, 1985), 111; Tonkin, "Boundaries of History in Oral Performance," 278.

performers exhibit spontaneous flexibility in how they recite and reenact an oral tradition in any particular instance, they are regularly corrected if the audience perceives them to have altered or misconstrued its essentials.

To appreciate the full significance of the audience's role in oral performance, we have to once again step outside of our customary modern, Western literary paradigm and remember that the activation of mutually shared ideas in oral communities is not primarily about disseminating information but about keeping a tradition—and a social identity—alive and relevant within the community.[131] In such a context, the community has great investment in preserving the essential elements of the historically oriented tradition that narrates their social origin and identity. In fact, Jawaharlal Handoo goes so far as to argue that this dynamic provides oral communities with "strong internal controls over misrepresentation, incorrect and unshared historical narration," and tends to make the oral tradition "quite resistant to distortion, even when compared with written history."[132]

While we have no reason to think that writing was altogether absent in the early church, it was nevertheless an orally dominant community and thus must be understood in the light of what we know about such communities. In this light, we must judge the creative-prophets thesis to be fundamentally misguided. As much as they emphasized the reality of the Spirit speaking to them in the present, given the data, we cannot easily imagine the earliest Christian communities allowing prophets to freely invent the Jesus traditions that constituted their very origin and identity.

To be sure, given what we know of orally oriented communities, we can perhaps conceive of the earliest Christians accepting prophetic *applications* and *expansions* of teachings of Jesus that already functioned as authoritative tradition within the community. This seems to be what is happening in Revelation 3:20–21 (cf. Luke 12:36; 22:29) and 16:15 (cf. Luke 12:39). But the supposition that communities received as authoritative altogether new material on the teachings or deeds of Jesus and then fused them with their orally transmitted memory of Jesus is difficult to square with certain dynamics that we find among both historical and religious traditions within orally dominant cultures.

If we had overwhelming independent evidence that prophets in the early church operated in the way form critics have imagined, we might be forced to conclude that the earliest Christian communities were simply idiosyncratic among oral communities in this regard. But as we have seen, not only is there no overwhelming evidence in support of this suggestion, but there is rather compelling evidence against it.

131. E. Bakker, "Activation and Preservation: The Interdependence of Text and Performance in an Oral Tradition," *Oral Tradition* 8 (1993): 9.

132. J. Handoo, "People Are Still Hungry for Kings: Folklore and Oral History," in *Dynamics of Tradition: Perspectives on Oral Poetry and Folk Belief*, ed. L. Tarkka (Helsinki: Finnish Literature Society, 2003), 70.

Absence of Early Church Issues

Finally, if it is true that early church prophets regularly spoke with the voice of the risen Jesus to address issues the church was facing, and if these sayings were eventually retroactively placed into the mouth of the earthly Jesus, then we should expect to find many—if not most—of the issues the early church faced being addressed by Jesus in the Gospels. Unfortunately for the creative-prophets thesis, this is simply not the case. To be sure, in a few instances, such as in Matthew 18:20, we can imagine this. But such cases are relatively rare.

For example, a central issue the early church had to wrestle with concerned the extent to which Gentiles needed to become "Jewish" when they became Christians. Did they need to be circumcised and obey food regulations when they aligned themselves with the Christian faith? Remarkably, we find no mention of this issue among the teachings of Jesus in the Gospels. Nor do we find any mention of how glossolalia should function within a community, how congregations should be organized and run, what role women can have within the church, what is appropriate attire for men and women in church, or whether Christians can eat meat offered up to idols. Yet we know from Paul's letters that each of these were issues with which the early church wrestled. If prophets were speaking on behalf of Jesus to give authoritative direction to the early church on particular matters, the virtual silence of the Jesus of the Gospels on these issues is puzzling. Moreover, if creative prophets were not prophetically speaking "words of the risen Jesus" on obviously important, relevant, and controversial matters such as these, one wonders what issues they presumably *did* address.[133]

Summary

In this chapter, the remaining three classic form-critical assumptions—assumptions often used to support the legendary-Jesus thesis—have been evaluated and found wanting. Against the form-critical assumption that eyewitnesses played no regulative role in the oral period of the early church, both recent studies on oral tradition and the New Testament itself suggest that eyewitnesses played an important role in the transmission and regulation of the oral Jesus tradition. Against the supposed universal developmental "laws" of oral tradition assumed by early form critics, the evidence forces us to conclude that these "laws" were largely born of an anachronistic literary paradigm, supported with circular reasoning, and based on inadequate field research. Finally, against the supposition that the oral Jesus tradition was heavily indebted to the inspired sayings of creative prophets, we find no clear evidence prophets functioned in this way in the early church, and

133. This question has been pressed by numerous scholars; see, e.g., Witherington, *Christology of Jesus*, 4; C. Blomberg, "Form Criticism," in *Dictionary of Jesus and the Gospels*, ed. J. B. Green, S. McKnight, and I. H. Marshall (Downers Grove, IL: InterVarsity, 1992), 246.

instead find good arguments against this proposal. The fact that orally dominant communities tend to have a vested interest in protecting their historically rooted traditions against substantial modification counts against this thesis, as does the fact that most issues we know the early church wrestled with are absent in the Jesus tradition that came to be recorded in the Gospels.

Part 4

The Synoptic Gospels
as Historical Sources for Jesus

Assessing the Evidence

Whatever one thinks of the content and reliability of oral and/or written pre-Gospel traditions, the issue of the extent to which canonical portraits of Jesus are historical or legendary obviously comes down to our estimation of the reliability of the canonical Gospels themselves. Thus, in part 4 of this work we investigate issues surrounding the historical reliability of the canonical Gospels—with a focus on the Synoptic Gospels.

The first issue surrounds what *kind* of text the Gospel writers intended to create. Legendary-Jesus theorists argue either that the Gospels were not intended to be read as biographies and/or histories or that, even if they were intended to be read as such, this does not increase our confidence in their historical reliability. We will explore issues surrounding the genre and nature of the Gospels in chapter 8.

Next, we must address three preliminary issues pertaining to the historical assessment of the Synoptic Gospels. Hence, in chapter 9 we explore the important issues of (1) where the burden of proof should lie as we assess the Gospels; (2) what methodology is most appropriate for evaluating the Gospels, given that they are written with an oral register; and (3) the extent to which we can be confident the documents we possess today allow us to reconstruct something very much like the originals.

Finally, in chapter 10, we will apply to the Gospels six final questions historians typically ask of an ancient document when assessing its historical reliability: (1) Does the document include self-damaging details? (2) Does the document include nonideologically motivated incidental details and/or casual information? (3) Is the document internally consistent? (4) Does the document contain inherently implausible events? (5) Do other literary works of the day corroborate the claims of the document? And, (6) does archaeological evidence corroborate the claims of the document?

To the genre question we now turn.

8

THE GENRE AND NATURE
OF THE CANONICAL GOSPELS

DID THE GOSPEL AUTHORS INTEND TO WRITE
HISTORICALLY RELIABLE ACCOUNTS?

The reliability of the canonical Gospels has been a subject of vigorous debate over the last several hundred years. The debate has largely revolved around questions pertaining to such things as sources, interrelations, genre, redaction, theology, internal consistency, and external corroboration with respect to the four Gospels. In this final section of this work, we will argue that, while some of these issues remain unresolved, we nevertheless have reason to conclude *on strictly historical grounds* that the Synoptic Gospels are generally reliable, thus providing us, at the very least, with a generally accurate portrait of the ministry and teaching of Jesus.

The present chapter will focus on the issue of genre and therefore on the question of whether the Gospel authors intended their works—among other things—to be read as historically reliable accounts. Clearly, if it can be shown that the authors of these works were not concerned with providing historically reliable information, our assessment of the reliability of these works will be more negative than if it can be shown that their intentions did include this goal.[1]

---

1. Given space considerations, we will be treating the Gospels under broad, thematic categories that focus on the specific issue of their historical reliability. At the outset we should emphasize that in its initial usage within the earliest church, "the gospel" (*to euangelion*) referred to "*oral proclamation* of the

We will begin with an overview of the major proposals put forth by scholars regarding the genre of the Gospels. We will then assess each of these proposals, exploring the possibility that the Gospels are best understood as sui generis, ancient biographies, ancient histories, pieces of ancient fiction, or examples of ancient Jewish midrash. Finally, we will further explore the nature of the Gospels by reconsidering them within their original orally/aurally dominant context.

An Overview of the Major Proposals

The concept of "genre" can be defined as "the conventional and repeatable patterns of oral and written speech, which facilitate interaction among people in specific social situations."[2] New Testament scholars have proposed a number of theories regarding the genre of the Gospels, each bringing its own possible challenges to the historical reliability of the Gospel portraits of Jesus. We will begin by reviewing and assessing five proposals that have exercised significant influence in scholarly circles.

"Gospel" as a Unique Genre

Beginning with the early form critics, many New Testament scholars have argued that there is no ancient text type that closely corresponds to a Gospel. Rather, the early Christian Gospels are "sui generis"—literally, "one of a kind."[3] In essence, this view developed naturally from several convictions almost universally shared by early form critics.

First, it was believed that the Gospels are unsophisticated, popular works with no real connection to Greco-Roman literature. Second, it was held that the Gospel authors were primarily collectors of the oral Jesus tradition, not authors of literature

---

significance of the death and resurrection of Jesus, *not to a written account* of the story of Jesus," as Graham Stanton has noted; *Jesus and Gospel* (New York: Cambridge University Press, 2004), 52 (emphasis added). This means that the "four Gospels" as canonical texts must be understood—as they were in the early church—against the backdrop of the "one gospel" of Jesus Christ that found its primary expression in the oral tradition that proclaimed "God's one glad tiding concerning Jesus Christ" (ibid., 59). In other words, the Gospel writers were recounting and inscribing *the* gospel, not creating *a* gospel. This point is well stated by M. Hengel in *The Four Gospels and the One Gospel of Jesus Christ: An Investigation into the Collection and Origin of the Canonical Gospels*, trans. J. Bowden (Harrisburg, PA: Trinity, 2000), see esp. chap. 5. This point will become important in our own proposal for understanding the nature of the Gospels later in this chapter.

2. J. L. Bailey, "Genre Analysis," in *Hearing the New Testament: Strategies for Interpretation*, ed. J. B. Green (Grand Rapids: Eerdmans, 1995), 200. The issue of the genre of the four Gospels is usually raised first and foremost with respect to Mark's Gospel, since most (but not all) scholars believe this Gospel was written first and used in the composition of Matthew and Luke.

3. K. L. Schmidt was the first to make a sustained case for this position; see "Die Stellung der Evangelien in der allgemeinen Literaturgeschichte," in *Eucharisterion*, ed. H. Schmidt (Göttingen: Vandenhoeck & Ruprecht, 1923), 50–134. Schmidt was responding to C. W. Votaw's claim that the Gospels are a variety of ancient popular biography.

in their own right. And, finally, it was widely assumed that the driving motivation behind the writing of the Gospels was not literary, but "kerygmatic." That is, the Gospels were designed to proclaim the life, death, and resurrection of Jesus for the purpose of convincing people he was the Son of God.[4] Given these assumptions, the form critics concluded that the Gospels were best classified as sui generis.

For many years this view was the dominant position within New Testament circles, and it continues to be held by a number of scholars, both liberal and conservative.[5] In the hands of more liberal scholars—Bultmann for example—this view can be combined with a highly skeptical view toward the historical reliability of the Gospels. Thus for Bultmann, the Gospels represent a unique popular-level genre, but one whose content was characterized largely as "mythological" in nature.

"Gospel" as Biography

Many contemporary scholars argue that, while the Gospels certainly have some distinctive aspects to them, they can nevertheless be classified as ancient biographical writings. There is, however, much less agreement about the precise type of ancient biography the Gospels represent.

A number of scholars have argued that the Gospels should be classified as "aretalogy." The late Morton Smith, a leading advocate of this thesis, has defined the ancient aretalogy as "a miracle story or a collection of miracle stories" whose primary purpose was "praise of and propaganda for the deity supposed to have done the deeds."[6] The deity in question was typically a godlike being in human form who was given the designation *theios aner*, or "divine man." Examples of such miracle-working "divine men" from the ancient pagan world include Pythagoras, Empedocles, Asclepius, and, most important for our purposes, Apollonius of Tyana (discussed in chap. 3). It is argued that, at the very least, the Gospels are closer to such aretalogies than "to any other ancient non-Christian works that we know of."[7]

---

4. This led to the famous description of Mark as "a passion narrative with an extended introduction," as noted by H. Koester, *Ancient Christian Gospels: Their History and Development* (Philadelphia: Trinity, 1990), 26.

5. See, e.g., respectively J. Fossum and P. Munoa, *Jesus and the Gospels: An Introduction to Gospel Literature and Jesus Studies* (Belmont, CA: Wadsworth, 2004), 9–12; R. Guelich, "The Gospel Genre," in *The Gospel and the Gospels*, ed. Peter Stuhlmacher (Grand Rapids: Eerdmans, 1991), 173–208.

6. M. Smith, "Prolegomena to a Discussion of Aretalogies, Divine Men, the Gospels and Jesus," *JBL* 90 (1971): 176.

7. Smith, "Prolegomena to Aretalogies," 196. See also M. Hadas and M. Smith, *Heroes and Gods: Spiritual Biographies in Antiquity* (New York: Harper & Row, 1965); H. Koester, "One Jesus and Four Gospels," *HTR* 61 (1968): 230–36. Several scholars have modified this thesis and argued that Mark, the first Gospel, is actually a sort of "reverse aretalogy." That is, its purpose was to combat an earlier "divine man" interpretation of Jesus that had become popular within Christian circles. The classic statement of this view is T. Weeden, *Mark—Traditions in Conflict* (Philadelphia: Fortress, 1971). See also J. Z. Smith, "Good News Is No News: Aretalogy and Gospel," in *Christianity, Judaism and Other Greco-Roman Cults, Studies for Morton Smith at Sixty*, ed. J. Neusner (Leiden: Brill, 1975), 1:35.

This thesis obviously requires that we accept that the Gospel authors would have been open to being positively influenced by paganism in their search for a model by which to imagine and articulate the significance of Jesus. Thus, in the words of Morton Smith, we must accept that "it is plausible both to suppose that there was some radical difference between Christianity and the other forms of first-century Judaism" and we must "look for the source of this difference in the Graeco-Roman culture and the continuing Semitic paganism of first-century Palestine."[8]

A second form of ancient biography that some have argued is close to the genre of the Gospels is that of ancient writings "that call themselves 'lives' (Greek, *bioi*; Latin, *vitae*)," more commonly known today as "popular biographies."[9] According to Charles Talbert, the single, essential generic marker of the *bios* genre is that it "presents a highly selective, often anecdotal account of an individual's life with everything chosen to illuminate his essential being. An ancient biography consists of information about a significant person, selected so as to reveal what sort of person he really is."[10]

There is significant disagreement as to what this classification entails in terms of the historical reliability of the Gospels. Those on the more skeptical end of the continuum emphasize that the ancient Greco-Roman genre of *bios* was influenced by idealistic impressions of what a great man should be, was generally used for rhetorical and propaganda purposes, and was clearly biased in its one-sided praise of the particular subject. It has been argued that such factors "inevitably led to the inclusion of an indeterminate amount of fictional elements."[11] Thus, the categorization of the Gospels as ancient popular biographies does not rule out the legendary-Jesus perspective. Indeed, some would argue it supports it.

8. Smith, "Prolegomena to Aretalogies," 194.

9. C. H. Talbert, "Once Again: Gospel Genre," *Semeia* 43 (1988): 54. Previously, C. H. Votaw had defended this view in "The Gospels and Contemporary Biographies in the Greco-Roman World," *American Journal of Theology* 19 (1915): 45–73, 217–49; reprinted as *The Gospels and Contemporary Biographies in the Greco-Roman World* (Philadelphia: Fortress, 1970). The thesis had been routinely dismissed until Talbert resurrected and refined it in *What Is a Gospel? The Genre of the Canonical Gospels* (Philadelphia: Fortress, 1977).

10. Talbert, "Once Again," 56. Talbert notes that ancient "history" and "biography" can be differentiated as follows: "Whereas history focuses on the distinguished and significant acts of great men in the political and social spheres, biography is concerned with the essence of the individual" (ibid., 55). A number of scholars have accepted and refined the *bios* genre thesis in various ways. See, e.g., D. E. Aune, "Greco-Roman Biography," in *Greco-Roman Literature and the New Testament*, ed. D. E. Aune (Atlanta: Scholars Press, 1988), 107–26; R. A. Burridge, *What Are the Gospels? A Comparison with Graeco-Roman Biography*, 2nd ed. (New York: Cambridge University Press, 2004); D. Frickenschmidt, *Evangelium als Biographie: Die Vier Evangelien im Rahmen antiker Erzählkunst* (Tübingen: Franke, 1997); P. L. Shuler, *A Genre for the Gospels: The Biographical Character of Matthew* (Philadelphia: Fortress, 1982). While the focus in the field today is upon the Greco-Roman biography, others have suggested a specifically Jewish biographical connection. Klaus Baltzer, for example, argues that the Gospels represent an example of Jewish "ideal biography"; see *Die Biographie der Propheten* (Neukirchen-Vluyn: Neukirchener, 1975).

11. Aune, "Greco-Roman Biography," 110.

"Gospel" as History

A third genre some scholars have identified as reflective of the Gospels is ancient historiography.[12] By all accounts, the strongest parallels between the Gospels and ancient histories are found in the two-volume work, Luke-Acts.[13] Among other things, the form and nature of the two prefaces are arguably similar to what we find in ancient histories, as is Luke's interest in historical chronology and his manner of speech construction.[14]

While many in this camp understand this identification as enhancing the historical reliability of Luke-Acts, others argue that such a conclusion is unwarranted. Rather, they maintain that ancient historiography was itself highly unreliable. They are quick to note that there was widespread mistrust of historians in the ancient world. While Lucian (*How to Write History*, 39, 51) states that truth alone is what the historian aspires to, Seneca reveals that, at least in the minds of some ancients, "it was axiomatic that historians are liars."[15]

Some have argued that a critical investigation of ancient histories suggests that Seneca's skeptical stance is justified. Bernard Lewis, for example, has argued that the content of these histories was "invented" at least as often as it was "remembered."[16] So too, T. P. Wiseman has argued that ancient historians exagger-

---

12. For example, Francis Watson identifies the Gospels as "narrated history"; see *Text and Truth: Redefining Biblical Theology* (Grand Rapids: Eerdmans, 1997), 33. M. C. Moeser, has recently argued that Mark's wider "host genre" is that of "apocalyptic historical monograph"; see *The Anecdote in Mark, the Classical World and the Rabbis* (New York: Sheffield Academic Press, 2002), 249.

13. See, e.g., D. L. Balch, "Comments on the Genre and a Political Theme of Luke-Acts: A Preliminary Comparison of Two Hellenistic Historians," in *SBLSP 1989*, ed. D. J. Lull (Atlanta: Scholars Press, 1989), 343–61; idem, "The Genre of Luke-Acts: Individual Biography, Adventure Novel, or Political History?" *Southwestern Journal of Theology* 33 (1991): 5–19; idem, "*METABOLE POLITEION*: Jesus as Founder of the Church in Luke-Acts: Form and Function," in *Contextualizing Acts: Lukan Narrative and Greco-Roman Discourse*, ed. T. Penner and C. Vander Stichele (Atlanta: Scholars Press, 2003), 139–88; D. Marguerat, *The First Christian Historian: Writing the "Acts of the Apostles"* (New York: Cambridge University Press, 2002); T. Penner, *In Praise of Christian Origins: Stephen and the Hellenists in Lukan Apologetic Historiography* (New York: Clark, 2004); G. E. Sterling, "Luke-Acts and Apologetic Historiography," in *SBLSP 1989*, 326–42. In his book, *The New Testament in Its Literary Environment* (Philadelphia: Westminster, 1987), D. E. Aune treats the Gospels under the category of Greco-Roman biography (chap. 2), but then goes on to devote two chapters to Luke-Acts as an example of Greco-Roman "general history" (chaps. 3–4).

14. See E. Haenchen, *The Acts of the Apostles*, trans. B. Nobel and G. Shinn, with R. McL. Willon, 14th ed. (Oxford: Blackwell, 1971), 136–37; D. L. Jones, "Luke's Unique Interest in Historical Chronology," in *SBLSP 1989*, 378–87; W. J. McCoy and B. Witherington, "In the Shadow of Thucydides," in *History, Literature and Society in the Book of Acts*, ed. B. Witherington (New York: Cambridge University Press, 1996), 16n63, 24–32.

15. T. P. Wiseman, "Lying Historians: Seven Types of Mendacity," in *Lies and Fiction in the Ancient World*, ed. C. Gill and T. P. Wiseman (Austin: University of Texas Press, 1993), 122.

16. B. Lewis, *History Remembered, Recovered, Invented* (Princeton: Princeton University Press, 1975). See also E. Hobsbawm and T. Ranger, eds., *The Invention of Tradition* (New York: Cambridge University Press, 1983); A. I. Baumgarten, "Invented Traditions of the Maccabean Era," in *Geschichte—Tradition—Reflexion: Festschrift für Martin Hengel zum 70. Geburtstag*, ed. H. Cancik, H. Lichtenberger,

ated or minimized facts and included fictional tales in their narratives as suited their own purposes. In other words, he argues, ancient "history" is actually just another category of ancient "literature."[17] If this generally negative assessment of ancient histories is accepted, then classifying Luke or any other Gospel as ancient history does nothing, in and of itself, to enhance our estimation of its general reliability.

"Gospel" as Fiction

Fourth, and more recently, a number of scholars have argued that the Gospels are best understood in terms of ancient "fiction."[18] For example, in his book *Gospel Fictions*, the literary critic Randel Helms argues that the Gospels "are largely fictional accounts concerning a historical figure, Jesus of Nazareth, intended to create a life-enhancing understanding of his nature." In fact, he argues, they are "the supreme fictions of our culture."[19] Though some continue to use the term "fiction" loosely to stand for any literature they judge to be making false historical claims, a number of scholars who classify the Gospels as "fiction" generally hold that the Gospel authors were *intentionally* writing fiction and assumed their work would be read as such.

There is no consensus among scholars within this camp as to what exact *kind* of fiction the Gospels are intended to be. Candidates include "folktale,"[20] "story-

---

and P. Schäffer (Tübingen: Mohr Siebeck, 1996), 1:197–210. Lewis describes the aim of invented history as "to embellish—to correct or remove what is distasteful in the past, and to replace it with something more acceptable, more encouraging, and more conducive to the purpose in hand" (*History Remembered*, 56–57).

17. Wiseman is a champion of those who claim that ancient rhetoric so thoroughly infects Greco-Roman historiography as to render it little more than a subgenre of fictional literature. See *Clio's Cosmetics: Three Studies in Greco-Roman Literature* (Leicester: Leicester University Press, 1979). Another leading voice in this regard is that of the literary critic A. J. Woodman, *Rhetoric in Classical Historiography: Four Studies* (London: Croom Helm; Portland, OR: Areopagitica, 1988). P. G. Walsh traces the rhetorical degeneration of ancient historiography to the influence of Isocrates. See *Livy: His Historical Methods and Aims* (New York: Cambridge University Press, 1961), 23.

18. For example, F. Kermode, *The Genesis of Secrecy: On the Interpretation of Narrative* (Cambridge, MA: Harvard University Press, 1979); M. A. Tolbert, *Sowing the Gospel* (Minneapolis; Fortress, 1989). Kermode's identification of Mark as fiction comes as one instance of his more general literary-theoretical critique of historical writings as simply literary devices and rhetoric that are, in fact, "benign deceit" (p. 122).

19. R. Helms, *Gospel Fictions* (Amherst, NY: Prometheus, 1988), 10, 11. See also idem, "Fiction in the Gospels," in *Jesus in Myth and History*, ed. R. J. Hoffmann and G. A. Larue (Amherst, NY: Prometheus, 1986), 135–42. Helms argues that the primary method of fictionalizing in the Gospels involves writing seemingly historical accounts about Jesus that are actually fictions based upon various passages in the Old Testament. Robert Funk also seems to suggest that the Gospel writers are largely "writers of fiction." See "On Distinguishing Historical from Fictive Narrative," *Forum* 9 (1993): 191.

20. For example, D. Brewer, "The Gospels and the Laws of Folktale," *Folklore* 90 (1979): 39. Allen Dundes argues that calling the Gospels "folktales" is "misguided," since folktales are *by definition* fictional (p. 18). Dundes himself argues that the category of "folklore" best encompasses the biblical texts, pointing

telling,"[21] "myth,"[22] "legend,"[23] "historical novel,"[24] "fantasy,"[25] "comedy,"[26] and
even "joke."[27] But several recent proposals seem to have gained more attention
and thus warrant comment.

A proposal that has won the approval of some scholars is that the Gospels
(and Acts) are related to the ancient "ideal romance" novels.[28] Richard Pervo, for
example, has argued that "Matthew, Mark, Luke and John . . . can be understood

out (interestingly enough) that folklore does not preclude historical veracity; see *Holy Writ as Oral Lit: The Bible as Folklore* (New York: Rowman & Littlefield, 1999), 10–11.

21. The Jesus Seminar has explained the activity of the Gospel writers in terms of the universal phenomenon of "storytelling," emphasizing the "storyteller's license," which allowed them to "freely invent" Jesus tradition. See R. W. Funk, R. W. Hoover, and the Jesus Seminar, *The Five Gospels: What Did Jesus Really Say?* (San Francisco: HarperSanFrancisco, 1993), 29–30.

22. For example, B. L. Mack, *A Myth of Innocence: Mark and Christian Origins* (Philadelphia: Fortress, 1988); idem, *Who Wrote the New Testament? The Making of the Christian Myth* (San Francisco: HarperSanFrancisco, 1995); G. A. Wells, *The Jesus Myth* (Chicago: Open Court, 1999); Northrop Frye, *Words with Power: Being a Second Study of "The Bible and Literature"* (New York: Harcourt, Brace & Jovanovich, 1990), xxi, 139. A. B. Lord also characterizes the Gospels as a type of "myth," but he clearly states that, under his definition—myth as "sacred narrative"—it is wrong to say that myth is necessarily fiction as opposed to historical fact; see "The Gospels as Oral Traditional Literature," in *The Relationships among the Gospels: An Interdisciplinary Dialogue*, ed. W. O. Walker (San Antonio: Trinity University Press, 1978), 38.

23. R. M. Price, *The Incredible Shrinking Son of Man: How Reliable Is the Gospel Tradition?* (Amherst, NY: Prometheus, 2003), 21.

24. T. R. Wright, "Regenerating Narrative: The Gospels as Fiction," *Religious Studies* 20 (1984): 389–400.

25. G. Aichele, "The Fantastic in the Discourse of Jesus," *Semeia* 60 (1992): 53–66. Aichele argues that Mark's presentation of Jesus is, technically speaking, "fantastic" in nature. While Matthew and Luke serve to "de-fantasize" Mark's portrayal, John later "re-fantasizes" Jesus, though in a more subtle and sophisticated manner than Mark's original fantasy (pp. 63–64).

26. S. B. Hatton, "The Gospel of Mark as Comedy," *Downside Review* 120 (2002): 33–56; D. O. Via, *Kerygma and Comedy in the New Testament: A Structuralist Approach to Hermeneutics* (Philadelphia: Fortress, 1974). Via sees Mark as patterned after Hellenistic comedy, though his language actually shifts to tragi-comedy, given the centrality of the passion in Mark.

27. J. Z. Smith, "Good News Is No News," 38. Smith writes: "The 'gospel' as I have described it stands in the closest relation to the joke. . . . Given the religious situation which confronted the man of late antiquity . . . such frivolity is, in fact, transcendence" (p. 38).

28. At the center of the discussion are the five ancient Greek "ideal romance" novels that have survived: Achilles Tatius's *Clitophon and Leucippe*, Chariton's *Callirhoe*, Heliodorus's *An Ethiopian Tale*, Longus's *Daphne and Chloe*, and Xenophon's *An Ephesian Tale*. The "comic romances," such as Lucian's *Ass*, Apuleius's *Metamorphoses*, and Petronius's *Satyricon*, seem to garner less comparisons with the Gospels. On the ancient novels, see E. H. Haight, *Essays on Ancient Fiction*, reprint ed. (Freeport, NY: Books for Libraries, 1966); R. F. Hock, "The Greek Novel," in *Greco-Roman Literature and the New Testament*, 127–46; J. R. Morgan, "Make-believe and Make Believe: The Fictionality of the Greek Novels," in *Lies and Fiction in the Ancient World*, 175–229; J. R. Morgan and R. Stoneman, eds., *Greek Fiction: The Greek Novel in Context* (London: Routledge, 1994); N. Holzberg, *The Ancient Novel: An Introduction* (London: Routledge, 1995); G. Schmeling, ed., *The Novel in the Ancient World* (New York: Brill, 1996). While a number of scholars are exploring ways in which the ancient novel can shed light on Gospel studies (i.e., in terms of illuminating a common historical-cultural background, etc.), most have stopped short of claiming that the Gospels are *representative* of the novel genre. See R. F. Hock, J. B. Chance, and J. Perkins, eds., *Ancient Fiction and Early Christian Narrative* (Atlanta: Scholars Press, 1998); see also the thematic

as fictional biographies roughly analogous to the *Alexander-Romance*, the *Life of Aesop*, or Philostratus' account about Apollonius of Tyana."[29] In the eyes of some, the connection between the ancient Greek romance novels and the Gospels is made more plausible in light of one theory of the origin of the ancient novel that traces its genesis back to sacred religious texts—perhaps even to the mystery religions themselves.[30]

Another recent proposal that falls within the "fiction" camp and has generated some discussion comes from Dennis MacDonald, a member of the Jesus Seminar. He argues that Mark intentionally modeled his Gospel upon, and in the process directly borrowed from, Homer's *Odyssey* and *Iliad*. "Mark," he writes, "wrote a prose epic modeled largely after the *Odyssey* and the ending of the *Iliad*. . . . The earliest evangelist was not writing a historical biography, as many interpreters suppose, but a novel, a prose anti-epic of sorts."[31]

MacDonald concludes his study by suggesting that, in light of Mark's creation of "theological fiction," the "'Gospel truth' is not a deposit of historically reliable data concerning Jesus but a process of generating more humane, ethical, beauti-

---

issue devoted to this topic in *Perspectives in Religious Studies* 29 (2002). Most of the essays in these two works would fall within this category.

29. R. Pervo, "The Ancient Novel Becomes Christian," in *The Novel in the Ancient World*, 689. Pervo's thesis was first developed as an exploration of the genre of Acts in "The Literary Genre of the Acts of the Apostles" (ThD diss., Harvard Divinity School, 1979). It was later revised and published as *Profit with Delight: The Literary Genre of the Acts of the Apostles* (Philadelphia: Fortress, 1987). See also S. P. and M. J. Schierling, "The Influence of the Ancient Romances on Acts of the Apostles," *Classical Bulletin* 54 (1978): 81–88.

30. This theory was originally put forward by K. Kerenyi in 1927 and was developed by R. Merkelbach beginning in the 1960s. On the Kerenyi-Merkelbach thesis, see G. Anderson, "Myth and Mystery," in *Ancient Fiction: The Novel in the Graeco-Roman World* (Totowa, NJ: Barnes & Noble, 1984), 75–87; R. Beck, "Mystery Religions, Aretalogy and the Ancient Novel," in *The Novel in the Ancient World*, 131–50; C. Ruiz-Montero, "The Rise of the Greek Novel," in *The Novel in the Ancient World*, esp. 76–80.

31. D. R. MacDonald, *The Homeric Epics and the Gospel of Mark* (New Haven: Yale University Press, 2000), 3, 7. MacDonald argues that Mark is an example of a "transvaluative hypertext" in relation to Homer—i.e., a text that both plays off another text (the "hypotext"), and yet seeks to substitute its values for those of the original text. He proposed the Homeric interpretation of Mark to the Jesus Seminar in two unpublished papers presented at the October 1992 and March 1993 meetings of the Seminar. In the second paper, in which he argues that Mark's episode of Jesus walking on the water (Mark 6:45–52) is taken directly from Homer, MacDonald states: "I have removed oral tradition entirely from my model insofar as I suspect that no one had heard of Jesus walking on the water until Mark wrote this story" ("Tracking Jesus the Hydrapatetic," 2). See also MacDonald, "Secrecy and Recognition in the *Odyssey* and Mark: Where Wrede Went Wrong," in *Ancient Fiction and Early Christian Narrative*, 139–53. MacDonald has gone on to broaden his application of the Homeric paradigm, arguing that the author of Luke-Acts included stories meant to be read as "fictions crafted as alternatives to those of Homer and Vergil" ("Paul's Farewell to the Ephesian Elders and Hector's Farewell to Andromache: A Strategic Imitation of Homer's *Iliad*," in *Contextualizing Acts: Lukan Narrative and Greco-Roman Discourse*, ed. Todd Penner and Caroline Vander Stichele [Atlanta: Scholars Press, 2003], 203). See esp. MacDonald, *Does the New Testament Imitate Homer? Four Case Studies from the Acts of the Apostles* (New Haven: Yale University Press, 2003). For a similar approach, one arguing that Luke-Acts is modeled not on Homer but rather on Virgil's *Aeneid*, see M. P. Bonz, *The Past as Legacy: Luke-Acts and Ancient Epic* (Minneapolis: Fortress, 2000).

ful, and inspiring myths."[32] Of course, as MacDonald notes, the Homeric thesis forces the conclusion that "the primary cultural context of the Gospel of Mark [is located] in Greek religious tradition, not in Judaism."[33]

By contrast, Michael Vines has recently argued that it is the ancient *Jewish novel* that best sheds light on the genre of Mark.[34] But whether Greco-Roman or Jewish, once the Gospels are cast as fictional novels of any type, their portrait of Jesus is poised to be judged as largely, if not totally, lacking a basis in history.

"Gospel" as Midrash/Pesher

A fifth genre proposal is closely related to the Gospels-as-fiction proposal, yet distinct enough to be considered in its own right. Some have argued that the Gospels are best understood as examples of Jewish midrash. In brief, midrash is an ancient Jewish form of scriptural commentary that enabled ancient Scriptures to speak to contemporary situations.

Scholars have identified two broad types of midrashic exegesis: overt/explicit and covert/implicit. Overt/explicit midrash begins with an explicit citation of the Old Testament text to be interpreted (the lemma) followed by the commentary on that passage (the midrash). Covert/implicit midrash is much more subtle. Often, it reframes a portion of the Old Testament in a contemporary setting. As Craig Evans notes, "The very manner in which the biblical narrative is retold in these writings brings to light new insights and new teachings. Its purpose is, in effect, to update Scripture."[35]

Virtually all New Testament scholars recognize that the authors of the Gospels made use of covert/implicit midrashic techniques to varying degrees and in various ways. But defenders of the Gospels-as-midrash thesis go far beyond this and claim that the Gospels themselves are to be understood wholesale as examples of covert/implicit midrash.[36] From this perspective, most, if not all, aspects of

---

32. MacDonald, *Homeric Epics*, 190.

33. Ibid., 189. In a similar vein, R. D. Kotansky argues that Mark reflects Greco-Roman myth, particularly the myth of Heracles. See his "Jesus and Heracles in Cadiz (*ta Gadeira*): Death, Myth and Monsters at the 'Straits of Gibraltar' (Mark 4:5–5:43)," in *Ancient and Modern Perspectives on the Bible and Culture: Essays in Honor of Hans Dieter Betz*, ed. A. Yarbro Collins (Atlanta: Scholars Press, 1998), 160–229.

34. M. E. Vines, *The Problem of Markan Genre: The Gospel of Mark and the Jewish Novel* (Atlanta: Society of Biblical Literature, 2002). Vines has in mind such "Jewish novels" as Esther, Susanna, and Daniel 1–6. He uses Bakhtin's genre theory and the idea of the "chronotype" to make his case. Alternatively, C. M. Thomas, in the published reworking of her Harvard dissertation, recently has argued that the Gospels are closer in form to ancient historical and "nationalistic" novels (e.g., those of Alexander, Nektanebos, Ninos, and Jewish novellas such as Joseph and Aseneth). See *The Acts of Peter, Gospel Literature and the Ancient Novel* (New York: Oxford University Press, 2003).

35. C. A. Evans, "Midrash," in *Dictionary of Jesus and the Gospels*, ed. J. B. Green, S. McKnight, and I. H. Marshall (Downers Grove, IL: InterVarsity, 1992), 546.

36. See, e.g., J. Drury, "Midrash and Gospel," *Theology* 77 (1974): 291–96; M. D. Goulder, *Midrash and Lection in Matthew* (London: SPCK, 1974). J. D. M. Derrett states that Mark is a "gigantic midrash"; see *The Making of Mark: The Scriptural Bases of the Earliest Gospel* (Shipston-on-Stour: Drinkwater,

the Gospel portrait of Jesus are actually ways of bringing to life Old Testament stories and teachings.

Obviously, this thesis seriously undermines any claim that the Gospels provide historically reliable information about Jesus. Earl Doherty, for example, argues that Mark's portrait of Jesus is—*in its entirety*—a fictional construction out of the Jewish Scriptures.[37] In his view, we cannot even conclude that a first-century Jesus ever existed.

Another exponent of the Gospels-as-midrash thesis is the Australian scholar Barbara Thiering. According to Thiering, the Gospel writers made use of a method of encoded biblical interpretation known from the Dead Sea Scrolls as "pesher" (literally the Hebrew term for "interpetation"). As a method of interpreting the Old Testament, pesher is quite similar to midrash (hence our classifying it under the Gospel-as-midrash category).[38] Thiering argues that the Gospels are actually pesharim from Qumran. As such, they primarily seek to disclose to the skilled reader the history of the Qumran community.[39] When Thiering unravels this code for the reader, some interesting things emerge concerning Jesus.[40]

Among other things, Thiering claims the properly decoded pesher-Gospels reveal that Jesus was not crucified in Jerusalem, but at Qumran. He did not die on the cross but was drugged and later regained consciousness with the help of Judas Iscariot's medical knowledge. He was later married to Mary Magdalene, fathered three children, divorced her, and married another woman. Thus, according to Thiering's reading, the Gospels represent at one and the same time a fictionalization of Jesus (the surface meaning) and a supposedly historically accurate record of Jesus in pesher code.

Is the Concept of Genre Still Applicable?

Before turning to an analysis of these proposals, a preliminary word is in order. In our twenty-first-century, postmodern context, it is no longer taken for granted that the concept of "genre" can even function in a meaningful sense. A number of literary scholars today, most notably literary deconstructionists, have argued that the very attempt to fit literature into genre-types is misguided. It is, they argue, an

---

1985), 1:38; similarly D. Miller, *The Gospel of Mark as Midrash on Earlier Jewish and NT Literature* (Lewiston: Mellen, 1990).

37. E. Doherty, "The Gospels as Midrash and Symbolism," in *The Jesus Puzzle: Did Christianity Begin with a Mythical Christ?* (Ottawa: Canadian Humanist Publications, 1999), esp. 225–39.

38. For the distinctives of pesher, see T. H. Lim, *Pesharim* (New York: Sheffield Academic Press, 2002).

39. B. Thiering develops this theory in several works, including *Redating the Teacher of Righteousness* (Sydney: Theological Explorations, 1979); idem, *The Gospels and Qumran: A New Hypothesis* (Sydney: Theological Explorations, 1981); idem, *The Qumran Origins of the Christian Church* (Sydney: Theological Explorations, 1983).

40. B. Thiering, *Jesus and the Riddle of the Dead Sea Scrolls: Unlocking the Secrets of His Life Story* (San Francisco: HarperSanFrancisco, 1992).

artificial construct imposed on literature that always says more about the person or group doing the classifying than it does the literature being classified.[41]

While a full-fledged defense of the category of genre lies outside the scope of this present work, we should at least register our agreement with the vast majority of New Testament scholars in holding that the concept of genre is still necessary and valuable to literary studies.[42] At the same time, the very fact that so many specialists disagree on the genre of the Gospels is enough to indicate a significant element of truth in the postmodern suspicion of this category. At the very least, this lack of scholarly consensus should serve as a reminder that the genre categories within which we try to understand the Gospels reflect *our* attempts to understand and recover ancient literary sensibilities. Hence, humility dictates that we allow for a good bit of complexity and subtlety as we attempt to categorize the Gospels and other ancient texts.[43]

In keeping with this, we will argue that while important aspects of the Gospels appear to be sui generis in nature, other aspects fit quite well with the ancient biographical genre, other aspects (especially in Luke-Acts) with ancient historiography, and still others with ancient midrash. The one proposal that finds no support, we argue, is viewing the Gospels as examples of intentionally crafted ancient fiction. We shall argue that the manner in which the Gospels incorporate elements from these four distinct genres is more easily understood once we fully appreciate the oral register of the Gospels. Most importantly for our purposes, we shall argue that the sui generis, biographical, historical, and even midrashic aspects of the Gospels tend to *support* rather than *undermine* the historical intentionality of the Gospel authors, especially when their works are viewed as oral recitations, and against the background of what we have already learned about oral traditions

41. E.g., Jacques Derrida suggests that since genres are always-already hybrid in nature—and thus are not "pure"—they cannot truly be classified; see "The Law of Genre," *Glyph* 7 (1980): 207–9.

42. With E. D. Hirsch (*Validity in Interpretation* [New Haven: Yale University Press, 1967]) and Jonathan Culler (*Structuralist Poetics: Structuralism, Linguistics, and the Study of Literature* [Ithaca, NY: Cornell University Press, 1975]) we would appeal to the idea of genre as a system (or sets) of expectations, the sort of mutual expectations that form what Heather Dubrow has described as a "generic contract" between the author and reader (*Genre* [New York: Methuen, 1982]). Ever since David Hellholm's 1982 essay, the field of genre criticism in biblical studies has had a shared baseline from which to discuss the matter. While scholars may move beyond it, Hellholm's tripartite division of genre into *content* (the propositional aspect), *form* (the utterance aspect; i.e., oral or written, etc.), and *function* (the "illocutionary/perlocutionary" aspect) has provided a shared conceptual model for many in the field. See Hellholm, "The Problem of Apocalyptic Genre and the Apocalypse of John," in *SBLSP 1982*, ed. K. H. Richards (Chico, CA: Scholars Press, 1982), 160. For a solid defense of the concept of genre and its use in biblical studies, see G. R. Osborne, "Genre Criticism—Sensus Literalis," in *Hermeneutics, Inerrancy and the Bible*, ed. E. D. Radmacher and R. D. Preus (Grand Rapids: Academie, 1984), 165–89. For a helpful introduction to the practice of New Testament genre criticism, see J. L. Bailey, "Genre Analysis," in *Hearing the New Testament: Strategies for Interpretation*, ed. J. B. Green (Grand Rapids: Eerdmans, 1995), 197–221.

43. For a recent statement on the complexity and subtlety required when exploring the Gospel genre, see R. Hurley, "Le genre 'evangile' en fonction des effets produits par la mise en intrigue de Jesus," *Laval Theologique et Philosophique*, 58 (2002): 243–57.

in orally dominant cultures. Having said this, we turn now to critically assess the merits of each proposal.

Are the Gospels Sui Generis?

There are two points we wish to make in response to the view that the Gospels are sui generis in nature. First, if David Hellholm is correct that genre involves aspects of content, form, and function—and we believe that he is—then it seems undeniable that there is a sui generis dimension to the Gospel genre. At the very least, it is hard to deny that the specific *content* of the Gospels is, in an important sense, unique. In the words of David Aune, "The unique character of the Gospels lies primarily in the uniqueness of their content, determined by their subject: Jesus of Nazareth. . . . No Greco-Roman biography depicts a life even remotely comparable to that of Jesus."[44] While there are significant literary parallels to the Gospels in terms of their form and function (see below), there is no clear parallel to this unique content, for (as we have argued in chap. 3) there is no real parallel to this historical person.

Not only this, but the very fact that the authors identify their work as "gospel" sets them apart. The term is tied to the Old Testament's Isaianic promise of "good news" (Isa. 40:9; 52:7; 61:1), which Mark associates with Jesus Christ at the beginning of his work (Mark 1:1–3). This means that the Gospels are fundamentally rooted in a Jewish worldview and are self-consciously working within a promise/fulfillment schema that serves to explicate God's salvation-historical dealings with humanity through his Messiah, Jesus Christ.[45] There is no known parallel to this in the ancient world, and inasmuch as the analysis of the Gospels as sui generis highlights this fact, it is, we believe, to be embraced.

But accepting that the Gospels are to this extent sui generis does not in any way suggest that they are not historically trustworthy, and this is our second point.[46] As noted earlier, those who assume that the sui generis analysis entails a skeptical view of the Gospels do so only because of assumptions they hold about the oral

---

44. Aune, "Greco-Roman Biography," 122; see also idem, "The Gospels: Biography or Theology?" *Bible Review* 6 (February 1990): 18.

45. Points also emphasized by E. E. Ellis, *The Making of the New Testament Documents* (Boston: Brill, 1999), 5–6; Guelich, "Gospel Genre," 195–98; T. Thatcher, "The Gospel Genre: What Are We After?" *Restoration Quarterly* 36 (1994): 137–38. J. D. Crossan appears to view the term "gospel" as reflecting a broad generic sense of "news" understood as "good" from a particular perspective; see *The Birth of Christianity* (San Francisco: HarperSanFrancisco, 1998), 21, 101. One certainly can hold that the term "gospel" signals the delivery of "news" to those previously unaware of the message (e.g., J. P. Dickson, "Gospel as News: *euaggel-* from Aristophanes to the Apostle Paul," *NTS* 51 [2005]: 212–30) without thereby disconnecting it from its explicitly Isaianic context and content. See N. T. Wright, "A New Birth? An Article Review of John Dominic Crossan's *The Birth of Christianity*," *SJT* 53 (2000): 75–76.

46. Hence, even some staunchly conservative scholars accept that the Gospels are sui generis. For example, Ellis, *Making of the New Testament*, 5; Guelich, "Gospel Genre," 202.

tradition behind the Gospels. With Bultmann and most early form critics, they assume that the oral Jesus tradition lacked any historical or biographical interest, was incapable of passing on extended narratives, and lacked any eyewitness influence. But in our prior consideration of this oral tradition, we have shown these assumptions to be without foundation (chaps. 6–7).

Once these assumptions are abandoned, there is no reason to conclude that the unique content of the Gospels undermines their historical reliability. To the contrary, on the basis of our analysis of the oral Jesus tradition, we would argue that we have good reasons to conclude that their unique content is solidly rooted in history. We will further explore this claim later in this chapter when we reconsider the Gospels in their original orally oriented context.

The Gospels and Ancient Biography

We turn now to consider whether the Gospels are ancient biographies. We will consider first the view that they are aretalogies and then the view that they are examples of Greco-Roman *bios*.

The Gospels as Aretalogies

While the proposal to view the Gospels as aretalogies enjoyed significant popularity in the 1960s, it finds very few defenders today, and for good reason. Foremost among its problems is that even defenders of the proposal concede there is very little evidence that the category of "aretalogy" ever formed a distinct genre of literature in the first century.[47] In fact, Morton Smith, one of the proposal's most ardent defenders, compares the evidence out of which he constructs the genre of aretalogy to "the practice of reconstructing a lion from a single claw."[48]

While there were certainly miracle workers in the ancient world and texts written about them, it has been argued that the claim of a specific "aretalogical" genre is little more than a modern scholarly construction by which to interpret the Jesus of the Gospels against the background of the supposed pagan, miracle-working "divine man."[49] In any case, it must at the very least be conceded that if

47. On the problems associated with the claim of a distinct aretalogical genre comparable to the Gospels, see D. L. Tiede, *The Charismatic Figure as Miracle Worker* (Missoula, MT: Scholars Press, 1972), 1–13; H. C. Kee, "Aretalogy and Gospel" *JBL* 92 (1973): 402–22; idem, "Synoptic Studies," in *The New Testament and Its Modern Interpreters*, ed. E. J. Epp and G. W. MacRae (Philadelphia: Fortress, 1989), 253–54; J. P. Meier, *A Marginal Jew*, vol. 2: *Mentor, Message, and Miracle* (New York: Doubleday, 1994), 595–601.

48. M. Smith, "Prolegomena to Aretalogies," 174.

49. This negative assessment regarding a first-century genre of aretalogy, coupled with our assessment of the *theios aner*/divine man concept in reference to Jesus (see chap. 3), leads us to conclude that no real evidence exists that a significant faction of the early church interpreted Jesus in the category of a Greco-Roman "divine man," and thus there is no reason to see Mark—or any of the Gospels—as an anti-, or "reverse," aretalogy. This theory requires us to see Mark as critical of Jesus's miracles, which is

we cannot be confident of a distinct aretalogical genre, we can hardly be confident about the proposal that the Gospels were modeled after it.

But even if for the sake of argument we grant that there is a discernible aretalogical genre the Gospels can be compared to, the proposal is still encumbered with serious difficulties. For one thing, the proposed examples of aretalogies simply do not provide any clear parallels to the Gospel genre. True, both genres involve a person performing supernatural feats, but after this the differences speak far more loudly than the similarities.

For example, unlike the proposed aretalogies, the Gospels display an explicit concern for "historical developments."[50] Additionally, aretalogical tales associate the miracles of a hero with his virtue (*arête* in Greek means "virtue"/"strength"), while the miracles of Jesus never serve this function. Rather, they are inextricably bound up with a Jewish apocalyptic eschatology, demonstrating the in-breaking of the kingdom of God to a world previously dominated by Satan.[51] Therefore, there is no reason to look beyond the confines of the first-century Jewish world as a context within which to make sense of Jesus's miracles as presented in the Gospels.[52]

Along with this, there is no reason to think that the first-century Palestinian world was influenced in a positive direction by Greco-Roman "divine man" concepts, as we have argued in chapter 2. The historical constraints of first-century Jewish monotheism simply cannot be underestimated here.[53] If anything, the presence of supposed "divine men" in the pagan world would have tended to foster more, not less, commitment to

simply not the case. Both Jesus and the disciples are presented as involved with healings and exorcisms, and in nothing like a negative light. The Q tradition views exorcisms as evidence of the kingdom's presence in Jesus's ministry (Q/Luke 11:20), and, as Kee notes, Mark and Q are in agreement here ("Synoptic Studies," 254).

50. A. Cook, *History/Writing: The Theory and Practice of History in Antiquity and Modern Times* (New York: Cambridge University Press, 1988), 159.

51. As argued by Kee, "Aretalogy and Gospel," 417–19; A. Pilgaard, "The Hellenistic *Theios Aner*—A Model for Early Christian Christology?" in *The New Testament and Hellenistic Judaism*, ed. P. Borgen and S. Giversen (Aarhus, Denmark: Aarhus University Press, 1995), 22–28.

52. See C. Brown, "Synoptic Miracle Stories: A Jewish Religious and Social Setting," *Forum* 2 (1986): 55–75; E. Eve, *The Jewish Context of Jesus' Miracles* (Sheffield: Sheffield Academic Press, 2002); Meier, *Marginal Jew*, 2:970; G. H. Twelftree, *Jesus the Miracle Worker: A Historical and Theological Study* (Downers Grove, IL: InterVarsity, 1999), 258–77; idem, "The Miracles of Jesus: Marginal or Mainstream?" *JSHJ* 1 (2003): 104–24. Here, Wendy Cotter's argument, that we must presume a broad Greco-Roman worldview (whatever that is) as background to Jesus's miracles rather than a Jewish apocalyptic conceptual context, is simply unsustainable; see "Cosmology and the Jesus Miracles," in *Whose Historical Jesus?* ed. W. E. Arnal and M. Desjardins (Waterloo, ON: Wilfrid Laurier University Press, 1997), 118–31. Her understanding of the nature of worldviews and their expression in generic forms is fundamentally flawed (e.g., p. 130). N. T. Wright's more nuanced and sophisticated approach would serve as a corrective; see *The New Testament and the People of God* (Minneapolis: Fortress, 1992), part 2, esp. 47–80.

53. With regard to the Jewish concept of "Son of God," see, e.g., A. E. Harvey, "Son of God: The Constraint of Monotheism," in *Jesus and the Constraints of History* (Philadelphia: Westminster, 1982), 154–73; J. K. Hoffmeier, "Son of God: From Pharaoh to Israel's Kings to Jesus," *Bible Review* 13 (June 1997): 44–49, 54; and esp. M. Hengel, *The Son of God: The Origin of Christology and the History of Jewish-Hellenistic Religion*, trans. J. Bowden (Philadelphia: Fortress, 1976).

creational monotheism among first-century Jews. On top of all this, no aretalogical tale depicts the hero as being martyred.[54] For good reason, therefore, this proposal has been abandoned by the vast majority of contemporary scholars.

The Gospels and the Greco-Roman Bios

In contrast to the Gospels-as-aretalogy thesis, the literary parallels between the Gospels and Greco-Roman *bios* are quite impressive, as the work of Talbert, Shuler, Burridge, Aune, Frickenschmidt, and others has shown. The question is: are these parallels sufficient to warrant classifying the Gospels as examples of this genre, *pure and simple*, or do they suggest something beyond this?

The problem with the proposal is that, for all the ways in which the Gospels parallel Greco-Roman *bios*, everyone concedes they have elements that are not typical of this genre. Hence, those scholars who argue that the Gospels should fall into this generic classification have to stretch the definition of the genre to the point that, it could be argued, its distinctiveness as a genre is threatened.[55] Others argue that the Gospels should be understood as a unique subtype of Greco-Roman *bios*, while still others contend that the Gospels should be understood as a sort of "mixed" genre, one that contains significant influence from and/or parallels to Greco-Roman *bios* but cannot be properly located exclusively within this genre.[56]

Our own sense is that the most fruitful approach is this latter one. While the Gospels clearly share some of the formal and functional features of Greco-Roman *bios*, and thus can be profitably compared with that genre at certain points, they also contain aspects of ancient historiography, as well as some unique features that derive from their apocalyptic Jewish-Christian matrix and the nature of the oral tradition that gave birth to them.

In our estimation, the classicist Albrecht Dihle captures the situation quite accurately. In his widely regarded study of the Gospels and Greek biography, he

---

54. Meier, *Marginal Jew*, 2:600; Kee, "Synoptic Studies," 253–54. Meier summarizes the evidence well: "Hence, in the period prior to or during Jesus's lifetime, there is no basis for equating an aretalogy with a biography of a *theios aner*, marked by miracle-working" (*Marginal Jew*, 2:600).

55. For example, Talbert has provided a laundry list of elements that are "accidental" to the genre, and only a single characteristic that is "essential" ("Once Again," esp. 55–60).

56. Among those who conclude for the former are Aune, *New Testament in Its Literary Environment*, 46; idem, "The Gospels: Biography or Theology?" 14; L. W. Hurtado, *Lord Jesus Christ: Devotion to Jesus in Earliest Christianity* (Grand Rapids: Eerdmans, 2003), 282; W. S. Vorster, "Gospel Genre," in *Anchor Bible Dictionary*, ed. D. N. Freedman (New York: Doubleday, 1992), 2:1079. Those who conclude for the latter perspective include Guelich, "Gospel Genre"; J. P. Meier, "Matthew, Gospel of," in *Anchor Bible Dictionary*, 4:623; P. Stuhlmacher, "The Genre(s) of the Gospels: Response to P. L. Shuler," in *The Interrelations of the Gospels*, ed. D. L. Dungan (Leuven: Peeters, 1990), 489; Thatcher, "Gospel Genre," 130–34. That the line separating these two views is quite thin is evident in the fact that adherents of either view are often found making qualifying statements that sound as if they are members of the other camp. The differences are largely matters of emphasis and nuance. In this light, one can appreciate the conclusion of D. A. Carson, D. J. Moo, and L. Morris: "The question as to whether the Gospels are biographies or are unique is little more than a question of semantics" (*An Introduction to the New Testament* [Grand Rapids: Zondervan, 1992], 47).

concludes, "There is nothing against reading, and hence against describing, the Gospels as biographies, provided one misunderstanding is excluded: by doing so one has not said anything about their peculiar genre in the strict sense of the word."[57] Supporting this conclusion, Dihle reminds us that the Greco-Roman world contained non-*bios* texts that nonetheless possessed "biographical" content.[58] He also reminds us that the examples of Greco-Roman *bios* that we possess tend to presuppose an inherent anthropological-ethical theory, one in which human nature is not affected by the surrounding forces of history.[59] This assumption, however, is "worlds apart from the premises of the gospel literature."[60] Additionally, Dihle argues that the Gospel genre—whatever else it is—is intimately involved with historiographical interests (especially as evidenced in Luke).[61]

For all these reasons, we agree with Dihle that the Gospels are best understood as literature that *includes* biographical features but cannot be reduced, pure and simple, to the genre of Greco-Roman *bios*. Charles Fornara makes a related point: "The influence of *biography* (i.e., the genre) is best kept separate from the frequent expression of 'biographical interest' in historiography generally. Natural interest of this type, transcending genre, is found in a wide variety of historical works of the Greco-Roman world."[62]

For our purposes, the central issue is how this assessment positively and/or negatively affects our understanding of the historical intentionality of the Gospel authors. As we have seen, skeptical scholars want to argue that the tendentious, propagandistic, even fictional nature of *bios* renders its content historically suspect. If this is true, the recognition of a significant parallel between the Gospels and Greco-Roman *bios* does not help—if anything, it undermines—our confidence in the veracity of the Gospels' portrait of Jesus. Three things can be said in response to this.

Greco-Roman Bios *and Ancient Historiography*

No doubt Thomas Carlyle overstated the case when he said that "biography is the only true history."[63] But it is also possible to contrast these two genres in a way that leads to a false disjunct. It can be argued that, in their search for a definable

57. A. Dihle, "The Gospels and Greek Biography," in *The Gospel and the Gospels*, 361.

58. Ibid., 362, 373. This sort of observation has led some to question whether there really was a commonly recognized *bios* genre in the Greco-Roman world. Fossum and Munoa, for example, argue that "a *bios/vitae* was not defined as a genre by the ancients and stands as a category delineated only by contemporary scholars" (*Jesus and the Gospels*, 12). See also Dihle, "Gospels and Greek Biography," 373–74.

59. Dihle, "Gospels and Greek Biography," 369–71. C. W. Fornara reminds us that ancient biography "cannot be understood except with reference to its origin in ethical preoccupations" (*The Nature of History in Ancient Greece and Rome* [Berkeley: University of California Press, 1983], 184–85). Thatcher argues that ancient writers themselves tended to see a stronger connection between history and *bios* than do many scholars today; "Gospel Genre," 132–33.

60. Dihle, "Gospels and Greek Biography," 382.

61. Ibid., 379–81, 385–86.

62. Fornara, *Nature of History*, 185.

63. Cited in D. Henige, *Oral Historiography* (New York: Longman, 1982), 106.

genre for the Gospels, some scholars have contrasted the ancient genres of *bios* and history to an unfortunate degree.[64] Instead, the ancient sources themselves suggest that the distinction between these two genres was often quite vague, at least with regard to form and function.[65] The one area where the distinction seems to have been clear concerns their respective content.

As Plutarch notes, biography, unlike history, is typically less concerned with great public deeds and more concerned with the subject's character, a character that is often best elucidated in the more trivial events of life.[66] Even here, however, the distinction is far from absolute. For as Lucian reveals, ancient historians were turning out works that would be difficult to distinguish from Plutarch's definition of biography.[67] And, as Tom Thatcher notes, the distinction between great and trivial events was often relative to the eye of the beholder.[68]

In this light, it seems that while we can generally *distinguish between* history and *bios*, we are not warranted in *contrasting* these two genres too sharply in terms of their historical intentionality. As David Aune notes, Greco-Roman biography was "intrinsically concerned with *history*."[69] However effective or ineffective any historical or biographical author may have been in achieving it, it seems that authors in *both* genres were to a significant degree concerned to report the past *as it actually took place*. And it seems that their audience read these works with this expectation.

Why a Bios-*like Genre?*

Second, we need to explore why early Christians might have appropriated a genre with *bios*-like aspects. In our estimation, Talbert offers some helpful insights on this question. He argues that "biographical narration was employed because it provided a controlling context not only for individual traditions but also for various types of traditions. In doing so, it served to protect both against the subversion of the gospel and against reductionism."[70]

By "subversion" Talbert means "an interpretation of the Jesus tradition that altered what mainstream Christians regarded as their true meaning," and by "reductionism" Talbert refers to "an interpretation of the Jesus tradition that absolutizes a part of the gospel and treats it as though it were the whole."[71] In other

---

64. For example, Talbert, "Once Again," 55–56.

65. As Thatcher has demonstrated from the works of Plutarch, Polybius, and Livy ("Gospel Genre," 132–35).

66. Plutarch, "Alexander and Caesar," 1. See P. Cox, *Biography in Late Antiquity* (Berkeley: University of California Press, 1993), 12. Fornara puts it simply: "History portrays the deeds of a man (or men). Lives delineate character" (*Nature of History*, 185).

67. Lucian, *How to Write History*, 7–9.

68. Thatcher, "Gospel Genre," 134.

69. Aune, *New Testament in Its Literary Environment*, 64 (emphasis in text).

70. Talbert, "Once Again," 62.

71. Ibid., 62, 64.

words, a *bios*-like genre was chosen to prevent distortions of the Gospel that had been orally passed down for decades. Among other things, this means that it was chosen *to preserve the accuracy of the tradition*.

Talbert's thesis takes on more plausibility and significance when we understand it in the light of our previous reflections on the oral Jesus tradition. Contra scholars such as Kelber and Funk, neither Mark nor the other three Gospel authors were creating a new "domesticating" genre. Rather, they were embarking on the written textualization or "literaturization" of a narrative oral gospel tradition that was already in place.[72] Their concern to prevent the "subversion" and "reduction" of this narrative reflects a desire to conserve the essence of the traditional context in which the oral text had always been transmitted, whether implicitly or explicitly. It is difficult to see how they could have done this without producing a *bios*-like type of literature.

Bios, *Bias, and Historical Intent*

Third, it cannot be denied that ancient biographies often contain bias, propaganda, exaggeration, error, and outright fabrication. Hence, it cannot be denied that acknowledging the historical intentionality of the *bios* genre and the *bios*-like quality of the Gospels does not in and of itself argue for the historical reliability of the Gospels. At the same time, no one would want to argue that *modern* biographers are altogether free from bias, propaganda, exaggeration, error, and sometimes even outright fabrication. As Stephen Oates notes with regard to contemporary biographies, "The process of selection, of deciding which details and quotations should be used and which should be discarded, depends upon the biographer's interpretation of character and career, his sense of significance, and his intentions and insights."[73]

It is undeniable that biographical writing, like historiography, always involves an irreducibly subjective element. Yet, we know of no one who is suggesting we throw out all contemporary biography as a historical source on generic grounds alone. And if we are not willing to do so with contemporary biographical writings, it seems unwarranted to do so with ancient biographical writings.

The fact that ancient Greco-Roman biographical works sometimes contain exaggerations, biases, and even fabrications does not mean that the authors did not *intend* to communicate factual history, or that readers of ancient biographies did not understand them to communicate factual history. Authors at times may have carried out this commitment poorly, but the fact that their choice of genre committed them to this *goal* already places important constraints on how freely they could comfortably treat their material. For these reasons, we believe David Aune is correct in concluding that the Gospels' connections with the *bios* genre suggests that the Gospels' authors "wrote with historical intentions."[74] The extent to which

---

72. Here we are borrowing Aune's term (*New Testament in Its Literary Environment*, 65–66).

73. S. B. Oates, *Biography as History* (Waco: Markham, 1991), 11.

74. Aune, *New Testament in Its Literary Environment*, 64.

they were effective at achieving this goal must be decided on other grounds, but the fact that they had these intentions is important in and of itself, for it means, at the very least, that we must take their historical claims seriously.

The Gospels and Greco-Roman Historiography

As we noted above, a number of scholars have argued that the Gospels (especially Luke-Acts) are best understood as examples of Greco-Roman history.[75] As with the *bios* genre, we shall argue that, while there are strong parallels between the Gospels—especially Luke—and Greco-Roman history, this ancient genre does not fully capture the Gospel genre.

The Case for Classifying the Gospels as Greco-Roman Histories

Again, the case for classifying the Gospels as some form of Greco-Roman history is made primarily on the basis of Luke-Acts. There are two main lines of argumentation used to support this contention.

First, the form and nature of Luke's two prefaces, his interest in historical chronology, and his speech construction fit well within the Greco-Roman historiographical genre.[76] Second, some argue that "Luke and Acts *must* be treated as affiliated with one genre."[77] Since Acts is clearly an example of Greco-Roman history, it is argued, the Gospel of Luke must be considered the same. David Aune speaks for a number of scholars when he concludes: "Luke does not belong to a type of ancient biography for it belongs with Acts, and Acts cannot be forced into a biographical mold."[78]

Not everyone is persuaded by these arguments. For example, while the Gospel of Luke certainly reveals that the author is deeply interested in historical matters (i.e., no other Gospel writer goes to the lengths Luke does to explicitly correlate

75. For a helpful annotated bibliography on Luke-Acts and ancient history, see J. B. Green and M. C. McKeever, *Luke-Acts and New Testament Historiography* (Grand Rapids: Baker Academic, 1994). There are a number of subcategories within this wider genre, and there is no consensus as to what subcategory the Gospels should be placed in. Some of the more noteworthy candidates include: "apologetic historiography" (e.g., G. E. Sterling, "Luke-Acts and Apologetic Historiography," in *SBLSP 1989*, 326–42; idem, *Historiography and Self Definition: Josephus, Luke-Acts and Apologetic Historiography*, NovTSup 64 [Leiden: Brill, 1992]); "institutional history" (H. Cancik, "The History of Culture, Religion, and Institutions in Ancient Historiography: Philological Observations concerning Luke's History," *JBL* 116 [1997]: 673–95); "political history" (Balch, "Genre of Luke-Acts"—though see Balch's recent shift in "*METABOLE POLITEION*"); "general history" (Aune, *New Testament in Its Literary Environment*, chaps. 3 and 4); and historical "monograph" (M. Hengel, *Between Jesus and Paul*, trans. J. Bowden [Philadelphia: Fortress, 1983], 99).

76. See, respectively, Haenchen, *The Acts of the Apostles*, 136–37; Jones, "Luke's Unique Interest in Historical Chronology"; McCoy and Witherington, "In the Shadow of Thucydides," 16n63, 24–32.

77. Aune, *New Testament in Its Literary Environment*, 80 (emphasis in text).

78. Ibid., 77.

events in the Gospel tradition with persons and events in the wider Greco-Roman world), some argue that this in and of itself does not demonstrate that Luke is consciously writing in a purely "historiographical" vein.[79] A text—ancient or modern—can be broadly historical in orientation and interest without being an intentional instance of the genre "history" per se.[80]

Others find fault with additional arguments used to support an understanding of Luke as ancient history. For example, the often-made claim that the prefaces of Luke and Acts reveal it to be a work of ancient historiography has been called into question by the extensive work of Loveday Alexander. Alexander argues that a comparison of the Lukan prefaces with Greco-Roman literature turns up a match, not with historiographical texts, but rather with what she terms the "scientific tradition" or "technical prose." She identifies this tradition with "the working handbooks and teaching manuals of a variety of technical subjects" from the working world of the "crafts."[81] Thus, Luke seems to have more in common with "engineers and medical writers who represent these 'craft' traditions" than he does ancient historians.[82]

79. M. Lombardi has recently argued that for all of the similarities between Luke's Gospel and the ancient genres of Greco-Roman and Jewish biography and/or historiography, Luke exhibits a clear generic autonomy and innovation in the shaping of the text. He argues that this innovation is motivated by his concern to demonstrate the historical truth of the gospel, anchored in eyewitness testimony; see "Aspetti innovative della diegesi nel Vangelo di Luca," *Orpheus* 23 (2002): 50–73.

80. For example, Fornara (*Nature of History*, 1) notes that examples of Greek and Latin "historical writing" that show concern for "the establishment or the preservation of some part of the record of the past" can actually be divided into at least five different genres—one of which is "history" per se—each with its own rules, conventions, and foci. We would argue that in terms of the broad concern for historical interest of one sort or another, even more genres could be added to the collection, including "gospel."

81. L. C. A. Alexander, "Formal Elements and Genre: Which Greco-Roman Prologues Most Closely Parallel the Lukan Prologues?" in *Jesus and the Heritage of Israel: Luke's Narrative Claim upon Israel's Legacy*, ed. D. P. Moessner (Harrisburg, PA: Trinity, 1999), 20. See Alexander's comprehensive work on this subject: *The Preface to Luke's Gospel: Literary Convention and Social Context in Luke 1:1–4 and Acts 1:1* (New York: Cambridge University Press, 1993), a revision of her 1978 Oxford PhD dissertation. See also idem, "Luke's Preface in the Context of Greek Preface-Writing," *NovT* 28 (1986): 48–74; idem, "The Preface to Acts and the Historians," in *History, Literature and Society in the Book of Acts*, 73–103. While one can quibble with whether Alexander has chosen the most illuminating rubric for this genre—"scientific tradition" (a point Daryl Schmidt raises in "Rhetorical Influences and Genre: Luke's Preface and the Rhetoric of Hellenistic Historiography," in *Jesus and the Heritage of Israel*, 28n3)—her clear descriptions of the type of writings she is referring to serves to clear up any misunderstanding. Some scholars who have committed themselves to the position that Luke-Acts is representative of Greco-Roman history have taken issue with Alexander's conclusions. See, e.g., Aune, "Luke 1:1–4: Historical or Scientific *Prooimion?*" in *Paul, Luke and the Graeco-Roman World: Essays in Honor of Alexander J. M. Wedderburn*, ed. A. Christopherson et al. (Sheffield: Sheffield Academic Press, 2002), 138–48. On prefaces in Greco-Roman historiography see D. Leeds, "Prologue-Form in Ancient Historiography," in *ANRW* 2.1.2:842–56.

82. Alexander, "Formal Elements and Genre," 20. Some argue that Alexander has underplayed the parallels between Luke and other ancient historians. See, e.g., P. M. Head, "Papyrological Perspectives on Luke's Predecessors (Luke 1:1)," in *The New Testament in Its First Century Setting: Essays on Context and Background in Honour of B. W. Winter on His 65th Birthday*, ed. P. J. Williams et al. (Grand Rapids: Eerdmans, 2004), 30–45.

With regard to the claim that Luke's genre is determined by Acts, some have pointed out that the claim holds only if one is convinced not only that Luke and Acts derive from the same author but also that this author intended both works to represent a single genre. Both claims have been disputed, however.[83] Instead, it has been argued that Acts was intended as a "sequel" to Luke rather than a "second volume."[84] Hence, even if Acts is regarded as a work of historiography, it does not follow that Luke is to be regarded as such.

Whatever we make of these disputes, it cannot be denied that in both the Gospel of Luke and in Acts the author does exhibit a profound historical interest. Indeed, this broader historical interest is, if to a less explicit extent, exhibited in the other three Gospels as well. To the thinking of some, the dominance of this historical interest should move us to see the Gospels more along the lines of ancient historiographical writings than along the lines of biographies.[85] That is to say, they have more in common with Thucydides than with Philostratus.

Our own sense is that, while the Gospels evince a clear concern with passing on reliable historical information, it is difficult to classify them—even in the case of Luke—as ancient historiography *pure and simple*. There is a parallel sensibility here with our previous conclusion regarding the Gospels and biography. With John Dominic Crossan, we would argue that with respect to genre, the "Gospels are not history, though they contain history. They are not biography, though they contain biography. They are gospel—that is, good news."[86]

83. Mikeal Parsons and Richard Pervo have vigorously criticized the view that Luke-Acts must constitute a single genre. They demonstrate that one can hold strongly to the authorial identity and theological coherence of Luke-Acts, while rejecting their generic equivalence. One of their central arguments is that the phenomenon of "Luke-Acts" as an unquestioned hyphenated entity is a relatively recent scholarly construction. In early Christianity the idea of this single genre, two-volume work was anything but obvious. See, e.g., R. Pervo, "Must Luke and Acts Belong to the Same Genre?" in *SBLSP 1989*, 309–16; idem, "Israel's Heritage and Claims upon the Genre(s) of Luke and Acts: The Problems of a History" in *Jesus and the Heritage of Israel*, 127–43; M. C. Parsons, "The Unity of Luke-Acts: Rethinking the *Opinio Communic*," in *With Steadfast Purpose: Essays on Acts in Honor of Henry Jackson Flanders, Jr.*, ed. N. H. Keathley (Waco: Baylor University Press, 1990), 29–53; M. C. Parsons and R. I. Pervo, *Rethinking the Unity of Luke and Acts* (Minneapolis: Fortress, 1993); also D. W. Palmer, "Acts and the Historical Monograph," *TynB* 43 (1992): 373–88.

84. Pervo, "Israel's Heritage," 142.

85. So dominant is this interest that Albrecht Dihle concludes, "One must therefore claim the canonical Gospels, and certainly not only the synoptic Gospels, as witnesses for a special kind of historical thought, which separates them from Greek biography, despite the interests of both of them in biographical details. This interest was historically, and in the final analysis, not biographically motivated" (Dihle, "Gospels and Greek Biography," 381). Albert Cook broadens this claim to the New Testament as a whole: "Every section of the New Testament sets out its presentation so that it is all sited in history and dependent on a historical sequence.... Thus the sense and senses of the New Testament are derived from a temporal sequence of public import; they satisfy a definition of history.... [T]he preponderant historical focus of the New Testament ...[is] so obvious as to be taken for granted" (*History/Writing*, 159–60). In this sense, Cook argues, a historiographical intentionality links any number of ancient texts from Thucydides to the Gospels.

86. Crossan, *Birth of Christianity*, 21. Again, while we agree with this particular statement of Crossan's, we would see the context and content of this "good news" as explicitly tied to the Isaianic vision (i.e., Isa. 40:9; 52:7; 61:1–3).

For our purposes, however, the important point is not merely the resolution of the genre question. Rather we must go on to ask: What implications does the fact that the Gospel authors demonstrate a clear *historical* intent have for our assessment of their historical reliability?

Is Ancient Historiography Largely Unreliable?

Some scholars argue that ancient historiographers, on the whole, are largely unreliable and not to be trusted. To the degree that the Gospels reflect historical concerns and techniques, this broader criticism of ancient Greco-Roman historical writings can be used to undermine confidence in them prior to giving them a fair hearing. In response to this common critique of ancient historical texts, we offer the following reflections.

First, there is in many academic quarters a certain prejudice against ancient historiography because it was "premodern." The assumption is that, in contrast to the present time, ancient authors were not critical of their sources, relied on hearsay, and often accepted myth as fact (e.g., incorporated reports of the supernatural into their accounts). While such things undoubtedly can be detected at times within ancient historical writings—as they can within relatively recent historical accounts—this is not the end of the story. As Glenn Chestnut has documented, "There was also a good deal of skepticism within the Graeco-Roman historiographical tradition."[87]

From Herodotus to Polybius to Pliny the Elder, miracle claims, for example, were open to serious questioning. With Thucydides, we find virtually the entire idea of the miraculous rejected. "Drawing on the rich intellectual resources of the humanistic and scientific rationalism of fifth-century Athens," Thucydides developed a historiographical method characterized by "freedom from mytho-poetic ways of thinking, critical realism, an 'eager generality,' and an inclination to penetrate rationally to the underlying order of things."[88]

---

87. G. Chestnut, "The Pagan Background," in *The Christian and Judaic Invention of History*, ed. J. Neusner (Atlanta: Scholars Press, 1990), 38. See also: A. H. McDonald, "Herodotus on the Miraculous," in *Miracles: Cambridge Studies in their Philosophy and History*, ed. C. D. F. Moule (New York: Morehouse-Barlow, 1965), 83–91; T. R. Tholfsen, "Thucydides and Greek Rationalism," in *Historical Thinking: An Introduction* (New York: Harper & Row, 1967), 18–26.

88. Tholfsen, "Thucydides," 18. Emilio Gabba has argued that the historical rigor of Thucydides had, short of Polybius, little actual influence in terms of restraining the fictive liberties of ancient historians; see "True History and False History in Classical Antiquity," *Journal of Roman History* 71 (1981): 50–62. However, two responses are in order. First, Gabba represents one polar position on this question. Others have argued that Thucydidean standards were not only known but also functioned as something of a goal of many ancient historians; see B. Witherington, "Addendum" to W. J. McCoy's "In the Shadow of Thucydides," in *History, Literature and Society in the Book of Acts*, 27. Second, regardless of how widespread Thucydides's influence was, the only pertinent question for our purposes is whether the type of rigor exhibited by Thucydides with respect to the faithful reporting of the past is exemplified in the Gospel authors' historical intentions. With respect to Luke, at least, Witherington argues that this comparison is defensible (see "Addendum," 23). A number of scholars have favorably compared Luke's method of speech

With regard to the first century in particular, Gerald Downing's survey of attitudes toward magic and miracles serves to unmask the false dichotomy between the premodern and modern worlds vis-à-vis their credulity toward the miraculous. Downing demonstrates that "the level of belief—or suspension of disbelief—seems to have been not much different from what we find today for belief in alternative medicines, belief in ley-lines, belief in visitors from outer space, or belief in the free market economy."[89]

In other words, like most people today, most ancient historiographers accepted the *possibility* of miracles. But there is no reason to conclude from this that either ancient historiographers or modern people are necessarily credulous or unreliable. It simply means that the worldview of ancient historiographers, as well as most modern Western people, is not as narrow as those skeptics who assume a priori that miracles never occur and who judge anyone who says otherwise to be credulous, "premodern," and uncritical.[90] In either case—when assessing the historical claims of an ancient historian or their dismissal by a naturalistic skeptic—something like the open historical-critical method discussed in chapter 1 offers a methodological paradigm for navigating such waters.

Second, some adopt a highly skeptical stance toward ancient historiography because of its associations with rhetoric.[91] Ancient Greeks and Romans generally assumed that history writing "ought to be truthful, useful, and entertaining."[92] To the thinking of some today, usefulness and entertainment often, if

construction with that of Thucydides, including F. F. Bruce ("[Luke's speeches in Acts] are Thucydidean in the proper sense"), "The Acts of the Apostles: Historical Record or Theological Reconstruction?" *ANRW* 2.25.3:2582; and C. J. Hemer, *The Book of Acts in the Setting of Hellenistic History*, ed. C. H. Gempf (Tübingen: Mohr Siebeck, 1989), 420–21. See also A. W. Mosley, "Historical Reporting in the Ancient World," *NTS* 12 (1965–1966): 10–26.

89. G. Downing, "Magic and Skepticism in and around the First Christian Century," in *Making Sense in (and of) the First Christian Century* (Sheffield: Sheffield Academic Press, 2000), 221. A similar point is made by L. Degh and A. Vazsonyi, "Legend and Belief," in *Folklore Genre*, ed. D. Ben-Amos (Austin: University of Texas Press, 1976), 113. Degh and Vazsonyi (pp. 112–15) also note the existence of a generally neglected—but quite common—genre of folk legend known as the "negative legend" (or "anti-legend"). The negative legend reports an ostensibly "supernatural" occurrence that is then debunked by supplying a rational, natural explanation for the phenomenon. The presence of negative legends within folk traditions is just one example that undercuts the false assumption that the "folk" are generally naive and gullible with respect to reports of supernatural occurrences. On the negative/anti-legend see also Degh and Vazsonyi, "The Dialectics of the Legend," *Folklore Preprint Series* 1/6 (December 1973): 12–14; J. Vlach, "One Black Eye and Other Horrors: A Case for the Humorous Anti-Legend," *Indiana Folklore* 4 (1971): 97–102.

90. For two contemporary philosophical investigations of miracles, both of which take them seriously, see T. C. Williams, *The Idea of the Miraculous: The Challenge to Science and Religion* (New York: Macmillan, 1990); and J. Houston, *Reported Miracles: A Critique of Hume* (New York: Cambridge University Press, 1994).

91. See, e.g., A. J. Woodman, *Rhetoric in Classical Historiography*; K. S. Sacks, "Rhetorical Approaches to Greek History Writing in the Hellenistic Period," *SBLSP 1984*, ed. K. H. Richards (Chico, CA: Scholars Press, 1984), 123–33.

92. Aune, *New Testament in Its Literary Environment*, 95.

not usually, trumped the concern for truthfulness. While this was undoubtedly the case at times, we must be careful not to overgeneralize this point. As J. L. Moles observes, "Some [ancients] write historiography according to rhetorical prescriptions, some do not."[93] Hence, on the question of how much accuracy (if any) was sacrificed for rhetorical purposes, each historian's work must be assessed independently.

At the same time, M. J. Wheeldon makes the valuable point that even those historians who closely follow the literary and rhetorical conventions of their day should not be held suspect for this reason alone.[94] In the ancient Greco-Roman view, exercising one's rhetorical skills to entertain and motivate readers was not viewed as competing with a concern for accuracy. As A. W. Mosley demonstrated decades ago, many ancient historians were at least as serious about the historical accuracy as they were with the rhetorical excellence of their writing.[95] The notion that faithful historical reconstruction is intrinsically at odds with a concern for rhetoric and vice versa is a peculiar modern/postmodern assumption the ancients simply did not share.[96]

93. J. L. Moles, "Truth and Untruth in Herodotus and Thucydides," in *Lies and Fiction in the Ancient World*, 118. This point also is emphasized by H. F. North, "Rhetoric and Historiography," *Quarterly Journal of Speech* 42 (1956): 234–42; and Witherington, "Addendum," 29–30. One does not have to buy into a full-blown "two schools" theory—i.e., Isocrates's pro-rhetoric school of historiography vs. Aristotle's anti-rhetoric school of historiography—to appreciate this point. At the very least, one can legitimately differentiate between "more scientific and more sensational approaches," as Clare Rothschild notes; see *Luke-Acts and the Rhetoric of History: An Investigation of Early Christian Historiography* (Tübingen: Mohr Siebeck, 2004), 76.

94. See M. J. Wheeldon, "'True Stories': The Reception of Historiography in Antiquity," in *History as Text: The Writing of Ancient History*, ed. A. Cameron (Chapel Hill: University of North Carolina Press, 1989), 31–63.

95. Mosley, "Historical Reporting."

96. As noted previously, the view that rhetorical and historical interests cannot coincide stems primarily from the influence of postmodern literary critics. See Moles, "Truth and Untruth," 89–92; E. D. Hirsch, "Back to History," in *Criticism in the University*, ed. G. Graff and R. Gibbons (Evanston, IL: Northwestern University Press, 1995). This movement seeks to foist its own rhetorically inclined interests onto all human writing, past and present, and in the process rides roughshod over the ancient authors' intentions—in this case, over the intentions of those who strove to provide an accurate reconstruction of the past. E. D. Hirsch ("Back to History," 193) has (somewhat cynically) noted that the impetus behind this move is understandable, given that in literary-critical circles the more "traditional" ways of construing interpretation have largely been hashed over ad nauseum, and that new dissertation topics and research projects have to be found in order to keep the literary-critical enterprise and its institutions afloat. The reduction of all things written to merely the "rhetorical" certainly creates new realms for literary-critical scholars to practice their discipline, but it comes only as they plunder the riches of other, once autonomous disciplines—in this case ancient history. Here, the cost of "institutional homeostasis" and self-preservation comes at too high a methodological cost—namely, the practical rejection of the ancient voice regarding the past. For a discussion of ancient genres that depend upon a generic contract wherein veracity is presumed, see E. L. Bowie, "Lies, Fiction and Slander in Early Greek Poetry," in *Lies and Fiction in the Ancient World*, 1–37. See also M. Flower, "Theopompus, Isocrates and the Myth of Rhetorical History," in *Theopompus of Chois: History and Rhetoric in the Fourth Century BC* (Oxford: Clarendon, 1994), 42–62.

Third, some argue for a skeptical stance toward ancient historians on the ground that, as a matter of empirical fact, we simply know they generally were not accurate. T. P. Wiseman presents the cumulative case for this view when he identifies seven ways in which ancient historians were accused—even in their own day—of "lying."[97] It seems to us that, at least at points in his essay, his case backfires. Space allows us to mention only two examples.

First, Wiseman grants that most of his critique of ancient historians could be applied to modern historians as well. He quotes the great historian of Rome, R. Syme, who said, "To become intelligible, history has to aspire to the coherence of fiction, while eschewing most of its methods. There is no choice, no escape." In this sense, modern historians are just as much "fabricators and creators of illusion" as ancient historians.[98] The point Syme is making, of course, is that all historians, ancient or modern, must of necessity be highly selective in *what* they record and at least somewhat creative in *how* they record it. They have to weave together a seamless narrative from a state of affairs that was much more complex and far less seamless. Invariably, much, if not most, of the complexity of how things actually unfolded has to be ignored while the remainder the historian attends to has to be, to some degree, "spun" with "the coherence of fiction." Selectivity, shaping, rhetoric—all of it is there in modern as well as ancient history.

Wiseman forcefully makes this case but then in the next breath tries to undermine it by stating ways in which ancient historians could "lie" that are no longer acceptable for modern historians. He is correct in noting that certain literary conventions were allowed in the ancient world that are no longer used today—for example, the use of a travel narrative against which to paint historical events. It is not clear, however, that this fact alone should negatively affect our estimation of their general reliability. Once the particular literary conventions of an ancient culture are understood and taken into account—just as we must do with contemporary historiographical conventions—we find that ancient historians are, generally speaking, no more prone to "lying" than are their contemporary counterparts. But, in any case, the other "types of mendacity" Wiseman accuses ancient historians of are hardly lacking among modern historians. The use of rhetoric, tendentiousness, and underelaboration, for example, are hardly endangered species among modern historians. In sum, therefore, it seems we have little reason to be significantly more suspicious of ancient historians than we are of modern historians. Of course, we should be critical of *both*. But accepting a critical stance is very different from accepting a skeptical-dismissive stance.

Second, the fact that Wiseman cites ancient sources against ancient historians to make his case presupposes that at least *some* ancients knew and cared about doing what we would call "good" history. This alone is enough to establish that we

97. Wiseman, "Lying Historians."
98. Ibid., 125–26; citing R. Syme, *Roman Papers 4* (Oxford: Oxford University Press, 1988), 19; idem, *Roman Papers 6* (Oxford: Oxford University Press, 1991), 164.

The Synoptic Gospels as Historical Sources for Jesus

cannot make sweeping generalizations about the unreliability of "ancient history." Rather, we must consider each historian and each work on its own merits. In what can be considered the most serious theoretical discussion of historiography that survives from the ancient world—Lucian's *How to Write History*—the author emphasizes that the historian must "sacrifice to Truth alone."[99] So apparently at least *some* ancient historians knew and cared about such things.[100]

The Gospel Genre and Historical Intention

Along with most other New Testament scholars, we cannot endorse the view that Luke's Gospel can be classified as an example of ancient historiography, pure and simple, but we believe it does have strong ties to the genre of ancient historiography (as each of the Gospels do with the Greco-Roman *bios* genre). In our view, this enhances our estimation of Luke's historical intent more than it undermines it. (Something similar may be said for the other Gospels insofar as they too parallel the genre of ancient historiography.) As we have shown, ancient historians clearly intended to write history, and there is hardly more reason to be skeptical about their intent and/or ability to do so competently than there is about modern historians, once their literary conventions and culturally accepted measures of preciseness are taken into account. To this general assessment we add two more specific observations.

The first is related to Willem van Unnik's insightful study of how ancient historians understood their work, based on Lucian's *How to Write History* and Dionysius of Halicarnassus's *Letter to Pompei*. From these two works van Unnik formulates "ten rules" of ancient historiography. Ancient historians were expected to (1) choose a noble subject; (2) choose a subject that would be useful to the intended audience; (3) be impartial and independent in researching and composing their history; (4) construct a good narrative with an especially good beginning and ending; (5) engage in adequate preparatory research; (6) use good judgment in the selection of material, exemplifying appropriate variety; (7) accurately and appropriately order one's material; (8) make the narrative lively and interesting; (9) exercise moderation in topographical details; and (10) compose speeches appropriate to the orator and the rhetorical situation.[101]

---

99. Wiseman, "Lying Historians," 122.

100. We can also mention a third area in which Wiseman's analysis might be said to backfire. His final example of "historical mendacity" of which ancient historians were accused in their own time was underelaboration and lack of detail (Ibid., 146). It is interesting that while ancients may have seen this as deception, we today, with our acute awareness of the impossible complexity of the real world and thus the inevitable selectivity of all historiography, would be more inclined to see this as perhaps an example of just the sort of discriminating restraint that tends to characterize modern critical historiography.

101. W. C. van Unnik, "Luke's Second Book and the Rules of Hellenistic Historiography," in *Les Actes des Apotres: Traditions, Redaction, Theologie*, ed. J. Kremer (Leuven: Leuven University Press, 1979), 37–60.

Recently, Daniel Marguerat has analyzed Luke's history writing in the light of Unnik's "ten rules" and has arrived at the following conclusion:

> Comparison of Luke-Acts with the list of historiographical norms confirms that the Lucan writing corresponds to standard Graeco-Roman historiography. We . . . find that Luke follows eight of the ten rules: his transgression of the other two (the first and third) points us toward the specificity of Luke's project. The instructions observed by Luke are also followed by the majority of historians of Hellenistic Judaism, especially Flavius Josephus.[102]

Luke's apparent violation of rule number one is instructive. Rather than a culturally appropriate noble subject, Luke and his fellow Gospel writers chose as their central focus the life of a Galilean carpenter who was eventually crucified as a false messiah and blasphemer—hardly a "noble subject." In fact, as G. W. Bowersock notes, the Gospel writers present Jesus as something of a pathetic antihero—at least as the accounts would have been read through the eyes of those holding to Greco-Roman virtues—a point capitalized on by Celsus in his critique of Christianity a century later.[103] The point to glean from this is that, however much personal convictions and evangelistic aspirations drive their writings, the Gospel authors seem unwilling to rewrite Jesus's own history in order to put him in a light favorable to the very culture they are trying to persuade.

The significance of this cannot be overstated. If the general historical quality of the Gospels suggests their historical claims must be taken seriously, this all-important sui generis component of the Gospels argues for it all the more. For it raises, once again, the question of how we are to explain the surprising, countercultural, even embarrassing, portrait of Jesus we find in all four Gospels. Given that it flaunts and even offends both Greco-Roman and specifically Jewish sensibilities, the most plausible explanation is one that traces the historical inspiration for this most unlikely of messiah figures to the life of Jesus himself.

Second, in a recent study of Luke-Acts in light of ancient historiography and its rhetoric, Clare Rothschild has concluded that many of the elements within Luke-Acts that have previously been considered corrupting "theological" intrusions into his historiography

> are actually, first and foremost, historiographical techniques functioning in this capacity as the author's "available means of persuasion"—Aristotle's famous definition of rhetoric (*Rh*. 1.2.1). As rhetorical "means of persuasion," these techniques function as proofs in an argument for the work's authentication to potential converts from more critical intellectual milieus.[104]

---

102. Marguerat, *First Christian Historian*, 14.

103. G. W. Bowersock, *Fiction as History: Nero to Julian* (Berkeley: University of California Press, 1994), 74–75.

104. Rothschild, *Luke-Acts and the Rhetoric of History*, 291.

Rothschild's wider study of Greco-Roman historiography shows that with the rise of a class of pseudohistorians—mediocre writers with an eye for the sensational and with less concern for accuracy—it became necessary for serious historians to find a way to communicate to their readers that they did not belong to this class. In this context, a "rhetoric of historiography" arose that was designed to ensure and persuade the reader that the author was a serious historian. Among these common rhetorical techniques were the inclusion of historical prologues, the use of stylistic imitation and recurrence patterns, and an emphasis on eyewitnesses. Rothschild demonstrates that Luke made good use of these techniques.

Rothschild's study effectively serves to challenge those who pit serious historiography against rhetoric. To the contrary, she shows that historiographical rhetoric was the means by which sound ancient historians assured the reader that the account could be trusted. With regard to Luke, she concludes: "With such care devoted to credibility, the survival of such a secure and rational account would have been all but guaranteed."[105]

While it remains for us to examine more particular arguments for and against the historical veracity of the Gospels, our analysis of the parallels and connections between the Gospels and the genre of ancient historiography has served to suggest that we should approach the historical claims of these documents with an open mind rather than an overly skeptical disposition.

---

105. Rothschild, *Luke-Acts and the Rhetoric of History*, 293. While we certainly appreciate Rothschild's important work on the interface of ancient historiography and rhetoric, we would suggest that she too often assumes that the use of a rhetorical convention is "nothing but" a rhetorical convention. For example, in her treatment of the historical convention of appealing to eyewitnesses (autopsy) in order to authenticate the work, she assumes that the presence of such a convention counts against the actual fact of eyewitnesses. Thus, she concludes, against Samuel Byrskog's work, that despite their pretense to eyewitness grounding, "no traces of eyewitness reports remain" (p. 223n39). Again, in answer to the question of whether any of the Gospel writers were eyewitnesses of the events they narrate, she argues, "Clearly, they were not" (p. 226). Against Rothschild, we would suggest that the presence of a historical convention that emphasized eyewitnesses would naturally lead to *the actual importance of eyewitnesses*, thus supplying the motivation to locate and transmit their historical remembrances, precisely as the early Jesus tradition suggests was the case. Not only this, but Rothschild would have done well to consider more carefully Byrskog's work on oral history in particular, and orality studies as they relate to the Jesus tradition in general. For all of its value, we submit that Rothschild's work is still overly indebted to the modern "literary-paradigm" of New Testament studies. From the perspective of the literary paradigm, eyewitness claims can easily be dismissed as "nothing but" a form of literary-rhetorical convention. From an orality-based paradigm, however, such claims suggest an anchoring in oral history, as Byrskog's work demonstrates. See *Story as History—History as Story: The Gospel Tradition in the Context of Ancient Oral History* (Boston: Brill, 2002). In a context where an oral hermeneutic predominates—such as the world within which the canonical Gospels were situated—the idea of the "strong tradition-bearer" is highly relevant to the question of eyewitnesses. See John D. Niles, *Homo Narrans: The Poetics and Anthropology of Oral Literature* (Philadelphia: University of Pennsylvania Press, 1999), 173–93. The same sort of critical questions can be raised with respect to Rothschild's easy dismissal of the "we" passages in Acts as trading in nothing but rhetorical "fantasy" (pp. 264–67). The gist of Rothschild's work comports well with the claim of Mary Katherine Hom that, in Luke's writings, history, theology, and artistry are not antithetical but mutually enriching; see "Luke as Historian, Theologian, and Artist in Luke 6:12–9:50," *Evangelical Journal* 21 (2003): 32–43.

The Gospels and Ancient Fiction

We turn now to examine the view that the Gospels intentionally were written as fiction. We will first consider the Gospel-as-romance-novel proposal, centering our discussion around the work of Richard Pervo. Then we will consider the Gospel-as-epic-novel proposal of Dennis MacDonald.[106]

The Gospels as Romance Novels

Pervo builds his case for viewing the Gospels as ancient romance novels largely on his analysis of the book of Acts and its connection with the Gospel of Luke. His argument that Acts should be read as an ancient romance novel rests on two lines of argumentation.

First, Pervo argues that there are so many flagrant historical inaccuracies and improbabilities in Acts that no ancient author of Luke's literary abilities could have done such a poor job if he was actually trying to write factual history. Second, Pervo argues that, as with other ancient novels, Acts is filled with the sort of entertaining literary features that would have served to keep the attention of ancient readers of fiction. There are six arguments that we believe suffice to undermine Pervo's case and/or seriously call into question the Gospel-as-romance-novel thesis as a whole.

First, Pervo has simply not made his case that Acts is filled with historical inaccuracies—and certainly not to the point that we should conclude that Luke did not intend to write actual history. As one reviewer has noted, Pervo works "more by assertion than argument."[107] While space does not permit an assessment of the general historical reliability of Acts, we will simply note that, on our reading, there are few alleged inaccuracies in Acts that cannot be accounted for, while there are numerous points where claims can be substantiated—often down to minute detail.[108] But even among those scholars who are generally skeptical of the reliability

---

106. We are not discussing in this section those scholars who call the Gospels "fiction" but by it mean either (1) consciously fraudulent accounts meant to deceive readers into thinking they were factual accounts (this would be hoax, not fiction) or (2) accounts believed and intended to be factual by their authors, though they were misled by their uncritical, "primitive" worldview (this would be simply mistaken history). It is the claim of intended "fiction" that we consider here. We should also note that we will not be examining every subgenre of fiction that has been proposed for the Gospels. We shall consider only the several that are most common and/or influential, and suggest that our basic approach to them could be similarly applied to arguments claiming that the Gospels represent some other sort of fictional genre. One of the specific claims we will not have space to consider is the suggestion that the Gospels represent examples of "fantasy." For a brief but helpful critique of this approach, see J. Dewey, "Response: Fantasy and the New Testament," *Semeia* 60 (1992): 83–90.

107. D. E. Johnson, review of *Profit with Delight*, by R. Pervo, *Westminster Theological Journal* 52 (1990): 379.

108. The historicity of Acts remains an issue of contention within the scholarly guild. The infamous textual conundrum has made the question more complex. Despite some who argue to the contrary (e.g., J. Read-Heimerdinger, *The Bezan Text of Acts: A Contribution of Discourse Analysis to Textual Criticism*

of Acts, very few see the alleged difficulties as so numerous and flagrant that they warrant the conclusion that Luke was intending to write fiction.

Second, the argument that Luke's literary techniques count against his historical interest is rooted in the assumption that rhetorical and historical concerns cannot successfully coexist in the same author and same work. But, as we have already argued, ancients certainly did not work with this assumption. As David Aune has argued, ancient historians were committed to being truthful *and* entertaining.[109] Unfortunately, Pervo virtually neglects this feature of ancient historiography. As Marion Soards observes, "Many—perhaps most or all—[of] the common characteristics Pervo identifies between Acts and the ancient novel may be located in [the] ancient historians whom Pervo basically ignores."[110]

One example must suffice here. One of the literary motifs that some have used to connect Acts with the ancient novel is that of the "travel" or "voyage" theme. From Homer's *Odyssey* to the romance novels of Chariton and Xenophon, the travel motif plays an important role in fictional accounts. So too, in both Luke's Gospel (Jesus's final journey to Jerusalem) and Acts (e.g., the journey of Paul to Rome), the various episodes of the text are woven around a travel theme. Does this mean that Luke's writings are fictional? Not at all. As Loveday Alexander reminds us, "Romance does not have a monopoly on voyage

---

[Sheffield: Sheffield Academic Press, 2003]; J. Rius-Camps and J. Read-Heimerdinger, *The Message of Acts in Codex Bezae: A Comparison with the Alexandrian Tradition*, vol. 1: *Acts 1.1–5.42: Jerusalem* [New York: Clark, 2004]), the best evidence remains with the consensus view that the Alexandrian textual tradition is, generally speaking, to be given more weight than the so-called Western tradition, of which Bezae is a prime example. See, e.g., S. E. Porter, "Developments in the Texts of Acts before the Major Codices," in *The Book of Acts as Church History: Text, Textual Traditions and Ancient Interpretations*, ed. T. Nicklas and M. Tilly (New York: de Gruyter, 2003), 31–67.

Some scholars have grown weary of the debate on this matter and have moved on to purely literary/theological/sociorhetorical questions. Others take up the historicity issue, only to conclude that Acts is largely unreliable. The most recent enterprise that takes this direction is the Acts Seminar, one of Robert Funk's follow-up projects to the Jesus Seminar. The results of the Acts Seminar have been published in various issues of *Forum* (beginning in the Spring 2000 issue). For example, in the first session of the Acts Seminar, "none of the stories that came before the seminar were deemed historical as stories" (D. E. Smith, "Preface," *Forum* 3 [2000], 7).

A good number of scholars, however, take the historicity of Acts quite seriously. See, e.g., Bruce, "The Acts of the Apostles," 2569–2603; J. A. Fitzmyer, *The Acts of the Apostles* (New York: Doubleday, 1998), 124–27; W. W. Gasque, "The Historical Value of Acts," *TynB* 40 (1989): 136–57; C. J. Hemer, *The Book of Acts*; M. Hengel, *Acts and the History of Earliest Christianity*, trans. J. Bowden (Philadelphia: Fortress, 1979); D. L. Jones, "Luke's Unique Interest in Historical Chronology," 378–87. Much of this material is summarized in Boyd, *Cynic Sage or Son of God? Recovering the Real Jesus in an Age of Revisionist Replies* (Grand Rapids: Baker Academic, 1995), 247–66. A very helpful article on this matter—a methodological ground-clearing exercise of sorts—is provided by C. H. Talbert, "What Is Meant by the Historicity of Acts?" in *Reading Luke-Acts in Its Mediterranean Milieu* (Boston: Brill, 2003), 197–217. From our perspective, Talbert's methodological proposal—when viewed in light of an appropriate approach to the supernatural (e.g., see chap. 1 above)—can lead to a generally positive assessment of the historicity of Acts.

109. Aune, *New Testament in Its Literary Environment*, 95.

110. M. Soards, review of *Profit with Delight*, by R. Pervo, *JAAR* 58 (1990): 309.

narratives."[111] After all, some people *actually did travel* in the ancient world! More to the point, Paul's letters reveal that he traveled a great deal—and in a way that corresponds quite well with the general sense of Luke's account of his travels in Acts. Hence, there is no good reason to think Luke's travel motif is nothing more than a fictional narrative framework.

Third, it is significant that many of the things that are typically found in ancient romance novels are absent in both Acts and the Gospels. For one thing, these works are altogether devoid of any romance! Nor are there any sexual dalliances, exotic encounters with bandits, or explicit and lavish details of persecutions and executions. While Pervo argues that someone with Luke's obvious literary ability could not have intended to write actual history while making so many mistakes, we would argue that someone of Luke's obvious literary ability could not have possibly missed so many literary opportunities if he was *trying to write a novel*.

Fourth, the genre signal sent by the prefaces of both Luke and Acts counts strongly against viewing these works as fictional. These are examples of "technical prose," as Loveday Alexander has argued.[112] They indicate, at the very least, that Luke is intending to recount history, not write fiction.

Fifth, if Acts was indeed intended to be fictional, it is somewhat surprising that no one in the early Christian community ever read the work as such. James Dawsey rightly asks, "If the Acts of the Apostles were the creative [i.e., fictional] work of an author, why would it not have suffered the same fate as the Acts of Paul?"[113]

Sixth, and finally, it is not insignificant to note that, while there were certainly antecedents, the distinct genre of romance novel did not appear until the reign of Nero and became widespread only after this point.[114] Hence, if there is a line of influence to be posited between the Jesus stories in their oral and written form and romance novels, it seems more likely it would run from the Jesus stories to

111. L. Alexander, "'In Journeyings Often': Voyaging in the Acts of the Apostles and in Greek Romances," in *Luke's Literary Achievement: Collected Essays*, ed. C. M. Tuckett, JSNTSup 116 (Sheffield: Sheffield Academic Press, 1995), 38. See also idem, "Narrative Maps: Reflections on the Toponymy of Acts," in *The Bible in Human Society: Essays in Honor of John Rogerson*, ed. M. D. Carroll R., D. J. A. Clines, and P. R. Davies, JSOTSup 200 (Sheffield: Sheffield Academic Press, 1995), 17–45.

112. Alexander concludes, "Within the epistemological space created by Luke's preface, there is no real room for doubt as to the broadly factual status of his narrative" ("Fact, Fiction, and the Genre of Acts," *NTS* 44 [1998]: 399).

113. J. Dawsey, "Characteristics of Folk-Epic in Acts," *SBLSP 1989*, 318. This point is well taken. In his recent essay, "The Ancient Novel Becomes Christian," Pervo devotes two paragraphs to the Gospels, one paragraph to Acts, and a full eighteen pages to the five later "Acts" (Andrew, John, Paul, Peter, and Thomas) and other later and obviously fictive legendary accounts.

114. Bowersock, *Fiction as History*, 124. Antecedents include "Homeric tales, Ctesias's Persian fantasies, Xenophon's *Cyropaideia*, Hellenistic travel literature, and the lost lubricities of the short Milesian tales" (p. 124). But, as Bowersock emphasizes, when the new fictional literature of the romance novel emerges, it is "a wholly new phenomenon in Graeco-Roman literature" (p. 124). Christopher Gill reminds us, for example, that the "distinction between factual and fictional discourse, which is familiar to us, has no obvious equivalent in Plato's framework" ("Plato on Falsehood—not Fiction," in *Lies and Fiction in the Ancient World*, 40).

the romance novels and not the other way around—a point G. W. Bowersock has effectively argued.[115]

Mark as Epic Novel

A second proposal that portrays the Gospels as fiction sees Mark as intentionally modeled after Homer's *Odyssey* and *Iliad*. In the words of Dennis MacDonald, the primary exponent of this perspective, Mark was "not writing a historical biography ... but a novel, a prose anti-epic of sorts."[116] His work, like the work of Homer, is intended to be an inspiring myth.[117] Robert Price, a defender of a radical form of the legendary-Jesus thesis, concludes that MacDonald's work has convincingly shown that Homer was a "major source" for the Gospel authors, particularly Mark and Luke.[118] We contend there are at least ten considerations that call his thesis into question. The first seven concern MacDonald's methodology, while the last three concern the content of his thesis.

METHODOLOGICAL PROBLEMS

Perhaps the most fundamental methodological problem with MacDonald's approach is that he has set things up so that not only do supposedly positive parallels and allusions support his theory, but so also do *contrasts* between Homer and Mark. These contrasts are counted as evidence of Mark's conscious "transvaluation" of Homer.[119] Thus *both similarities and differences are taken as evidence of Mark's use of Homer*, which means, of course, that his thesis is rendered virtually unfalsifiable.[120]

Second, many of MacDonald's suggested parallels seem quite forced. For example, he argues that Mark's account of the transfiguration of Jesus is "an episode

115. In Bowersock's opinion, the stories of Jesus "inspired the polytheists to create a wholly new genre that we might call romantic scripture. And it became so popular that the Christians, in turn, borrowed it back—in the *Clementine Recognitions* and in the massive production of saints' lives" (*Fiction as History*, 143). The fact that Pervo and others reverse this relationship is, in Bowersock's eyes, both "implausible for chronological reasons" and, unfortunately, reminiscent of the similar move made a century ago by the history of religions school in which the relationship between Christian and pagan rites and utterances "obscured influences in the reverse direction" (ibid., 139n43, 127). Specifically, Bowersock demonstrates that Eucharist-like similarities—including the motif of cannibalism—between Christianity and the pagan novels are best explained as the latter being influenced by the former (pp. 125–39). With regard to Pervo in particular, Bowersock writes: "No one seems to have asked whether Acts, whatever its genre, could itself have influenced the novelists. Once again we have the familiar failure to look for the impact of Christianity on polytheist culture" (ibid., 139n43).

116. MacDonald, *Homeric Epics*, 3, 7.

117. Ibid., 190.

118. Price, *Incredible Shrinking Son of Man*, 31.

119. In MacDonald's words, his sixth criterion by which he identifies Mark's use of Homer suggests that we must be aware of "differences between texts" since they may actually provide "evidence of emulation" (*Homeric Epics*, 9).

120. Several reviewers have pointed out this fundamental problem; e.g., M. M. Mitchell, "Homer in the New Testament," *JR* 83 (2003): 252, 254; S. Dowd, review of *Homeric Epics and the Gospel of Mark*, by D. MacDonald, *CBQ* 63 (2001): 156.

modeled after Odysseus's demonstration of his identity to Telemachus." The evidence for this connection is that both scenes involve the revelation of an identity and bright, clean clothing. The parallel is tenuous, to say the least.

Third, MacDonald tends to minimize, and often ignores altogether, the far clearer parallels and possible literary lines of influence on Mark from Old Testament texts. For example, Mark's transfiguration account has much more in common with the Mount Sinai narrative in Exodus than it does Homer's account of Odysseus's self-revelation. So too, while MacDonald argues that Mark's stilling of the storm account is a play off of Homer's tale of Aeolus's bag of wind, he relegates to a footnote the significant verbal and thematic parallels between this account and the Old Testament narrative of Jonah as given in the Septuagint.[121] Yet, as Margaret Mitchell notes, the parallels between Mark's account and the Old Testament's account of Jonah "go far beyond any of the parallels with Homeric texts" listed in MacDonald's book.[122] This penchant to find parallels in Homer rather than in the Old Testament is surprising, given that Mark was writing from within a first-century, monotheistic Jewish context. One would think it rather obvious that if we are looking for possible sources of literary inspiration for Mark, we should first look to the Old Testament before turning to Homer or any other Greco-Roman source.

A fourth methodological problem with MacDonald's approach concerns his criterion of "analogy." In his view, the more often a particular episode in Homer was used by others in the ancient world in general, the more likely it would be consciously taken from Homer by Mark to be used in his anti-epic.[123] But why should we assume this? Could not one just as easily argue *the opposite*—namely, the more an episode was used by others in the ancient world in general, the more likely it is that the motif had become a cultural commonplace and thus the less likely it is that Mark—or anyone else writing in the first-century Mediterranean world—is directly and *consciously* dependent on Homer per se when putting it to use?[124]

Fifth, even when it can plausibly be argued that there are similarities between any two literary texts, this does not necessitate the conclusion that one author borrowed from the other. To borrow Samuel Sandmel's famous phrase, it seems that MacDonald is indulging himself in "parallelomania."[125]

Sixth, even if, for the sake of argument, we grant that Mark imitated Homer at points, this fact in and of itself does not necessarily lead to the conclusion that Mark was thereby writing fiction. One could plausibly argue that Mark saw

121. MacDonald, *Homeric Epics*, 174.
122. Mitchell, "Homer in the New Testament," 253.
123. MacDonald, *Homeric Epics*, 8.
124. A point noted by Dowd, review of *Homeric Epics*, 156.
125. S. Sandmel, "Parallelomania," *JBL* 81 (1962): 1–13. M. Hooker raises this question in a review of *Homeric Epics and the Gospel of Mark*, by D. MacDonald, *JTS* 53 (2002): 198. See chap. 3, where we discussed this problem in relation to those who view the Jesus story as a "hero myth."

in certain aspects of Jesus's life incidents and episodes that paralleled or echoed Homeric themes and allowed the parallels to shape the telling of the Jesus story. While we personally do not see any evidence of this, someone who does perceive such parallels (e.g., MacDonald) should at least countenance this possibility and wrestle with the potential implications.[126]

Seventh, although MacDonald admits that there may be historical elements in Mark—a point that would at least serve to complexify, if not undermine, his theory—he provides no serious identification and consideration of these elements. Nor does he suggest how one might detect these elements as opposed to the elements of Homeric fiction.[127]

PROBLEMS WITH THE CONTENT OF MACDONALD'S THESIS

Beyond these methodological problems, MacDonald's thesis runs into difficulties in terms of its specific content.

First, MacDonald has not adequately explained *why* Mark would want to create a theological fiction patterned after Homer. As Margaret Mitchell observes, "It remains unintelligible (or, at least, unelucidated here) why a Hellenistic (Jewish?) author would link his hero Jesus with wily, ironic Odysseus, a figure of much-debated character flaws."[128] Not only this, but if MacDonald's thesis is correct, we must seriously wonder why any Jewish-Christian audience would find a hero modeled after Odysseus attractive, let alone compelling enough to live and die for. Indeed, if the whole work were intended to be read as theological fiction, it is not altogether clear what embracing Mark's Homeric mythic vision would look like. What exactly did the early Christians preach and put their lives on the line for—if they were aware that the Gospel they proclaimed and "believed" was largely, if not totally, rooted in a Homeric myth?[129]

This leads to a second and very significant problem with the content of MacDonald's thesis. As a matter of historical fact, neither the early Christians nor anyone up to very recent times ever thought of interpreting Mark or any other Gospel as intentional fiction, let alone as fiction patterned after Homer's *Odyssey* and *Iliad*. MacDonald himself writes, "Readers for two thousand years apparently have been blind" to the fact that Mark was writing a fictional "prose anti-epic of sorts."[130] One wonders how everyone got it wrong for so long.

This problem is particularly acute since, to make his larger case, MacDonald argues that "ancient authors could expect the readers to draw connections to

---

126. One can make a serious comparison of Mark with a Greco-Roman literary form without thereby undercutting its historicity. See, e.g., G. G. Bilezikian, *The Liberated Gospel: A Comparison of the Gospel of Mark and Greek Tragedy* (Grand Rapids: Baker Academic, 1977).

127. A point highlighted by Mitchell, "Homer in the New Testament," 255.

128. Ibid., 254. This problem is also emphasized by Dowd, review of *Homeric Epics*, 197.

129. For a related argument on a broader scale, see R. Trigg, "Tales Artfully Spun," in *The Bible as Rhetoric: Studies in Biblical Persuasion and Credibility* (New York: Routledge, 1990), 117–32.

130. MacDonald, *Homeric Epics*, 7.

Homer that are invisible to us."[131] However, by his own admission, *no one did*. As Karl Sandnes has pointed out, MacDonald's thesis about Mark is missing at least one essential element: in the ancient world when one text was imitating another—even in an exercise in transvaluation—the subtle moments of emulation were accompanied by very clear moments of "advertised intertextuality," moments in which the emulation exercise was "broadcast in ways that alerted the reader."[132] These clear moments of advertised emulation are missing from Mark's Gospel. It seems Mark's alleged allusions to Homer were as "invisible" to his original audience, and even his fellow Gospel authors, as they are to all modern scholars—*except* MacDonald. This obviously begs the question of whether it is all other readers throughout history, on the one hand, or MacDonald himself, on the other, who missed Mark's real intention. In our view—particularly given the significant problems noted above—it is far more plausible to suppose the latter rather than the former.

Finally, MacDonald's theory requires that we accept that Mark was a rather savvy, sophisticated literary critic who lived in the world of irony and textual finesse. But this hardly comports with what we know of the first-century Christian community, which, as we have argued, was orally dominant in its communicative style. MacDonald's "Mark" seems much more at home in a postmodern, literary-critical milieu—MacDonald's own context—than he does in the first-century Christian community.[133] Maurice Casey's observation, drawn from another context, most likely applies to MacDonald's thesis as well: "The portrayal of [Mark] as flimsy post-70 fiction is the unsatisfactory consequence of reading it in light of literary theory which has emerged from the study of modern fiction."[134] In light of all these concerns, we conclude that MacDonald's thesis, while highly provocative, is ultimately unsuccessful.

The Gospels and Jewish Midrash/Pesher

The final proposal we will consider is that the Gospels should be understood as a form of Jewish midrash. While almost all New Testament scholars grant that there are midrashic aspects within the Gospels, few accept the thesis that substantial

131. Ibid., 171.

132. K. O. Sandnes, "*Imitatio Homeri?* An Appraisal of Dennis R. MacDonald's 'Mimesis Criticism,'" *JBL* 124 (2005): 732.

133. See the relevant comments of Dowd, review of *Homeric Epics*, 198; Mitchell, "Homer in the New Testament," 250. MacDonald's thesis depends upon a presumption of the type of schooling—including the fundamental availability of Homeric texts—accessible to people like Mark and his audience. But with Hooker (review of *Homeric Epics*, 198) we must ask what evidence exists to imagine that Mark was "that kind of cultured writer."

134. M. Casey, *Aramaic Sources of Mark's Gospel* (New York: Cambridge University Press, 1998), 259–60.

portions of the Gospels, if not the Gospels as a whole, should be understood as examples of midrash genre per se. There are good reasons for this. We offer five arguments that we believe undermine the Gospels-as-midrash thesis, and two that address the more specific Gospels-as-pesher-code thesis of Barbara Thiering.

Assessing the Gospels-as-Midrash Thesis

First, it is worth noting that, as "creative" as some ancient Jewish approaches to Scripture could be, there was also a strong tradition of Jewish exegesis that insisted that Old Testament texts should be interpreted according to their original literary context. Through his exhaustive research into this area, David Brewer has concluded that two approaches to biblical exegesis were represented in the pre-70 CE Jewish world.[135]

The "nomological" approach, championed by the pre-70 CE scribal tradition, viewed Old Testament texts as law and generally held that proper exegesis must interpret these texts within their literary contexts while avoiding secondary allegorical meanings beyond the plain surface meanings of the texts. On the other hand, the "inspirational" approach, adopted by a variety of exegetical contemporaries of the scribes—including the Qumran exegetes and Philo—viewed the Old Testament predominantly as living prophecy. While not entirely ignoring the original literary context of particular texts, they were willing to discover secondary meanings independent of the plain meaning of the texts when they believed the Holy Spirit inspired them to do so.

The conclusion Brewer's research leads to is that pre-70 CE Jewish exegesis was not as imaginative as it is sometimes made out to be. Especially in the "nomological approach, there were identifiable and effective forces at work that served to check and balance countervailing tendencies toward de-contextualized, allegorical interpretation."[136] To whatever degree the Gospels were influenced by the first-century Jewish *scribal* tradition—which they clearly seem to be—this "nomological" hermeneutic could, to one degree or another, be expected to tame any competing tendency toward a full-blown allegorical "midrash" approach.

Second, even the more imaginative, midrashic, "inspirational" exegesis does not serve as an adequate foundation for the Gospel-as-midrash thesis. Jewish exegetes in this school were driven by what can be called a "fulfillment hermeneutic." That is, they tended to use midrashic techniques to correlate current historical events, or anticipated future events, with Old Testament texts as a means of bringing out

---

135. D. I. Brewer, *Techniques and Assumptions in Jewish Exegesis before 70 CE* (Tübingen: Mohr Siebeck, 1992). For a summary comparison of the two approaches, see 215–22.

136. Brewer writes: "The results are unexpected and conflicting with the generally held assumption that the scribes, like the rabbis after 70 CE, frequently interpreted the OT without regard to context, [and] found hidden meanings by means of allegory or atomistic exegesis. . . . The absence of these types of exegesis has been demonstrated not only by their total absence from more than 100 examples of scribal exegetical argument, but also by demonstrating that the scribes had a coherent approach to Scripture which entails the rejection of such methods" (*Techniques and Assumptions*, 223).

the perceived biblical significance of those events. Sometimes Old Testament texts would be "creatively" reframed to accommodate this correlation, but rarely were contemporary events *fabricated* to accommodate this correlation. Thus, as Shani Berrin notes, "An essential feature of *pesher* is the application of the base text to *historical reality*."[137] Yet, according to the Gospels-as-midrash thesis, many of the accounts of Jesus in the Gospels were simply *invented* to correlate with various Old Testament passages. For this there is no clear precedent in first-century Jewish exegetical practice, a point that cannot help but call this thesis into question.[138]

We may with justification appreciate certain aspects of the midrashic-like creativity by which the Gospel authors attached biblical significance to various aspects of Jesus's life—for example, the slaughter of the innocents (Matt. 2:17–18; cf. Jer. 31:15), Jesus's betrayal (John 13:18; cf. Ps. 41:9), and his being given sour wine to quench his thirst (John 19:28–29; cf. Ps. 69:21). But this is very different from saying that these events were *fabricated* in order to "fulfill" these biblical passages.[139] To the contrary, the fact that the Gospel authors found any messianic significance in otherwise obscure Old Testament texts such as these—texts that, as far as we know, prior to the Gospels were never read as messianic or predictive in

137. S. Berrin, "Qumran Pesharim," in *Biblical Interpretation at Qumran*, ed. M. Henze (Grand Rapids: Eerdmans, 2005), 114. As Berrin notes (p. 114n11), some have claimed that while this tie to the historical is characteristic of pehsarim, this does not necessarily hold true for all Jewish midrash. However, L. H. Silberman (following I. L. Seeligman) argues that a similar historicizing tendency characterized midrash as well; see "Unriddling the Riddle: A Study in the Structure and Language of the Habakkuk Pesher [1QpHab]," *Revue de Qumran* 3 (1961–62): 326.

138. J. B. Green writes of the "substantial work of the last decade on the hermeneutics of late Judaism, specifically on the question of whether the creation of current history from Old Testament texts was an accepted and widely practiced phenomenon. In fact, while more work needs to be done, study of *pesherim* texts from Qumran, post-biblical historiography, and selected apocalyptic writings is already suggesting that the direction of influence was *from event to biblical text*" (review of *The Cross That Spoke*, by J. D. Crossan, *JBL* 109 [1990]: 257–58 [emphasis in text]). Using both literary-critical analysis and historical evidence, M. A. Powell has effectively argued against Spong's claim that the Gospel writers intended—and the original audiences understood—that the Gospels were to be read as metaphorical exercises in midrash; see "Authorial Intent and Historical Reporting: Putting Spong's Literalization Thesis to the Test," *JSHJ* 1 (2003): 225–49. C. H. Dodd had already argued along these lines in *Historical Tradition in the Fourth Gospel* (New York: Cambridge University Press, 1963), 48–49, and *The Apostolic Preaching and Its Development* (London: Hodder and Stoughton, 1936), 53. Similarly, R. T. France has argued that it appears actual events influenced midrash rather than that midrash fostered the fabrication of events; see "Jewish Historiography, Midrash, and the Gospels," in *Gospel Perspectives*, vol. 3: *Studies in Midrash and Historiography*, ed. R. T. France and D. Wenham (Sheffield: JSOT, 1983), 119–20.

139. In an important observation, D. J. Moo notes that the "fabrication of recent history" thesis is based on the supposition that New Testament authors felt compelled to demonstrate Jesus's fulfillment of every Old Testament messianic prophecy. But there is little evidence that the authors were guided by such a presupposition. Instead, it appears that "the prophecies which were important were determined by the life of Jesus" (*The Old Testament in the Gospel Passion Narratives* [Sheffield: Almond, 1983], 380). As we shall argue more fully below, three other considerations also strongly support Moo's contention: (1) most of the "messianic" texts the Gospel authors cite were not regarded as such by the culture; (2) the way in which Jesus "fulfills" these Old Testament texts is often tenuous and awkward; and (3) the messianic portrait of Jesus these authors supposedly constructed was radically countercultural.

their original contexts—is best explained on the assumption that these events *did actually occur.* If the Gospel authors were going to invent a Jesus along midrashic lines in order to bring to light certain Old Testament texts, they wouldn't have had to stretch as far as they seem to have stretched, in these instances, to do so. In other words, had the Gospel authors invented a Jesus along midrashic lines, he could have been made to "fulfill" Old Testament texts much more obviously and much less awkwardly than what we often find in the Gospels.

To give just one example, John depicts the episode of a guard giving Jesus sour wine as a fulfillment of Scripture (John 19:28–29). It seems clear that John is referring to Psalm 69, where David says of his enemies, "They gave me poison for food, and for my thirst they gave me vinegar to drink" (v. 21). Now, since there is nothing remotely predictive about this passage, it seems very unlikely anyone would have felt the need to fabricate a current event to "fulfill" it. But even if someone had felt such a need, why would that person have Jesus drink sour wine instead of vinegar, as the Old Testament text says? Even more puzzling, why would the writer have Jesus "fulfill" the second half of the verse *but not the first?* Why is there no account of Jesus being given poison for food, if indeed the ostensively historical account is being created out of this passage?

But if we assume Jesus had, as a matter of historical remembrance, been given sour wine to quench his thirst, we can begin to understand why a disciple might have found significance in the fact that David had experienced similar treatment at the hands of his enemies a millennium earlier. Jesus "fulfilled" the verse, not by experiencing something that was previously predicted, but in the sense that his experience brings out in a superlative way the significance of what David previously experienced. Jesus is the supreme example of the kind of mistreatment God's servants, like David, sometimes receive. In any case, we find it far more likely that the midrashic techniques we find in the Gospels are used to interpret events that had taken place in history than that they represent fabricated events to awkwardly and partially "fulfill" Old Testament passages.

Third, something similar may be said about the Qumran pesharim in particular. While some scholars have argued that authors of the Qumran texts invented events and people to illuminate a certain understanding of biblical texts, more are now arguing that the Dead Sea Scrolls actually suggest "the Qumranites were concerned with real people and events."[140] That is, as with the Gospel authors, the Qumran community tended to use pesher to *interpret* historical events/persons

140. Lim, *Pesharim*, 67. Lim refers here especially to Pesher Nahum's references to Demetrius and Antiochus (4QpNah frags. 3–4, col. 1). As Lim notes, these references in Pesher Nahum provide "the clearest indication that the pesherist was interested in history" (p. 64). P. R. Davies is one example of a scholar who denies that pesharim refer to actual people and events. See *Behind the Essenes: History and Ideology in the Dead Sea Scrolls* (Atlanta: Scholars Press, 1987). For Lim's assessment of Davies, see *Pesharim*, 68. For an example of an author working toward a mediating position, see J. H. Charlesworth, *The Pesharim and Qumran History: Chaos or Consensus?* (Grand Rapids: Eerdmans, 2002). Charlesworth offers a brief summary of three perspectives on history and the Qumran pesharim on pp. 4–5.

as fulfilling Scripture, not to *fabricate* events/persons to fulfill Scripture. As James Charlesworth notes, Qumran pesharim "are biblical commentaries in the sense of fulfillment hermeneutics. They reveal primarily the way Qumranites viewed their recent past by finding meaning for their own lives [in the Scriptures]." They looked for ways in which the Scriptures "had been fulfilled in the life and history of their own special Community."[141] Hence, even if we were to grant that the Gospels used—or even are examples of—pesher, this would not necessarily warrant denying the essential facticity of the Jesus who undergirds them.[142]

At the same time, however, *there is no compelling reason to think that the Gospels are examples of the midrash or pesher genre*—this is our fourth argument.[143] As Timothy Lim observes, pesher, while "neither generic nor unique," is distinctive both in terms of "structure and content," and this distinctiveness "should not be homogenized into an undifferentiated Jewish-Christian biblical interpretation by its application to exegesis of the New Testament that may have some superficial similarities."[144] Those who too easily equate the Gospels with midrashic exegesis of the Old Testament tend to ignore the fundamental difference between ancient Jewish approaches to the biblical texts as opposed to how they approached their own recent history. Borrowing categories from contemporary oral tradition studies, one could compare this to the confusion of oral tradition and oral history.[145] In the end, contrary to the Gospels-as-midrash thesis, the Gospels show a demonstrated concern for the reporting and interpreting of actual recent history.

Additionally, as David Brewer has demonstrated, while New Testament authors at times reflect the influence of a more creative, "inspirational" manner of interpreting Old Testament texts (e.g., ways in which Jesus "fulfilled" Old Testament passages), they can also, in keeping with the first-century "nomological" orientation, reflect more of a concern for the context and plain meaning of Old Testament texts than the Gospels-as-midrash thesis would lead us to expect.[146]

141. Charlesworth, *Pesharim and Qumran History*, 5–6.

142. As F. F. Bruce argues, to whatever degree the Qumran pesher style of exegesis offers us an analogy to the Gospels, "it lends no support to the view that the evangelists engaged in free redactional activity uninhibited by historical fact" ("Biblical Exposition at Qumran," in *Studies in Midrash and Historiography*, 98).

143. See the intriguing argument put forth by P. S. Alexander, "Midrash and the Gospels," in *Synoptic Studies*, ed. C. M. Tuckett (Sheffield: JSOT, 1984), 1–18, esp. 10–11.

144. Lim, *Pesharim*, 83.

145. See R. T. France, "Postscript: Where Have We Got to and Where Do We Go from Here?" in *Studies in Midrash and Historiography*, 298. An example of this methodological confusion—one that results in claims that explicitly and needlessly undermine the historical veracity of the Gospels—can be found in G. W. E. Nickelsburg, *Ancient Judaism and Christian Origins: Diversity, Continuity, and Transformation* (Minneapolis: Fortress, 2003), 24–28. Nickelsburg falls into hasty generalizations about oral history, and carelessly equates the Jesus tradition with "storytelling," which, he claims, "understands truth in a freer and richer way than the recounting of facts, events and propositions" (p. 27).

146. Brewer, *Techniques and Assumptions*, 224. This is not to say that the New Testament authors were as tied to the original context/meaning as are most exegetes today. We are simply making a comparative claim here.

What is more, the Gospels do not reflect the formulaic pesher style employed at Qumran. As N. T. Wright argues in connection with Thiering's thesis, *"There is nothing in the writing of actual 'pesher'-style works which corresponds in any way to what we find in the gospels."*[147] And finally, the Gospels incorporate a number of features—not least of which are their biographical and historical interests—that cannot easily be reconciled with the view that they are examples of substantially fictionalized midrash.

Fifth, in light of these weaknesses of the Gospels-as-midrash thesis, the question must be raised as to why certain scholars have made this claim. Mark Allan Powell has recently—and, we would add, correctly—provided a response to this question. In his analysis of John Shelby Spong's version of this claim, Powell points out that virtually all of the Gospel narratives identified by Spong as fabricated midrash have one thing in common:

> a portrayal of events that would have no adequate scientific explanation; they all involve instances of what is sometimes called "the supernatural" or "the miraculous". . . . Basically, Spong's position seems to be this: Events that cannot happen, did not happen. But the evangelists were not liars (or fools). They never intended for us to read these stories as literal history. They intended us to read them as midrashic folklore. This seems like Bultmann *redivivus*.[148]

One of the main problems with this thesis, of course, is that—unlike the post-Enlightenment Spong—most first-century Jewish readers would have had no problem believing in the reality of literal miracles. Powell concludes that the

> literary-critical analysis of the Gospels *as literature* reveals that the implied readers of these narratives are expected to receive them as narrative reports of events that actually transpired in history. . . . In short, the historical evidence does not support Spong's claim that the Gospel's original readers would have understood accounts of spectacular events as metaphorical midrash *as opposed to* literal historical reporting.[149]

Responding to Thiering's Gospels-as-Pesher Thesis

Finally, a brief word must be said in response to Barbara Thiering's particular thesis that the Gospels should be understood as Qumranic pesher. Two arguments suffice, we believe, to lay the theory to rest.

---

147. N. T. Wright, *Who Was Jesus?* (Grand Rapids: Eerdmans, 1992), 27 (emphasis in text). See also E. W. Larson, "Are the Dead Sea Scrolls Christian?" *Near Eastern Archaeology* 63 (2000): 170–71. C. M. Pate has recently favorably compared Matthew and pesher, but he is quite explicit that this comparison is one of a "broad connection" suggested by the fact that both "adapt and apply the Old Testament to their communities, perceived by them as eschatological in scope" ("The Hermeneutic of Restoration: Matthew, Pesher and the DDS," in *Communities of the Last Days: The Dead Sea Scrolls, the New Testament and the Story of Israel* [Downers Grove, IL: InterVarsity, 2000], 86).

148. Powell, "Authorial Intent," 228, 229.

149. Ibid., 236–37 (emphasis in text).

First, Thiering's whole project presupposes an inaccurate understanding of pesher. As we have noted, in general, pesher functioned as a form of biblical commentary that served to make Old Testament texts relevant to the contemporary situation, a situation that was believed to be on the brink of the eschaton. Thiering's thesis, however, treats pesher as if it were a complex method for writing current history *in code*. The pesher texts we have from Qumran were designed, in a sense, to *decode* Old Testament texts in order to make them understandable to the contemporary audience. By contrast, Thiering's approach assumes that the authors of pesher were *coding* their messages so that the surface meaning actually *hides* the true interpretation. The code would take centuries—and Barbara Thiering—before it would be unlocked. This is a very idiosyncratic view of pesher, to say the least, and one that the actual pesher texts of Qumran do not exhibit.[150]

Second, Thiering claims that the Dead Sea Scrolls' "Teacher of Righteousness" was John the Baptist, and the "Wicked Priest" was Jesus. Unfortunately for her thesis, archaeological and paleographical evidence, together with radiocarbon dating have led virtually all scholars to conclude that the bulk of the Qumran texts were composed approximately two hundred years before the ministries of John or Jesus.[151] As Joseph Fitzmyer states, views such as Thiering's "ride roughshod over the archaeological, palaeographical, and radio carbon dating of the evidence that clearly pinpoints most of the QS [Qumran scrolls] to the pre-Christian centuries."[152] Though Thiering's remarkable thesis still seems to enjoy a certain

---

150. Larson, "Are the Dead Sea Scrolls Christian?" 171. R. Burridge, noting that Thiering has failed to persuade scholars, refers to her theory as "fantasy"; see review of *Jesus and the Riddle of the Dead Sea Scrolls*, by B. Thiering, *Sewanee Theological Review* 36 (1993): 437, 439. One can also add here the fact that the Gospels simply do not offer enough genre/stylistic similarity to the Qumran pesher to be considered examples of the genre. See S. E. Witmer, "Approaches to Scripture in the Fourth Gospel and the Qumran *Pesharim*," *NovT* 48 (2006): 313–28.

151. For a helpful summary of the dating evidence, see J. VanderKam and P. Flint, *The Meaning of the Dead Sea Scrolls* (San Francisco: HarperSanFrancisco, 2002), 20–33, and esp. 325–27. Beyond Thiering, one other exception to this consensus is R. Eisenman, *James the Brother of Jesus: The Key to Unlocking the Secrets of Early Christianity and the Dead Sea Scrolls* (New York: Penguin, 1997). Eisenman also argues that the Dead Sea Scrolls are intimately tied to early Christianity. In fact, he attempts to make the case that James, the brother of Jesus, is the "Teacher of Righteousness" mentioned in the scrolls, while the "Wicked Priest" is Ananus who put James to death in 62 CE, and the "Man of Lies" is none other than the apostle Paul. For a brief but helpful critique of Eisenman's theory, see Larson, "Are the Dead Sea Scrolls Christian?" 68–70.

152. J. A. Fitzmyer, *Responses to 101 Questions on the Dead Sea Scrolls* (New York: Paulist, 1992), 110. See also Wright, *Who Was Jesus?* 26; VanderKam and Flint, *Meaning of the Dead Sea Scrolls*, 326–27. Thiering, Eisenman, and associates continue to attempt to undermine the dating consensus by attacking the common radiocarbon dating results. See, e.g., G. Rodley and B. Thiering, "Use of Radiocarbon Dating in Assessing Christian Connections to the Dead Sea Scrolls," *Radiocarbon* 41 (1999): 169–82; J. Atwill and S. Braunheim, with R. Eisenman, "Redating the Radiocarbon Dating of the Dead Sea Scrolls," *Dead Sea Discoveries* 11 (2004): 143–57. Nonetheless, the vast consensus is arrayed against them. See S. Ivy et al., "Radiocarbon Dating of Fourteen Dead Sea Scrolls," *Radiocarbon* 34 (1992): 843–49; A. Jull et al., "Radiocarbon Dating of Scrolls and Linen Fragments from the Judean Desert," *Radiocarbon* 37 (1995): 11–19; idem, "Radiocarbon Dating of Scrolls and Linen Fragments from the Judean Desert," *Atiqot* 28

appeal among more popular audiences, especially people with a proclivity to conspiracy theories, it has for good reason gained no allegiance in the scholarly community.[153]

In light of all this, we conclude that, while the Gospels do, at times, exhibit midrashic and perhaps even persher-like literary techniques, they cannot be said in any substantive ways to be composed as midrash or pesher in terms of their genre classification. Moreover, even the midrashic or pesher features the Gospels exhibit do not necessarily undermine the historicity of the events they depict with these features. To the contrary, they tend to argue for it, given that if they were inventing a story to fulfill Scripture, we would expect that the "fulfillments" would in many cases be much more natural than what we actually find. We can explain why the authors were so creative in utilizing Old Testament texts *given that what they say happened actually did happen*. But we cannot easily envision them fabricating what they say happened solely on the basis of the Old Testament texts they utilize.[154]

The Gospels as Oral Recitations

To summarize our conclusions on the Gospel genre to this point, there is no evidence that the Gospels were written as literary fiction, whether romance novel,

---

(1996): 85–91; and esp. G. Doudna, "Dating the Scrolls on the Basis of Radiocarbon Analysis," in *The Dead Sea Scrolls after Fifty Years*, ed. P. Flint and J. VanderKam (Leiden: Brill, 1998), 1:430–71.

153. Thiering is not the only contemporary scholar who attempts to find ingenious "codes" within the Gospels based upon supposed first-century Jewish exegetical techniques. E.g., in a recent book, John Dart—former religion writer for the *Los Angeles Times*—argues that the original Gospel of Mark can be reconstructed from our canonical Mark, fragments of Luke, and Morton Smith's Secret Gospel of Mark fragment. This reconstruction project is possible once one realizes that Mark utilized a complex chiasmus style of writing that structures the entire Gospel, both on the micro and macro levels. Beyond the facts that (1) macro-chiasmus is hardly an established feature of first-century writing, and (2) chiasmus itself is not discussed in ancient rhetorical texts until the fourth century, the exegetical gymnastics and special pleading needed to make the theory work testify more to Dart's creativity than to Mark's. See Dart, *Decoding Mark* (Harrisburg, PA: Trinity, 2003). For two insightful critiques of Dart's book, see the reviews by M. Schuler and L. Blumell in the online *Review of Biblical Literature* 9 (2004) (www .bookreviews.org).

154. As noted above, Moo has raised the question of whether the Gospel authors fabricated materials for their passion narratives in order to create "fulfillments" of Old Testament prophecies. His conclusion is that "no instance in which [the creation of ostensive historical materials designed to 'fulfill' OT prophecies] is the most probable explanation has been discovered in the course of this investigation" (*Old Testament in the Gospel Passion Narratives*, 379). See also France, "Postscript," 291; J. D. G. Dunn, *Unity and Diversity in the New Testament*, 2nd ed. (Philadelphia: Trinity, 1990), 99. France writes: "The evidence suggests that it is more satisfactory to explain these features as the result of a deliberate presentation of existing traditions in light of a deliberate 'fulfillment' than as indicating that the story itself was created out of the Old Testament texts. To observe a strong scriptural colouring, in other words, is not to settle the question of the origin of the traditions. The question remains, which came first, the tradition or the scripture?" ("Postscript," 296). We believe the cumulative evidence has generally settled that question.

Homeric transvaluation, or fictionalized Jewish midrash. Describing the actual nature of the genre is a bit more complex. While the Gospels may not be fully captured by the genre of ancient biography, they nonetheless are biographical in nature. Similarly, while the Gospels—even Luke—may not be reduced to historiography, pure and simple, still they are clearly historical in their intent. The Gospels appear to be unique—sui generis—in certain senses, particularly with respect to their content. Most important, the messianic fulfillment of the Isaianic promise of "good news," fleshed out with categories derived from the world of Jewish apocalyptic soteriology, sets these narratives apart from all others in the ancient world.

However, before drawing the discussion of the Gospel genre to a close, we must consider a final facet of the Gospels that has all too often been neglected in modern scholarship. Regardless of where one comes down on the question of the specific literary genre of the Gospels, these texts will be fundamentally misconstrued unless it is recognized that they emerge from, and are intended for, a predominately oral/aural environment. The Gospels will be properly understood by the post-Gutenberg, highly literate world of contemporary scholarship only when it is remembered that they were consciously composed primarily for the purpose of oral recitation and aural reception.[155]

On the Nature of Orally/Aurally Oriented Written Texts

As contemporary orality-literacy studies have demonstrated, orality and literacy are able to interact in ways much more complex and fascinating than many scholars in the past have imagined.[156] Homeric scholar Egbert Bakker has provided an

155. While most of the work done on this matter to date has focused on the Gospel of Mark, we suggest that similar—if less obvious—cases can be made for the other Gospels as well.

156. Our thoughts on the orality-literacy interface have been shaped by a wide range of interdisciplinary studies. Among the most helpful, we would include: M. C. Amodio, *Writing the Oral Tradition: Oral Poetics and Literate Culture in Medieval England* (Notre Dame, IN: University of Notre Dame Press, 2004); E. J. Bakker, *Poetry in Speech: Orality and Homeric Discourse* (Ithaca, NY: Cornell University Press, 1997); idem, "How Oral Is Oral Composition?" in *Signs of Orality: The Oral Tradition and Its Influence in the Greek and Roman World*, ed. E. A. MacKay (Boston: Brill, 1999), 29–37; E. Fantham, "Two Levels of Orality in the Genesis of Pliny's *Panegyricus*," in *Signs of Orality*, 221–37; G. R. F. Ferrari, "Orality and Literacy in the Origin of Philosophy," *Ancient Philosophy* 4 (1984): 194–205; R. Finnegan, "Literacy versus Non-Literacy: The Great Divide?" in *Modes of Thought: Essays on Thinking in Western and Non-Western Societies*, ed. R. Horton and R. Finnegan (London: Faber and Faber, 1973), 112–44; J. M. Foley, "Oral Tradition into Textuality," in *Texts and Textuality: Textual Instability, Theory and Interpretation*, ed. P. Cohen (New York: Garland, 1997), 1–24; idem, "What's in a Sign?" in *Signs of Orality*, 1–27; M. Gagarin, "The Orality of Greek Oratory," in *Signs of Orality*, 163–80; I. Hofmeyr, "John Bunyan, His Chair, and a Few Other Relics: Orality, Literacy, and the Limits of Area Studies," in *African Words, African Voices: Critical Practices in Oral History*, ed. L. White et al. (Bloomington: Indiana University Press, 2001), 78–90; L. Honko, J. Handoo, and J. M. Foley, eds., *The Epic: Oral and Written* (Mysore, India: Central Institute of Indian Languages, 1998); T. M. Lentz, *Orality and Literacy in Hellenic Culture* (Carbondale: Southern Illinois University Press, 1989); W. Oesterreicher, "Types of Orality in Texts," in *Written Voices, Spoken Signs: Tradition, Performance, and the Epic Text*, ed. E. Bak-

insightful framework by which to understand some of the potentialities of this interaction. Bakker begins by making a helpful distinction between the medium of communication, on the one hand, and what he refers to as the conceptional nature of that communication, on the other.[157] In terms of its *medium*, a communicative act is either oral (spoken) or literate (written) in form. However, in terms of *conception*—the linguistic/hermeneutical strategy and style of a communicative act—the oral-literate distinction is not a simple binary relationship, but rather forms a continuum. In other words, in terms of its *conception*, a communicative act can be more or less "oral" or "literate."

One important implication of this distinction is that medium and conception are separable. Thus, a communicative act may be written in medium but can remain largely "oral" in its conception.[158] Bakker notes the implications:

ker and A. Kahane (Cambridge, MA: Harvard University Press, 1997), 190–214; K. O'Brien O'Keeffe, *Visible Song: Transitional Literacy in Old English Verse* (New York: Cambridge University Press, 1990); C. O'Danachair, "Oral Tradition and the Printed Word," *Irish University Review* 9 (1979): 31–41; J. P. Small, *Wax Tablets of the Mind: Cognitive Studies of Memory and Literacy in Classical Antiquity* (New York: Ro-Hedge, 1997); B. Stock, *Listening for the Text: On the Uses of the Past* (Baltimore: Johns Hopkins University Press, 1990); C. J. Swearington, "Literate Rhetors and Their Illiterate Audiences: The Orality of Early Literacy," *PRE/TEXT* 7 (1986): 145–62; A. Sweeney, *A Full Hearing: Orality and Literacy in the Malay World* (Berkeley: University of California Press, 1987); D. Tannen, ed., *Spoken and Written Language: Exploring Orality and Literacy* (Norwood, NJ: ABLEX, 1982); R. Thomas, *Literacy and Orality in Ancient Greece* (New York: Cambridge University Press, 1992); idem, *Oral Tradition and Written Record in Classical Athens* (New York: Cambridge University Press, 1989); R. Whitaker, "Orality and Literacy in the Poetic Traditions of Archaic Greece and Southern Africa," in *Voice into Text: Orality and Literacy in Ancient Greece*, ed. I. Worthington (New York: Brill, 1996), 205–17; I. Worthington, "Greek Oratory and the Oral/Literate Division," in *Voice into Text*, 165–77.

Two of the most common problems in orality-literacy studies of the past have been (1) the assumption of a "great divide" between oral and literate cultures vis-à-vis modes of cognition, etc., and (2) the unfortunate tendency to make hasty generalizations about all orally dominant contexts (whether about their oral traditions or their written texts) based upon a very small number of actual field studies. The first problem largely has been put to rest in the field today (see Finnegan's landmark essay, "Literacy versus Non-Literacy: The Great Divide?"), although shadows of it do persist when scholars create more subtle sets of false binary oppositions between aspects of orality and literacy (e.g., pristine indigenous "oral" cultures vs. modern, elitist, colonialist "literate" cultures). A recent example of this unfortunate tendency may be detected in certain contributions to two recent volumes edited by J. A. Draper, *Orality, Literacy and Colonialism in Antiquity* (Atlanta: Society of Biblical Literature, 2004); and *Orality, Literacy and Colonialism in Southern Africa* (Atlanta: Society of Biblical Literature, 2004). Terence Ranger points out several of these binaries in his "Commentary" in the second volume (pp. 236–37, 247). The second problem remains a constant threat. In an attempt to avoid this common pitfall, the following general observations about the nature of orally/aurally oriented written texts have been gleaned from a good range of studies done within a wide variety of contexts.

157. Bakker, *Poetry in Speech*, 7–9; idem, "How Oral Is Oral Composition?" 29–33. Bakker takes this distinction from P. Koch and W. Oesterreicher, "Sprache der Nähe—Sprache der Distanz," *Romanistisches Jahrbuch* 36 (1985): 15–43. See also Oesterreicher, "Types of Orality," 190–96.

158. This insight explains the many, sometimes paradoxical sounding, phrases that scholars have coined to try to capture the "oral"-like aspects that can be found within written texts—e.g., "literate orality," "written orality," "oral manuscript culture," "rhetorical culture," "transitional literacy," "oral residue/habits/orientation/techniques," etc.

An important consequence of the conceptional understanding of "oral" is not only that the orality of a discourse is perfectly compatible with writing; equally important, especially for the study of how oral traditions are recorded, is that the very notion of writing is sensitive to the new understanding of "oral." Often we talk about writing as if it is a monolithic concept, but in reality writing runs the gamut of the whole oral-literate continuum.[159]

What Bakker refers to as the "conceptional" dimension of a communicative act is closely linked with the idea of linguistic *"register."*[160] Wulf Oesterreicher has proposed that the most characteristic difference between oral and literate conceptions/registers is best captured using the metaphor of spatial proximity. He suggests that informality and "immediacy" characterize the oral conception/register, while more elaborate styles of communication characterized by formality and "distance" typify the literate conception/register.[161]

There is a growing consensus that the widespread flourishing of a highly literate register did not begin with the move from an oral to a scribal culture. Rather, this significant moment in communicative history comes with the move from a scribal world of handwritten texts to a post-Gutenberg world of fixed printed type.[162] Within any given culture, it appears that it is with the advent and proliferation of the fixed print medium that the reading strategies of written texts fundamentally change. In the ancient scribal world, reading remained largely a public, communal act of oral recitation and aural reception. When one knew that his or her text would be read aloud and thus heard by the audience, the communicative strategies and linguistic register of one's written text remained fundamentally "oral" in nature. With the advent of the printing press, however, silent individual reading eventually became the norm, and texts acquired an increasingly "literate" register.

Elizabeth Einstein succinctly captures the essence of this transition when she notes that "learning to read is different from reading to learn."[163] That is to say, one can be quite versatile with the written medium and thus "literate" in the traditional sense (with respect to medium), and yet still think and communicate within the stylistic world of an informal, "immediate," oral conception/register. It is with the advent and availability of fixed print and the enthronement of

159. Bakker, "How Oral Is Oral Composition?" 31.

160. On the concept of linguistic "registers" see Foley, "What's in a Sign?" 11; S. Niditch, "Oral Register in the Biblical Libretto: Towards a Biblical Poetics," *Oral Tradition* 10 (1995): 387–408.

161. Oesterreicher, "Types of Orality," 194. On other common characteristics of an oral register/style, see Gagarin, "Orality of Greek Oratory," 168–73.

162. P. J. J. Botha, "Mute Manuscripts: Analysing a Neglected Aspect of Ancient Communication," *Theologia Evangelica* 23 (1990): 41; J. Dewey, "The Gospel of Mark as an Oral-Aural Event: Implications for Interpretation," in *The New Literary Criticism and the New Testament*, ed. E. Struthers Malbon and E. V. McKnight (Sheffield: Sheffield Academic Press, 1994), 148–49; B. B. Scott, "Blowing in the Wind: A Response," *Semeia* 65 (1994): 182.

163. E. L. Einstein, *The Printing Press as an Agent of Change: Communications and Cultural Transformations in Early Modern Europe* (New York: Cambridge University Press, 1979), 1:65.

silent, individualistic, "reading to learn" strategies in the modern world that a momentous shift in communicative conception/register takes place. As Joanna Dewey reminds us: "Modern readers can stop and reflect on the text at any point; ancient hearers could not. We can reread and check back; they could not. We read silently and alone; they heard it spoken in community." As Dewey goes on to note, "New Testament scholars are just beginning to explore the issues of how oral/aural/textual media of antiquity influenced composition and reception of particular ancient texts."[164]

The Gospels as Orally/Aurally Oriented Texts

It is important to remember that for the earliest Christians, the term "gospel" was used to refer to the "oral proclamation of the significance of the [life,] death and resurrection of Jesus, not to a written account of the story of Jesus."[165] While the term "gospel" was eventually also applied to written texts that contained the story of Jesus, the term never ceased being used to refer to the oral proclamation. It has retained this dual-purpose semantic range to this day. But we must always remember that in the beginning was the "gospel" as Good News proclaimed *orally*.[166]

In our estimation, many of the conundrums New Testament scholarship has created for itself arise from the fact that this fundamental point often has been given insufficient attention. From textual ("lower") criticism to literary-historical ("higher") criticism, modern, post-Gutenberg biblical scholarship has tended to approach the written Gospels from within a decidedly "literary paradigm"—the natural paradigm of the modern, Western, academic "print culture." This perspectival bias, rooted in a print mentality, has had unfortunate effects upon much New Testament scholarship as it concerns the nature of the written Gospels.[167] This has happened in (at least) two different but closely related ways.

164. Dewey, "Gospel of Mark as an Oral-Aural Event," 147–48.
165. Stanton, *Jesus and Gospel*, 52.
166. There is debate as to who initially transitioned the word "gospel" to indicate a written text. For Mark (1:1), "gospel" still refers to the proclamation, while Luke and John never use the noun in their texts. H. Koester has argued that most likely it was Marcion who first transitioned the term; see "From the Kerygma-Gospel to Written Gospels," *NTS* 35 (1989): 361–81. Stanton (*Jesus and Gospel*, 56–59) has recently made a case for considering Matthew as the instigator. While Matthew understands Jesus's teachings and kingdom deeds as "gospel" (4:23; 9:35), he adds "this" to Mark's "the Gospel" at 24:14 and 26:13, which may suggest that he sees his own writing as a "Gospel" (a move fueled by his need to distinguish his writing from Mark's and thus requiring a term for their generic type). This strikes us as loading more freight upon Matthew's redactional gloss than is merited. Recently, J. A. Kelhoffer has proposed that this transition took place sometime after Matthew but before the Didache (and thus Marcion). See "'How Soon a Book' Revisited: *EUAGGELION* as a Reference to 'Gospel' Materials in the First Half of the Second Century," *ZNW* 95 (2004): 1–34.
167. Among those scholars who have warned of the dangerous effects of this bias are T. E. Boomershine, "Peter's Denial as Polemic or Confession: The Implications of Media Criticism for Biblical Hermeneutics," *Semeia* 39 (1987): 47–68; Botha, "Mute Manuscripts"; Dewey, "Gospel of Mark as an Oral-Aural

On the one hand, fueled by the early form-critical approach, scholars in the first half of the twentieth century tended to compare the Gospels' compositional method and style to modern literature and found them to be rather crude and unsophisticated. On the other hand, by the end of the twentieth century and under the influence of new literary approaches to the Scriptures, the pendulum had swung to viewing the Gospels as sophisticated literary works (e.g., MacDonald's "Mark-as-Homeric-epic" thesis discussed above). In both cases, however, the predominant media context from which the tools of literary analysis were drawn was the modern scholar's own print-based literary world. In both cases, the actual media world within which the New Testament authors lived and moved and wrote their texts was—however unintentionally—ignored.

Even for the few voices crying for a fundamental reevaluation, the attempted escape from the vortex of the modern, print-based literary paradigm was, at times, unsuccessful.[168] Vernon Robbins perceptively writes:

> The problem is that a discussion of "print culture" appropriate for our time has been imposed onto the first centuries of the common era in such a manner that the relations between oral and written culture during early Christian times is badly misconstrued. . . . The confusion arises through a failure to recognize the pervasiveness of rhetorical culture throughout Mediterranean society during the Hellenistic period.[169]

Robbins highlights the significance of this observation when he goes on to demonstrate that in "rhetorical cultures"—cultures not devoid of writing but yet dominated by orality—the recording of words in a written text is commonly the result of what can be called "recitation composition," as opposed to the word-

---

Event"; and esp. W. Kelber, *The Oral and the Written Gospel: The Hermeneutics of Speaking and Writing in the Synoptic Tradition, Mark, Paul, and Q* (Philadelphia: Fortress, 1983).

168. The paradigm case is found in the work of Werner Kelber. Although Kelber warned others against the print mentality, he nonetheless remained captive to it in important ways. See the critiques by Boomershine, "Peter's Denial"; J. Dewey, "Mark as Aural Narrative: Structures as Clues to Understanding," *Sewanee Theological Review* 36 (1992): 54–55; V. K. Robbins, "Writing as a Rhetorical Act in Plutarch and the Gospels," in *Persuasive Artistry: Studies in New Testament Rhetoric in Honor of George A. Kennedy*, ed. D. F. Watson (Sheffield: Sheffield Academic Press, 1991), 144.

169. Robbins, "Writing as a Rhetorical Act," 144. Robbins defines "rhetorical culture" as an environment where "oral and written speech interact closely with one another" (p. 145). Elsewhere Robbins described a rhetorical culture as one where "speech is influenced by writing and writing is influenced by speaking" ("Progymnastic Rhetorical Composition and Pre-Gospel Traditions: A New Approach," in *The Synoptic Gospels: Source Criticism and the New Literary Criticism*, ed. C. Focant [Leuven: Leuven University Press, 1993], 113). Several decades ago W. J. Ong identified the importance of "rhetorical culture," a phenomenon he described as "basically oral culture shrouded in writing" (*Romance, Rhetoric and Technology: Studies in the Interaction of Expression and Culture* [Ithaca, NY: Cornell University Press, 1971], 261; on rhetorical culture see 1–3, 25–28). We believe Bakker's concepts of "media" versus "conception" and Foley's explication of linguistic "register" best capture this crucial phenomenon; see Bakker, "How Oral Is Oral Composition?"; Foley, "What's in a Sign?"

for-word "copying" of a more technical verbatim "scribal" mind-set.[170] Broadly construed, recitation composition can be understood as a method of transmitting a text (whether oral or written) that allows for a significant degree of creative, rhetorical *flexibility in wording* even while it strives to faithfully preserve the essential (i.e., illocutionary) meaning of the original text.[171]

As Robbins uses the terms, it is this flexibility to record the text either verbatim or in different words that distinguishes recitation composition from a more rigid, verbatim "scribal" strategy of composition. In other words, recitation composition—while a communicative approach that makes use of a written medium—nonetheless remains rooted in, and indebted to, an essentially oral conception/hermeneutic.

This oral conception/hermeneutic was easily maintained, despite the written medium, for at least three reasons. First, that which was being recorded was typically *rooted in prior oral composition/tradition*.[172] Second, the very act of composing a written text usually involved *oral dictation*.[173] And third, the final written product was generally used *as the basis for future oral performances and aural receptions*. In other words, the written composition itself was both born out of, and in turn gave birth to, oral performance. And, like oral performance—and thus quite unlike what typically transpires within a rigidly "scribal" or, even more so, a modern *"print"* culture—the recitation composition "contained as much or as little verbatim reproduction as was congenial to the writer."[174] Robbins summarizes this essential characteristic when he writes, "There is no embarrassment with extensive verbatim reproduction, yet there is no commitment to verbatim copying. This, I submit, reveals the presence of 'recitation composition' as a guiding principle."[175]

170. Robbins, "Writing as a Rhetorical Act," 145. Robbins's identification of a fourfold typology is extremely helpful here. Often the typology is reduced to three options: "oral," "manuscript," and "print" cultures. But here the important difference between rhetorical and scribal cultures is lost when blended under the larger rubric of "manuscript" culture—see, e.g., D. Brewer, "The Gospels and the Laws of Folktale," 38. However, Robbins's ideal-typical "rhetorical culture" vs. "scribal culture" divide could lead to the false assumption that all scribes were uniformly and rigidly (in his terms) "scribal" in their orientation to the texts with which they worked. If nothing else, the manuscript tradition of the New Testament demonstrates that this is clearly *not* the case.

171. More narrowly and technically, it can be defined as the attempt to record "the assigned chreia very clearly in the same words or in others as well" (R. F. Hock and E. N. O'Neil, *The Chreia in Ancient Rhetoric*, vol. 1: *The Progymnasmata* [Atlanta: Scholars Press, 1986], 95).

172. For a perceptive essay on the ways in which a written text can be influenced by orality, see Foley, "Oral Tradition into Textuality."

173. On the oral dictation of ancient written texts, see H. Gamble, "Literacy, Liturgy, and the Shaping of the New Testament Canon," in *The Earliest Gospels: The Origins and Transmission of the Earliest Christian Gospels—The Contribution of the Chester Beatty Gospel Codex P45*, ed. C. Horton (New York: Clark, 2004), 30–31; A. B. Lord, "Homer's Originality: Oral Dictated Texts," *Transactions of the American Philological Association* 84 (1953): 124–34; Thomas, *Literacy and Orality*, 91. As Lord states, "The moment of dictating is the moment of creation of our texts from the past. The more we know about that moment, the greater will be our understanding of those texts" ("Homer's Originality," 134).

174. Robbins, "Writing as a Rhetorical Act," 147.

175. Ibid., 155.

When a recitation composition deviates from verbatim reproduction, the change can be other than merely ad hoc. On the one hand, as Jocelyn Small reminds us, "Classical authors generally do not check [quotations] for accuracy for [several reasons] . . . : the logistical problems of using ancient texts, the widespread belief in the excellence of their memories, and a lack of any real concern for verbatim accuracy."[176]

On the other hand, verbal variations *can* also represent conscious rhetorical strategies. Three of the most common techniques of verbal variation are abbreviation, expansion, and commentary. Thus, deviation from verbatim recitation often—though not always—serves a strategic purpose.[177] This is the media world of rhetorical culture and recitation composition. *And this appears to be the media world of the Gospels.*[178] The commonalities among and differences between the four written Gospels can be considered from a new perspective once we understand them functioning along the lines of ancient recitation compositions.

Thus, once again, the Gospels can be easily misconstrued by modern readers if they forget that the Gospels were primarily intended *to be performed orally and heard aurally in a communal setting*, not read privately and silently by isolated individuals. Indeed, it appears that within the ancient Mediterranean world, the private, silent reading of texts was relatively rare.[179] Generally speaking, our contemporary mode of reading the biblical texts was unknown to most in the ancient world. To assume that the original authors and audience would have engaged a written text as we do is dangerously anachronistic, or, as Boomershine says, it is an example of "media eisegesis."[180] In propagating this media confusion,

176. Small, *Wax Tablets*, 219–20. On this phenomenon in the ancient world, see also N. Yamagata, "Plato, Memory, and Performance," *Oral Tradition* 20 (2005): 117–19, 121, 125.

177. For discussion see Robbins, "Writing as a Rhetorical Act," 155–67.

178. Robbins notes that Mark, Matthew, and Luke have each "proceeded according to the guidelines of recitation composition" rather than mere copying (ibid., 153). For a complementary study of some of the unique dynamics that occur when the worlds of orality and literacy meet and cohabitate, see Sweeney, *A Full Hearing*. Some of Sweeney's methodological observations (see esp. chap. 1: "Predecessors and Presuppositions") could profitably be considered by New Testament scholars and applied to the Gospel tradition.

179. While there is debate on just how common the silent reading of texts was in the ancient world, the relatively low literacy rate in the ancient Mediterranean world leads to the unavoidable conclusion that most people, of necessity, engaged texts orally/aurally. Regarding the silent reading debate, earlier in the twentieth century several scholars argued that silent reading was virtually unknown in the ancient world. See, e.g., J. Balogh, "Voces Paginarum," *Philologus* 82 (1927): 84–109, 202–40; G. L. Hendrickson, "Ancient Reading," *Classical Journal* 25 (1929): 182–96. Further studies have demonstrated that the issue is more complex than previously portrayed. See W. P. Clark, "Ancient Reading," *Classical Journal* 26 (1931): 698–700; E. S. McCartney, "Notes on Reading and Praying Audibly," *Classical Philology* 43 (1948): 184–87; B. M. W. Knox, "Silent Reading in Antiquity," *Greek, Roman, and Byzantine Studies* 9 (1968): 421–35; F. D. Gilliard, "More Silent Reading in Antiquity: *Non omne verbum sonat*," *JBL* 112 (1993): 689–96; A. K. Gavrilov, "Techniques of Reading in Classical Antiquity," *Classical Quarterly* 47 (1997): 56–73; M. F. Burnyeat, "Postscript on Silent Reading," *Classical Quarterly* 47 (1997): 74–76.

180. Boomershine, "Peter's Denial," 65.

we miss important possibilities and constraints that attach to ancient texts that were designed to be read—that is, *performed*—aloud.

The Gospels as Oral Recitation

Mark, which most argue was the earliest of the four canonical Gospels and a partial template for Matthew and Luke, shows clear signs of being designed for oral recitation and aural/auditory consumption.[181] For example, Joanna Dewey has noted that the book of Mark is notorious for its resistance to being "outlined" in a linear fashion by scholars. Dewey suggests this can be accounted for by understanding it as structured as a sort of nonlinear tapestry created for oral/aural performance.[182] Her analysis of Mark reveals a structuring method that "corresponds very closely" to Eric Havelock's description of "oral methods of narrative development."[183] "The basic principle," Havelock writes, "can be stated abstractly as variation within the same."[184] Havelock points out that oral composition

> operates on the acoustic principle of the echo. . . . The same compositional principle [the echo principle] extends itself to the construction of the tale as a whole; it will avoid sheer surprise and novel inventions. . . . The basic method for assisting the memory to retain a series of distinct meanings is to frame the first of them in a way which will suggest or forecast a later meaning which will recall the first without being identical with it.[185]

In light of these observations, Dewey makes a convincing textually based case—focusing upon Mark's parallel and concentric/chiastic structures—for understanding this Gospel as designed for oral recitation and aural reception.

Similarly, Christopher Bryan effectively demonstrates that both in terms of its narrative structure and its compositional style Mark shows all the evidences of being written for oral recitation.[186] Bryan concludes his study by asking, "Was

181. The most obvious settings for the oral performance of the Gospels are liturgical and/or ritual contexts—i.e., the gathering of the early Christian community for worship, baptism, etc. (see 1 Thess. 5:27; Col. 4:16; 1 Tim. 4:13; Rev. 1:3). Hengel (*Four Gospels and the One Gospel*, chap. 4) proposes a liturgical context, as does Gamble ("Literacy, Liturgy," 32–35). Whitney Shiner, however, suggests a ritual context, particularly baptism; see *Proclaiming the Gospel: First-Century Performance of Mark* (New York: Trinity, 2003), 48–49.

182. J. Dewey, "Mark as Interwoven Tapestry: Forecasts and Echoes for a Listening Audience," *CBQ* 53 (1991): 221–36.

183. Ibid., 234.

184. E. Havelock, *Preface to Plato* (Cambridge, MA: Harvard University Press, 1963), 147.

185. E. Havelock, "Oral Composition in the *Oedipus Tyrannus* of Sophocles," *New Literary History* 16 (1984): 182, 183.

186. By "compositional style" Bryan refers to such things as Mark's preferences for narrative over unadorned propositions, the concrete and visual over the abstract, hyperbole and overstatement over measured and balanced observation, and confrontation and controversy over docile dialogue. C. Bryan, *A Preface to Mark: Notes on the Gospel in Its Literary and Cultural Settings* (New York: Oxford University Press, 1993); see Part II: "Was Mark Written to Be Read Aloud?" 67–171.

Mark written to be read aloud?" He answers this question with a resounding yes. "Mark," he adds, "was designed for oral transmission—and for transmission as a continuous whole—rather than for private study or silent reading."[187]

When we examine Mark's structural arrangements, again and again we find ourselves dealing with broad thematic effects that would emerge naturally in the course of a performance of the whole, but that can hardly emerge otherwise. Subsequent examination of the details of Markan style, and even his use of Scripture, all reinforce this impression.[188] Based on these observations, a growing number of scholars are convinced that Mark's Gospel was intentionally designed to be read aloud as a single, continuous performance-event.[189] We may with confidence

187. Ibid., 152.

188. Bryan has focused on the manner in which Mark's use of the Old Testament betrays its design as a text for oral/aural performance in "As It Is Written: Notes on the Essentially Oral Characteristics of Mark's Appeal to Scripture," *Sewanee Theological Review* 36 (1992): 78–90.

189. See esp. Shiner, *Proclaiming the Gospel.* See also R. Horsley, *Hearing the Whole Story: The Politics of Plot in Mark's Gospel* (Louisville: Westminster/Knox, 2001), 53–78; E. Best, "Mark's Narrative Technique," *JSNT* 37 (1989): 43–58; Boomershine, "Peter's Denial," 51–55; P. Botha, "The Historical Setting of Mark's Gospel: Problems and Possibilities," *JSNT* 51 (1993): 38–40, 54; idem, "Mark's Stories of Jesus' Tomb and History," *Neotestamentica* 23 (1989): 196–201; Brewer, "Gospels and the Laws of Folktale," 38–39; R. H. Stein, "Is Our Reading of the Bible the Same as the Original Audience's Hearing It? A Case Study in the Gospel of Mark," *JETS* 46 (2003): 63–78; B. Standaert, *L'Évangile selon Marc. Composition et genre Litteréraqire* (Nimmegen: Stichting Studentenpers, 1978). Although Joel Marcus (*Mark 1–8,* Anchor Bible 27 [New York: Doubleday, 2000], 68) sides with Standaert, he offers the conclusion rather tentatively, given that the length of Mark would make one wonder if such a long tract would have been read in a single service. This hesitation, however, is fueled by anachronism. In the ancient Mediterranean world—where neither a roast beef in the oven nor the kickoff of an NFL game made the congregation nervous if the service lasted more than an hour—a narrative the length of Mark's easily would have been performed during a single gathering of the community. As we noted in chap. 6, oral narratives much longer than Mark's are routinely performed to this day in certain cultures.

Incidentally, the fact that Mark and the other Gospels were written for oral performance does not necessarily mean that their authors did not make use of any written sources in their composition. A. B. Lord's notorious essay in which he argued for the oral composition of the Gospels presses this question ("The Gospels as Oral Traditional Literature," 33–91). Charles Talbert's strong reaction against Lord's theory is representative of those who espouse any written source theory. See "Oral and Independent or Literary and Interdependent? A Response to Albert B. Lord," in *Relationships among the Gospels,* 93–102. There is no little irony in the fact that, when Lord—whose theories have been so widely embraced as helpful for our understanding of the oral Jesus tradition—was finally invited to weigh in on the Gospels themselves, he saw no reason to posit a written source-critical theory but rather saw the similarities between the Synoptic Gospels as quite readily explained in purely oral terms. More recently, an interdisciplinary study (New Testament and experimental psychology) has argued that most of the Synoptic parallels can be readily explained on the grounds of memorized oral tradition. See R. K. McIver and M. Carroll, "Experiments to Develop a Criteria for Determining the Existence of Written Sources, and Their Potential Implications for the Synoptic Problem," *JBL* 121 (2002): 667–87. While it is certainly not necessary to dismiss the two-source theory entirely, we would argue that once one breaks free of considering the Gospels from within the dominant literary paradigm, a new appreciation for the role of oral tradition in Gospel studies—including its role in explaining the Synoptic interrelationships—is an obvious consequence. We find James Dunn's recent thoughts to be pointing in the proper direction; see *Jesus Remembered,* 222–23.

conclude that the other canonical Gospels also would have had as their primary audience a gathering of the Christian community wherein the Gospel would be read aloud. They each show internal signs of being designed for oral recitation. Both the narrative structure and stylistic features characteristic of texts intended for oral recitation are evident in each of the Gospels.[190]

This conclusion, based upon literary signals within the Gospels themselves, is further confirmed by the fact that the culture in which Christianity was birthed was an orally dominant one. The vast majority of people in the first-century Greco-Roman world would access the Gospels only through the oral/aural medium. We must therefore understand that, from the beginning, the "gospel" primarily was intended to be heard by those who had "ears to hear."

Summary

We conclude that the Gospels are best understood as recitation compositions rooted in the oral Gospel tradition, texts that, while informed by historical and biographical interests, are nonetheless distinctive enough to warrant their classification as a unique genre—"Gospel." As orally oriented texts, they were always intended to undergo various "re-oralizations" within the context of the early Christian communities.[191] They arose from, and were designed to constantly return to, an oral milieu. Though written, they were intended to preserve the fundamentally oral orientation that characterized "the gospel" proclaimed from the beginning, while preventing it from being subverted or distorted (Talbert). To whatever degree the Gospel authors made use of certain available literary genres in the writing of their texts (biography, historiography, midrash, etc.), these generic features did not displace the orally oriented conception/hermeneutic that gave birth to them.

190. On Matthew as designed for oral performance, see, e.g., G. Stanton, *A Gospel for a New People: Studies in Matthew* (Louisville: Westminster/Knox, 1993), 73–75; M. Knowles, "Reading Matthew: The Gospel as Oral Performance," in *Reading the Gospels Today*, ed. S. E. Porter (Grand Rapids: Eerdmans, 2004), 56–77. On each of the four Gospels as documents intended to be read aloud in liturgical settings, see the insightful thoughts of Hengel, *Four Gospels and the One Gospel*, chap. 4: "The Cross-Check: the Origin of the Collection of the Four Gospels and the Christian Book Cupboard." See also S. Byrskog, "History or Story in Acts—A Middle Way? The 'We' Passages, Historical Intertexture, and Oral History," in *Contextualizing Acts*, esp. 268–69. As Shiner notes, texts the length of Matthew and Luke were commonly delivered orally in the first century (*Proclaiming the Gospel*, 48). On the continued presence of aids to memory in the Synoptics, see A. D. Baum, "Bildhaftigkeit als Gedächtnishilfe in der synoptischen Tradition," *Theologische Beiträge* 35 (2004): 4–16.

191. We take the term "re-oralization" from M. A. Mills, "Domains of Folkloristic Concern: The Interpretation of Scriptures," in *Text and Tradition: The Hebrew Bible and Folklore*, ed. S. Niditch (Atlanta: Scholars Press, 1990), 232. With David Aune (*New Testament in Its Literary Environment*, 65–66), one could also speak of the "literaturization" of the oral Gospel tradition, as long as one is careful not to import anachronistic elements from our modern literary context into one's use of the term here.

As examples of the impulse behind the ancient recitation composition, they are designed to preserve and express the oral Jesus tradition.[192]

Acknowledging the oral/aural context of the canonical Gospels helps explain their peculiar fusion of written genres. And when this insight is combined with the findings on the historical intentionality of community-defining oral traditions discussed previously (chaps. 6–7), this insight has important implications for our assessment of the Gospels. Given their place in the wider oral tradition, given their oral registers, given their Jewish-rooted sui generis elements along with their biographical and historiographical elements, we have every reason to conclude that, among other things, the authors of these works intended to recall and communicate reliable information about Jesus. How well they delivered on this intention is the subject of the two remaining chapters of this book.

192. L. W. Hurtado captures this dynamic when he writes: "The Gospels are organically connected to the oral tradition about Jesus and reflect wider tastes and trends in Greco-Roman culture [e.g., *bios* literature, etc.]" ("The Gospel of Mark: Evolutionary or Revolutionary Document?" *JSNT* 40 [1990]: 19). Hurtado (following John Kloppenborg) correctly insists—contra Werner Kelber—that it is illegitimate to pit Q (as an "oral genre") against Mark (as the domestication-through-textualization of the oral genre). He argues that Q is already a "literary work" with historicizing, *bios* tendencies (pp. 18–19). While we agree that Kelber's artificial splitting of Q (and we would add Paul) vs. Mark is misguided, we would equally want to argue it from the other direction—like Q, Mark retains the characteristics of an oral sensibility, as does, in their own ways, Matthew, Luke, and John.

9

EVALUATING THE SYNOPTIC GOSPELS AS HISTORICAL SOURCES

METHODOLOGICAL ISSUES AND PRELIMINARY CONSIDERATIONS

Thus far we have argued that the Gospel genre signals, among other things, a clear intention to transmit reliable history about Jesus. This brings us to a final question: How well did the Gospel authors fulfill this intention? This is the question we will seek to answer in the last two chapters of this book.

In this chapter we will address three foundational/methodological issues and explore three preliminary questions pertaining to the assessment of the historical veracity of any ancient work. The first methodological issue concerns whether the burden of proof should be placed upon those scholars who claim an ancient document is trustworthy or upon scholars who allege that an ancient document is untrustworthy. Specifically, we will reconsider the widespread historical-critical assumption that the data within the Synoptic Gospels are to be considered historically unreliable until proven otherwise.

The second foundational issue related to evaluating the Synoptic Gospels concerns the question of methodology per se. The question is this: What methodology is appropriate for assessing the overall reliability of ancient historical works and, more specifically, testing large-scale hypotheses about the Jesus of history? This is an especially important question since, we suggest, many of the seeds of contemporary skepticism concerning the Synoptics are rooted in certain a priori methodological assumptions.

The final foundational issue we will briefly address concerns the textual attestation of the Synoptics. Obviously it makes no sense to explore seriously the question of the historical reliability of an ancient work unless we are confident that, from the texts in hand, we can reconstruct a reasonably close approximation of what was originally written.

After addressing these three foundational issues, we will turn to three preliminary historiographical questions that must be faced when assessing ancient documents, and thus the Synoptic Gospels. First, did the author write with historical intent? Second, was the author in a position to report reliable history? And finally, to what extent did the author's bias affect the reliability of the report? The first question has already been addressed in chapter 8, so our response here will be by way of summary. The second and third questions, however, will explore new ground and therefore be discussed at greater length. All of this will set the stage for the final chapter in which we will consider and apply six historiographical criteria—criteria involving both internal and external evidence—that will have a direct bearing upon our assessment of the historical reliability of the Synoptic Gospels' portrait(s) of Jesus.

The "Burden of Proof" Issue

The first issue that must be addressed—for it will affect one's estimation of all other particular issues surrounding the reliability of the Synoptic Gospels—is where the burden of proof should lie as we assess the historicity of these works. Should the burden of proof lie on those who claim that any given aspect of the Synoptic tradition is historically *unreliable*? Or should it lie on those who argue that any given aspect of this tradition is in fact *reliable*?

The Skeptical Position

As we have seen throughout this study, with respect to the Gospels, the default setting for many critical New Testament scholars today—and certainly all legendary-Jesus theorists—is one of skepticism. In the view of these scholars, the sheer fact that the Synoptics contain miracle reports is enough to shift the burden of proof to anyone who would claim these documents are reliable. In this view, a historical-critical scholar cannot, as a matter of principle, accept as historical reports of supernatural occurrences.

Beyond the miraculous, however, there are other aspects of the Synoptic Gospels that are believed to justify taking an overall skeptical posture toward them. Jesus Seminar participant Robert Miller, for example, specifies four features that incline many critical scholars to place the burden of proof on anyone who wants to argue that any particular aspect of the Gospels is historically reliable.[1]

First, each of the canonical Gospels leaves out important details of Jesus's life, focusing almost exclusively on the last few years. Second, the Gospels often contradict one another. Third, redaction criticism has demonstrated that the Gospel authors creatively shape and augment the traditional material they use in very significant ways according to their own theological biases and community needs. And fourth, the Jesus tradition incorporated into the four Gospels makes no distinction between the words and deeds of the earthly Jesus and those of the risen Christ, often retrojecting the latter onto the former. In other words, much of the material in the Gospels that *looks* historical is actually the product of the imagination of early Christians, especially of early church prophets.

In this and the final chapter of this work, each of Miller's concerns will be considered. In the end we will conclude that none of them, in fact, undermines the essential historical reliability of the Synoptic portrait(s) of Jesus. However, these very considerations have led others to conclude that "*the nature of the synoptic tradition is such that the burden of proof will be upon the claim to authenticity.*"[2] As Robert Price puts it, "A heavy burden of proof rests on anyone who would vindicate the [canonical Gospels'] material as genuine."[3]

The Jesus Seminar has codified this conviction as the seventh of their "Seven Pillars of Scholarly Wisdom." The introduction to *The Five Gospels* states:

> The seventh and final pillar that supports the edifice of contemporary gospel scholarship is the reversal that has taken place regarding who bears the burden of proof. It was once assumed that scholars had to prove that details in the synoptic gospels were *not* historical. . . . The current assumption is more nearly the opposite and indicates how far scholarship has come since Strauss: the gospels are now assumed to be narratives in which the memory of Jesus is embellished by mythic elements that express the church's faith in him, and by plausible fictions that enhance the telling of the gospel story for first-century listeners who know about divine men and miracle workers firsthand. Supposedly historical elements in these narratives must therefore be demonstrated to be so.[4]

1. R. J. Miller, *The Jesus Seminar and Its Critics* (Santa Rosa, CA: Polebridge, 1999), 29–34.

2. N. Perrin, *Rediscovering the Teaching of Jesus* (New York: Harper & Row, 1967), 39 (emphasis in text). Similar perspectives are expressed by E. Käsemann, "The Problem of the Historical Jesus," in *Essays on New Testament Themes* (London: SCM, 1964), 34; J. M. Robinson, *A New Quest of the Historical Jesus* (London: SCM, 1959), 38–39n1; K. Grayston, "Jesus: The Historical Question," *Downside Review* 95 (1977): 262.

3. R. M. Price, *The Incredible Shrinking Son of Man: How Reliable Is the Gospel Tradition?* (Amherst, NY: Prometheus, 2003), 19. For Price, this burden is so unbearable that, in the end, we must face the likelihood that "the historical Jesus will have shrunk to the vanishing point" (p. 354). As we have already seen, this sort of radical methodological skepticism has led Price to a "Jesus agnosticism"—he is uncertain whether there ever was a historical Jesus. See Price, *Deconstructing Jesus* (Amherst, NY: Prometheus, 2000), 17.

4. R. W. Funk, R. W. Hoover, and the Jesus Seminar, *The Five Gospels: The Search for the Authentic Words of Jesus* (San Francisco: HarperSanFrancisco, 1993), 4–5. This position is expressed by a number

Another way of expressing this skeptical perspective is to say that, with regard to reconstructing the historical Jesus, a scholar cannot claim to "know it if you cannot show it" and "cannot use it if you do not prove it."[5] In this view, *nothing* should be accepted as historical unless it is substantiated with "evidence and convincing arguments." In other words, as Robert Miller puts it, "No scholar whose method is truly historical can use any gospel material for a portrait of the historical Jesus unless he has demonstrated its historical reliability."[6] Miller even goes so far as to argue that something should be accepted as historical "only if there is no other reasonable way to account for its presence in the gospels." Miller admits that "this principle produces minimalist results" but nevertheless contends that "such is the burden of proof that must be shouldered if we are to move beyond wishful thinking and arrive at anything approaching 'assured' conclusions."[7]

Is this skeptical stance toward the Gospels justified? In what follows we shall argue that (1) there is no warrant for the left-most wing of New Testament scholarship to claim that their approach is *the* truly scholarly or critical approach; (2) the concerns to keep historical scholarship "objective" can be better addressed by not adopting an a priori default setting of skepticism toward the Gospels; (3) the a priori skeptical stance toward the Gospels is not adequately aware of how it is driven by its own set of (anti-)religious and philosophical presuppositions; and (4) recent findings in orality-literacy studies must be centrally factored into any discussion of where the burden of proof lies in historical-critical research into the Gospels.

The Lack of Scholarly Consensus

Despite the frequent claim of legendary-Jesus theorists that the skeptical position on the burden-of-proof question is a necessary element of truly "critical" scholarship—a settled component of "scholarly wisdom"—there are, as a matter of fact, many solid, critical, New Testament scholars who do not adopt it. Indeed, a wide range of scholars have argued precisely the opposite—that the burden of

---

of Jesus Seminar members in their individual works. See, e.g., L. C. McGaughy, "Words before Deeds: Why Start with the Sayings?" *Forum*, n.s., 1 (1998): 394; R. J. Miller, "Historical Method and the Deeds of Jesus: The Test Case of the Temple Destruction," *Forum* 8 (1992): 15. Co-convener of the Seminar, J. D. Crossan, is willing to say that for those sayings that he deems as deriving from the earliest stratum (30–60 CE), "everything is [assumed] original until it is argued otherwise." Yet Crossan seems to reaffirm the Seminar's position on the burden of proof when, even for this earliest stratum, he decides (in the name of methodological rigor) to drop any singly attested datum from consideration. With this move, the burden of proof remains largely on the tradition, though it may shift for multiply attested first stratum data. See *The Historical Jesus: The Life of a Mediterranean Jewish Peasant* (San Francisco: HarperSanFrancisco, 1991), xxxii–xxxiii.

5. Miller, *Jesus Seminar*, 35–37; see also idem, "Back to the Basics: A Primer on Historical Method," *Fourth R* (November–December 1998): 14.

6. Miller, "Back to the Basics," 14.

7. Miller, *Jesus Seminar*, 15.

proof should remain on those who claim that any given portion of the Gospels is not reliable.[8]

For example, Joachim Jeremias has argued that "in the synoptic tradition it is the inauthenticity, and not the authenticity, of the sayings of Jesus that must be demonstrated."[9] And no less an authority than W. G. Kümmel argues that, with respect to the sayings of Jesus, it is a "false methodological principle" to place the burden of proof on those who argue for their authenticity rather than the other way around.[10] Others, such as E. P. Sanders, have argued for a sort of mediating position, which holds that the burden of proof "falls on the one who argues a case," whether it be for or against the authenticity of any given segment of the gospels.[11] Others add that the burden of proof should be considered flexible, shifting in the course of scholarly debate.[12] This diversity of perspectives on the burden-of-proof question among reputable New Testament scholars serves

8. Beyond Jeremias and Kümmel (noted below), see S. C. Goetz and C. L. Blomberg, "The Burden of Proof," *JSNT* 11 (1981): 39–63; R. E. Brown, "After Bultmann, What?—An Introduction to the Post-Bultmannians," *CBQ* 26 (1964): 27; L. T. Johnson, *The Real Jesus: The Misguided Quest for the Historical Jesus and the Truth of the Traditional Gospels* (San Francisco: HarperSanFrancisco, 1996), 5; D. Lührmann, "Die Frage nach Kriterien für ursprüngliche Jesusworte—eine Problemskizze," in *Jesus aux origines de la Christologie*, ed. J. Dupont (Gembloux: Duculot, 1975), 70; I. H. Marshall, *I Believe in the Historical Jesus* (Grand Rapids: Eerdmans, 1977), 199–200; G. R. Osborne, "History and Theology in the Synoptic Gospels," *Trinity Journal* 24 (2003): 6; E. Schillebeeckx, *Jesus: An Experiment in Christology*, trans. H. Hoskins (New York: Crossroad, 1991), 83, 87; R. H. Stein, "The 'Criteria' of Authenticity," in *Gospel Perspectives*, vol. 1: *Studies of History and Tradition in the Four Gospels*, ed. R. T. France and D. Wenham (Sheffield: JSOT, 1980), 225–63. In light of his methodological proposals and his adoption of the "principle of inclusion of data," N. T. Wright apparently assumes the burden lies with those who would question the data of the tradition. See *The New Testament and the People of God* (Minneapolis: Fortress, 1992), 98–109.

9. J. Jeremias, *New Testament Theology*, trans. J. Bowden (New York: Scribner's Sons, 1971), 1:37.

10. W. G. Kümmel, "Norman Perrin's 'Rediscovering the Teachings of Jesus,'" *JR* 49 (1969): 60–61. Kümmel had argued this methodological point earlier in "Jesusforschung seit 1950," *Theologische Rundschau* 31 (1965–66): 43.

11. E. P. Sanders, *Jesus and Judaism* (Philadelphia: Fortress, 1985), 13. Here, Sanders is following M. Hooker, "Christology and Methodology," *NTS* 17 (1970–71): 485; see also idem, "On Using the Wrong Tool," *Theology* 75 (1972): 580. Others advocating this type of stance include M. E. Boring, "The Historical-Critical Method's 'Criteria of Authenticity': The Beatitudes in Q and Thomas as a Test Case," *Semeia* 44 (1988): 19; B. F. Meyer, *The Aims of Jesus* (London: SCM, 1979), 83, 277n8; W. Marxsen, *The Beginnings of Christology: A Study of Its Problems* (Philadelphia: Fortress, 1969), 8; J. P. Meier, *A Marginal Jew*, vol. 1: *Rethinking the Historical Jesus* (New York: Doubleday, 1991), 183; G. Theissen and D. Winter, *The Quest for the Plausible Jesus: The Question of Criteria*, trans. M. E. Boring (Louisville: Westminster Knox, 2002), 204. Not surprisingly, some scholars who hold this view argue that the whole "burden of proof" question for Jesus studies is largely irrelevant and needlessly distracting (e.g., Boring, "Historical-Critical Method's 'Criteria,'" 19n20).

12. See, e.g., H. K. McArthur, "The Burden of Proof in Historical Jesus Research," *ExpT* 82 (1971): 116–19; J. Caba, *De los evangelios al Jesus historico* (Madrid: Biblioteca de autores cristianos, 1971), 393; Meyer, *Aims of Jesus*, 81–87. McArthur argues that in the face of three or more lines of independent attestation for a pericope, the burden then shifts to those who would claim inauthenticity. Caba argues that double attestation may accomplish the shift. See also the above comment on Crossan (n4).

to reveal that—contrary to the claim of the Jesus Seminar—there is, in fact, no settled scholarly consensus on the issue.

It is worth noting that this lack of consensus regarding burden of proof is by no means restricted to New Testament scholarship. It is also found in contemporary historical scholarship in other fields.[13] To illustrate, at one extreme we find Louis Gottschalk maintaining that "even the most genuine of documents should be regarded as guilty of deceit until proven innocent."[14] Representing a very different perspective, however, is the respected Josephus scholar T. Rajak, who operates on the principle that "as long as what Josephus tells us is *possible*, we have no right to correct it."[15] Between these two extremes we find scholars such as David Fischer who, similar to E. P. Sanders, argues that the burden of proof lies on anyone making a historical claim, whether for or against the authenticity of any particular segment of a historical work. Fischer calls this "the rule of responsibility."[16]

In our estimation, there are valid concerns that lie behind each of these perspectives. Those who place the burden of proof on all who argue for the reliability of a document, or any passage within a document, are legitimately concerned with distancing critical scholarship from the historical naïveté of the past that led many to uncritically accept reports as factual, especially when they had a vested religious and/or political interest for doing so. They rightly want to keep historical research as rigorously critical, "objective," and disciplined as possible.

Those who argue that all ancient documents deserve an a priori vote of confidence are legitimately concerned to avoid descending into an abyss of hyper-skepticism, one fueled by a chronocentric hubris that believes the only people interested in, and capable of, transmitting reliable history have been Western scholars of the last several hundred years.[17] Realistically assessing how difficult (if not impossible) it is in most cases to *prove* historical reliability, some of these scholars are concerned to avoid having the discipline of historiography collapse in on itself. For, as N. J. McEleney has argued, unless one presumes that documents

13. In fact, beyond historical studies, debates about the nature of the "burden of proof" can be found in any number of disciplinary contexts, including philosophy, medical ethics, and, of course, the manifold world of legal conundrums. For example, K. M. Parsons, *God and the Burden of Proof: Plantinga, Swinburne and the Analytic Defense of Theism* (Buffalo, NY: Prometheus, 1989); D. S. Davis, "Shifting the Burden of Proof," *Second Opinion* 18 (1993): 31–36; A. Makhijani, "The Burden of Proof," *Bulletin of the Atomic Scientists* 57 (July/August 2001): 49–55; C. Heweston and A. Khan, "The Burden of Proof," *The Lawyer* 17 (June 16, 2003): 27–28.

14. L. Gottschalk, *Understanding History: A Primer of Historical Method* (New York: Knopf, 1963), 144.

15. T. Rajak, *Josephus: The Historian and His Society* (Philadelphia: Fortress, 1984), 16. Similarly, J. M. Wallace-Hadrill, in dealing with centuries-old reports of Viking raids, concludes that, in the absence of obvious exaggeration, "I give them the benefit of the doubt" (*The Vikings in Francia* [Reading, UK: University of Reading, 1975], 8).

16. D. H. Fischer, *Historians' Fallacies: Toward a Logic of Historical Thought* (New York: Harper, 1970), 48, 63.

17. This point is emphasized by Kümmel, "Jesu Antwort an Johannes den Täufer," *in Heilsgeschehen und Geschichte* (Marburg: Elwert, 1978), 2:177–200.

that claim to report history generally do so in a reasonably reliable way (after all due consideration is given to the reporter's limitations, biases, etc.), it is difficult to see how any "historiography, ancient or modern, would win acceptance." Hence, he argues, a historian should accept "the word of the reporter unless he has reason not to do so."[18]

Finally, those advocating a middle-ground position appear to be attempting to balance these legitimate, though tensive, methodological concerns. We suggest that a more satisfactory approach to the burden-of-proof issue is possible as one seeks to embrace each of these concerns without setting them up as either/or propositions.

The A Priori and A Posteriori Burdens of Proof

Our second, yet closely related, response to the a priori skeptical posture toward the Gospels is that the legitimate concern to avoid historical naïveté can more adequately be addressed by means other than an a priori shifting of the burden of proof to the texts themselves. With respect to the burden-of-proof debate in contemporary New Testament studies, we suggest that all too often proponents of the various positions are simply talking past one another, using the phrase "burden of proof" in an equivocal fashion. This problem is related to the fact that the field of history has borrowed the term "burden of proof" ("*onus probandi*") from the semantic world of the law court.[19] In this legal context, the judge determines which claims are to be accepted by the court as true and which require proving. As James Cargile has noted, when the notion of the "burden of proof" is detached from its original legal setting and is relocated to other fields, certain problems arise—not least of which is "unclarity."[20] While this is not the place to offer a full-scale analysis of the problem, we propose that two distinct methodological concerns be recognized regarding the burden of proof as it relates to the historical assessment of a document. We can best do this by distinguishing between two logically distinct critical moments.

The first moment is what we will refer to as the "a priori burden of proof." With this term we want to signal the claim—one we advocate—that the initial burden of proof lies with *any* historian making *any* claim, positive or negative, about the reliability of a document or a passage within a document. In the words of Cargile, the principle operative in this first logical moment is that "when someone positively asserts p, he acquires the obligation to defend his claim."[21] As a guiding historical-critical principle, this moment fosters an a priori default setting wherein competing, legitimate methodological concerns are held in balance, while ensuring

18. N. J. McEleney, "Authenticating Criteria and Mark 7:1–23," *CBQ* 34 (1972): 446.
19. For a very helpful introductory philosophical analysis of the broad notion of the "burden of proof," see J. Cargile, "On the Burden of Proof," *Philosophy* 72 (1997): 59–83.
20. Ibid., 60.
21. Ibid., 62.

that each historian is responsible to make his or her case without committing the fallacy of the presumptive proof.[22] We suggest that it is in terms of what we are calling the a priori burden that the methodological intuitions of E. P. Sanders, David Fischer, and others are most appropriately located and understood.

As scholarly research and debate takes place in a given field, however, a general sense of where the burden of proof lies with respect to a particular document (or parts thereof) may settle out in one direction or the other. Here the individual historian, and perhaps the entire scholarly guild, reaches a conclusion regarding the reliability, or unreliability, of a document or passage. To the extent that the historian becomes convinced one way or the other, the burden of proof naturally shifts in the historian's mind to anyone who would argue against his or her position. The general sense of a document's historical reliability that derives from the actual in-depth study of the text in question leads to what can be called the a posteriori burden of proof. This constitutes what we can refer to as the second logical historiographical "moment" vis-à-vis the burden question.

It is conceivable, of course, that the historian may conclude that even the a posteriori burden remains finely balanced. But in such a case, the reasons that drive this conclusion are not a priori and methodological, as with the a priori burden, but rather are tied to the fact that the data itself underdetermines the location of the a posteriori burden. Thus, whereas the assignment of the a priori burden of proof is a methodological given, assigning the a posteriori burden always requires careful, judicious assessment. And given that conclusions regarding the a posteriori burden are generally tied to probabilistic assessments of complex data, it is not surprising that various scholars will disagree on where the a posteriori burden of proof lies in any given case.

This two-part analysis of the burden of proof allows us both to affirm and yet to appropriately qualify the claim of Stewart Goetz and Craig Blomberg that "there is no mediating position" on the question of where the burden of proof lies with respect to a historical document.[23] In our view, Goetz and Blomberg are correct as it concerns the a posteriori assessment of the burden of proof (except for those seemingly "finely balanced" cases). Over time, scholars do tend to arrive at either a generally positive or negative assessment of a document's historical reliability. But with regard to what we are calling the a priori burden of proof—the first logical moment—a methodological "mediating position" of

22. Interestingly, even Seminar spokesman Robert Miller affirms this position and equalizes the burden (contrary to the Jesus Seminar's "seventh pillar") when he writes, "The burden of proof falls on the one who makes a claim" ("Historical Method and the Deeds of Jesus," 28). See also Miller, "Back to the Basics," 14. It is important to note that, even if there were to emerge in the future something like a disciplinary consensus on the Gospels, this would not affect the placement of the a priori burden of proof for the individual scholar vis-à-vis any particular claim. As Cargile notes: "It is sometimes said that one who makes a claim contrary to received opinion has the burden of proof. . . . But it is not being opposed to popular opinion that should bring the burden, but rather, being committed to a position" ("Burden of Proof," 67–68).

23. Goetz and Blomberg, "Burden of Proof," 46.

sorts is precisely what is called for, and what a truly critical historical method would seem to require.

Getting Honest about Presuppositions

This brings us to our third response to the a priori skeptical stance toward the Gospels adopted by many contemporary New Testament scholars. Though it is rarely explicitly addressed among academic historians, it is undeniable that the religious and philosophical presuppositions historians bring to their discipline significantly affect their a priori stance toward the documents they study, and thus the location of the a priori burden of proof vis-à-vis those documents.[24] As historians like R. J. Shafer have noted, even seemingly mundane historical issues can quickly become entangled with one's personal worldview and values:

> The historian's own sense of values, we must emphasize again, affects his own search for evidence and his understanding of that evidence. . . . To be sure, as we have said before, certain facts can be treated almost without reference to values; e.g., the date of John Adams' death, or the weight of a nuclear weapon, or the time required for a given journey to the moon. Such matters can, however, by linkage with other events, objects, and ideas enter into considerations involving value judgments; they may even be turned into aspects of a metaphysical question.[25]

Clearly, the discipline of history cannot be divorced from the reality that those engaging in the discipline infuse their research and evaluations with their personal religious and philosophical presuppositions—their worldviews. This observation is especially relevant when we are talking about the study of ancient history, for here the evidence one has to work with is generally more meager. In such instances, one's presuppositions about what is and is not possible/plausible tend to play an even more decisive role.[26] This will naturally be the case when the text under consideration is informed by a worldview that is in conflict with that held by a contemporary scholar—for example, the worldview of the Synoptics in which miracles were deemed to be possible.

As Henk De Jonge and others have argued, the contemporary "quest for the historical Jesus"—the search for the man behind the presumably "mythic" portrayal of the Gospels—primarily was launched in the seventeenth century, not because newly discovered evidence called for it, but because the appropriation of

---

24. For an example of historical Jesus scholarship that is quite aware of these sorts of connections, see Theissen and Winter, *Quest for the Plausible Jesus*, 48, 56, 75–76, 110, 123.

25. R. J. Shafer, ed., *A Guide to Historical Method*, rev. ed. (Homewood, IL: Dorsey, 1974), 38, 39.

26. G. Y. Okihiro notes that the influence of a historian's "worldview or theory [i.e., philosophy] of history" upon the scholar's historical conclusions tends to increase as the number of available historical sources diminishes: "Historical debate is fueled by the scarcity of reliable evidence—the lesser the amount of reliable evidence, the greater the dependence on theory and the greater the dependence on theory, the greater the opportunity for debate" ("Oral History and the Writing of Ethnic History: A Reconnaissance into Method and Theory," *Oral History Review* 9 [1981]: 33).

a new, "naturalistic" worldview *required it*.[27] Formerly, the premodern Western worldview found nothing intrinsically implausible about reports of miracles, and thus placed the burden of proof on anyone who would argue against the reliability of the canonical Gospels. Conversely, the modern naturalistic worldview that arose out of the scientific revolution and the ensuing Enlightenment found these reports intrinsically implausible, if not outright impossible, and thus set about to reconstruct a more plausible historical reconstruction of Jesus—a Jesus more consistent with modern, naturalistic presuppositions and plausibility structures. This remains the predominant worldview that drives the legendary-Jesus project. With N. T. Wright, we would suggest that much of what goes on today within historical Jesus studies is "largely the projection of an undiscussed metaphysic."[28]

The covert influence of an unarticulated metaphysic is not found merely among more conservative scholars. It is just as clearly seen in the writings of many legendary-Jesus theorists. For example, despite the fact that the first page of the Jesus Seminar's publication, *The Acts of Jesus*, claims that a "critical scholar" is one whose conclusions are "not determined by theological considerations," we must remember that this Seminar was founded by Robert Funk, who, at its inaugural meeting, explicitly called for these same critical scholars collaboratively to create a "new gospel."[29] Indeed, "theological considerations" can be found in a variety of guises and quarters.

Similarly, when Funk announces that "the God of the metaphysical age is dead" and that "there is not a personal god out there external to human beings and the material world," one can hardly help but suspect that this article of faith might influence his scholarly assessment of the Gospels along the way.[30] So too, when Crossan admits, with admirable forthrightness, that his "theological presupposition" is that "God does not operate [by miraculous intervention]," or when Roy Hoover announces that "the ancient world's concept of God is as impossible to maintain in the modern world as is its concept of the cosmos," one cannot help but conclude that these faith-presuppositions will influence, if not significantly

27. Henk De Jonge writes: "Reimarus' understanding of the Gospels did not primarily stem from a close investigation of the differences between these four books. It was the other way around: the stimulus came from Reimarus' philosophical ideas [i.e., Deism]" ("The Loss of Faith in the Historicity of the Gospels: H. S. Reimarus [CA 1750] on John and the Synoptics," in *John and the Synoptics*, ed. A. Denaux [Leuven: Leuven University Press, 1992], 417).

28. Wright, *New Testament and People of God*, 31. This has been true from the beginning of the historical-critical enterprise. See De Jonge, "Loss of Faith in the Historicity of the Gospels," 409–21; D. Pailin, "The Supposedly Historical Basis of Theological Understanding," in *The Making and Remaking of Christian Doctrine: Essays in Honour of Maurice Wiles*, ed. S. Coakley and D. Pailin (Oxford: Clarendon, 1993), 213–37.

29. R. W. Funk and the Jesus Seminar, eds., *The Acts of Jesus: The Search For the Authentic Deeds of Jesus* (San Francisco: HarperSanFrancisco, 1998), 1; R. W. Funk, "The Issue of Jesus," *Forum* 1 (1985): 12.

30. R. W. Funk, "The Mythical Matrix and God as Metaphor," *Forum*, n.s., 3 (2000): 395. In another context, Funk writes, "We now know that Jesus is not literally God" ("Issue of Jesus," 12).

determine, what these scholars find plausible or implausible in the Gospels, at least as it concerns their reports of the supernatural.[31]

Lloyd Geering, himself a member of the Jesus Seminar, frankly observes:

> At [the Jesus Seminar's] core is a group of scholars who are well aware that the real world is the global secular world. . . . [I]t is not the Jesus who was elevated into a mythical heaven who is of relevance to us; it is Jesus the fully human person. . . . While traditional Christians have deplored the removal of the mythical Christ as a great loss, it is actually turning out to be a great gain.[32]

Geering clearly is not describing what is true about the "real world"; rather, he is prescribing what he and most in the Jesus Seminar *believe* is true about "the real world"—namely, that it is a "global *secular* world." As we argued in chapter 1, most people around the world, and even most modern Westerners, do not embrace a secular, naturalistic worldview. Nor do many of us find the "Jesus who was elevated into . . . heaven" irrelevant or find that the "removal of the mythical Christ" is a "great gain." Whether he is aware of it or not, Geering is speaking on behalf of a particular faith-based community—yet presenting it as though it alone was the community of enlightened scholars who, in contrast to the rest, see reality as it *really* is. In any case, in light of expressions of faith commitments such as these, the claim that these "critical" scholars do not allow "theological considerations" to drive their scholarly work—while the rest of us do—seems, at best, naive.

For our part, we have revealed from the outset the presuppositions we bring to our work. Because of our own experiences, as well as for other reasons, the authors of this work—similar to a vast number of people throughout history—are convinced a personal God exists who is always active in the world, sometimes in a supernatural way. In this light, it is not surprising that we are open to finding the portrait(s) of

31. J. Crossan, *Will the Real Jesus Please Stand Up? A Debate between William Lane Craig and John Dominic Crossan*, ed. P. Copan (Grand Rapids: Baker Academic, 1998), 61; R. Hoover, "Realities and Illusions: Resurrection and Life after Death," *Forum*, n.s., 3 (2000): 299–300. Elsewhere Crossan states: "Jesus' divine origins are just as fictional or mythological as those of Octavius. Neither should be taken literally, both must be taken metaphorically" ("A Tale of Two Gods," *Christian Century* [December 15, 1993], 1275). For an assessment of the religio-philosophical presuppositions that drive Crossan's rejection of the bodily resurrection of Jesus, see P. R. Eddy, "Response" [to William Lane Craig's "John Dominic Crossan on the Resurrection of Jesus"], in *The Resurrection: An Interdisciplinary Symposium on the Resurrection of Jesus*, ed. S. T. Davis, D. Kendall, and G. O'Collins (New York: Oxford University Press, 1997), 280–86.

32. L. Geering, "The Legacy of Christianity," in *The Once and Future Jesus*, ed. R. W. Funk et al. (Santa Rosa, CA: Polebridge, 2000), 143–44. So too, Arthur Dewey, another member of the Jesus Seminar, acknowledges the theological nature of the Seminar's work when he notes that "from its outset in 1985 the Jesus Seminar has been implicitly engaged in the task of Christology" ("Some Ragged Lines: From Christology to Christopoetics," *Forum*, n.s., 3 [2000], 307; see also 314–15). Dewey seems less aware of the always-already-present religio-philosophical presuppositions that drive such a task, and the need for a healthy hermeneutic of self-suspicion at this point.

Jesus as depicted in the Gospels to be quite plausible.[33] Indeed, it is our conviction that, given our a priori openness to the realm of the supernatural, there are very good reasons for accepting the Gospels' portrayals of Jesus as rooted in history.

In any event, it should be obvious that we are not asking that anyone pretend to abandon personal religious and philosophical presuppositions when debating issues surrounding the Gospels. To the contrary, we are asking that scholars *not* pretend to have abandoned them. We are asking that these presuppositions, rather than being concealed, be made explicit and brought to the table *as part of the scholarly debate*. What has, to this point, been largely a matter of undiscussed metaphysics must be made part of the discussion within the guild if we are to move beyond the impasse of the current "liberal-conservative" divide in Gospel scholarship. Our historiography of the New Testament world cannot be advanced responsibly apart from a guildwide wrestling with the issues of a critical philosophy of history and the attendant religio-philosophical presuppositions that always-already guide our approach to these questions.

To put these deep-seated concerns on the table for discussion will allow us to consider and assess not only the particular arguments used to support an interpretation of the historical data, but also the religious and philosophical presuppositions that invariably play a decisive role in how each scholar interprets the data. While assessing religious and philosophical presuppositions is difficult, it is not impossible. And, at the very least, it allows others to call to accountability those who would be inclined simply to assume that their particular religio-philosophical presuppositions are correct and/or that only those who embrace their presuppositions are capable of a truly "critical" historiography. In this sense, we wholeheartedly agree with Jesus Seminar member Stephen Patterson, who has recently called Jesus scholars to "be honest with one another about biases and presuppositions (as has often not been the case)."[34]

The Oral versus Literate "Registers" of Written Texts

Our fourth and final response to the a priori skeptical stance toward the Gospels is that it has tended to operate from the perspective of a literary dominant paradigm rather than an orally dominant paradigm. Not only is its a priori burden of proof stance saturated with a worldview that cannot help but dismiss from the start the supernatural reports contained in the Gospels, but its a posteriori burden

33. As noted in chap. 1, this is our application—ironic as it is—of Troeltsch's principle of analogy. It is worth noting here again that Walter Wink, a Jesus Seminar member who apparently has had similar experiences of the supernatural, states that these experiences have led him to reject a number of the skeptical conclusions of his fellow Seminar members on these matters. He perceptively concludes: "People with an attenuated sense of what is possible will bring that conviction to the Bible and diminish it by the poverty of their own experience" (W. Wink, "Write What You See," *Fourth R* [May/June 1994]: 6).

34. S. J. Patterson, "History and Theology: A Reflection on the Work of the Jesus Seminar," *Forum*, n.s., 3 (2000): 366.

of proof stance is heavily indebted to "assured results" that are largely dependent on a misunderstanding of the nature of these first-century documents.

We must recall that in orally dominant cultures, orality and literacy interact in ways that are much more complex than most scholars in the past have imagined. Again, in light of Egbert Bakker's distinction between the *medium* of communication and the *conceptional nature* of communication, we can see that many New Testament scholars have missed this important differentiation, and have therefore assumed that the *written* texts of the Gospels will, on a *conceptional* level, function roughly similar to post-Gutenberg *literary* works.[35] Bakker and others have shown that this is simply not the case.

In our estimation, these observations have monumental ramifications for our assessment of the reliability of the Gospels. When we fail to fully appreciate the significant difference between our post-Gutenberg world and the rhetorical culture of the first-century Mediterranean world—a world in which the literate medium was, for the most part, conjoined with an oral register—we inevitably impose our own literate register and commensurate criteria upon these texts. As Bakker notes, we tend to anachronistically approach ancient texts "without questioning or rethinking any of our common literate assumptions" about their conceptional dynamics.[36]

Our contention is that some of the reasons scholars give for adopting a skeptical stance toward the Gospels vis-à-vis the burden of proof can be traced to the fact that they have read and assessed these texts through the lens of a literary paradigm. Criteria that may well be appropriate to texts written with a literate register are illegitimately imposed on texts written with an oral register/conceptionality—and so, not surprisingly, these texts come up short. As John Harvey has noted, "Many of the so-called 'assured results' of modern OT and NT scholarship are based on presuppositions more appropriate to the silent print culture of the nineteenth and twentieth centuries than to the rhetorical culture in which the documents were produced."[37] However, when the Gospels are read as inscribed oral performances

---

35. Even as astute and passionate a spokesperson for the cause of orality in Gospel studies as Werner Kelber missed this fact in his early work by assuming that an ancient written text functions similarly to the written text of our modern, literate world. Again, this assumption also had the unfortunate consequence of fostering the now notorious idea of a "great divide" between oral and written sources. See W. Kelber, *The Oral and the Written Gospel: The Hermeneutics of Speaking and Writing in the Synoptic Tradition, Mark, Paul, and Q* (Philadelphia: Fortress, 1983).

36. E. J. Bakker, *Poetry in Speech: Orality and Homeric Discourse* (Ithaca, NY: Cornell University Press, 1997), 23–24. Similarly Walter Ong writes of the distorting effects of the "relentless domination of textuality in the scholarly mind" in *Orality and Literacy: The Technologizing of the Word* (New York: Methuen, 1982), 10.

37. J. D. Harvey, "Orality and Its Implications for Biblical Studies: Recapturing an Ancient Paradigm," *JETS* 45 (2002): 109. Similar concerns are voiced by J. Dewey, "The Gospel of Mark as an Oral-Aural Event: Implications for Interpretation," in *The New Literary Criticism and the New Testament*, ed. E. Struthers Malbon and E. V. McKnight (Sheffield: Sheffield Academic Press, 1994), 147–48; W. H. Kelber, "Jesus and Tradition: Words in Time, Words in Space," *Semeia* 65 (1994): 140–41, 154. Such concerns are reflected in other disciplines as well. With respect to the way in which contemporary "scriptocentrism" (p. 3) has

primarily designed for re-oralization, as texts that presuppose an ongoing context of authoritative oral tradition, good reasons arise to suggest the need for a reassessment of their historical intention and reliability. Just such a reassessment is the subject of the remainder of this chapter and the chapter to follow.

On Methodology

The second foundational issue we need to address is closely related to the first. It concerns the methodology of analysis that is appropriate to the Gospels. Over the last half century, and largely under the influence of Bultmann's form-critical enterprise, much New Testament scholarship—including, especially, that wing of scholarship that embraces the legendary-Jesus thesis—has employed a methodology that largely consists of the microanalysis of small, independent units of tradition. This approach is epitomized in the method of the Jesus Seminar, which commenced with an eight-year project of voting on the authenticity of individual sayings of Jesus. The problems with this approach to the Gospels are numerous. We shall note two.

The Problem of Circularity

One of the chief problems with this analytic methodology is that, while it is offered as a way to move from small-scale, inductive studies to a general conclusion about the reliability of a Gospel's portrait(s) of Jesus, in actual practice the numerous decisions about the authenticity of individual units are always-already being influenced by each scholar's intuitions about who Jesus actually was. Theissen and Winter have correctly assessed this hidden circularity:

> Methodologically, judgments about the authenticity of individual traditions by no means stand at the beginning of the effort to reconstruct a picture of the historical Jesus, as though we could then inductively piece together a comprehensive picture. It is rather the case that judgments about individual traditions are dependent on a comprehensive picture of Jesus, however vague and open this picture may be. To a great extent, historical Jesus research consists of the testing and refining of such preliminary comprehensive images.[38]

---

blinded scholars to a proper understanding of African oral texts, see K. Barber and P. F. de Moraes Farias, eds., *Discourse and Its Disguises: The Interpretation of African Oral Texts* (Birmingham, UK: Centre of West African Studies, 1989). In this volume, for example, Elizabeth Tonkin notes: "All the people who study orality in universities are profoundly literate, so consciously literate and unconsciously oral that I believe we really do not know how to study oracy. So I am asking what experiences and expectations we must unlearn, as well as what features we must train ourselves to notice, if we are to unmask the literate disguises of discourse" ("Oracy and the Disguises of Literacy," in *Discourse and Its Disguises*, 39). Tonkin offers this challenge to scholars who study African oral tradition. We suggest it must be just as forcefully applied to scholars who study the oral Jesus tradition and even the written Gospels, indebted as they are to an oral register.

38. Theissen and Winter, *Quest for the Plausible Jesus*, 201. This point is equally emphasized by N. T. Wright in his plea for a method that focuses upon large-scale historical hypotheses and verification, as

We would add to this only that each scholar's guiding, intuited, comprehensive image of Jesus is inextricably connected to that scholar's intuitions about the general historical reliability of the Gospels. One's guiding image of Jesus and sense of the historicity of the Gospels is typically more *influential upon*—rather than *influenced by*—one's "inductive" study of individual units of tradition. In fact, in terms of method, the tendency to focus on authenticating isolated, detached sayings of Jesus is a natural reaction within a scholarly environment where *a generally skeptical stance toward the Gospels themselves already reigns*.[39] Thus, most skeptical Jesus studies that focus on assessing the authenticity of individual sayings do not *end* by demonstrating the general unreliability of the Gospels. Rather, they *begin* by assuming it.

Authenticity Criteria and Their Problems

Second, virtually every one of the "authenticity criteria" that have been used to guide decisions on the individual, isolated units of the Jesus tradition have come under serious criticism. For example, the criterion that perhaps has been most influential in undermining the reliability of the Synoptic Jesus tradition is the notorious "double dissimilarity" criterion.[40] This criterion in essence states that our confidence in the authenticity of any particular saying of Jesus must decrease to the extent that the saying in question is similar to teachings of traditional Judaism, on one hand, and similar to what we would expect the earliest Christians to have believed, on the other. In other words, only those sayings that look like things a traditional Jew or an early Christian would *not* say can confidently be ascribed to Jesus. In all other cases, all other things being equal, we should conclude for safety's sake that the teaching was borrowed by early Christians from traditional Judaism or imaginatively created by the early church and retroactively placed in the mouth of Jesus. Not surprisingly, very few Synoptic sayings attributed to Jesus pass the test.[41]

The criterion has been heavily criticized, and for good reason. To cite just one objection, since Jesus was Jewish, and since he was, at the very least, the primary influence in what earliest Christians believed, it seems a bit unreasonable to approach with suspicion all sayings attributed to him that sound Jewish and/or like something early Christians would have believed. Intentionally or not, the criterion presupposes, and then reinforces, an image of the original Jesus that is both *non-Jewish* and *non-Christian*.

---

opposed to small-scale assessments of individual sayings; see *The New Testament and the People of God*, 98–109.

39. A point noted by N. T. Wright, *Jesus and the Victory of God* (Minneapolis: Fortress, 1996), 543.

40. In the famous essay that is said to have inaugurated the new quest, Ernst Käsemann explicitly affirms the double dissimilarity criterion ("Problem of the Historical Jesus," 37). For an excellent history and critique of this criterion, see G. Theissen and D. Winter, *The Quest for the Plausible Jesus*, parts 1–3.

41. Indeed, Robert Price argues that "every single one [of the sayings] . . . fails, and must fail, the criterion of dissimilarity" (*Incredible Shrinking Son of Man*, 17–18).

Other commonly employed authenticity criteria have their own problems. For example, for any single isolated unit, the criteria of "Aramaic traces" or "Palestinian environment" always underdetermine the question since it can always be argued that the Aramaism or the Palestinian flavor could as easily have been a creation of the early, Aramaic-speaking, Palestinian church as it could an original saying of Jesus. Even such a stalwart criterion as "multiple independent attestation"—the criterion that has been called "the most objective of the proposed criteria"—has its problems.[42] On the one hand, the question of "independence" is not easily settled and depends upon always-hypothetical reconstructions of literary relations. On the other hand, scholars as diverse as C. F. D. Moule and Werner Kelber have raised serious questions about any historical method that would a priori dismiss singly attested materials in the Jesus tradition.[43]

Finally, even apart from the inherent problems of the criteria themselves, there is the disturbing fact that scholars applying the same criteria to the same individual units of tradition reach wildly different conclusions with respect to the authenticity question. This once again suggests that it is not so much the criteria themselves as it is the intuited, comprehensive image of Jesus—in tandem with each scholar's a priori estimation of the overall reliability of the Gospels—that largely determine the authenticity of individual units of tradition.[44] This suggests that there is something seriously amiss in the (supposedly) purely inductive methodology of analyzing individual units of tradition as a means of arriving at "assured" and "objective" results. Indeed, it suggests that the notion that scholars are working from small, inductive studies to arrive at a comprehensive reconstruction of the historical Jesus is largely an illusion. Again, in point of fact, the influence seems primarily to work in the opposite direction.

Moving forward Methodologically

We do not believe that this critique necessarily implies that we must accept that Jesus scholarship is a hopelessly subjective enterprise. Naturally, scholars bring to their work their own intuitions about who the historical Jesus was. But this only leads to a dangerously subjective fideism if we pretend that our *intuited images* of Jesus are the *result* of our research rather than its *starting point*.

The way to avoid this danger—so far as we can see, the only way to keep any semblance of objectivity in our scholarship—is to make our intuitions about the historical Jesus as explicit as possible at *the start* of our research and consider them *initial hypotheses to be tested* rather than pretending we have no comprehensive

42. H. K. McArthur, "Basic Issues: A Survey of Recent Gospel Research," *Interpretation* 18 (1964): 48. For a brief survey of its criticisms, see Stein, "'Criteria' of Authenticity," 230–33.

43. C. F. D. Moule, *The Phenomenon of the New Testament* (Naperville, IL: Allenson, 1967), 71; Kelber, "Jesus and Tradition," 147. Crossan adopts the methodological practice of "bracketing" singularly attested units; see *Historical Jesus*, xxxii–xxxiii.

44. A conclusion also reached by G. Van Oyen, "How Do We Know (What There Is to Know)? Criteria for Historical Jesus Research," *Louvain Studies* 26 (2001): 264–65.

image of the historical Jesus until we "discover" one through our "critical," small-scale investigations. Proceeding in this way also requires that we begin discussing historical criteria that are appropriate for accessing and verifying large-scale hypotheses about Jesus, while at the same time interacting with the concrete data of the tradition. Toward this end, the recent criteriological proposals of Wright, Theissen and Winter, and Stanton are, in our estimation, on the right track (i.e., simplicity, inclusion, double dissimilarity-similarity, historical plausibility, embarrassment, aftermath, etc.).[45]

In light of all this, we could summarize the methodological approach we believe to be most appropriate to the Gospels with respect to the historicity of their various portraits of Jesus by making the following four points.

1. It is the responsibility of all scholars who approach the Gospels to accept the a priori burden of proof with respect to any claim made, whether positive or negative. Practically speaking, this does not mean that they must begin their study as if no prior consideration and historical assessment had occurred on their topic of focus. It does, however, call for scholars to clearly delineate and defend the prior historical work/conclusions upon which they are building.

2. It is the responsibility of scholars to make explicit, and open for critical debate, the religio-philosophical presuppositions that inform their historical method, as well as the comprehensive image of Jesus they want to test.

3. The study of Jesus is best served as scholars employ criteria that are designed for investigating large-scale hypotheses about Jesus, since it is no longer credible to claim that one is merely "discovering" an image of Jesus by focusing on individual, isolated units of the tradition.

4. In the end, scholars should explicate via historical argumentation where their own study has led them vis-à-vis their assessment of the a posteriori burden of proof with respect to a certain Gospel and/or a certain portion of a Gospel.

For our part, we have already argued for an "open" historical-critical methodology, one for which reports about supernatural events are not necessarily ruled out of court (chap. 1). Thus we do not find the portraits of Jesus in the Gospels to be inherently implausible. When we combine this with the evidence and arguments regarding the Torah-true, monotheistic Jewishness of first-century Palestine (chap. 2), the distinctness of certain aspects of the early Christian movement (chap. 3), the evidence from non-Christian Greco-Roman sources and from Paul (chaps. 4–5),

45. Wright, *New Testament and the People of God*, 104–7; Theissen and Winter, *Quest for the Plausible Jesus*; G. Stanton, *The Gospels and Jesus*, 2nd ed. (New York: Oxford University Press, 2002), 174–77. We are in agreement with Wright when he argues that it is time to adopt a historical methodology that both honors and balances the criteria of "simplicity" and "inclusion" (i.e., "getting in the data"). The skeptical tendency to rush to a decision of "early church creation" for much of the tradition utterly neglects the criterion of inclusion and often disregards the criterion of simplicity. For other recent statements in support of this methodological trajectory, see D. C. Allison, *Jesus of Nazareth: Millenarian Prophet* (Minneapolis: Fortress, 1998); J. D. G. Dunn, *Christianity in the Making*, vol. 1: *Jesus Remembered* (Grand Rapids: Eerdmans, 2003), 174–254; K. Snodgrass, "The Gospel of Jesus," in *The Written Gospel*, ed. M. Bockmuehl and D. A. Hagner (New York: Cambridge University Press, 2005), 32.

the findings on the nature of the oral Jesus tradition (chaps. 6–7), and the genre and nature of the Gospels (chap. 8), we believe we are well on the way to establishing a broad cumulative case for general reliability of the Synoptic portrait(s) of Jesus. Hence, it seems to us—from where we stand—that the a posteriori burden of proof lies with the one who wishes to argue against the general reliability of the images of Jesus offered in the Synoptic Gospels.

Testing the Synoptics' Portait(s) of Jesus

In what follows we will continue to test our view of the reliability of the Gospels, particularly the Synoptics. The criteria we will use for our assessment largely arise from the wider field of historiography. Our goal is to subject the Gospels to the same criteria other ancient works are customarily evaluated by with respect to their historical reliability. However, before embarking on this final venture, there is one further foundational matter to consider. Given that the texts in question are products of the pre-Gutenberg world of scribal manuscripts, we must first raise the question of whether, from the texts we possess, we are able to reconstruct a reasonably faithful representation of the original writings. We must, therefore, briefly discuss the textual attestation of the Gospels.

Textual Criticism

The Inevitability of Textual Corruption

Textual criticism is "foundational to all study of the New Testament," since "one cannot hope to produce fruitful work without a reliable text."[46] The issue is important since, prior to the invention of the printing press, manuscripts had to be copied by hand, thus allowing significant opportunity for copying errors and intentional alterations to take place. The fact that the Gospels, like many other ancient texts, were originally written without word breaks and with little-to-no punctuation made it easy for scribes to lose their place and either duplicate or delete words within the text. Beyond these factors, as New Testament textual critic Michael Holmes notes, "Fatigue, poor eyesight or hearing, or simple stupidity could also contribute to errors in copying."[47]

On top of unintentional errors of copying, we know that scribes sometimes consciously altered—or in their minds "corrected"—manuscripts for a variety

---

46. M. W. Holmes, "Textual Criticism," in *Interpreting the New Testament: Essays on Methods and Issues*, ed. D. A. Black and D. S. Dockery (Nashville: Broadman & Holman, 2001), 63. For helpful orientations to the issues of New Testament textual criticism, see Holmes, "Textual Criticism"; B. M. Metzger, *The Text of the New Testament: Its Transmission, Corruption and Restoration*, 2nd ed. (New York: Oxford University Press, 1968); K. Aland and B. Aland, *The Text of the New Testament*, 2nd ed., trans. E. F. Rhodes (Grand Rapids: Eerdmans, 1989).

47. Holmes, "Textual Criticism," 47.

of reasons. These include attempts to correct spelling and grammar problems, attempts to correct perceived historical, geographical, or doctrinal errors, and attempts to harmonize perceived inconsistencies (either within a Gospel or between Gospels).[48] In any event, the one thing that virtually could be counted upon when a lengthy ancient text was copied by hand was that the human scribe would not reproduce an identical replica of the original text.

These considerations leave room for the charge that the New Testament documents have been *significantly* corrupted. Thus, some maintain that the extant copies of the Gospels (and/or the entire New Testament) are, in significant respects, different from the originals.[49] Charges of even more severe textual corruption have been a staple of Islamic apologetics, conspiratorial theorists, and various New Age advocates for some time. The claim that the New Testament has been significantly corrupted has recently been given a tremendous boost in popular culture by playing a central role in Dan Brown's bestselling novel, *The Da Vinci Code*.[50]

In what follows we argue that, while the field of New Testament textual criticism may not be the "safe" discipline it was once thought to be—a haven for biblical scholars from challenges to personal theological and faith commitments—there are good reasons for thinking we can confidently reconstruct the essence of the original texts of the Gospels.[51]

The Quantity of Extant Ancient Manuscripts

There are at least four lines of evidence that come into play in the textual reconstruction of ancient manuscripts.[52] The first concerns the *quantity* of ancient manuscripts attesting a document's textual transmission. Obviously, the greater

---

48. On the varieties of scribal changes to texts, see Metzger, *Text of the New Testament*, 186–206.

49. See, e.g., B. D. Ehrman, *The Orthodox Corruption of Scripture: The Effect of Early Christological Controversies on the Text of the New Testament* (New York: Oxford University Press, 1993); and, more recently, idem, *Misquoting Jesus: The Story behind Who Changed the Bible and Why* (San Francisco: HarperSanFrancisco, 2005).

50. D. Brown, *The Da Vinci Code: A Novel* (New York: Doubleday, 2003).

51. E. J. Epp has stated that New Testament text criticism never was a theologically "safe" discipline, at least for those who thought through the implications of the numerous textual variations. See "The Multivalence of the Term 'Original Text' in New Testament Textual Criticism," in *Perspectives on New Testament Textual Criticism: Collected Essays, 1962–2004* (Boston: Brill, 2005), 591–92.

52. Recent decades have seen an ongoing methodological debate within New Testament text-critical circles concerning the most appropriate manner in which to reconstruct the original texts from the numerous manuscript variants. In what follows, it will be clear that we would align ourselves with those who argue for a "reasoned eclecticism," where both external (the date and provenance of a text, etc.) and internal (conformity with the author's style, vocabulary, and theology, known scribal habits, etc.) evidences are taken seriously. On the three broad approaches, see M. W. Holmes, "Reasoned Eclecticism," in *The Text of the New Testament in Contemporary Research: Essays on the Status Quaestionis*, ed. B. D. Ehrman and M. W. Holmes (Grand Rapids: Eerdmans, 1995), 336–60; the relevant essays in D. A. Black, ed., *Rethinking New Testament Textual Criticism* (Grand Rapids: Baker Academic, 2002); E. J. Epp, "Textual Criticism," in *The New Testament and Its Modern Interpreters*, ed. E. J. Epp and G. W. MacRae (Philadelphia: Fortress, 1989), 92–97.

the quantity of copies of an ancient manuscript we possess, the greater the potential database for our textual comparisons and reconstructions. Hence, the more confident our conclusions tend to be.

As has often been noted, in this respect the text of the New Testament is far and away the best attested work from the ancient Greco-Roman world. In the words of E. J. Epp, the sheer quantity of extant manuscripts is literally "a genuine embarrassment of riches."[53] We possess roughly 5,500 ancient Greek manuscripts of the New Testament, either in fragments or in whole.[54] In addition, we possess thousands of ancient translations (Latin, Syriac, Coptic, Armenian, Georgian, Arabic, etc.) of the New Testament, as well as countless citations by early Christian writers.[55] In fact, even if we possessed no ancient manuscripts of the New Testament, most of it could be reconstructed from the numerous citations by Christian writers of the first several centuries.[56] As Epp has noted, given the sheer quantity of extant New Testament manuscripts, it is virtually certain that "the original reading in every case is somewhere present in our vast storehouse of material."[57]

By comparison, among the next best attested ancient works is Homer's *Iliad*, for which we have about seven hundred published papyri manuscripts.[58] Among the Greek tragedies, the most abundant in extant manuscripts are those of Euripides, which number about four hundred. With respect to ancient historical works, we possess nine Greek manuscripts of Josephus's *Jewish War*, about twenty manuscripts of Livy's Roman history, ten good manuscripts of Caesar's *Gallic War*, and one ninth-century manuscript of Tacitus's *Annals* (books 1–6).[59] Obviously, the New Testament is in a class by itself in terms of the wealth of our textual database.

---

53. Epp, "Textual Criticism," 91.

54. These include papyri, unicals, minuscules, and lectionaries. On the extant Greek manuscripts, see Holmes, "Textual Criticism," 48–49; Metzger, *Text of the New Testament*, 36–67; Aland and Aland, *Text of the New Testament*, 72–184; and J. K. Elliott, *A Bibliography of Greek New Testament Manuscripts*, 2nd ed. (New York: Cambridge University Press, 2000).

55. For a summary of extant early translations and patristic citations, see Holmes, "Textual Criticism," 49–50; Metzger, *Text of the New Testament*, 67–92; Aland and Aland, *Text of the New Testament*, 171–221.

56. There are, of course, important methodological issues involved in such a project. On the complexities, possibilities, and challenges of identifying (what would become) New Testament texts in early Christian writings, see A. F. Gregory and C. M. Tuckett, "Reflections on Method: What Constitutes the Use of the Writings That Later Formed the New Testament in the Apostolic Fathers," in *The Reception of the New Testament in the Apostolic Fathers*, ed. A. F. Gregory and C. M. Tuckett (New York: Oxford University Press, 2005), 61–82.

57. Epp, "Textual Criticism," 91.

58. M. L. West, *Studies in the Text and Transmission of the Iliad* (Leipzig: Saur, 2001), 87. In this volume, West has provided the most complete catalog to date of the *Iliad* papyri (see pp. 86–138). He reports on the 704 published papyri as well as an additional 840 unpublished papyri from Oxyrhynchus currently housed at the Ashmolean Museum in Oxford.

59. On these comparisons of other ancient texts, see Metzger, *Text of the New Testament*, 34; Epp, "Textual Criticism," 91; F. F. Bruce, *The New Testament Documents: Are They Reliable?* (Downers Grove, IL: InterVarsity, 1960), 16. Metzger offers some relevant thoughts in an interview; see L. Strobel, *The*

At the same time, it must be said that the sheer number of extant copies of a manuscript does not in and of itself ensure that it can confidently be reconstructed. As Holmes notes, "Ten thousand copies of a mistake do not make it any less a mistake."[60] Thus, we need to turn to three other relevant lines of evidence.

The Dating of Extant Manuscripts

All other things being equal, it is reasonable to assume that the greater the time span between the original autograph and a given copy of the text, the greater the likelihood that textual corruptions have crept into the transmission process. If a variant reading is consistently supported by earlier manuscripts, there is good reason—all other things being equal—to consider it authentic. Conversely, if a variant is not found in earlier manuscripts, one must doubt its authenticity—again, all other things being equal.[61]

Once again, compared to other ancient texts, the relatively brief chronological distance between the writing of the New Testament documents and our earliest available manuscripts is very impressive. Epp reminds us that the "riches in NT manuscripts, however, are not only in their *quantity* but also in their *quality*"—that is, the abundance of relatively early texts.[62] Our earliest fragment of a Gospel text—the famous John Rylands papyrus fragment ($\mathfrak{P}^{52}$)—is generally dated to the first half of the second century (ca. 125).[63] Of the more than eighty New Testament papyri, over twenty containing portions of one or more of the Gospels can be dated to the third and fourth centuries. Five virtually complete texts of the New Testament date from the fourth and fifth centuries. By contrast, the earliest copy of Homer's *Iliad* we possess dates approximately nine hundred

---

Case for Christ: A Journalist's Personal Investigation of the Evidence for Jesus (Grand Rapids: Zondervan, 1998), 57–66.

60. Holmes, "Textual Criticism," 55. This fact shows that the "Majority text method" of textual reconstruction—which bases its judgments primarily on the attestation of the greatest number of manuscripts—is problematic. Conservative apologists have often made much of the number of manuscripts. Given that a textual corruption can be copied endlessly, the number of copies of a text, while an important consideration, is certainly not in itself decisive.

61. It is important to note that it is not simply the date of a manuscript that matters, but the date of the manuscript from which it was copied. For example, MS 1739 (tenth century) was copied from a fourth-century manuscript.

62. Epp, "Textual Criticism," 91 (emphasis in text).

63. The dating of $\mathfrak{P}^{52}$ at ca. 125 is fairly uniform across the ideological spectrum; e.g., W. L. Petersen, "The Genesis of the Gospels," in *New Testament Textual Criticism and Exegesis: Festschrift J. Delobel*, ed. A. Denaux (Leuven: Leuven University Press, 2002), 35; G. Stanton, "Early Christian Preference for the Codex," in *The Earliest Gospels: The Origin and Transmission of the Earliest Christian Gospels—The Contribution of the Chester Beatty Gospel Codex P45*, ed. C. Horton (New York: Clark, 2004), 46. The claim of C. P. Thiede that a Greek copy of Matthew preserved in the Magdalen College library at Oxford dates to the second half of the first century has been rejected by most text critics, conservative and liberal alike. For Thiede's case, see *Rekindling the Word: In Search of Gospel Truth* (Valley Forge, PA: Trinity, 1995). For a solid rebuttal to Thiede, see G. Stanton, *Gospel Truth? New Light on Jesus and the Gospels* (Valley Forge, PA: Trinity, 1995), 11–19.

years after the original. Most of our extant texts of Euripides were produced in the Byzantine era. The single manuscript of Tacitus's *Annals*, books 1–6, dates to the ninth century, while the sole manuscript of books 11–16 was copied in the eleventh century.[64]

The Geographical Distribution of Manuscripts

A third important text-critical consideration involves the geographical distribution of a text. In general, the wider the distribution of an ancient manuscript, the greater the likelihood of discovering independent lines of witness.[65] This is significant since, as textual critics establish the genealogical relationships between textual families, independent families can act as controls upon one another's variant readings. Unlike many ancient texts, the relatively early proliferation of New Testament texts throughout the Mediterranean world, both in their original Greek form and in a variety of translations, affords a remarkable geographical distribution and diversity with which to work. Here too the New Testament has far and away better attestation than any other ancient work.

Transcriptional and Intrinsic Considerations

Fourth, and finally, textual critics assess the relative quality of a manuscript by evaluating it in the light of ancient scribal tendencies and practices (transcriptional considerations) as well as the scribal idiosyncrasies and issues of content that are specific to the text itself (intrinsic considerations).[66] In contrast to the first three text-critical considerations, there is an increasing amount of scholarly discussion regarding the implications of this last criterion, and especially over how it affects New Testament textual criticism. In light of our growing understanding of scribal tendencies and practices in the ancient world and in orally oriented cultures in general, some have begun to raise the question of whether it even makes sense to continue to talk about "original autographs."

Given the complex and fluid way ancient orally oriented texts interact both with the established oral tradition that gives rise to them (and into which they feed) and with other written texts, some have suggested that it is anachronistic and "post-Gutenbergian" to continue to speak of an "original text" that all copies are to be measured against.[67] Rather, it is argued that orally oriented written texts are

---

64. Metzger, *Text of the New Testament*, 34; Epp, "Textual Criticism," 91.

65. See Holmes, "Textual Criticism," 56–57; Metzger, *Text of the New Testament*, 209.

66. See Holmes, "Textual Criticism," 57; Metzger, *Text of the New Testament*, 209–11.

67. Those who work from a more stringent postmodern perspective tend to question the stability of any textual tradition, arguing instead for a nonauthorial, multiple-text approach that emphasizes a "democratic pluralism" with respect to the text-critical enterprise; see D. C. Greetham, "Textual Scholarship," in *Introduction to Scholarship in Modern Languages and Literatures*, ed. J. Gibaldi (New York: Garland, 1992), 112. For a helpful introduction to this perspective, see P. Cohen, "Textual Instability, Literary Studies, and Recent Developments in Textual Scholarship," in *Texts and Textuality: Textual Instability, Theory and Interpretation*, ed. P. Cohen (New York: Garland, 1997), xi–xxxiv. D. Henige—a specialist on African

living things, functioning much more like dynamic oral traditions than fixed-type documents. Thus, as Rosalind Thomas notes, "Even when a text is available and adherence to it required, its transmission is not necessarily through the written word itself, but it can be oral with the text as a distant mnemonic aid."[68] According to some, this suggests that the very idea that there is something particularly pristine about the "first time" a tradition is written down (assuming we can even delineate "*the* first time") is a post-Gutenberg retrojection that causes scholars who live in a modern, highly literate world to ask all the wrong questions—such as, how close are our copies to "the original"?

On top of this, some have argued that even if one insists on pursuing the issue of the proximity of copies to "the original," the "degree of variation" found in the textual traditions of the Gospels in particular renders this project problematic.[69] Bart Ehrman argues along these lines when he notes the frequent "orthodox corruption of scripture," wherein

> proto-orthodox scribes of the second and third centuries occasionally modified their texts of Scripture in order to make them coincide more closely with the christological views embraced by the party that would seal its victory at Nicea and Chalcedon."[70]

Of course, textual critics have noticed these features of the manuscript tradition for years.[71] What Ehrman and others are suggesting, however, is that most scholars to date have not taken seriously enough the implications of these features as it concerns the recovery of the hypothetical "original text." In response, we offer three considerations.

---

oral tradition—has broadened skepticism about the stability of tradition to *any* type of communicative transmission of information, whether oral or written; see "Survival of the Fittest? Darwinian Adaptation and the Transmission of Information," *History in Africa* 30 (2003): 157–77. Epp has raised the question of the difficulty of the notion of an "original text" within New Testament studies in "Multivalence of the Term 'Original Text,'" 551–93 (though in our perspective he has significantly overcomplexified the problem). D. C. Parker has clearly posed some of the related textual issues with respect to the Gospels; see *The Living Text of the Gospels* (New York: Cambridge University Press, 1997), 184–96.

68. R. Thomas, *Oral Tradition and Written Record in Classical Athens* (New York: Cambridge University Press, 1989), 49.

69. Parker, *Living Text*, 197.

70. Ehrman, *Orthodox Corruption*, 275. In a recent book—a revision of his dissertation done under Ehrman—W. C. Kannaday broadens Ehrman's thesis by exploring a variety of early scribal modifications of the Gospel manuscripts motivated by "apologetic interests." See *Apologetic Discourse and the Scribal Tradition: Evidence of the Influence of Apologetic Interests on the Text of the Canonical Gospels* (Atlanta: Scholars Press, 2004).

71. The entire enterprise of textual criticism is predicated upon the fact that manuscripts of the same text vary among themselves. The work of E. G. Turner showed decades ago the wide range of variants that are possible among early (e.g., mid-third-century BCE) Greek papyri; see *Greek Papyri: An Introduction* (Oxford: Clarendon, 1968).

Adaptation of Living, Textualized, Orally Oriented Traditions

First, as we have already argued, it cannot be denied that our growing awareness of the nature of ancient scribal traditions and practices in rhetorical cultures has forced on us the realization that Western scholars have, on the whole, tended to view ancient textual traditions and practices through the lenses of their own modern, highly literate, academic world. The model of fixed, stable, textual reproduction is the aspiration and achieved result of the post-Gutenberg world, but it is not necessarily an aspiration shared by scribes within orally dominant cultures. Indeed, the study of scribal habits in rhetorical cultures, where the written medium and the oral conception interact in complex, living ways, has brought to light the remarkably different aesthetics at play in ancient textual reproduction.[72]

We suggest that this dynamic explains in large measure the phenomenon we find in the textual tradition of the Gospels. In the orally dominant milieu of the early church, it would have been quite sufficient that any particular written copy of a Gospel reflected the essence of the countless, communally controlled, orally performed variants of that Gospel—that is, "what was *said* and *heard*" of this Gospel on a regular basis.[73] Whether or not a document was a meticulously copied, exact reproduction of another written text would have, in general, been less important in this orally/aurally oriented milieu than it is in our post-Gutenberg world. In fact, as foreign as it may be to those of us who habitually approach texts with a literary conception, in the context of rhetorical cultures such as the early church, ordinary protocol would include allowing scribes to amend texts in order to render them more faithful to the wider tradition out of which they emerged.

This is not to say that we find no conservative ancient copyists of the New Testament who strove to produce exact replicas of their texts. For example, $\mathfrak{P}^{75}$ demonstrates that ancient scribes could copy a text with a high degree of accuracy. In addition, as Eldon Epp reminds us, there is evidence that "standardized procedures were in existence already in the late first or early second century for the transmission of Christian texts" (the codex form, *nomina sacra* techniques, evidence for the existence of scriptoria, etc.).[74] Nonetheless, the scribal mind-set

---

72. On the ancient Greco-Roman world, see, e.g., J. Small, *Wax Tablets of the Mind: Cognitive Studies of Memory and Literacy in Classical Antiquity* (London: Routledge, 1997), 219–20; Thomas, *Oral Tradition and Written Record*, 47–48, 59; idem, *Literacy and Orality in Ancient Greece* (New York: Cambridge University Press, 1992), 93; N. Yamagata, "Plato, Memory, and Performance," *Oral Tradition* 20 (2005): 111–29. From the context of contemporary Malay, see A. Sweeney, *A Full Hearing: Orality and Literacy in the Malay World* (Berkeley: University of California Press, 1987), 28–30. This awareness is growing among biblical scholars as well. See, e.g., R. Horsley, "Oral Tradition in New Testament Studies," *Oral Tradition* 18 (2003): 35; S. Niditch, "Oral Tradition and Biblical Scholarship," *Oral Tradition* 18 (2003): 44; E. Ulrich, "Our Sharper Focus on the Bible and Theology Thanks to the Dead Sea Scrolls," *CBQ* 66 (2004): 2–4.

73. Sweeney, *A Full Hearing*, 28.

74. E. J. Epp, "The Significance of the Papyri for Determining the Nature of the New Testament Text in the Second Century: A Dynamic View of Textual Transmission," in *Gospel Traditions in the Second*

and practices within a rhetorical culture generally conceived of texts differently than the modern approach with its invariant fixed-type texts. The ancient scribal approach makes sense if the written text was originally intended primarily to serve as an inscribed preservative and mnemonic aid for future oral/aural performances within the custodial community.

Such a concept is obviously alien to the modern, highly literate academic world of textual criticism. As Rosalind Thomas notes, "For the silent reader and scholar, the written text is all-important, because there is nothing else."[75] However, in an orally oriented world wherein written texts are naturally born of, and surrounded by, a communally shared, authoritative oral tradition, for any single written instantiation of that tradition, "small variations in unimportant words did not matter."[76] Thus, while we can certainly regard many of the variations that crept into the textual tradition in the first centuries of the church as nothing more than ordinary human errors, we need not view the manner in which scribes consciously modified texts as intentional distortions. To be sure, the changes *were* sometimes intentional. But in the orally dominant context within which the scribes worked, these modifications were adaptations of a living, relatively stable (vis-à-vis ancient standards of precision) tradition, not "distortions" of an "original autograph."[77]

THE NATURE AND SCOPE OF THE INTENTIONAL MODIFICATIONS

This brings us to our second response to the claim that the "degree of variation" in early Gospel manuscripts prevents us from arriving at an adequate approximation of the "original text." The fact is that, consistent with the way oral performers tend to modify traditions that, communally speaking, are both sacred and identity-forming in nature, the vast majority of scribal modifications of the written Gospels are relatively minor. Thus, rarely do we find copyists substantively altering the core message of any Gospel passage. Rather, it seems that the "fixed-yet-flexible" nature of religious oral traditions was to some extent carried over into the way early scribes copied the Gospel manuscripts.

New Testament textual critic Frederik Wisse nicely captures the balance presented by the actual evidence. On the one hand, he notes, there is clear evidence of occasional scribal modification of texts, including omissions, word changes, and, at times, interpolations. On the other hand, the omissions are best character-

---

Century: Origins, Recensions, Text, and Transmission, ed. W. L. Petersen (Notre Dame, IN: University of Notre Dame, 1989), 101–2.

75. Thomas, *Literacy and Orality*, 93.

76. Thomas, *Oral Tradition and Written Record*, 48. The issue of "relevant precision," which is crucial to this matter, is considered in chap. 10.

77. J. D. G. Dunn captures this dynamic well when he writes: "The first written versions of the oral Jesus tradition would be oral performances in writing. . . . In the ancient world, written tradition could be as variable as oral tradition" ("On Faith and History, and Living Tradition: In Response to Robert Morgan and Andrew Gregory," *ExpT* 116 [2004], 19). See also Dunn, *Jesus Remembered* (Grand Rapids: Eerdmans, 2003), 202n158.

ized as "minor," while the interpolations are almost always limited in scope.[78] For example, in the Gospels themselves, there are only two instances of what could be considered major interpolations—namely, the well-known cases of Mark 16:9–20 and John 7:53–8:11. Wisse concludes his study with a significant observation:

> Though the evidence before Irenaeus is very difficult to evaluate, there is no indication that the Gospels circulated in a form different from that attested in the later textual tradition. . . . [T]he claims of extensive ideological redaction of the Gospels and other early Christian literature runs counter to all of the textual evidence.[79]

While acknowledging the sorts of variations one would expect of ancient scribal tradition, others such as Leon Wright, Peter Head, and Andrew Gregory have come to conclusions similar to that of Wisse. In the words of Head, the typical "improvements" made by early Christian scribes "have not affected the general reliability of the transmission of the texts [of the Synoptic Gospels] in any significant manner."[80]

It is interesting to note the qualified language used even by those scholars who push the textual instability thesis most strongly. For example, in stating his general thesis, the most that Ehrman is willing to claim is that such theologically inspired modification "occasionally" happened in the scribal tradition of the Gospels.[81] It thus seems that the charge that textual variants preclude working back to a reasonable approximation of the "original autographs" is an overly pessimistic interpretation of the actual textual data.

THE SIGNIFICANCE OF THE "ORIGINAL TEXT"

Third, while we certainly concur that scribes in rhetorical cultures would not have necessarily aspired to the degree of textual fixity characteristic of the post-Gutenberg world, we do not see that this implies that the notion of an "original text"—an autograph—is dispensable. True, neither the author(s) of the original work nor those who transmitted it likely would have viewed the "original" as the one, pure, unalterable version of the tradition(s) that the written work itself inscribes and expresses. Rather, it likely would have been viewed as a written version of the wider oral performative tradition of that Gospel, and thus as subject to appropriate modification in subsequent (oral or written) performances. Yet,

78. F. Wisse, "The Nature and Purpose of Redactional Changes in Early Christian Texts: The Canonical Gospels," in *Gospel Traditions in the Second Century*, 52.

79. Ibid., 51–52.

80. P. M. Head, "Christology and Textual Transmission: Reverential Alterations in the Synoptic Gospels," *NovT* 35 (1993): 129. See also L. Wright, *Alterations of the Words of Jesus as Quoted in the Literature of the Second Century* (Cambridge, MA: Harvard University Press, 1952), 116; A. Gregory, "An Oral and Written Gospel? Reflections on Remembering Jesus," *ExpT* 116 (2004): 9.

81. Ehrman, *Orthodox Corruption of Scripture*, 275.

this does not mean contemporary scholars are misguided in continuing to speak about the original autograph of a text.

In fact, we can discuss the extent to which scribes in the early church did or did not *modify* texts only by assuming that there was, in each case, an original written text to copy and, within limits, modify. There is an unfortunate tendency in our postmodern context to ignore the fact that, at the headwaters of an ancient textual tradition, lies an autograph, an "original text" that was first penned at a certain time on a certain day at a specific location. Within an orally dominant context, the very reason for inscribing such a text would have been to preserve in a fixed form the sacred oral Gospel tradition. While later oral or written recitations of this text may have been characterized by a degree of flexibility alien to our modern literate world, they nonetheless were designed faithfully to retain the propositioned essence of the inscribed tradition, if not always the exact words.

In light of all this, we conclude that an understanding of the textual transmission of written texts in rhetorical cultures explains the nature and scope of the ways in which early Christian scribes modified texts, while demonstrating that such textual modifications generally did not alter the substance either of the "original text," or, for that matter, the sacred oral Jesus tradition from which it arose.[82]

Did the Gospel Authors Intend to Transmit Reliable History?

Thus far we have seen that if ever we are warranted in accepting a contemporary version of an ancient work as reasonably close to its original, we are so with the canonical Gospels, and indeed with the entire New Testament. We now turn to evaluate the Synoptics by subjecting them to the same nine historical-critical questions historians customarily put to any ancient document as they seek to ascertain its historical reliability. The first three of these questions are preliminary in nature and shall be addressed presently. The last six shall be addressed in the next chapter.

The first of these preliminary questions has been dealt with earlier (see chap. 8) and thus may be assessed briefly, by way of review. It concerns the historical intentionality of the Gospel authors. Did they intend to transmit reliable history in their works? As we have seen, many contemporary New Testament scholars answer no. As Robert Funk declares, "The evangelists do not qualify as historians in the modern sense of the term."[83]

There is a sense in which this is true. In one sense the claim that the Gospel authors were not historians "in the modern sense of the term" is a truism. The Gospel

82. Again, Dunn correctly observes: "In the ancient world, written tradition could be as variable as oral tradition. But I would assert with equal vigor the alternative formulation: in the ancient world oral tradition could be as stable (reliable) as written tradition" ("On Faith and History," 19).

83. R. Funk, "On Distinguishing Historical from Fictive Narrative," *Forum* 9 (1993): 191 (see 190–91 for Funk's articulation of the criteria).

authors obviously do not write with the methods and motives that characterize modern critical historians. But this is true of any ancient writer. If we are going to dismiss the Synoptic Gospels on this count alone, we must conclude that we can learn next to nothing about history from any ancient historical document.

Though the Synoptics are clearly not examples of "historiography" in the modern sense of the term, the authors nevertheless consistently demonstrate a concern for transmitting actual history. As textualized oral recitations intended to express and reinforce the oral Jesus tradition, the Synoptics creatively combine elements from a number of genres—including ancient histories and biographies. Given the presence of these generic signals, we can conclude that, among other things, the Synoptic authors reveal a clear interest in reliably passing on information about Jesus's life and teachings. *In this sense* we must answer the question, "Did the Synoptic authors intend to record reliable history?" with a resounding *yes*.

Objections to this conclusion have not been particularly strong. Most are rooted in a lack of appreciation for the oral register of the Gospels—or, in other words, in a tendency to anachronistically impose a post-Gutenberg literary register and its criteria on these ancient texts. For example, Funk argues that whenever a narrative portrays the narrator as omniscient and/or as possessing unlimited knowledge of the past, present, and future, we must assume we are dealing with an essentially fictive narration.[84] According to Funk, since the Gospel authors frequently make use of this literary technique, their works must be judged to be largely fictional in nature.

The argument simply does not stand up to scrutiny, however. In orally orientated cultures, oral traditions—and the inscribed recitations of those traditions—frequently assume the type of creative voice and style that modern, highly literate scholars instinctively associate with a fictive literary genre. Yet, orality studies have confirmed over and over again that these traditions can, in fact, be examples of intentionally transmitted historical material. Indeed, as we have already shown, such studies frequently have confirmed that these traditions are capable of reliably transmitting historical material as well as (some would claim even *better* than) modern literate historians. In any event, we see, once again, how approaching ancient, orally conceived written texts from a post-Gutenberg, highly literary mentality can easily lead scholars to erroneous conclusions. The judgment that the Gospel authors did not intend to communicate reliable history is one of them.

Were the Gospel Authors in a Position to Record Reliable History?

The Traditional Authorship of the Gospels

A second preliminary issue historians typically explore when assessing the historical veracity of ancient documents concerns the extent to which the authors

84. Funk, "Distinguishing Historical from Fictive," 190–91.

were in a position to access and thus transmit reliable history. Were they themselves eyewitnesses of the events they record, or did they at least have access to sources that go back to eyewitnesses?

While the canonical Gospels themselves are anonymous texts, according to early Christian tradition each was written either by an eyewitness of Jesus's ministry (Matthew and John) or a close associate of a first-generation apostle (John Mark and Luke). While space does not permit a detailed consideration of the authorship of the Synoptic Gospels, it must be said that cogent cases have been made for the traditional authorship claims. This is especially true with respect to the Gospel of Mark, which—in light of the traditional claim of John Mark's historical connections with Peter's preaching and granting the two-source theory— also would put both Matthew and Luke in touch with an authoritative apostolic stream of tradition.[85]

There is also good evidence that the traditional attributions were attached to the four Gospels relatively early on. The practical needs of the church—for example, reading during community gatherings, church libraries and book cupboards, and early scribal activity—necessitated that the early church have an agreed terminology by which to distinguish the four Gospels.[86] It is also noteworthy that by the end of the second century, the traditional names were solidly established. This suggests that the traditional author-Gospel connections most likely were in existence by the early second century.[87] Also, in contrast to other writings that

85. The tradition of John Mark as author with a Petrine connection is unanimous in the early church, being noted by, e.g., Irenaeus, *Against Heresies*, 3.1.2 (ca. 180); Tertullian, *Against Marcion*, 4.5 (ca. 200); and Clement of Alexandria, *Hypotyposes* (ca. 200), according to Eusebius (*Ecclesiastical History*, 6.14.5–7). Papias is, of course, the earliest source. See below.

86. M. Hengel, "The Titles of the Gospels and the Gospel of Mark," in *Studies in the Gospel of Mark*, trans. John Bowden (Philadelphia: Fortress, 1985), 74–81; idem, *The Four Gospels and the One Gospel of Jesus Christ: An Investigation into the Collection and Origin of the Canonical Gospels*, trans. John Bowden (Harrisburg, PA: Trinity, 2000), chap. 4. That the Gospels were read in the early Christian worship service is attested in Justin Martyr, *1 Apology*, 67.3.

87. Hengel, "Titles of the Gospels," 67–72. T. K. Heckel has reaffirmed Hengel's conclusions in *Vom Evangelium des Markus zum viergestaltigen Evangelium* (Tübingen: Mohr Siebeck, 1999). See also T. C. Skeat, "Irenaeus and the Four-Gospel Canon," *NovT* 34 (1992): 194–99; R. A. Piper, "The One, the Four, and the Many," in *Written Gospel*, 269–71. Skeat has argued that three papyrus fragments ($\mathfrak{P}^4$, $\mathfrak{P}^{64}$, $\mathfrak{P}^{67}$) are, in fact, portions of a second-century four-Gospel codex; see "The Oldest Manuscript of the Four Gospels?" *NTS* 43 (1997): 1–34. G. Stanton has embraced and elaborated on this thesis; see "The Fourfold Gospel," *NTS* 43 (1997): 317–46. Recently, however, P. M. Head has questioned each of the planks upon which Skeat built his case in "Is P4, P64 and P67 the Oldest Manuscript of the Four Gospels? A Response to T. C. Skeat," *NTS* 51 (2005): 450–57.

D. C. Parker has challenged Hengel and Heckel on this point with respect to their use of certain papyri manuscripts—$\mathfrak{P}^{4, 64, 67}$ and $\mathfrak{P}^{66}$—to establish the early, consistent use of the traditional superscriptions. He argues that "the former is certainly and the latter probably from a later hand," and therefore, given that $\mathfrak{P}^{4, 64, 67}$ is a third-century text, it is actually evidence "pointing in the opposite direction"; review of *Vom Evangelium des Markus zum viergestaltigen Evangelium*, by T. Heckel, *JTS* 52 (2001): 299. Parker's own relevant conclusions are available in *Codex Bezae: An Early Christian Manuscript and Its Text* (New York: Cambridge University Press, 1992), 11–12. While Parker's manuscript evidence is important and

circulated in the second and third centuries, the authorship of the canonical Gospels was never disputed. This fact is difficult to explain if the documents originally circulated anonymously.[88]

The earliest source on the authorship of the canonical Gospels is Papias, a second-century bishop of Hierapolis in Asia Minor. His work, titled "The Interpretation of the Oracles of the Lord" and written sometime in the first half of the second century, is lost to us, but excerpts have survived within Eusebius's fourth-century *Ecclesiastical History*. As Robert Gundry has argued, there is good reason to date Papias's original text to the first decade of the second century (ca. 101–108).[89]

Papias reports that an "elder" named John—a figure that is best identified as the apostle John—passed on to him information about the authorship of the Second Gospel:

> Mark became Peter's interpreter and wrote accurately all that he remembered, not, indeed, in order, of the things said or done by the Lord. For he had not heard the Lord, nor followed him, but later on, as I said, followed Peter, who used to give teachings as necessity demanded but not making, as it were, an arrangement of the Lord's oracles, so that Mark did nothing wrong in thus writing down single points as he remembered them. For to one thing he gave attention, to leave out nothing of what he had heard and to make no false statements in them.[90]

In our estimation, the widespread rejection of this report of Papias within critical New Testament circles is largely unwarranted.[91] Several decades ago, in

---

serves to force a reassessment of Hengel and Heckel's arguments at this specific point, it certainly does not settle the issue. The existence of a manuscript ($\mathfrak{P}^{4,64,67}$) that betrays a later superscription addition in and of itself tells us nothing. This data must be interpreted. One can interpret this as evidence that there was no settled title for the text when it was copied. However, one can also imagine a situation where a text is copied, its identity and its title well known, and yet for whatever reason the original copyist fails to affix the superscription—a decision that is remedied by a later hand. Despite Parker's claim, with respect to $\mathfrak{P}^{66}$ the question is still quite unsettled. Even Parker seems less certain about this judgment in his own book, where he concludes that "perhaps" the title was a later addition (*Codex Bezae*, 11). In any case, Parker's data does not, in itself, overturn the other lines of evidence for the relatively early appearance of the traditional titles.

88. See Hengel, "Titles of the Gospels," 74–81; idem, *The Four Gospels and the One*, chap. 4. Hengel (*Four Gospels*, 80) writes: "Another argument [for the authorship of John Mark] is that this writing, quite novel in earliest Christianity, managed to establish itself in the communities and to be used extensively by such self-confident authors as Luke and the author of the First Gospel . . . only because a recognized authority and not an anonymous Gentile Christian, i.e., a Mr. Nobody in the church, stood behind it."

89. R. Gundry, *Mark: A Commentary on His Apology for the Cross* (Grand Rapids: Eerdmans, 1993), 1026–34.

90. Eusebius, *Ecclesiastical History*, 3.39.15; we have taken the translation from J. Marcus, *Mark 1–8* (New York: Doubleday, 2000), 21–22. For the case that Papias's "elder" John is to be identified with the apostle John, see C. S. Keener, *The Gospel of John: A Commentary* (Peabody, MA: Hendrickson, 2003), 1:95–98; and esp. Gundry, *Mark*, 1026–45.

91. A. C. Perumali poses the question well in the title of his article: "Are Not Papias and Irenaeus Competent to Report on the Gospels?" *ExpT* 91 (1980): 332–37. Gundry offers a sustained argument

a landmark interdisciplinary symposium on the Gospels, noted classics scholar George Kennedy challenged New Testament scholars to take the report of Papias much more seriously.[92] In his written response, Reginald Fuller initially expressed his "greatest surprise" over the weight Kennedy placed on external evidence regarding the authorship of the Gospels. However, in light of Kennedy's case, Fuller goes on to concede:

> New Testament scholars generally have not taken the external evidence (especially that of Papias) seriously enough.... As a result of Kennedy's essay and the subsequent discussion, New Testament scholars have been challenged to take more seriously the external evidence regarding the origin of the gospels than they have been wont to do in the past.... [T]hey must henceforth exercise great caution when they spin off theories about the internal evidence that flatly contradict the external evidence.... This should be one item for the agenda of future studies of the relationships among the gospels.[93]

While few have heeded Fuller's call, there is little reason not to. Once Papias's remark is taken seriously, we submit that it provides rather compelling grounds for accepting John Mark as in fact the author of the Gospel attributed to him, which, in turn, links his Gospel with the witness of Peter.

Also, it is difficult to explain how the Second Gospel, if it originally circulated anonymously, would have acquired the authorial attribution it did, since (John) Mark hardly would have been a figure of choice had someone been fabricating an authoritative author from scratch. Even Werner Kümmel—who in the end rejects the traditional ascription (largely due to what we consider to be a misunderstanding of the nature of the oral Jesus tradition behind Mark)—grants the force of this argument.[94] But there is more. Not only is John Mark an obscure non-apostle

---

for taking Papias's report on Mark very seriously; see *Mark*, 1026–45. His arguments are reproduced in *Matthew: A Commentary on His Handbook for a Mixed Church under Persecution*, 2nd ed. (Grand Rapids: Eerdmans, 1994), 609–20. As Gundry himself notes in his preface to the second edition, those who have disagreed with his positive assessment of the Papias tradition have tended to ignore his actual arguments—or, alternatively, have dismissed them without either full engagement or offering substantive counterarguments in response (*Matthew*, xii).

92. G. Kennedy, "Classical and Christian Source Criticism," in *The Relationships among the Gospels: An Interdisciplinary Dialogue*, ed. W. O. Walker (San Antonio: Trinity University Press, 1978), 125–55.

93. R. H. Fuller, "Classics and the Gospels: The Seminar," in *Relationships among the Gospels*, 178, 183. While there is still a great deal of unargued resistance to the Papias tradition, there are also signs that some are beginning to grant the early external evidence the respect it deserves. See, e.g., M. N. Sabin, *Reopening the Word: Reading Mark as Theology in the Context of Early Judaism* (New York: Oxford University Press, 2002), chap. 1; C. E. Hill, "Papias of Hieraplois," *ExpT* 117 (2006): 309–15.

94. W. G. Kümmel, *Introduction to the New Testament*, 17th rev. ed., trans. H. C. Kee (Nashville: Abingdon, 1975), 97. Kümmel seems to reject the claim of John Mark as author largely based upon his assumption that the complex nature of the tradition history behind the Second Gospel would preclude a direct Peter-John Mark-Second Gospel line of influence (pp. 95–96). However, this type of assumption is rooted in a far too simplistic, monochromatic, and now outdated view of oral tradition. Beyond this, Kümmel's other reasons for rejecting John Mark as author (p. 97)—supposedly blatant geographical

who, in himself, provided no eyewitness support—even worse, he was known in the tradition as a deserter of Paul (Acts 13:13; 15:36–39). Moreover, according to the second-century Anti-Marcionite Prologue, Mark was described as "stump-finger"—because his fingers appeared to be too short for his body. And yet, though one in that culture might think that Mark would be less than *physically* suited to the task of Gospel authorship, the tradition never balks at this fact.

Given the very good reasons that the early church would have had for not identifying a Gospel with someone like John Mark, one is left wondering just what would have led them to do so had the ascription not been there from the beginning. John Mark is no "Matthew," no "John," not even a "Luke"—that is, a respectable, if largely unknown, associate of Paul's. Rather, like Luke, he is a largely unknown, but unlike Luke, much of what is known is not respectable. In fact, one can argue that the most plausible explanation for the attribution of this Gospel to Mark is that something like the Peter-John Mark-Second Gospel connection was both rooted in history and known as a fact in the early church.[95] In the end, the case for John Mark as author of the Second Gospel

---

blunders, misunderstandings of Jewish customs, etc.—have all been adequately rebutted. See, e.g., the works of Gundry and Hengel noted above and our own comments in the next chapter.

95. A number of scholars have argued against a Petrine connection to John Mark and/or the Second Gospel. Related to this, some have claimed there is no good reason to put either Peter or John Mark in first-century Rome—the traditional setting for their association. See, e.g., P. J. Achtemeier, "Mark, Gospel of," in *ABD*, ed. D. Freedman (New York: Doubleday, 1992), 4:542–43; G. A. Wells, *Can We Trust the New Testament? Thoughts on the Reliability of Early Christian Testimony* (Chicago: Open Court, 2004), 115–39; M. D. Goulder, "Did Peter Ever Go to Rome?" *SJT* 57 (2004): 377–96.

In response, it should be noted that the Peter-Rome connection is relatively early and strong, with much of it being unconnected to anything like a later papal apologetic. For example, the tradition of Peter's martyrdom at Rome is attested as early as 1 Clement (5:4–7; 6:1) and Ignatius (*Epistle to the Romans*, 4:2–3), and is widely held after that (e.g., Irenaeus, *Against Heresies*, 3.3.2; Eusebius, *Ecclesiastical History*, 2.25.7). The Peter-Mark connection is also attested by Justin's note that Mark 3:16–17 represents "recollections of Peter" (*Dialogue with Trypho*, 106.3).

Much of the negative case here is based upon an argument from silence—silence in such early texts as Paul's letters and Acts—a silence that is maintained well into the second century. But here, as is commonly the case, the argument from silence is notoriously difficult to assess. This is particularly so when the supposed "silence" is clearly broken by 1 Peter 5:13. Of course, skeptics will argue that 1 Peter may well have provided the ambiguous data from which to fabricate the tradition of Peter in Rome in the first place, and thus provides no historical testimony to this traditional claim. However, this response is largely ad hoc and represents little more than special pleading. Whereas some skeptics suggest that the "Babylon = Rome" interpretation of 1 Peter represents a later interpretation imposed on the text, we have independent evidence for this connection in the book of Revelation (14:8; 16:19; 17:5; 18:1–24).

Beyond this, Hengel has offered a strong critique of the claim that Papias's source—or even Papias himself—invented the Peter-John Mark-Second Gospel connection based on knowledge of 1 Peter 5:13, calling the idea "nonsense"; see "Literary, Theological, and Historical Problems in the Gospel of Mark," in *The Gospel and the Gospels*, ed. P. Stuhlmacher (Grand Rapids: Eerdmans, 1991), 233n56. As noted above, there is good evidence that Papias is in touch with earlier tradition, not simply inventing his information out of thin air. Only a hyperskeptical methodology could dismiss the evidence that Papias is in touch with prior tradition. But this means that Papias's sources could not have derived their Peter-Mark theory from 1 Peter 5:13, since Papias's source would have been "synchronous with the origin of 1 Peter under

may not merely be one "plausible" account among many. Instead, it may be the only truly plausible account by which to explain the rather curious data of the tradition itself.

Were They in a Position to Transmit Reliable History?

However, even if the case for the traditional Markan authorship is not granted, we *still* have good reason for concluding that the author of Mark—and thus the other Synoptics—was very much in touch with early Jesus tradition, and thus was in a position to record reliable history. Even on the most liberal dating of the Gospels, they were written within forty to seventy years after the events they record, with Mark (on the two-source theory) being the earliest and eventually providing source material for Matthew and Luke. From what we know about the reliability patterns of orally transmitted traditions, this actually is a rather insignificant span of time—one that, technically speaking, puts us in touch with "oral history" rather than "oral tradition" per se.[96] A broad range of studies—from ancient Greece to nineteenth-century Serbo-Croatia to contemporary Africa—have all confirmed that orally oriented historical traditions (both oral and written in medium) of relatively recent events—within roughly 80 to 150 years of the event recorded—tend to be quite reliable.[97]

Domitian (81–96) or soon after him. Both traditions are independent and provide reciprocal confirmation" (Hengel, "Literary, Theological, and Historical Problems in the Gospel of Mark," 233n56). Hengel's argument, of course, depends on a late first-century date for 1 Peter. While some conservative scholars would debate this, it has become the standard view in critical New Testament scholarship, and thus is most likely held by the critical scholar who is questioning the tradition as found in Papias.

A number of scholars have demonstrated that a very good case can be made on textual grounds that the Second Gospel does in fact betray a Roman provenance. See, e.g., C. C. Black, "Was Mark a Roman Gospel?" *ExpT* 105 (1993): 36–40; B. J. Incigneri, *The Gospel to the Romans: The Setting and Rhetoric of Mark's Gospel* (Boston: Brill, 2003). (While much of Incigneri's argument for Rome is tied to his rather idiosyncratic dating, other lines of evidence that he offers can be disentangled from his dating thesis.)

Finally, for some, even when the evidence for a direct connection between Peter and the Second Evangelist/Gospel appears inconclusive, there remains a strong argument for a decisive Petrine influence upon this Gospel, one that is noticeable when it is compared with the letter of 1 Peter. See C. C. Black, *Mark: Images of an Apostolic Interpreter* (Columbia: University of South Carolina Press, 1994), 206–9; J. H. Elliott, *A Home for the Homeless: A Sociological Exegesis of I Peter, Its Situation and Strategy* (Philadelphia: Fortress, 1981), 270–88.

96. As David Henige notes, technically speaking, "to qualify for the sobriquet [i.e., "oral tradition"], materials should have been transmitted over several generations" ("Oral, but Oral What? The Nomenclature of Orality and Their Implications," *Oral Tradition* 3 [1988]: 232). Many scholars go on to distinguish more recent orally transmitted traditions as "oral history." On the early gospel tradition as oral history, see S. Byrskog, *Story as History—History as Story: The Gospel Tradition in the Context of Ancient Oral History* (Boston: Brill, 2002).

97. See respectively: W. Kullmann, "Homer and Historical Memory," in *Signs of Orality: The Oral Tradition and Its Influence in the Greek and Roman World*, ed. E. A. MacKay (Boston: Brill, 1999), 96–97; B. A. Stolz, "Historicity in the Serbo-Croatian Heroic Epic: Salih Ugljanin's 'Grcki rat,'" *Slavic and Eastern European Journal* 11 (1967): 423; J. Vansina, "Afterthoughts on the Historiography of Oral Tradition,"

Thus, simply by virtue of the fact that the authors of the Synoptics served as tradents within the ancient oral Jesus tradition, we have reason to believe they would have been in a position to write reliable history had they intended to—and all indications are they did intend just that. Regardless of the authorship debate, the current consensus on the first-century dating of the Synoptics, combined with the internal and external evidences to be discussed in the next chapter, suggest that the Synoptic authors were, in fact, in touch with reliable tradition, and thus were in a good position to record reliable history about Jesus.

How Much Did the Theological Commitments of the Gospel Authors Affect Their Portrayal of Jesus?

The final preliminary question commonly investigated by critical historians exploring the historical reliability of ancient documents concerns authorial biases. How much did the bias of an author affect the author's perspective of what happened? Did an author have a motive for intentionally distorting the past? Is the author's work more a piece of ideologically driven propaganda than an accurate recounting of the past? To address these questions in relation to the Synoptic Gospels is to enter into the realm of redaction criticism.

The Challenge of Redactional Criticism

The individual perspectives and biases of the Gospel authors have been studied over the last sixty years under the guise of "redaction criticism."[98] In the words of Norman Perrin, redaction criticism "is concerned with studying the theological motivation of an author as this is revealed in the collection, arrangement, editing, and modification of traditional material, and in the composition of new material or the creation of new forms within the traditions of early Christianity."[99]

For the most part, redaction criticism has operated on the assumption of the two-source solution to the Synoptic problem, allowing scholars to discern Matthew's and Luke's distinctive theological biases on the basis of how they uniquely redact the Markan and Q material. In contrast to the earlier form critics, redaction

---

in *African Historiographies: What History for Which Africa?* ed. B. Jewsiewicki and D. Newbury (Beverly Hills, CA: Sage, 1986), 109–10.

98. Just as three German scholars launched the form-critical study of the Gospels earlier in the century, so three German New Testament scholars shaped the rise of redaction criticism shortly after World War II: Günther Bornkamm (generally considered the first true redaction critic), Hans Conzelmann, and Willi Marxsen. Marxsen gave the new type of critical method its name—*Redaktionsgeschichte.* On the rise and method of redaction criticism, see N. Perrin, *What Is Redaction Criticism?* (Philadelphia: Fortress, 1969); J. van Seters, "An Ironic Circle: Wellhausen and the Rise of Redaction Criticism," *ZAW* 115 (2003): 487–500; R. H. Stein, *The Synoptic Problem: An Introduction* (Grand Rapids: Baker Academic, 1987), 231–63.

99. Perrin, *Redaction Criticism,* 1.

critics have insisted that the Gospel authors should be viewed not merely as passive editors of a tradition but as creative authors in their own right. Consequently, and also largely in contrast to earlier form critics, redaction critics have emphasized the need to engage and explain the "final form" of the Gospels rather than simply analyzing the discrete units that comprise them.

In our estimation, this break from certain tendencies within classical form criticism has been a healthy corrective in New Testament studies. The critique of form criticism's tendency to atomize the study of the Gospels was much needed. The recognition that the Gospel writers were authors in their own right and not merely passive editors of a tradition was long overdue. And, on the other side of things, the emphasis on the distinctive theological perspectives of each Gospel author was a healthy corrective to the traditional tendency to read these texts in the light of one another, emphasizing the unifying features of the Gospels at the expense of their significant distinctives.

At the same time, the methodology of redaction criticism has often intensified the skeptical stance of some toward the Gospels. The emphasis on the creativity of the Gospel authors, combined with the emphasis on the theologically motivated nature of their writings, has led many to conclude that the writers were willing to distort and even fabricate supposedly historical events on the basis of their own literary and theological designs and/or the needs of their respective communities. Perrin, for example, writes, "In our view Mark is a significant and creative literary figure . . . , and after several generations of being read mistakenly, as an historian, he has earned the right to be read as a theologian."[100] Clearly for Perrin and others, taking Mark or other Gospel authors seriously as creative authors and/or theologians (note the identification) means rejecting the traditional idea that they were also interested in, and committed to, preserving the essential historical data of the Jesus tradition with which they worked. So it is that Robert Funk argues that the Gospels are largely fictive on the grounds that "the writers are emotionally involved: they believe fervently in the story they are telling, which means they are not impartial observers."[101] Similarly, the Acts Seminar concluded that "in the Gospel of Luke, the author's use of Mark often involved creating new stories to fit his theological program."[102] At least six considerations serve to call into question the manner in which redaction-critical studies have been used to undermine the historicity of the Gospels.

Authorial Bias and Historical Accuracy

First, if Funk's "bias" argument against the Gospels were carried through consistently, all historical reporting by people who fervently believed and were emotionally invested in what they report would have to be dismissed. Histori-

---

100. Perrin, *Redaction Criticism*, 53.
101. Funk, "Distinguishing Historical from Fictive," 191.
102. "The Acts Seminar: Voting Records, Fall 2002," *Forum*, n.s., 5 (2002): 118.

cal information often is initially reported by those who fervently believe what they report. Since the hypothetical ideal of the historian as a detached, objective observer is a rather modern concept (some would argue, a modern *myth*), it is hard to imagine ancient reporters passing on material they *did not* in some sense passionately care about.

Moreover, it is virtually impossible to imagine certain events being reported by anyone, ancient or modern, in an emotionally detached manner. Consider, for example, Holocaust survivors reporting what transpired in Nazi concentration camps. While historians always must take their limitations and biases into consideration, can anyone imagine dismissing the basic reliability of the survivors' various reports on the grounds that they were, "emotionally involved" and believed "fervently in the story they [were] telling"?[103] If what they are reporting is remotely close to what actually happened, would it not be positively bizarre if they were *not* "emotionally involved" and believed "fervently in the story they [were] telling"?

So it is, we contend, with the Gospel authors. If the Jesus they knew was remotely like the Jesus they report, we cannot imagine them being anything other than "emotionally involved" and invested in "the story they [were] telling." Indeed, it is difficult to understand why they wrote what they wrote unless they were passionately committed to the story they were telling. For given the religious-political environment they were ministering in, these authors would have known that proclaiming this message would likely instigate hostility from both Jews and Romans—which, of course, it did.

The Impossibility of Pure Objectivity

Second, if the postmodern turn has taught us anything, it is that there is no such thing as an unbiased, objective author/reader. To write or research *anything* is to do so *from a distinct perspective*, complete with already-established assumptions that frame everything that is experienced, remembered, spoken, and heard. And this is as true of Robert Funk as it is of any conservative scholar or ancient author.[104] Yet, this does not keep always-already biased skeptical scholars from believing that *their* readers should take *their* reconstructions and conclusions as more or less reliable reflections of the past. If the particular biases of these contemporary scholars do not prevent *them* from doing (what they want others to accept as) reliable history, why should we think that the bias of the Gospel authors prevents them from communicating generally reliable history? In our postmodern context, it seems that hermeneutical humility should lead us to grant to ancient

---

103. Again, using the phraseology of Funk, "Distinguishing Historical from Fictive," 191.

104. Ironically, Funk is a paradigm example of just such a personally biased scholar. On the one hand, he argues for the importance of scholarly objectivity, defining true critical scholarship as that which is "not determined by theological considerations" (*Acts of Jesus*, 1). On the other hand, in his opening address to the Jesus Seminar, in the manner of a "true believer," he explicitly makes a fervent (a)theologically driven plea for a "new gospel" ("Issue of Jesus," 12).

authors the same possibilities-amid-fallibilities we grant to ourselves. Certainly they, like us, are biased. Yet they, like us, are capable of communicating more or less reliable history when they want to.

Bias, which is inevitable, does not necessarily undermine accuracy, whether we are talking about the bias of modern historians, Holocaust survivors, or ancient writers. As H. E. W. Turner has pointed out, "There is nothing anti-historical in writing history from a standpoint."[105] Indeed, if part of the bias of the Gospel authors includes an interest in preserving actual history, as we have argued is the case (e.g., Luke 1:1–4), the emotional investment of the authors may actually *enhance* their reliability. As with Holocaust survivors, their fervent belief in the story they tell and emotional investment in reporting it like it happened may well have motivated them to do the work necessary to get the story right.

The Highly Speculative Nature of Redaction Criticism

Third, to date the practice of redaction criticism has not had enough in the way of methodological constraints to keep it from indulging in unverifiable hypotheses and uncontrolled speculation. As R. P. C. Hanson has pointed out, "There is no statement attributed to Jesus in the whole gospel whose origin it is not easy to explain by a theological motive in the mind of the evangelist or his predecessors if the critic is determined to find one."[106] Given this, it is easy to see how the unrestrained creation of speculative hypotheses has grown to the point it has. Once any given piece of data in the Gospels can be a priori rejected as historical and explained as a theological fabrication, there is very little *certain and stable* historical data left by which to constrain the speculation. Virtually *anything* becomes historically possible, since the data presented can always be reduced to fabrication and legend whenever necessary.

Redaction criticism also tends to foster unbridled speculation about the redactional histories of various texts. The triple-layered Q hypothesis with its multistratified Q community put forward by Burton Mack and others is a case in point.[107] C. C. Black emphasizes the problem here when he observes that redaction critics are "compelled to engage in often highly speculative conjectures about the history of traditions *behind* the Evangelist, assumptions unamenable to empirical analysis yet invariably determinative of that researcher's exegetical or methodological results."[108]

105. H. E. W. Turner, *Historicity and the Gospels: A Sketch of Historical Method and Its Application to the Gospels* (London: Mowbray, 1963), 64.

106. R. P. C. Hanson, "The Assessment of Motive in the Study of the Synoptic Gospels," *Modern Churchman* 10 (1967): 255.

107. B. Mack, *The Lost Gospel: The Book of Q and Christian Origins* (San Francisco: HarperSanFrancisco, 1993). Mack borrows the triple-layered Q redactional theory from J. Kloppenborg, *The Formation of Q: Trajectories in Ancient Wisdom Collections* (Philadelphia: Fortress, 1987).

108. C. C. Black, "The Quest of Mark the Redactor: Why Has It Been Pursued, and What Has It Taught Us?" *JSNT* 33 (1988): 30; see also Black's survey and insightful assessment of redaction criticism:

Worth noting in this regard is a well-known comment by C. S. Lewis. In his famous essay, "Fern-seed and Elephants," Lewis reflects upon the times when his own literary works had been subjected to redaction-critical assessments by his contemporary reviewers, that is, times when reviewers attempted speculatively to reconstruct the genesis and development of his works. Lewis responds,

> My impression is that in the whole of my experience not one of these guesses has on any one point been right; that the method shows a record of one hundred per cent failure. You would expect that by mere chance they would hit as often as they miss. But it is my impression that they do no such thing. I can't remember a single hit. . . . What I can say with certainty is that they are usually wrong. And yet they would often sound—if you didn't know the truth—extremely convincing.[109]

This is enough to render the enterprise of speculating on the redactional motives and moves of the Gospel authors and the redactional histories of their writings suspect. But Lewis goes on to note that his reviewers had advantages that contemporary New Testament scholars do not have with regard to the biblical texts. For example, Lewis's reviewers shared the same culture and language as Lewis, something that is not true of critics of the New Testament. This strongly suggests that speculations about the redactional histories of ancient texts have far less likelihood of being correct than the speculations about Lewis's writings proffered by contemporary reviewers. And this cannot help but call the whole enterprise into question.

Yet, remarkably enough, the more extreme redaction critics, and especially those who employ redaction criticism in defense of the legendary-Jesus thesis, typically exhibit very little tentativeness in presenting their speculative reconstructions. Furthermore, it appears that often the rhetoric of confidence is rooted less in inevitable conclusions drawn from the literary evidence than in the simple fact that the speculations are inherently unfalsifiable. As Lewis himself notes—with no small tinge of sarcasm—"remember, the Biblical critics, whatever reconstructions they devise, can never be crudely proved wrong. St. Mark is dead. When they meet St. Peter there will be more pressing matters to discuss."[110]

Anachronistic Aspects of Redaction Criticism

Fourth, throughout this work we have had a number of occasions to note how New Testament criticism has often gone awry when it has not adequately considered the significant differences between orally oriented texts, on the one hand, and fixed-print texts with a decidedly literate conception/register, on the other.

The Disciples according to Mark: Markan Redaction in Current Debate (Sheffield: Sheffield Academic Press, 1989).

109. C. S. Lewis, "Fern-seed and Elephants," in *Fern-seed and Elephants and Other Essays on Christianity*, ed. W. Hooper (London: Fontana/Collins, 1975), 115.

110. Lewis, "Fern-seed," 118.

The same problem arises in connection with redaction criticism. From its inception, redaction criticism has tended to read ancient texts with the sensibility and tools appropriate to modern, highly literate texts. Indeed, as John van Seters has argued, the very idea of a "redactor" is largely a nineteenth-century anachronism foisted back upon the biblical world.[111]

The fact is that the discipline of redaction criticism is steeped in a post-Gutenberg understanding of texts. It has operated on the assumption that people in the first century approached writing roughly the same way modern people do. But this, we have seen repeatedly, is a fundamentally flawed assumption.[112] As Mark Amodio has forcefully noted:

> Our status as *homo legens* and our habit of imposing contemporary interpretive strategies upon the written remains of the past has led many myopically to assume that medieval [and, we would add, first-century] habits of mind and procedure parallel our own literate ones. . . . We have habitually judged all texts against the standard of our tradition's idiosyncratic, literate poetics, no matter how impertinent that poetics may be to the texts at hand.[113]

With respect to New Testament studies, Pieter Botha highlights one aspect of this important difference between an oral and literate poetics vis-à-vis redaction criticism. With regard to the former, he writes: "The issue of tradition and redaction simply disappears: it is not possible to think in those terms within an oral poetics."[114]

Moving to a very practical consideration, the discipline of redaction criticism has tended to overlook the physical constraints of the materials used for writing in the first century (e.g., the cumbersomeness of scrolls, writing on one's lap as opposed to a desk, etc.). While contemporary scholars can easily scan back and forth over a document on a desk, meticulously inspecting how its author uses words, concepts, and traditional material, ancient authors could not. Consequently, ancient "redactors" would have relied much more on their memory to access written material than on an inspection of a text in front of them.[115]

---

111. J. van Seters, "The Redactor in Biblical Studies: A Nineteenth Century Anachronism," *Journal of Northwest Semitic Languages* 29 (2003): 1–19. See also idem, "Ironic Circle." J. L. Ska has responded to van Seters in "A Plea on Behalf of the Biblical Redactor," *Studia Theologica* 59 (2005): 4–18.

112. P. J. J. Botha has critiqued the assumption that "because some *wrote*, that activity is directly comparable to *our* writing today"; see "Cognition, Orality-Literacy, and Approaches to First-Century Writings," in *Orality, Literacy and Colonialism in Antiquity*, ed. J. A. Draper (Atlanta: Scholars Press, 2004), 63.

113. M. C. Amodio, *Writing the Oral Tradition: Oral Poetics and Literate Culture in Medieval England* (Notre Dame, IN: University of Notre Dame Press, 2004), 11. This concern is a common one among those who work at the intersection of the oral and literate worlds. For example, T. M. Lentz writes: "Scholars have made much of the fact that the ancients clearly 'wrote' discourse because we have the extant evidence. . . . The unstated assumption was that the ancients were writers in the modern sense of the term" (*Orality and Literacy in Hellenic Greece* [Carbondale: Southern Illinois University Press, 1989], 103).

114. P. J. J. Botha, "Mark's Stories of Jesus' Tomb and History," *Neotestamentica* 23 (1989): 201.

115. Small, *Wax Tablets*, 219–20; Yamagata, "Plato, Memory, and Performance," 117–18.

From another angle, the discipline of redaction criticism has not adequately internalized the fact that orally oriented texts were used largely as preservation tools and memory cues for future oral/aural performances, not as closely and constantly consulted texts in the way we often use them in the modern, literate world.[116] Just as variants within the manuscript tradition of the Gospel of Mark suggest that its scribes were often as dependent upon their memory of the oral performance of Mark as they were the written texts itself,[117] so, we suggest, the Gospel writers were in all probability as dependent upon their *memory of the public readings of their written sources*—which they would have heard, in various forms, countless times—as they were upon close readings of those sources when they composed their own texts (and perhaps more so).

If this is true, then what appears to the modern redaction critic as a conscious, theologically motivated divergence on the part of Matthew or Luke from Mark is, in many instances, likely to reflect nothing more than an unconscious paraphrase or a more familiar variant available in the wider tradition. In other words, given our understanding of how texts function in rhetorical cultures, we have every reason to assume that divergences between the Gospels generally are due to the fact that *the semantic contract of the ancient world allowed greater flexibility in recounting a source than we in the modern, literate world are accustomed to.* Without at all denying the unique theological perspectives of each Gospel author, we must in this light conclude that reading a self-conscious theological and/or polemical motive into differences between the Gospels must, often times, be judged to be anachronistic and unhelpful.[118]

116. That, in an orally oriented context, written texts are primarily used as preservation tools and occasionally consulted mnemonic aids to oral/aural performance has been argued by a wide variety of scholars from various disciplines. See, e.g., W. H. Kelber, *The Oral and the Written Gospel*, xxiii; R. Scodel, "Homeric Signs and Flashbulb Memories," in *Epea and Grammata: Oral and Written Communication in Ancient Greece*, ed. I. Worthington and J. M. Foley (Boston: Brill, 2002), 99–116; Thomas, *Literacy and Orality*, 90–93; idem, *Oral Tradition and Written Record*, 21, 49. Rosalind Thomas reminds us that even with the ancient historians (she mentions Herodotus and even Thucydides, generally speaking) we tend to find "a fairly simple use of written texts," which is "symptomatic of the relatively unsophisticated approach to written documents of the time" (*Oral Tradition and Written Record*, 90).

117. A point noted by J. Dewey, "The Survival of Mark's Gospel: A Good Story?" *JBL* 123 (2004): 505.

118. The basic problem here is that orally oriented written texts allow contemporary scholars to impose "modes of mircoanalysis" upon them that are entirely foreign and inappropriate, and yet which are natural to the modern critic. As C. J. Swearingen observes, such microanalysis is "constitutive of literate values and literate linguistic bias." Modern scholars can easily forget that what one can "look for with a transcription in hand, and what one 'notices,' 'remembers' or 'understands' in a *viva-voce* exchange are of necessity different, but for multiple reasons, and not just because of a difference in medium" ("Literate Rhetors and Their Illiterate Audiences: The Orality of Early Literacy," *PRE/TEXT* 7 [1986], 153). Thus, one characteristic of an orally oriented text is its "lack of precision" compared with modern literate texts; see M. Gagarin, "The Orality of Greek Oratory," in *Signs of Orality*, 166. Quite unconsciously, then, contemporary redaction critics tend to read the Gospels with a level of linguistic and compositional precision that, while natural for themselves and necessary for their complex redactional hypotheses to fly, is nonetheless treating the Gospels in an amazingly anachronistic fashion. Here, Rosalind Thomas's

The Constraints of Orally Oriented Texts

Closely related to this is a fifth consideration: redaction criticism has tended to neglect the constraints that are placed on texts written for oral delivery and aural reception. As we have noted a number of times, the Gospel authors composed their texts with the awareness that they would primarily be recited aloud—often from memory and thus not verbatim—to mostly illiterate audiences. Illiterate, orally oriented, tradition-centered people simply do not *hear* with the same literary precision and subtlety that modern, text-centric scholars *read*.[119] And this fact alone changes everything for a theory and method of textual composition. It shows, once again, how anachronistic it is to instantly read theological polemics into the variations found between the Gospels.

One rather clear example of such modern "overreading" of the Gospels via redaction-critical analysis can be seen in the work of Werner Kelber—a fact that is somewhat ironic given that Kelber is one scholar who has attempted to take the orally oriented nature of the Gospels very seriously. Kelber reads Mark as self-consciously constructing an anti-Petrine polemic in his Gospel. Specifically, he argues that Mark's negative portrayal of Peter and the disciples is a critique both of the Jewish-Christian community centered in Jerusalem and of the oral gospel tradition that they represent.[120]

Unfortunately, Kelber's interpretation of Mark is based upon a close text-centric reading that is quite implausible given the original aurally receptive audience. As Thomas Boomershine has demonstrated,

> When the narrative is read aloud in a manner as close as possible to the patterns of oral recitation implicit in the narrative, the anti-Petrine interpretation is much less probable. The reason is the difference in psychological distance to the text and, in this story, to Peter that is required for oral recitation in contrast to silent reading.[121]

Aspects of a narrative that may suggest explicit textual tensions and pointed polemics to modern, highly literate readers closely studying the text in silence

---

observation concerning orally oriented texts in classical Athens is equally applicable to the Gospels: "The oral context may alter the content and significance of the written word considerably. . . . They are not simply written documents in our sense, and we may misinterpret their content, omissions, and their very importance if we take them to be that" (*Oral Tradition and Written Record*, 93–94).

119. This general point has been effectively applied as a critique by Sean Freyne to John Kloppenborg Verbin's masterful but very text-centric redactional analysis of Q; see Freyne, "In Search of Q: A Conversation with the Work of John S. Kloppenborg," *Proceedings of the Irish Biblical Association* 25 (2002): 127.

120. See Kelber, *The Kingdom in Mark: A New Place and a New Time* (Philadelphia: Fortress, 1974); and idem, *The Oral and the Written Gospel*, 97, 130.

121. T. E. Boomershine, "Peter's Denial as Polemic or Confession: The Implications of Media Criticism for Biblical Hermeneutics," *Semeia* 39 (1987): 59. Thus Boomershine concludes: "Kelber has collapsed 1900 years of media development into a forty year period in the first century" (p. 60). Joanna Dewey raises similar issues in "Mark as Aural Narrative: Structures as Clues to Understanding," *Sewanee Theological Review* 36 (1992): 54–55.

simply would not be *heard* as such by people experiencing the narrative in a community context of oral recitation and aural reception. The observation made by Amin Sweeney with regard to contemporary Malay orally oriented texts is equally relevant to Gospel studies: "An aurally consuming, nonliterate postulated audience ... places constraints on the level of complexity possible in a written text."[122] In this sense, whereas the classical form critics tended to underestimate the literary achievement of the Gospel authors, redaction critics have tended to overestimate them, finding vast amounts of carefully plotted polemical subtlety, rhetorical complexity, and theological nuance where, most likely, little exists to be found.[123] It is the natural constraints, both of medium and conception, in an orally oriented culture that largely have been missed in the skeptical conclusions of contemporary redaction critics.

The Retrojection of Highly Literate Aesthetic Goals

Sixth, all too often redaction critics seem to assume their highly literate aesthetics, values, and goals were shared by the ancient Gospel authors. Within modern, literate culture the production and reception of texts are "intensely private, highly idiosyncratic, and highly unconventional" endeavors.[124] The modern literary paradigm values originality and novelty. Unlike the aesthetic that guides the ancient, orally oriented author, modern authors are typically praised for "the unique ways in which they produce original creations or for their additions to and novel reshaping of inherited material."[125]

In sharp contrast to this, oral tradents, while valued for the relatively creative retelling of their traditional materials, are not quick to create new material and/or pass off untraditional material as "tradition." Both their guiding poetics and their interactive, traditionally formed audience tend to dampen such ventures.[126] This forces on us the conclusion that the hermeneutical paradigm and guiding poetics that shape the minds of contemporary redaction critics are largely alien to the authorial mind-set and goals of the ancient Gospel authors.

122. Sweeney, *A Full Hearing*, 306.

123. Thus, W. R. Telford writes of the "tendency" among those New Testament scholars who favor contemporary literary-critical methods "to over-estimate Mark's achievement" ("Mark and the Historical-Critical Method: The Challenge of Recent Literary Approaches to the Gospel," in *The Synoptic Gospels: Source Criticism and the New Literary Criticism*, ed. C. Focant [Leuven: Leuven University Press, 1993], 501). Similarly, from the perspective of understanding the orally dominant context of Mark's Gospel, Botha can conclude that Mark "has no complicated message" ("Mark's Stories," 201).

124. Amodio, *Writing the Oral Tradition*, 5.

125. Ibid.

126. Seen in this context, the generally conservative treatment of sources by the Gospel authors can be better recognized and appreciated. On the generally conservative tendencies in Mark, see, e.g., E. Best, "Mark's Preservation of the Tradition," in *Disciples and Discipleship: Studies in the Gospel according to Mark* (Edinburgh: Clark, 1986), 31–48; in Matthew, see, e.g., R. C. Beaton, "How Matthew Writes," in *Written Gospel*, 116–34, esp. 120–21, 134.

The Need for a New Orally Oriented Redaction-Critical Approach

In our estimation, if redaction criticism is to have a future in New Testament studies, redaction critics are going to have to seriously rethink their methodology in light of the emerging interdisciplinary findings on orally oriented written texts. Among other things, they will have to take seriously the fact that the modern "text-centric" approach tends naturally to treat ancient orally oriented texts in an anachronistic fashion.[127] They will have to appreciate the fact that to understand orally oriented texts one must understand and apply the notion of "traditional referentiality," wherein dense idiomatic expression is the assumption and "only the properly prepared audience is equipped to understand."[128] As Foley notes, "Traditional referentiality enables an extremely economical transaction of meaning, with the modest, concrete part standing for a more complex whole. *Pars pro toto* is the fundamental principle."[129] In other words, if redaction criticism is to have a future—and we certainly believe it should—it will need to appropriate what Foley calls a "composite poetics," one that "takes account of both traditional character and what some have construed as 'literary' quality" of *written texts indebted to an oral register*. To date such an approach has proven to be "elusive," as Foley again observes.[130]

Along these same lines, if redaction criticism is going to be reconciled with insights emerging from contemporary orality studies, critics will have to seriously reevaluate the common assumption that individual first-century oral tradents would have felt entitled to transgress the tradition by drastically modifying its contents or even fabricating new units of tradition wholesale. They also will have to abandon the assumption that alterations made by ancient authors to their sources were primarily intended to transform or subvert those very sources. The operation of traditional referentiality in orally dominant cultures largely undercuts both assumptions.

In reality, were tradents to deviate seriously from the tradition, whether through oral/aural performance or written record designed for future re-oralizations, they would quite naturally be corrected by their audiences, given that a traditional audience fundamentally relies on the wider, shared tradition to make sense of any particular performance event. In an orally oriented context, each text (oral or written) is but "a thin slice of the tradition's vast, rich, and unchartable narrative possibilities."[131] Following the hermeneutic of oral performance and its virtually

---

127. Foley, "What's in a Sign?" in *Signs of Orality*, 10.

128. Ibid., 7.

129. Ibid., 11.

130. Ibid., 6.

131. Amodio, *Writing the Oral Tradition*, 14. This observation, made with respect to the poetics of medieval England, applies equally to other orally oriented texts such as the Gospels. For example, John's comment (John 21:25) that all the world could not hold the books that could be written about Jesus reflects this ancient attitude, one often missed by us modern, literate readers, who respond to John's comment by (silently!) saying to ourselves: "Come on, John—surely you exaggerate!"

unlimited possibilities, the number of variations that written textual performances could take are literally endless, *yet, at the same time, unequivocally bounded by tradition*. Unless the future of redaction criticism includes appropriating these and related insights, it risks becoming an antiquated discipline, wrecked upon the shoals of historical and media anachronism.

Summary

In this chapter we have suggested that the confusing equivocation connected with the "burden of proof" debate can largely be avoided by distinguishing the a priori from the a posteriori burden of proof. The former is a methodological principle that should be embraced by all New Testament scholars. The latter reflects the studied, provisional conclusion about the general reliability of a text. As we have seen, the latter is, in fact, directly influenced not only by one's historical research, but also by the religious and philosophical assumptions—together with the intuited comprehensive picture of Jesus—one brings to the text in question. If New Testament scholarship is going to continue to claim to strive for objectivity, all of this must be made explicit and made part and parcel of the scholarly discussion.

We have further argued that the method we employ to move forward in our assessment of the reliability of the Gospels should be fashioned after the method used by historians in other areas. Rather than pretending that we are arriving at a comprehensive picture of Jesus by analyzing isolated, individual units of tradition—a methodology that already is prejudiced in a skeptical direction and is problematic on other accounts—we should treat the Synoptics as we would any other ancient texts.

When we do this—and when we consistently evaluate them by the standards of their own orally dominant culture rather than by our own highly literate context—we find they give evidence of plausible grounds for affirming their authors' intent and ability to reliably report on the historical events with which they are concerned. Moreover, when evaluated as orally oriented texts, we find nothing in them that would lead us to conclude that their biases prevented them from accurately communicating on historical matters. Having addressed the foundational issues of the burden of proof, methodology, and textual attestation of the Gospels, and having addressed the three preliminary questions of authorial historical intent, authorial capacity to report history, and authorial bias, we now turn to several more specific questions regarding the actual content of the Gospels.

10

THE SYNOPTIC TRADITION AND THE JESUS OF HISTORY

COMPLETING A CUMULATIVE CASE FOR THE RELIABILITY OF THE SYNOPTIC PORTRAIT(S) OF JESUS

In the previous chapter we addressed three methodological issues and three preliminary questions related to the evaluation of the reliability of the Gospels. In this final chapter we will apply to the Synoptic Gospels six broad diagnostic questions historians routinely ask of ancient documents in order to assess their historical reliability.[1] As before, our focus will be mostly on Mark, since it is

---

1. These questions and concerns are methodological commonplaces within the field of historiography. See, e.g., R. J. Shafer, ed., *A Guide to Historical Method*, rev. ed. (Homewood, IL: Dorsey, 1974), 157–58; L. Gottschalk, *Understanding History: A Primer on Historical Method* (New York: Knopf, 1963), 150; G. J. Renier, *History: Its Purpose and Method* (New York: Harper & Row, 1950), 108–10, 162–65. They represent two broad types of evidence and corresponding tests: "internal evidence/tests," which involves the consideration of issues within the text itself (e.g., internal self-consistency within the document, etc.), and "external evidence/tests," which consider whether the text is corroborated by additional evidence external to the text itself (i.e., other literary evidence, archaeological evidence, etc.). On these two categories of evidence/criteria, see also B. M. Metzger, *The Text of the New Testament: Its Transmission, Corruption and Restoration*, 2nd ed. (New York: Oxford University Press, 1968), 209–11; B. Allen and W. L. Montell, *From Memory to History: Using Oral Sources in Local Historical Research* (Nashville: American Association for State and Local History, 1981), 71–87; C. Sanders, *An Introduction to Research in English Literary History* (New York: Macmillan, 1952), 142–61.

widely regarded as the forerunner and primary source of the other two Synoptics. The six questions we will explore vis-à-vis the Synoptics are: (1) Does the document(s) include self-damaging details? (2) Does the document(s) include incidental details and/or casual information characteristic of historical reminiscences? (3) Does the document(s) show evidence of a broad internal consistency? (4) Does the document(s) contain inherently improbable events? (5) Does external literary evidence corroborate the document(s)? And, (6) does external archaeological evidence corroborate the document(s)? Again, the purpose here is to make a general assessment of the nature and historical quality of the Synoptic Jesus tradition in order to ascertain whether the broad contours—the essential portraiture(s)—of Jesus found in this tradition can plausibly be said to be rooted in history. While a variety of smaller-scale matters will be considered along the way, each question is designed to assist the construction of this broader, cumulative-case project.

Inclusion of Self-Damaging Details?

The presence of self-damaging details in a document usually suggests to historians that the author was willing to risk damaging his own cause for the sake of remaining faithful to history.[2] Thus, all other things being equal, the presence of such material in a document should increase our confidence in its historical veracity.

In Gospel research this test often has been termed the "criterion of embarrassment." The reasoning behind the criterion is that early Christians would not have invented material that was counterproductive to their cause—material that put Jesus or themselves in a negative light, made them vulnerable to the criticism of opponents, and so on. To the contrary, one would be inclined to think that over time Christians would have tended to minimize or expunge altogether aspects of the tradition that were problematic. This criterion often has been used as part of an argument to identify authentic individual sayings of Jesus.[3] In evaluating how the Gospels fare on the question of the inclusion of self-damaging material, three points are worthy of consideration.

2. As Louis Gottschalk (formerly professor of history, University of Chicago) has noted in his primer on historical method: "More dependably, when a statement is *prejudicial* to a witness, his dear ones, or his cause, it is likely to be truthful" (*Understanding History*, 161).

3. John Meier lists the criterion of embarrassment among what he considers to be the five "primary" criteria of historicity; see *A Marginal Jew: Rethinking the Historical Jesus*, vol. 1: *The Roots of the Problem and the Person* (New York: Doubleday, 1991), 168–71. Others who rank this criterion among the most reliable include G. Stanton, *The Gospels and Jesus*, 2nd ed. (New York: Oxford University Press, 2002), 175; G. Theissen and D. Winter, *The Quest for the Plausible Jesus: The Question of Criteria*, trans. M. E. Boring (Louisville: Westminster Knox, 2002), 239–40 (which they term "resistance to tendencies of the tradition").

The "Softening" of Troubling Material within the Synoptic Tradition

A convincing case can be made that, in the course of its transmission, the Synoptic tradition tended to "soften" troubling and embarrassing material, as we would expect in any ancient tradition. Consider, for example, the various accounts of Jesus's baptism by John. This account would have been problematic for early Christians. After all, John's baptism is explicitly said to be a baptism of repentance, thus a baptism intended *for sinners* (Mark 1:4; Matt. 3:1–2, 6). Additionally, the very fact that Jesus was baptized by John raises the question of whether John was actually greater than Jesus. Interestingly enough, there is no account of Jesus or anyone else baptizing John. Nevertheless, the Gospel of Mark boldly and tersely records Jesus's baptism by John, without in any respect softening its problematic implications with any sort of theological apologetic (Mark 1:4–11).

On the assumption of the two-source theory, Matthew and Luke appropriated Mark's account. Both retain the baptismal account but seem to soften its embarrassing features to some degree. Matthew offers his readers a theological apologetic by explaining that John initially refused to baptize Jesus, wanting instead to be baptized by Jesus. John relented only after Jesus insisted, cryptically adding that it was "proper" for them to "fulfill all righteousness" (Matt. 3:13–17). Luke can be read as going yet a step further, locating the baptism after John's arrest and never explicitly mentioning who baptized Jesus (Luke 3:19–22). While our focus is on the Synoptics, we might here simply note that John arguably softened the tradition further still. He retains the account of the witness of God from heaven and the descending dove upon Jesus, but does not even mention Jesus's baptism itself (John 1:29–34).

In light of this, it seems clear that the episode of Jesus's baptism (and a number of other accounts) underwent a softening in the transmission of the earliest Jesus traditions. At the same time, we have to be careful not to retroject a post-Gutenberg, literate conception onto the Gospels and/or the traditions they express. Given the orally orientated nature of these works and the culture in which they were produced, it is not necessarily the case that, in each instance, Matthew or Luke had a hard copy of Mark's Gospel in front of them that they consciously modified to soften its embarrassing features. Rather, for any given case, it is just as likely that this softening of the tradition is a result of Matthew or Luke inscribing one of the countless performative variations available within the wider authoritative tradition.

Moreover, given the oral register that likely would have characterized the communicative world of the early church, one must be careful to avoid reading too much into this tendency within the tradition. Given the fixed-yet-flexible nature of oral traditions, it is unlikely anyone in the earliest Christian communities would have found much significance in these modifications since it is highly unlikely that either these orally oriented tradents or their audiences were engaged in close, literary readings and comparisons. When the Gospel of Matthew was being read and heard, for example, no one was consciously comparing it to the different nuances found within the traditions represented by the Gospel of Mark, or Luke, or John. Thus we should be cautious in imagining a consciously contrastive, let alone explicitly polemical, motive behind these alterations. There simply would have been far too many performative variations within the various communities for this sort of critical exercise to be commonplace in the early church.

Nevertheless, as we now compare the Synoptic Gospels, we can plausibly discern the sort of softening that characterizes most traditions, ancient and modern. Given the subjective dimension in how material is selected and recounted, this tendency is almost unavoidable. But for this very reason, it says a lot about an author's and/or a tradition's commitment to accuracy when they nevertheless retain potentially self-damaging elements. It therefore becomes difficult to doubt the early church's tradition about Jesus's baptism by John, especially as it is found in Mark.

The Prevalence of Self-Damaging Material

Second, for our purposes it is important to note that the embarrassing account of Jesus's baptism in Mark and, to a lesser extent, in the subsequent Gospels, is by no means an isolated case in the Synoptic tradition. To the contrary, the Synoptics are brimming with "embarrassing" material, which we not only cannot imagine early Christians inventing, but which we might have expected the earliest traditions to drop—were they not so invested in retaining historically rooted information about Jesus.[4] For example, among the embarrassing material in Mark's Gospel, we find that:

- Jesus's own family questioned his sanity (3:21)
- Jesus could not perform many miracles in his own town (6:5)
- Jesus was rejected by people in his hometown (6:3)
- some thought Jesus was in collusion with, and even possessed by, the devil (3:22, 30)
- Jesus at times seemed to rely on common medicinal techniques (7:33; 8:23)
- Jesus's healings were not always instantaneous (8:22–25)
- Jesus's disciples were not always able to exorcise demons (9:18) and Jesus's own exorcisms were not always instantaneously successful (5:8)
- Jesus seemingly suggested he was not "good" (10:18)
- Jesus associated with people of ill repute (2:14–16)
- Jesus was sometimes rude to people (7:27)

4. One must, of course, be careful here. As John Meier has warned, what we might consider embarrassing may in fact not have been embarrassing in a first-century Mediterranean context. As an example, Meier proposes Jesus's "cry of dereliction" from the cross (*Marginal Jew*, 1:170–71).

- Jesus seemed to disregard Jewish laws, customs, and cleanliness codes (e.g., 2:23–24)
- Jesus often spoke and acted in culturally "shameful" ways (e.g., 3:31–35)
- Jesus cursed a fig tree for not having any fruit when he was hungry, despite the fact that it was not even the season for bearing fruit (11:13–14)
- the disciples who were to form the foundation of the new community consistently seemed dull, obstinate, and eventually cowardly (e.g., 8:32–33; 10:35–37; 14:37–40, 50)
- Jesus was betrayed by an inner-circle disciple (14:43–46), and Peter denied any association with him (14:66–72)

On top of all this, we must remember that the Gospel of Mark, and each subsequent Gospel, is centered on the fact that Jesus was crucified by the Romans. It is hard to imagine a more effective way to convince people in a first-century Jewish context that someone is *not* the Messiah than by telling them that the would-be savior was executed by Israel's military oppressors! To go further and tell them that this would-be savior died a cursed death on a tree would make the sales pitch all the worse (cf. Deut. 21:22–23). The fact that the *Gospel of Thomas* has no crucifixion shows us that it was possible to write a "gospel" without mentioning this infamous moment. Thus, the fact that the Synoptic tradition not only continues to mention the crucifixion but also makes it a centerpiece of its message must be taken as evidence that the earliest Christians, including the authors of the Synoptic Gospels, remained willing to acknowledge, remember, and boldly proclaim the single most embarrassing historical fact associated with their fledgling movement. This is the very sort of self-damaging material historians typically look for in assessing the veracity of ancient works, and Mark is literally packed with it.

It is important to note not only that the presence of self-damaging material testifies to the historicity of these individual pericopes within Mark, but also that the sizeable amount of this material found in this Gospel and the *broad pattern* that it forms leads to a more general conclusion. John Meier draws out the implications of this pattern:

> The fact that embarrassing material is found as late as the redaction of the Gospels reminds us that besides a creative thrust there was also a conservative force in the Gospel tradition. Indeed, so conservative was this force that a string of embarrassing events (e.g., baptism by John, betrayal by Judas, denial by Peter, crucifixion by the Romans) called forth agonizing and varied theological reflection, but not, in most cases, convenient amnesia. In this sense, the criterion of embarrassment has an importance for the historian far beyond the individual data it may help to verify.[5]

---

5. Meier, *Marginal Jew*, 1:170. While we affirm Meier's insight here, in our own estimation this sort of evidence for the broad conserving trend in the Synoptic tradition is underappreciated by Meier at various points in his multivolume Jesus project.

The Omission of Relevant Issues

Third, while Mark and the other Gospels (including John) include material one might have expected them to omit, they also omit material one might have expected them to include. If the Gospel authors (and the traditions they drew from and fed back into) were more interested in creating a Jesus who was relevant to their needs than they were in remembering what Jesus actually said and did, we would expect to find many things said by Jesus that are conspicuous by their absence. But neither Mark nor the other canonical Gospels have Jesus addressing many issues we know plagued the earliest Christian communities.

For example, we read in these works nothing about the issue of how "Jewish" Gentiles must become when they join the Jesus movement. Nor do we find anything about how "spiritual gifts" such as glossolalia are to be used, how congregations are to be organized and run, what role women can have within the community, what is appropriate attire for men and women in church, or what attitude disciples should have toward meat offered to idols. Had the early tradents generally been inclined to invent Jesus material relevant to their particular concerns, rather than hold as sacred what in fact he did say, *these are precisely the sorts of issues we would have expected the Jesus of the Gospels to address.*[6] That the Gospel tradition retains an amazing amount of embarrassing material on the one hand, and so often fails to insert material that clearly would have been of benefit on the other, testifies to their generally strong interest in, and commitment to, preserving early Christian memory of the earthly Jesus. Scholars who adopt a skeptical stance toward the Gospels, including most legendary-Jesus theorists, rarely give these considerations their due weight.[7]

In our estimation, by any fair application of standard historical methodology, the wealth of self-damaging material and the omission of material that would have met practical needs of the church should, at the very least, play a role in shifting the a posteriori burden of proof to those who would treat the Synoptic Jesus tradition—and especially Mark—as generally unreliable.

Inclusion of Incidental Details and/or Casual Information?

A second standard historiographical question used to assess the historical veracity of ancient documents is: "Did [the author] give incidental or casual information,

6. For discussion see B. Witherington, *The Christology of Jesus* (Minneapolis: Fortress, 1990), 4; C. Blomberg, "Form Criticism," in *Dictionary of Jesus and the Gospels*, ed. J. B. Green et al. (Downers Grove, IL: InterVarsity, 1992), 246.

7. For a laudable exception, see R. Pesch, *Das Markusevangelium*, 2 vols. (Freiburg: Herder, 1976–77).

almost certainly not intended to mislead?"[8] All other things being equal, the inclusion of nonideologically motivated incidental detail or "local color" in a document tends to bolster a historian's confidence of an author's historical intentions and commitment. Especially with respect to texts written within a generation of the events recorded, it may even suggest that the author is an eyewitness—particularly if the author claims as much—or that the author is in touch with eyewitness tradition.

Could Such Details Be Fictional Embellishments?

Of course, it is always possible that what appears to be incidental detail or casual information could in fact be nothing more than a redactional gloss created precisely to give a fictional narrative a realistic feel. For this reason, Meier classifies the criterion of "vividness of detail" as a "secondary" or even "dubious" criterion.[9] In our estimation, there may well be more to this criterion than Meier and others have granted, especially as it concerns the Gospel of Mark.[10]

Decades ago, the widely respected form critic Vincent Taylor made two observations that are pertinent to this issue.[11] First, Taylor noted that a number of the details found in Mark give no evidence of being redactional glosses and serve no obvious redactional purpose in Mark's narrative (e.g., 4:36).[12] He thus became convinced that their presence in Mark could best be explained by concluding that these elements were part of the tradition Mark relied upon. Second, Taylor noted that at key points in Mark's Gospel, moments of high drama where one might expect Mark to embellish his account with details (if that in fact is what he was up to), Mark's narrative actually tends to *lack* vivid detail—for example, the choosing of the Twelve (3:13–19), the priestly plot against Jesus (14:1–2), the betrayal of Jesus by Judas (14:10–11). In fact, with his typically terse prose, Mark misses many opportunities to do precisely what skeptics suggest he and other early Christian tradents specialized in—rampant and creative embellishment of the tradition. This is an important point, since historians rightly can become suspicious if they find "*excessive* detail and elaboration" in an account.[13]

Taylor's observations rarely have been given serious consideration in academic circles. First, they were overshadowed by the dominance of certain Bultmannian form-critical assumptions, assumptions that have since been shown to be seriously flawed (see chaps. 6 and 7). Following this, and in reaction to form criticism, Taylor's perspective was again overshadowed by the dominance of the redactional

8. Shafer, ed., *Historical Method*, 157.

9. Meier, *Marginal Jew*, 1:180.

10. We are not suggesting that Mark is filled with this type of material; merely that enough exists to raise the present consideration.

11. V. Taylor, *The Gospel according to St. Mark*, 2nd ed. (New York: St. Martin's, 1966), 135–49.

12. Ibid., 274.

13. B. M. Ross, *Remembering the Personal Past: Descriptions of Autobiographical Memory* (New York: Oxford University Press, 1991), 164 (emphasis added). Here Ross is summarizing an insight drawn from M. Bloch, *The Historian's Craft* (New York: Knopf, 1953).

critical assumption that, since the Gospel authors were creative authors in their own right, they were quick to embellish their received traditions with fictional glosses. However, as discussed in the last chapter, many of the redaction-critical assumptions that generated this skepticism have been shown to be anachronistic and/or problematic on other grounds. For this reason, we contend that it is time to seriously reconsider Taylor's observations.[14]

The point here is not that the presence of incidental detail in any given passage *necessarily* demonstrates the reliability of that particular passage, for clearly it does not.[15] The point rather is that when a work such as Mark's Gospel does at certain points exhibit these features without any clear hint of a redactional motive, this becomes one more indicator that the author may well be presenting traditional material originally derived from an eyewitness perspective.[16] Again, this consideration is particularly relevant for relatively recent traditions—within one generation or so of the original events—as is the case with the Gospels. In arguing this we are simply trying to treat the Gospels the way historians generally treat ancient documents. Except in cases where one is dealing with a hoax or a fictional genre, the general assumption is that the inclusion of realistic detail in a relatively recent historical narrative signals an author's and/or a tradition's intention to transmit factual data.[17]

In this light, it seems fair to say that when we are dealing with recent works that appear to be concerned with conveying actual historical events, and when

---

14. Meier argues that, in light of the results of redaction criticism and the general dismissal of Petrine influence upon Mark, "Taylor's arguments do not seem as strong today as they might have appeared in the early fifties" (*Marginal Jew*, 1:181). As an updated corrective, we would say that, in light of more recent orality oriented critiques of redactional-critical study of the Gospels and of a much-needed reassessment of the value of oral tradition in general—and Mark's connections to it in particular—Taylor's arguments seem *stronger* today than they did in the early 1950s when Bultmann's shadow loomed larger than life.

15. A point well noted by J. B. Green, "The Book of Acts as History/Writing," *Lexington Theological Quarterly* 37 (2002): 121. Recent memory studies stress a similar point—the *vividness* of a personal memory does not necessarily indicate the *accuracy* of that memory; see S. Engel, *Context Is Everything: The Nature of Memory* (New York: Freeman, 1999), 15–16. For example, recent study of "flashbulb memories" demonstrates the complexities involved; see E. Winograd and U. Neisser, eds., *Affect and Accuracy in Recall: Studies of "Flashbulb" Memories* (New York: Cambridge University Press, 1992).

16. See, e.g., the recent study of "local color" in Luke's narration of Acts 13–14: C. Breytenbach, *Paulus und Barnabas in der Provinz Galatien: Studien zu Apostelgeschichte 13f.; 16,6; 18,23 und den Adressaten des Galaterbriefs* (Leiden: Brill, 1996).

17. As H. Jason notes, "The nearer, better known, and more everyday the historical and geographical setting of the tale, and the nearer its actors to the narrator's personal experience, the more 'real' the happening of the tale will appear to the narrator" ("Concerning the 'Historical' and the 'Local' Legends and Their Relatives," in *Toward New Perspectives in Folklore*, ed. A. Paredes and R. Bauman [Austin: University of Texas Press, 1972], 144). Related to this is the observation (based on experimental data) of Marcia Johnson and Carol Raye that externally generated memories (i.e., actual experiences)—as opposed to internally generated memories produced by imagination—are commonly characterized by spatial, temporal, and sensory attributes. See "Reality Monitoring," *Psychological Review* 88 (1981): 67–85. If one wants to challenge this ostensive claim about "reality" in the face of what appears to be a clear and conscious signal of the author/narrator, the burden of proof should decisively rest upon that person's shoulders.

these works include nonideologically motivated incidental detail and seemingly casually recounted information, the burden of proof should lie on any scholar who wants to reject these elements merely as fictional. To dismiss such detail with a wave of the redactional hand is to treat the Gospels more skeptically than historians generally treat other ancient documents.

Detail in the Gospels

As a matter of fact, the Synoptics, as well as John, do contain some detail and casual information (e.g., Mark 4:36). Moreover, some of this detail has been independently confirmed to reflect the situation of first-century Palestine.[18] Not infrequently, scholars outside the field of New Testament studies have appreciated the significance of this more than scholars within the field. For example, Wolfgang Schadewaldt, a respected classical philologist and Homeric scholar who has focused upon issues of authenticity in his own field, writes:

> As a philologist, someone who has acquired some knowledge of "literature," I am particularly concerned here to note that when we read the Synoptic Gospels, we cannot be other than captivated by the experiential vividness with which we are confronted.... I know of no other area of history-writing, biography or poetry where I encounter so great a wealth of material in such a small space.[19]

Paul Merkley has raised the question of how it is that numerous historians, classical scholars, and others outside the discipline of New Testament studies have so often come to much more optimistic estimations of the Synoptics' reliability than New Testament specialists. He notes, for example, the vast rift that separated Rudolf Bultmann and Eric Auerbach on the question of the concern for history on the part of the Gospel authors.

> What does it mean that Rudolf Bultmann and Eric Auerbach have before them the same texts, and are impelled by the same passion for truth—and that one can announce with scholarly sobriety that the authors under review (the gospel-writers) are utterly without interest in historical detail; and the other, on the same sober tone, that the detail of place, setting, characterization and so on is so massive and so obtrusive that we must concede that we are at the source of all the realistic literature of our civilization?[20]

18. Various small-scale studies have demonstrated the historical value of certain details in the Gospel tradition. See, e.g., D. L. Bock, "Jewish Expressions in Mark 14.61–62 and the Authenticity of the Jewish Examination of Jesus," *JSHJ* 1 (2003): 147–59; G. Theissen, *The Gospels in Context: Social and Political History in the Synoptic Tradition*, trans. L. M. Maloney (Minneapolis: Fortress, 1991).

19. W. Schadewaldt, "The Reliability of the Synoptic Tradition," in M. Hengel, *Studies in the Gospel of Mark*, trans J. Bowden (Philadelphia: Fortress, 1985), 102.

20. P. Merkley, "The Gospels as Historical Testimony," *EQ* 58 (1986): 335–36. Referring to E. Auerbach, *Mimesis: The Representation of Reality in Western Literature*, trans. W. Trask (Garden City, NY: Doubleday, 1957).

With Merkley, it seems to us that this difference largely can be explained as resulting from a bias many New Testament specialists have toward the Gospels. For a variety of reasons, they approach these works with a more skeptical attitude than historians generally approach ancient works.

The Presence of Aramaisms

Since we are concerning ourselves with details within the Synoptics, it is appropriate to note that these works contain a number of Aramaic words and expressions.[21] Occasionally, one can also detect signs of an Aramaic substratum behind the Greek. For example, when Jesus says that the Pharisees "strain out a gnat but swallow a camel" (Matt. 23:24), it seems apparent that he was making a play on words in an Aramaic original, since the Aramaic for "gnat" (*galma*) and "camel" (*gamla*) are so similar.

This phenomenon has led some to consider the presence of Aramaisms as a positive authenticity criterion. Others, however, have heavily criticized this criterion, arguing that since presumably a good number of early Christians were Palestinian, Aramaic-speaking Jews, the presence of an Aramaism cannot be used to authenticate a saying as originating with Jesus per se. That is to say, any particular Aramaism in the Gospels can be explained as originated from later Christians rather than from Jesus himself. Even Joachim Jeremias, one of the prime champions of this criterion, recognized that the mere presence of an Aramaism could not prove the authenticity of an independent unit of tradition.[22]

However, if we once again step back from an atomistic analysis of individual pericopes and take a broader perspective of the Synoptics—an approach that is more appropriate to testing large-scale hypotheses about a comprehensive image of Jesus—the Aramaic criterion arguably acquires some significance. The broad pattern of Aramaisms found in the Synoptic tradition becomes part of the cumulative case that helps establish the location of the a posteriori burden of proof. At the very least, the widespread presence of Aramaisms, together with other details that point to a first-century Palestinian environment, testifies to the likelihood of the relatively early origin of these traditions, as well as to the generally conservative nature of the transmission of these traditions.[23] While no single saying or episode

21. For example, *talitha cum* (Mark 5:41), *ephphatha* (Mark 7:34), *golgotha* (Mark 15:22), *bar* (Matt. 16:17).
22. J. Jeremias, *The Problem of the Historical Jesus*, trans. N. Perrin (Philadelphia: Fortress, 1964), 18.
23. On Aramaisms, Semitic poetry and/or a likely Aramaic substratum for the Gospel tradition, see M. Black, *An Aramaic Approach to the Gospels and Acts* (Oxford: Clarendon, 1967), esp. 50–185; J. Jeremias, *New Testament Theology: The Proclamation of Jesus*, trans. J. Bowden (New York: Scribner, 1971), 3–37; J. A. Fitzmyer, *A Wandering Aramean: Collected Essays* (Missoula, MT: Scholars Press, 1979), 1–27; M. Casey, *Aramaic Sources of Mark's Gospel* (New York: Cambridge University Press, 1998). On the admitted difficulty of determining the existence and extent of Semitisms in the tradition, see E. C. Maloney, *Semitic Interference in Marcan Syntax* (Chico, CA: Scholars, 1981). On the criterion of Palestinian environment, see J. Jeremias, *The Parables of Jesus*, 3rd ed., trans. S. H. Hooke (London: SCM, 1972), 11–12; R. H. Stein, "The 'Criteria' of Authenticity," in *Gospel Perspectives*, vol. 1:

can definitively be authenticated by this consideration alone, this is the sort of evidence one would expect to find if the tradition did indeed stem from the time of Jesus. Conversely, it is not the sort of evidence one would expect to find if the Synoptic Jesus tradition was significantly indebted to the creative, legend-making imaginations of non-Palestinian and/or non-Aramaic-speaking Christians from the mid-to-late part of the first century.

The Inclusion of Personal Names

Another potential signal of the presence of tradition rooted in eyewitness reporting involves the inclusion of personal names attached to a relatively recent historical tradition within an orally oriented context. Right up to today, as the phenomenon of "urban legends" reveals, "a hallmark of *legendariness*" is the avoidance of identifying particular named persons as eyewitnesses of the event in question.[24] Thus, anonymity (i.e., "it happened to a friend of a friend . . .") naturally attaches to fictive legends, while the naming of known people (people who can actually be questioned as to the veracity of the report) tends to signal eyewitness accounts.

There is good evidence that just such signals are indicated by the inclusion of certain names in the Synoptic tradition. In a recent study, Richard Bauckham has provided a detailed and insightful assessment of the presence and use of names in the Synoptic Gospels.[25] He documents that, while later extracanonical gospels invent names for characters that are anonymous in the Synoptic tradition, the Synoptic tradition itself *works in the opposite direction* (assuming, once again, the two-source theory). Among the Synoptic Gospels there is "an unambiguous tendency toward the elimination of names."[26] Indeed, oddly enough, "in no case does a character unnamed in Mark gain a name in Matthew or Luke."[27]

Specifically, Matthew and Luke both retain Mark's use of a name in four cases (Simon of Cyrene, Joseph of Arimathea, Mary Magdalene, and Mary the mother of James and Joses). In one case Luke retains a name while Matthew changes it (from Matthew to Levi). In one case Luke retains a name while Matthew drops it (Jairus). And in four cases Matthew and Luke drop the name found in Mark (Bartimaeus, Alexander, Rufus, and Salome).[28] Given this tendency toward eliminating names, and given that many of the Gospel characters appear anonymous

---

Studies of History and Tradition in the Four Gospels, ed. R. T. France and D. Wenham (Sheffield: JSOT, 1980), 236–38.

24. Ross, *Remembering the Personal Past*, 182. Here Ross is discussing an observation of J. H. Brunvand on urban legends; see *The Choking Doberman and Other "New" Urban Legends* (New York: Norton, 1984), 51.

25. R. Bauckham, "The Eyewitnesses and the Gospel Traditions," *JSHJ* 1 (2003): 28–60.

26. Bauckham, "Eyewitnesses," 47. Bauckham notes that this fact "refutes Bultmann's argument [i.e., of the tendency toward elaboration], so long as one accepts Markan priority (as Bultmann did)."

27. Ibid., 47.

28. For a detailed chart of this data, see ibid., 44–46.

from the beginning, Bauckham argues that we have good grounds for concluding that "these names in the Gospel narratives belong to the original form of the
tradition."[29] Indeed, Bauckham argues that the presence of names in the Synoptic
tradition can, in most cases, be best explained by supposing that these characters
were specifically remembered because they were eyewitnesses of the traditions
to which their names were attached, and continued to testify to these traditions
throughout their lifetimes.

For example, Bauckham argues that the naming of Cleopas in Luke 24:18 is
best explained by assuming that the information contained in this passage derives from Cleopas. The narrative itself does not require a name, and in fact his
companion in the account remains anonymous. Why is this? Given the rarity of
this name, Bauckham argues that Cleopas should be identified with the Cleopas
whose wife Mary was at the cross (John 19:25). Moreover, according to Hegesippus,[30] Cleopas was the brother of Jesus's father, Joseph. As a relative of Jesus and an
eyewitness of the resurrected Jesus, Cleopas would have been a respected tradent
in the early Christian communities. This would easily explain why his name was
retained in the tradition. Bauckham persuasively outlines a number of similar cases
for considering named characters as eyewitness tradents, including the women at
the cross and tomb, Simon of Cyrene and his sons, and certain named recipients
of Jesus's healings (Jairus, Bartimaeus, Lazarus).

Bauckham's thesis also plausibly explains why certain names were dropped from
the tradition over time. Once an eyewitness tradent was deceased, or if a living
tradent was not known to a particular community, there would be no reason to
retain the name in the tradition. Thus, for example, Mark mentions by name not
only Simon of Cyrene, but also his two sons, Alexander and Rufus (15:21). Both
Matthew and Luke, however, retain Simon's name but, curiously enough, drop the
names of his sons (Matt. 27:32; Luke 23:26). Bauckham argues that, given that
Mark does not overly use names, the mere fact that Mark expected his audience
to know Simon's sons does not in and of itself adequately explain the inclusion
of their names in the tradition.[31] Rather, what explains the inclusion of these
names is that "Mark is appealing to Simon's eyewitness testimony, known in the
early Christian movement not from his own firsthand account but from that of
his sons."[32] After the sons died, or in communities that were unacquainted with
these sons, there would no longer be any purpose for including their names.

If Bauckham is on the right track—and we strongly suspect he is—not only
are we afforded a new appreciation of the way in which concrete details in the

29. Ibid., 49.

30. Eusebius, *Ecclesiastical History*, 3.11; 4.22.4.

31. We would add that the sheer fact that Mark expected his audience to know the sons of Simon
of Cyrene is historically significant, apart from the issue of *why* Mark mentions them. Among other
things, it suggests that Mark is writing for an audience not more than one generation removed from the
events he records.

32. Bauckham, "Eyewitnesses," 55. See the full-scale study in idem, *Jesus and the Eyewitnesses*.

Synoptic tradition constitute evidence of historical remembrance, but the details themselves may well identify eyewitness tradents who were known to testify to the circulating accounts attached to their names.

The Question of Internal Consistency

A third standard historiographical question used to assess the historical veracity of a document is: "Are there inner contradictions in the document?"[33] Generally speaking, one could expect that fabricated or simply mistaken accounts would tend to include more inconsistencies than truthful, accurate accounts. Hence, in the absence of other contravening factors, the internal consistency of a document contributes to a positive estimation of a document's historical reliability. In the case of the Synoptic Gospels, we can ask this, not only of each Gospel individually, but also of the shared Synoptic tradition represented by the three Gospels together. Thus, in this section we will consider the question of a broad consistency both within and between the Synoptic Gospels.

Do the Synoptic Gospels Contradict One Another?

Everyone acknowledges the obvious fact that the Synoptics (over and against John) have a great deal in common and thus are, in broad strokes, consistent with one another. But this very commonality highlights their notable differences—differences that include what many scholars describe as sheer contradictions. For example, Kümmel has argued that

> the Gospels differ from one another sharply in both form and content. The infancy stories in Mt and Luke contradict each other in essential features. . . . The genealogy of Mt (1:1 ff) and that of Luke (3:23 ff) are wholly different, and the two are irreconcilable. Nor do the resurrection stories represent a unified tradition. . . . And of the material concerning the public activity of Jesus . . . there are differences at every step.[34]

No contemporary New Testament scholar is more adept at sniffing out supposed contradictions within and between the canonical Gospels than legendary-Jesus

---

33. Shafer, ed., *Historical Method*, 158.

34. W. G. Kümmel, *Introduction to the New Testament*, 17th ed., trans. H. C. Kee (Nashville: Abingdon, 1973), 43–44. So too, Bart Ehrman argues that while the differences between the Synoptic Gospels are sometimes merely a matter of "simple shifts in emphasis," at other times they constitute "irreconcilable conflicts" (*The New Testament: A Historical Introduction to the Early Christian Writings*, 3rd ed. [New York: Oxford University Press, 2004], 55). The postmodern turn has served only to heighten the sensitivity of scholars to differences, tensions, ruptures, and aporias in and between the Gospels. For example, postcolonial theorist R. S. Sugirtharajah argues that "subjecting the Bible to a postcolonial scrutiny does not reinforce its authority, but emphasizes its contradictory content" (*Postcolonial Criticism and Biblical Interpretation* [New York: Oxford University Press, 2002], 101).

theorist Robert Price. For example, while many scholars have held that the gene-alogies in Matthew and Luke are irreconcilable, Price goes further and argues that they both contradict Mark and are, in all probability, *both* inauthentic. Interpreting Mark 12:35–37 to be an apologetic for Jesus *not* being a descendant of David, Price writes:

> It is just impossible to reconcile the two tables, though the desperate have tried. . . . No doubt neither genealogy is genuine. If it were only that they contradict each other, one of them might still be authentic, but the point is that both alike are rendered spurious by the witness of Mark 12:35–37. . . . If Jesus were known to have been descended from David, would anyone have wasted time trying to show it was alright for him not to be?[35]

A list of some of the better-known issues within the Gospels that have elicited charges of internal inconsistency or comparative contradiction would include the following:

- "doublets" within a Gospel, where it appears that one historical event has been recorded as two separate events (e.g., the two feedings of the masses in Mark 6:33–44 and 8:1–9)
- unexplainable omissions or additions within parallel passages (e.g., Matthew's [5:32; 19:9] addition of the exception clause to Mark's [10:11–12; followed by Luke 16:18] unqualified prohibition against divorce)
- chronological conflicts (e.g., Matthew's collapsing of Mark's two-day fig tree scenario into a seemingly instantaneous, one-day episode [Mark 11:12–14, 20–21 vs. Matt. 21:18–22])
- instances of apparently mutually exclusive reports (e.g., did Jesus tell his disciples to take a staff and sandals as Mark reports [Mark 6:8–9], or *not* to take them as Matthew reports [Matt. 10:9–10]?)

Taking a Broad Approach

One way of responding to this charge is to attempt to show that specific instances of alleged contradictions within and between the Gospels are in fact only apparent. This has been the customary approach of Christian apologists throughout history. As important as it is to engage specific texts in this respect, given space

---

35. R. M. Price, *The Incredible Shrinking Son of Man: How Reliable Is the Gospel Tradition?* (Amherst, NY: Prometheus, 2003), 49. Price argues, "Mark, whether or not he realized the implications, has preserved a bit of apologetics that presupposed that Jesus was not a descendant of David" (p. 51). In response to this particular argument, we would simply note that few scholars agree that Mark 12:35–37 indicates that Mark saw Jesus as a non-Davidic messiah. Pointing out the "contradictions" in and between the Gospels is a common tactic among secular apologists at war with the Christian faith. For a rather exhaustive list of alleged contradictions, see C. D. McKinsey, *The Encyclopedia of Biblical Errancy* (Amherst, NY: Prometheus, 1995).

considerations and our overall objectives for this book, this is not the approach we will take here. Since our present concern is with the *general* reliability of the Synoptics and, more specifically, with assessing where the a posteriori burden of proof might lie vis-à-vis our stance toward these three works, our approach will be broader and thus more modest. However, our proposal offers a number of broad considerations that can serve to add weight to the more common small-scale arguments in defense of the internal consistency of the Gospels.

In brief, our argument will be that once a standard historiographical approach to the Synoptic Gospels is adopted, once they are granted a reasonably sympathetic interpretation when possible, and once we thoroughly locate these works in the orally oriented environment from which they arose, the level of consistency and (at least apparent) inconsistency we find within and between them is at least on a par with what one finds in other works whose general reliability historians are willing to grant. In other words, even if one grants that some of the apparent inconsistencies within and between the Gospels are currently irresolvable, this, alone, does not undercut the clear signs of their generally reliable nature.

On the Legitimacy of Harmonization

To begin, we must note that most of the specific problems within and between the Gospels that many contemporary scholars find to be so decisive in undermining their credibility as historical works have been considered since the second century and discussed throughout church history.[36] However plausible or implausible we may judge various attempted solutions to these problems, thinkers within the Christian tradition have always felt the need to respond to these difficulties by offering ways in which they can be resolved.[37] What has changed in modern times is not that we have discovered new contradictions within and between the Gospels. Rather, what has changed is that most critical scholars, especially those who constitute the left-most wing of New Testament scholarship, now reject the legitimacy of even *trying* to harmonize these ostensive conflicts.

This much has been more or less true since the beginning of the quest for the historical Jesus. Hermann Reimarus, generally regarded as the "father" of the quest,

36. See R. M. Grant, *The Earliest Lives of Jesus* (New York: Harper, 1961).

37. For several more recent treatments that offer specific responses to tensions and problems within the Gospels, see C. Blomberg, *The Historical Reliability of the Gospels* (Downers Grove, IL: InterVarsity, 1987), 113–52; S. L. Bridge, *Getting the Gospels: Understanding the New Testament Accounts of Jesus' Life* (Peabody, MA: Hendrickson, 2004); N. Geisler and T. Howe, *When Critics Ask: A Popular Handbook on Bible Difficulties* (Wheaton: Victor, 1992); W. C. Kaiser et al., *Hard Sayings of the Bible* (Downers Grove, IL: InterVarsity, 1996); R. H. Stein, *Interpreting Puzzling Texts in the New Testament* (Grand Rapids: Baker Academic, 1996), parts 1–2. On the resurrection accounts, see J. Wenham, *Easter Enigma: Are the Resurrection Accounts in Conflict?* 2nd ed. (Grand Rapids: Baker Academic, 1992). For recent thoughts on three of the perennial conundrums arising within the Gospels, see D. Instone-Brewer, "The Two Asses of Zechariah 9:9 in Matthew 21," *TynB* 54 (2003): 87–98; S. W. Need, "Bethlehem: Was Jesus Born There?" *Modern Believing* 44 (2003): 38–45; B. W. R. Pearson, "The Lucan Censuses, Revisited," *CBQ* 61 (1999): 262–82.

boldly asserted that "the four evangelists cannot possibly be harmonized. Their contradictory accounts betray that the Gospels are not based on facts."[38] Prior to Reimarus multitudes of very intelligent people looking at the very same data had come to the opposite conclusion. What accounts for this difference? Henk De Jonge perceptively addresses this question when he writes:

> From the structure of Reimarus' argumentation it is clear that the discrepancies among the Gospels did not themselves lead him to his radically skeptical view of the Gospels as historical sources. Rather it was the other way around: it was his and others' a priori scepticism [sic] about the trustworthiness of the Gospels ... that made the well-known discrepancies suddenly seem irreconcilable.[39]

De Jonge goes on to trace out the source of this skepticism:

> Why did Reimarus assume a priori that the Gospels were untrustworthy and could not provide the basis for a reliable harmonistic reconstruction of Jesus' life and teaching? The reason is that Reimarus was a deist. ... Now that Reimarus no longer wanted them to be reconcilable, they *were* irreconcilable.[40]

In other words, the skeptical conclusions announced by Reimarus primarily were rooted in naturalistic religious and philosophical assumptions he *brought to* his investigations, not in evidence he found *as a result of* his investigations. And so it has continued in certain circles of New Testament research to the present. Ways of reconciling conflicts within and between the three Synoptic Gospels have become implausible, not because they are inherently so, but because the naturalistic worldview that has been enshrined in the historical-critical method, and the a priori skeptical stance toward the Gospels it inspires, makes these conflicts *seem* irresolvable.

This is not to suggest that skeptical scholars have not *at times* had good reason for rejecting particular attempts to harmonize Synoptic accounts. It must be granted that, usually in an effort to defend a certain fundamentalist understanding of "inspiration" or "inerrancy," some well-intentioned people have occasionally offered harmonizations that are decidedly implausible. The now-classic example of this is Harold Lindsell's desperate suggestion that the differences between the Gospel accounts of Peter's denial of Jesus could be harmonized by positing six different denials![41] Only those invested in preserving a doctrine of inerrancy that is indebted to a modernist, literary paradigm in tandem with a rigidly literalistic, genre-insensitive hermeneutic would be driven to such mental gymnastics. But

---

38. Cited in H. De Jonge, "The Loss of Faith in the Historicity of the Gospels: H. S. Reimarus (ca. 1750)" in *John and the Synoptics*, ed. A. Denaux (Leuven: Leuven University Press, 1992), 409.

39. Ibid., 415.

40. Ibid., 416–17.

41. H. Lindsell, *The Battle for the Bible* (Grand Rapids: Zondervan, 1976), 174–76.

there is no reason to assume at the outset that all proposed harmonizations must be as obviously theologically motivated or as clearly implausible as Lindsell's. Such a generalization would be as unwarranted in New Testament studies as it would be in other areas of historiography.

For example, those who attempt to argue that the Holocaust never took place have sometimes proposed preposterous harmonizations of discordant data to make their case. Yet, World War II historians do not reject the method of harmonization as a reaction to this abuse of the method, for they understand what some New Testament scholars apparently need to be reminded of: that harmonization, properly understood, is *absolutely necessary* for responsible, critical historiography. The reason is that rarely do we find multiple witness reports to the same event that do not contain at least some apparent contradictions.[42] Hence, the standard historiographical assumption, one that should be applied to the study of the Synoptics, is that apparently conflicting historical data deserves to be read as sympathetically as possible—including responsible attempts to harmonize the data—before being dismissed as irresolvable and thus unhistorical.

On the Need for Harmonization

Apparent contradictions are so common when multiple witnesses report on the same event that journalists, investigators, and historians customarily grow suspect that witnesses are not truly independent if there are no apparent discrepancies between their accounts. From the discrepant reports on Alexander the Great by Arrian and Plutarch, to the differing accounts of Hannibal crossing the Alps by Livy and Polybius, to differing accounts of Kennedy's assassination, up to this week's news magazines, discrepancies of one type or another are the norm—which means attempts at harmonization must be the rule as we try to discern "what actually happened."

Several contemporary illustrations may be helpful. First, in the course of arguing for the importance of applying a careful method of harmonization within New Testament studies, J. P. Holding analyzes three separate news stories as reported in *Time* and *Newsweek* magazines.[43] He quickly identified apparent contradictions—not

---

42. The importance of clear definition with respect to harmonization is emphasized by Craig Blomberg in his helpful essay, "The Legitimacy and Limits of Harmonization," in *Hermeneutics, Authority and Canon*, ed. D. A. Carson and J. D. Woodbridge (Grand Rapids: Academie, 1986), 139–74. In what follows we are indebted to a number of Blomberg's insights on harmonization. As we use the term, "harmonization" simply refers to the proposal of a scenario(s) under which apparently conflictive elements that purport to refer to the same event are shown to be *plausibly* reconcilable.

43. J. P. Holding used the issue of each magazine published for September 30, 1996. For his original analysis see "Harmonization: The Issue of Complementary Accounts—Part I," www.tektonics .org/harmonize/lincoln01.html. See the section titled "Harmony #1—Current Events." We have checked the original news articles, and except for a page number error and the confusing of the magazine sources for one story, Holding's report of the data appears accurate. For an insightful and relevant comparison of the similarities and differences between journalism and oral history, see M. Feldstein, "Kissing Cousins: Journalism and Oral History," *Oral History Review* 31 (2004): 1–18.

unlike the type of things skeptical scholars identify as irreconcilable in the Gospels.[44] Now, no reasonable contemporary reader who was made aware of these discrepancies would, on this count alone, conclude that either *Time* or *Newsweek* (or both) was hopelessly unreliable or fictional in nature. They would—and should—instead consider harmonizing strategies before dismissing the reports. And such strategies are readily available. We could consider the perspectival limitations of the sources and reporters, the differing standards of linguistic precision, the differing assumptions about the social context and knowledge of the intended audiences, and any number of other factors that could easily make reports of the same event *appear to us* as contradictory at points.

Holding carried out the same exercise with even more stunning results on four separate twentieth-century biographies of Abraham Lincoln. None of these biographies had been unduly criticized by experts as being unreliable, yet by engaging in an unsympathetic reading and comparison of these works—similar to the way many skeptical New Testament scholars read and compare the Synoptics—Holding was able to disclose significant "irreconcilable contradictions" between them. In reality, most of the "contradictions" were only apparent, but they could be shown to be such only by engaging in a bit of sympathetic harmonization of the accounts. Examples like this demonstrate that a hypercritical historical methodology is just as damaging to good "critical" historiography as is a naively uncritical approach.

A particularly fascinating illustration of the need to explore creative harmonization possibilities before concluding for irreconcilable differences comes from historians Barbara Allen and William Montell. In their book on methodology for conducting local historical research, Allen and Montell investigated two different accounts of the 1881 lynching of two young men—Frank and Jack McDonald ("the McDonald boys")—in Menominee, Michigan. One account claimed that the boys were hung from a railroad crossing, while the other claimed they were strung up on a pine tree. The accounts seemed hopelessly contradictory until Allen and Montell discovered old photographs that showed the bodies hanging *at different times from both places*. As macabre as it is, the McDonald boys apparently had first been hung from a railroad crossing, then taken down, dragged to a pine tree, and *hoisted up again*.[45] Sometimes reality is stranger—and more gruesome—than fiction.

This particular episode is all the more interesting because it bears a certain resemblance to the apparently conflicting accounts of Judas's death. Matthew tells us Judas hung himself (Matt. 27:5), while Luke states he "fell headlong, his body burst open and all his intestines spilled out" (Acts 1:18 NIV). Skeptics have consistently belittled the harmonizing proposal that perhaps Judas hung himself

---

44. In one case, for example, reported numerical estimates could be interpreted as diverging by a factor of 1,000. *Time* (p. 42) reported that "24,000" US troops were in the area when a cache of chemical weapons was destroyed, while *Newsweek* (p. 38) reported the number as "up to 25,000."

45. Allen and Montell, *From Memory to History*, 77.

from a tree, and either the limb or the rope he hung from broke, causing him to fall. Yet such a proposal seems less far-fetched than what in fact turned out to be true about the double hanging of the McDonalds. Were it not for the discovered photographs, historians who treated the differing traditions of the boys' tragic hanging as skeptically as many New Testament critics treat the Gospels would be insisting that at least one of the accounts *must* be wrong. In fact, however, both were accurate.

As a final illustration, the necessity of engaging in harmonization attempts was recognized by film writer and director John Cameron while working on the script for his blockbuster movie *Titanic*. In a documentary interview on the making of his film, Cameron explained that he discovered numerous conflicts in the available eyewitness reports about what happened on the *Titanic*'s fateful voyage. Some of these reports were given in court under oath, and there was absolutely no reason to doubt their essential veracity. Yet, as is typical of multiple eyewitness accounts, these reports contained a variety of apparent contradictions. Despite these conflicts, however, Cameron reported that he found enough in common among the reports to start reconstructing the main lines of what actually happened.[46]

This is how good, critical history should be done—whether we are talking about the sinking of the *Titanic*, the life of Alexander the Great, the hanging of the McDonald boys, or the life of Jesus Christ. In virtually all cases of independent reports of a single event, we should *expect* to find some apparent conflicts. This highlights the important notion of "the double-edged role of similarity" in historical accounts.[47] According to historian Marc Bloch, this is the idea that, particularly with respect to historical documents, there is "the similarity [i.e., internal consistency] which vindicates and that which discredits."[48] The type of similarity/consistency that "discredits" is, of course, that which is *so similar* that one cannot avoid the conclusion one is dealing with "intentional imitation and even forgery."[49] At the very least, accounts that have no significant differences or apparent contradictions naturally raise the suspicion that they are not independent of one another. When sympathetically considered, apparently conflictive independent accounts of the same event—accounts that naturally inscribe and reflect the unavoidable differences of human perception, perspective, precision, description, and so on—often can legitimately and appropriately be harmonized in order to construct the essence of what actually happened. From our perspective, it seems about as unreasonable to reject the general reliability of the Synoptic Gospels on the grounds that they apparently contradict one another at certain points as it would be to reject the essential reliability of the apparently contradictory reports of the *Titanic*, Alexander the Great, Hannibal, the MacDonald boys, or countless other examples of generally acknowledged historical events that could be given.

46. J. Cameron, interview for "Titanic: Breaking New Ground," a televised documentary, aired on March 24, 1998.
47. Ross, *Remembering the Personal Past*, 164.
48. Cited in Ibid.
49. Ibid.

The bottom line, as Gilbert Garraghan explains in his *Guide to Historical Method*, is that "almost any critical history that discusses the evidence for important statements will furnish examples of discrepant or contradictory accounts *and the attempts which are made to reconcile them*."[50] As Allen and Montell note:

> Rarely is one single informant able to recount all details surrounding a specific event of years ago. But when enough people are interviewed, trends develop, patterns unfold, and truth emerges. . . . Divergent accounts are not necessarily in disagreement with each other, although they may sometimes seem to be, on the surface.

Each divergent account, they add, "represents truth as known by its narrator. A close analysis of each text will often demonstrate that it represents that portion of the story with which the narrator could naturally identify through personal or ancestral association."[51]

"Harmonization" Strategies of the Skeptical Mind

Interestingly enough, even those skeptical scholars who claim to reject a harmonizing method cannot, in fact, escape it. Often they engage in extraordinary attempts to harmonize conflicting data. For example, in one currently fashionable image of Jesus—that of a radically hellenized Cynic philosopher with little that is religiously Jewish about him—the evidence for the thoroughly "Jewish" nature of first-century Palestinian Judaism must be explained away (harmonized, if you will) to comport with the thesis of a largely non-Jewish Jesus. So too, the strained attempts to reconcile the New Testament data with the "radical early Christian diversity thesis," speculative efforts to redactionally stratify Q and reconstruct the "history" of its community, and attempts to prioritize (both chronologically and ideologically) the *Gospel of Thomas* over the canonical Gospels all in their own ways incorporate harmonizing strategies.

Indeed, we submit that these attempts to harmonize conflicting data often are as speculative and historically implausible as anything Harold Lindsell or any other fundamentalist ever proposed. John Meier has rightly called to task the "hilarious mental acrobatics" of certain "fundamentalists" with respect to their harmonization efforts.[52] However, such intellectual antics are hardly characteristic of "fundamentalists" of a conservative stripe alone. "Fundamentalists" and their "mental acrobatics" can be found at both ends of the ideological spectrum. In both cases, correctives are in order and a renewed commitment to a historically

---

50. G. Garraghan, *A Guide to Historical Method* (New York: Fordham, 1946), 314 (emphasis added). See also J. Topolski, *Methodology of History* (Warsaw: PWN—Polish Scientific Publishers, 1976), 471–73.

51. Allen and Montell, *From Memory to History*, 76–77. See also J. Vansina, *Oral Tradition* (Chicago: Aldine, 1961), 138–39.

52. Meier, *Marginal Jew*, 1:197.

responsible approach to the attempted harmonization of apparently conflictive data within the Gospel tradition is called for.

The Nature of "Consistency" in an Orally Dominant Environment

As in all issues surrounding our understanding of the New Testament, it makes all the difference whether we approach the apparent conflicts within and between the Synoptics with a clear vision of their orally oriented nature or whether we anachronistically approach them from our own post-Gutenberg, literary paradigm. In what follows, we offer six points that flesh out how approaching these texts as born of an orally oriented environment affects our understanding of whether their differing accounts can, and should, legitimately be harmonized.

A Presupposed Oral-Traditional Background

To begin, it is important to keep in mind that, like all written texts in rhetorical cultures, the Gospels presuppose a broader, unstated, authoritative oral tradition in all that they present.[53] While the "performance"—whether oral or written—is the "enabling event" in orally dominant cultures, the tradition itself is the "enabling referent."[54] Yet, due to the limiting factors of any single performance—whether oral or written—most of what is important is not explicitly stated. Here, *metonymy*—a "mode of signification wherein the part stands for the whole"—is not an occasional, stylistically driven literary technique, as it is with modern authors.[55] Instead, as John Miles Foley observes, it is "the fundamental principle" of efficient and effective communication in a dominantly oral/aural environment.[56] This is why, as Rosalind Thomas has argued, we will never

---

53. Also relevant to the considerations of this issue is the notion of the "framing" of discourse, i.e., the metacommunicative, mutually shared knowledge-schemas and structures of expectation that frame all human interaction. Consideration of framing is central to all discourse analysis. For example, what outsiders (modern scholars) perceive as gaps, aporias, discontinuities, and contradictions within the Gospels no doubt tells us much more about the imposition of modern, text-centric interpretive frames forced upon the text than it does about how the texts would have been understood by the original community with its shared frame of metacommunicative reference. On this important concept of "framing," see D. Tannen, ed., *Framing in Discourse* (New York: Oxford University Press, 1993). We would add that this sort of consideration is all the more important in an orally dominant environment, which—in comparison to a highly literate context—tends to place "considerable importance on the specificity of words and phrases from a locality" (P. Nanton, "Making Space for Orality on Its Own Terms," in *The Pressures of the Text: Orality, Texts, and the Telling of Tales*, ed. S. Brown [Birmingham, UK: Centre of West African Studies, 1995], 86).

54. J. M. Foley, "What's in a Sign?" in *Signs of Orality: The Oral Tradition and Its Influence in the Greek and Roman World*, ed. E. A. MacKay (Boston: Brill, 1999), 11.

55. J. M. Foley, *Immanent Art: From Structure to Meaning in Traditional Oral Epic* (Bloomington: Indiana University Press, 1991), 7. See idem, "Selection as *pars pro toto*: The Role of Metonymy in Epic Performance and Tradition," in *The Kalevala and the World's Traditional Epics*, ed. L. Honko (Helsinki: Finnish Literature Society, 2002), 106–27.

56. Foley, "What's in a Sign?" 11. This phenomenon appears to be ubiquitous within orally oriented contexts. For examples from Greece and the Arctic, respectively, see A. Caravelli, "The Song beyond the

accurately interpret ancient documents if we understand them to be anything like autonomous, self-sufficient works.[57] Documents with an oral conception/register almost always "recorded the relevant facts very partially . . . relying on a background of memory and witnesses."[58]

All of this means that if harmonization is appropriate—even necessary—as an aspect of good historical methodology in general, *it is all the more so when we are dealing with texts written in orally dominant cultures such as that of the Synoptic Gospels*. It means we have to understand that, unlike written accounts produced within a highly literate context, the various episodes recorded in the Gospels very likely were *intentionally written and consciously received as* what we would consider fragmentary in nature—as composed of "parts" of the Jesus tradition that were intended to signal the "wholes" that stood behind them. They were designed primarily to call to memory through narrative allusion and traditional referentiality a much broader, shared oral history, anchored by the testimony of trusted witnesses. While texts characterized by a literate conception are meant primarily to "convey information," texts such as the Gospels driven by an oral conception are intended to "activate" the shared, orally transmitted knowledge of the community—knowledge that was profoundly constitutive of the community's very identity.[59]

These observations reveal that the basic assumption that fuels responsible harmonization attempts—the awareness that texts that offer apparently conflicting data may represent partial, fragmentary, allusive retellings of a richer, denser, well-known account—is precisely what is intentionally at work in orally oriented texts like the Synoptic Gospels. If ever we should be willing to entertain responsible attempts to harmonize conflicting data, therefore, it is with orally oriented texts such as these. And in this light we have no choice but to conclude that the refusal of skeptical scholars to take seriously responsible attempts at harmonization of apparently discordant Synoptic accounts constitutes a dogmatic stance that is fundamentally opposed to the orally oriented nature of the Synoptic texts.

Song: Aesthetics and Social Interaction in Greek Folksong," *Journal of American Folklore* 95 (1982): 129–58; K. Rasmussen, *The Netsilik Eskimos: Social Life and Spiritual Culture*, reprint ed. (New York: AMS, 1976), 321.

57. Rosalind Thomas notes that ancient documents "presuppose knowledge which is simply remembered and not written down." Far from being autonomous works, as texts with literate registers tend to be, ancient works "cannot perform their task without backing from non-written communication." Hence, she concludes, "It becomes difficult to separate oral and written modes in any meaningful sense except in the most basic one (i.e., what was written down and what was not). *It is surely only our modern confidence in and obsession with the written text which see documents as entirely self-sufficient*" (*Literacy and Orality in Ancient Greece* [New York: Cambridge University Press, 1992], 76 [emphasis added]).

58. Ibid., 76–77.

59. See E. J. Bakker, "Activation and Preservation: The Interdependence of Text and Performance in an Oral Tradition," *Oral Tradition* 8 (1993): 5–20; N. Tisani, "Classified Material in Oral Tradition: Its Survival and Transmission," in *Oral Tradition and Its Transmission: The Many Forms of Message*, ed. E. Sienaert, M. Cowper-Lewis, and N. Bell (Durban, South Africa: University of Natal, 1994), 169.

It demonstrates, once again, how fundamentally rooted in a literary paradigm contemporary New Testament scholarship tends to be. It demonstrates, in this case, that skeptical scholars can easily retroject their modern, literate-dominant assumptions about autonomous texts with a literary register onto an alien textual world, a world where harmonistic hearing/reading strategies would have been assumed on the part of all involved, authors and hearers/readers alike.

These observations of course do not necessarily imply that if we had access to the broader oral tradition of the early Christians all apparent conflicts would instantly be resolved. It is entirely possible that various traditions modified their contents in ways that at points flatly contradict other traditions, even by ancient standards. But it does imply that modern scholars should not assume that what appears to us to be a contradiction *could not* be responsibly reconciled if we had access to the broader tradition the written Gospels emerged from and always-already assume. And, therefore, it implies that we should not belittle plausible proposals as to how apparent conflicts might be harmonized by appealing to the broader, presupposed oral tradition shared by the Gospels' original audience(s). To the contrary, it suggests that responsible critical scholarship attempting to understand the Synoptics must consider imaginative explorations of this broader traditional background to be central to its task.

On "Remembering Things" in Orally Oriented Contexts

A second aspect of orally oriented written texts that pertains to the issue of harmonization is that, in such texts—as in the oral traditions from which they emerge and into which they feed—the focus of memory is generally on *things*, not *words* (i.e., on illocutions, not locutions). As Tony Lentz has demonstrated in relation to the orality-literacy dynamic of ancient Greece, remembering the subject matter conveyed by words was extremely important for ancients; retaining the exact words a tradent used to convey the subject matter generally was not.[60]

Among other things, this suggests that scholars who strive to recover Jesus's *ipsissima verba* instead of his *ipsissima vox* are, in most cases, pursuing the wrong quarry. While we can expect to find the essential *voice* of Jesus in the early church's tradition, we cannot, apart from certain cases (e.g., mnemonically driven aphorisms, sayings anchored in sacred ritualistic settings, etc.), suppose early Christians would have been invested in preserving the *exact words* of Jesus. It also suggests that we are missing the mark if we suppose there to be any genuine conflict between the sometimes remarkably (from our perspective) different ways the Gospels record Jesus's teachings or the events of his life.

---

60. T. M. Lentz, *Orality and Literacy in Hellenic Greece* (Carbondale: Southern Illinois University Press, 1989), 92. See also F. A. Yates, *The Art of Memory* (Chicago: University of Chicago Press, 1966), 29–31. The same point is made in a very different oral context by W. T. Wallace and D. C. Rubin, "'The Wreck of the Old 97': A Real Event Remembered in Song," in *Remembering Reconsidered: Ecological and Traditional Approaches to the Study of Memory*, ed. U. Neisser and E. Winograd (New York: Cambridge University Press, 1988), 303.

For example, while modern, highly literate people might find a discrepancy between the way the Gospel authors recite the words spoken by God at Jesus's baptism (Matt. 3:17 // Luke 3:22 // Mark 1:11), it is unlikely any ancient person would have so much as noticed this difference—or wondered about it if they did. So too, modern, highly literate folk might find a "contradiction" between one Gospel author's recording of Jesus telling his disciples to wear sandals (Mark 6:9), while the others have him forbidding them (Matt. 10:10; Luke 10:4). But it is very unlikely any ancient person would have been concerned in the least with this. More likely, what would matter to them was the fundamental point of the passage—the essential content—not the particular way it was expressed.[61]

Schematic Wholes over Discrete Facts

Closely related to the focus on things over words within orally dominant cultures is the fact that such cultures tend to trade in the composition, preservation, and consumption of schematic wholes, as opposed to autonomous, discrete details.[62] A schematic approach is not less historical than one centered on discrete, isolated facts. Each approach has its strengths and weaknesses, historiographically speaking. But the Gospels' orientation toward schematic wholes as opposed to discrete, isolated facts has led some New Testament scholars to perceive conflicts between them that would not have been viewed as such by the original authors and audiences of these works.

61. Augustine recognized this point long ago; see Stein, *Interpreting Puzzling Texts*, 26–28. While this certainly is not the only line of response to this famous conundrum, it is one aspect that is important to consider. The same could be said for many other "discrepancies" between the Gospels. For example, Stephen Barton raises the problem of the verbal discrepancies between the Gospels with respect to the inscription on the titulus affixed to Jesus's cross. Mark reads, "The King of the Jews" (15:26); Matthew reports, "This is Jesus, the King of the Jews" (27:37); Luke has, "This is the King of the Jews" (23:38); and John reads, "Jesus of Nazareth, the King of the Jews" (19:19). Barton concludes: "It is surprising, given all the eyewitnesses to the crucifixion, that there is such variety" ("The Believer, the Historian and the Fourth Gospel," *Theology* 96 [1993]: 292). In response, we would say there is no surprise here at all. The remembrance of essential things over specific words explains the divergences quite adequately. If verbatim reproduction of exact words is the test of historicity, then the Gospels—and most written texts derived from orally dominant cultures—fail the test. We suggest, however, that this is a modern, literate precision standard anachronistically imposed upon texts written in an oral conception/register. On the ancient precision standard/goal as "gist," see J. P. Small, *Wax Tablets of the Mind: Cognitive Studies of Memory and Literacy in Classical Antiquity* (New York: Routledge, 1997), 193–96, 200.

62. For a clear explication of this phenomenon drawn from contemporary Malay culture, see A. Sweeney, *A Full Hearing: Orality and Literacy in the Malay World* (Berkeley: University of California Press, 1987), esp. 8–12, 272, 297–98, 305. While Sweeney's study was completed before Foley's breakthrough concept of traditional referentiality was widely recognized, it nicely complements and confirms Foley's thesis.

To apply this consideration to one example in New Testament studies: Bultmann and the early form critics who followed him contended that only small units get transmitted, since oral traditions are incapable of passing on extended narratives. But, as we have already shown, they had it exactly wrong (see chap. 6). Generally speaking, explicit and implicit extended narratives functioning as integrated schematic complexes are precisely the sorts of things that are viewed as most essential to orally oriented traditions.

This helps explain the "fixed-yet-flexible" dynamic at work within the communicative moments of orally oriented cultures. The general framework of Jesus's life is relatively fixed, together with the essential data that structures this framework and infuses it with significance. But within this fixed context, certain elements of the *expression* of known detail is more or less flexible—so long as it expresses the essence of the overall schemata. James Dunn nicely summarizes this dynamic, including the elements of expression that an orally dominant community would have viewed as flexible in nature:

> The differences introduced by the Evangelists, whether as oral diversity or as literary editing, are consistently in the character of abbreviation, omission, clarification and explanation, elaboration and extension of motif. The developments often reflect the deeper faith and insight of Easter; that is true. But they do not appear to constitute any radical change in the substance or character or thrust of the story told.[63]

Once again, the contemporary skeptical approach that sees contradictions and reads intentional polemics into so much of the divergent detail within the Synoptics is shown to be rooted in a literary paradigm that is foreign to the Gospels themselves.

"Relevant Precision" in an Orally Oriented Context

Every cultural-linguistic context operates under its own specific and shared conventions of "relevant precision." Even within a single culture, conventions of relevant precision differ across subcontexts. That is, cultural presuppositions about linguistic precision will vary depending upon whether, for example, one is in the context of a medical diagnosis, a courtroom trial, a sporting event, a weather report, or an episode of family reminiscing. Paul Drew observes that the

> effectiveness, accuracy, adequacy, appropriateness and so on of such outcomes as these rely upon a property of language used in these settings—the *relevant precision* with which some states of affairs are described and reported. In all forms of interaction and in whatever contexts, a certain appropriate or relevant degree of precision is required in how people describe what they did, felt, heard, experienced, observed, can see in front of them, and the like.[64]

63. J. D. G. Dunn, *Christianity in the Making*, vol. 1: *Jesus Remembered* (Grand Rapids: Eerdmans, 2003), 224.

64. P. Drew, "Precision and Exaggeration in Interaction," *American Sociological Review* 68 (2003): 917 (emphasis in original). The point we are making in this section could be developed significantly by exploring the broader observations of speech-act theorists concerning the context- and purpose-dependent nature of all language. Particularly relevant to our immediate concerns are: E. Goffman, "Felicity's Condition," *American Journal of Sociology* 89 (1983): 1–54; H. Sacks, "Everyone Has to Lie," in *Sociocultural Dimensions of Language Use*, ed. M. Sanches and B. G. Blount (New York: Academic Press, 1975), 57–79; K. DeRose, "The Ordinary Language Basis for Contextualism, and the New Invariantism," *Philosophical*

Thus, relevant precision refers to "the selection of the type, or the degree of specificity, of a description that is relevant and appropriate in the circumstances in which it is produced."[65]

To take an example from our contemporary Western culture, modern meteorological linguistic convention makes use of the terms "sunrise" and "sunset" to designate the times of the day, in any given locale, when the rotation of the earth either allows or blocks the sun's illuminating rays. In terms of technical, literal precision, the two terms are profoundly problematic. For several centuries now, we have known that the sun itself does not "rise" or "set," but rather the earth itself rotates. And yet, despite the heliocentric convictions of modern meteorological science, every newspaper and weather forecaster continues to use these terms without hesitation. They "do the job," despite the fact that they represent a loose—even factually inaccurate, taken literally—use of linguistic precision. The "relevant precision" required for the reporting of the quite specific and factual data of when the earth's rotation will allow or block the sun's rays permits this flexible use of language. And anyone who would feel the need to alert the local newspapers or television stations to inform them that they are several hundred years out of date with respect to their theories of astronomy would not be met with appreciation for their powers of conceptual precision. Rather, they would either be dismissed as a prankster, or, perhaps, considered a foreigner from an alien sociolinguistic context.

As Drew notes, to apply culturally foreign standards of precision and exactness in a given context would rightly be considered "inappropriate, disruptive, even pathological."[66] For purposes of communicative efficiency, the tendency within human interactions is to assume that "only as much detail or precision *as is relevant* need be provided." And, of course, the all-important quality of relevance here is both culturally (broadly) and situationally (narrowly) specific. Among other things, relevance is gauged by the cultural context of the interaction, the specific intentions of the interlocutors, and the implicit semantic contracts at work within that cultural-linguistic system. In any interactional context, efficiency of communication is always balanced by situation-appropriate limits with respect to verbal license.

This general consideration of relevant precision can be applied to our study of the Gospels as we note one common characteristic of interactive communication in an orally dominant setting. As a wide range of studies have shown, communication within an oral conception/register—both in its oral and written modes—tends to operate with much less stringent standards of linguistic precision than does,

---

Quarterly 55 (2005): 172–98; and esp. H. P. Grice, "Logic and Conversation," in *Syntax and Semantics*, vol. 3: *Speech Acts*, ed. P. Cole and J. L. Morgan (New York: Academic Press, 1975), 41–58.

65. Drew, "Precision and Exaggeration," 917. This fits well with Grice's ("Logic and Conversation," 45–46) "Cooperation Principle," which calls upon interlocutors to provide the quantity of information—and no more—that is relevant to the specific conversational context.

66. Ibid., 923.

say, the modern, Western, highly literate academic world.[67] Unfortunately, for over two centuries of critical New Testament studies, Western academics have often read and judged the Gospels through the lenses of their culture's standards of relevant precision. Or as J. P. Holding has aptly put it, all too often the Gospel authors "are signators to a semantic contract that Westerners haven't even read."[68] Modern skeptics of the Gospels would certainly take offense if someone from another time and place belittled them for holding to a pre-Copernican universe based upon the ubiquitous use of the terms "sunrise" and "sunset" within our culture—and rightly so. But rarely have they considered that they are doing the same sort of thing to the narratives of the Gospels. Drew reminds us of what skeptics of the Gospels often have forgotten: "Indeed to insist on greater precision [than was intended or necessary for a given interactional context] would be sanctionable, pedantic, or intrusive."[69] The practical fallout from all this is that the significantly different standards of relevant precision between the first-century, largely peasant Mediterranean world and the contemporary Western academic worlds goes a long way toward explaining why skeptical scholars charge the orally oriented Gospels with "error" and "contradiction"—and why so many of these charges are, culturally speaking, unimpressive and inappropriate.

CHRONOLOGICAL REORDERING IN ORAL PERFORMANCES

Yet a fifth way in which orality studies should affect our understanding of alleged contradictions within and between the Synoptics, as well as the enterprise of proposing ways of harmonizing these conflicts, concerns the loose way these works order their material. Scholars in the modern historiographical world are deeply concerned with reconstructing the chronological order of discrete historical facts. But we now know that such a concern is largely foreign to people in orally dominant cultures.

Saad Sowayan's insightful study of Arabic historical narrative in the oral mode is instructive at this point. Sowayan demonstrates that these narratives are designed as *suwalif*—meaning, literally, "to have happened in the past." In sharp contrast to the widespread assumption of Western scholars that oral traditions tend to lack genuine historical interest, Sowayan shows that the traditional narratives he studied were centered on "historical events and biographical or social circumstances connected with the immediate, or remote, past."[70] Yet, he also demonstrates that the order in which events are presented in any given oral performance has more

---

67. See, e.g., M. Gagarin, "The Orality of Greek Oratory," in *Signs of Orality*, 166.

68. J. P. Holding, "Precisely the Opposite: On Gospel Details and Precision in Narratives," www .tektonics.org/harmonize/gospelprecision.html.

69. Drew, "Precision and Exaggeration," 937. Drew's comment continues: "To challenge such claims might be to flout one of Goffman's 'felicity conditions,' and thereby to risk 'disconfirming that we are sane.'" For Erving Goffman's remark, see his helpful article "Felicity's Condition," 48.

70. S. A. Sowayan, *The Arabian Oral Historical Narrative: An Ethnographic and Linguistic Analysis* (Wiesbaden: Harrassowitz, 1992), 19.

to do with the "process of remembering" on the part of the performer than it does with the order in which events actually took place. "As one remembers," he says, "one narrates. . . . Once the narrative begins, it can be developed in any of several possible directions, depending upon the performance context."[71]

Sowayan fleshes out the nature of these historically oriented oral recitations:

> The linear string of [a performed narrative's] episodes and the establishment of connections between events is complex and trying. The task is made more difficult by the fact that various events are intertwined like a grid, forming a complex network of episodes interconnected in a crisscross fashion. Actually, a long narrative is a cluster of smaller narratives which are imbedded and interlinked with each other. The swarming of the various narratives to the narrator's mind as he starts, and the disentanglement of the various episodes as they come in the way of one another and crowd in his breast . . . can be likened to the flocking of thirsty camels to the drinking-trough. . . . At times, stories come in the way of one another and the narrator may find himself compelled to suspend an ongoing story in the middle to tell a different one. . . . This is because narratives are plentiful and interconnected.[72]

Numerous orality studies have found a similar pattern.[73] Unless they are familiar with it, this sort of nonlinear, creative flexibility in how material is presented may strike scholars who operate within the assumptions and precision standards of a literate conception as necessarily involving historical inaccuracies and contradictions. What this phenomenon signals, however, is just how different the assumptions, criteria, and precision standards of an oral conception—as opposed to a modern, highly literate conception—can be with respect to the accurate recording of history.

We have every reason to believe that this sort of oral conception would have characterized the approach to history of the tradents of the Synoptic Jesus tradition. While the Gospels are written texts, their treatment of chronology more or less reflects this sort of oral sensibility. The authors freely rearrange events and sayings. At times they appear to collate and/or divide up events. Sometimes this technique seems to be driven by topical concerns. But, for all we know, at other times they may do so simply because this is how the material came to mind as they were composing their works. In any event, *by the standards of orally dominant cultures*, the fact that events and sayings are ordered in markedly different ways in each Gospel does not constitute a "contradiction," and does not, in any relevant

71. Ibid., 22.

72. Ibid., 23.

73. For example, in the context of a study of Yoruba tradition, Robin Law concludes, "It is important that each event occurred . . . , but the precise chronological sequence in which they occurred is normally unimportant." Significantly enough, he adds, "Literate historians, in contrast, are sometimes almost obsessively concerned with sequence and chronology" ("How Truly Traditional Is Our Traditional History? The Case of Samuel Johnson and the Recording of Yoruba Oral Tradition," *History in Africa* 11 [1984]: 198).

sense, compromise the genuineness of the historical interest or capabilities of the Synoptic authors.

To illustrate, modern, literate-minded scholars who operate with the truism that "without chronology there is no history"[74] may be inclined to see a contradiction between Matthew and Mark's differing accounts of the cursing of the fig tree, since, as we noted earlier, the former collapses a two-day fig tree scenario into a one-day affair (Mark 11:12–14, 20–25 vs. Matt. 21:18–22). Some may even be inclined to conclude that one or both of these works are not historical, since we cannot reconstruct the "actual" chronology of events. Others may be inclined to go further yet and read polemical motives into Matthew's alteration of Mark. Conversely, some conservative Christian apologists, working with the very same modern (and thus anachronistic) historical and literary assumptions as their skeptical interlocutors, may be inclined to propose highly implausible ways of harmonizing the accounts in order to demonstrate that these Gospels can meet the requisite precision standards of our contemporary academic context.

If we keep in mind that both these works were written with an oral conception, however, none of this is necessary or warranted. The two different reports are "harmonized" simply by understanding the nature of oral recitation and accepting that they were written to be heard against a much broader, richer, authoritative oral-traditional context. Most likely, we have here an instance of chronological compression, a phenomenon quite common within orally dominant contexts (i.e., the well-known practice of "telescoping"). And all of this is rendered intelligible— quite apart from intricate and anachronistic redactional theorizing—by reading the Gospels in light of the patterns and practices of historical remembrance common to orally oriented cultures. We may *guess* at why these alterations were made. But, for all we know, the explanation goes no deeper than that this is how the material presented itself to the tradent's mind at the time of writing. Be that as it may, one thing is clear: we entirely misunderstand the text if we suppose differences like this necessarily constitute "contradictions," are primarily polemically motivated, or undermine the essential historical veracity of these reports.

Jesus as an Itinerant Preacher

A sixth and final implication of orality studies for our understanding of apparent conflicts within and between the Gospels centers on the ministry of Jesus himself. Because the modern critical study of the Gospels has been driven by a literary paradigm that has determined both the questions that are asked and the answers that are given, insufficient attention has been paid to the realities and

---

74. That is, "pas d'histoire sans chronologie" (Y. Persons, "Tradition orale et chronologie," *Cahiers d'Etudes Africaines* 11/7 [1962]: 463). However, even among contemporary historians there is the recognition that chronological ordering is not the only manner of historiographical presentation. See J. Gorman, *Understanding History: An Introduction to Analytical Philosophy of History* (Ottawa: University of Ottawa Press, 1992), 62–63; R. Gruner, "Comment on Mandelbaum on Narratives," *History and Theory* 2 (1969): 275–77.

constraints that would have characterized Jesus's ministry *as an itinerant preacher/ prophet* within an orally dominant culture.[75] Far too few contemporary scholars have considered seriously enough the implications of the fact that Jesus's ministry would have been characterized by multiple oral performances of the same—or at least very similar—material. Werner Kelber hits the mark when he states,

> Reiteration and variation of words and stories must be assumed for Jesus' own proclamation. Multiple, variable renditions, while observable in tradition, are highly plausible in Jesus' own oral performance. . . . What if Jesus himself spoke sayings and stories more than once, at different occasions, and in different versions?[76]

In light of what we now know about orally dominant contexts, Kelber goes on to answer his own question:

> There is every reason to assume . . . that repeated renditions characterized Jesus' speech habits. The point is worth stressing because our search for the *ipsissimum verbum* and the *ipsissima structura* has imprinted upon our minds the model of singular verbal originality. Oral redundancy bears no resemblance to the idea of duplication inherent in print. The latter takes pride in the uniformity of textual productions modeled on *the* original, while repetition in oral aesthetics involves variation. Repetitions almost always vary, and hence are rarely literal repetitions. In face-to-face communication, the rhetorical doctrine of efficaciousness prevails over standards of exactitude.[77]

So too, N. T. Wright notes the "enormous implications . . . this has for synoptic criticism" when he argues that "within the peasant oral culture of his day, Jesus must have left behind him not one or two isolated traditions, but a veritable mare's nest of anecdotes, and also of sentences, aphorisms, rhythmic sayings, memorable stories with local variations, [etc.]."[78] Among other things, this means that most of the variations of Jesus's teachings found in the Synoptics—variations that modern, literate-minded scholars tend to explain by appealing to the redactional and/ or polemical motives of the authors—are as easily explained as oral variations performed by Jesus himself.[79] While critics sometimes read very sophisticated redactional motives into the different versions of Jesus's teaching on the great banquet feast, his parable of the talents, his teachings on the beatitudes, and so

75. A point forcefully made by N. T. Wright, *Jesus and the Victory of God* (Minneapolis: Fortress, 1996), 170–71. See also M. F. Bird, "The Purpose and Preservation of the Jesus Tradition: Moderate Evidence for a Conserving Force in Its Transmission," *Bulletin for Biblical Research* 15 (2005): 170–71.

76. W. Kelber, "Jesus and Tradition: Words in Time, Words in Space," *Semeia* 65 (1994): 146.

77. Ibid., 150. G. Kennedy confirms this assessment; see "Classical and Christian Source Criticism," in *The Relationships among the Gospels: An Interdisciplinary Dialogue*, ed. W. O. Walker (San Antonio: Trinity University Press, 1978), 142.

78. Wright, *Jesus and the Victory of God*, 170.

79. Ibid., 170; see also 632–33.

on, it is just as likely that Jesus simply gave this teaching in different ways at different times.[80]

To a priori reject such an explanation for these sorts of parallels and "doublets" in the Synoptic tradition, as many skeptical scholars do, is to "simply have no historical imagination for what an itinerant ministry, within a peasant culture, would look like."[81] Certainly it is possible that in any given case the "doublet" phenomenon in the Gospels is due to the artistic device of *iterata* (repetition).[82] But it is also very possible that any particular "doublet" or parallel simply is a result of the fact that itinerant oral performers like Jesus of necessity repeated themselves quite frequently, and did so with the "fixed-yet-flexible" style that tends to characterize oral traditional material.

ON ACKNOWLEDGING WHAT WE CANNOT KNOW

One important implication of understanding the Gospels as oral recitations, and therefore as writings with an oral register, is that it forces us to acknowledge that, separated as we are from the immediate community of the early church, much of the background data of oral tradition that was assumed as a referent for the Gospel authors largely has been lost to us. For this reason, even someone as close to the first-century Christians in time and culture as Celsus can find an array of problems in the Gospels. Though he was part of an orally dominant culture himself, Celsus was in most respects as removed as we are from the integrated schemata of oral tradition that was shared by first-century Christians. Like so many contemporary New Testament scholars, Celsus was an unsympathetic outsider evaluating a religion primarily on the basis of its written texts, without the benefit of the rich oral tradition and shared communal knowledge that would have provided the illuminating context to the often apparently conflictive data in the texts. And so, not surprisingly, Celsus's evaluation was mostly negative—as is the evaluation of many contemporary scholars for precisely the same reason.

So it will necessarily be for any unsympathetic reader who refuses to imaginatively explore the possible contours of the often-opaque oral world of the first-century Christians and their traditions about Jesus. It is frustrating for some to have to admit that this oral world is now largely lost to us and that we are forced to imaginatively speculate about it to make sense of the texts before us. But to imagine instead that because we possess the texts we do, we possess the data necessary to

---

80. Indeed, though nothing of significance hangs on this, it is not impossible that the previously mentioned variations on Jesus's instructions to his disciples to take sandals (Mark 6:8–9) or to forgo them (Matt. 10:9–10) may in fact go back to two different sets of instructions given to his disciples on two different occasions (see Blomberg, *Historical Reliability*, 144–46). It would be advisable for New Testament scholars, who are generally an imaginative bunch, to use this historical imagination to consider the wide variety of quite interesting and often different things that an itinerant prophet-teacher could end up saying to his disciples over the course of several years as his movement develops.

81. Wright, *Jesus and the Victory of God*, 171.

82. As noted by Schadewaldt, "Reliability of the Synoptic Tradition," 101.

pass an unsympathetic judgment upon the early Christians' ability to faithfully record history is, in our opinion, an instance of cultural insensitivity and hubris. Given that, unlike our modern, highly literate context, the early Christian communities would have stored most of their knowledge in the receptacles of memory and oral performance—receptacles that we now have no access to except for the brief written oral recitations that have come down to us—it is, in all probability, not *they* who were in the historical dark about Jesus, but rather *we* are.

To conclude this section, it is clear that by literate-minded, modern historiographical standards, the Synoptics can be read as containing many "contradictions" within and between themselves. What we have been arguing, however, is that evaluating them by these standards constitutes an anachronistic misunderstanding of the very texts themselves. Judged by the conventions and constraints of their own orally dominant cultural context, and read sympathetically with an imaginative appreciation for the broad oral tradition they were written to express, the Gospels can be seen as exhibiting the sort of broad internal consistency that suggests that the authors both intended to faithfully record the essential aspects of Jesus's life and teaching, and that—as far as we can tell—they were quite successful at doing so.

Inclusion of "Inherently Improbable Events"?

A fourth important question typically asked of ancient documents as historians assess their historical reliability is: Does the document report events or make claims that "seem inherently improbable: e.g., contrary to human nature, or in conflict with what we know"?[83] This common way of posing the issue should strike us as problematic, however, for it leaves unanswered the question of how we can, with any degree of objectivity, decide what is and is not "plausible" and/or who gets to decide "what we know."[84]

With this criterion we come once again to what we suspect is a driving force behind—and a fundamental problem of—the legendary-Jesus theory. However

---

83. Shafer, ed., *Historical Method*, 157.

84. For example, Allen and Montell (*From Memory to History*, 79) offer as one historical test "whether or not the information provided in a given text is logical." They never explore the complex problem of "whose logic" is allowed to pass judgment on whose. This problem has led W. H. McNeill to conclude that historical truths "are what historians achieve when they bend their minds as critically and carefully as they can to the task of making their account of public affairs credible as well as intelligible to an audience that shares enough of their particular outlook and assumptions to accept what they say. The result might best be called mythohistory perhaps . . . for the same words that constitute truth for some are, and always will be, myth for others, who inherit or embrace different assumptions and organizing concepts about the world" (cited in Ross, *Remembering the Personal Past*, 166). One does not have to adopt McNeill's proposal of "mythohistory" in order to acknowledge that the worldview presuppositions and plausibility structures scholars bring to their historical research generally will play a determinative role regarding what they will allow the data to "possibly" suggest.

well the Synoptics pass other tests for historical reliability, the events they record are, for many modern academic scholars, simply *too implausible* to be accepted as historical. This criterion, therefore, trumps the others—though it is arguably the most subjective of the standard criteria used by historians to access histori-cal veracity. Some scholars simply write as if they just "know" that God (if he exists) does not actually become human and no amount of historical evidence can demonstrate otherwise. Such scholars just "know" that babies cannot ever be conceived in virgins, people do not ever rise from the dead, and people with leprosy are never instantaneously healed. Thus, these scholars just "know" that ancient or contemporary texts that say otherwise simply are trading in narrative fictions—all arguments to the contrary notwithstanding.

We have addressed this issue at length in chapter 1. Hence, a few brief points by way of review will suffice for our present response. As we previously argued, this a priori naturalistic stance toward all supernatural claims is a metaphysical assumption, accepted on faith, nothing more. There are no compelling philo-sophical, logical, or historical arguments that justify one in assuming—let alone require one to take—this stance. Moreover, this assumption has not been shared by most people throughout history and still is not shared by most people today— including those who make up contemporary Western culture. The claim that the naturalistic posture is warranted because "people do not experience miracles today" is weak since (1) this use of the principle of analogy is problematic on a number of counts and (2) many people do, as a matter of fact, report experiences of the supernatural today. The fact that naturalistic scholars uncritically dismiss all these experiences—as they do all reported supernatural experiences of the past—simply testifies to their dogmatic commitment to naturalism.

We also argued previously that this naturalistic posture is arguably ethnocen-tric and chronocentric, since it is rooted in the assumption that the particular post-Enlightenment, Eurocentric, academic perspective of a rather small tribe of Western scholars is superior to all others. In the name of the privileged perspective of this tribe, these scholars dismiss all claims of the supernatural—and reject as historically reliable all texts that contain these claims. Finally, this viewpoint is then presented as the one truly "critical" and "scholarly" perspective.

While there certainly is a need for the plausibility criterion in assessing the historical veracity of ancient texts (as well as modern reports), we have to be guarded in our use of it since it is the most subjective of the criteria. Even as the authors of a classic textbook on historical methodology present this criteria, they warn that the historian "should temper his skepticism with a bit of humility. The history of science," they remind us, "is a history of changing ideas about what is possible and what is impossible, and the evidence of an extremely improbable event just might be confirmed by further investigation."[85] This is a good piece of methodological advice for New Testament scholars to consider as well. Cer-

85. Shafer, ed., *Historical Method*, 42.

tainly, critical historical methodology should prefer "natural" explanations over "supernatural" ones, all other things being equal. But when purely naturalistic explanations seem unable to deal fairly with the evidence at hand, we believe a truly "critical" stance, combined with intellectual and cultural humility, should incline the historical scholar at least to be open to the possibility that something "out of this world," so to speak, has taken place.

Our own conviction is that if scholars are genuinely open to the possibility that the Gospel portrait of Jesus is *possible*, an assessment of all available evidence in this light will lead them to the conclusion that the historical veracity of this portrait is not only possible but most *plausible*. To state it differently, we believe that once the "plausibility" criterion is no longer used as an a priori naturalistic filter imposed upon the data, and once we allow the techniques and standards of historical reporting/precision of the orally oriented ancient world to guide our reflection, the evidence itself offers good reasons to conclude that the a posteriori burden of proof is justly shifted to those who wish to argue that the Synoptic portrait(s) of Jesus is not substantially reliable.

External Corroboration: Literary Evidence

Two final questions customarily asked by historians assessing a document's historical reliability focus not upon internal characteristics of the document itself, but rather upon external evidence.[86] They involve the assessment of external *literary* evidence on the one hand and *archaeological* evidence, on the other. Hence, we are interested here in assessing the extent to which ancient literary works and archaeological evidence supports, or undercuts, the general reliability of the Synoptic Gospels.

To address the literary question first, we have already seen (chap. 4) that there is very little by way of ancient literary evidence for or against the reliability of the Synoptic Jesus tradition. This should come as no surprise, however, since the vast majority of all that was written in the ancient world has perished. Not only this, but those who wrote history in the ancient Roman world generally did so under the authority of governing officials and thus typically recorded only items relevant to the administration they worked for. Since the earliest Jesus movement was a small, sectarian group originating in a rather remote region of the Roman

---

86. M. Howell and W. Prevenier, summarizing criteria offered by two classical texts on historical method, go so far as to say that "the source whose account can be confirmed by reference to outside authorities in some places can be trusted in its entirety if it is impossible similarly to confirm the entire text" (*From Reliable Sources: An Introduction to Historical Methods* [Ithaca, NY: Cornell University Press, 2001], 70). While we would suggest this is far too broad of a generalization, the point stands that external corroboration of a source at certain points adds a broad credibility to the document, including those points at which external sources are not available for comparison. At the very least, external corroboration begins to shift the a posteriori burden of proof to those who want to question the source's reliability.

Empire, and since new religious movements were not uncommon in the ancient world, we should not expect either Jesus or the movement he birthed to have caught the attention of ancient historians.

Nevertheless, as we also argued in chapter 4, while relevant literary evidence is meager, it is not nonexistent. And the little we do find helps to corroborate some claims made in the Gospels. The following are the pieces of evidence discussed in chapter 4 that we found most plausibly support aspects of the early Jesus tradition.

- It is possible that in the mid-50s a Roman historian named Thallus attempted to explain away the odd, prolonged darkness that took place during Jesus's crucifixion.

- The letter of Mara bar Serapion to his son sometime in the second or third century possibly suggests that at least some non-Christians in the ancient Roman world did not doubt that Jesus existed. Indeed, at least some viewed Jesus in a rather positive light and believed he was condemned unjustly.

- Pliny's letter to Hadrian in 110 CE reveals the speed with which the early Christian movement spread throughout the Roman Empire and indicates that both Christians and non-Christians assumed that Jesus was a historical person. It also confirms that among the earliest Christians Jesus was worshipped as divine and adherents were willing to die for their faith.

- The historian Suetonius plausibly confirms Luke's account of the expulsion of Jews from Rome in 49 CE.

- Celsus's second-century attack on the Jesus movement shows not only that opponents of Christianity accepted that Jesus existed, but also that they did not doubt that he performed what appeared to be supernatural feats.

- A text from Lucian of Somosata suggests that critics of Christianity in the second century did not question that Jesus existed and that he was crucified.

- The Roman historian Tacitus confirms that Jesus died by crucifixion during the reign of Tiberius (14–37 CE) and during Pilate's governorship (26–36 CE). He also gives evidence that by the time of Nero's persecution, the Christian movement had been in existence for some time and that these first- and second-generation disciples were willing to endure torture and execution for their faith.

- It is more probable than not that two passages from Josephus give evidence that a first-century Jewish historian accepted that (1) Jesus existed, (2) had a brother named James, (3) was a teacher, (4) performed what appeared to be supernatural feats, (5) was crucified under Pilate, and (6) had followers who continued to have "affection" for him after his death.

Though somewhat meager and of varying degrees of value, this external evidence is arguably more plentiful than we might expect and is consistent with, and largely confirmatory of, things we find in the Synoptic Gospels. At the very least, it buttresses, to some extent, the claim that the burden of proof should lie on any who argue against the general reliability of the Synoptics rather than on those who defend its reliability.

External Corroboration: Archaeological Evidence

Finally, historians typically inquire into the extent to which the material remains of the culture in question supports or challenges the reliability of an ancient text. There has been a significant amount of data arising from archaeological research in ancient Palestine over the last several decades that potentially has implications for our assessment of the Gospels. In fact, Sean Freyne has gone as far as to say that "due largely to developments in the discipline [of archaeology], we are now in a position to write Renan's 'fifth gospel' in ways and in details that he could never have imagined."[87]

Of course, since archaeological artifacts are no more self-interpreting than ancient texts, and since religious and philosophical presuppositions play such a decisive role in New Testament studies, one should not be too surprised to discover that there is a remarkably wide range of opinions, not only about how various archaeological data should be interpreted, but even about how this data should or should not be integrated with the textual evidence for the early Jesus movement.[88] Because of space limitations, we cannot even begin to enter into the details of this complex discussion. What it means, however, is that we must be hesitant to place too much weight on any particular find, whether this be to

87. S. Freyne, "Archaeology and the Historical Jesus," in his *Galilee and Gospel: Collected Essays* (Tübingen: Mohr Siebeck, 2000), 160.

88. For a spectrum of views on the prospects and tensions between the worlds of text and artifact for historical Jesus studies, see J. D. G. Dunn, "On the Relation of Text and Artifact: Some Cautionary Tales," in *Text and Artifact in the Religions of Mediterranean Antiquity: Essays in Honour of Peter Richardson*, ed. S. G. Wilson and M. Desjardins (Waterloo, ON: Wilfrid Laurier University Press, 2000), 192–206; D. E. Groh, "The Clash between Literary and Archaeological Models of Provincial Palestine," in *Archaeology and the Galilee: Texts and Contexts in the Graeco-Roman and Byzantine Periods*, ed. D. R. Edwards and C. T. McCollough (Atlanta: Scholars Press, 1997), 29–37; R. A. Horsley, "The Historical Jesus and Archaeology of the Galilee: Questions from Historical Jesus Research to Archaeologists," in *SBLSP 1994*, ed. E. H. Lovering (Atlanta: Scholars Press, 1994), 91–135; J. L. Reed, "Galilean Archaeology and the Historical Jesus," in *Archaeology and the Galilean Jesus: A Re-examination of the Evidence* (Harrisburg, PA: Trinity, 2000), 8–12; J. F. Strange, "First-Century Galilee from Archaeology and from Text," in *SBLSP 1994*, 81–90 (a modified version of this conference paper by the same title appears in *Archaeology and the Galilee*, 39–48). This tension is not unusual and is generally found whenever there is an attempt to compare oral and/or literary historical data with archaeological data. On the similar, and instructive, debate with respect to Africa's past, see P. Robertshaw, "Sibling Rivalry? The Intersection of Archaeology and History," *History in Africa* 27 (2000): 261–86.

argue for or against the reliability of the Synoptic tradition. In what follows we will simply mention eight examples and/or categories of archaeological data we believe to one degree or another supports a positive assessment of the reliability of the Synoptic tradition.

1. In our estimation, among the most significant archaeological findings in recent years are those that have established just how "Torah true" first-century Palestine was, despite (and perhaps partly because of) the spread of Hellenism.[89] As discussed in chapter 2, we have found that coins minted by Herod in first-century Galilee avoid human representations, suggesting the population remained sensitive to traditional Jewish interpretations of the second commandment. The material used for ceramic wares conforms to Levitical laws. We find ritual bathing pools throughout the region.[90] There is a conspicuous absence of pork bones in the area at this time. And burial sites in Palestine reflect distinctive Jewish practices (i.e., the presence of ossuaries).

In our estimation, discoveries such as these are significant not only because they help to confirm aspects of the Synoptic portrait of first-century Palestine, but even more so because they serve as strong evidence against the claim made by many legendary-Jesus theorists, that first-century Palestinian Jews were religiously hellenized to the point that they could have easily and naturally generated and/or accepted a legend about a miracle-working divine man.

2. Recent excavations of Bethsaida confirm that the Gospel depiction of this city as a fishing village existing on the north shore of the Sea of Galilee is accurate.[91] Also, a jar with a cross was discovered in 1994 and dates sometime before 67, plausibly providing a mid-first-century testimony to the newly born Jesus movement, which was, interestingly enough, centered on a crucified Messiah.[92]

3. In 1986, a sunken fishing boat that dates from the first century was found in the Sea of Galilee. Galilean archaeologist Jonathan Reed has noted that the boat, measuring 8.2 by 2.3 meters, "could certainly hold thirteen people," the number of people necessary for Jesus and his twelve disciples to cross the Sea as mentioned a number of times in the Gospels.[93] Not only this, but the boat's rather shallow draft (1.2 meters) comports well with Mark's report that, in the midst of

89. With respect to this claim, beyond the many sources cited in chap. 2, see also Freyne, "Archaeology and the Historical Jesus," 176–82.

90. Reed, "Galilean Archaeology," 117.

91. For brief summaries of the excavations of Bethsaida and Khirbet Cana, see J. H. Charlesworth, "Jesus Research and Near Eastern Archaeology: Reflections on Recent Developments," in *Neotestamentica et Philonica: Studies in Honor of Peder Borgen*, ed. D. E. Aune, T. Seland, and J. H. Ulrichsen (Boston: Brill, 2003), 55–57; J. J. Rousseau, "The Impact of the Bethsaida Finds on Our Knowledge of the Historical Jesus," in *SBLSP 1995*, ed. E. H. Lovering (Atlanta: Scholars Press, 1995), 187–207; J. J. Rousseau and R. Arav, "Bethsaida," in *Jesus and His World: An Archaeological and Cultural Dictionary* (Minneapolis: Fortress, 1995), 19–24.

92. Rousseau, "Impact of the Bethsaida Finds," 204.

93. J. D. Crossan and J. L. Reed, *Excavating Jesus: Beneath the Stones, behind the Texts* (San Francisco: HarperSanFrancisco, 2001), 3. See S. Wachsmann, "The Galilee Boat," in *Archaeology and the Bible: The*

a storm, the boat began to founder as it filled with water (Mark 4:37).[94] The boat thus provides some confirmation of the historical plausibility of two aspects of the Jesus tradition.

4. In 1962, a Latin inscription of the Roman prefect Pontius Pilate was discovered at Caesarea Maritima, confirming that this man reigned in the position ascribed to him by the Synoptics.[95]

5. The entombed remains of a first-century crucified man in Palestine were discovered in 1968. The find confirms aspects of the biblical account of Jesus's crucifixion and refutes the argument—yet espoused by Crossan—that we cannot expect a Jewish victim of crucifixion to have been granted a proper burial in a private tomb, as the Gospels claim of Jesus (Mark 15:42–47).[96]

6. In 1990, an ossuary was discovered in a burial cave south of Jerusalem's Old City. The limestone ossuary was uncharacteristically ornate, signaling ownership by a wealthy family. Etched rather crudely into its side in Aramaic is the name "Caiaphas." While there is obviously room for debate here, a number of leading scholars have concluded that the ossuary most likely once contained the bones of the high priest who, according to the Gospels, presided over the Jewish trial of Jesus.[97]

7. In Capernaum, a simple first-century house was discovered beneath a fourth-century house-church that was itself buried beneath a fifth-century octagonal church structure. On the walls of one of the rooms of the first-century structure are inscribed a variety of Christian invocations that date from the second century. Clearly, Christians in the early centuries of the church knew there was something significant about this first-century house. A number of reputable scholars, rang-

---

Best of BAR, vol. 2: *Archaeology in the World of Herod, Jesus, and Paul*, ed. H. Shanks and D. P. Cole (Washington, DC: Biblical Archaeological Society, 1990), 208–23.

94. J. H. Charlesworth, "Archaeological Research and Biblical Theology," in *Geschichte—Tradition—Reflexion: Festschrift für Martin Hengel zum 70. Geburtstag*, ed. H. Cancik, H. Lichtenberger, and P. Schäfer (Tübingen: Mohr Siebeck, 1996), 1:12.

95. See Crossan and Reed, *Excavating Jesus*, 2.

96. See J. D. Crossan, *Who Killed Jesus? Exposing the Roots of Anti-Semitism in the Gospel Story of the Death of Jesus* (San Francisco: HarperSanFrancisco, 1995), 163–68. For a case against Crossan's thesis that the burial of Jesus in a private tomb was a fabrication of the early church, see P. R. Eddy, "Response [to W. L. Craig's "John Dominic Crossan on the Resurrection of Jesus"]," in *The Resurrection: An Interdisciplinary Symposium on the Resurrection of Jesus*, ed. S. T. Davis, D. Kendall, and G. O'Collins (New York: Oxford University Press, 1997), 277–80.

97. For a list of some of these archaeologists, see C. A. Evans, *Jesus and the Ossuaries* (Waco: Baylor University Press, 2003), 107. Crossan and Reed make the connection explicit and without qualification (*Excavating Jesus*, 2). See also Charlesworth, "Archaeological Research," 25. Among those who emphasize that we can never be certain about this connection—which, of course, is a historical truism—see H. K. Bond, *Caiaphas: Friend of Rome and Judge of Jesus?* (Louisville: Westminster John Knox, 2004); Evans, *Jesus and the Ossuaries*, 104–12. Evans admits his "substantial doubt" (p. 107) at this point, a doubt that goes so far as to judge the connection as possible but not probable (p. 123). It is interesting to note here that the positions of Crossan and Reed vs. Evans demonstrate that the common expectation that "conservatives" always defend such claims, while "liberals" always deny them is not a law of New Testament studies!

ing across the conservative-liberal spectrum, argue this is most likely the home of the apostle Peter, the very place Jesus used as a base of operations for his Galilean ministry (Mark 1:29–35; 2:1; Matt. 4:13; 8:14–16).[98]

8. Some reputable scholars, including James Charlesworth, argue that we have good grounds for accepting that Jesus was crucified on the rock now located inside the Church of the Holy Sepulchre.[99] The site, though rooted deeply in tradition, often has been dismissed because it appeared to lie within the city walls. But, at least to the thinking of some scholars, more recent evidence suggests this site would not have been within the city walls in the 30s of the first century.

Finally, a word about the notorious "James ossuary" is in order. In 2002, an ossuary was discovered with the words, "James, son of Joseph, brother of Jesus," etched on it. Within a short time, the ossuary was being countenanced as "the first archaeological link to Jesus and his family."[100] News of this find burst onto the scene in November of 2002 with an article by the renowned paleographer Andre Lemaire, published in the *Biblical Archaeology Review*. Lemaire concludes his article by arguing that "it seems very probable that this is the ossuary of the James in the New Testament. If so, this would mean that we have here the first epigraphic mention—from about 63 CE—of Jesus of Nazareth."[101] Lemaire's article included a copy of an affirmative assessment of the box completed by the Geological Survey of Israel (Ministry of National Infrastructures).[102] Following this, a team from the Royal Ontario Museum in Toronto examined the ossuary and its inscription and also determined it to be authentic.

However, subsequent inspections have called these original assessments into question. The Israel Antiquities Authority (IAA) has argued that, while there is good evidence that the ossuary itself is authentic, the inscription is a later

98. J. Murphy-O'Conner concludes: "The most reasonable assumption is the one attested by the Byzantine pilgrims, namely that it was the house of Peter in which Jesus may have lodged.... Certainly, nothing in the excavations contradicts this identification" (*The Holy Land*, 4th ed. [New York: Oxford University Press, 1998], 220). Crossan and Reed rank the locating of Peter's house as third among their "top ten archaeological discoveries" pertaining to Jesus (*Excavating Jesus*, 2, 3). This identification is also defended by J. Strange and H. Shanks, "Has the House Where Jesus Stayed in Capernaum Been Found?" in *Archaeology in the World of Herod, Jesus, and Paul*, 188–99. Charlesworth concurs; see "Jesus Research," 61–62. For an example of a dissenter, see J. Taylor, *Christians and the Holy Places: The Myth of Jewish-Christian Origins* (Oxford: Clarendon, 1993), 284–94.

99. Charlesworth, "Jesus Research," 51. See also D. Bahat, "Does the Holy Sepulchre Church Mark the Burial of Jesus?" in *Archaeology in the World of Herod, Jesus, and Paul*, 248–66; M. Broshi, "Evidence of Earliest Christian Pilgrimage to the Holy Sepulchre Comes to Light in Holy Sepulchre Church," in *Archaeology in the World of Herod, Jesus, and Paul*, 267–69. For dissenters, see J. J. Rousseau and R. Arav, "Golgotha, Traditional Site," in *Jesus and His World*, 112–18.

100. H. Shanks and B. Witherington, *The Brother of Jesus: The Dramatic Story and Meaning of the First Archaeological Link to Jesus and His Family* (San Francisco: HarperSanFrancisco, 2003). The ins and outs of the James ossuary saga up to 2003 are recounted in the first part of this book.

101. A. Lemaire, "The Burial Box of James the Brother of Jesus," *BAR* (November/December 2002): 33.

102. Ibid., 29.

forgery.[103] Indeed, they have charged the antiquities collector who brought the box forth with producing a forgery. The crucial issues dividing experts in the field center on whether the inscription reflects an authentic first-century Aramaic script, and whether the patina—the thin covering on the surface of the etching caused by aging—is authentic or an (initially) impressive forgery.

The fact that experts in the field are divided over their assessments of these issues is intriguing. Understandably, it has led some to suspect that factors other than an objective assessment of evidence may be influencing the players in this debate. Obviously, if the James ossuary is confirmed as authentic, this could have significant religious implications—implications that may be influencing the examiners in one direction or the other.[104] What is more, the fact that the James ossuary emerged, not by careful extraction by an archaeologist from an excavation site, but from the often shady world of the antiquities market, leaves a cloud of suspicion hanging over it in the eyes of many professionals. Thus, on two separate counts—religious and professional—the James ossuary finds itself caught in the crossfire of turf wars and human emotion. Unfortunately, such a context is not conducive to a fair and clearheaded assessment of an ancient artifact.[105]

Of course, even if the ossuary's inscription is authentic, this does not prove the box held the bones of the brother of Jesus mentioned in the New Testament.[106] On the one hand, it is significant that, most likely, a brother of the deceased would be mentioned on an ossuary only if he were relatively well known. Therefore we would have to ask ourselves how probable it is that there was more than one man *named James* who was the *son of a Joseph* who had a *well-known brother named Jesus* during the rather short interval of time in pre-70 Palestine when ossuaries were used. Such considerations lead some scholars, including Lemaire, to conclude that if the inscription of this ossuary is indeed authentic, in all probability it contained the bones of Jesus's brother.[107] Nonetheless, the debate at present continues, and no firm conclusions can be drawn.

We conclude this section by noting that while archaeological evidence is, by its very nature, often ambiguous, and thus while it is hard to ever rise much above the

103. Conclusions in the words of several of the individual IAA team members are available in H. Shanks, "The Storm over the Bone Box: Ossuary Update," *BAR* (September/October 2003): 30.

104. It is interesting to note that one of the members of the IAA team, whose instructions included a warning to consider nothing but the objective data, prefaced his conclusion with this caveat: "Even if the ossuary is authentic, there is no reason to assume the deceased was actually the brother of Jesus" (Shanks, "Storm," 30).

105. While the final scholarly jury is still out on this one, the sort of evenhanded tone and careful assessment that the field can benefit from can be seen in Craig Evans's recent consideration of various inscriptional and ossuary evidence in *Jesus and the Ossuaries*. Kudos to Evans and Baylor University Press (Carey Newman) for the publication of this book. For Evans's treatment of the James ossuary, see pp. 112–22.

106. A point argued by J. Magness, "Ossuaries and the Burials of Jesus and James," *JBL* 124 (2005): 154.

107. Lemaire, "Burial Box," 33.

"more or less probable," it seems to us that archaeological discoveries, especially over the last few decades, have on the whole served to enhance our confidence in the general reliability of the Gospels. Again, while we think it unwise to place much weight on this, the evidence may nevertheless function as part of the cumulative case for the general reliability of the Synoptic tradition. At the very least, it serves to buttress the claim that the burden of proof should lie on anyone who wishes to argue that the general portrait of Jesus offered in the Synoptic Gospels is not historically trustworthy.

Excursus: Geographical/Cultural Blunders in Mark?

In this final section, we will address two additional, broadly related issues that often are raised against the claim of the reliability of the Synoptic Jesus tradition. The first involves the claim that the Synoptic tradition—particularly as it is represented in Mark—contains "numerous geographical errors."[108] The four most commonly cited instances of geographical error in Mark are: (1) In 5:1, Mark pictures the "country of the Gerasenes" as on the coast of the Sea of Galilee; however, Gerasa is over thirty miles southeast of the Sea. That there is a geographical problem at this point in Mark is obvious from the variants in the manuscript tradition that try to smooth it out and from Matthew's attempt to fix the problem by changing it to "Gadarenes" (8:28), since Gadara—though it is over five miles from the Sea—is at least closer than Gerasa.

(2) In 6:45, Mark claims that Jesus sent his disciples to "the other side" of the Sea of Galilee "toward Bethsaida"—referring presumably to Bethsaida Julias on the northeast side of the lake in what is now the Golan Heights. However, later in 6:53, Mark describes Jesus and the disciples, having weathered a storm, as finally "crossing over" the Sea and landing at "Gennesaret," which is back on the west side of the lake, several miles southwest of Capernaum. Apparently the author does not know the geography of the lake well enough to know that Bethsaida and Gannesaret are on opposite sides of the north end of the lake.

(3) In 7:31, Mark seems to depict Sidon as south of Tyre, which of course it is not. He then goes on to claim that the Sea of Galilee was in the region of the Decapolis, when actually it is to the northwest of this region.

(4) In 10:1, Mark describe Jesus going from Galilee "to the region of Judea, [and] beyond the Jordan." The variants in the manuscript tradition point out the problem, and there is a debate as to which represents the original text. A major question is whether the "and" (*kai*) reflects Mark's original text. In either case, so

---

108. Kümmel, *Introduction to the New Testament*, 97. This is a common argument in the literature. See, e.g., P. Achtemeier, "Mark, Gospel of," in *ABD*, ed. D. N. Freedman (New York: Doubleday, 1992), 4:542; K. Niederwimmer, "Johannes Markus und die Frage nach dem Verfasser des zweiten Evangeliums" *ZNW* 58 (1967): 178–82; D. Nineham, *Saint Mark* (Philadelphia: Westminster, 1978 [1963]), 40; G. A. Wells, *The Jesus Myth* (Chicago: Open Court, 1999), 15–16.

the argument goes, there is a geographical blunder. Without the "and," the text seems to say that Judea is beyond (i.e., east of) the Jordan, which it is not. If the "and" is retained, it seems to say that Jesus went first to Jerusalem and then out "beyond the Jordan" (i.e., into the region of Peraea, east of the Jordan). The expected route, however, would be the reverse: Jews on pilgrimage from Galilee to Jerusalem would often travel east of the Jordan down to Jericho to avoid Samaria. Thus the text should have depicted Jesus as traveling beyond the Jordan on his way to Judea/Jerusalem.

In response, we want to suggest that plausible ways of reading Mark exist for each of these instances that do not involve charging Mark with geographical inaccuracy. In fact, once the anachronistic application to Mark's account of modern conventions of geographical specificity and reporting method is called into question, the plausibility factor only increases.

Mark 5:1 and the "Gerasenes" Conundrum

Various proposals have been offered to reconcile the manuscript variants connected with this text. Given the two-source theory and strong textual evidence (i.e., early Alexandrian and Western manuscripts), the original text of Mark did read "Gerasenes" (followed by Luke in 8:26; modified by Matthew to "Gadarenes" at 8:28).[109] There is no avoiding the fact that the textual variants and the variations between the Gospels themselves point to a complex problem. Neither Gerasa nor Gadara is on the coast of Galilee. Neither provides a setting that would allow a herd of pigs to run into the sea. A third name in the text tradition turns up: "Gergasenes." While some have conjectured that this variant originated with Origen, others—Robert Gundry, for example—have demonstrated that a plausible case can be made for taking the "Gergasenes" variant as reflective of the original.[110] Intriguingly, near the modern town of Khersa (Kursa/Kersi) on the east side of the sea, there is a steep slope that ends less than fifty yards from the sea. Within two miles of this site, cave tombs have been located. It is also interesting that a fifth-century chapel was located here, suggesting that the site held significance for the early church.[111] This location would easily fit the topography of the exorcism account found in the Gospels. Several plausible explanations have been proposed to explain how the original site of Khersa could have resulted in the complex manuscript tradition that we find. As Gundry has demonstrated, a case can be made for identifying modern-day Khersa with ancient Gergasa. Identifying Gergasa as the original site is one way of explaining the early presence in the manuscript tradition of this relatively obscure site. As Gundry notes, the accidental dropping of the

109. B. M. Metzger, *A Textual Commentary on the Greek New Testament* (New York: United Bible Societies, 1971), 23–24, 84.
110. See, respectively, Nineham, *Saint Mark*, 153; R. H. Gundry, *Mark: A Commentary on His Apology for the Cross* (Grand Rapids: Eerdmans, 1993), 255–57.
111. Rousseau and Arav, "Gadara, Kursi," in *Jesus and His World*, 98.

second "g" sometime in the copying history would produce "Gerasa."[112] The fact that both Gerasa and Gadara were larger and better-known could explain why, as scribal activity continued along in time beyond Palestine, it would have been easy to replace the relatively unknown name with a more familiar one.[113] In this scenario, the geographical ignorance lies not with Mark but with later copyists. Given the undeniable variations in the manuscript tradition, this is not merely an ad hoc proposal, but rather one plausible way of interpreting the complex data. It should also be noted that each of the Greek manuscript variants could plausibly be understood as reflecting the attempt of a translator to render an Aramaic original—perhaps *KRS* or *GRS*.[114]

Another possible explanation of the data that both affirms the more common scholarly conclusion that "Gerasa" was the original reading, and yet renders Mark's original report as historically accurate, begins by noting that the text may well be read as saying "in the territory/vicinity of Gerasa," and that in verse 20, the former demoniac is reported as proclaiming amidst the Decapolis. As R. T. France and others have noted, it may be that Mark is loosely using the name "Gerasa" to designate the wider region, since it was a leading city of the Decapolis, and the northwest region of the Decapolis can be understood as extending to the shores of the Sea of Galilee.[115]

Mark 6:45 and the Sea Incident

The textual evidence is strongly in favor of the inclusion of the seemingly troubling phrase "toward Bethsaida," the problem being that if they were heading to Bethsaida, which is on the east side of the lake, why do they eventually arrive at Gennesaret, on the west side (6:53)?[116] In order to alleviate this problem, some have conjectured that there was a second town named Bethsaida on the west side of the lake. But there is no real evidence for this, and it is difficult to believe the author would have simply written of "Bethsaida" if there were two different towns on the lake that would need to be differentiated. Another response, however, both fits the real-life context of the narrative, and would also alleviate the charge of geographical confusion. In the narrative, between the statement of the intended destination of Bethsaida in 6:45 and the statement of the actual destination of Gennesaret in 6:53, the disciples encounter a storm during their boat voyage. In fact the episode is told for this very reason—a strong storm arises and Jesus meets them, walking on the water, to calm their fears. A number of commentators have

112. Gundry, *Mark*, 256.

113. An observation with which—following Gundry, *Mark*, 256—B. Witherington concurs in *The Gospel of Mark: A Socio-Rhetorical Commentary* (Grand Rapids: Eerdmans, 2001), 180n141.

114. Witherington, *Gospel of Mark*, 180.

115. R. T. France, *The Gospel of Mark: A Commentary on the Greek Text* (Grand Rapids: Eerdmans, 2002), 227.

116. On the ancient locations—and implications for Jesus research—of Bethsaida and Gennesaret, see Rousseau and Arav, "Bethsaida," and "Gennesareth," in *Jesus and His World*," 19–24, 109–10.

pointed out that if the storm was accompanied by a strong east wind, it could well be the case that a small boat that started out for Bethsaida on the east side would have ended up in Genessaret on the west side.[117] Some scholars have objected that, since the episode ends with the wind dying down, there is no reason they would have not continued on to Bethsaida.[118] However, we would suggest that this objection, while logically possible, hardly enters into the actual experience of a group of traumatized, water-logged men on a small boat who just narrowly escaped being drowned. Perhaps stepping onto firm terrain and drying out were more pressing priorities at that moment than turning the boat back into the sea! Once the possibility of a Peter-John Mark connection is entertained, there is no problem imagining that this particular event would have made quite an impression on Peter, would have come out in numerous oral retellings (even down to the details of where they were headed and where, after the storm, they actually landed), and eventually recorded in Mark's gospel. This is, in fact, the very type of memorable personal experience that would have lent itself to inclusion in Petrine oral tradition.

Mark 7:31 and Jesus's Journey from Tyre

As Joel Marcus notes, "If Mark's wording is meant to describe a direct journey, it implies that Sidon and the Decapolis are on a line from Tyre to the Sea of Galilee"—which of course they are not.[119] But that is one fairly significant "if"! Instead of assuming that is Mark's intent and charging him with geographical error, why not give the author the benefit of the doubt and consider the possibility that he was not trying to describe the most time-efficient way of getting from Tyre to the Sea of Galilee? A host of scholars have shown how historically unimaginative this skeptical conclusion is, once it is remembered that Jesus is trying to conduct an itinerant preaching mission, not break a land travel-time record. As John Painter notes, "After all, Jesus was engaged in a mission, not attempting to travel as quickly as possible from A to B."[120] In fact, the description would suggest that Jesus was taking a circuitous route through largely gentile areas, eventually bringing him back to the Sea of Galilee. Incidentally, some have argued that this verse shows that Mark pictured the Sea of Galilee as "in the midst of" the Decapolis, which it is not. However, as Gundry effectively shows, this is both an uncharitable and

117. For example, H. B. Swete, *The Gospel according to St. Mark*, 3rd ed. (Grand Rapids: Eerdmans, 1951 [1909]), 129–30; France, *Gospel of Mark*, 264. See also Gundry's insightful comments on this question in *Mark*, 338–40.

118. For example, J. Gnilka, *Das Evangelium nach Markus* (Benziger: Neukirchener, 1978), 1:266; J. Marcus, *Mark 1–8: A New Translation with Introduction and Commentary* (New York: Doubleday, 2000), 422.

119. Marcus, *Mark 1–8*, 472.

120. J. Painter, *Mark's Gospel: Worlds in Conflict* (New York: Routledge, 1997), 116. See also M. Hooker, *The Gospel according to Mark* (Peabody, MA: Hendrickson, 1991), 185; France, *Gospel of Mark*, 300; Gundry, *Mark*, 386–88; Witherington, *Gospel of Mark*, 233n108.

an unlikely interpretation of Mark. Rather, the "in the midst of" (*ana meson* with the genative) attaches to Jesus's journey, not the Sea of Galilee.[121]

Mark 10:1 and Jesus's Journey to Jerusalem

Once again, plausible explanations for this verse are available, explanations which also offer a charitable reading of the text, including the author's geographical knowledge. It can, of course, be read as Mark not knowing that the regions of Judea and the Transjordan are distinguishable, or that Jesus went through Judea to get to the Transjordan and not the other way around, which it should have been. However, it can also be read (1) as Mark placing Jesus's final and ultimate destination—Judea, that is, Jerusalem—first for rhetorical emphasis, or (2) as Mark noting that, once he went to Judea, Jesus also made a missional visit beyond the Jordan while in the southern regions. In conclusion, various scholars have provided plausible historical answers to these geographical conundrums, and none of them precludes a Palestinian Jew like John Mark from authoring them, or from possessing an accurate (by ancient standards and conventions) knowledge of Palestinian geography.

Mark 7:3–4 and Ancient Jewish Hand-Washing Customs

A second line of criticism involves the pointing out of ostensive errors on Mark's part vis-à-vis ancient Jewish customs. A common example of this claim involves the author's statement that hand washing was a purity rite kept by "Pharisees" and "all Jews" (7:3–4). In fact, according to the Torah, the only class of people who were called to practice hand washing observances were priests (Exod. 30:18–21; 40:30–32; Lev. 22:1–16). And it was not until post-70 Rabbinic Judaism that Jews began a wider practice of hand washing. Thus, Nineham, for example, quickly concludes that "the story as it stands can hardly be historical."[122]

In response, several things can be said. While it is true that, as far as the Torah is concerned, the only people who must perform ritual hand washings are priests, there is reason to suggest that by the first-century, the Pharisees—who had as their ideal something like the "priesthood of all believers"—were encouraging all Jews to keep the cultic purity rites of the priests, and that ritual hand washing would have been one of their teachings. Along similar lines, Gundry has made a plausible case for the claim that ritual hand washing may well have been far more widespread in first-century Jewish culture than many have realized.[123] Furthermore, even apart from these considerations, the conclusion that Mark is flat-out "wrong" on this point simply because he makes the claim for "all Jews" is achieved only as one anachronistically forces upon Mark modern historical/semantic conventions

121. Gundry, *Mark*, 387–88.

122. Nineham, *Mark*, 193. See also Niederwimmer, "Johannes Markus," 183–85; Wells, *Jesus Myth*, 16.

123. Gundry, *Mark*, 358–60.

and precision standards quite alien to those operating within the ancient Jewish world. "All Jews" may well be a classic case of Jewish hyperbole, simply making the point that Jews were often known for their hand washing. In fact, the (ca. second-century BCE) Jewish text *Epistle of Aristeas* (305) makes the very same claim—that "all Jews" followed the custom of hand washing. In any case, there are plausible explanations for Mark's comment that stop short of accusing him of "error."

Conclusion: The Synoptic Portrait(s) of Jesus and the a Posteriori Burden of Proof

We close by asking: Is the thrust of the legendary-Jesus thesis—that the general portrait(s) of Jesus provided in the Synoptic Gospels is substantially legendary—the most plausible reading of the historical data? In light of all we have considered in this work, we conclude that the answer must be in the negative.

To summarize our broad cumulative case for the historicity of the essential portrait(s) of Jesus found in the Synoptic Gospels—and against the legendary-Jesus thesis—the general religious environment of first-century Jewish Palestine would not have provided a natural environment for birthing a legend/myth centered around a recent, Torah-trumping, cruciform-messianic God-man. Fundamental countercultural and embarrassing features of the Jesus story provide further evidence against the Synoptic portrait(s) being significantly legendary. The claims that Jesus's identity was inextricably bound up with that of Yahweh-God and that he should receive worship, the notion of a crucified messiah, the concept of an individual resurrection, the dullness of the disciples, the unsavory crowd Jesus attracted, and a number of other embarrassing aspects of the Jesus tradition are difficult to explain on the assumption that this story is substantially legendary. The fact that this story originated and was accepted while Jesus's mother, brothers, and original disciples (to say nothing of Jesus's opponents) were still alive renders the legendary explanation all the more implausible. In our view, it is hard to understand how this story came about in this environment, in such a short span of time, unless it is substantially rooted in history.

Moreover, attempts to argue against the historicity of the Jesus tradition on the basis of the alleged silence of Paul or ancient secular writers have not been forceful. Paul's letters reveal that Paul and his audiences believed Jesus lived in the recent past and that they knew a good deal about the events of Jesus's life, as well as his teachings. And while there is little found in ancient secular writings that pertain to the early Christian movement, there is more than we might expect, and what does emerge tends to confirm aspects of the Jesus tradition.

Beyond this, much of what we have learned about oral traditions in orally dominant cultures over the last several decades gives us compelling reasons to accept the earliest traditions about Jesus as having been transmitted in a historically reliable fashion. Considerations from studies on ancient historically oriented traditions support the view that these authors wrote with historical intent and, by ancient standards, historical competency.

Finally, as we have seen in the last two chapters, the Synoptics themselves give us plausible grounds for accepting that the basic portrait(s) of Jesus they communicate is substantially rooted in history. Yes they are "biased," but no more so than many other ancient or modern historical writers whom we typically trust. They include a wealth of self-damaging detail, as we have noted. They also contain the sorts of non-ideologically driven incidental details and casual information historians typically look for as evidence of historical interest. They are seen to be reasonably consistent once we understand them as texts operating with an oral rather than a literate conception/register, and when assessed within the constraints of the precision standards of ancient orally oriented cultures. The claims they make are not implausible, unless, of course, one rules out the possibility of the supernatural from the beginning. And while there is relatively little literary or archaeological evidence that unambiguously supports the reliability of these works, there is some, which is more than we might reasonably have expected for texts of their date and sociocultural provenance.

Where does all this leave us? We suggest that these lines of evidence, viewed from the standpoint of an "open" historical-critical method, provide reasonable grounds for the conviction that the portrait(s) of Jesus in the Synoptic Gospels substantially is rooted in history. At the very least, this probability is greater than the probability of any competing hypothesis, which leads us, at minimum, to the conclusion that the a posteriori burden of proof should be born by those who claim the Synoptic Gospels are unreliable vis-à-vis their essential representations of Jesus.

In this vein, we find ourselves concurring with the recent assessment of James Dunn, when he writes:

> If we are unsatisfied with the Jesus of the Synoptic tradition, then we will simply have to lump it; there is no other truly historical or historic Jesus. . . . [T]he quest has been too long captivated by the will-o-the-wisp of a historical Jesus, an objective artifactual figure buried in the Gospels and waiting to be exhumed and brandished aloft, as different from the Jesus of the Gospels—not fully realizing the less the reconstructed Jesus owed to the Synoptic picture of Jesus, the more it must be expressive of the agendas of the individual questers.[124]

---

124. J. D. G. Dunn, *A New Perspective on Jesus: What the Quest for the Historical Jesus Missed* (Grand Rapids: Baker Academic, 2005), 34. Our conclusion with respect to the Synoptics in general coincides with that of Craig Keener's regarding Matthew. Keener writes, "My own judgment, after working through the Synoptic pericopes and comparing how Matthew and Luke adapt Mark, supports this assignment of the burden of proof to those skeptical of Matthew's historical accomplishment. Nevertheless, in many cases inadequate historical evidence remains to make a clear historical judgment in either direction" (*A Commentary on the Gospel of Matthew* [Grand Rapids: Eerdmans, 1999], 24). Similarly, our conclusions parallel those proposed in Bird's recent study of the Jesus tradition; see "Purpose and Preservation of the Jesus Tradition."

Our historiographical conclusions, of course, do not yet come close to the surrendered, trusting relationship to the living Christ that lies at the heart of the Christian faith. But no amount of strictly historical reasoning or evidence can take one to *that* point. At best, historical reasoning can point in a more or less probable direction. To speak now as Christian theologians: the Holy Spirit, personal commitment, and covenant trust must carry one the rest of the way. If this work has, to any extent, helped to clarify the solid historical grounds for this faith response, it has served its purpose.

Index of Scripture and Ancient Writings

General Index

Abogunrin, S. O., 22n21
Abrahams, R., 253n57
Acts, book of, 330–31n88, 337–38. *See also* Luke, Gospel of: Luke-Acts
Acts Seminar, 338n108, 397
Adonis, 92n1, 135, 141, 143
Africa, historians of/historiography of, 22n21, 86n96, 261, 262, 434n73, 442n88
Agapius, 193–94
Aichele, G., 315n25
Akenson, D. H., 210n21
Albl, M. C., 250n52
Alexander, L., 328, 338–39
Alexander the Great, 61, 62, 101, 423, 425
Allen, B., 424, 426
Allison, D. C., 230–31
Alver, B., 297
Amodio, M. C., 401
Ananus, the high priest, 187–89
angels, 30, 74, 106, 128, 162, 208n16
    watchers, 125
Angus, S., 135
anthropology, 71, 253, 261n82, 262, 263, 264, 266, 273, 293n90
anti-language. *See* orally-dominant/oriented cultures: and anti-language
anti-legend. *See* legend: anti-legend
apocalyptic eschatology. *See* Judaism: apocalyptic eschatology; Paul the apostle: and apocalyptic eschatology
Apollonius of Tyana, 31, 32, 138, 151–54, 311, 316
Apollos, 206
Appleby, J., 17n8

Aquinas, T., 283
Aramaic, 113, 446, 449
archaeological evidence, archaeology, 30, 35, 105, 109, 115, 116, 117, 120, 121, 246, 440, 442–47, 453
Archelaus, 120
Aristobulus I, 117
Aristotle, 335
Arrian, 423
Artapanus, 131, 141
Asclepius, 311
Assmann, J., 277n23
astrology, ancient, 30
    within ancient Judaism, 105, 122–28
Athens, 66, 330, 403n118
Attis, 30, 135, 137, 143, 146
Auerbach, E., 415
Aune, D. E., 313n13, 320, 323, 325, 326, 327, 338, 360n191
authenticity criteria, 377–79
    aftermath, 379
    Aramaic traces, 378, 416–17
    double dissimilarity, 377
    double dissimilarity-similarity, 379
    embarrassment, 379, 408–11
    historical plausibility, 379
    inclusion, 379
    multiple independent attestation, 378
    Palestinian environment, 378
    simplicity, 379

Baal, 30n35, 137, 144
Bailey, J. L., 319n42

Bailey, K. E., 238n1, 262n84
Baird, J. A., 303n128
Bakker, E. J., 254n60, 257, 266n97, 351–53,
    355n169, 375
Baltzer, K., 312n10
Bandstra, B., 94n8
baptism, 142
Barker, M., 94, 100, 106n53
Barnabas, 215, 222
Barstad, H. M., 145n39
Bartlett, Sir F., 276, 278, 280–82
Barton, S., 430n61
Bauckham, R., 94, 97, 129–30, 290–91, 417–18
Bauer, B., 24, 159n78
Bauer, G. L., 159n78
Bauer, W., 135n3
Bauman, R., 264n86
Baur, F. C., 43n7, 135n3
Becker, C., 278
Beissinger, M. H., 148n50
Ben-Amos, D., 148
Berger, P. L., 73, 79, 80, 81
Berrin, S., 345
Bethsaida, 443, 447, 449–50
Biddle, J., 92n1
Bilde, P., 185n61
Bilezikian, G. G., 342n126
biography, Greco-Roman, 35, 152, 312, 320,
    323–27
    conserving function of, 325–26
    and Greco-Roman historiography, 324–25
    and historical intent, 326–27
    See also Synoptic Gospels: genre/nature of:
    biography/bios
Bird, M. F., 453n124
Black, C. C., 399
Blackburn, B., 130n149, 131
Blomberg, C. L., 14n2, 305n133, 370, 423n42,
    437n80
Boman, T., 255–56, 275n16
Bonaparte, N., 61, 62, 149
Bond, H., 197–98
Boomershine, T., 248, 249n46, 357, 403
Borg, M., 26n28, 48n21, 77
Boring, M. E., 298n110, 302n122–23
Bornkamm, G., 396n98
Bostock, D. G., 137n14
Botha, P. J. J., 258, 401, 404n123
Bousset, W., 93, 135
Bovon, F., 267
Bowersock, G. W., 108, 335, 339n114, 340
Bowlin, J., 72

Bowman, A. K., 243–44
Boyd, G. A., 26n28, 129, 161n81, 290n75
Bradley, F. H., 43, 44, 54n32
Brewer, D., 344, 347
Brewer, W., 281
Broer, I., 212
Brown, D., 381
Bruce, F. F., 331n88, 347n142
Bryan, C., 358–59
Bulatao, J., 68n61
Bultmann, R., 13n1, 25, 31n38, 44, 45, 46, 47,
    51, 56, 57n41, 73, 74, 75, 76, 79, 93, 145n38,
    207, 237n1, 238, 240, 252, 269–72, 278, 291,
    292–94, 296, 298, 311, 321, 348, 376, 413,
    414n14, 415, 430n62
    post-Bultmannian tradition, 25, 271, 283, 289
    See also demythologization; form criticism/
    critics
burden of proof, 35, 188, 414n17
    a priori, 84–85, 87, 369–71, 374, 379, 406
    a posteriori, 370, 374–75, 379, 380, 406, 412,
    416, 421, 440, 452–54
    and the Synoptic Gospels, 307, 363–76, 447,
    452–54
    lack of consensus, 366–69
    and religio-philosophical presuppositions,
    371–74, 442
    skeptical position, 364–66
    and their oral register, 374–76
Burridge, R. A., 323, 349n150
Bush, D., 141
Butler, T., 283
Byrskog, S., 288–90, 336n105

Caba, J., 367n12
Caesarea Maritima, 182, 444
Caiaphas, 132, 444
Cameron, J., 425
Campbell, J., 31n36
Campbell, S., 279n34, 280, 284
Capernaum, 444, 447
Capes, D., 94
Cargile, J., 369, 370n22
Carlyle, T., 20, 324
Carr, D. M., 247n40
Carrell, P., 94
Carson, D. A., 323n56
Casaubon, I., 134n2
Casey, M., 94, 96n12, 343
Cattell, M. G., 277
Celsus, 32, 92n1, 134n2, 139, 154, 166, 177–78,
    190, 198–99, 335, 437, 441